EXPLORATION OF THE SOUTH SEAS IN THE EIGHTEENTH CENTURY

EXPLORATION OF THE SOUTH SEAS IN THE EIGHTEENTH CENTURY

Rediscovered Accounts

Edited by
Sandhya Patel

Volume I
Samuel Wallis's Voyage Round the World
in the *Dolphin* 1766–1768

LONDON AND NEW YORK

First published 2017
by Routledge
2 Park Square, Milton Park, Abingdon, Oxon OX14 4RN

and by Routledge
711 Third Avenue, New York, NY 10017

Routledge is an imprint of the Taylor & Francis Group, an informa business

Editorial material and selection © 2017 Sandhya Patel; individual owners retain copyright in their own material

All rights reserved. No part of this book may be reprinted or reproduced or utilised in any form or by any electronic, mechanical, or other means, now known or hereafter invented, including photocopying and recording, or in any information storage or retrieval system, without permission in writing from the publishers.

Trademark notice: Product or corporate names may be trademarks or registered trademarks, and are used only for identification and explanation without intent to infringe.

British Library Cataloguing in Publication Data
A catalogue record for this book is available from the British Library

Library of Congress Cataloging-in-Publication Data
A catalog record for this book has been requested

ISBN: 978-1-8489-3070-4 (Set)
ISBN: 978-1-138-68985-5 (Volume I)
eISBN: 978-1-315-53736-8 (Volume I)

Typeset in Times New Roman
by Apex CoVantage, LLC

Publisher's Note

References within each chapter are as they appear in the original complete work

CONTENTS

VOLUME I

List of Illustrations and Annexes	vii
Preface	xiii
Introduction	xv

Samuel Wallis's Voyage Round the World in the
Dolphin 1766–1768   1

VOLUME II

List of Illustrations	vii
Introduction	ix

Voyage Round the World Performed under the Direction of
Captain Etienne Marchand in the *Solide* of
Marseilles 1790–1792   1

ILLUSTRATIONS AND ANNEXES

1. *Whitsunday Island Discovered on Whitsunday Onboard his Majestys Ship Dolphin 1767. Lat:d 19:°26' S. Long:d 137:56 West from London. Variation 6:00 E* (Pilot)
   Courtesy of the State Library of New South Wales   xli
2. *Queen Charlotte's Island Discovered On board His Majestys Ship Dolphin on June the Ninth 1767. In Latitude 19:18 South. Long. 138.04 West from London, Variation 5:°40' Easterly* (Pilot)
   Courtesy of the State Library of New South Wales   xlii
3. *His Royal Highness Duke of Gloucesters island (Paraoa) discovered on the Twelfth day of June 1767 Onboard his Majestys ship Dolphin. Lat:d 19:121* S Long: 140:04 W from London Variation 6:00 Easterly* (Pilot)
   Courtesy of the State Library of New South Wales   xliii
4. *The Right Hon:ble the Earl of Egmonts (Vairaotea) Island discovered on the eleventh day of June 1767 Onboard his Majestys ship Dolphin in Latitude 19:°20' South Longitude 138:30 West from London; Variation 5:° 20' E* (Pilot)
   Courtesy of the State Library of New South Wales   xliv
5. *His Royal Highness the Bishop of Osnaburg's Island Discovered Onboard His Majestys Ship Dolphin on this 18th Day of June 1767 Latitude of [...] Longitude 147:30 West from London* (Pilot)
   Courtesy of the State Library of New South Wales   xlv
6. *His Most Sacred Majestys King George the Third Island with the Harbour of Port Royal which was discovered Onboard his Majestys Ship the Dolphin on the Nineteenth day of June 1767 Lying in the Latitude of 17:°29' South, Longitude 150:00 West from London by severall Observations variation of the compass 6:00 Easterly* (Pilot)
   Courtesy of the State Library of New South Wales   xlvi

ILLUSTRATIONS AND ANNEXES

7   *A Plan of Port Royal Harbour on the NE side of King Georges Island in Latitude 17:°29' South, Longitude from London 150:00 West, by Observation; Variation 6:00 Easterly* (Pilot)   xlvii
    Courtesy of the State Library of New South Wales
8   Untitled (Pilot)   xlvii
    Courtesy of the State Library of New South Wales
9   Untitled (Pilot)   xlviii
    Courtesy of the State Library of New South Wales
10 *His Royal Highness the Duke of York's Island Discovered the 25th of June 1767 Onboard his Majestys Ship Dolphin. In Latitude of 16:16* S. Variation 5:°40' East. Longitude West from London by Observation 150:°16 W* (Pilot)   l
    Courtesy of the State Library of New South Wales
11 *Sir Charles Saunders Island Discovered Onboard his Majesty's Ship Dolphin on the 28th Day of July 1767. In the latitude of 17:28* South. Longitude 151:04 West from London by Observation Variation of the Compass 6:08 Easterly* (Pilot)   li
    Courtesy of the State Library of New South Wales
12 *The Right Honb:le Lord Howes Island discovered Onboard his Majestys Ship Dolphin on the 30th July 1767 in the Latitude of 16:46* South. Variation 7:52 Easterly. Longitude from London by Observation 154:13 Westerly* (Pilot)   li
    Courtesy of the State Library of New South Wales
13 *Scilly Islands Discovered Onboard his Majestys Ship Dolphin on the 31:st July 1767 Lying in the Latitude of 16:28* S:° Long:d 155:30 W from London. Variation 7:20 Easterly* (Pilot Book)   lii
    Courtesy of the State Library of New South Wales
14 *The Honble Augustus Keppel's Island Discovered Onboard His Majestys Ship Dolphin on the 13:th day of August 1767 In Latitude 15:54* S Longitude from London by Observation 177:00 Westerly. Variation 11:36 Easterly* (Pilot)   lii
    Courtesy of the State Library of New South Wales
15 *Boscawen's Island Discovered onboard His Majestys Ship Dolphin on the August 13:th 1767. Lying in the Latitude of 15:50* South. Variation 11:44 E. Longitude of 175:09 West from London* (Pilot)   liii
    Courtesy of the State Library of New South Wales
16 *Wallis Islands Discovered on the 17 Day of August 1767 Onboard His Majestys Ship Dolphin, it lying in the Latitude of 13:18* South & Longitude Observed 177:00 West from London Variation of the Compass 10:00 E* (Pilot)   liii
    Courtesy of the State Library of New South Wales

ILLUSTRATIONS AND ANNEXES

Annex A

A1 Illustration on the back cover of Volume II of Wallis's log:
A ground plan & elevation of the Queens House at King Georges Island in the South Seas in July 1767. This House is 327 feet long, forty two feet wide, thirty feet high in the middle, and twelve feet at the ends and sides. It stands upon thirty nine posts on each side and fourteen support the middle. It hath a bamboo railing two feet high between the side posts and another comes down from the thatch of three or four feet more so there is about six feet clear lvi
Courtesy of the State Library of New South Wales

Annex B

B1 First page of the Sketchbook showing the *Dolphin* surrounded by ships and in sight of land lvii
Courtesy of the State Library of New South Wales

Annex C

C1 Second page of the Sketchbook showing the *Dolphin* most probably in company with the *Swallow* lviii
Courtesy of the State Library of New South Wales

Annex D

D1 Third page of the Sketchbook showing the *Dolphin* from two perspectives lix
Courtesy of the State Library of New South Wales

Annex E

E1 Last page of the Sketchbook showing the boat rowing back to the ship lx
Courtesy of the State Library of New South Wales

ILLUSTRATIONS AND ANNEXES

Annex F

F1 This drawing is labelled: *A Ground Plan; and Perspective View of the Queens House, at King Georges Island, Lying in Lat:^{d} 17:30 S and Longitude of 150:00 West from London. This House is 327 feet Long and forty two feet Broad it is supported in the Middle by fourteen Pillars and Thirty Nine at the Sides, is thirty feet high in the Middle and Twelve feet high at the Sides. Discovered by his Majestys Ship Dolphin on the 24. of June 1767. Done by Sam: Wallis. 1767* (Series 2)   lxi
Courtesy of the State Library of New South Wales

Annex G

G1 Drawing of Wallis Island (Series 2)   lxii
Courtesy of the State Library of New South Wales

Annex H

H1 *Whitsunday Island*   lxiii
Courtesy of the National Library of Australia
H2 *Osnaburg Island*   lxiii
Courtesy of the National Library of Australia
H3 *Otaheiti or King Georges Island*   lxiv
Courtesy of the National Library of Australia
H4 *York Island*   lxiv
Courtesy of the National Library of Australia
H5 *Saunders Island*   lxv
Courtesy of the National Library of Australia
H6 *Howe Island*   lxv
Courtesy of the National Library of Australia
H7 *Keppel Island*   lxvi
Courtesy of the National Library of Australia
H8 *Wallis Island*   lxvi
Courtesy of the National Library of Australia
H9 Untitled drawing   lxvii
Courtesy of the National Library of Australia

Annex I

I1 This image is dated 26th June 1767 (Series 4) and is of St George's Island, though this is not specified on the back of drawing   lxviii
Courtesy of the National Library of Australia

ILLUSTRATIONS AND ANNEXES

Annex J

J1	*Whitsunday: Island*	lxix
	Courtesy of the British Library	
J2	*Queen: Charlotte's Island*	lxix
	Courtesy of the British Library	
J3	*Duke: of Gloucester's Island*	lxx
	Courtesy of the British Library	
J4	*Lord: of Egmont's Island*	lxx
	Courtesy of the British Library	
J5	*Bishop of Osnaburg's Island*	lxxi
	Courtesy of the British Library	
J6	*Sir Charles: Saunders's Island*	lxxi
	Courtesy of the British Library	
J7	*King: Georges Island*	lxxii
	Courtesy of the British Library	
J8	*A Survey of Port Royal King Georges Island In the South Seas*	lxxiii
	Courtesy of the British Library	
J9	*A View of Port Royal Bay at Georges Island* [drawing of the *Dolphin* at anchor in Port Royal with the Queen's house in the background]	lxxiv
	Courtesy of the British Library	
J10	*Duke of York's Island*	lxxiv
	Courtesy of the British Library	
J11	*Admiral: Boscawen's Island*	lxxv
	Courtesy of the British Library	
J12	*Admiral: Keppel's Island*	lxxv
	Courtesy of the British Library	
J13	*Captain Wallis's Island*	lxxvi
	Courtesy of the British Library	
J14	*Lord: Howes Island*	lxxvi
	Courtesy of the British Library	
J15	*Scilly Isles*	lxxvii
	Courtesy of the British Library	

Annex K

	Extracts from Captain Wallis's Journal (British Library RP 9327)	lxxviii
	Courtesy of the British Library	
17	Samuel Wallis by Henry Stubble	1
	Courtesy of the National Library of Australia	
18	The first page of the fair copy of the *Dolphin* logs	7

19	Wallis's calculations as they appear in the PL.	278

Annex L

L1	*A Table of the Latitudes Observ'd and Longitudes West from London both by Account & Observation of all the Places His Maj:^s Ship was at, or saw in late Voyage in the Years 1766, 1767 & 1768* Reproduced in Hawkesworth	557

PREFACE

Captain Cook bestrides the history of Europe's exploration of the Pacific like a colossus. His achievements were extraordinary, well known and certainly far too many to list here. His three great voyages began an intense maritime examination of this dauntingly large ocean, often carried out by officers that he had trained in his methods, and by the officers that they in turn trained: officers such as William Bligh, who trained Matthew Flinders, or George Vancouver, surveyor of the north-west American coastline, who trained William Broughton, who went on to explore the Sea of Japan. Cook's Pacific researches inspired the state-sponsored voyages of other countries, commanded by those such as Lapérouse of France and Malaspina of Spain. Such was the dominance of Cook, however, that the achievements of those who followed him could be seen as little more than footnotes to history. However, since the closing decades of the last century scholarship has been bringing those voyages to the fore once more and producing a steady flow of critical editions of journals and published voyage narratives, and this resurgence has introduced a far more sophisticated understanding of the voyages, their aims and the encounters between explorers, islanders and first peoples.

The same reappraisal has also increased knowledge of those European voyages that took place before Cook, bringing greater insights into the ways in which mariners such as Anson, Byron, Wallis, Carteret, Surville, de Fresne and Bougainville played their parts in shaping Europe's understanding of the Pacific. Two defining moments in the history of Pacific exploration were the "discovery" of Tahiti by Samuel Wallis in 1767, and the arrival of Louis-Antoine de Bougainville shortly after Wallis had returned to England. Although Cook's name has been inextricably linked to the discovery of Tahiti, his formative encounters there can only be understood properly by examining those before him. This has not been unproblematic, for Wallis's journal has never been published in full, although a heavily edited and shortened version was published in John Hawkesworth's compilation of Byron, Wallis, Carteret and Cook's expeditions, *An Account of Voyages Undertaken . . . in 1772*. Descriptions of the first meetings between Europe and Tahiti have up to now had to rely on the journal of Wallis's sailing master, George Robertson.

As we approach the 250th anniversary in 2017 of the arrival of Wallis in Tahiti, Sandhya Patel's excellent and informative critical edition of Samuel Wallis's journal rights this historical wrong and makes an important contribution to research on the early European voyages. It provides a thoughtful reappraisal of Wallis, his voyage and his achievements. Her introduction carefully unpicks the tangled web of British motives for and expectations of his voyage, while the charts and sketches produced by Wallis and Midshipman George Pinnock make interesting comparisons with the surveys and drawings of Cook's voyage. Patel's edition makes a fascinating and revealing study of an important but neglected voyage.

Nigel Rigby
National Maritime Museum

INTRODUCTION*

1. The People

Publication of key voyaging manuscripts has contributed to the burgeoning of worldwide scholarship in various fields in a recognised, long-term manner. Many of what may be called the primary sources in this field have already been made available. Most new publications today are versions of former editions which have limited or non-existent accessibility. Samuel Wallis though was the first Englishman to come across what are today known as the Society Islands in the South Pacific, specifically Tahiti, but his ship's logs and the related iconography have never been published. These records may however be understood as key sources. They attest to the very first encounter between Europeans and Tahitians, but the *Dolphin* papers also undoubtedly posted markers for ensuing texts, namely Cook's, as he voyaged with the documents in the *Endeavour*. The Polynesian archipelagos subsequently grew into objects of textual and iconographical discourse over the years and the Wallis papers may very well be located at the heart of these evocative constructs.[1]

Samuel Wallis was born in April 1728 at Fentonwoon in Cornwall and died in 1795 in London. He was a mariner all his life, principally in the Royal Navy. At 20, he was promoted to Lieutenant, serving on HMS *Anson*, HMS *Gibraltar* and then HMS *Torbay*, the flagship of Rear Admiral Boscawen's fleet engaged in an expedition against the French in 1756. That same year, he was given command of the sloop *Swan*.[2] He was actively involved in the manoeuvres in North

---

* Full bibliographical details are given in the footnotes (rather than in a final list) throughout this volume in order to further simplify the reading of the log, which may be complex as it is because of the unusual tabular format. I chose not to include an index as referencing proved difficult due to the note-like stylistics of the log.
1 The reaction in Britain and in Europe as a whole to the discovery of the South Sea islands, specifically Tahiti, "discovered" by Captain Samuel Wallis, has been amply documented and analysed over the years by eminent scholars such as Bernard Smith, Greg Dening, Anne Salmond, Nicholas Thomas, Glyndwr Williams, Vanessa Smith to name but a few.
2 He had under him a certain John Rickman who was to sail with Captain Cook many years later on the latter's third voyage round the world.

INTRODUCTION

America, and in 1757 he captained HMS *Port Mahon*, sailing as part of Admiral Holbourne's fleet to Halifax. Captain of the *Prince of Orange* from 1758 to 1763 in Canada, he sailed under the command of Vice-Admiral Charles Saunders. There is little information as to his doings between 1763 and 1766 but his experience in the Royal Navy until this latter date was one of active service involving combat and conflict in often difficult conditions.[3]

Between 1766 and 1768 Wallis undertook a two-ship exploratory expedition round the world in HMS *Dolphin* in company with the *Swallow*.[4] This voyage's objectives were completely at odds with the more military purposes of his past engagements in the Americas. During this expedition Wallis's immediate naval history was nevertheless omnipresent as some of the islands he discovered in the South Seas were named by him after the various commanding officers (Keppel, Boscawen, Saunders) of the fleets he had been closely associated with. Why Wallis decided to take up an exploratory mission after an eventful, active career in the Royal Navy, and why he was chosen to do the job, is unclear. Hugh Carrington[5] considers that perhaps Boscawen's previous interest in Wallis and his authority as member of the Privy Council and Lord Commissioner of the Admiralty had been useful in the appointment. The fact that Boscawen was from Cornwall, like Wallis himself, may most certainly have weighed in the balance for his former appointments,[6] but not necessarily as regards this particular one as Edward Boscawen died in 1761 and his posthumous influence may have played little or no part in the choice of Wallis for the voyage. Glyndwr Williams points to the fact that thanks to Wallis's previous "meritorious" service, Sir Charles Saunders, Second Lord at the time (and very briefly First Lord of the Admiralty in 1766) suggested that he be the man to lead the expedition. There is however little documentary evidence as to the reasoning behind the choice of Wallis. Like Williams, Helen Wallis,[7] though further underlines the role which John Byron himself played in the undertaking as a whole, whilst acting as possible advisor to Lord Egmont, the then First Lord. This might explain the new Pacific bent, rather than the South Atlantic and Northwest Passage orientations of Byron's 1764–1766 circumnavigation which immediately preceded Wallis's

---

3 See Glyndwr Williams, "Wallis, Samuel (1728–1795)", *Oxford Dictionary of National Biography*, Oxford University Press, 2004, online edition, Jan 2008 [http://www.oxforddnb.com/view/article/28578, accessed 15 March 2016]. Also http://southseas.nla.gov.au/biogs/P000407b.htm. There is no published biography of Samuel Wallis.

4 See Hugh Carrington's detailed description of the *Dolphin* in *The Discovery of Tahiti. A Journal of the Second Voyage of the HMS Dolphin round the World By George Robertson 1766–1768*, Hakluyt Society, 1948, p. xxxii–xxxv.

5 *Ibid.*, p. xxxv.

6 Clive Wilkinson suggests that "The Boscawens were already an important and popular family in local politics, especially as the Admiral could provide places and career opportunities for local sons, creating what his wife termed 'a little navy of your own making'". Clive Wilkinson, "Boscawen, Edward (1711–1761)", *Oxford Dictionary of National Biography*, Oxford University Press, 2004, online edn., Jan 2008 [http://www.oxforddnb.com/view/article/2931, accessed 3 March 2016].

7 Helen Wallis, *Carteret's voyage round the world, 1766–1769*, Cambridge, Hakluyt Society, 1965.

voyage to the South Seas. Alexander Dalrymple may also have been a proponent in putting forward this latter perspective according to H. Wallis, who has discussed the aims behind the fitting-out of such an expedition in her exhaustive consideration of the Admiralty sources.[8] She makes it clear that there were political as well as scientific concerns in the pushing forward of such a project in spite of internal Cabinet opposition to the voyage, notably in terms of the competition between the French and the British for the Falklands chain. This though does not explain why Wallis was singled out as commander of the expedition and Captain of the *Dolphin* on her second voyage of exploration around the world, the first being that of Byron. Neither do we know why he decided on pursuing his career thus after having played a preponderant role in naval warfare. The end of the Seven Years War, and the fact that Wallis was, at 38 years old,[9] in poor health (documented by himself in the ships' logs, and in George Robertson's journal of the voyage – see transcription), perhaps making him unfit for continued service even in (relative) peacetime, may have been an important factor in the decision.

John Byron had thus captained the *Dolphin* on her first voyage of exploration round the world from 1764 to 1766. Byron had already had an eventful naval career[10] and as Commodore of the *Dolphin* and *Tamar* two-ship expedition, he was charged with a political mission to reconnoitre the Falklands and to sail in search of Pepys Island and of the Northwest Passage. Gallagher in his *Introduction* to Byron's journal sets out in detail the Admiralty "subterfuge" involved in keeping the geographically-strategic objectives secret but considers nevertheless that like the second *Dolphin* expedition led by Wallis, the first had as its principal objective "the advancement of trade – particularly in the Pacific – not discovery for the sake of adding to human knowledge [which] was behind not only this voyage in 1764, but also that of Wallis and Carteret in 1766."[11] Byron's instructions make it clear that *Lands and Islands of great extent hitherto unvisited by any European Power may be found in the Atlantick Ocean between the Cape of Good Hope and the Magellanick Streight.* He was to search for these lands and exhaustively survey the Falkland Islands. He was also to closely examine the western coast of *the Countrey of New Albion in North America first discovered and taken possession of by Sir Francis Drake in the Year 1579 [which] has never been examined with that care which it deserves, notwithstanding frequent recommendations of that Undertaking by the said Sir Francis Drake, Dampier, & many other Mariners of great experience, who*

---

8 *Ibid.*, p. 103.
9 Cook (date of birth 27th October 1728) was born the same year as Wallis.
10 See Robert E. Gallagher, *Byron's Journal of his Circumnavigation* (1764–1766), Cambridge, Hakluyt Society, 1964.
11 *Ibid.*, p. xxxi. See also pp. xxxii–xxxvi. Wallis conversely makes very little reference to the economic gain to be obtained by discovery. His principal concerns seem rather more pragmatic focusing on where and how ships can "recruit" on such long voyages round the world. Robertson on the other hand is interested in discussing the advantages of various sites as potential, perhaps prosperous colonies.

INTRODUCTION

have thought it probable that a passage might be found between the latitude of 38° and 54° from that Coast into Hudson's Bay.[12] Advances in the policy of exploration were complemented by technological innovation as the *Dolphin* was sheathed in copper in an attempt to prevent shipworm. Randolph Cock[13] dates such experiments as beginning in earnest in the mid-eighteenth century, though wooden, lead and brass lining of ships' bottoms had been under way, unsuccessfully and sporadically, for hundreds of years. After several quite successful trials at the beginning of the 1760s, the *Dolphin* and *Tamar* were reinforced with copper bottoms in an attempt to modernise maritime exploratory initiatives.[14] Byron on this first voyage of exploration did not manage to find the mythical Pepys Island. Neither did he proceed along Californian shores to the northwest coast of America. This was however because he chose not to pursue these objectives. Gallagher notes that the reasons for ignoring orders, given in a letter to Lord Egmont on the 22nd of June 1765, are "unsatisfactory." He argues that the "driving" reason for instead continuing across the Pacific ("discovering" several atolls previously sighted) was a desire to fall in with the mythical Soloman Islands.[15]

Thus, this first *Dolphin* voyage has been understood as a failure in terms of the objectives assigned to it. Byron's journal remained unpublished, except in the truncated form which appeared in John Hawkesworth's *Voyages*[16] in 1773. Cock[17] though considers that "credit" must be given to this *Dolphin* voyage and the ensuing one as they were "precursors" to the infinitely successful Cook voyages. He pinpoints the "consensus" of historians of exploration of the Pacific which has led to an elision of the results of the expeditions which, if not in keeping with official expectations, were nevertheless considerable: *Notwithstanding the virtual unanimity of the condemnation of Byron and Wallis, it does not square with either the evidence of their achievements, or with the opinion of their contemporaries.* Cock's analysis singles out for example the innovative dimension of Byron's rapid circumnavigation and the discovery of six islands.[18]

---

12 *Ibid.*, p. 9.
13 Randolph Cock, 'The Finest Invention in the World': The Royal Navy's Early Trials of Copper Sheathing, 1708–1770", *The Mariner's Mirror*, 87:4, November 2001, pp. 446–459.
14 Four years later and after one intermediate report, on Wallis' return from his circumnavigation, the Admiralty was convinced of the efficacy of the process. See Cock, *Ibid.*, pp. 454–456.
15 *Ibid.*, pp. l–lvii.
16 *An Account Of The Voyages Undertaken By The Order Of His Present Majesty For Making Discoveries In The Southern Hemisphere, And Successively Performed By Commodore Byron, Captain Carteret, Captain Wallis, And Captain Cook, In The Dolphin, The Swallow, And The Endeavour: Drawn Up From The Journals Which Were Kept By The Several Commanders, And From The Papers Of Joseph Banks, Esq.; By John Hawkesworth, Ll.D*, 1773.
17 See Randolph Cock, "Precursors of Cook: The Voyages of the Dolphin 1764–1768", *The Mariner's Mirror*, 85:1, February 1999, pp. 30–52.
18 Cock (1999), *op. cit.*, p. 3. Gallagher underlines here that two of these discoveries were already known (p. lii).

INTRODUCTION

The *Dolphin* set off for a second circumnavigation immediately after Byron's return in May 1766. Cock, like H. Wallis, suggests that the reasons behind this precipitate, second ostensibly exploratory expedition, were on the whole strategic, the British fearing French expansion and appropriation of the southern continent in the Pacific.[19] The second voyage was also to be a two-ship expedition (the *Dolphin* and the *Swallow* captained by Carteret who had only just returned home having sailed with Byron as Lieutenant of the *Dolphin*). Wallis's instructions[20] were as follows:

To
Cap.n Wallis, Commander   Egmont
of his Majesty's Ship Dolphin   Cha.s Saunders
                                    C. Townshend

Whereas nothing can redound to the honour of this Nation as a Maritime Power, to the dignity of the Crown of Great Britain, and to the advancement of the Trade and Navigation thereof, than to make Discoveries of Countries hitherto unknown; And whereas there is reason to believe that Land or Islands of Great extent hitherto unvisited by any European Power may be found in the Southern Hemisphere between Cape Horn and New Zeeland, in Latitudes convenient for Navigation, and in Climates adapted to the produce of Commodities useful in Commerce; and whereas His Majesty taking the same into His Royal Consideration, and conceiving no conjuncture so proper for Enterprises of this nature as a time of profound Peace, hath signified unto us (by the Earl of Egmont) His Pleasure that an attempt should forthwith be made to discover & obtain a complete knowledge of the Land or Islands supposed to be situated in the Southern Hemisphere as before-mentioned. We have in consequence thereof, caused the Swallow Sloop to be fitted victualled and stored in all respects proper for such an Undertaking, and, confiding in your Skill and Prudence have thought fit to entrust you with the Conduct thereof. –

You are therefore hereby required and directed to proceed to the Isle of Madeira with the said Ship and Sloop (and the Prince Frederick Victualling Storeship – whose Commander is directed to obey your Orders and there take on board without loss of time such Quantities of Wine as may be necessary for their respective Companies, and such Refreshments as you shall be able to procure for them.

You are then to put to Sea and proceed to St. Iago one of the Cape de Verde islands for farther Refreshments, if necessary, and from there to some convenient Port to complete your Wood & Water and take such Supplies of Provisions out of the Victualling Storeship as the Dolphin and Swallow can conveniently stow.

Having so done you are to direct Lieu.t Brine, who has the Command of the Victualling Storeship, to proceed with her to Port Egmont on the North Side of

---

19 Cock (1999), *op. cit.*, p. 5. Again Wallis is not very forthcoming as regards the political implications of his voyage and attending discoveries.
20 Adm. 2/1322, National Archives, London, UK.

INTRODUCTION

Falklands Isles, and follow such Orders as he shall receive from Cap.ⁿ Macbride of the Jason, or the Commanding Officer of his Majesty's Ships there, for his farther proceedings.

You are then to proceed with the Dolphin and Swallow round Cape Horn, or through the Streights of Magellan, as you shall find most convenient, and stretch to the Westward about One Hundred and Twenty Degrees of Longitude from Cape Horn, losing as little Southing as possible, in search of the Land or Islands supposed to be in that part of the Southern Hemisphere which is beforementioned, unless you shall discover such Land or Islands in a shorter Run, or shall have been father to the Northward than you might reasonably have expected; in the former of which Cases you are carefully and diligently to investigate and explore the Lands or Islands that you have discovered so long as your Provisions and Water will admit of it, reserving a sufficient quantity to bring you round Cape Horn to Port Egmont, or to carry you to some European Settlement in the East Indies; And in the latter Case, viz. that of being driven farther to the Northward than you might reasonably have expected, if from the State of your Provisions you find that you have a sufficient Quantity left to enable you to proceed to Port Egmont, or the Coast of Brazil, you are to return to England round Cape Horn standing as much to the Southward as you can in your way to the Cape, being the most probable method of discovering the Continent or Land before mentioned, if there be any, & you should have missed it by your having been driven too far to the Northward in your former Tract.

You are to get the best information you can of the Genius, Temper and Inclinations of the Inhabitants of such Land or Islands as you may discover that have not been visited by any European Power, and to endeavour by all proper means to cultivate a Friendship and alliance with them, making them Presents of such things as may be acceptable to them (we having caused the sum of Five Hundred Pounds to be advanced to you to provide yourself with proper Quantities and Assortments for that purpose) inviting them to Trade, and shewing them every kind of Civility and Regard; taking care however if they are numerous not to be surprised by them, but to be always upon your guard against any Accidents. You are moreover to endeavour to make Purchases and with the consent of the Inhabitants – take Possession of convenient Situations – in the Country in the name of the King of Great Britain; But if no Inhabitants are found on the Land or Islands discovered, you are, in such Case, to take possession of such Lands or Islands for His Majesty by setting up proper Marks & Inscriptions as first Discoverers and Possessors.

You are carefully to observe the Latitude & Longitude in which such Land or Islands as you may discover are situated, and to observe the height, direction & course of the Tydes & Currents, the Depth & soundings of the Sea, the Shoals & Rocks, the Bearings of Head Lands, variation of the Needle, and the Trade Winds, or Winds that generally prevail in different seasons and you are to survey and make Charts & Plans of the Coasts, Harbours, Bays, Inlets &ᶜᵉ. of all such Land or Islands as you shall discover, taking care not to omit any thing that may be useful to Navigation.

INTRODUCTION

You are also to observe the nature of the Soil, and the various kinds of Trees, Fruits, Grains &^{cc}. that it produceth, the Beasts & Fowls that inhabit or frequent such Land or Islands and the Fishes that are to be found in the Rivers, Harbours, or on the Coasts thereof, and in what quantities, that you may be enabled upon your return to give us full information of the same: And in case you find any Mines, Minerals or valuable Stones, you are to bring home with you specimens of each and transmit them to our Secretary in order that we may cause them to be properly examined.

But if contrary to expectation you shall not have discovered the Land or Islands supposed to lye in the Southern Hemisphere as before mentioned, in stretching to the Westward as above directed, You are then either to return to England round Cape Horn, or to stand to the North West until you get into the Latitude of 20° South in search of Land or Islands that have not hitherto been discovered, and upon your arrival in the Latitude if you find the condition of the Ship and the Sloop, and the State of their Provisions & Health of their Men will admit of your proceeding any farther upon Discoveries of the like nature, You are at liberty to do so, taking care to reserve a sufficient Quantity of Provisions to enable you to proceed to China or some of the European Settlements in the East Indies, which you are in that case to do, in order to give your Men such Refreshment as they may stand in need of, and to put the Ship & Sloop into condition to return to England. And having so done, you are without loss of time to return to England round the Cape of Good Hope, and transmit to our Secretary for our information an Account of your arrival & proceedings.

But for as much as in an Undertaking of this import and nature several Emergencies may arive and to be foreseen and therefore not to be provided for by Instructions beforehand, You are in all such cases to proceed in such a manner as you shall judge most likely to attain the Object thereof.

And in case of your in ability to carry the foregoing Instructions into execution by any accident whatsoever, you are to be careful to leave them with the next Officer in Seniority to yourself, who is hereby authorized and required to execute them in the best manner he can. Given – the 16th of August 1766.

The previous objectives, those of Byron, had been reworked, and the Pacific had become now the focus of a national exploratory enterprise. This change in perspective was of course ultimately successful as in the wake of Byron and Wallis, James Cook was in the ensuing decade to appropriate the principal Pacific land masses (Australia and New Zealand) and archipelagoes.

The *Dolphin*[21] and the *Swallow* sailed from Plymouth on the 21st August, 1766, refreshing at Madeira and St Jago and crossing the Atlantic. After four months of weaving their way through the Magellan Straits, the ships separated and the

---

21 For a detailed review of the *Dolphin's* crew taken from the muster role (ADM 36/7580) see http://www.captaincooksociety.com/home/detail/muster-records-for-the-royal-navy-ships-of-james-cook-1763–1780.

Dolphin continued on alone into the South Seas into largely uncharted waters. This separation was most probably due to the fact that the ships were unequally matched. Helen Wallis has shown that Carteret was very aware of the poor state of his vessel, he was "appalled" even at how unfit she was for such an expedition, though how far they were going to go remained secret until well after the two ships had sailed. His doubts were entirely justified. The *Dolphin* was better equipped and provisioned, and sailed faster.[22] The careful record in the logs,[23] noting when the *Swallow* was in company or not, is evidence of how she lagged behind. In the summary of the voyage in the opening page of the rough log, Wallis (presumably) describes the separation:

> On Wednesday December the 17th at 8 PM anchored under Cape Virgin Mary at the entrance of the Straights of Magellan the 18th PM entered the Straights the 27th: Anchord at Port Famine January 18th 1767, sailed from Port Famine in company with the Swallow, the Prince Frederick storeship sailed from thence the 17:th for Port Egmont Sunday April 12 at 1 PM got round the islands of Direction and entered the South Sea. We lost sight of the Swallow about two hours before this under Cape Pillar; & the weather looking very greasy & blowing very fresh from the SW and WSW was obliged to carry all the sail we could to get of the shore.

Previously, on the 11th of August, even before taking to the high seas, Wallis loses *sight of the Swallow* for the first time on the 13th. On the 26th and 27th, the *Dolphin* waits for the Swallow to catch up, the logs note that they . . . *carry very little sail as the Swallow can scarce keep company.* The next day the *Dolphin* shortens sail and in the days to come, constantly adjusts her speed in order to stay in company. On September 22nd, the *Dolphin* and the *Swallow* are no longer in view of one another. On November 17th and 18th, Wallis's mounting impatience is apparent in the terse: *Light airs & fair saw two sails in the NW steering to the NE, bore down to the Swallow & the storeship I ordered them to keep near us and . . . we being to windward bore down to the Swallow & store ship & told them to keep near us.* During the passage through the Straits, there is an almost daily record of the *Swallow's* progress and the final entry in the rough log, Wallis describes the separation thus:

> Cape Pillar SW half a mile, the Swallow about six miles a stern – Little wind was obliged to make all the sail I could to get without the Streights mouth as I found the current set the ship over to the North shore – At 10 would have shortened sail for the Swallow but was obliged to carry to

---

22 See H. Wallis, *op. cit.*, p. 3.
23 See the *Papers* section in this introduction for a detailed description of the logs.

INTRODUCTION

weather the Islands of Direction & we could not fetch into the Streights again this was the opinion of myself & the officers.

Captain Carteret and the *Swallow* are practically never mentioned again. The *Swallow* was slow and difficult to handle and in the Straits she was ominously close to being wrecked several times. Whether this was entirely due to her unwieldiness remains questionable. When Wallis writes of ordering the *Swallow* to remain in sight, both Gore[24] and Molineux[25] in their journals point out that she did not take "notice" of the signal and that it had to be repeated three times.[26]

After the forced separation, Wallis continued his route and there followed a chain of discoveries from the 6th June, 1767 onwards, culminating in the sighting of Tahiti on the 19th June, 1767, the ship making sail WSW *toward land we discovered*. On the 28th July, Wallis left Tahiti and the exploration of the South Seas was resumed. The discovery of King George's Island was to prove particularly useful as future expeditions into the South Pacific, notably Cook's, would take on wood and water there so avoiding disease and death and allowing further investigation with renewed vigour. Wallis went on to discover six more islands and atolls. His decision not to double back and return on a different track to Cape Horn or the Straits (as his instructions allowed him to do) is clearly set out and justified by the state of the ship:

> The boat being returned with the before mentioned account, the ship leaking & the rudder shaking the stern much, and not knowing what damage she may have received in her bottom and it being the depth of winter, and must expect very bad weather to go round Cape Horn, or to gain the Streights of Magellan, and if her leak should prove worse (which it had hitherto done when it blows hard) we should have no where to push to and if we should luckily get well round the Cape yet we must refresh somewhere and in all probability we shall sooner be home by way of the Cape of Good Hope, as we may recruit at Tinian & Batavia, whereas our watering here would take up a considerable time and much fateague. Therefore having considered all these things and many more and having so good an account of the refreshments that may be had for any future expedition that may be made to this part of the world, I thought it most prudent and more for the benefit of his Majestys service to make the best of my way to Tinian, Batavia & to Europe and if we found the ship not in a condition to proceed we had in a manner a certainty of saving our selves & perhaps of getting refitted as from hence to Batavia is a calm sea.

---

24 John Gore, Master's mate on the *Dolphin*, sailed with Cook on the *Endeavour* voyage on his return.
25 Robert Mollyneaux or Molineux (spelt thus in his log), AB, also went on to sail with Cook.
26 See the entry for December 16th, 1766 in the transcription.

INTRODUCTION

The ship reached Tinian on September 19th, 1767, a little over three weeks after leaving Tahiti. After almost a month at Tinian, the ship sailed for Batavia and anchored in the Road on the 1st December, 1767. After a week of taking onboard refreshments, Wallis continued through to Princes Island where he anchored on the 16th December, 1767. On the 21st, the sick list is long and Wallis notes that:

> When we sailed from Princess Island we had a larger sick list than we have had for many months – there being sixteen on it – yet five of them were accidents and many hath been in a low week way for near twelve months – by the the 1:t of January our sickness increased to that degree being fevers & fluxes we had no less than forty men down and had buryed three, those that were down in a very low weak condition and quite disponding as the ship hath been so very healthy during the voyage.

The ship itself is again described as taking in water and Wallis attributes this to the wet weather.[27] The actual cleanliness on board is emphasised as are the precautions taken to avoid sickness including isolating those who are ill and disinfecting the water with a red-hot iron. The *Dolphin* anchors at the Cape on February 6th, 1768, the crew is still in poor health and Wallis himself is so weak that he leaves the ship on arrival and comes back onboard on the 27th February: *I being very ill was put onshoar and carried up the country about eight miles where I continued all the time we lay there and went of rather worse than I came onshoar*. The ship sojourns at the Cape for a month until the 5th of March. The run home to England was relatively straightforward and Wallis even indulges in a little policing (in keeping with his past naval experience) as on approaching the Scilly Islands:

> at ½ past saw a ship in chace of a sloop & fired severall guns at her, we bore away & at 3 fired a shott at the the chace & br:t her to. The ship to windward being near to the chace sent her boat onboard & soon after came on board Capt: Hammond of his Majestys sloop Savage & told me that the vessel was in company with an Irish wherry but on his coming near them they on discovering him to be a man of war, took different ways, the wherry hauld the wind & this bore away, he heuld the wind but found that he could not gain ground bore away, and luckily I came in the way & stopt her as he found he scarce gained any of her. She was laden with tea brandy and other goods from Bascoe in France a bound to Bergen in Norway if a SW course would carry him there. She belongs

---

27 Wallis had previously discovered a large tear under the copper sheathing during the stopover at Tinian (as a result of running aground on the Tahitian reef) and this was thought to be the explanation for the ship making so much water. Due to inadequate repairs the *Dolphin* continued to be subject to leaks for the whole of the duration of the voyage home.

to Liverpool, called the Jenny, Robert Christian Master. She having the before named goods on board in small bags, detained her to send to England – Fresh gales – both ships in company.

Wallis goes on shore at Hastings on the 20th May, 1768 and sets out for London with all the logs and journals in hand.

This voyage was then a two-year navigation, like the Byron expedition, and as mentioned above, Cock (1999) has shown that this expedition, like Byron's, has been overlooked in terms of its contribution to British exploration of the South Seas:

> ...the editor of his master's journal pronouncing that 'Wallis had not shown great regard for his instructions nor conspicuous initiative; and the results of the voyage must have disappointed its promoters', whilst Wallis suffered from 'a deficiency in enterprise and intellectual curiosity'. Basil Greenhill asserted that 'Captain Samuel Wallis returned to England in 1768, the latest of the long series of unsuccessful explorers of the South Pacific', Glyndwr Williams considered Wallis's voyage 'as unenterprising as Byron's', and Beaglehole conceded only that 'though a good commander was not a gifted explorer.'[28]

Suggesting that Wallis's voyage was significant in geographical terms, as regards the documentary sources resulting from the voyage which Cook was to make immediate use of during the *Endeavour* voyage, in terms of technical, nautical innovation but also of the health record, Cock argues for a reconsideration of the status of both *Dolphin* crossings.[29] He affirms that *historians have been guilty of viewing the voyages of 1764–68 with hindsight, and, consciously or not, belittling the progress made by Cook's predecessors, and therefore exaggerating the extent of his own.*[30] Publishing the *Dolphin* papers may then be a means of allotting the voyage its proper place within the British annals of the history of exploration.

2. The Papers

The *Dolphin* voyages commanded by Byron and then by Wallis were perhaps thus neglected because there was no direct publication of the journals immediately

---

28 Cock (1999), *op. cit.*, p. 30.
29 *Ibid.*
30 *Ibid.*, p. 1. In reference works such as the *Oxford Encyclopedia of Maritime History*, for example, Wallis is mentioned in implicitly negative terms: "Wallis's route across the Pacific Ocean brought him to Tahiti. Significant as this find would prove for subsequent maritime exploration and for the career of Captain James Cook, Wallis returned to England believing that he had made an infinitely greater one. In the days before reaching and after leaving Tahiti, he and his crew thought that they saw the cloud-hung fringe of Terra Australis, but because of the danger of exploring an unknown

after the voyage, particularly as the reports of Wallis's circumnavigation were not narrative accounts as such. In terms of the textual record, the papers (in libraries and museums all over the world) comprise two complete logbooks (all the entries seem to be in the same handwriting), one fair copy and one partial record also described as being a logbook.

The main body of this transcription is of what may be considered as the "rough" log as it is the immediate though abbreviated record of the voyage, where notes instead of narration take precedence. It is perhaps the *in situ* source par excellence as far as the connotative values of the seas, voyages and encounters are concerned. It is possibly the "pristine" document in the "archetypal form."[31] This source (ML) is held by the the State Library of New South Wales.[32] This log is signed by Samuel Wallis.

The second log book, also signed by Wallis, is held at the National Archives in London (PL).[33] This copy seems to be a neater, better-executed version of the ML and all the differences between the two are noted in the footnotes to the transcription.

The third log is a fair copy[34] in copperplate script. It contains some entries and annotations in free hand, most probably Wallis's, which perhaps indicate that he supervised the copying of the logbooks or possibly even made the duplicate himself.[35] The signed fair copy differs from the logs in that the formatting is different (two days per vertical page instead of three in the logs) and records fewer wind directions. When this copy was made is difficult to assess but it may very well have been before the logbooks were handed to the Admiralty as the coordinates and distance travelled every day are practically identical to those recorded in the two logs.

The fourth log (BL – held by the British Library) is a partial record signed by Wallis, almost identical in content to the other logs. The formatting here differs, there is no hourly record but rather a day-to-day account and the vertical columns

---

shore with only one ship, he decided that 'it was too hazardous . . . to coast the Continent' (which they had then actually in view). And afterwards [they] thought [it] most prudent on their Return, not to take Notice that they had Ever seen it at all". Where this quote comes from is unclear in the entry, but it is not to be found in the *Dolphin* logs transcribed here and signed by Samuel Wallis.

31 Percy Guy Adams, *Travel Literature and the Evolution of the Novel*, Lexington, University Press of Kentucky, 1983), p. 64.

32 State Library of New South Wales, Sydney, Australia, Ms Safe 1/98. High quality online images of all the pages of the log have been made available by the Mitchell Library very recently. This log is referred to as the ML in this introduction and in the transcription. The National Maritime Museum also holds photocopies of the ML (MRF/9 and PGR/9).

33 National Archives, London, England, Adm 55/35. This log is referred to as the PL in this introduction and in the transcription.

34 Alexander Turnbull Library, Wellington, New Zealand, qMS-2114. High quality online images of all the pages of the log have been made available by the Library very recently. This log is referred to as the FC in this introduction and in the transcription.

35 The logs books are subtly different and show the complex processes involved in representing voyage identities and politics.

are headed Year, Month & Day, Winds, Course, Distance, Latitude, Longitude, Variation and Thermometer.[36] This log is in the same handwriting as the others which is very regular with practically no crossing-out (which indicates perhaps that it was copied for the *Prince Fredrick* to take back to England). Why the format differs from the others in this partial log, and why the daily note of the temperature appears in only this account, is uncertain. These pages are pasted into a large book and are followed by George Pinnock's (Midshipman) charts and drawings of the islands discovered in the South Seas (see next section on *The Pictures*).[37]

The editing and publication of the shipboard journals (very rarely logs) of exploration were mandated by the Admiralty, even if unauthorised sometimes anonymous accounts regularly appeared in print. One of several reasons for this drive toward publication in the latter part of the eighteenth century was that it represented a means of establishing and validating imperial claims in the eyes of foreign competitors. Other more prosaic but prime, material considerations consisted in tapping into the enthusiasm of the educated public who made up the majority of the buyers of such publications considering the popularity of travel literature at the time. Why the *Dolphin* account, even reworked by Wallis, went unpublished for so long is difficult to explain (as is the case with the iconography of the voyage). Was it perhaps considered as minor compared to the wealth of information and more practised images brought back by Cook so soon afterwards? The only official relation of Wallis's voyage was the one contained in Hawkesworth's *Voyages* or in full: *An Account Of The Voyages Undertaken By The Order Of His Present Majesty For Making Discoveries In The Southern Hemisphere, And Successively Performed By Commodore Byron, Captain Carteret, Captain Wallis, And Captain Cook, In The Dolphin, The Swallow, And The Endeavour: Drawn Up From The Journals Which Were Kept By The Several Commanders, And From The Papers Of Joseph Banks, Esq.; By John Hawkesworth, Ll.D. In Three Volumes*, first published in 1773, which was five years after Wallis's return home (and two years after Cook's *Endeavour* voyage). Volume 1 reproduces abridged and amended accounts of the Byron, Wallis and Carteret voyages. Volumes 2 and 3 are the reports of the *Endeavour* voyage.

For publication, as far as the *Dolphin* texts were concerned, various narrative strategies to rework the form and contents of the logs were used by Hawkesworth,[38]

---

36 Whereas the other logs contain as headers: Hour (H), Knots (K), Fathom (F), Course and Wind.
37 This log (which runs from 21st August, 1766 to 14th January, 1767) and the charts are held at the British Library, London, AD MS 15499. The log, signed by Samuel Wallis, was most probably sent back to England on the Prince Frederick store ship. This source will be referred to as the BL. The drawings though were most probably made onboard ship by George Pinnock. The British Library (RP 9327) also holds a copy (the originals are in a private collection) of extracts from the *Dolphin* logs in a "secretarial hand." The catalogue dates the copy to 1780. See Annex K for a transcription of these extracts.
38 Occasionally, some of the pages of the PL are annotated in pencil and these notes are described in the catalogue as being those of Hawkesworth.

notably an intermediary first person narrator.[39] This narratological appropriation of the Captain's voice was destined to afford more "entertainment" to the reading public.[40] As an unfortunate result, a process of fictionalisation of the voyage (and of the South Seas) could be said to have come into effect based on the editor's and the reading public's exigencies, and thanks to the nature of the discoveries made in this Ocean. As Batten[41] argues in his influential work on travel writing, literary convention acting on the navigators' facts (as recorded in the logs) did not alert the readers to the derived untruthfulness of the published narrative, but rather made what they understood as instruction, pleasing. This fictionalising tendency is fully apparent in the adaptation of the *Dolphin* papers by Hawkesworth in spite of the fact that in the *Introduction* to the compilation, Hawkesworth in his own words describes the sources used to draw up the account as "authentic" (which was indeed true), insisting on the "fidelity" with which he relates the events. He argues that the various commanders authorised his representation of the "facts" in question. Furthermore, he purports to correct past mistakes and establish truths – to scientise the account as it were. The ensuing discussion in his *Introduction* is centred on considering the correct chronology of the relations, on the usefulness of including sentiment, comment, hypotheses, the disadvantage of a summary or digest, and a dissertation on whether to use the first or the third person. In terms of the final content, the fact that Hawkesworth uses several manuscripts, notably Robertson's, to publish a compilation is perhaps instrumental in the mythopoetical process. By combining two or more perceptions with the added contribution of hindsight, as Hawkesworth was writing up Cook's journals and deconstructing Wallis's manuscripts at the same time, the legitimacy of Hawkesworth's relations of the *Dolphin* voyage is of course open to question. The textual embroidering produces what may be argued as an impression of the voyage – a fiction made up of a series of nonfictional accounts because the views of Wallis and Robertson may have converged, however, to cite Johnson on the subject of multiple points of view, they (views) may also have been irreconcilably contrary.

The writing up of journals once back home or on long stretches of the voyages, as with the "painting up" of sketches made in the field, were most certainly creative processes[42] where in the text at least, the protagonist/narrator becomes "aware of [his] own involvement" as in fiction because these documents were reflexive constructions and were sometimes written with an audience in mind, the Admiralty being the addressee.[43] Nevertheless, referring to the initial record of the

---

39 See Carol E. Percy's discussion of Hawkesworth's reworking of the Cook logs and journals in "In the margins: Dr Hawkesworth's editorial emendations to the language of Captain Cook's voyages", *English Studies*, 77:6, 1996, pp. 549–578.
40 See Hawkesworth, *op. cit.*, p. 4.
41 See Charles Batten, *Pleasurable Instruction*, University of California Press, 1978.
42 Adams, *op. cit.*, p. 79.
43 The poem in Wallis' honour in the ML may be considered as an example of this type of consideration.

sea voyage, here the *Dolphin* logs, is as far back as one can go. In the logs as the primary source, the South Seas as well as the sea and the sea voyage (as they were understood and experienced on a pragmatic quotidian level), may be considered as being at their most reliable, but these sources remained unpublished. Hawkesworth's *Voyages* conversely is at the other end of scale, more a secondary source, creatively based on the logs, but in the guise of a primary record of events, both nationally and internationally, as for example the compilation was translated into Dutch, French,[44] German[45] immediately afterwards in 1774 and then into Italian in 1784.[46] Various collections of voyages also took up Hawkesworth's accounts over the years.

Specifically, as concerns the *Dolphin* expedition, Hawkesworth proceeded to "compress" the voyage, perhaps rendering it even more insignificant when compared to the longer account of Cook's three-year circumnavigation. For example, the editor of *Voyages* makes away with seventeen days on shore from the 28th December, 1766 to the 14th January 1767, when Wallis is busy preparing the ships for the voyage through the Straights. This passage was a long and difficult maritime trek and constitutes an essential element in a full rendition of the sea voyage as such. The climate namely the cold and the wet, the currents and the dangers of shoals are detailed in the logs and form part of the "distancing" process which makes for a clearer understanding of the voyage. This is not so in *Voyages* except when there is "story value" in the proceedings. The attention paid to "seatime" is not as pronounced as that allotted to the "event". Elements of drama like storms are recorded for interest[47] but observations made during the night for example are all excluded in Hawkesworth's version of the voyage, thus accelerating time, manipulating attention and reducing the understanding of the duration and distance covered. Where Wallis notes wind, course, speed, depth and

---

[44] *Relation des voyages entrepris par ordre de Sa Majesté Britannique actuellement régnante pour faire des découvertes dans l'hémisphère méridional, et successivement exécutés par le commodore Byron, le capitaine Carteret, le capitaine Wallis et le capitaine Cook ... rédigée d'après les journaux tenus par les differens commandans et les papiers de M. Banks, par J. Hawkesworth, traduite de l'anglois,* translated by Anne-François-Joachim Fréville and Jean-Baptiste-Antoine Suard, Saillant and Nyon, and Panckoucke, 1774.

[45] *Geschichte der See-Reisen und Entdeckungen im Süd-Meer welche auf Befehl Sr. Großbritannischen Majestät unternommen, und von Commodore Byron, Capitain Wallis, Capitain Carteret und Capitain Coockim Dolphin, der Swallow, und dem Endeavour nach einander ausgeführt worden sind : aus den Tagebüchern der verschiedenen Befehlshaber und den Handschriften Joseph Banks Esq. in drey Bänden verfaßt : Mit vielen ... Kupfern und einer Menge von See- und Land-Charten,* translated by Johann Friedrich Schiller, Haude and Spener, 1774.

[46] *Storia dei viaggi intrapresi per ordine di S.M. Britannica dal capitano Giacomo Cook [microform]: ricavata dalle autentiche relazioni del medesimo: con una introduzione generale contenente la notizia dei più celebri viaggi precedent,* Portrait and atlas containing 52 engraved plates and charts. 13 vols. 8vo. Naples. From Edward Cox's *A Reference Guide To The Literature Of Travel Including Voyages, Geographical Descriptions, Adventures, Shipwrecks and Expeditions,* 1935.

[47] Hawkesworth, *op. cit.*, p. 366.

the lie of the land, Hawkesworth summarises "we stood off and on all night".[48] After leaving the Straits of Magellan, almost two whole months of voyaging, across rough South Seas, are glossed over in *Voyages* in a series of brief elliptic paragraphs referencing the growing sickness on board and generating the effects suggested above. After forty days of navigation, with the gradual amelioration in the weather with the hard gales and violent cold turning into light airs and fair weather, the logs record the first reference to the South Seas: *saw a few flying fish, these being the first ones we have seen in the South Seas* (21st May, 1767). When land is finally sighted on the 6th June, 1767, after fifty-six days at sea, the ML is brief and precise and there is no mention of any joy, noting only *at noon saw it off the deck bearing WNW 5 or 6 leagues low land into two hummocks in the middle.* The PL and FC, perhaps later amended copies, are a little more forthcoming with: *at half past noon Jonathon Puller (seaman) called out land from the mast head in the WNW – at noon saw it plainly off the deck it was a low island bearing WNW distance about 5 or 6 leagues – fine pleasant gale & hazey, all the sick overjoyed at our discovery as were likewais the well.* Hawkesworth describes *the joy which every one felt at this discovery conceived by those only who have experienced the danger, sickness and fatigue of such a voyage* (*Voyages*, 423). Each entry adds more narrative polish to the initial entry in the ML.

Overall, Wallis's discovery of the chain of islands becomes in Hawkesworth a series of discoveries interspersed with little "seatime" and much detail about people and place – their physical appearance, the construction of the canoes, the "repositories of the dead" of which the log makes only brief but nevertheless pertinent mention. The five days of sailing from the Whitsun and Charlotte's Islands are hardly mentioned, but the discoveries of other islands, the events, dominate the narrative. The logs are on the contrary cartographies of the navigation, interspersed with discoveries, which interrupt the seatime, and not as in *Voyages*, where seatime is more a series of brief interludes, necessary to authenticate the story. Thus, the account of the sojourn at Tahiti makes up a large, material part of Hawkesworth's narrative of the circumnavigation of 637 days, though it covers only 32 days. This privileging of the stay at Tahiti in terms of reading time, is justified first by the fact that it was "discovered", and that secondly without their discovery Wallis would certainly have lost a number of his crew due to illness. But this slowing down of narrative tempo, where the event receives extended attention, is also a feature of fiction and novels in particular producing a magnifying effect as the event takes on major importance.

Furthermore, within this mythopoetic perspective, the events recounted in the *Dolphin* logs are associated with an overwhelming concern for survival (in spite of more descriptive *Remarks* sections), for water and food, meat and vegetables. Each daily entry notes the tonnage of water taken on board and is a catalogue of the number of hogs the people obtained and how the meetings with the Queen,

---

48 *Ibid.*, p. 371.

as she is called, resulted in better market days. For example, the Queen comes on board five times during the whole of Wallis's stay at Tahiti. Wallis makes it clear after the first three visits (the last two being on the 26th and 27th July, the day the *Dolphin* leaves Tahiti), the *ship's company never wanted a fresh meal* (13th July), that *the gunner sent off more stock than any day before* and that there were *fruits of all sorts in great abundance*. The primary record is obviously based on vital economics and is much less orientated towards social perspectives. The South Seas become though in Hawkesworth an arena for the building of interpersonal relationships, especially between the Captain and the Queen, both amicable, or more, and belligerent, more rarely pragmatic as in the logs. This in itself of course contributes to broadening the understanding of the peoples and places encountered, but the form of the narration of these relationships, characterised by the use of reduction and amplification of time and events, and of course in terms of content embellishment and omission, undoubtedly contributes to a fictionalising of the South Seas, producing mythologies which came to be associated inextricably with the interpersonal.

Once the *Dolphin* leaves King George III Island, Hawkesworth's account is again shorn of seatime as if the climax of the story had been reached. For example, Wallis sails to Tinian and camps on shore for 27 days, having spent 55 consecutive days at sea after leaving Tahiti. The company as well as Wallis are ill and the ship is leaking severely. These 80 or so days are condensed into a few pages in *Voyages* and the time on shore to five or six paragraphs. Narrative time then is again compressed as it would be in fiction but "should" not be in an "authentic" account to quote Hawkesworth, where the essence of the voyage lies precisely in this specific rapport between time and distance. Adrien Pasquali[49] interestingly argues that movement produces distance and the speed at which this distance is covered might determine the nature of the vision of new spaces. In other words, the speed, in the accounts in terms of the narrative technique, at which the places, or peoples, are reached, determines perceptions of them, where excessive speed creates blurred and fragmentary visions due to the perception of distance as being reduced.

For decades and even centuries though, *Voyages* has been in the privileged position of primary material as far as Wallis is concerned. The *Dolphin* accounts, like the others, were subjected to the fictionalising processes in Hawkesworth, discussed above, but unlike them, there was never any counterbalancing access to the veritable papers. Byron, Carteret and Cook's manuscripts were published in time by the Hakluyt Society.[50] Only the Wallis texts were forgotten, perhaps due to their unusually "nautical" nature, which is the log format and the lack of a narrativised journal. The format of the logs, with their associated emphasis on the reduced speed and great distances travelled, induces a specific understanding of

---

49 Adrien Pasquali, *Le Tour des Horizons*, Paris, Klinckseick, 1994, pp. 3–29.
50 By Robert Gallagher, Helen Wallis and John Beaglehole respectively.

the voyage and subsequently of the places visited and the people encountered, and visions of the seas and sea voyages. This second voyage of the *Dolphin* around the world from June 1766 to June 1768 was documented once by Hugh Carrington in his transcription of George Robertson's journal.[51] Carrington considers that the logs were "a mass of indigestible nautical material" and that Robertson's narrative journal is on the contrary an account of his "fears and anxieties, his hopes and joys in simple language and in perfect freedom." This of course overlooks the retrospective, rewriting processes as far as Robertson and many others were concerned. It also disregards the importance of logs in describing other than personal mental states. Clive Wilkinson[52] is very clear on the research potential of such "indigestible" or "dry" contents and makes a convincing case for a better understanding of the *striking impression of the vastness and emptiness of the oceans* (which we have argued is imperceptible in edited, published accounts such as Hawkesworth's) which in fact improves historical insights into routes and times of sailings. Wilkinson also makes it clear that in areas such as medical history (relationship of climate variability and infectious disease) as well as environmental history,[53] the study of logbooks can be of great value. He notably argues that:

> The large-scale study of many logbooks in the age of sail can give a number of insights into the history and development of navigational science and the corresponding responses to technological innovation. Conducted on a multi-national level, logbook studies provide the opportunity for comparative research between the naval and mercantile services of competing maritime powers. The information on navigation, much of it in tabular form, might not lend itself easily to the historian more often used to narrative accounts but will, with careful analysis and observation, demonstrate the increasing knowledge of mariners and the efficiency of sailing vessels in crossing vast tracts of ocean.[54]

During this "new" age of exploration of the South Seas, Wallis seems to have been the only navigator not to have written a complementary journal in a pronounced narrative form, as did Byron before him, and as Cook was to do after him. This transcription reproduces the tables and "terse" entries of the various logbooks of

---

51 Carrington, *op. cit.*, p. xlv.
52 See "The Non-Climatic Research Potential of Ships' Logbooks and Journals," *Climatic Change*, 73, 2005, pp. 55–167.
53 "Logbooks have proved an essential resource for the study of historical marine climatology and the only resource that can give high-resolution daily and even hourly meteorological data over the oceans. Equally, logbooks provide a unique place to begin to study the environmental history of the oceans and seas. Not only does the plotting of hundreds of ship tracks clearly indicate how the ocean and atmosphere circulations were exploited but, more important to the historian at least, it indicates how those circulations were perceived and understood." *Ibid.*, p. 65.
54 *Ibid.* p. 158.

INTRODUCTION

this the second *Dolphin* voyage with a view to stressing the considerable results of the voyage in spite of possible reservations as to the formatting which in Wilkinson's view "might not lend itself easily to the historian more often used to narrative accounts but will, with careful analysis and observation, demonstrate the increasing knowledge of mariners and the efficiency of sailing vessels in crossing vast tracts of ocean".[55]

3. The Pictures

The Wallis papers, in addition to the logs and the fair copy, also include five series of drawings of the atolls and islands[56] discovered during the voyage despite the fact that there was no official artist on board, as was the case on Cook's ensuing expeditions. This primary material is little-known and is for the most part published here for the first time.

In Volume 1 of the ML, there is a page of views of Cape Blanco and Port Desire and a page with three unsigned drawings of fish – two of a flying fish. In the second volume of this log (back cover) there is a drawing of the Queen's house in Tahiti entitled *A ground plan & elevation of the Queens House at King Georges Island in the South Seas in July 1767. This House is 327 feet long, forty two feet wide, thirty feet high in the middle, and twelve feet at the ends and sides. It stands upon thirty nine posts on each side and fourteen support the middle. It hath a bamboo railing two feet high between the side posts and another comes down from the thatch of three or four feet more so there is about six feet clear* (Annex A).

The State Library of New South Wales also holds a sketchbook kept during the voyage which contains twenty drawings in ink, two on one page (referred to as Series 1 in this introduction). Each page is numbered and initialled SW (Samuel Wallis) and dated 1766.[57] The sketches are in fine detail and show the *Dolphin*, flags and pennants flying, initially surrounded by other vessels and with land in

---

55 *Ibid.*
56 Wallis provides a list of the islands visited at the beginning of the ML: "June 6 made Charlotte & Whitsun Islands, June the 11:[th] sailed by Prince Will:[m] Henry's Island, the 12 passed by the Duke of Gloucester's Island, the Princess of Brunswick and Prince Henry's Islands, the 17 made the Bishop of Osnaburg. The 19:[th] discovered King George the Thirds Island. the East end; the 21:[st] anchord about the middle of the Island, the 23 anchord in Port Royal Harbour near the West end of King Georges Island, and four leagues from the Duke of Yorks Island. And the next day continued here until the 27:[th] day of July and then sailed Westward, the 28 from ½ past Noon until six in the evening off the Duke of Yorks Island and the next day at Noon passed by Admiral Saunders Island. July the 30:[th] passed by Lord Howes Island, & the 31:[st] were entangled from four in the afternoon untill – with the Dangerous Reefs & the Islands of Scilly. August the 14:[th] & 15, pass'd by Boscawens, & Keppels Islands. August 17:[th] pass'd by Wallis's Island." This catalogue is slightly different from the table given in the FC, reproduced in Hawkesworth's *Voyages*.
57 This sketchbook is available online: http://www.acmssearch.sl.nsw.gov.au/search/itemDetailPaged.cgi?itemID=844600. Two of these sketches are reproduced in Gallagher's edition of the Byron journal (*op. cit.*).

xxxiii

sight, probably at the moment of departure. The drawings read like a chronology, the other ships become fewer in number and smaller in size as graphically the *Dolphin* makes sail and starts on her voyage. Only once is the *Dolphin* shown in company, most probably with the *Swallow*.[58] The sea is generally calm or very calm (Wallis sketches the reflection of the ship in the water in the latter case) but in one of the drawings, the only labelled one in the whole series, the *Dolphin* is pictured as driving dangerously near a bluff (Oznaburg Island) in a storm.[59] Wave formations and the strength of the wind are represented by the state of the pennants and the flag. In the final drawing, the boat is shown as rowing back to the ship[60] but none of drawings shows islands or atolls in full.

The State Library also holds an album (loose leaves) of twelve wash drawings (Series 2) all signed Sam:¹ Wallis, Sam: Wallis, or S: Wallis and dated 1767.[61] Eleven of these show the atolls and islands discovered and named by Wallis and there are two of Queen Charlotte's Island. The illustrations are representations of the bays and passages into the lagoons of the atolls but they also provide information as to the characteristics of the flora of the various landfalls. The very first representations of islander material culture are also identifiable in the frequent depictions of canoes but also in the sustained focus on the Queen's house (of which the preliminary sketch is to be found in the ML – Annex A above). This is also the only image of an islander (reworked in Series 3 discussed below) that Wallis presents.[62] This series does not contain a drawing of Port Royal at King George's Island. All the drawings feature the *Dolphin* in a prominent, central position at anchor opposite the shore and are headed by a title in a scroll and the coordinates of each island are given except for in one of the two of Queen Charlotte's Island.[63]

---

58 See Annexes B, C and D.
59 This drawing is labelled *In a Swell off Oznaburg Island. June 1767 – in the South Seas.*
60 See Annex E.
61 This album is available online: http://www.acmssearch.sl.nsw.gov.au/search/itemDetailPaged.cgi?itemID=422946
62 See Annex F.
63 In the Library catalogue, the titles of this group of twelve drawings are as follows (Wallis omits the apostrophes):

- *Whitsunday Island Latitude 19°: 26'S. Long.:^{d} 137° : 56'W*; signed S. Wallis. June 1767;
- *A View of Queen Charlotts Island, Lat:^{d} 19°: 18'S, Long: 138°:2? W*, signed Sam: Wallis June 1767
- *Her Majesty Queen Charlottes Isle*, signed S: Wallis 1767
- *The Earl of Egmonts Island, in Lat:^{d} 19°:20'S Long: 138:30 W of London*, signed Sam:¹ Wallis
- *His Royl: Highness the Duke of Glocesters Island In Lat: 19 : 11 S Long: 140 :04 W from London*, signed by Sam: Wallis 1767.
- *His Roy: Highness the Duke of Cumberlands Island. Lat: 19 : 18 S. Long 140 : 36 West of London. / Roy: Highness Prince W:^{m} Henrys Island. Lat:^{d} 19 : 00 S Long:^{d} 140 : 06 West of London*, signed Sam:¹ Wallis 1767.
- *His Royal Highness the Duke of Yorks Island. Lying in Lat: 17 : 30 South, Long: 150 : 16 West from London*, signed Sam:¹ Wallis 1767;

INTRODUCTION

The script is not copperplate and it seems likely that the headings are in Wallis's handwriting. The words are often crowded into the allotted space and the letters are irregular in size.[64] The drawings adorned with these banners may indicate Wallis's first attempts at preparing for publication.

In addition, the National Library of Australia holds a collection of nine drawings from the *Dolphin* voyage (Series 3). These drawings are signed but not dated. Eight of these are of the atolls and islands discovered (this time including Tahiti) and they are again finely detailed, but they are enclosed within a simple, blackline, rectangular border.[65] The name of each atoll or island is formally inscribed at the bottom of each drawing outside the enclosed area in copperplate script.[66] This may then show Wallis's decision to adopt a more pragmatic approach to the question of potential publication as this time he decides on simpler titles perhaps better suited to the reproduction process, eliminating long headings, the coordinates and banners, hence clarifying understanding of the drawings by a possibly unversed viewing public. The ninth drawing is untitled and in a different format with a patterned border identical to borders of the drawings in Series 4 discussed below, but it is unsigned. This drawing may be of Queen Charlotte's Island or of Whitsunday Island if we consider its resemblance to the three in the Series 2.[67]

The Alexander Turnbull Library in New Zealand also holds a collection of 11 ink-and-wash drawings (Series 4). This is the only series which has been described and analysed. Marian Minson discusses these drawings in detail and starts by suggesting that though Wallis's writings have been repeatedly published,[68] the artwork has not been studied and is not known. If we consider however the original

- *The Right Hono:*^{b} *Lord Visc: Howes Island lying in Lat:*^{d} *16 : 46. S. Long.:*^{d} *154 : 13.W from London*, signed Sam:^{l} Wallis 1767;
- *Boscawens Isle. Lati:*^{d} *15 : 50 S. Long 175 : 09. W (Aug 13. 1767* marked in above the title within the scroll), signed Sam: Wallis;
- *The Hono.:*^{b} *Augustus Keppel's Island Lying in the Latitude of 15 : 54 S. Long.:*^{d}. *175 : 12 W from London (Aug. 13. 1767* marked in pencil under the scroll), signed Sam: Wallis 1767
- *Wallis Island. in Latitude 13°: 18' South, and Long: 177 : 00 West from London. Variation 10.0. East.*, signed by Sam:^{l} Wallis 1767;
- *A Ground Plan; and Perspective View of the Queens House, at King Georges Island, Lying in Lat:*^{d} *17:30 S and Longitude of 150:00 West from London. This House is 327 feet Long and forty two feet Broad it is supported in the Middle by fourteen Pillars and Thirty Nine at the Sides, is thirty feet high in the Middle and Twelve feet high at the Sides. Discovered by his Majestys Ship Dolphin on the 24. of June 1767. Done by Sam: Wallis. 1767*

64 See, for example, Annex G depicting Wallis Island.
65 They were most probably originally loose leaves but have been pasted onto card and collected together in an album.
66 See Annex H – *Whitsunday Island, Osnaburg Island, Otaheiti or King Georges Island, York Island, Saunders Island, Howe Island, Keppel Island, Wallis Island* – followed by the untitled drawing.
67 See Marian Minson, *The Art of Exploration: Samuel Wallis and the First Drawings of the Society Islands*, Turnbull Library Record, Vol. 44, 2012. Minson suggests it may be of Queen Charlotte's Island (p. 6).
68 *Ibid.*, p. 3.

"papers," that is the logs and fair copy, which are published here for the first time, then both text and image have been neglected in editorial and perhaps academic terms. The only published account of Wallis which Minson mentions is in the Hawkesworth compilation (discussed earlier). Thus, the textual record as well as the rich graphic complement, the papers and the pictures, relating the 1766–68 *Dolphin* voyage have been overlooked.

Minson provides a careful description of Series 4:

"The drawings are similar in subject matter. Each is drawn from aboard the Dolphin, but includes the ships with the flags flying, moored in the foreground against a background of a Pacific Island or atoll. Eight show the Society Islands. Most include canoes and houses of local people; most show coconut palms. A lot of care has been taken with tiny details and with recording minute variations from area to area. Weather and sea conditions are included, the majority showing a fine day with little wind and fine seas." In Series 4, the drawings are all untitled and were most probably done by Wallis (though they are unsigned) as they are very similar in terms of style to those in the other collections (which are signed).[69]

Much of Minson's analysis is related to correctly identifying the islands portrayed in the pictures. She points to the errors in the labels (in pencil on the back of each drawing) and rectifies according to the coordinates given in the logs, to the descriptions which Wallis gives of the islands and by referring to Series 2 and 3.[70]

Minson also very interestingly discusses the timing issues related to the artwork, that is when Wallis did the various series and in what order. In her study, she concludes that some of the drawings in Series 4 may have been done *in situ*, and others retrospectively, perhaps even once the ship returned to England. For example she suggests that the drawing of Queen Charlotte's Island does not show the Union Jack and assumes that *he [Wallis] drew it on the first day (7th June) before the flag was planted, that is in situ.*[71] But if he drew it on the first day, how is the mislabelling to be explained as Minson also puts forward the idea that because

---

69 *Ibid.*
70 *Ibid.* Minson provides the following titles and corrections of the pencil notes on the back of each drawing:

- *Queen Charlottes Island* – present-day Nukutavake (labelled *Egmont Island*)
- *Egmonts Island* – present-day Vairaatea (labelled *Queen Charlotte's Island*)
- *Prince William Henry's Island* – present-day Nengonengo (labelled *Gloucester Island*)
- Osnaburg island – present-day Mehetia (labelled *Whitsunday Island*)
- *King George's Island* – present-day Tahiti
- *Duke of Yorks Island* – present-day Moorea
- *Sir Charles Saunders Island* – present-day Maiao (labelled W*hitsunday Island*)
- *Lord Howe's Island* – present-day Maupihaa
- *Boscawen's Island* – present-day Tafahi (labelled Osnabruge Island)
- *Keppel Island* – present-day Nuiatoputapu
- *Wallis Island* – present-day Uvea

71 *Ibid.*, p. 6.

most of the drawings in Series 4 are incorrectly labelled (by Wallis presumably) on their reverse sides in pencil, this is evidence of errors due to the distance in time and space (the drawing being done in England) from the actual event of discovery and encounter?

Further, this time as regards Series 3, only one wrong identification is referred to by Minson and this "appears"[72] to be incorrect as regards the "Whitsunday Island" drawing – it should read Queen Charlotte's Island (according to Minson). But on close study of the Series 3 drawing in question, it is not necessarily clear that the drawing has been erroneously labelled if we compare it to those of Queen Charlotte's Island and Whitsunday Island in Series 2.

Similarly, according to Minson, the drawing of St George's Island in Series 4,[73] on the other hand may have been completed after the fact, on the ship *after peace had been restored*[74] (the annotation on the back of the drawing dates it 26th June, 1767), as Wallis was most probably busy elsewhere on that particular day of battle and that *he included large numbers of canoes retrospectively.*[75] Thus, this would be another drawing *in situ* by Wallis in the days following the battle. But at the same time, Minson also points to the fact that Wallis remained on board for most of the voyage as he was unwell and that this situation was not conducive to the execution of minute drawing detail in the various collections. This latter argument in Minson's view may then be considered as evidence in favour of deferred representation (once back in England?). Again in rather contradictory terms, she also suggests that all "drawings in the Antipodean collections have the appearance of being groups of secondary copies, done in England shortly after the voyage."[76] What she calls "ornamental peripheral details", that is banners, decorative borders, inscriptions in a copperplate hand and even signatures, were most likely added in England in preparation for publication. It is worth noting here that even if in poor health, Wallis did for example spend time on shore, at Tinian or at the Cape of Good Hope where for example the *Dolphin* sojourned from the 6th to the 27th of February 1768: *I being very ill was put onshoar and carried up the country about eight miles where I continued all the time we lay there and went of rather worse than I came onshoar* (PL and FC). He could then have made copies during these sojourns on shore and added the ornamental detail. So again, the question of when these drawings were done remains undecided. The order and dates of execution suggested by Minson's analysis (Series 2 followed by Series 4, Series 3 being the final version for putative publication – which never took place)[77] remains open

---

72 *Ibid.*
73 See Annex I.
74 *Ibid.*
75 *Ibid.*
76 *Ibid.*, p. 7.
77 *Ibid.*, p. 7: "Another feature of secondary copies is the gradual alteration and sometimes reduction of detail as they are developed from the primary drawing made in sight of the subject to later copies. There is minor variation in the three sets of drawings, and only the National Library of

to question.⁷⁸ Minson's general conclusion seems valid however, namely that all three series were based on originals or what she calls "prototype sketches" which seem to have disappeared.⁷⁹ This volume, along with little-known texts, presents two series of sketches which may perhaps be considered possible primary material which Wallis used to "draw up" Series 2–4 presented above.

On board the *Dolphin* was an essential aid to navigation, *The English Pilot, The Third book, Describing the sea-coasts, capes, head-land, streights, soundings, sands, shoals, rocks and dangers, the islands, bays, roads, harbours and ports in the oriental navigation . . ./ collected for the general benefit of our own countrymen*. This large, published work was seemingly used by Wallis as a sketch book and he used the blank verso sides of the printed maps and instructions in the *Pilot* to draw up his voyage round the world.

The drawings⁸⁰ in this *Pilot* were themselves very probably copied from the charts which George Pinnock drew and signed. These latter drawings are held, along with the BL, in London.⁸¹ The BL is an abridged account of the full length logs and begins on the 21ˢᵗ August 1766 when the *Dolphin* leaves Plymouth (see *papers* section in this introduction). Wallis initials the final entry and closes the textual record. There follows a small drawing of a thermometer (which explains the focus on the temperature readings in the preceding pages) and a sketch of a *Sling Used by the Patagons* (both unsigned). The charts which follow

---

Australia's set shows generally fewer features, for example in the way the verdure is depicted, or in the number of canoes; the copies in the State Library of New South Wales have consistently reliable titles, suggesting more accuracy in copying from the originals, at least for the inscriptions. The careful and precise quality of the drawings is consistent across the three collections."

78 Another interesting consideration concerns the titles of Series 3. Except for King George's Island, all the others are shorn of nobility with the absence of the Lord, Earl, Bishop, Admiral, Honourable and simpler than the initial, long explanatory labels. But these may have been unlikely final titles considering the care Wallis took in honouring his past and possibly future patrons during the voyage in naming his discoveries after them. It is possible that in Series 4, the body and periphery of the drawings were completed but the titles were pending. Minson also suggests that the NLA version may be the final version because it is labelled Otaheite or King Georges Island and that Otaheite was the "preferred name of Cook and all who followed him." The difficulty in determining the order of completion of the Series works is again here very apparent. Did Wallis wait five years for the account of Cook's voyage by Hawkesworth in 1773, in which the putative preferred name comes to the fore, before drawing or labelling Series 3? Or did he have early access to Cook's journals (which is unlikely)? Another possibility is that he read the anonymous account of the voyage published immediately after Cook's return in 1771, and then he did Series 3 and labelled the most important drawing of the collection Otaheite or King Georges Island as a result, again waiting four years. But in this anonymous relation Otahitee is used, but so is George's Island or King Georges Island. Wallis himself also uses Otaheiti in the PL in the pages of the *Remarks* section (see transcription). It is therefore difficult to determine which of the two series was the final one.

79 Minson, *op. cit.*, p. 68. The proto-sketches for the drawings of the ship in Series 2–4 may perhaps be understood as being those in the sketch book.

80 Reproduced here courtesy of the State Library of New South Wales.

81 ADM 15499 (British Library) © The British Library Board. There are twenty-two sketches in all but only the fifteen of the islands and atolls are reproduced here (see Annex J).

are signed by Pinnock (George Pinnock or Geo. Pinnock), Midshipman on the *Dolphin*. There are two studies, one of a tree (not reproduced here) and one of the *Dolphin* at anchor in Port Royal Harbour, in addition to a survey of Port Royal.[82] The others are very clear contours within rhumb lines of all the islands discovered by Wallis. They are "framed" with scales and North arrows. Pinnock meticulously dots the barrier reefs surrounding most of them. He also specifies watering places, rocks and ponds. He occasionally sketches clumps of trees. The only image of the islanders is a seemingly finished work entitled *A View of Port Royal Bay at Georges Island* in which manned canoes are shown in the bay and alongside the *Dolphin*. The Queen's house is also disproportionally large and placed very near the shore. The fact that Wallis in Series 2 uses the same scroll detail as Pinnock (or perhaps vice versa), is possibly indicative of the collaborative nature of the artwork as a whole. It is also worth noting that in Series 2, the only drawing missing is one of Port Royal Harbour, here presented by Pinnock. The correspondence between Pinnock's charts and Wallis's drawings is very clear and it may be assumed that the *Pilot* drawings of the atolls and islands were based on Pinnock's, as the former are more elaborate versions of the latter (except the *View* described above).

The drawings in the *Pilot* can be divided into several categories. The first category comprises charts of bays and harbours in the Straits of Magellan. This group of ink drawings (not reproduced here) are of the various bays and harbours the *Dolphin* put into or passed by in the passage through the Straits. Pinnock does not draw charts of these places. Wallis and/or Pinnock (as these drawings are unsigned), show the coastal outlines, indicate the coordinates, the depth of the water, the reefs, rocks and weeds, the wooding and watering places available and occasionally include remarks on the tides. The titles of the drawings are sometimes long and explanatory, for example *A Plan of Swallow Harbour (opposite Cape Notch) on the South Shore in the Streights of Magellan it is a very convenient place to recruit it, & if I was to go thro' the Streights I would endeavour to refit at that place and only stop for water & refreshments in passing by other places*. These sketches were most probably then not only "personal" records because they provide instructions and advice for future navigators. They were not necessarily destined for publication either, for the same reasons. This group relays a pragmatic, rather less aesthetic approach (the latter identifiable in Series 2–4), in

---

82 The drawings reproduced in Annex J are labelled as follows: *Whitsunday: Island, Queen: Charlotte's Island, Duke: of Gloucester's Island, Lord: of Egmont's Island, Bishop of Osnaburg's Island, Sir Charles: Saunders's Island, King: Georges Island, A SURVEY OF PORT ROYAL KING GEORGES ISLAND ISLAND IN THE SOUTH SEAS, A View of Port Royal Bay at Georges Island* [drawing of the *Dolphin* at anchor in Port Royal with the Queen's house in the background], *Duke of York's Island, Admiral: Boscawens Island, Admiral: Keppels Island, Captain Wallis's Island, Lord: Howes Island, Scilly Isles. A View of Port Royal Bay at Georges Island* was published by Carrington (*op. cit.*). Hawkesworth also had access to Pinnock's charts as *Voyages* presents two engravings obviously based on Pinnock's work entitled *Chart of Cocos Island, called by C. Wallis Boscowen, and Traitors Island, called by Wallis Keppel* and *Chart of Wallis's Island*.

picturing the voyage. They also demonstrate how every step of the maritime way was important in relating the story of a voyage.

The second category comprises two unsigned drawings: *A Plan of St Jago or rather the Bay of Port Praya in one of the Cape de Verd Islands Lying in the Latitude of 14:53* North. Long:^{d} from London 22:56 West. Variation 9:00 West* and *A Plan of Tinian Road where the Dolphin lay at anchor in the year 1767 and lost an anchor & cable by the coral rock as we had sounded under we judged we were in good ground –*

Latitude Observed –
Longitude Observed from London –
Variation of the Compass –.

These two drawings are interesting in that they are plans but they also show relief (cliffs and slopes) and also the camps (tents) and buildings (the fort). They are a mix of chart and figurative drawing, perhaps by Pinnock himself. In the *Plan of Tinian Road*, the place names seem to be in distinctive squared lettering, which is much like the script used by Pinnock to label his charts. The main title though seems to be in Wallis's handwriting.

The third category is the most significant as possible source material for the supposed secondary copies in Series 2, 3 and 4 described above. These drawings may perhaps be understood as the elusive proto-sketches, along with Pinnock's charts, which Minson supposed had been made but was not able to locate. The fact that they are in the *Pilot* attest perhaps to their informal, veritable *in situ* status. There are sixteen sketches in all, thirteen are of the newly discovered atolls and islands, two are studies of Port Royal (unsigned) and one is a plan of the aforesaid harbour (unsigned). They are all topographical representations but in the compound iconographical style detailed above – that is sometimes with the architectural and vegetal features shown in skewed perspective. Some of them are enclosed in rectangles, (precursors to the later Series?) and rhumb lines cross whole or part of the pages. The North arrow is a fleur-de-lys. All these features are more or less common to Pinnock's sketches. The *Dolphin* is not figured in these *Pilot* drawings as she is in Series 1, 2, 3 and 4.

As they appear in the *Pilot*, the first drawing is unsigned and is of Whitsunday Island (Pinaki). The title, the coordinates and the scale are given in the middle of the drawing. Trees (coconut trees as well as two clumps of indeterminate ones) and two huts are depicted. The coral reefs are also shown. The 7th June entry in the ML copy of the log describes this first landing in these terms:

> Remarks made at the first of the Whitsun Isles – at 2 PM hoisted all the boats out & sent Lieu:^{t} Furneaux with Proper Petty Officers & men armed to make a landing on the 2 Islands which they with much difficulty effected on account of the Surf which runs very high every where – at 7 they returned and made me the following report : that the Island was

of a circular form with a large lagoon in the middle but both ends were guarded with large reefs of rocks that they found it impossible to get a passage thro' them; that there was ten or a dozen neat little habitations and one canoe built and more on the stocks that the habitants had but just gone he supposed by seeing their tools laying in confusion the tools consisted chiefly of shells and fish bones, he saw no kind of metal, the canoes were neatly sew'd together & their hutts very decent & clean he left every thing in the same manner he found it – and gathered scurvy grass of which there was great plants and a few cocoa nutts. At day light in the morning sent him with the boats to get off more refreshments but after trying in every part that seemed practible he returned at eleven o clock without landing the surf running so high that the boats could not venture near the shore

The outline of Whitsunday Island is almost identical, but not quite, to that in Pinnock's drawing. The clumps of trees are in the same positions, as are the houses and the asterisks denoting the reefs. The title is not though in the squared lettering characteristic of Pinnock's charts (which is the case for all the drawings in this category) and Wallis most probably added it later and included the coordinates and the date of discovery. It is thus unclear who actually did the drawing itself (it was very likely Pinnock).

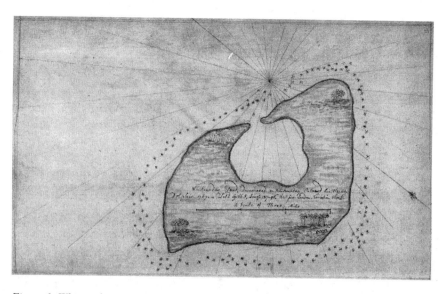

Figure 1 Whitsunday Island Discovered on Whitsunday Onboard his Majestys Ship Dolphin 1767. Lat:d 19:°26' S. Long:d 137:56 West from London. Variation 6:00 E (Pilot)

Courtesy of the State Library of New South Wales

INTRODUCTION

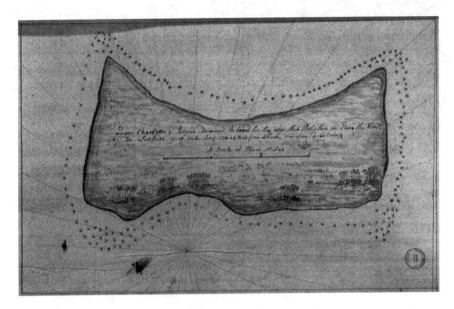

Figure 2 Queen Charlotte's Island Discovered On board His Majestys Ship Dolphin on June the Ninth 1767. In Latitude 19:18 South. Long. 138.04 West from London, Variation 5:°40' Easterly (Pilot)

Courtesy of the State Library of New South Wales

The second drawing is of Queen Charlotte's Island and the sketch is relatively accurate in terms of the actual shape (the size of the atoll is slightly overestimated). Like Pinnock's sketch, this drawing shows the reefs and indicates the trees and the position of four huts. There is no sign of the islanders (which is a characteristic of the *Dolphin* iconography) or the canoes, in spite of the fact that this is where the very first, rather fraught encounter with the South Sea islanders takes place, as the ML relates on the 8th June:[83]

> Little wind & fair standing off & on near the second island, the boats inshore great many inhabitants on the beach at 1 the boats returned having purchased from the inhabitants about sixty cocoanuts for which gave them nails, bill hooks, hatchetts &:[ce] they would not suffer the people to land – except two who they soon put into the boat again – stood off and on all night at daylight sent the boats with an Officer to endeavour to get more cocoa nutts & scurvy grass. the natives had launched for double canoes and were embarked on board of them, on our approach they

---

83 Wallis even goes on shore and spends the afternoon on Queen Charlotte's Island (once the initial skirmishes are over), though he does not say if he surveyed the island.

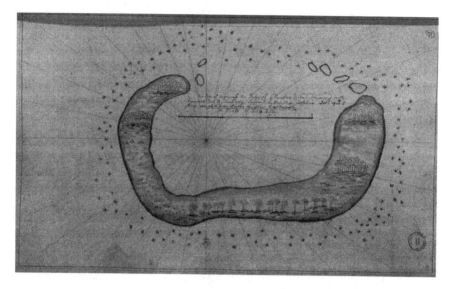

Figure 3 His Royal Highness Duke of Gloucesters island (Paraoa) discovered on the Twelfth day of June 1767 Onboard his Majestys ship Dolphin. Lat:d 19:121* S Long: 140:04 W from London Variation 6:00 Easterly (Pilot)

Courtesy of the State Library of New South Wales

landed, but on the boats going to windward of them they all embarked & set sail and steer'd away WSW until we lost sight of them

The drawing of Duke of Gloucester's Island, is again almost identical to Pinnock's, and it is relatively accurate, the actual coordinates are latitude 19°14' and longitude 140°69', 3.75 miles in breadth. Again, the islanders who come down to the shore on that day, apparently armed, are not shown.[84]

The fourth unsigned drawing of the Earl of Egmont's Island shows canoes for the first time, four drawn up on the beach. Pinnock's drawing, almost identical in form, does not include canoes. Wallis recounts the sighting in the 11th June entry in the ML:

at ½ past 3 the new island bore from the East end of it SE about one mile at this time we were abreast of seven sail of double canoes that were

---

84 ...saw an island bearing WSW – stood for it at 4 ran past it twas not a quarter of a mile broad and four or five mile long and the back of it was made a circle by a reef of rocks that went round it, where the sea beat very high – we saw here about sixteen inhabitants the island seem'd full of wood & stones – low with the waters edge – not one cocoa nut tree on it – ran within musquett shot of the shoar, no soundings nor any place to anchor in there being a very great surf on every part of the beach – I saw no canoes & very few hutts on the shore – the people seem to be the same in manner & complexion as those in the other islands – came down to the waterside with fine & long pikes . . . (ML).

INTRODUCTION

hauled up on to the beach and were the same people that left Charlott Island, the people all sitting on the beach & their things just taken out of their canoes – could see no place to anchor in and a very great surf running on the shoar very few huts on the island and no cocoa nutt trees – & the island quite narrow & rocky under the trees not sandy like the last island – the wind likewais blowing fresh I stood from the island and brought to.

The next drawing of Osnaburg Island presents a scale of 1 mile (as opposed to the three mile scales in the preceding drawings). Again, the estimation of the breadth of the island is a very reasonable inference. Pinnock's chart includes clumps of trees which are not shown in this *Pilot* drawing. Again Wallis's people land and there are inhabitants but these sketches do not represent the sometimes fleeting, tense first encounters:

the boats landed on the island but in so bad a place that it was with great difficulty the inhabitants were standing off about two hundred men weomen & children – all well look'd stout people – the women handsome & dress'd in white, on the boats coming to a grapnell the weomen the island on showing some beads & trinketts were in a great haste to

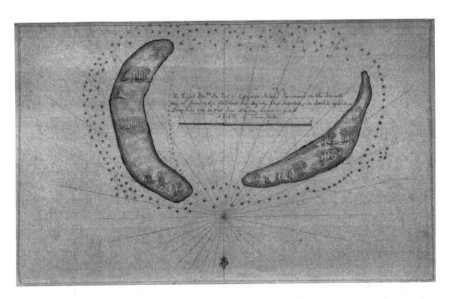

Figure 4 The Right Hon:ble the Earl of Egmonts (Vairaotea) Island discovered on the eleventh day of June 1767 Onboard his Majestys ship Dolphin in Latitude 19:°20' South Longitude 138:30 West from London; Variation 5:° 20' E (Pilot)

Courtesy of the State Library of New South Wales

come to the boats but the men prevented them & sent up the cliff. they made signs that they would bring fowles cocoa nutts hogs &:ᶜᶜ but after waiting several hours not one came & the woods inaccessible the boats returned and we sailed from the island – at noon the boats laying at a grapnell under a rock close in shore – on the SW side of the island – the island in the middle bore NEBE distance two miles – the island I named the Bishop of Osnaburgs Island.

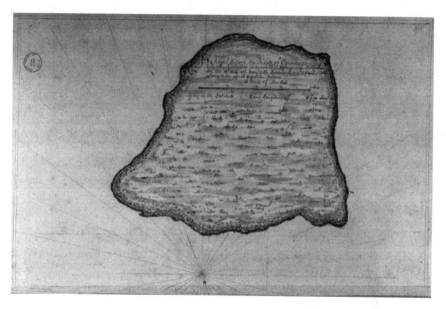

Figure 5 His Royal Highness the Bishop of Osnaburg's Island Discovered Onboard His Majestys Ship Dolphin on this 18ᵗʰ Day of June 1767 Latitude of [...] *Longitude 147:30 West from London (Pilot)*
Courtesy of the State Library of New South Wales

The drawing of King George's Island, very like Pinnock's, comes next on a double blank page of the *Pilot*. The contour of the island is again a very reasonable appraisal but there is no scale. The coral reefs are indicated and various key sites are named after the officers or according to events, Hutchingson Point, Robertson Point, Furneaux Point, Harrisons Island, Dolphin Reef. These labels seem to be in Wallis's hand and not in Pinnock's distinctive square script. This is the first of the signed *Pilot* drawings. The signature Sam: Wallis is in a different, darker ink but it appears under the title and not in the bottom right-hand corner as in some of the drawings in the Series (see above). Wallis may have added the signature later and so his part in the artistic endeavour remains uncertain.

INTRODUCTION

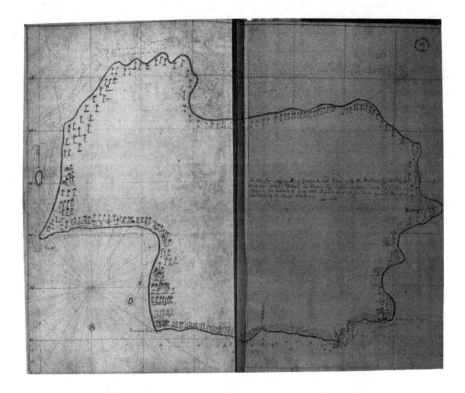

Figure 6 His Most Sacred Majestys King George the Third Island with the Harbour of Port Royal which was discovered Onboard his Majestys Ship the Dolphin on the Nineteenth day of June 1767 Lying in the Latitude of 17:° 29' South, Longitude 150:00 West from London by severall Observations variation of the compass 6:00 Easterly (Pilot)

Courtesy of the State Library of New South Wales

A detailed chart of Port Royal Harbour (unsigned) with a scale follows. Seven structures of varying sizes (much like the Queen's House) are detailed as are the varying depths of the water, the channels and the anchoring places (very likely labelled in Pinnock's script). This chart also shows the *Dolphin* for the first time opposite the largest house.

There are also two untitled studies and four other very basic, obviously unfinished attempts (not reproduced here) at drawing the Tahitian coastline, perhaps in view of a final, publishable picture. In the first drawing, there is no title, no signature, no North arrow. The page is nevertheless gridded as a drawing aid for perspective and scale. Thus, in these successive drawings in the *Pilot*, the *Plan* slowly progresses and the emergence of the focus of the Library Series becomes apparent as instead of paring down the detail to its basics (see above), the artwork effects a telescopic approach, drawing in more salient features, creating as it were

INTRODUCTION

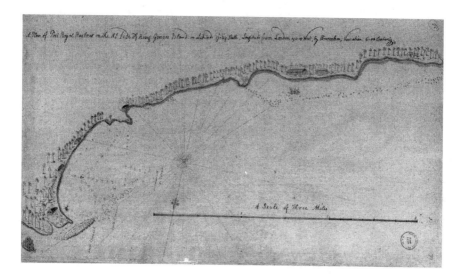

Figure 7 A Plan of Port Royal Harbour on the NE side of King Georges Island in Latitude 17:°29' South, Longitude from London 150:00 West, by Observation; Variation 6:00 Easterly (Pilot)

Courtesy of the State Library of New South Wales

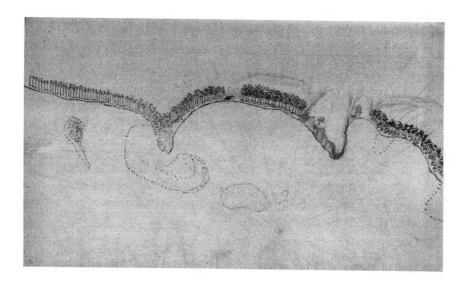

Figure 8 Untitled (Pilot)

Courtesy of the State Library of New South Wales

INTRODUCTION

Figure 9 Untitled (Pilot)
Courtesy of the State Library of New South Wales

the objects of interest, which were then taken up in the ensuing drawings of Port Royal. The ship gains prominence as does the distinguishing feature of One Tree Hill (so-called by Cook) and the Queen's House.

The artist here again is probably Pinnock as this drawing seems to be a precursor (uncharacteristically as his BL drawings seem primarily to be less elaborate than the *Pilot* iconography) to his *View* (see Figure 9), though he does not detail houses other than the principal Queen's house. Pinnock's *View*, is thus a "close-up", the one drawing without rhumb lines or the North arrow. He draws in nine manned canoes which do not appear in the *Pilot* book versions. Pinnock also very interestingly inserts the title in a banner, as in all the sketches in ML Series 1, the latter signed by Samuel Wallis. Wallis may then have copied and appropriated Pinnock's initial style and drawings. In the Series 3 version of the *Dolphin* at anchor, Wallis seems to partially reproduce Pinnock's *View* and depicts only one major structure, the Queen's House, and the ship. The manned canoes are more numerous than in Pinnock, the people represented as black dots in order to relay information as to canoe size but also as to the number of adversaries which the *Dolphin* had to struggle against on the day of battle. The hills acquire contours and gardens cultivated on the slopes are sketched in, the trees on the shore become more distinctive. The Series 4 version, with even more canoes and a wider perspective may have been the final version of this whole progression which seems to gain in precision and develop peripheral ornamentation, perhaps contrary to Minson's suggestion that the simpler the drawing, the more suited it is to publication. Unfortunately, the final published version however was not to be any of Pinnock's or Wallis's careful individual or collaborative attempts. Rather, Hawkesworth who obviously had access to some or all of the primary material chose to go from simple to complex in dramatic fashion by publishing *A Representation of the attack of Captain Wallis in the Dolphin by the natives of Otaheite*[85] in *Voyages* in which he conceives of a title and a scenario which neither Pinnock nor Wallis envisaged in their draughtsmanship or in their artwork. The engraving is a composite representation integrating the existing text and images to produce a new appraisal of contact and conflict. The *Dolphin*, the Queen's House, the wooded slopes, One Tree Hill and the manned canoes come together to constitute a scene of confrontation. The ship, with her intricate rigging and great cabin windows, in central position, fires her guns at the incongruously turbaned Tahitians in their single, double and canopied canoes. The black dots in Pinnock's and Wallis's rather more pacific renditions are fleshed out and detail is added, but not necessarily accurately.

Similarly, the drawings of the Queen's House are also reworked, first by Wallis himself and then by Hawkesworth. The very first sketches in the *Pilot* may be understood as exemplars of technical drawing only (there seems to have been several of these types of constructions according to the initial depictions). In the ML (Annex A), Wallis presumably is careful to produce an almost architectural blueprint of the house. There is no pictorial reference at all to the encounter between the Queen and the English in this technical drawing. In Series 2 (Annex F), the sketch is drawn up with a more elaborate background, the flora is carefully detailed, the house goes from having 40 supporting pillars to 37. And the Queen, the only image of a South Sea islander in the *Dolphin* iconographical collection, is in perhaps incidental pride of place in the image. She proffers a symbol of peace and the Englishmen appear small in size as compared to the majestic and overly tall Queen (in unwitting contradiction perhaps of accepted colonial codes). The title however remains almost the same as in Annex A, focusing on the technical aspects of the building and not on the fictitious site of encounter. In Series 3 and 4, this then fleeting interpersonal perspective disappears to the advantage of the view of the bay and the canoes, privileging once again the technological identities of the voyage. Hawkesworth chooses to re-introduce the interpersonal and bring in a new colonial dimension in commissioning the engraving *A representation of the surrender of the island of Otaheite to Captain Wallis by the supposed Queen Oberea*. The house with the pillars, the marines at attention, the Queen in robes carrying the symbol of peace are all elements taken from the originals. The basics though were added to, and Captain Wallis makes his appearance, as does the Queen's entourage. Based on the textual record (all the logs), the meeting with Wallis was not an act of surrender as the title of the engraving indicates, and never took place in these conditions.

To return to the remainder of the third category *Pilot* drawings, there are a further seven sketches of the other atolls and islands which Wallis discovered. All

---

85 See http://nla.gov.au/nla.pic-an9185012.

INTRODUCTION

the long titles are signed by the Captain. In the double-page drawing of *His Royal Highness the Duke of York's Island Discovered the 25th of June 1767 Onboard his Majestys Ship Dolphin. In Latitude of 16:16* S. Variation 5:°40' East. Longitude West from London by Observation 150:° 16 W,* Pinnock's template is reproduced but the form of the mountains inland, as seen from the sea, are represented, most certainly aids for the drawing up of the more elaborate views of the coastline to come. Again the shoreline is depicted in detail as concerns the vegetation and the buildings (but the reefs are not shown, as in Pinnock's version). The other six sketches include one of the Scilly Islands. This atoll is described thus: *at six the Eastermost land NEBN 3 leagues breakers to the S:°ward of it NW four or five leagues and breakers every where about it. Very squally dirty weather, kept turning to windward all night. At daylight crowded sail to get round these sholes and at nine got round them named them Scilly Islands, it being a group of islands and shoals that are very dangerous as the shoals are so far of every way that a*

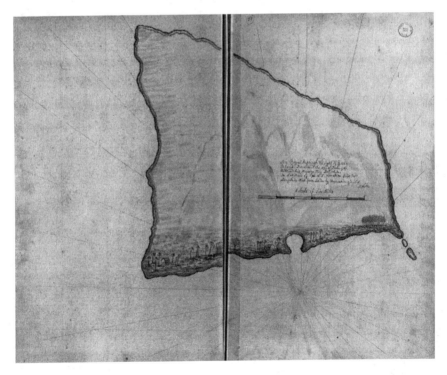

Figure 10 His Royal Highness the Duke of York's Island Discovered the 25th of June 1767 Onboard his Majestys Ship Dolphin. In Latitude of 16:16* S. Variation 5:°40' East. Longitude West from London by Observation 150:°16 W (Pilot)

Courtesy of the State Library of New South Wales

INTRODUCTION

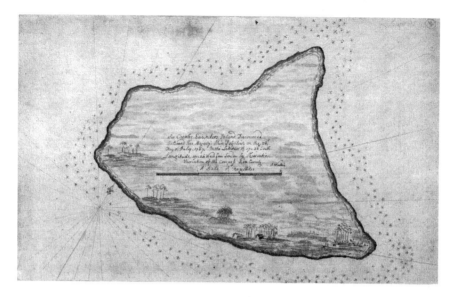

Figure 11 Sir Charles Saunders Island Discovered Onboard his Majesty's Ship Dolphin on the 28th Day of July 1767. In the latitude of 17:28* South. Longitude 151:04 West from London by Observation Variation of the Compass 6:08 Easterly (Pilot)

Courtesy of the State Library of New South Wales

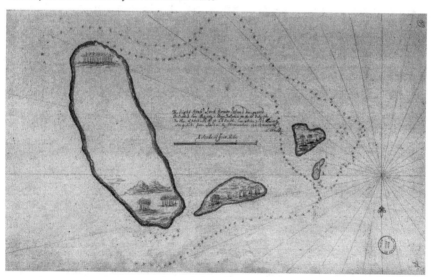

Figure 12 The Right Honb:le Lord Howes Island discovered Onboard his Majestys Ship Dolphin on the 30th July 1767 in the Latitude of 16:46* South. Variation 7:52 Easterly. Longitude from London by Observation 154:13 Westerly (Pilot)

Courtesy of the State Library of New South Wales

INTRODUCTION

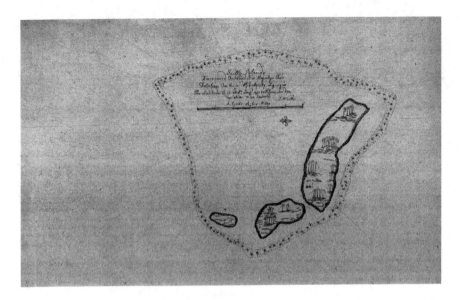

Figure 13 Scilly Islands Discovered Onboard his Majestys Ship Dolphin on the 31:ˢᵗ July 1767 Lying in the Latitude of 16:28* S:° Long:d 155:30 W from London. Variation 7:20 Easterly (Pilot Book)

Courtesy of the State Library of New South Wales

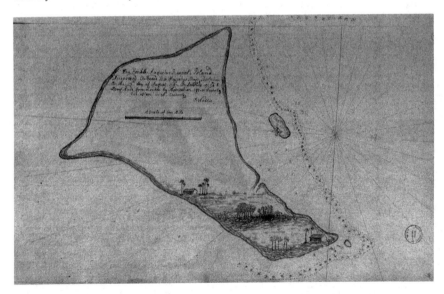

Figure 14 The Honᵇˡᵉ Augustus Keppel's Island Discovered Onboard His Majestys Ship Dolphin on the 13:ᵗʰ day of August 1767 In Latitude 15:54* S Longitude from London by Observation 177:00 Westerly. Variation 11:36 Easterly (Pilot)

Courtesy of the State Library of New South Wales

lii

INTRODUCTION

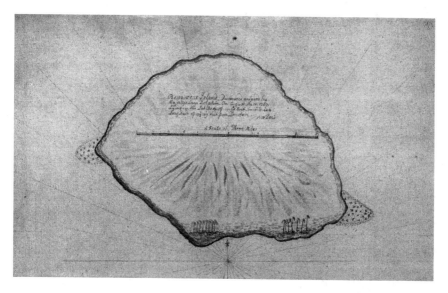

Figure 15 Boscawen's Island Discovered onboard His Majestys Ship Dolphin on the August 13:th 1767. Lying in the Latitude of 15:50* South. Variation 11:44 E. Longitude of 175:09 West from London (Pilot)
Courtesy of the State Library of New South Wales

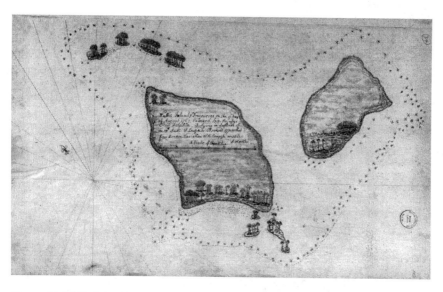

Figure 16 Wallis Islands Discovered on the 17 Day of August 1767 Onboard His Majestys Ship Dolphin, it lying in the Latitude of 13:18* South & Longitude Observed 177:00 West from London Variation of the Compass 10:00 E (Pilot)
Courtesy of the State Library of New South Wales

INTRODUCTION

Drawings	ML	Pinnock's Sketches	Pilot Book	Series 1 (20 drawings) Sea-and-shipscapes	Series 2 (12 drawings)	Series 3 (9 drawings)	Series 4 (11 drawings)
Whitsunday Island		✓	✓✓✓		✓		✓✓
Queen Charlotte's Island		✓✓	✓✓✓		✓✓ (2 drawings)	✓	
Earl of Egmont's Island		✓✓	✓		✓✓		
Duke of Gloucester's Island		✓✓			✓		
Duke of Cumberland's Island							
Prince William Henry's Island		✓✓					
Osnaburg's Island		✓✓✓	✓✓✓			✓✓	✓✓✓✓
King George's Island		✓✓✓✓	✓✓✓✓		✓	✓✓✓	✓✓✓✓
Duke of York's Island		✓✓	✓✓				
Sir Charles Saunders' Island		✓✓	✓✓		✓✓		
Lord Howe's Island		✓	✓✓✓		✓✓✓	✓✓	✓
Boscawen's Island			✓				
Scilly Isles							
Keppel's Island							
Wallis's Island							
Queen's house	✓						
Canoe	✓						
Fish							

clear night or hazey weather one might run on them without seeing land.[86] All the sketches are very reasonable estimates of size and shape considering that the *Dolphin* did not reconnoitre them in detail. None of the drawings feature canoes or people (even though, as mentioned above, there was encounter and exchange).

The *Pilot* thus contains an iconographical catalogue of the *Dolphin's* voyage round the world which might comprise the source, proto-material for the Library series. The table presents a summary of the contents of the various collections of drawings which George Pinnock and Samuel Wallis were closely connected with, not including the charts and maps by Robertson for example, which remain to be categorised and associated with the results of the *Dolphin* voyage. The table also suggests a tentative timeline of the order of execution of the artwork where Pinnock's work and the *Pilot* drawings, the most representative of the South Sea discoveries, may have served as studies for more elaborate charts and illustrations with a view to publication.

In addition to the concern for the compilation of a textual record, shown by the making of careful copies of the logs which this transcription highlights, that Wallis was also deeply interested in constituting an iconographical archive of the *Dolphin* voyage is clear. Fittingly, Henry Stubble's portrait of Wallis[87] shows the Captain sitting at a table, simply drawing, without the added adornment of plentiful gold braid, books and charts to identify him as the proficient navigator and explorer he must have been.

---

86 In the PL and the FC.
87 The entry in the ODNB reproduces a black and white photograph of another portrait (artist unknown) of Wallis. This photograph is held at the National Portrait Gallery (Reference Negative 27302) but the whereabouts of the original are unknown.

INTRODUCTION

Annex A

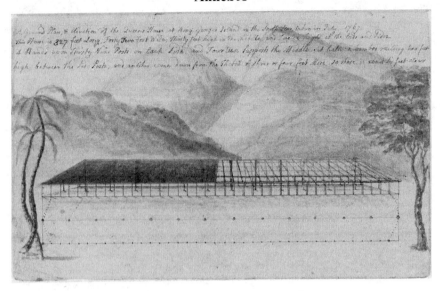

Figure A1 Illustration on the back cover of Volume II of Wallis's log:

A ground plan & elevation of the Queens House at King Georges Island in the South Seas in July 1767. This House is 327 feet long, forty two feet wide, thirty feet high in the middle, and twelve feet at the ends and sides. It stands upon thirty nine posts on each side and fourteen support the middle. It hath a bamboo railing two feet high between the side posts and another comes down from the thatch of three or four feet more so there is about six feet clear

Courtesy of the State Library of New South Wales.

INTRODUCTION

Annex B

Figure B1 First page of the Sketchbook showing the *Dolphin* surrounded by ships and in sight of land

Courtesy of the State Library of New South Wales.

INTRODUCTION

Annex C

Figure C1 Second page of the Sketchbook showing the *Dolphin* most probably in company with the *Swallow*.

Courtesy of the State Library of New South Wales.

INTRODUCTION

Annex D

Figure D1 Third page of the Sketchbook showing the *Dolphin* from two perspectives. Courtesy of the State Library of New South Wales.

INTRODUCTION

Annex E

Figure E1 Last page of the Sketchbook showing the boat rowing back to the ship.
Courtesy of the State Library of New South Wales.

INTRODUCTION

Annex F

Figure F1 This drawing is labelled *A Ground Plan; and Perspective View of the Queens House, at King Georges Island, Lying in Lat:^{d} 17:30 S and Longitude of 150:00 West from London. This House is 327 feet Long and forty two feet Broad it is supported in the Middle by fourteen Pillars and Thirty Nine at the Sides, is thirty feet high in the Middle and Twelve feet high at the Sides. Discovered by his Majestys Ship Dolphin on the 24. of June 1767. Done by Sam: Wallis. 1767* (Series 2)

Courtesy of the State Library of New South Wales.

INTRODUCTION

Annex G

Figure G1 Drawing of Wallis Island (Series 2)
Courtesy of the State Library of New South Wales.

INTRODUCTION

Annex H

Figure H1 Whitsunday Island
Courtesy of the National Library of Australia

Figure H2 Osnaburg Island
Courtesy of the National Library of Australia

Figure H3 Otaheiti or King Georges Island
Courtesy of the National Library of Australia

Figure H4 York Island
Courtesy of the National Library of Australia

INTRODUCTION

Figure H5 Saunders Island
Courtesy of the National Library of Australia

Figure H6 Howe Island
Courtesy of the National Library of Australia

INTRODUCTION

Figure H7 Keppel Island
Courtesy of the National Library of Australia

Figure H8 Wallis Island
Courtesy of the National Library of Australia

Figure H9 Untitled drawing
Courtesy of the National Library of Australia

INTRODUCTION

Annex I

Figure 11 This image is dated 26th June 1767 (Series 4) and is of St George's Island, though this is not specified on the back of drawing.

Courtesy of the National Library of Australia

INTRODUCTION

Annex J

The Pinnock Charts are labelled as follows:

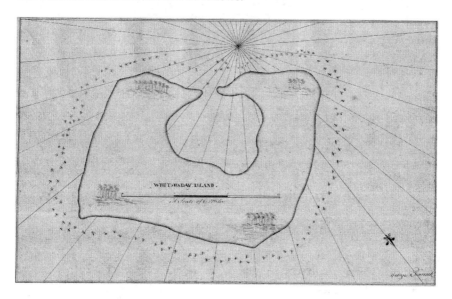

Figure J1 Whitsunday: Island
Courtesy of the British Library

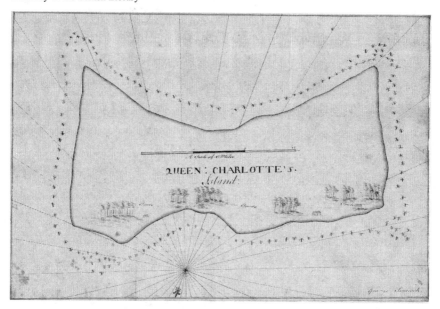

Figure J2 Queen: Charlotte's Island
Courtesy of the British Library

INTRODUCTION

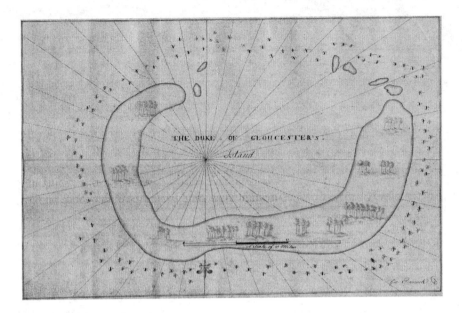

Figure J3 Duke: of Gloucester's Island
Courtesy of the British Library

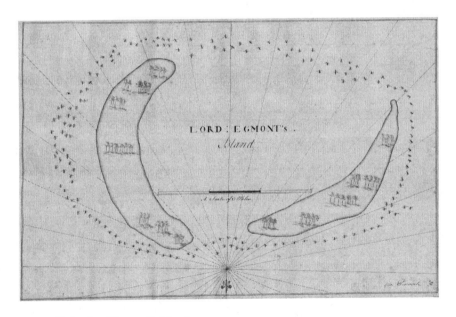

Figure J4 Lord: of Egmont's Island
Courtesy of the British Library

INTRODUCTION

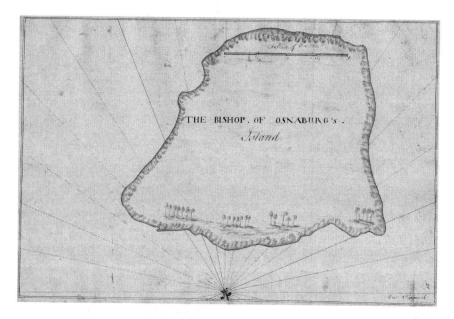

Figure J5 Bishop of Osnaburg's Island
Courtesy of the British Library

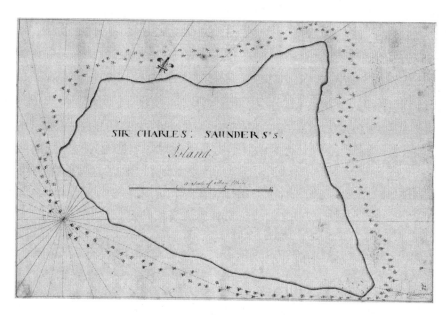

Figure J6 Sir Charles: Saunders's Island
Courtesy of the British Library

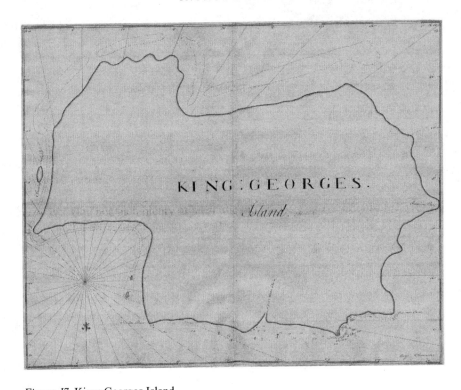

Figure J7 King: Georges Island
Courtesy of the British Library

INTRODUCTION

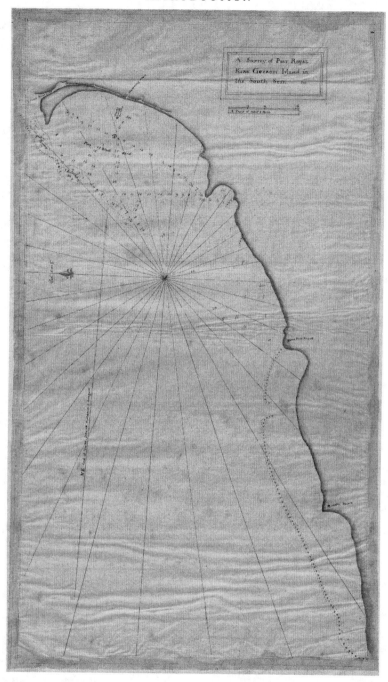

Figure J8 A Survey of Port Royal King Georges Island In the South Seas
Courtesy of the British Library

Figure J9 A View of Port Royal Bay at Georges Island [drawing of the *Dolphin* at anchor in Port Royal with the Queen's house in the background]

Courtesy of the British Library

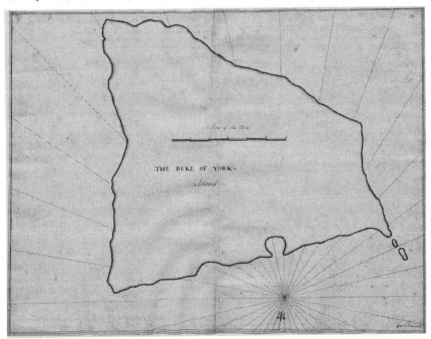

Figure J10 Duke of York's Island

Courtesy of the British Library

INTRODUCTION

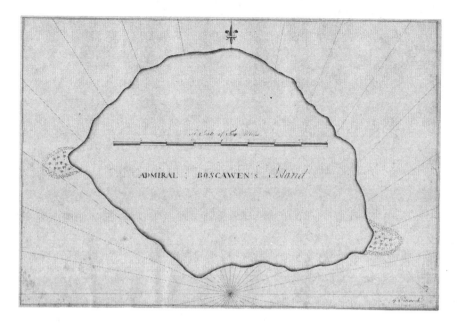

Figure J11 Admiral: Boscawen's Island
Courtesy of the British Library

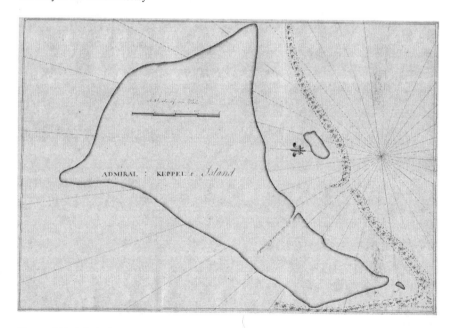

Figure J12 Admiral: Keppel's Island
Courtesy of the British Library

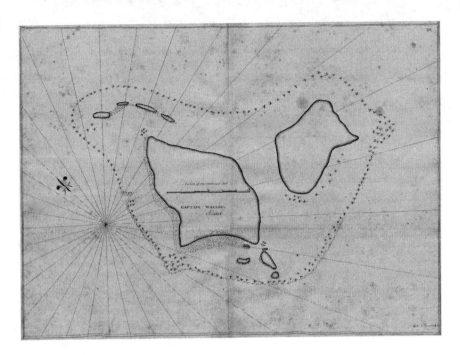

Figure J13 Captain Wallis's Island
Courtesy of the British Library

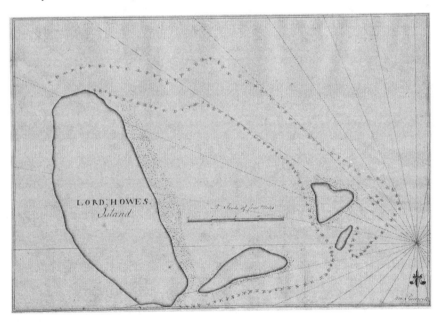

Figure J14 Lord: Howes Island
Courtesy of the British Library

INTRODUCTION

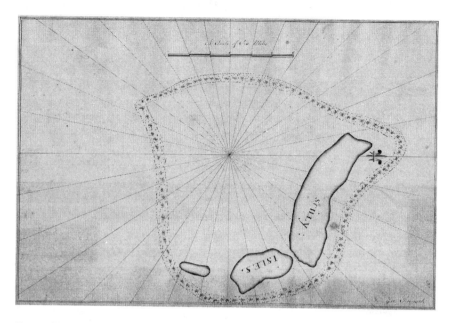

Figure J15 Scilly Isles
Courtesy of the British Library

INTRODUCTION

Annex K

1

Extracts from Captain Wallis's Journal (British Library RP 9327)
Courtesy of the British Library
   Aug.t 1766

21st. Sailed from Plymouth in company with the Swallow Sloop and Prince Frederick Store ship.
Sept. 8th. Arrived at Madeira. Got refreshments water and wine.
12th. Sailed from Madeira.
15th. Saw the Island of Palma.
21st. Saw Island of Sal.
22nd. Lost company with the Swallow.
23rd. Past Bonavista. saw the Isle of May. joined the Swallow.
24th. Arrived at Port Praya in the Isle of St Jago. Got refreshments.

2

28th. Sailed past the Isle of Fuego.
Oct. 7th. Sawe Coast of Brazil, along which we sailed.
8th. Passed Cape Blanco, Penguin Isle and Port Desire.
10th. Passed St Juliano.
12th. Cape Beachy-Head. Cape Fairweather.
17th. Anchored in a Bay close under Cape Virgin Mary. Saw a great many men on the shore with horses, calling and waving to us. – Went on shore with a strong party. – Made signs to the people to come and sit down in a semicircle which they did cheerfully – Gave them several toys &tc, which they took with great joy – endeavoured to make them understand we wanted fresh Meat, and offered them hatchets, bill-hooks &tc. But they would not comprehend us, but yet seemed very desirous of the hatchets.

3

Dec.r 1766. – Every man had his horse, with saddle, stirrups and bridle – The Men wore wooden spurs, except one who had a large pair of Spanish spurs, brass stirrups, and Spanish scimetar, but did not appear of any greater authority than the others. –

On measuring them with a rod, found one six feet seven, several six feet 5 & 6 inches; but the greater part about six feet, well made and robust, cloathed with skins sewed together and tied round their middle, and a large kind of drawers and buskins – Every one had a sling, which consists of two stones, as big as a fist, covered with leather and tied together with a Thong about 8 feet long. This they are very dexterous in throwing, and will

4

1766 make both the stones hit a small mark at fifteen yards distance.

They had ostriches tied to their saddles which they eat raw, and offered us some. – We stayed 4 hours among them and offered to take some of them on board. – most of them were desirous to go – took 8 on board – who did not seem astonished at the ship, but excessively pleased with a looking-glass, and surprized at the animals on board, particularly 3 guinea hens, and turkies. They eat any thing but would drink nothing but water – gave each a canvas bag with a number of odd things in it – about noon made signs to them that they must go on shore – Found it difficult to get them to leave the ship –

5

Decr 1766. They would steal anything they could lay hold of, but if seen would give it up gain quietly; one of them would not be prevailed on to go till he had got a pair of shoes and buckles. Most of them had their faces painted whimsically with red circles about their eyes, and the girls had their eye lids painted black. They continually repeated the word Chevow, which seemed to be their salutation : likewise the word Capitane, but did not seem to understand any Spanish or Portugueze.

They repeated English very distinctly.

Several of them had beads, and red baize, similar to that I gave them, which I conclude was given them by Mr Byron –

18th Weighed and made sail – came

6

Decr 1766

to an Anchor again farther on, about 3 miles from the shore – Saw a number of people. And this being the exact place where Mr Byron saw the tall men, sent a boat to reconnoitre them- brought back word they were the same we had seen yesterday, with a greater number: that they were very desirous of coming off, and those who had been on board yesterday waded into the sea to come to us; but our people could not make them bring provisions – They had a great number of women children and dogs with them.

25th. Anchored under Elizabeth Island, in the Streights of Magellan.

27 Anchored in Port Famine Bay – Good water and with wild vegetables at Port Famine, and excellent fish caught

7

Decr 1766

in the Bay. The Crew at their arrival looked very pale and meagre and many of them had the scurvy but in a fortnights time by being on shore, eating a great deal of vegetable food and being very cleanly, of which the greatest care was taken, they were perfectly recovered.

Jany 1767

17th The Store Ship, being now emptied, sailed for Falklands Islands –

18th Sailed with the Swallow. We were from this time so

April 10th in the Streights, labouring with every kind of difficulty and danger, – winds and currents continually against us, exposed to the most violent Sto rms coming in sudden squalls and Gusts from the mountains without any warning, often unable to get any

April 1767

8

Anchorage, and in constant expectation of being dashed against the perpendicular rocks, which form the coast of both sides. At such times as we were obliged to the still, we got vegetables and fish, by which means our men continued pretty free from scurvy, but were disordered with fatigues colds and fluxes. The farther you advance in the Straights, the more mountanous, desolate and dreary the country is, and barren to the greatest degree. The Natives who are but few, seem to be the most wretched of human beings. We saw them three or four times. They are low in stature and sometimes quite naked, at other times covered with seals skins, the rotten flesh and blubber of which they chiefly live upon. Our people gave them some fish they

9

April 1767

had just caught, which they immediately eat raw, beginning at the head, and eating to the tail, bones, scales, fins and all. They would eat any thing but would drink nothing but water. Their canoes were very clumsily made. They were armed with bow and arrows and javelins pointed with flint, with which they struck seals, penguins, &^tc. They were excessive chilly and most of them had their eyes very red and so owing to their being constantly crowding over a smoaky fire. They smell most insupportably strong.

April 11th. We got out of the Streights and in order to do this were obliged to carry so much sail, that we lost sight of the Swallow; and bad weather coming on we were forced to get as good an offing as we could, and never saw

10

April 1767

anything more of her.

May 3rd.

Kept to the Westward *during this interval* as much as possible but found so great a sea and such bad weather, and our ship so deep, that we saw no chance of making any progress in the latitude we then were in, so ran down to the Northward, into latitude 22 and the bore away to the West. We met with such terrible seas ever since we came out of the Straights, and such a violent swell from the South West that the ship being pretty Loose and open in her upper works the men had been constantly wet in their beds, by which numbers of them were very ill with colds and some with scurvy. We passed the spot where Davis's Land is marked and cruised several days for it, but could not find it. One afternoon we fancied we saw high Land to the Eastward and stood for it till sun-set, when it still continuing to have the same appearance, we stood on till two in the morning when we could see nothing; and having run 18 Leagues we hauled our wind: the next morning was very clear and we saw nothing. We had now fine weather with South and East winds. Our people recovered of their disorders but began to grow ill of the scurvy.

11

June 1767

6th. Discovered a small island – Bore up to it and saw another island at a small distance from the first: Sent of the 2 Lieutenant to rennoitre the first, who found it a small flat place, producing nothing but cocoa nuts and scurvy-grass, without fresh water or anchorage. There were some people on it., who on the boats approach, put off in two canoes and made for the other Island.

8th Sent a Boat to the other Island, where the natives stood on their guard and did not chuse our people should land but brought them some water and cocoa nuts with which they waded to them, and our people gave them nails, hatchets, &^{tc}.

9th When our people went back they found seven large canoes with two masts in each lying in the surf and the people by them, who beckoned to our men to go higher up, which they did and landed when the natives embarked in their canoes and were joined by two more and sailed quite away, steering W.S.W. This Island was sandy and level, full of trees, but not many cocoanut trees or underwood. The people were

12

June 1767

intirely gone, and had left little behind them, but for 4 or 5 canoes and some tools made with shells and stones sharpened. Could find no anchorage, so stood on and off while we sent our people on shore to get water, and what refreshments they could, with strict orders not to do any damage to the canoes, huts or trees, leaving several things, such as hatchets, nails, beads, glass bottles, and shillings and six pence's and half-pence, together with the ships name, and time of our coming. We called this island Queen Charlotte's Island and the first Whitsunday Island

11th. Came to another island or rather a cluster of islands, where we found our friends from the other island with their canoes. They came close down to the waterside with long pikes in their hands and some firebrands, dancing in a strange manner, and making a noise: there were several women and children who stayed with the canoes which were hauled upon the shore. We guessed these might be in all 80. These Islands were low, full of trees but no cocoas, sandy not green as Charlotte's Island under the trees: so narrow that we could see through from one side to the other: There is

13

June 1767

No anchorage near, they being surrounded with a platform Rock, beyond which no sounding. Finding no prospect of an advantage to be got here, we passed on calling this Egmont's Island. The inhabitants appeared a handsome, well made people of a reddish colour.

12th. Passed another Island in every respect like the last, at one end of which we saw about 16 inhabitants. Called this Gloucester Island.

13th. Passed another Island surrounded with breakers, Called this Cumberland Island

14th. Passed another, which we called Prince William Henry's Island.

17th. Saw a high land at a distance, came to it and sent a boat on shore, which brought back word that there was no anchorage and the island difficult to access: that there were several large canoes and a great number of people, more in all probability than the island which was very small could support. They brought a few provisions, for which they had trafficked with the natives. While they were doing this, the boat was fastened to a grapnel, and they had thrown a warp on shore which the natives took hold of and held. They had no

14

June 1767

Weapons among them except some white sticks, which were held by people who seemed to be in authority and who kept the others back. Upon our men giving them looking-glasses, toys &tc. the women all came running down to the water but the men drove them back. Soon after a man came slily round a rock, and dived and weighed the grapnel and at the same time the natives made an attempt to draw the boat on shore. But on our people firing a musquet they all desisted and our men finding they could get nothing more then came away; we called this Osnaburg Island.

18th. Discovered very high Land, lay to in the night.

19th. At day break found ourselves surrounded by some hundreds of canoes, with different numbers of men, from one to ten in them, hallowing and making strange noises. The land appeared very high in the peaks, the sides of the hills looked cultivated and the shore full of houses and people. It was level near the waterside, and full of cocoa trees. From the sides of the mountains we saw several large rivers. – Several of the people came on board. On shewing them fowls and hogs, they

17

June 1767

made signs that they had such things, but on being shewn goats and sheep, they ran away and jumped overboard with fear but afterwards came back. We made them signs to bring us necessaries but they did not seem to understand, and were chiefly employed in Stealing what they could; one of them snatched a laced hat off a Midshipmans head, and jumped overboard with it.

20th. Sent our boats out to look for anchorage which they could not find thereabouts. A number of natives in their canoes, gathered about our boats and attacked them with stones but on the ships bearing down and firing over them and the boat firing once and wounding one man, they retired.

21st. Sailed along the shore in search of anchorage. Found anchorage – numbers of the natives came and brought fowls hogs and Fruit which we bought of them. Sent our boat towards the shore to reconnoitre: they were gain attacked by the natives, and fired over their heads which they did not mind so were forced to wound some on which they desisted. And still kept trading with the ship.

16

June 1767

Sent the boats again to sound and get some water. Some thousands of the people collected on the beach, where there was a fine stream of fresh water. The natives took their water vessels and returned two of them filled and kept the others. Seemed to want to entice our people on shore – the women acted every lewd gesture imaginable for that purpose. Our people found the ship might lie within two cables length of the shore.

22d. Intended to run in and anchor here, but standing out in order to get more Windward, discovered a bay round a point for which we stood. Just as we were entering it, unfortunately ran foul of a rock of coral tho' we had two boats sounding ahead: lay some time in great danger, but got off without mischief; got into the bay and anchored.

23d. Began to warp the ship up the bay to get near the shore – A great number of Boats gather'd about the Ship, many of them with a Dozen Men in each and ballasted with round Pebble stones. Then came others who had women with them, who made all kinds of lascivious gestures and all the boats crowded round the ship, the people

17

June 1767

playing on flutes, blowing shells, and singing with hoarse voices. At last a – sitting on a Canopy, fixed up in a large Canoe, came near the ship, and gave a bunch of red and yellow feathers to one of our men, and pushed off again: as soon as he had done that, he flung a branch of cocoa tree up into the air, on which a shower of stones was instantly poured into the ship from every side and all the Canoes at once moved towards the ship. I ordered the guard to fire, and two quarter-deck guns loaden with small shot were discharged amongst them: this checked them a moment, but they soon came on again, on which we fired our great guns, some among the canoes, others at a part of the shore where there were a number of canoes taking in men and coming off towards us. Upon this fire they desisted and pulled away-

We ceased firing on which they hoisted white streamers in their boats, and collected again together, and attacked us with stones of two pound weight, which they threw very dexterously with slings, and began to approach the ships bow, where they had probably observed no shot were fired. – Two guns were immediately run out there, and fired

18

June 1767

and one of the shot having hit the principal canoe, and cut her in sunder they all dispersed and in half an hour there was not a canoe to be seen – We warped the ship up, and anchored about a cable and half from the shore, close to a watering place.

24th. Sent boats to reonnoitre the whole bay and to fix a landing place opposite to the ship.

25th. Took possession and hoisted a staff and Pendant, and called the Island St George's Island. Tasted the water of the river, which does not fall into the bay, but empties itself round the point, found it good. Saw two old men on the other side in a suppliant posture – beckoned them over – One came on his hands and knees – tried to make him sensible they had used us ill, and that we only came for refreshments and shewed him what we would give in exchange – left some things with him and came away the Pendant remaining flying. Soon after the old man danced round the pendant staff for a considerable time, then threw down the boughs, the retired, and came forward again in a suppliant posture with a dozen of the inhabitants who would come up close to it but when the wind moved it would retire

19

June 1767

With great precipitation – Soon after they brought down two hogs, which they laid down at the foot of the staff, and after a while brought them down to the water and put them in a canoe, and the old man brought them to the ship. – when he came alongside he gave in several Plaintain leaves making a speech with every leaf, and then gave in the two hogs. He would take nothing. In the night we heard the noise of many conch's Drums and wind instruments.

26th. Saw no people. The Pendant taken away – Sent the people on shore with casks to begin water – the old man with a few of the people came down and brought some things, but kept on the opposite side the river. About – we discovered from the ship many thousands of people, pushing down from all sides, among the woods towards our people and a great number of Canoes coming round each point into the bay. Sent to order the people off – They were forced to leave the Casks which the natives took possession of with great rejoicing. In the mean time, the number of canoes increased amazingly, the

20

June 1767

inhabitants keeping pace with them on the shore, and getting into them as fast as they could, carrying large bags on board with them. As they were now making to the Ship and there was no room to doubt of their hostile purpose, I ordered some guns to be fired each way at them which immediately put them to flight; those nearest running on shore and the others pushing away out of the beach. We then fired into the woods, which they soon quitted and assembled in a prodigious multitude on the hills behind, where the women and children were as they thought in great security I ordered four guns to be let down as low as possible, and fired that way – Two of the shot fell close to a tree where numbers of them were sitting, which so alarmed them, that in a few minutes there was not one to be seen. I then sent the carpenter on shore and cut to pieces all the Canoes that were lying there, to the amount of fifty – many of them were sixty feet long and three broad and were lashed two together, and filled with stones and slings – about two hours afterwards, ten of the natives came down to the beach with green boughs

21

June 1767

Which they stuck up and retired – Then came down again, and brought Hogs and Dogs, with their legs tied, and cloth which they left, making signs for us to take it – Sent and fetched the hog but left the other things – Left Hatchets and Nails in the place, which the natives would not touch, because we had not taken all their things – Sent and fetched the cloth & Dogs away, on which they took our things and rejoiced much – Sent and brought away our water casks, which were not damaged.

27th. Sent people on shore to water – the old man came down again to them – our people shewed him the stones that had been flung, and endeavoured to convince him that we meant them no harm, but were forced to act as we did. He turned to the other people and made a long and vehement discourse to them showing the stones, slings &tc. much in the same manner we had shewed him. We then shook hands and embraced, and settled to traffick for Provisions, we to remain on our side the stream, and they on theirs. On this regulation great quantities of Provisions were soon brought down –

22

June 1767

Appointed an Officer to command on shore and manage the intercourse – sent all the sick on shore, and erected a tent for them – The old man kept near us, and was very helpful.

28th. Sick people recovered very fast – From

29th

July 6th. Continued in the same way – Had not such plenty of meat, the old man not appearing – Examined the ships bottom, found she had received no damage and was as clean as when she came out of dock – The old man returned – had been up the country to make the people come down to trade with us. –

7th. The price of things much raised, by the sailors having stole so much Iron work from the ship – The natives now require a long spike for what they took a small nail for before.

10th. Some of the natives who seemed above the common sort, came off in our boat to the ship, where they had some presents and were sent on shore again.

13th Gunner came on board with a tall well looking woman, seemingly about 45 years of age with a very majestic mein. She was just come to the shore, and he seeing great respect paid her, made her

23

July 1767

some presents; in return she invited him to her habitation, about two miles up the valley, and gave him some large hogs; then came with him on board. She was quite free and easy while in the ship. I made her a present of a large blue mantle tied with ribbons, and several beads. Seeing I had been ill she invited me on shore. I made signs I would come the next day.

14th. I went on shore for the first time, when the Queen (as she appeared to be) soon came – She made her people carry me, and others who were weak from illness cross the river and quite to her house, which was very large and well built. She seemed to have a number of guards and domesticks living within. The sides were chiefly open: but she had another large one near it, that was closed up with lattice work. There was a great multitude of people around us but on her waving her hand they withdrew. As we approached the habitation, a great number of Men and Women came court to meet her, whom she brought to me, and making signs that they were her relations, she made them all kiss my Hand. Then coming

24

July 1767

in the house, she made us all sit down, and four young girls took off my shoes and stockings, and my coat, and then gently rubbed the skin with their hands. They did the same for the Lieutenant and Purser, who were both ill; but did not trouble those who appeared well. After about half an hour, they dressed us again. The Queen then took some pieces of their cloth, which she made us put on. Upon our taking leave, she ordered a large sow and Pigs to be taken down to the Boat, and accompanied us thither herself. And as I chose to walk alone rather than be carried she took hold of my arm and lifted me over any difficult place with as much ease as I should have done a child.

15th. Sent the gunner on shore with some presents to the Queen. He found her giving an entertainment to near a thousand people. She distributed the messes to them herself; after which she sat down by herself in a high place, and her attendant women came and fed her. She only opening her mouth. She ordered a mess for the Gunner, which he said he though consisted of Fowl –

25

July 1767

small, mixed with apples, and seasoned with salt water. –

16th. Great complaints that the trade is spoiled by large spikes which the sailors steal from the ship, and carry on shore to give the women; by which means they will part for nothing but for twice as much as first.

17th Sent the Lieutenant with a strong   and the boats along shore to reconnoiter. They went about six miles, found the country very pleasant, populous and the people very civil. Fine anchorage to the shore the whole way.

18th. And

19th. The Queen having been absent some days is returned.

20th. The Queen came on board, and stayed most part of the day. The Master went on shore with her in the evening; on landing, she took him by the hand, and made a long speech to the natives, – him up to her house and cloathed him in her dress.

23rd. The Queen came on shore and invited us on shore, whither we went; she made us sit down, and took our hats, and tied bunches of feathers in them

26

July 1767

and put large wreaths of hair, knotted and braided round our necks, which she seemed to tell us was her own hair, and her own work – I endeavoured to make her understand that in seven days we should depart: she understood me immediately, and made signs that we should stay twenty days, and that we should go up into the country with her for a few days I made her understand that we must go at the time first mentioned, on which she sat down and cried bitterly.

24th. The Gunner desired some presents for the old man, who had been very useful, and who he thought would let his son go with us – sent some accordingly.

25th. Sent the Queen two turkies, two Geese, three Guinea hens, a cat big with kitten, some China Glass bottles, shirts, needles, thread, cloth, Ribbons, iron pots, scissors, knives and spoons and about sixteen different sorts of garden seeds, which we planted for her, and shewed her the method, – some that we had planted at first, were now come up and very flourishing. Sent Mr Gore, with the two Marines, and forty seamen, up the country to make

27

July 1767

observations on the soil and produce and went on shore with Mr Harrison, observe and eclipse of the sun which I had foretold to the people, who were gathered in great numbers to see it. After we had made our observations, let the Queen and her attendants look thro' the glass to their utter astonishment. Afterwards invited the Queen and her Company to Dinner on board, which they accepted, only the Queen would not eat nor drink: The others eat very heartily but would drink only water. In the evening when Mr Gore and his Company were returned we landed the Queen &tc. Mr Gore gave me a written account of his expedition, which is subjoined.

26th. Queen came on board in the morning but went back soon after. Many new more inhabitants seem to be come from the country, several of them persons to whom great respect is shewn by the others. In the afternoon the Queen came again on board with the old man, bringing some very fine fruit. She made us signs to stay ten days longer, while she went up the country to bring us more things – we shewed her that we must go the next day

28

July 1767

On which she wept much; then made signs to know when we should come back we answered in fifty days, at which she seemed pleased, but wanted us to fix our return in thirty days. At night she could scarce be prevailed on to go on shore, but lay down upon the arms chest, and cried for a long time; but at length went away. We had lost the old mans son for some days, tho' he made signs that he was gone up into the country to take leave of his friends, and would return to go with us, which however he did not. –

27th. Made our preparations for sailing, and sent the barge and cutter to fill the empty casks. They found the shore covered with people, so that they declined landing, till the Queen came forward and called to them, making the multitude retire beyond the river. When they had done their business she would have come off with them, but the officer having orders to bring nobody off could not admit her. On which she immediately launched one of her own largest canoes and came to the ship attended with about 15 more canoes. She came onboard crying much, and staid about an hour when a breeze springing up, we were

29

July 1767

obliged to take our leave of her. She quitted us with great affection as did all her attendants, embracing us all round in the most affectionate manner. Soon after she had left us, it fell calm on which the canoes returned to the shore, the Queens was made fast to one of the ports, she came and sat in the head of it, she crying. We made her a number of presents of everything we could useful which she accepted, yet seemed to make very little account of them. At length, a fresh gale sprung up, and the ship now being at some distance from the shore and the sea beginning to run rather high, she shook us all round by the hand, and put off and returned to the shore

At the time we left this island we – the greatest stock of fresh provisions –, water that we could possible stow; and our men healthy, except myself and the first Lieutenant, who recover but slow.

28th. Passed along another island much resembling Georges Island in appearance and population but much smaller, full of fine harbours and good anchorage: But it being so – other island and the people continually passing from one to the other in their

30

July 1767

canoes, we did not think it necessary to go on shore here, especially as the weather was growing bad. Called this the Duke of York's Island.

29th. Passed another island six miles long with few inhabitants on it, and in every respect much inferior to those we had left. We did not stop but called it Sir Charles Saunders's Island.

31 Passed a small poor island, without any anchorage about it, and scarce any appearance of cultivation or inhabitants except a smoak we perceived at one end. This we called Lord Howe's Island. In the evening saw land but found it of dangerous approach on account of shoals and rocks, kept off till next morning

Aug.t 1st. Sailed by this land, which we found to be a group of islands, mixed with shoals and rocks called them Scilly Islands

2nd. One of the seamen fell from the Main yard and was killed.

14th. Discovered two islands, called the first Boscawen's, and the other Keppel's islands. Passed by Boscawen's which did not seem promising, and bore for Keppel's –

15th. Sent our boats to inspect this island, they found very indifferent anchorage, but a tolerable good watering place. They got

31

Aug.¹ 1767

two fowls and some fruit. About fifty inhabitants came down on the shore, and stood looking, but would not come nearer than 100 yards. Two canoes came likewise with the six men, who seemed peaceably inclined, they had all lost the first joints of their little fingers, were clothed with Matt; but in make and complection, were much like the people of Geroge's Island. When our people were coming away, there of the men from these canoes, came into our boat, but when they had got about half a mile, they suddenly jumped overboard and swam away. Upon considering all circumstances, we now determined it would be best to return by the way of the Cape of Good Hope; and that we might refresh better at Tinian, and at Battavia, than by stopping here : So made sail and bore away.

16th. Saw land in the evening.

17th. Sent the Master to inspect it, who found it in every respect similar to the last seen. Met with some inhabitants with whom he trafficked, but could not get any provisions from them. They were clothed like the last, only rather worse, and seemed very treacherous, and ill designing, tho' not openly hostile. The shore appeared tolerably

SAMUEL WALLIS'S VOYAGE ROUND THE WORLD IN THE *DOLPHIN*, 1766–1768

Figure 17 Samuel Wallis by Henry Stubble
Courtesy of the National Library of Australia

[1]Dolphins Loggbook. Put in Commission the 19th Day of June 1766 at Deptford. came out of the dock the 8:th[2] of July 1766, sailed to Long Reach the 26:th July 1766, from Long Reach to the Nore the 1:st, 2:d, 3:d of August. Sailed from the Nore for the Downs in company with the Swallow sloop the 11:th of August where we anchored at night, next day we sailed from the Downs for Plymouth being 12:th of August, and arrived at Plymouth the 16:th of August, 1766; Sailed from Plymouth in company with the Swallow sloop and Frederick Victualler August the 21:st 1766. Arrived at Madeira Monday Sep.r 8:th at 6 PM; Sailed from thence Friday the 12:th at 8 AM; Pass'd by the Island of Palma Sep:r the 15:th at Noon. Wednesday September 24 at 3 PM anchored at Port Praya in S:t Jago one of the Cape de Verd Islands and on Sunday Sep:r 28 at 1 PM sailed from Port Praya; October 22:d crossed the Equinox. On Sunday December the 7:th at 6 AM saw the land near Cape Blanco in Patagonia South America. On Wednesday December the 17:th at 8 PM anchored under Cape Virgin Mary at the entrance of the Straights of Magellan. the 18:th PM entred the Straights the 27:th Anchord at Port Famine January 18:th 1767, sailed from Port Famine in company with the Swallow, the Prince Frederick storeship sailed from thence the 17:th for Port Egmont Sunday April 12 at 1 PM got round the Islands of Direction and enterd the South Sea. we lost sight of the Swallow about two hours before this under Cape Pillar; & the weather looking very greasy & blowing very fresh from the SW and WSW was obliged to carry all the sail we could to get of the shore. June 6 made Charlotte & Whitsun Islands, June the 11:th sailed by Prince Will:m Henry's Island, the 12 passed by the Duke of Gloucester's Island, the Princess[3] of Brunswick and Prince Henry's Islands, the 17 made the Bishop of Osnaburg. The 19:th discovered King George the Thirds Island. the East end; the 21:st anchord about the middle of the Island, the 23 anchord in Port Royal Harbour near the West end of King Georges Island, and four leagues from the Duke of Yorks Island. And the next day continued here until the 27:th day of July and then sailed Westward, the 28 from ½ past Noon until six in the evening off the Duke of Yorks Island and the next day at Noon passed by Admiral Saunders Island. July the 30:th passed by Lord Howes Island, & the 31:st were entangled from four in the afternoon untill – [4] with the Dangerous Reefs & the Islands of Scilly. August the 14:th & 15, pass'd by Boscawens, & Keppels Islands. August 17:th pass'd by Wallis's Island September the *(sic)* pass'd by the Piscadore Islands; September the 20 we anchored at Tinian, and on the 17 of October we sailed from thence, October the 29 we pass by the

---

1 This is the transcription of the log held at the Mitchell Library, Sydney, and will be referred to in this volume as the ML. The second log is in the Public Records Office, London and will be referenced as the PL. The third is the FC, or fair copy, held at the Alexander Turnbull Library in Wellington, New Zealand. This particular entry in the ML does not appear in the two other logs.
2 Wallis usually, but not always, inserts a colon between the number and the superscript when writing dates. We have followed the log and the colon is sometimes included and at other times omitted.
3 Throughout the log, the island is referred to as *Prince* of Brunswick Island.
4 Illegible (…will indicate illegible script in the rest of this transcription).

Basshee Islands. November the 3, 4, & fifth entangled with dangerous shoals in the Chinese Seas November the eighth pass'd by the island of Pulo Condore, the 14:th passed by the islands of Pulo Condore, Aroa and Pesang. The 23:d entered the Streights of Banca; and on the first day of December arrived at Batavia and sailed from thence the eighth, anchord at Princess Island December 16:th and sailed from thence the 20:th of December 1767. On January the 31 1768 we saw the land of Monopotapa and on the 6:th of February 1768 we anchord in Table Bay at the Cape of Good Hope sailed from on the 24:th passed by the island of Ascension; on the 28:th of March 1768, we crossed the Equinox. April the 25:th pass'd by the Western Islands, May the fourteenth pass'd by Scilly Islands, and May the nineteenth anchord in the Downs, having been absent from England 638 days. But it must be remarked that we lost one day, so on the thirteenth day of March – we having completed 360 degrees of west longitude – we added a day from from Sunday March the thirteenth – we made it Monday March the fourteenth – so in fact by our sea account we were only 637 days from the time we weigh'd from Plymouth to our anchoring in the Downs – but we did not sail from Plymouth Sound untill nine in the morning of the 21:st of August 1766, and anchor'd in the Downs at 4 in the morning in the morning of the nineteenth of May 1768, so in fact we were only 636 days on our voyage – and – were not two years in commission being commissioned the nineteenth day of June 1766 – & paid off the fourth of June 1768 –

From a small island to the SE.t end of S.t Georges there is deep water all the way over to Tower Hill within a ½ mile in a bay the E.t part of which made by an other island 30 fathom where a ship might stop a tyde, it being soft ground you may go within a ships length of the South point of the island. T. Hill. There being 20 f.m water, from which to the S.ºE.t point of Hintow there is deep water no ground 55 f.m and room enough to sail till you come within a mile of hintow where is 40 f.m from thence to – 40, and within ¼ of a mile to the E:tward 17f and within two ships length to the S:d 30f. and all the way from thence toward the SW Point of Hintow 42. 43 f.m and no ground 55f.m when within a ½ mile of the Point from which over to the Deadman about mid channel 35f.m about ¼ mile of 50f.m and about ½ a mile off the Island to the W:d 34f.m about a ⅓ oft the way to the tryangle 20 f.m ⅔ D.t 18 f.m about a ships length to the Eastward of the Δ 11f.m, 10f.m ½ 9, gap 11 W Δ 20 good mid chanel from the larboard point & castle 11fm:[5]

---

[5] On this page, a pencilled note in the ML most probably by library staff indicates that this page was found loose and inserted at this point in the log in November 1961.This may be the note which Robertson refers to as lost in his journal (see *The Discovery of Tahiti*, op cit.)

Week day	Mon Day	Wind	Remarks Onboard His Majestys Ship Dolphin, Captain Samuel Wallis Commander. Commencing June 19:th 1767–[6]
June Thursday	1766 19		This day I was appointed to the command of his Majestys ship Dolphin, & Lieu:^{t} Will:^{m} Clarke to be first Lieutenant[7].
Friday	20	North	Moderate & cloudy. This day went to Deptford with Lieu:^{t} Clarke, & hoisted the pendant onboard his Majestys Ship Dolphin in the dock where she lay to be repaired. began to enter seamen – was directed by the Secretary of the Admiralty to enter no servant for my self or other officer onboard but to compleat the ship with 147 able seamen & three Widdows Men[8], in all 150.[9]
Saturday	21	NE	Moderate & fair employed as before, raising men
Sunday	22	East	Light airs, victualed & kept the men onboard the sheer hulk[10]
Monday	23	SW	Ditto weather
Tuesday	24	SW	Fresh breezes & cloudy[11]
Wednesday	25	SW	Moderate weather
Thursday	26	SSW	Ditto weather –

(opposite page of journal)

6 Minor differences (spelling and formulation) between the logs will not be catalogued here. Elements which may shed light on shipboard organisation, on the reporting of various incidents at sea, of encounters, contact and conflict will be noted. The page formatting of all three logs is similar. In the header of the FC, the name of the Captain was presumably initially omitted, and then later added in less formal script, most probably by Wallis himself (see Figure 18). The FC also begins with a table of latitudes and longitudes (see Annex L).

7 "This day the right Honourable the Lords of the Admiralty were pleased to appoint me to the command of his Majestys Ship Dolphin, lying in dock at Deptford where I went & hoisted a pendant oboard her, & began to enter seamen having orders to enter no boys for my self or any of the officers. Ships repairing in the dock." PL. Here the PL and the ML differ in that the PL log begins with a more sustained homage to hierarchy than the ML log which attests to the fact that the PL was written after the ML.

8 In William Burney's 1815 *A New Universal Dictionary of the Marine*, a "modernized and much enlarged" version of Falconer's opus, Widows' men is "An appellation given to a cetain number of men, according to circumstances, in every hundred of which the complement of the ship shall consist who are directed by Act of Parliament to be borne on all his Majesty's ships' books as able seamen the produce of whose wages, and the value of whose provisions, are applied to the relief of poor widows of commissioned and warrant officers in the Royal Navy. For the due performance of this benevolent scheme, every captain, or other officer, commanding any of his Majesty's ships or vessels of war, is directed to enter on the books of the ship or vessel he commands, as part of her complement, one or two (as the clerk of check shall inform him that circumstances require) fictitious names in every hundred men of her complement . . ."

9 "Had the appointment of all the officers" added in the FC in less ornate script.

10 This entry is truncated to "Fair weather" in the PL and the FC. A sheer hulk was a service platform described by Falconer "an old ship of war, fitted with an apparatus, to fix or take out the masts of his majesty's ships, as occasion requires. The mast of this vessel is extremely high, and withal properly strengthened by shrouds and stays, in order to secure the sheers, which serve, as the arm of a crane, to hoist out or in the masts of any ship lying

June Friday	1766 27	SW	Moderate & cloudy weather, employed in raising seamen. Ship refitting in the dock —[12]
Saturday	28	Ditto	Light airs with rain, received fresh beef for the ships company —[13]
Sunday	29	Ditto	Rainy weather
Monday	30	WSW	Moderate & fair [14]
July Tuesday	1766 1st	SW	Moderate & fair
Wednesday	2	NE	Fresh breezes & rainy
Thursday	3	NNE	Ditto weather
Friday	4	WNW	Cloudy weather –
Saturday	5	NW	Ditto weather
Sunday	6	Ditto	Ditto weather
Monday	7	variable	Light airs & fair employed as before —[15]

Figure 18 The first page of the fair copy of the *Dolphin* logs[16]

alongside. The sheers are composed of several long masts, whose heels rest upon the side of the hulk, and having their heads declining outward from the perpendicular, so as to hang over the vessel whose masts are to be fixed or displaced. The tackles which extend from the head of the mast to the sheer-heads, are intended to pull in the latter towards the mast-head, particularly when they are charged with the weight of a mast after it is raised out of any ship, which is performed by strong tackles depending from the sheer-heads. The effort of these tackles is produced by two capsterns, fixed on the deck for this purpose."

11 Robertson in his journal indicates that the Dolphin was "getting a thorough repair." (Carrington, op. cit., p.3)
12 This entry is truncated to "Moderate weather" in the PL and the FC.
13 "Light airs with some rain, the ships company were supplied with fresh beef, & ordered to be served it whilst we lay here –." PL and FC.
14 "Moderate & fair still employed in raising seamen." PL and FC.
15 "Light airs & fair employed in raising seamen & fitting the ships rigging." PL and FC.
16 Courtesy of the Alexander Turnbull Library, Wellington, New Zealand.

Week day	M: Day	Wind	Remarks onboard his Majestys ship Dolphin –
July Tuesday	1766 8	variable	Fresh gales & squally with hard rain, at 2 PM fine pleasant weather – at 3 PM hauled the ship out of the dock & got her alongside the sheer hulk a got in the fore & main masts, AM took in 45 tons of shingle ballast –
Wednesday	9	Ditto	Moderate & cloudy employed in rigging the ship took in the mizen mast.[17]
Thursday	10	SE SSW	Fresh breezes & rainy employed in rigging the ship
Friday	11	variable	Moderate with rain, employed as before
Saturday	12	SW	Moderate & fair, taking in officers stores & provisions[18]
Sunday	13	Westerly	Light airs & fair
Monday	14	variable	Fresh breezes & rainy employed as before –[19]
Tuesday	15	Ditto	Rainy employed in stowing the hold, shipwrights still at work in the ship –
Wednesday	16	Ditto	Rainy employed as yesterday

(opposite page of journal)

Week day	M: Day	Wind	Remarks &:ce
July Thursday	1766 17	variable	Moderate & fair employed in recovering stores and provisions and stowing them away
Friday	18	D.°	Ditto weather
Saturday	19	D.°	Ditto weather
Sunday	20	D.°	Rainy, latter fair. Got off the booms, stowing the hold & fitting the ship, read the Articles of War &:ce to ships company –[20]
Monday	21	SW	Moderate & fair the shipwrights finished their work. Bent the sails & got the boats off –[21]
Tuesday	22	variable	Moderate & cloudy – employed in getting ready to fall down the river[22]
Wednesday	23	D:°	Moderate & cloudy the ship near completed both with men and stores –
Thursday	24	D.°	Set up all rigging fore & aft. Sent to the Navy Board for the Pilot
Friday	25	D:°	Fresh breezes with rain latter cloudy got all ready to drop down the river, at AM a pilot came onboard & took charge of the ship –

---

17 "Moderate & cloudy employed in rigging the masts." PL and FC.
18 Truncated entry here: "Fair weather." PL and FC.
19 "Fresh breezes & rainy, employed in getting onboard stores & provisions, rigging & fitting the ship, & raising men." PL and FC.
20 Here Wallis is more formal in his approach and specifies that he reads the Articles of War & Abstract of the Act of Parliament." PL and FC.
21 The ship is "near compleated with men & stores" at this stage. PL and FC.
22 The shipwrights having finished their work leave the ship according to the PL and FC.

Week day	M:°Day	Wind	Remarks &:ᶜᵉ⁻
July Saturday	1766 26	SW	Fresh breezes & fair, at 1 PM cast off from the sheer hulk at Deptford, & made sail down the river, at 5 PM anch.ᵈ & moor'd at Long Reach in five fathom water muddy. Employed in rounding the cables –
Sunday	27	Ditto	Employed in getting onboard provisions & other stores & stowing them betwixt decks –
Monday	28	Ditto	Squally with some rain – employed in getting onboard gunners stores – dryed the sails
Tuesday	29	West WSW	Cloudy with rain received Gunners stores, a still & a copper oven & some mathematical instruments[23]
Wednesday	30	Ditto	Fresh gales, received 10 HH:ˢ of malt; employed in getting off guns & gunners stores –
Thursday	31	SW	Received all the powder & Gunners stores (120 half barr.ˡˢ) employed in getting reading to sail – The Adm:ʸ sent orders to Lieu.ᵗ[24] to convey the ship to the Nore –
August Friday	1766 1	variable calm	Mod:ᵉ & fair came onboard a Pilot & took charge of the ship, AM at 8 unmoored & weighed, at 11, it falling calm anchor'd abreast of Norfleet Chalk Wharf in 2 fm: water
Saturday	2	variable	First part foggy latter fair. At 10 AM weigh'd at Noon abreast of the Hope Point

(opposite page of journal)

Week day	M: Day	Wind	Remarks &:ᶜᵉ⁻
August Sunday	1766 3	East WNW	Mod:ᵉ & cloudy at 4 PM anchor'd in 7 fm: water abreast of Lee Town. At 5 AM weigh'd and at 8 anchor'd at the Nore, where we moor'd in 8 fm: water, the Nore Light NW¼W & Sheerness WSW¼W about four miles –
Monday	4:ᵗʰ	West	Fresh breezes & cloudy put the ship into sea victualing employed in putting the ship into order.[25] Found here his Majestys Sloop Swallow.
Tuesday	5	WNW	Moderate & fair received from Chatham beer and provisions & from Sheerness several kinds of stores.[26] Pass'd by his majestys Victualler Prince Frederick –

(*Continued*)

23 The PL and FC also list "a theodlit, sextant, telescope, & measuring chains & ten half Hhds of malt." Robertson (Carrington, op. cit, p.5) notes two new invented compasses for taking azemuths & amplitudes and the other for taking in boats to try the currents, both invented by Dr Knight. There were also "two fine globes" on board. There is also a thermometer onboard (mentioned and drawn by Pinnock in the blank pages of the incomplete log of the *Dolphin* voyage signed by Samuel Wallis (BL). In this log, Wallis records daily temperatures, which he does not do elsewhere.
24 Clarke in the PL.
25 "Received fresh mutton from Lee." PL and FC.
26 Both the PL and the FC note reception of a new davit (spelt David in the PL).

Week day	M: Day	Wind	Remarks &:ce–
Wednesday	6	ESE	Mustered birth'd & quartered the ships company and put everything at rights.[27]
Thursday	7	variable	Read the Articles of War & Act of Parliament. Sailed the Prince Frederick Victualler. the Clk of the Cheque mustered.
Friday	8	Easterly	Employed in getting the ship ready for sea
Saturday	9	SSE	Moderate & cloudy, received some water & beer from Chatham NB: we received fresh beef or mutton every meat day since the 30:th of June –
Sunday	10:th	NE	Fresh breezes, at 9 PM received my orders from the Adm:y in London and at 4 AM set out for Sheerness where I arrived Sunday at 6 in the evening –

Week day	M: Day	Wind	Remarks onboard his Majestys Ship Dolphin
August Monday	1766 11	NBE	at 4 AM unmoored at 10 weighed in company with his Majestys sloop Swallow whom I had given orders to put himself under my command.[28] at noon we were abreast of the Spoil Buoy.
Tuesday	12	NNW	Light breezes & fair running over the flats. at 8 PM anchor'd in the Downs discharged the Pilot & got of a six oar'd cutter.[29] fired the evening & morning gun. AM weigh'd in company with the Swallow at Noon Beachy Head NWBW½W six leagues. The Swallow in company[30]
Wednesday	13	variable	Calm & hazey moderate fresh gales, latter moderate breezes. at 8 PM Beachy WBN 3 leagues, at 8 AM Dunnose NBE 3 leagues and the Needle Point North – lost sight of the Swallow –
Thursday	14	variable	Moderate and cloudy at 8 AM Peverell Point NBW three leagues. at Noon the Bill of Portland bore NW 4 leagues –
Friday	15	variable	Moderate & cloudy weather, at 9 PM Portland Lights EBN three leagues. at Noon the Bill of Portland bore about E¾S four or five leagues –

---

27 "... our incouragement will intirely depend on our success in discovering a place of consequence in the South Seas. This is but very poor incouragement to set out on so dangerous a voyage, and I have reason to believe that few on bd if any, would willingly go this voyage if they knew the uncertain footing that we are going on." Robertson (Carrington, op. cit., p.4).
28 This detail concerning the command of the *Swallow* is missing in both the PL and the FC.
29 Pinnace in the FC.
30 Robertson is already (he wrote up his journal retrospectively) aware of the Swallow (like the *Prince Frederick*) being a very "dull sailor" (Carrington, op. cit., p. 5).

Week day	M: Day	Wind	Remarks &:ce –
August Saturday	1766 16	variable	Fresh breezes and cloudy, latter moderate & fair. At 7 the Rams Head N½West 3 leagues. at 9 the Bolt Tail NEBE 2 miles, past by his Majestys ship Burford – At 8 AM anchor'd and moor'd in Plymouth Sound in 6½ fm: water; Mount Batten NBE Withy Hedge SEBS & Drakes island NW½N found here his Majestys ship Burford & in Hamoze Lord Edgcombes flagg flying onboard the Hero – we saluted with 13 guns which was returned – found the Prince Frederick store ship at anchor in – water –
Sunday	17	NNE	Moderate & cloudy employed in getting onboard stores from the Victualling Office and dock yard – anchor'd here his Maj. Sloop Swallow –
Monday	18	North	Employed as yesterday secured some mosquetons & powder[31]
Tuesday	19:th	NW	Completed our water beer & other provisions received a Serjeant & twelve marines.[32] Ten half Hh:s of malt, three thousand weight of portable soup, a bale of cork jackets, surgeons medecines and an extra quantity of the surgeons own purchasing both of medecines & necessarys which I gave him leave to store in my cabbin, there being no other part of the ship where to put it in – every officers cabbin & my steerage & state room being full of stores &:ce[33]
Wednesday	20:th	SSE East ENE	at 1 PM received my sailing orders from the Admiralty command and sent orders for this ship sloop Swallow & P: Frederick Victualler to do the same & put themselves under my command[34]

---

31 "... twelve musquetoons, some powder & musquet balls." PL and FC.
32 The PL and FC indicate "from sick and hurt" at this point.
33 "A.M. Came onboard a Serjeant Corporal & 12 marines." Molineux (Mate).
34 The entry in the PL and the FC is longer (corresponding to 19th and 20th August in the ML) and continues: "... AM unmoord the ship and got all ready for sea at noon the Commissioners came off & paid the ships company two months in advance – The Surgeon informed me that he would purchase an extra quantity of medecines & necessaries which might be of infinite service if the ships company were sick and in a place where those things could not be come at. if we find room anywhere in the ship to stow them away, every part of her being so full he could not find room; I gave him leave to put them in my cabbin. the steerage & state rooms being full of slops & portable soup – the extra medecines and necessaries consisted of severall large boxes." In the FC, there are additional annotations in free hand: in pencil "took my leave of Rev:d M:r Thomas Hearle & M:rs Hearle" and a list in ink "The officers names who sailed in the Dolphin –
    Sam:l Wallis
    Captain Will:m Clarke, & Tobias Furneaux 2:d Lieutenants
    George Roberston Master, John Hutchingson Surgeon
    Harrison Gunner (in pencil)

On board his Maj:^{s} ship Dolphin –
Remarks Thursday August 21: 1766 1

H	K	F	Course	Wind
1				
2				
3				
4				
5				
6				
7				
8				Calm
9				
10	Madeira			19
11	S:^{t} Jago At S:t Jago		3	13
12	To Virgin Mary Port Famine			81 10
1	At Port ---			21
2	Cape Pillar	84		
3	Whitsun & Queen Charlottes Is	56		
4	K Georges Isle At anchoring			13 4
5	Remained at Georges Isle	33		
6	To Tinian	55		
7	At Tinian			27
8	Batavia			16
9	Princess Isle	13		
10	Cape England			47 75
11				638
12				491-1
		22.31		

at anchor^{35} in Plymouth Sound – moderate and fair the
Commissioner paid the ships company two months advance

Light airs

Foggy weather

Ships	Commandors	Guns	Men
Dolphin	Cap:^{n} Wallis	24	150
Swallow	Cap:^{n} Carteret	14	90
P:^{ce} Frederick	Lieu:^{t} Brine	6	24

At 4 made the signal & weighd in company with his Majestys
sloop Swallow, and Prince Frederick Victualler they being
under my command –

at noon moderate & hazey
in company as above –

The Eddy Stone bore ESE 4 or 5 miles^{36}

John Harrison Purser, [added in black ink the following] thro whose means we took the longitude by taking the distance of the sun from the moon – and working it according to D/r Masceline method which we did not understand."

The Reverend Mr Thomas Hearle and his wife whom Wallis mentions here were most probably his wife's (Betty Wallis, née Hearle) uncle and aunt. Thomas Hearle was also Betty's guardian. Betty's father was John Hearle and on his death Thomas, his brother (along with the widow and a certain John Rogers), had become her and her sisters' guardian.

35 "at single anchor" in the PL and the FC. When at sea, the ML is formatted horizontally with three days per page. The PL is also formatted horizontally with four days per page, the FC is divided into two days per page. The five ruled columns on the left of each page of all the Wallis logbooks are headed H (hour of the 24- hour day), K (knots indicating the speed of the ship), F (fathoms indicating depth), Course and Wind. These headers have been omitted in the ensuing transcription as they are a constant feature of all logbooks in general and Wallis's in particular.

36 "five miles" in the PL.

On board his Maj:ˢ ship Dolphin –
Remarks Friday August 22: 1766 2

1	4		West	ESE	
2	3	4			moderate & clear weather
3	3	3			
4	3	4	WBS		
5	4	2			the Lizard bore WBN 2 or 3 leagues
6	4	2			
7	5	1	WBS½S		
8	5				the Lizard Lights NNW½W Dis:ᵉ 37
9	4	3			Lizard Lat: 50:00 N.
10	4			SE	Lon:ⁿ from London 5:14 W
11	4	3			
12	5			SSE	
1	4	3			
2	4	4			
	5	2			
	4			South	variation p:ʳ amplitude 21:°00' W –
5	3				
6	2	1			
7	3	2			
8	4	4			
9	1		NNW	West	moderate & fair weather the Swallow sloop & P:ᵉ Frederick in comp.
10	2		NBW	WBN	
11	3		SWBW	NWBW	
12	2		SWBS	WBN	

Course	Dist:ᶜᵉ	Latitude in	Longit:ᵘᵈᵉ made	M: Dist:ᶜᵉ
S39:°00'W	50	49:22*N	0:49'W	31W

The Lizard bore N39:°10' Distance 17 leagues –

37 Distance 4 leagues in the PL.

On board his Maj:ˢ ship Dolphin –
Remarks Saturday August 23: 1766 3

H	K	F	Courses	Winds	Remarks
1	2	4	SBE	SWBW	
2	2		SBW	WBS	Moderate & fair, saw an East India Ship laying too[38] stood for her soon after she made sail – bore down to the Swallow & store ship
3	5	4			
4	4	2			
5	3		SE	WSW	
6	6	4	South	WSW	
7	4		SSE	SW	Close reeft tops:ˢ & down top gall: yards
8	5		SE½S		
9	3	5	WNW	SW	Taken aback
10	3		NWBW	SWBW	fresh gales with heavy rain and a great SW swell –
11	3				carried away the ftop:ˢ staysail stay fixed a new one –
12	2	2	SWBW	NW	Handed the fore top sail
1	2		WSW		
2	2	4	SWBW		
3	2	4	SWBW ½W		
4	2	4			Hard gales with a great sea in company as before –[39]
5	2	4	SWBW	NWBW	
6	3				
7	3	4			
8	3	3			
9	3	4	SW		
10	3	4	SW½W	WNW	
11	3	4			
12	3	4			

Course	Dist:ᶜᵉ	Latitude in	Longit:ᵘᵈᵉ made	M: Dist:ᶜᵉ
South	52	48:30*N	0:49W	31W

The Lizard bore N19:°00'E Dist 32 leagues

---

38 ". . . a French ship and a Dutch ship near her . . ." PL and FC.
39 "The Swallow sails wretchedly." PL and FC.

Remarks Sunday August 24: 1764

H	K	F	Course	Wind	Remarks
1	2	6	SWW	WNW	fresh gales with a great SW swell
2	2	2			
3	2	2			set the fore tops:[s] & out 3: reefs
4	2	5			Little wind
5	3		South	WBN	
6	3				
7	2	5	SWBS		
8	1	5			
9	1		SSW		
10	1				
11	1	4			
12	2				Light breezes & cloudy
1	2	4	SBE	SWBW	
2	3	4	SBE½E		
3	3	4	SSE	SW	
4	3	5	SEBS	SWBS	
5	2	4	West	SSW	handed the topsails
6	3	3	West		
7	2	4	W½N		
8	2	5			
9	1	4	WBN		hard gales
10	2	3	WNW		& squally, the ships in company as before
11	3	4			
12	3	4	WNW½N		

Course	Dist:[ce]	Latitude in	Longit:[ude] made	M: Dist:[ce]
S12:°50'W	23	48:30*N	0:49W	31W

Lizard bore N17:°45'E Distance 40 leagues

Remarks Monday August 25 5

H	K	F	Courses	Winds	Remarks
1	3	2	NWBW	SWBW	Strong gales with thick weather & a great SW swell – struck top gall masts & jib boom –
2	3	2	NW		
3	3	4	NWBN	WBS	
4	2	5	NNW		
5	2	3	NBW	WBN	made the signal and wore
6	3		SSW	West	set the fore topsail
7	3		SWBS	WBN	
8	3		SW½S		
9	3				moderate gales with a great Western swell
10	4				
11	3		SWBW	NWBW	
12	3				clear weather with a great swell
1	3		WSW½S	NW	
2	2	3			
3	2		WSW		
4	2	4			
5	4	3			set up the main rigging
6	3	4	WSW½S		moderate weather got up topgall masts & yards & let the reefs out
7	2	4	WSW		
8	2	4	WSW½W		
9	4				moderate & fair unbent the cables
10	3	4			In company as before –
11	3				Ship 14 miles to the Soward of reckoning.
12	3	2			

Course	Dist:^{ce}	Latitude in	Longit:^{ude} made	M: Dist:^{ce}
S27:°00'W	67	47:* 08N	1:°42'W	66W

The Lizard bore N21:°00'E Distance 61 leagues

EXPLORATION OF THE SOUTH SEAS

Remarks Tuesday August 26 1766 6

H	K	F	Course	Wind	Remarks
1	1	4	SWBW½		Light airs & fair
2	1	4			great rippling of a current
3	1	3			
4	1				
5			}		calm her head from the NW to the SE
6					
7	1		SWBW		
8					
9			}		calm her head from the SW to the SE
10					
11					
12					Bore away to the Swallow
1	1		SE	NW	
2	1		SBW	WBS	
3	2	2	South	WSW	
4	2	4	SBE	SWBW	
5	1	4	South		lay too for the Swallow
6			SBW off	SEBS	Light airs & fair weather
7	1		SBW	WBS	
8	1				
9	1				
10	1		NW	WSW	Light breezes in comp:^{y} as before
11	1				
12	1	4			

Course	Dist:^{ce}	Latitude in	Longit:^{ude} made	M: Dist:^{ce}
South	14	46:*54N	1:42W	66

The Lizard bore N19: 00E Distance 64 leagues

Remarks Wednesday August 27:ᵗʰ 1766 7

H	K	F	Courses	Winds	Remarks
1	1	2	WNW½N		Light breezes & fair weather making points & gaskets.
2	1	2			
3	1	2	NWBW		
4	1	5			pass'd by us a French & Portuguis ship
5	2	2	NW½W		
6	2	4			variation p:ʳ ampli:ᵈᵉ: 21:16 West
7	1				
8			NWBW	off NNW	Light airs & fair lay too for the Swallow
9					
10	1		NW	WSW	
11	2				
12	2	3	NW½W		
1	2	4	NWBW	SWBN	
2	1				
3	1	3			
4	1				
5	1	2	W	SSW	Fair weather –
6	1	2			
7	2	2	WBS	SBN	carry very little sail as the Swallow can scarce keep company₄₀
8	2	3	WSW	South	
9	4	1	WBS	SBE	Exercised small arms
10	3	2	WSW		In company as before
11	4		SW	SSE	
12	2	5	SW		

Course	Dist:ᶜᵉ	Latitude in	Longit:ᵘᵈᵉ made	M: Dist:ᶜᵉ
West	40	46:*54N	2:41W	106W

The Lizard bore N29:°50E Distance 72 leagues

---

40 "... but with all the sail they can press on her." PL and FC.

Remarks Thursday August 28 8

H	K	F	Courses	Winds	Remarks
1	3	2	SW½W	SSE	Moderate & clear
2	3		SWSBW	SBE	
3	3	2			Lay too for the Swallow, at the same time spoke with a French ship from Guadeloupe for Nantes
4	1				
5	2	2	WSW	South	
6	2				
7	1				
8	1				
9	1		WBN	SWBW	
10	1		WNW	SW	
11	1	3			
12	2		NWBN	SWBW	
1	2				Light airs
2	1	5			
3	2		NW	WSW	
4	2				variation p:r ampli:de 21° 30' West
5	2				
6	2				shortened sail for the Swallow
7	1				Moderate & cloudy
8	2				
9	2		SSW	West	
10	2	3	SW	NWBW	
11	2				Little wind & cloudy In company as before –
12	1	4			

Course	Dist:ce	Latitude in	Longit:ude made	M: Dist:ce
S72:°00'W	32	46:*45N	3:28W	136W

The Lizard bore N35:°00E Distance 79 leagues

---

41 According to John Gore and Molineux, this ship was bound for Bordeaux (28th August entry). John Gore's log contains very little description of the peoples encountered during the voyage but contains geographical material in detail.

Remarks Friday August 29:th 1766 9

1	2		SW	NWBW	
2	2	3			Light breezes & fair
3	2	4			
4	1	2			
5	1	2			
6	1	5			
7	2				
8	2	3			
9	1				
10	1	5			
11	2		SSW	West	
12	2	3			
1	2	4			
2	2	2			
3	3				
4	3				
5	2		SWBW	WBN	
6	2	3	SW½S		fair weather with Western swell
7	2		SW	WNW	
8	2				
9	3	4	SWBS		
10	3	5	SSW		In company as before —[42]
11	3	5			
12	2	2	SE		

Course	Dist:ce	Latitude in	Longit:ude made	M: Dist:ce
S ¼ W	59	45:*44N	3:32W	139W

The Lizard bore N28: 30E Dist:ce 97 leagues

---

42 A free-hand entry is inserted in the FC for this day: "Turned the hands up, put them at three watches, at the same time told them that they were to bring their hamacks on deck at 8 every morning that any man from this day forward who was dirty either in cloaths or person should be punished; for punctually observing this the people were divided into classes & put under the Lieu:t & Midshipmen who were to look over things every Monday morning. Gave orders that the Cook reported to the Officer of the Watch when he had cleand the coppers, when amid and foremost [. . .] allway to see the truth of it – further directed the Cook to put the fat of the beef & pork into a cask with stale urine to prevent people from using it. Recommended to the whole to live in harmony with each other and to bear their share of fatigue with cheerfulness & willingness & that they might be assured of every indulgence they merited—& thus we settled our setting off." (See also Carrington, op.cit., pp.64–65).

Remarks Saturday August 30:th 1766 (10)

H	K	F	Winds	Course	Remarks
1	3		SSW	West	
2	3		SW	WNW	Moderate & cloudy
3	4		SWBS	WBW	Saw a strange sail
4	2	4			
5	2	4			variation p:r ampli:de 19°16' West
6	2	3	SBW	WBS	
7	2	4			made the signal & tack'd
8	2	4			
9	1				
10	2	4	SSE	Variable	
11	1		NNW	SW	light airs & fair weather
12	2		WBN		
1	1		NWBW	SWBW	shortened sail for the swallow
2	1				
3	1		NW	WSW	
4	1				light airs & fair in company as before
5	1				
6	1				
7	1				
8	2				
9	1		SBE	SW	
10	1	2	SSE		
11	1		SE		
12	1		WBS	SBW	

Course	Dist:ce	Latitude in	Longit:ude made	M: Dist:ce
S15: 00W	23	45:°22*N	3:40W	145W

The Lizard bore N27:°30'E Distance 104 leagues

REDISCOVERED ACCOUNTS, VOLUME I

Remarks Sunday August 31: 1766 (11)

H	K	F	Courses	Winds	Remarks
1	1	3	SW½W	SSE	
2	1	4			
3	2	5	SW		Light airs & fair weather
4	2				
5	3		NWBN		opened a cask of pork N868: 300 pc^{es} one peice over –[43]
6	1		SW	WBS	bore down to the Swallow
7	2				set up the fore rigging –
8	1				
9	2	5		SE	
10	3	2			shortened sail for the Swallow
11	3	3			
12	3	4			
1	4	3			
2	4	2			
3	3	5			
4	4	5			
5	4	4			fresh breezes made more sail
6	6				
7	6	6		SEBE	variation p:^{r} ampli:^{de} 17° 38'West
8	5				
9	6				
10	7				thought we saw some land bearing SE
11	7	4			moderate gales hazey weather
12	7	3			in company as before

Course	Dist:^{ce}	Latitude in	Longit:^{ude} made	M: Dist:^{ce}
SWBS	90	44: 08*N	4:50W	195W

The Lizard bore N27:°30'E Distance 134 leagues

---

43 This type of detail is rarely reported in the PL or in the FC.

H	K	F	Courses	Winds	Remarks Monday September 1:st 1766 (12)
1	8		SW	ESE	Fresh breezes & cloudy
2	8				Sailing with the topsails on the caps to keep company with the Swallow
3	7	5			
4	7	3			pass'd by two ships sailing SW.
5	7	4			at ½ past 7 saw lights from the SBW to SSE – made the signal
6	7	4			and altered the course
7	7	2			at 9 the light at Cape Finistere[44]
8	6	4	SWBW		about 8 miles dist.ce 4 leagues
9	4		WNW		Cape Finistere Lat – 43:12 N
10	4		NWBW		Long:d – 9: 40 W
11	8				
12	10				
1		2	WSW	EBN	Made the signal & altered course
2	3	2			
3	6				
4	5	2			Fresh gales & hazey
5	8				Two strangers in sight
6	3	3			
7	6	4			
8	6	3			
9	6				Fresh breezes & hazey
10	6				In company as before –
11	6	4			
12	6				

Course	Dist:ce	Latitude in	Longit:ude made	M: Dist:ce
S54:00W	76	42: 28*N	1:21W	61W
			2:10 W	195
			7:00W	88
				283

Cape Finistère N54: 30'E Distance 28 leagues
Longitude made from Lizard 6 :50W[45]

---

44 Between Coranna and Cape Finistère (PL and FC).
45 "The Lizard bore N32:01E Dist:ce 181 leagues." PL

Remarks Tuesday Sep:ᵉʳ 2 1766 (13)

H	K	F	Courses	Winds
1	6	3	SW½W	ENE
2	6	5	SWBS	
3	6	4		
4	5	4		
5	5	5		
6	6	2		
7	6	2		
8	6	2	SW½W	
9	6	2	SWBS	
10	6	4		
11	6	2		
12	6			
1	6	4	NE	
2	7			
3	7	2		
4	6	5		
5	7			
6	7	3		
7	7	3		
8	7			
9	7	2		
10	7			
11	7	2		
12	7			

Fresh breezes & clear weather
In company with a french ship and snow from Bordeaux for Goree –

Ditto weather

Moderate & hazey. In company with then swallow. Pr.ᶜᵉ Frederick and two French ships

Course	Dist:ᶜᵉ	Latitude in	Longit:ᵘᵈᵉ made	M: Dist:ᶜᵉ
SBW½W	155	40: 00*N	2:22W	107W

Cape Finistère bore N29:15E Dist:ᶜᵉ 73 leag:ˢ[46]

---

[46] The PL and the FC continue to specify the direction and distance from the Lizard ("The Lizard bore N29:30E Distance 231 leagues).

Remarks Wednesday Sep:er 3 1766 (14)

H	K	F	Courses	Winds
1	5	4	SWBS	NE
2	5	5		
3	6			
4	5			
5	4	5		
6	4	2		
7	4	5		
8	4	2		
9	3	3		
10	3	2		
11	3			
12	3	3		
1	3			
2	3	4		
3	4			
4	3	4		
5	3	3		
6	3	4		
7	3	2		
8	3			
9	3			
10	3	2		
11	3	2		
12	2			

Moderate & hazey

Barometer 18:°15'

Barometer 18:°45'

variation p:r azim:t 15° 30'W

Light breezes. In company as before –

Course	Dist:ce	Latitude in	Longit:ude made	M: Dist:ce
SBW½W	90	38: 34*N	3:00W	136W

Cape Finistère bore N26: 00E Dis:t 103 leag:s[47]

---

[47] "The Lizard bore N28:15E distance 261 leagues." PL and FC.

H	K	F	Courses	Winds	Remarks Thursday Sep:ᵉʳ 4 1766 (15)
1	2	3	SWBS	SE	
2	2				Light airs & fair weather
3	2	2			
4	1			Calm	
5	1				Barometer 19:°15'
6	2				Variation p:ʳ ampl:ᵗ 16° 00'W
7	2	4			
8	2	2		NNE	
9	2				
10	2				
11	3				
12	3	5		ENE	
1	3	5			Barometer 20:°00'
2	4				
3	4	3			
4	4	2			
5	4				
6	3				
7	3				
8	3				
9	3				
10	3	2			
11	3	4			Light breezes In company as before
12	3	4			

Course	Dist:ᶜᶜ	Latitude in	Longit:ᵘᵈᵉ made	M: Dist:ᶜᶜ
SBW½W	65	37: 32*N	3:24W	155

Cape Finistère bore N24:°30'E Dist:ᶜᶜ 125 leagues⁴⁸

---

48 "The Lizard bore N27:30E distance 283 leagues." PL.

Remarks Thursday Sep:ᵉʳ 5   1766 (16)

H	K	F	Course	Wind
1	2	4	SWBS	NEBE
2	2	4		
3	2	3		
4	2	4		
5	3			
6	4	4		
7	4	4		
8	5	5		NE
9	4			
10	4			
11	4	4		
12	4	2		
1	4	5		
2	5			
3	5			
4	4	5		
5	4			
6	4			
7	4			
8	4			
9	3	3		
10	4			
11	4			
12	5			

Light breezes & clear weather

fired a gun & made the P:ᶜᵉ Frederick sign:ˢ to make more sail

bar: 19:40

bar: 19:05

Boyled 10 pounds of portable soup in the peoples pease[49]

Light breezes in company as before

Course	Dist:ᶜᵉ	Latitude in	Longit:ᵘᵈᵉ made	M: Dist:ᶜᵉ
SBW½W	96	36:02*W	3:59W	182

Cape Finistère bore N23:°00'E Dist:ᶜᵉ 155 leagues[50]

49 "Boiled 8 pounds of portable soup in the oatmeal & pease, which we shall continue to do on banyan days." PL and FC.

50 "The Lizard bore N27:00E distance 314 leagues." PL and FC. Banyan days were days without meat (see John Mack, *The Sea. A Cultural History*, London, Reaktion Books, 2011, p.190) who suggests that "banyan" was a reference to Indian vegetarianism.

Remarks Friday Sep:er 6 1766 (17)

H	K	F	Course	Winds	Remarks
1	3	4	SWBS	NE	Moderate & hazey
2	3	5	SW½W		
3	3	2			
4	3	3	Bar:	19:10	
5	3	4			Parted company with the two French ships
6	4				
7	4	2			variation p:r ampli:de 13°25' West
8	4	2			
9	4	4			caught a bonitta
10	4	3			
11	4				
12	5				
1	4	4			
2	5				
3	4	4		NNE	
4	4	5	Bar:	19:30	variation p:r am 12:15W
5	3	5			azm : 12:35
6	4	2		North	spoke a french schooner from Martineec for Bordeaux.
7	4	5			severall bonettas about the ship
8	4	4			caught one –
9	4	3			Moderate & fair bent the cables
10	4	4			In company as before –
11	4	2			Bent the cables –
12	5				

Course	Dist:ce	Latitude in	Longit:ude made	M: Dist:ce
SWBS	115	34:26*N	5:16W	246W

Cape Finistère N25:°00'E Dist:ce 194 leagues[51]

---

51 "The Lizard bore N 27:00 E distance 350 leagues." PL.

Remarks Sunday Sep:^er 7 1766 (18)

1	6		SW½W	NBE	
2	5	4			Moderate with squalls
3	6				
4	6			NEBN	
5	5	4	Bar	91:10	caught a bonetta
6	6				2:^d reeft the topsails
7	4				
8	5				
9	5				
10	4	2			
11	6				
12	6	5		NEBE	
1					
2					
3			UP NBW	off NWBW	
4					
5			Bar	19: 40	
6	5		WSW		
7	8				
8	4	4	WBS		Saw the Island of Porto Santo NBW ½ W 5 leagues
	4	3	West		
9	8	3			The body of Porto Santo NBW½W
10	8				Madeira East End W½S
11	6	4	SWBS		East end of Deserter SBW½W
12	6	3		NEBN	

Course	Dist:^ce	Latitude in	Longit:^ude made	M: Dist:^ce
S 32:00W	118	35:52*N	6:38W	316W

Cape Finistère bore N29:°00'E Dist:^ce 229 leagues
Longitude at Noon 16:°18' West from London[54]

---

52 This small sketch is labelled "Porto Santo Bearing West by Compass about Six Leagues Distance." Courtesy of the State Library of New South Wales.
53 Called Serteres in the PL and the FC.
54 The only entry here is "Porto Santo the middle NBW½W five leagues." PL. The PL log contains no sketches or drawings.

Remarks Monday Sep:ᵉʳ 8 1766 (19)

1	4	1	SWBW		NBE
2	4	2	SW½W		
3	8	2	WBN		
4	8	4			
5	7	3	WBS		NNE
6					
7	Long. Made from the Lizard to Madeira –	12:50 W 5:24 Lizard [...]	18:14 by [...] miles West	Lond. Madeira Merid: Dist: 575	
8					
9					
10					
11					
12					

Fresh breezes – the Swallow and Victualler in sight a stern – at 4 the SE end of Madeira bore W½N dis:ᶜ 2 leagues Ran between the East end of Madeira & the Deserters – A very clear passage – there is a low flat island with a needle rock at the Deserter that is next Madeira, and the end of Madeira is very ragged & rocky – you may go within two miles of either side or nearer if it requires it – at ½ past 4 the Needle at the innermost Deserter bore SE½E – the Brazen Head going into the Fenchale Road WBN½N, and the Rocky Point at the East end of Madeira opposite the Deserters NE½E – at six, anchor'd in Madeira Road, veer'd away & moor'd a cable each way in twenty four fm:ˢ water muddy ground. sent an officer to the Governor to let him know I wished to salute him if he could return an equal number of guns which he promised to do.

When moor'd the Brazen Head bore ESE, the Westmost land in sight W½N, & the Lose Rock NWBW½W, dis:ᶜᵉ of shoar about ½ of a mile, if we had been a cables length nearer the Loses I should have had a better birth at 8 the Swallow & Pr:ᶜᵉ Frederick anchor'd here at 6 saluted the Governor with 13 guns he ret:ᵈ equal N°[55]

---

[55] In the PL and FC there is an additional detail concerning the victualing and the ship's positions "Sent onshoar & got beef for this ship & the Swallow", and the following table:

M: Dist:ᶜᵉ	Latitude observed	Longit: made from London	Long: West from London	By an astro-nomical observa:ⁿ
558W	32:25 North	12:46 West	18:00	16:40 West

Week day	M:° Day	Wind	Remarks in Madeira Road (20) (1)
September 1766 Tuesday	9:th	N°erly	Fresh breezes and hazey weather sat up all the rigging fore & aft received fresh beef of which was served to the ships company Sent of fresh beef to the Swallow sloop[56]
			— longitude from Greenwich *
	Bar	20:00 20:00	Madeira Road lat – 32: 35N Astronomical observation long: – 6:40
Wednesday	10	Easterly	(21) (2) Moderate & cloudy sometime clear sent ashoar all our empty casks by thear boats to be filled the surf so great we could not use our own boats.[57] Received fresh beef sent to the Swallow – Saluted the Consul with 9 guns
	Bar	21:10 21:00	
Thursday 22 days out	11 Bar	Variable 22:30 21:45	(22) (3) Moderate breezes received all our water & of fresh beef sent to the Swallow.
Friday	12 Bar	ENE North 20:00 20:30	(1) Moderate weather. PM received four pipes and ten puncheons of wine for the ships company and quantity of onion sent part onboard the Swallow. At 4 AM made the signal and got under sail in company with the Swallow sloop & P:ce Frederick store ship – at Noon, Fenchall North 5 leagues the SE end of Deserters SBE½E * Latitude 32: 25 North[58]

56 "Fresh breezes & hazey. Set upall the rigging fore & aft, served fresh beef to the ships comp:y sent the boats for water but the surf was so great they could get none off." FC.

57 In the PL (and in the FC), Wallis uses a more narrative form: ". . . sent our empty cask onshoar to be brought of (spelt correctly in the FC – off) full by the Portuguese boats, the surf so great we can do nothing with our own boats . . ."

58 Corrected to 32:20 N in the PL and the FC (these types of corrections or modifications will no longer be referenced). Gore lists the provisions taken onboard: wine, apples, peaches, pears, onions, walnuts, oranges, lemons, chestnuts, figs, beef, pork, fowl, cabbages and sweet potatoes.

Remarks Saturday Sep:[r] 13: 1766 (2)

H	K	F	Courses	Winds	Remarks
1	1	4	SBW	WBS	Little wind & fair weather served onions to the ships company[59]
2	2				
3	2				
4	1	3	SSW	NNW	
5	1		Bar.	20:20	
6	1			20:35	
7	1				Madeira bore from NNW½W to NNE½E – Funchall N½E 8 leagues
8	1		SWBS	WEST	
9	1				
10	1				
11	1				
12	1		SSW ⌐		
1					
2					
3			⌐	Calm	
4					
5					Her head to the S:ward
6	1				
7	2	2	SWBS ⌐	SBE	Unbent the cables
8	2				
9	2				
10	3		SSN½W	ENE	
11	3				Served wine to the ships company
12	3				The Swallow & the P:[ce] Frederick in company

Course	Dist:[ce]	Latitude in	Longit:[ude] made	M: Dist:[ce]

The town of Funchall NBE½E Distance 14 leagues –

---

[59] "... divided all the onions amongst the ships company, each man had about seventeen pounds." PL and FC.

EXPLORATION OF THE SOUTH SEAS

Remarks Saturday Sept:r 14: 1766 (3)

1	1		SWBW	East
2	1			
3	1		SSW½W	
4	1	2		20:15
5	2			
6	2			NEBN
7	2			
8	2	4		
9	2	4		
10	2	5		
11	4			
12	4	4		NE
1	4	5		
2	4	2		
3	3	4		
4	4			21:15
5	3			
6	3	4		ENE
7	4			
8	3	5		
9	4	2		
10	4			
11	4	4		
12	4	3		

Course	Dist:ce	Latitude in	Longit:ude made	M: Dist:ce
S7°/10'W	120	30:*40 North	00:18W	15W

Light airs & fair
The high land of Funchall[60] bore NBE 16 leagues –

variation p:r ampl:de 15° 00' West
a strange sail pass'd by us Westward

Little wind and cloudy weather

Moderate & hazey In company as before

Madeira bore N7:00E[61] Distance 40 leagues –

---

60 "The high land of Madeira over Funchall . . ." PL.
61 Corrected to 7°10' in the PL.

Remarks Sep:ʳ 15: 1766 (4)

H	K	F	Course	Winds	Remarks
1	4	3	SSW½W	ENE	Moderate & cloudy[62]
2	4	4			
3	5	2			
4	5	3		21:00	
5	5				
6	5				
7	6				
8	6	4			Fresh breezes & fair
9	5				
10	5				
11	5	4			
12	6	4		East	
1	6	3			
2	5	4			
3	5	3		20:40	at 6 saw the Isle of Palma from SWBS to SBE Dn:ᵉ about 8 or 9 leagues
4	6				
5	9	5		EBN	
6	3	5	SW½W		Judge Palma to lay from Madeira S12:00W distance 81 leagues[63]
7	6				
8	7				
9	8		SWBS		Light airs the middle of Palma bore EBS distance five leagues.
10	7				
11	1				In company as before –
12	5		West		

Course	Dist:ᶜᵉ	Latitude in	[64]Longit:ᵘᵈᵉ made	M: Dist:ᶜᵉ
		28:*41 North	1:07W	58W

The Island of Palma bore from ENE to SE four leagues

---

62 Entry in free-hand in the FC: "Ordered that portable soup should be boiled every banyan day in the oatmeal wheat and pease during the voyage – & sent the same orders to the Swallow."
63 "I think the course from Madeira to Palma is S 12:00 W distance 81 leagues." PL and FC.
64 "from Madeira". PL.

Remarks Thursday Sep:[r] 16: 1766 (5)

H	K	F	Courses	Winds
1	4		West	NEBE
2				
3			up N off	NW
4	5		SW	20:40
5	6		SWBS	NEBE
6	4		SW½W	
7	4			
8	4			
9	2		SW	
10	1	3		
11	5			
12	5			
1	6			
2	5			
3	4			
4	5			
5	4	4		
6	5			
7			Up SE off	South
8	2		SSW	EBN
9	6	2		NE
10	6			
11	6	3		
12	7	4		ENE

Fresh breezes with a great SW swell I brought to for the Swallow she being becalmed under the land.

at 4 the middle of Palma East 6 leagues
variation p:[r] ampl:[de] 14:00W
Palma   Lat:[d] 28:40N
             Long: 17:36

Light airs
Fresh breezes

Fresh gales
Brought too for the Swallow

Made sail the Swallow & P:[ce] Fred:[k] in com:[y]

ship 15' to S:[d] fr the reckoning –
Fresh gales & squally

Course	Dist:[ce]	Latitude in	Longit:[ude] made[65]	M: Dist:[ce]
S29:°30'W	116	27:*00N	1:09W	59W

The Island of Palma bore N29:°30'E Dist:[ce] 39 leagues

---

65 "from Palma." PL and FC.

Remarks Wednesday Sept:^er 17th 1766 (6)

H	K	F	Course	Winds
1	7	3	SSW	ENE
2	6	4		
3	5			
4	6			20:40
5	5	4		
6	6			
7	5	4		
8	6	4		
9	5	2		
10	5	2		
11	6	4		
12	6	5		
1	5	2		
2	6			
3	6			20:15
4	6			East
5	6	4		
6	6	3		
7	7	2		
8	7			
9	7			
10	8			
11	7			
12	6	4		

Moderate Gales & cloudy
Boyled 9lb of portable soup amongst the peoples pease[66]

Close reefed the topsails

Ditto weather
The Swallow and store ship in company

Course	Dist:^ce	Latitude in	Longit:^ude made	M: Dist:^ce
19:08W	147	24:*36N	1:31W	81W

Palma bore N18:°25'E Dis:^ce 86 leagues

---

66 The PL and the FC do not note this measure (unlike Gore) and specify for this day "exercised small arms."

Remarks Thursday Sept:er 18 1766 (7)

H	K	F	Courses	Winds	Remarks
1	6	3	SW½W	ENE	Moderate & cloudy
2	5	5			
3	5	2			
4	5	4		20:15	
5	6	3			variation p:r az 12:33[67]
6	6				
7	7	2			
8	6	4			
9	5	5			
10	6				
11	7	3			
12	7	1		NE	
1	7	3			Moderate gales & cloudy
2	7	2			
3	6	5			
4	6	2		20:48	
5	6	2			
6	7	5			
7	7	5			
8	7	5			
9	7	4			
10	7	2			Fresh gales & hazey[68]
11	8				In company as before –
12	7	5			

Course	Dist:ce	Latitude in	Longit:ude made	M: Dist:ce
S15:°20'W	169	21:*54N	2:19W	125W

Palma bore N17:°05' Distance 142 leagues

---

67 "Exercised small arms." PL and FC.
68 "Saw a great number of flying fish & bonettos several of the former flew into the ship." Molineux.

Remarks Friday Sept:ᵉʳ 19:ᵗʰ 1766 (8)

H	K	F	Courses	Winds	Remarks
1	7		SSW½W	NEBN	Fresh gales & hazey
2	7	3			Exercised small arms
3	7	4			
4	7			21:15	
5	7	2			
6	7				variation p:ʳᵉ az:ᵗʰ 11:°40'W
7	7				
8	7				Caught several flying fish⁶⁹
9	7				
10	7				
11	6	4			
12	6	3		NE	
1	6	5			
2	6	3		22:00	
3	6				
4	6	2		EBN	
5	6	1			
6	5	6			
7	5	5			Boyled 9lb of portable soup.
8	5	5			shortened the distance 18 miles.
9	6				Judge the current hath set the ship NE⁷⁰
10	5	5			Mod: hazey. In comp:ʸ as before
11	5	5			saw two herons flying to the Eastward
12	5				a Tropic bird about the ship

Course	Dist:ᶜᵉ	Latitude in	Longit:ᵘᵈᵉ made	M: D
S17:°00W	138	19:*42N	3:02W	165W

Palma bore N17:°10' Distance 189 leagues

---

69 Omitted in the PL and the FC. Molineux specifies that "bonettas" were caught.
70 Omitted in the PL and the FC.

EXPLORATION OF THE SOUTH SEAS

Remarks Saturday Sep. 20 1766 (9)

H	K	F	Courses	Winds
1	6	3	SSW½W	ENE
2	6			
3	5	3		
4	5	3		23:05
5	5			
6	6			
7	5	2		
8	5			
9	5			
10	4	5		
11	5			
12	5	4		
1	5	2		23:10
2	4	5		
3	5	1		
4	5			
5	5	3		
6	5	4		
7	6			
8	5	4		
9	3			
10	2			
11	2			
12	1			

Mod: & cloudy

exercised great guns & small arms[71]

Many bonettos about the ship struck & caught with hook eight

Squally cleared of top:^{ls} set them again –
Found the current to set by compass SWBW – five fathoms an hour[72]

Swallow & store ship in company

Course	Dist:^{ce}	Latitude in	Longit:^{ude} made	M: Dist:^{ce}
SSW	112	17:*58N	3:45W	206W

Palma bore N18:00 dis:^{t} 224 leagues

71 The PL and the FC do not mention the small arms.
72 Omitted in PL and the FC. According to Molineux, the current was measured by the cutter.

Remarks Sunday Sep:ʳ 21 1766 (10)

H	K	F	Courses	Winds
1	2	3	SW½W	ENE
2	2	4		
3	2	3		
4	1	5		23:00
5	2	2		
6	2	3		
7	1	2		
8	1	3		
9	1	4		
10	1			
11	1			ESE
12	1			SE
1	2	2		
2	2			ENE
3	2			23:20
4	2			NEBS
5	3			
6	3			ENE
7	4		SW	
8	4			
9	2		SSE	
10	2			
11	1		SBW	
12	1			

Moderate & cloudy.

Caught a shark served it to the ships company —[73]

variat:ⁿ p:ʳ az 9:30W
at 8 saw the Isle of Sall bearing S½W
saw another isle bearing SBW½W

Light airs in company as before[74]

Course	Dist:ᶜᵉ	Latitude in	Longit:ᵘᵈᵉ made	M: Dist:ᶜᵉ
SSW	50	17:*13N	4:06W	226W

The Isle of Sal bore S¾ West dist:ᶜᵉ six leagues

---

73 ¾ of a pound per man according to the PL and the FC.
74 The PL and the FC do not include the sketch of the Isle of Sal.

H	K	F	Courses	Winds	Remarks Monday Sep: 22 1766 (11)
1	1		SSW	SE	Light airs
2					variat:ⁿ p:ʳ az 8:30W
3	1	4			at 6 the isle of Sal bore from S¾W to SSW Distance 6 or 7
4		3		22:30	leagues
5	1				
6	1				
7			Ships head SW		
8					
9			Ship head Eastward		
10					
11					
12	2		SE	SEBE	
1	1	2			
2	1			24:25	
3	2				
4	3	4			
5	4		SSE	NNE	variation 8:14W
6	5		Azm:ᵗ & amp:d		
7	4		08 :4W		
8	4				
9	4		Isle of Sall WNW 6 leag:ˢ		at 6 this morning saw nothing of the Swallow sloop.
10	4				
11	4	4			at noon in company with the store ship.
12	4	5	SBE	NNE	

Course	Dist:ᶜᵉ	Latitude in	Longit:ᵘᵈᵉ made	M: Dist:ᶜᵉ
S¾E	56	16:*18N	3:57W	218W

Island of Bonavista bore from South to WSW distance from the nearest shoar – 7 or 8 miles –

Remarks Tuesday Sep:ʳ 23 1766 (12)

H	K	F	Courses	Winds	Remarks
1	4		SE	NEBN	Mod. & hazey – at 2 sounded & had 15 fm: coral bottom, the East end of Bonavista West. 2 leagues. observed a reef stretching of the point ESE 4 miles – at the same time saw breakers without us bearing SE 3 miles. know not if it is a current or rock[75]
2	2				
	2		South		
3	2		SSBSE		
4	2	2	South	23:30	
	3		SWBS		
5	4				
6	4				
7	3	5			variation 9:10W
8	3				Bonavista NNW 3 leagues
9	4				
10	3	5			
11					made the sig:ˡ a bʳ; too
12					made the sig:ˡ & made sail
1			Up NEBE	off ESE	
2				23:10	
3					
4					at 6 the Isle of May W½SW dist:ᶜ 7 leagues
5	2		SWBS	NNE	variation 10:00W
6	4	2			
7	5	2			at ½ past 10, the West part of May North five miles
8	2		SWBW		a current sets to the Soward amongst these islands about 20 miles for 24 hours
9	8	3	WSW		The Swallow joined us.
10	5	5	West	North	
11	7		W½S	NBW	
12	7		West		Moderate & fair[76]

Course	Dist:ᶜᵉ	Latitude in	Longit:ᵘᵈᵉ made	M: Dist:ᶜᵉ
SSW	86	15:*00N	4:32W	252W

The West end of the Isle of May NE½E 9 leagues S° end of St Jago SWBW½W 4 leagues, the N:° most five leagues

---

75 ". . . at the same time observed a reef or a very great ripling stretching of the point about ESE – three miles and and at the same time saw breakers without us bearing SE about three miles, went between them and the shoar but had no soundings after hauling of half a mile – the store ship passed very near the breakers in the SE but had no soundings – yet they believe them to be dangerous." PL and FC.

76 "At noon, the W.end of the Isle of May bore NE½E 3 leagues." FC.

Remarks Wednesday Sep:r 24 1766 (13)

1	4			NNE
2	3			
3			1:07W	
4			4:05 W	24:00
5			18:14W	
6			23:56W	
7				
8		Longitude made from Madeira to Palma		
9		From Palma to S:t Jago		
10		Madeira in by reckoning		
11		Longitude of S:t Jago & by my account		
12				
1				
2				24:00
3				
4				
5				
6				
7				
8				
9				
10				
11				
12				West

Moderate & fair
at ½ past 3 anchord in Praya Road of the Isle of Jago in 8 fm: water sandy ground moord with a cable on the small & half a cable in the best bower to NNE, & small to the SSW –
The East point of the Bay EBS
the middle of the fort NWBN
the middle of the Island, WBN
& the West point of the Bay SWBW. The Swallow & the P Frederick anchord by us –

all night much lightning & rain AM – employed in getting off water[77]
Bent the sheet cable

found every where great quantities of purslane which gather and gave the ships company here was likewise plenty of goats oxen fowls, & fruit but our stay was so short that but small quantities came in, & that sold dear – oxen 12 Piastres 3 pieces peices Indian corn – 2.d pr. Pound –[78]

Latitude observed	Longit:ude from London
14:*53N[79]	23:00 West

---

77 ". . . sent to the commanding officer at the fort for leave to get off water & refreshments which he granted." PL and FC.

78 These details are not reported in the PL and in the FC. Wallis inserts a set of coordinates in both:

Long Lizard West of London	5:°14'
Madeira West of Liz:d by account	2:16
Palma West Madeira – by acc:t -	1:08
Port Praya West Palma	4:36
Port Praya Lon:d by acc:t from London	23:14 W

79 14:*54N in the PL and in the FC.

Week day	M:º Day	Wind	Remarks at S.ᵗ Jago (1)
Thursday	25	23:20 24:15 NE to NW	Rainy weather. Latter fair employed in watering the ship took out 1500 weight of bread from the store ship – received fresh beef from the shoar & 2 live oxen, dryd the sails[80]
Friday	26	23:00 23:40 NE	(2) Moderate & fair, employd watering got off four[81] live oxen, set up the rigging fore & aft, PM anchord here a Dutch India ship who saluted with 13 guns returned eleven –

Saturday	27	21:30 22:45 NE SSW	(3) Employed watering, PM unmoor'd & hove to half a cable on the best bower AM completed our water to 73 tons
			
			          Feet inc
			Ships draught of water forward 16 5
			        abaft 14 9
			
			[82]Every day whilst here hauled the sayne and served fish to the ships company – such as mullet, Old Wives, Snapper and many other kinds of fish –
			This being a sickly season – & the small pox plenty on the island made me to hurry away from hence fast as possible –[83]

---

80 "Served fresh beef to the ships company & sent part onboard the Swallow." PL and FC.

81 Eight in the PL and the FC.

82 "Soon after our arrival I learnt that this was the sickly season, and that the rain was so great that twas with diffuclty things could be brought from the country down to the ships, which made every thing very scarce & dear and what alarmed most was that the small pox raged to a great degree and was very fatal to the inhabitants, therefore no men were allowed to go onshore but what had the small pox, & those were not to go into any house.

 The seine was hauled twice every day & we caught abundance of fish such as mullet, snappers & old wives and in the valley where we got water we got prodigious quantities of very large & fine purslane growing wild of which I took off enough on our sailing to last the people above a week they eat it as salad and twas boiled in their broth and pease, & was very good." PL and FC.

83 Gore lists here the provisions taken onboard: beef, pork, fowls, turkeys, goats, oranges, limes, lemons, pineapples, coconuts, guava, papaya, Guinea hens, sugar and "tolerable good water", Indian corn, fish with hook and "scene". Molineux inserts a drawing of "Port Praya Bay in the Island of Sᵗ Jago" into his log.

EXPLORATION OF THE SOUTH SEAS

Remarks Sunday Sept:r 28 1766 (1)

H	K	F	Courses	Winds	
1					Little wind & fair made the sig:l & weigh'd in company with
2					the Swallow & P:ce Frederick –
3					unbent the cables & row'd the anchor
4	3		SBW	West	at 4 Port Praya N½W
5	1	4		23:10	variation p:r amp:de 8:22 West
6	1	4			at 6 Port Praya North Dis:ce 10 miles
7	1	2	SBE		the Peak of Fuego WNW 12 leagues
8	1				Jago lat.84S:t 14:°* 52 North
9	2		SSE		long:d – 22: 56 West
10	1	5			
11	1				
12	1	3	SEBS		
1	1				
2			Calm her head	S:°ward 22:45	Porto Prya in sight
3					variation p:r amplitude 7:50W
4				SEBS	
5	2		SWBS	SEBE	
6	3		SSW½W		
7	1	4			
8	1				Served fishin hooks & lines to the ships company –
9	2		SSW	SE	
10	2	2	SWBS	SEBS	
11	2				Little wind, the sloop & store ship in company –
12	2				

Course	Dist:ce	Lat:d in	Longit:ude made	M: Dist:ce
		14:*24N		

S:t Jago bore N¾E – Distance 10 or 11 leagues

---

84 These coordinates are omitted in the other logs. Hawkesworth adds a detail from Robertson's log (p.10) which does not appear in any of the Dolphin logs: "This day I ordered hooks and lines to be served to all the ship's company, that they might catch fish for themselves; but at the same time I also ordered that no man should keep his fish more than four and twenty hours before it was eaten, for I had observed that stale, and even dried fish, had made the people sickly, and tainted the air in the ship." All the quotes from Hawkesworth's *An Account Of The Voyages Undertaken By The Order Of His Present Majesty For Making Discoveries In The Southern Hemisphere* (1773), are taken from the *South Seas Project* transcriptions. http://southseas.nla.gov.au/journals/hv01/. Hawkesworth most probably had access to the PL and Robertson's journal, as the *Voyages* account, suposedly Wallis's, includes details from both.

Remarks Monday Sept:^r 29 1766 (2)

H	K	F	Courses	Winds	
1		4	SSW	SE	lights airs & fair
2		5			variation p:^r azim:^t ⎱ 9:18W
3		4			ampl:^{de} ⎰
4		5		23:55	at 6 the Burning Mountain on the Isle of Fuego NW½W 5
5	1	4			leagues
6	1		South ½ W		kill'd an ox – sent 170^{lb} of beef onboard the Swallow
7	1			EBS	
8	2	2			
9	1				
10	1				
11	1				
12	1			EBN	
1	1				Little wind & cloudy with some heavy showers –
2	1			23:05	
3	1				
4	2				
5	3				
6	3				
7	3				
8	2	4		EBS	
9	4	2			
10	5				
11	5	2			Little wind & fair, the Swallow a P:^{ce} Frederick in company[85]
12	5				

Course	Dist:^{ce}	Latitude in	Longit:^{ude} made	M: Dist:^{ce}
South	77	13:*36N	00:00	0

S:^t Jago bore North – Distance 26 leagues

---

[85] "Am afraid that we shall have a long passage to the Streights of Magellan, if they do not fall upon some method of trimming them to go better." Robertson (Carrington, *op. cit.*, p.10).

Remarks Tuesday Sept:ʳ 30 1766 (3)

H	K	F	Courses	Winds	Remarks
1	5		S½W	ESE	
2	5				
3	4				
4	3	4		24:00	Moderate breezes & fair
5	4	2		EBS	
6	4	4			
7	2				variation p:ʳ azimu:ᵗʰ 7:49 W
8	5				squally with rain –
9	3	4			variation p:ʳ ampl:ᵈᵉ
10	5				azim:ᵗ – 6:98 West
11	5	2			
12	5	3			
1	5	5			
2	5	5		23:30	
3	5	4			
4	5	5			
5	6				
6	5	5			out reefs
7	6				
8	5	2			
9	5	3			
10	5	5			
11	5	4			Fair weather in company as before
12	6				

Course	Dist	Lat in	Long: made	M: Dist:ᶜᵉ
South –	132	11:*24	00:10E	102

S:ᵗ Jago bore North – Distance 70 leagues

Remarks Wednesday October 1 1766 (4)

H	K	F	Courses	Winds	Remarks
1	5	5			
2	6				
3	6				Moderate & fair weather
4	6	2		24:00	
5	5		SBW	SEBE	
6	5	5			Kill'd an ox
7	4	2			
8	3				
9	5		SWBS	SEBS	
10	4		SSW½W	SE	
11	2				
12	2	4	SWBS		
1	2	5	SSW	SE	
2	3		SW	SSE	
3	2			24:00	
4	1	4			Squally with rain
5	2	5	SWBS	SEBS	
6	4		SW½S	SSE	
7	1	4	WSW		variation p:r amp:d 7:27W
8					sent 142lb of fresh beef to the Swallow[86]
9					
10	1	2	WBS	SBW	
11	1		West	SSW	
12	1		WBN	SWBS	Fair weather, in compy as before[87]

Course	Dis	Latitude in	Longit:ude made	M: D
S20:00W	50	10:*37N	00:7 West	7 West

S:t Jago bore North 2:00E – Distance 85 leagues

---

[86] "Kill'd an ox and sent part to the Swallow." PL and FC. It weighed 316 pounds according to Gore.
[87] "Exercised great guns & small arms." PL and FC.

Remarks Thursday Oct:er 2 1766 (5)

H	K	F	Courses	Winds	Remarks
1			calm	her	Light airs & fair weather
2			Head S°	Westerly	
3					
4					
5	1		S½W	NEBN	a great swell from the S: West
6	1	2		24:00	
7	1	4			
8	1				
9		5			Light airs
10		4			
11	2	4			
12		4		NE	
1	2	5			variation p; amp:de 7:°00 West
2	1	4		23:00	Exercised great guns & small arms[88]
3		4		North	
4		4			
5	1				
6	1				
7	1	2			
8	1	4			
9	1				
10	1				
11	1				In company as before
12		4			

Course	Dis	Latitude in	Long:d made	MD
SBSW	32	10:*66N	00:12W	11

S:t Jago bore North N2:°00E – Distance 97 leagues

---

[88] See preceding note. The days on which the arms are exercised vary (plus or minus one day) in the logs and will not be footnoted from this point onwards.

Remarks Friday Oct:er 3 1766 (6)

1					
2					Calm & fair weather killd & ox & sent part of it on board the Swallow
3				24:00	
4					Tryed the current found it set SBE about 6 fm:s p:r hour
5					
6				Calm the ships head to the Southward	Cloudy
7					caught three dozen of young dolphins & found them very
8					good – put a bit of fresh meat on a hook & just touched the
9					water with it & they catch greedily at it
10					the hook about the size of a whiting hook[89]
11					
12					
1			Ships head all round the compass		
2					
3					23:00
4	1		SWBW	South	Light airs
5	1	1	WSW		
6	1				
7	2		WSW½W		
8	2	3			
9	2	3	West	SSW	Exercised small arms.
10	2		SE½SE		
11	2				
12	2	4			Light airs & fair & Comp:y as before

Course	Dis	Latitude in	Long: made	MD
S½E	20	9:*46N	00:10W	9W

S:t Jago bore North N½E – Distance 102 leagues

---

[89] "Killed an ox, sent part to the Swallow a school of young dolphins about the ship try'd them with a hook and a bit of red rag on it, & bought three dozen and eight from the cabbin windows they weigh'd about a pound or more a piece & were very good." FC and PL.

Remarks Saturday Oct:er 4 1766 (7)

H	K	F	Courses	Winds	
1	2		SE½S	SWBS	
2	2				Light airs & fair
3	2				Exercised small arms
4	1	4		25:00	
5	3				
6	1		ENE	South	
7	1		North		Killd an ox supplied the Swallow with part
8	1		West		
9	1	3	SW		variation 5: 49W
10	1	2			
11	1		SWBS		
12	1	2	SBW	SEBE	
1	1				
2	1		SWBS	23:50	
3	1				
4	1		S½W	SBE	
5	1	5			
6	1				Exercised great guns & small arms
7	2				Light breezes & fair In comp:y as before
8	1	5		East	
9	1	5			
10	3	2			
11	4	2			
12	4				

Course	Dis:e	Latitude in	Long: made	MD
South	31	9:°*15N	00:10W	9 West

S:t Jago bore North N1:°10E – Distance 113 leagues –

Remarks Sunday Oct:er 5 1766 (8)

H	K	F	Courses	Winds	Remarks
1	3			East	
2	3				Light breezes & fair
3	2	4			Exercised small arms & great arms
4	2	3		23:55	variation p:r azi:t & amp:de 6:23W
5	3				
6	3	3			
7	3	4			
8	3	3		ENE	
9	2	5			
10	2	5			
11	2	4			
12	2	4			
1				Calm	
2	1	3	East	SSE	Squally with rain
3	1	3		23:00	
4	1				
5	1		EBN		
6					
7					
8			Calm the ships		
9			head to the		
10			S:°ward		
11					
12					Calm & cloudy In comp:y as before

Course	Dis:	Latitude in	Long: made	MD
SBE	34	8:*42N	00:4W	3W

S:t Jago bore North Distance 124 leagues

Remarks Monday Oct 6 1766 (9)

H	K	F	Courses	Winds	Remarks
1				Calm & cloudy weather	
2	1		SW	SSE	Bore down to the Swallow
3	1				
4				Calm	
5	3		S½W	NNE	Squally with heavy rain
6				24:05	
7					
8					
9	1		SW	SSE	much lightning to the S:°ward
10	1	5			
11	1	4	WSW		
12	1	5	W½S	SSW	
1					made the sig:ˡ & tack'd
2			S½W	West	
3				23:0	
4	2				
5					
6			ships head to S:°ward		
7					
8					Killed an ox sent part to the Swallow
9	2	2	NBE		Bore down to the Swallow
10	1				
11	1	5	SE	SSW	Light breezes & fair, in com:ʸ as before
12	2	3	South	WSW	

Course	Dis:ᵗ	Latitude in	Long: made	MD
S17:00N	19	8:*24N	00:09W	8: West

S:ᵗ Jago bore North– Distance 130 leagues

Remarks Tuesday Oc:ʳ 7 1766 (10)

1	1	3	S½W	WBN	
2	1	4	S½E		Light breezes & fair
3	1	3	S½		
4	1	4		24/30	
5	1	3			Read articles of war & act of parliament —[90]
6	1				
7	1		S½E		
8	1				Light airs
9	1		S½W		
10	1				
11	1	4			
12		5	SE	SSW	
1	2	5	SEBE	SWBS	
2	2	5		23/35	
3	2	5	SSE	SW	
4	2		SBE½E		
5	2	2	SSE		Little wind with a head swell
6	3	1			
7	2	3	SE½S		
8	3	3			
9	3		SE½S	SSW	
10	3		SE½S		
11	2		SSE		Fresh breezes & cloudy with a hard sea – In company as before
12	2	5	SEBS	SWBS	

Course	Dis:ᶜ	Latitude in	Long: made	M: Dis
SSE½E –	57	7:*34N	00:18E	19E

S:ᵗ Jago bore North 2:°00'W Distance 146 leagues

---

[90] Omitted in the two other logs.

Remarks Wednesday Oc:ʳ 8 1766 (11)

1	2	5	SEBS	SWBS	
2	3	2	SBE	SWBS	Squally with heavy rain
3	3		SE		saved two days rainwater –[91]
4	2		ESE	23:10	at 4 tack'd, thick foggy weather
5	1		WSW	Variable	fired a gun every hour[92]
6	1		WSW		
7	1		West	SSW	
8	2				
9	2	3	WBN	SWBS	at 8 moderate gales & hazy –
10	2				
11	2	3			
12	2	2	W½N	SSW	
1	1	3	West		Moderate & cloudy –
2	2	2		23:00	
3	3				
4	3				Fresh gales
5	2	4			At 6 bore away to joyn the Swallow[93]
6	2		WNW		
7	3	5			made the signal & wore
8	2	4			
9	2	4	SE½E		several swallows about the ship
10	2	3			Fresh gales & cloudy. In comp:ʸ as before –
11	3	2	SEBE	SBW	caught some Bonnetos
12	3				

Course	Dis	Latitude in	Long: made	M: Dis
S63:00W	22	7:*24N	00:00E	0 –

S:ᵗ Jago bore North – Distance 150 leagues

91 Five hogsheads (PL and FC).
92 ". . . 'till nine when it cleared up." PL and FC.
93 Omitted in the two other logs.

Remarks Thursday Oc:ʳ 9 1766 (12)

H	K	F	Courses	Winds
1	3	3	SEBE	SBW
2	3	3	SE	SSW
3	2	2		
4	2	3		24:00
5	2			
6	2		SEBE½E	SWBS
7	2	2	SE½E	SSW
8	2	2	SE	
9	2			
10	2	2		
11	3			
12	2	5		
1	4			23:30
2	3	5	SE½S	SWBS
3	2	3	SSE	SW
4	2	4	SEBS	SWBS
5	2	2		
6	2			
7	3	3		
8	3			
9	3		SE	SSW
10	3	3		
11	4			
12	3			

Fresh gales & cloudy with a great swell from the SW – Handed f tops:[1]

variation p:ʳ azum:ᵈᶜ: 5: 40W
Set fore topsail

Cloudy –

Rainy –

Moderate & fair in comp:ʸ as before

Course	Dis	Latitude in	Long: made	M: Dis
S78:°10E	64	7:*04N	1:01E	60E

S:ᵗ Jago bore N7:°15'W Distance 158 leagues

EXPLORATION OF THE SOUTH SEAS

Remarks Friday Oct:ʳ 10 1766 (13)

H	K	F	Courses	Winds	
1	3		SE	SSW	Fresh breezes & fair out reefs
2	3	5	SE½E	24:25	
3	3	3		SBW	Moderate & fair
4	3	4	SEBE	SBW	Gave to Captain Carterett a copy of the Admiralty orders, and orders rendez-vous &:ᶜᵉ from myself – together with the following draughts –
5	3		SEBE	SBW	
6	2	5	SEBE	SSW	
7	1	5	SE		Faulk Lands Islands
8	2	3			Port Egmont
9	3		SEBE		Port Desire
10	2	5			Entrance of Streight of Magellan
11	2				Streights of Magellan – Two
12	2		SEBE	SBW	Cape Quod
1	1	3	ESE½E		Long Beach
2	1	2		23:30	
3	1	3			Gave Lieu:ᵗ Brine his orders and instructions with the following draughts –
4	1	4	SE½E	SSW	
5	1	4			Falklands islands
6	1	5			Port Egmont
7	1	2			Port Desire
8	1	3			Streights of Magellan
9	1	4			Entrance of the Streights of Magellan
10	1				Light airs in comp:ʸ as before[94]
11	1				
12	1				

Course	Dis	Latitude in	Long: made	M: Dis
S53:°00'E	50	6:*34N	1:41E	100E

S:ᵗ Jago bore NBW Distance 171 leagues

---

[94] The corresponding entry in both the PL and the FC is brief ("Moderate & fair Light airs. In company as before.").

Remarks Saturday Oct:^{r} 11 1766 (14)

variation p:^{r} azy:th & amp:^{de}: 8:00W

H	K	F	Courses	Winds	Remarks
1	1	2	SEBS	SWBW	
2	1	2			
3					
4				24:30	
5	1	2			
6	1	2			
7	1				
8	1		SSE	SW	
9	1				
10	1				
11	1		S½W	West	Light airs
12	1				
1					
2				23:45	
3	1		SSE	SW	
4	1				Rainy
5	1				
6	1	3	S½W	West	Fair
7	2	4			cask of pork N 987. contents 314 short 3.
8	1		SSE	SW	
9	1		South		
10					Rainy
11	1		SW	SSE	Light airs & fair in comp:^{y} as before
12	1		WSW	South	

Course	Dis	Latitude in	Long: made	M: Dis
SEBS	36	6:04	2:02E	120E

S:^{t} Jago bore N12:°45'W Distance 182 leagues

Remarks Sunday Oct:ʳ 12 1766 (15)

1	1	3	SBE	SWBW
2	1	4	S½W	
3	1		South	WSW
4	1			24:30
5				
6				
7	1	3	SE	
8	1	4	SSE	
9	1	5		
10	2	4		
11	2	4		
12	1	5		
1	2		SEBS	SWBS
2	4		S½W	NW
3	5			23:00
4	3			
5	1	4		
6	1	2	South	
7	1			
8	1	4		
9	2	4	S½W	West
10	2	4	South	
11	2		SBW	
12	5			

Moderate & fair
variation p:ʳ azm: ᵗʰ 8:40 W
caught a large shark after hooking two four times he had a dolphin, two other large fish & some peices of pork in his belly one of the hooks was sticking in his jaws

1:ˡ reefs topsails

Fresh gales & dark rainy weath:ʳ
Fired a gun every hour till five[95]

caught a shark —
Rainy squally weather

Swallow & store ship in company
heavy rain fill'd all the empty casks with rain water saved ten days rain water[96]

Course	Dis	Latitude in	Longit:ᵘᵈᵉ made	M: Dist:ᶜᵉ
S18:30E	51	5:16N	2:18E	136

S:ᵗ Jago bore N13:°20'W Distance 198 leagues

---

[95] Until 6 in the PL and the FC and until 4 in Gore's log. No details as to the stomach contents of the shark are given.

[96] "Saved near three tuns of rain waterwhich keeps extremely well by keeping the bungs of the casks open but what was bunged up close stunk very bad so that it could not be drunk." Robertson (Carrington, op. cit., pp.10–11).

Remarks Monday Oct:ʳ 13 1766 (16)

1	2		SBW	NWBW
2	1	3		
3	1	4		NBW
4	1	4		21:20
5	1	5		WBN
6	1	4	SBE	SWBW
7	2			
8	2			
9	2			
10	2	5	SSE	SW
11	3		SEBS	
12	3		SE	
1	2		SSE	variable
2	2			21:40
3	1		SE	
4	1	2	SBE	SWBW
5	2	3		
6	2			
7	1	4	SBE½E	
8	2		SE	SSW
9	3			
10	3			
11	3		SE½S	
12	3		SE	

Little wind & rainy weather

Light breezes & fair

variation p:ʳ azm:ᵗʰ: 8:30W
opened a cask of beef N:°1292 cont: 167⁹⁷
short 3 pieces

Light breezes & fair

Course	Dis	Latitude in	Longit:ᵘᵈᵉ made	M: Dist:ᶜᵉ
S59:°00'E	45	4:*54E	2:°57'E	175E

S:ᵗ Jago bore N16:°20'W Distance 207 leagues

---

97 Omitted in the PL and the FC.

Remarks Tuesday Oct:r 14 1766 (17)

H	K	F	Courses	Winds	Remarks
1	2		SEBE	SBW	Light breezes & fair weather
2	2				
3	2	2	ESE	South	
4	1		EBS	23:20	Little wind with drizzling rain
5	2		West	SSE	reeft the topsails
6	1		EBS	SBE	
7	1	5			
8	2				
9					
10					
11					
12					
1					calm from 9 PM to 8 AM the ships head all round the
2				22:30	compass[98]
3					
4					
5					heavy rain with much lightning and thunder
6					caught a shark & shot two more but they got of the hook[99]
7					
8					
9					
10	1	3	SWBS	SEBS	Moderate & fair
11	1	3	SWBW	SBE	In company as before
12	2				

Course	Dis	Latitude in	Longit:ude made	M: Dist:ce
South	10	4:*44E	2:°57'E	175E

S:t Jago bore N16:°00'W Distance 210 leagues

---

98 The empty casks are filled with rainwater (Gore).
99 ". . . caught sharks enough to serve the ships company." PL and FC.

Remarks Wednesday Oct:[r] 15 1766 (18)

H	K	F	Courses	Winds	Remarks
1	1	2	WBS½S	S½W	
2	1	3	WBS	SBW	Light breezes & fair
3	2	2	W½S		
4	2		West	SSW	Bore down to the Swallow
5	1		NW	22:10	
6	4		SWBW	SBW	caught a shark 9 feet: 5 inches long
7	3				
8	2	4			
9	2	4	SW½S	SEBS	
10	2		SW½W	SSE	
11	2		SWBW	SBE	
12	2				Cloudy
1	2	5	ESE	South	Made the sig:[l] & tack'd[100]
2	1		SWBW	SBE	
3	2	2		22:30	
4	2				fair weather
5	4	4			
6	1	3			variation p:[r] azm:[th] 9:10W
7	1	2			
8	1	2			
9	2				Exercised great guns & small arms
10	2				Moderate breezes & fair
11	1	5			In company as before
12	1	2	WSW	South	

Course	Dis	Latitude in	Long:[de] made	M: Dist:[ce]
S63:°00	45	4:*24N	2:17E	135E

S:[t] Jago bore N12:°08'W Distance 215 leagues

---

100 Noted twice in the PL and the FC.

EXPLORATION OF THE SOUTH SEAS

					Remarks Thursday October 16 766 (19)
1	1	4	WSW	SW	Little wind & cloudy
2	2	5			Fresh breezes & rainy –
3	2		SBW	EBS	
4	4			21:50	variation – 9:46W
5	3	2			
6	2	4	SBW½W	SEBE	
7	2		SSW		Moderate & cloudy
8	2	3	SW	SSE	
9	2		SWBW	SBE	
10	2				
11	1	4			
12	1	3	SW	SSE	
1	2		SWBW	SBE	
2	2			22:10	variation p:r amp:de: 8:17W
3	2	2			
4	2	5			
5	2	4			Exercised great guns & small arms
6	2	3			
7	2	2			
8	2	4	SW½W		
9	2	2	SW	SSE	
10	2	3			Little wind & cloudy. In company with the Swallow & Prince Frederick
11	2	3			
12	2	3			

Course	Dis	Latitude in	Long made	M: Dist:ce
SW	46	3:*52N	1:45E	103E

S:t Jago bore N8:40W Dis:te 224 leagues

Remarks Friday Oct: 17 766 (20)

H	K	F	Courses	Winds
1	2	2	SW½W	SSE
2	2			
3	3		SWBW	
4	2	4	WSW½S	SBE
5	3			23:30
6	2		SW½W	
7	1	5	SWBW	
8	2			
9	1	4	WSW	South
10	1	3		
11	2			
12	2	2	WBS	SBW
1	2			
2	1	5		
3	1	5		
4	2	3	WBS	22:50
5	2		WBS	
6	2	5	West	SSW
7	1		SE	
8	2	4	SE½E	
9	2	2	SE	
10	3		SE½E	
11	2	5		
12	2	2		

Light breezes & fair weather

variation p:r amp:^{de} 9:30W.

variation p:^{r} azim:th : 9 :35W.

Little wind & fair –

In company as before –

Course	Dis	Latitude in	Long made	M: Dist:^{ce}
S59:°10'W	25	3:*40N	1:24E	82E

S:^{t} Jago bore N6:50W Distance 227 leagues

Remarks Saturday O:[b] 18 766 (21)

H	K	F	Course	Wind
1	3		SEBE	SBW
2	2			
3	2	2		
4	2	3	SE	SSW
5	1	4		24:00
6	1	5	SEBS	SWBS
7	1	5	SE	SSW
8	2	5	SEB½E	
9	3		SEBS	SWBS
10	2	2	SSE	SW
11	2	6	SSE½E	
12	2	6	SE½S	
1	3		SEBS	SSW
2	3	2	SE	SWBS
3	3	3	SEBE	SSW
4	3	4	SEBE½E	SBW
5	2	4	SEBE	23:00
6	2	3		
7	3			
8	3			
9	3	5	ESE	South
10	4		E½S	
11	3	5	EBS	
12	4			SBE

Moderate breezes & fair

Light breezes & cloudy in comp as before –

Course	Dis:	Latitude in	Long made	M: Dist:[ce]
S71:°00'E	64	3:*20N	2:24E	142E

S:[t] Jago bore NBW Distance 237 leagues

Remarks Sunday Oct:r 19 766 (22)

1	2	2	WSW½W	South	
2	2	1	WSW		Little wind & cloudy
3	2				
4	2	3		23:30	
5	2				variation p:r amp:dc : 10 :18W.
6	1	4	SWBW		a SE swell
7	1	5			
8	2	5			
9	3	3			
10	3	4			
11	3	5			
12	3				
1	2	4	SW	SSE	
2	2	3		22:45	
3	2	5	SW½W		
4	2	5			
5	2				
6	3				
7	3				
8	3		SW		variation p:r azim:th: 9 :00W
9	3				
10	3	4			
11	3	5			
12	3		SW½W		Fresh breezes In company as before

Course	Dis:	Lat:d in	Long. made	MD
S40:°15'E	67	2:*44N	1:28E	86E

S:t Jago bore N6:°45'W Distance 246 leagues

Remarks Monday October 20:[th] 766 (23)

1	2	5	SW½W	SSE	
2	5				Moderate & fair
3	3		WBN		
4	3		SW	23:0	bore down to the store ship
5	3				variation p:[r] Azum:[th]: 9:30W.
6	3				
7	2	5			
8	2	2			
9	3	3	SWBS		
10	2		WBN		
11	5		SW½S		bore down to the store ship –
12	2	4	SW		
1	3				
2	3			22:05	
3	3				
4	3		SW½W		
5	3	5			
6	3				
7	3		SWBW	SBE	
8	3		SW½W		variation p:[r] azumuth – 8:°00'W –
9	2	5			
10	2	2	SW		
11	2	2	SW½S	SEBS	[101]Served oyle to ships company
12	2	2	WBN		Little wind & fair in company as before
	1	4	SW	SSE	

Course	Dis:	Latitude in	Long. made	MDist:[ce]
SW½W	70	02:°*44N[h]	0:34E	32E

S:[t] Jago bore N2:°05'W Distance 258 leagues

---

101 "The butter & cheese being all expended began to serve oyle. Gave orders for the people to be served mustard & vinegar once a fortnight during the rest of the voyage." PL and FC.

Remarks Tuesday October 21 – 1766 (24)

H	K	F	Courses	Winds
1	3		SW½S	SSE
2	3			
3	3	2	SSW½W	
4	3	1		22:40
5	4		SWBS	SEBS
6	4			
7	2	3		
8	2	4	SSW	SE
9	3	4	SSW½W	
10	3	1		
11	3	4		
12	3	5		
1	3	5		
2	4			22:05
3	3			
4	2	2		
5	3		SWBW	SEBS
6	3	3		
7	3			
8	3			
9	3		SSW½W	
10	2	4	SSW	SE
11	3			
12	3			

Moderate and fair weather
served mustard & vinegar
several swallows about the ship

variation p:^{r} azum:th: 8:00W
a SE swell

Moderate & fair. In comp:^{y} as before
Bent new main fore & mis:^{n} topsails[102]

Course	Dis:^{t}	Latitude in	Long. made	MDist:^{cc}
SSW½W	75	0:*54N	0:81W	3W

S:^{t} Jago bore North Distance 280 leagues

---

[102] ". . . & set about repairing the old ones." PL and FC. Robertson also indicates that they were experimentally dipped in the sea to prevent mildew (Carrington, *op. cit.*, p.11).

Remarks Wednesday October 22 – 1766 (25)

H	K	F	Course	Winds	Remarks
1	2		SSW	SE	Moderate & fair weather
2	3				
3	4				saw a Man of War bird –[103]
4	4		SWBS	22:30	bore down to the store ship –[104]
5	3		WSW		variation p:^{r} azum:th: 8:05W –
6	3		SWBS		
7	4	4			
8	4			SEBS	
9	3	4			
10	3				
11	3	4			
12	3	5			
1	3	2			
2	3	2		22:30	
3	3		SSW½W	SE	
4	3				
5	3	3			
6	3	1			variation p:^{r} azum:th: 6:10N
7	2	6			Sailmakers employed in repairing the old topsails –[105]
8	3	3			
9	3	2			
10	3	3			Exercised great guns & small arms
11	3	3			fair weather in company as before
12	3				

Course	Dis:^{t}	Latitude in	Long. made	MDist:^{ce}
SW¾S	75	0:*54N	0:81W	3W

S:^{t} Jago bore N1:08E Distance 301 leagues

103 Omitted in the PL.
104 Omitted in the PL.
105 Mentioned in the 22nd October entry in the PL and FC. Hawkesworth: "On the 22d we saw an incredible number of birds, and among the rest a man of war bird, which inclined us to think that some land was not more than 60 leagues distant: this day we crossed the equator in longitude 23° 40' W."

REDISCOVERED ACCOUNTS, VOLUME I

Remarks Thursday Oct:ʳ 23 – 1766 (26)

H	K	F	Courses	Winds	Remarks
1	3	2	SSW½W	SE	Fresh gales & hazey 2: reeft top:ˡˢ
2	3	2			
3	3		SWBS		
4	3	3		22:15	variation p:ʳ azum:ᵗʰ 5:13W.
5	3	3	SSW		saw a vast number of birds a head which spread from SW to
6	3	4	SSW½W		SE they kept so far from the ship could not say what they
7	4		SSW		were but believe they were Boobies —[106]
8	3	5			
9	3	2			
10	3	3			
11	4				
12	3	4			
1	3				
2	3			22:30	
3	3				
4	3	2			
5	5	5			Sailmakers employed as before[107]
6	4	3			
7	4	3			Exercised small arms
8	4	4			
9	4	2			
10	3	3			fresh gales & cloudy
11	3	3			In company as before
12	3	5			

Course	Dis	Latitude in	Long. made	MDist:ᶜᵉ
SSW½W	84	1:*24N	1:28W	90W

S:ᵗ Jago bore N2:10E Distance 326 leagues

---

[106] "Saw a prodigious number of birds flying from the SW to the SE." PL and FC.
[107] Omitted in the PL.

Remarks Friday Oct:ʳ 24 – 1766 (27)

H	K	F	Wind	Course	Remarks
1	3	5	SSW½W	SE	Moderate & hazey
2	3	3			
3	5				
4	5	2		22/20	
5	5	3		SEBE	Fresh breezes with a SE swell
6	4	3			variation p:ʳ azum:ᵗʰ: 5:08 West.
7	3			SE	caught a dolphin
8	3	3			
9	3	3			
10	4	2			
11	4				
12	5			SEBE	Squally
1	5	4			
2	5	3		22:10	
3	4				
4	5			SE	
5	3	3			
6	4				variation p:ʳ azimuth – 4:25W
7	5	2			
8	5	5			sailmakers employed as before[108]
9	4	4			
10	4	1			Fresh breezes & fair
11	5				In company as before –[109]
12	4	5			

Course	Dis	Latitude in	Long. made	MDist:ᶜᵉ
SWBS	108	2:*54N	2:28W	150W

S:ᵗ Jago bore N8:00E Distance 360 leagues

---

108 Omitted in the PL and FC.
109 "Served brandy to ships company and reserved the wine for the sick & recovering." PL and FC.

Remarks Saturday Oc:ʳ 25 – 1766 (28)

H	K	F	Courses	Winds
1	5		SSW½W	SE
2	5			
3	5	2		
4	5	3		22:00
5	4	4		
6	4	3		
7	4	4		SEBE
8	4	4		
9	4			
10	5			
11	4	6		
12	4			SE
1	5			
2	5			21:40
3	4	2		
4	3	4		SEBE
5	4	4		
6	4	2		
7	4	3		
8	4	2		
9	4	5		
10	5			
11	4			SE
12	4			

Fresh breezes & fair weather

variation p:ʳ amp:ᵈᵉ: 3:45W

variation p :ʳ azum:ᵗ : 2:16W.
sail makers employed as before

Fresh gales & squally with a great SE swell – got down top gallant yards – in company as before

Course	Dis	Latitude in	Long. made	MD
S36:°00'W	110	4:*22S	3:°33'W	215W

S:ᵗ Jago bore N10:°36'E Distance 393 leagues

Remarks Sunday Oc:ʳ 26 – 1766 (29)

1	3	3	SSW½W	SEBE	Fresh gales & squally with a great swell from the SE –
2	4				
3	4	5		22:00	
4	4		NNW		Bore down to the P:ᶜᵉ Frederick she having carried away her
5	3		SSW		fore topsail yard –
6	2	5			variation p:ʳ amp:ᵈᵉ 2:40W
7	3				
8	4				
9	4				
10	4				
11	4	5			
12	3	5			
1	3	6			
2	4	6		22:00	
3	4				
4	3	4			
5	4	4			
6	3				
7	3	5			squally with rain
8	3	2			
9	2	5			
10	4				
11	4				fresh gales & cloudy In cm:ʸ as before
12	4				

Course	Dis	Lat:ᵈ in	Long. made	MDist:ᶜᵉ
S 24:°15'W	91	5:*44S	4: 12W	254W

S:ᵗ Jago bore N11:°40'E Distance 424 leagues

Remarks Monday Oc:ʳ 27 1766 (30)

H	K	F	Courses	Winds
1	3	5	SSW½W	SE
2	3	5		
3	3	5		
4				22:0
5		up	SSW off	SW
6	3	5	SSW	SE
7	4	3	SSW½W	
8	4			
9	4	3		
10	5			
11	4	2		
12	4			
1	4		SSW	ESE
2	4	2		
3	4			21:21
4	4			SEBE
5	4	5		
6	4	4		
7	4	4		
8	4			
9	5			
10	4	4		
11	4	5	SBW½W	
12	4			

Fresh breezes –
The store ship made the signal of distress brought too & sent a boat onboard of her with the carpenters & some of his crew, found that some of her men were sick and that she had sprung a leak under the larboard cheek sent a carpenter & five seamen to remain onboard her –[110]
at 5 made sail

Fresh gales & fair

variation p:ʳ az: 1:00 West.

Moderate & fair in comp:ʸ as before –

Course	Dis:ᵗ	Lat:ᵈ in	Long. made	MDist:ᶜᵉ
S29:°0'W	100	7:*11S	5:03W	304W

S:ᵗ Jago bore N12:°50'E Distance 456 leagues

---

[110] "At 3 the storeship made the signall of distress. Brought too and sent a boat with the carpenter onboard her. The boat returned & the carpenter informed me that she had sprung a leak under the larboard cheek forward and that it was impossible to do anything until we had better weather Lieu: Brine who commanded her said that his crew were sickly, that he feard twold be impossible to keep her in company with me without some help. That the fateague of the pumps and the constant standing by the sails had worn them down greatly. That their provisions was very indifferent and they had nothing but water to drink. On this I sent the carpenter and six seamen to assist in pumping and working the ship. At six made sail." PL and FC. In the FC the spelling has been corrected for words like fatigue and 'twould. Molineux points out that the five men would "assist at the pump." Robertson adds that the leak could not be stopped at sea and that the carpenter did not think it "very dangerous at present" (Carrington, *op. cit.*, p.12).

Remarks Tuesday Oct:ʳ 28 1766 (31)

H	K	F	Courses	Winds	Remarks
1	4		SBW½W	ESE	Fresh gales & hazey bent the old main topsail
2	4				2:ᵉ reeft the topsails¹¹¹
3	5				
4	5			22:30	variation p:ʳ amp:ᵈᵉ 1:40W
5	4				
6	3	5		SEBE	
7	4	2			
8	4	4			Fresh gales & cloudy
9	4	3			
10	3	5			
11	5				
12	4	4		ESE	
1	4	4			
2	4	3			
3	4			21:50	variation p:ʳ azum:ᵗʰ 00:44W
4	4				open'd a cask of pork. N 957. Contents 310 –
5	5				Punished Edmond Morgan for drunkenness & mutiny –
6	5	2		East	Bent the old fore topsail –
7	6				
8	6	4		EBS	
9	6				Fresh gales & fair
10	6				The Swallow & stroreship in comp:ʸ
11	6	3			set up the rigging
12	6				

Course	Dis	Latitude in	Long. made	MD
SSW	112	8:*54S	5:47W	347W

S:ᵗ Jago bore N13:40E Dist:ᶜᶜ 493 leag:ʳ

---

111 "In 2:ⁿᵈ reef fore top sail having otherwise (with the foresail) too much sail for the other ship to keep up." Gore.

Remarks Wednesday Oct:r 29 1766 (32)

H	K	F	Courses	Winds		
1	5	4	SBW½S	EBS		
2	5					
3	4	5				
4	5	2		22:55		Fresh breezes and fair
5	5	2				
6	4					
7	5					variation p:r amp:de 1:20W
8	4					
9	4	3				
10	4					
11	3	5				
12	3	3				
1	4	2				
2	3	5		21:55		
3	3	4				
4	3					
5	4					
6	5					
7	4	3				
8	3					
9	3					
10	2					
11	2					
12	2					Moderate & hazey[112]

Course	Dis:ce	Latitude in	Long. made	MDis:
SSW	93	10:*20S	6:24W	384W

S:t Jago bore N14:°15'E Dist:ce 521 leagues

---

112 "Set up all the rigging fore & aft." PL and FC.

Remarks Thursday 30 Oc:ʳ 1766 (33)

H	K	F	Courses	Winds	Remarks
1	3		SBW½W	ENE	
2	3		SW	SBE	Moderate & cloudy
3	2		SWBW		
4	2			25:00	Rainy weather
5	2		WBS	SBW	
6	1				
7	1	4			hook'd a very large fish which got from me[113]
8	1				
9	1		SWBW	SBE	
10	1		SBW½W	SE	Drizling rain
11	1			SEBE	
12					
1	1		SWBW	SBE	Light airs with drizling rain
2	2		SBW½W	ESE	
3	3	4		21:00	
4	3	5			
5	3	5		East	Little wind & fair
6	2				
7	1				
8	1	4			
9	1	4	SW		a Curlue about the ship –
10	2	4	SBW½W	ENE	Moderate & cloudy weather
11	3				In company as before –
12	4	4			

Course	Dis –	Latitude in	Long. made	MD
SSW½W	49	11:*04S	6:46W	406W

S:ᵗ Jago bore N14:°35'E Distance 535 leagues

---

113 Omitted in the PL and FC.

Remarks Friday 31 1766 (34)

1	3	4	SBW½W	East	Moderate & cloudy opened a cask of beef
2	3	5			
3	4				
4	4	3		22:30	variation p:^{r} az:th & amp:^{de} 1:00E
5	4				
6	4	3			
7	4	3			
8	4	5			Fresh breezes & clear
9	5	3			
10	5	4			
11	5	3			
12	5			ESE	
1	5	2			
2	5			21:30	
3	5	3			
4	5			East	
5	5				
6	5	3			variation p:^{r} az:th 1:30E
7	6				
8	6				
9	6				
10	6	3			Exercised small arms
11	6	3			In company as before
12	6	2		ESE	

Course	Dis	Latitude in	Long. made	MD
SBW½W	124	13:*02S	7:27W	446W

S:^{t} Jago bore N15:°00'E Distance 576 leagues

Remarks Saturday November 1: 1766 (35)

H	K	F	Courses	Winds
1	5	4	SBW½W	EBS
2	5	2		
3	4	5		
4	5	2		22:00
5	5			
6	5	2		
7	5			
8	5			ESE
9	5	2		
10	5			
11	4	4		
12	4	3		
1	5	3		
2	5			21:00
3	5			
4	4	3		
5	4			
6	4	4		
7	5	4		
8	5	5		
9	6	2		
10				
11				
12				

Fresh breezes & fair
Exercised great guns & small arms

Squally

In company as before

Course	Dis	Latitude in	Long. made	MD
SBW½W	129	15:*06S	8: 55W	483W

S:.ᵗ Jago bore N15:°05'E Distance 619 leagues

Remarks Sunday 2 Nov:ʳ 1766 (36)

H	K	F	Course	Winds	Remarks
1	5		SBW½W	ENE	
2	5				
3	5	4			Fresh breezes & fair wea:ʳ unbent the new miz:ⁿ tops:ˢ & bent
4	5	4		21:45	the old one it being repaired –[114]
5	5	3		East	
6	5	3			variation p:ʳ az:ᵗʰ & amp:ᵈᵉ 1:°00'E
7	5	4			
8	5	5			
9	5	5			
10	6				
11	6	2			
12	6			EBS	
1	6	2			
2	6	4		21:20	Reeved a new tiller rope the old one being stranded –[115]
3	6				
4	5	4			
5	5	6			
6	6				
7	6	3			variation p:ʳ az 1:°57'E
8	6	2			
9	6	4			
10	6				
11	6	4			
12	6				Fresh breezes[116]

Course	Dis:ᶜᵉ	Latitude in	Long. made	MDis:ᵉ
S18:00W	138	17:*17S	8: 50W	527W

S:ᵗ Jago bore N15:°20'E Distance 666 leagues

---

114 Omitted in the PL and FC.
115 Omitted in the PL and FC.
116 "Served wine to the ships company." Gore.

Remarks Monday Nov:^r 3 1766 (37)

1	6		SBW½W	EBS
2	6	2		
3	8	3		Fresh gales & cloudy weather
4	4		SBW½W	21:03
5	6	2		
6	6	5		
7	6	2		
8	7			
9	7			
10	7			
11	7			
12	6	4		
1	7			
2	5			20:55
3	6	2		
4	6			NE
5	5			Squally with rain[117]
6	5	3		
7	5	4		
8	5	2		
9	6	3		
10	6	4		
11	6	5		
12	6	4		

Course	Dis	Latitude in	Long. made	MDis:^e
SBW½W	149	19:*20S	10: 05W	597W

S:^t Jago bore N16:10E Distance 715 leagues

---

[117] "In company (as before (PL)) the Swallow & Prince Frederick." FC.

Remarks Tuesday Nov:ʳ 4 1766 (38)

H	K	F	Courses	Winds
1	6		SWBS	NEBE
2	6			
3	5	2		
4	6			20:40
5	6			
6	5	4		
7	5	4	W½S	
8	5	3		
9	5	4		
10	4	2		
11	4	4		
12	5	2		
1	6	2		
2	5	3		20:57
3	5	4		
4	6			NEBN
5	6			
6	6	2	SWBS	
7	6			
8	5	2		
9	5			
10	5			
11	5			NBW
12	5			

Fresh gales & cloudy rainy wea:ʳ with a great swell from the NE

Close reeft the topsails –

Fresh gales & hazey –

Saw great quantities of birds about the ship – like sheerwaters only browner –[118]
Fresh breezes –

Course	Dis	Latitude in	Long. made	MDis:ᶜ
S57:°10'	120	20:*32S	11: 51W	697W

S:ᵗ Jago bore N19:°10'E Distance 746 leagues

---

[118] "Saw a great number of sheerwaters and other birds about the ship". PL and FC (5ᵗʰ November entry).

Remarks Wednesday 5 Nov:ʳ 1766 (39)

H	K	F	Course	Winds	Remarks
1	3	3	SWBS	SEBN	Fresh gales & rainy weather
2	4				
3	4				Saved two tons of rain water during the rain
4	4	4		20:00	
5	5	3			
6	5	4		NEBE	
7	5	4			
8	5				Rainy weather with a great swell
9	6				
10	5	3			
11	5				
12	4			NEBN	
1	5				
2	4			19:50	
3	2	5			
4	3	2		NE	Moderate breezes with drizly rain & hazey weather
5	3	4			a great NE swell –
6	4				
7	4	5			
8	4				let out all the reefs
9	3				Moderate & fair In comp:ʸ as before
10	2	4			caught two sharks –
11	2	2			
12	2	2			

Course	Dis	Latitude in	Long. made	MDis:ᵉ
SWBS	99	21:*54S	12: 50W	752W

S:ᵗ Jago bore N18:°50'E Distance 780 leagues

Remarks Thursday 6 Nov:ʳ 1766 (40)

H	K	F	Courses	Winds	Remarks
1	2		SWBS	East	
2	2	3	SW	SSE	Fresh gales & squally weather
3	3	4			
4	3	2		20:05	
5	3		SWBS	SEBS	loose reefs the topsails
6	2	4	WBS		
7	5		SWBS		a great hard sea –
8	3				
9	3	2			Fresh gales & squally weather with a heavy head sea which
10	3	3			makes the ship labour much
11	2	4	SW	SSE	
12	2	3			
1	4		SW½S	SEBS	
2	3	2		20:00	
3	2	6	SWBS		
4	2	4			
5	3	4			Fresh gales & squally with a great swell & head sea – variat:ᵗⁿ
6	2	4			p:ʳ az:ᵗ 6°30'E
7	3				
8	3				
9	3				
10	3	2			
11	2	4	SW½S		
12	2	3			Fresh gales & cloudy – in company as before –

Course	Dis:ᵗ	Lat:ᵈ in	Long. made	M:Dis
S50:°00'W	75	22:*41S	13: 52W	810W

S:ᵗ Jago bore N19:°40'E Distance 805 leagues

Remarks Friday 7 Nov.ʳ 1766 (41)

H	K	F	Courses	Winds	Remarks
1	3		SW½S	SEBS	
2	3	3	SWBS	SE	Squally with light showers
3	3	3			
4	2	4		19:35	
5	3	4			Moderate & cloudy
6	5				
7	5		SSW½W		
8	5				
9	4				
10	4	5			
11	4	5			
12	3				Moderate breezes & fair weather
1	3	4			
2	3	5		19:05	
3	3				observed at 3 in lat:ᵈ 23:23 by ---
4	4	5			
5	4	2			variation p:ʳ amplitude 7:°00'E
6	4				
7	4	2			out reefs – unbent the courses & bent new ones –
8	4	3			
9	5				
10	5				
11	5				Moderate & fair¹¹⁹
12	4	3		NEBE	

Course	Dis	Latitude in	Long. made	M:Dis
SW	75	23:*48S	15: 04W	877W

S:ᵗ Jago bore N20:°40'E Distance 830 leagues

---

119 "The Swallow & Prince Fredrick in company." PL and FC.

Remarks Saturday 8 Nov 1766 (42)

H	K	F	Course	Winds	Remarks
1	4	3	SW½W	EBN	Moderate & fair
2	4	3			sounded with 160 fm: no ground
3	4	4			
4	4	3	SSW	19:15	got four guns into the hold[120]
5	5	4		ENE	
6	6				variation p:r azm – 7:20E
7	6	3			amp 7:00
8	5	5			
9	6				
10	6	2			
11	6	4			
12	6	5		NEBN	
1	6	2			
2	6			19:20	
3	6	4			
4	6	5		NBE	2:d Squally hazey weather
5	5	2			
6	5	3			
7	5				
8	5	4			
9	5	4			
10	5	4			
11	5	3			
12	6			North	Moderate gales & fair weather[121]

Course	Dis:	Latitude in	Long. made	MDis:ce
SSW¾W	144	25:*52S	16: 24W	950W

S:t Jago bore N21:°15'E Distance 875 leagues

---

120 Omitted in the PL and in the FC.
121 "In company as before." PL and FC.

Remarks Sunday 9th November 1766 (43)

H			Course	Wind	Remarks
1	6		SSW	NBE	Fresh gales & hazey –
2	6				
3	6	4			clear weather
4	5	5		20:05	
5	5	5			variation p:r azum:t & amp:de 8:12E
6	6				
7	5				
8	5	5			
9	5	2			
10	6	3			
11	6	4			
12	6	5			
1	6	2			
2	6	4		19:30	
3	6	3			variation p:r amplitude: 10:°10'E
4	5	4			p:r azum :th 10:00E
5	4	5			
6	4	4			saw some alcatrosses —[122]
7	5				
8	5	4			
9	6	2			
10	6	3			Moderate gales & hazey
11	6	4			In company as before
12	6	3			

Course	Dis	Latitude in	Long. made	MDist:
SSW½W	145	28:*00S	17: 40W	1018W

S:t Jago bore N21:°22'E Dis:t 923 leagues

---

[122] "... saw some large white birds with the tips of their wings black called Alcatross." PL and FC.

Remarks Monday Nov:ʳ 10 1766 (44)

H	K	F	Courses	Winds	Remarks
1	5	4	SSW	North	Fresh gales & hazey –
2	5	3			
3	5	4			
4	4			19:00	
5	4	4			
6	4	4			
7	4	4			
8	2				
	2	4	WBS	NBW	
9	2	5			
10	4				Foggy rainy weather
11	4	4			Drizzling rain & foggy fired a gun every hour till six[123]
12	3	4		NW	for the 11ᵗʰ
1	3	5			☾ from sun 118° 18: 3
2	3	4		19:55	semi diameter + 32
3	3	3			110: 50:
4	2		SSW½W		Effect of parallax — 117: 56
	2		SWBS		54
5	2	5		WNW	[...] ☾ lat 87:15 9.999950
6	3				Rad 10:
7	1	2	SBE	SW	∷ Co si θ dis ☾ --- 9.67018
8	1	4	EBS	SBE	to ☾ diff log:
9	3	2	SWBS	SE	27:56
10	3	3			90
11	4	4			30 117:56
12	4	5			3:27:56
					☉ Long: + 7: 19:25: 6 E
					☾ Long: 11.17.21: 6.E[124]

Course	Dis	Latitude in	Long. made	MDis:ᵗ
S43:15W	87	29:*02S	18: 47W	1077W

S:ᵗ Jago bore N21:°22'E Dis:ᵗ 944 leagues

---

123 "Lost sight of the Prince Frederick and fir'd a gun as a sig:ˡ to her at 3 saw her light and bore up for it at 4 fir'd another gun. Saw the Prince Fredrick ahead." Gore.
124 These calculations do not appear in the PL and in the FC.

Remarks Tuesday Nov:ʳ 11 – 1766 (45)

H	K	F	Courses	Winds	Remarks
1	4	4	SWBS	SE	
2	5				Moderate & fair
3	4	3			H M S
4	4	5		18:30	3: 33: 20 --- 39:55 --- 29°18'
5	4	4			Dist:ᶜᵉ from ☉ from ☾ 118:18:30
6	5				Equation of time 15m 39 slow
7	4	5			Long: in from London- 42:50
8	3	4			in fine – 2H: 51 M: 20 S
9	4				made the storeship sig: to come under our stern
10	5				worked the above observation a found us under
11	5				Long: ☾ p:ʳ observ. 11: 17:°21' 6ˢ
12	5	3		ESE	Long: p:ʳ tables 11: 17 21
1	3	2			so we judge our longitude in to be very true
2	2	3		18:20	
3	1				
4	1				variation as p:ʳ az:ᵐ 9:30 E
5	1				sent six men onboard the store ship to relieve those sent the
6	1				27: of Oct:ʳ
7	1				sent likewais 8 punc: & 143 iron hoops & received from her
8	1	2			25 bagg of bread
9	2				the Swallow likewais received provisions[125]
10	1			16:20	
11	1	4			saw some sea weeds
12	1	4		SE	Light airs & clear weather

Course	Dis	Latitude in	Long. made	MDis:ᵗ
SW	76	29:°*55S	19: 44W	1127W

S:ᵗ Jago bore N22:40E Distance 970 leagues

125 The entry in the other two logs is reduced to "Sent our boats onboard the P:ʳ Frederick with the carpenter to stop the leak but they could do very little toward it – compleated the Swallows & this ships provisions from the store ship and sent all our staves, iron hoops & oil jarrs on board the store ship." PL and FC. Gore specifies that grog was served to the ships company that day.

Remarks Wednesday Nov:r 12 – 1766 (46)

1	1	4	SWBS	NNE	Light airs & fair weather[126]
2	1	3			
3	1	4			
4	1	5		17 :50	saw a large turtle; & two alcatrosses & some oar weed –[127]
5	1				
6	1			North	
7	1	5			
8	1	5		NE	
9	2	3			
10	2				
11	1				
12	1				Light airs & small drizling rain
1					
2				Calm	her head to the SW
3					
4				18:05	
5	1				
6	1	6			
7	2	4			Light airs & foggy –
8	3				
9	2	6			The Swallow & storeship in comp:y
10	2	4			
11	2	2			Light airs & cloudy –
12	2			East	

Course	Dis	Latitude in	Long. made	MDis:t
SW¼S	40	30:°24'S	20: 15W	1154W

S:t Jago bore N23:00E Distance 984 leagues

---

126 ". . . sent six seamen and a carpenter in lieu of those who have been there they being much worn by pumping. The Surgeon went on board with some medecines to the sick there as severall are ailing and some of them have the appearance of the scurvy." PL and FC. Hawkesworth: "On the 12th, being now in latitude 30 south, we began to find it very cold; we therefore got up our quarter cloths, and fitted them to their proper places, and the seamen put on their thick jackets."

127 "Sounded with 180 fm: – no ground." PL and FC.

Remarks Thursday Nov:^r 13:th – 1766 (47)

H	K	F	Courses	Winds	Remarks
1	2	3	SWBS	SEBS	
2	2	4			Light breezes & cloudy
3	3				
4	5	6		19 :05	
5	5	6			variation p:^r azu:^m: 10:°47'E
6	6	3			
7	6	4	SWBS	SE	Fresh gales & cloudy
8	5				
9	5				
10	6				
11	5				
12	6			SEBE	
1	5			18:00	Fresh gales & cloudy weather
2	6				
3	6				
4	5				
5	6				
6	6				
7	6	3			
8	6	5			
9	7	2			Saw some birds & some weeds –¹²⁸
10	7				
11	7				Fresh gales & foggy weather
12	7		SSW½W	EBS	The ships in company as before

Course	Dis:^e	Latitude in	Long. made	MDis:^t
SW	132	31:°55'S	22: 12W	1254W

S:^t Jago bore N24:00E Distance 1025 leagues

---

128 "Sounded no ground with 150f:^s." PL and FC.

Remarks Friday Nov:r 14 – 1766 (48)

H	K	F	Wind	Course
1	7		SSW½W	EBS
2	8			
3	7	5		
4	7			
5	7	3		
6	7			
7	6		SSW	
8	5			
9	6			
10	4	3		
11	4			
12	3			SEBE
1	2	3		
2	2			17:00
3	3		SW	SSE
4	3	4	SWBS	SEBS
5	5		SSW½W	SE
6	4	2		
7	4	4		
8	5	4		
9	5	3	SSW	
10	5	2		
11	4	3		
12	5			

Fresh gales & hazey with drizzling rain

close reeft the topsails
saw several kinds of birds about the ship
Sheerwaters & albatrosses –[129]

Moderate & cloudy

Little wind

opened cask beef N 134. Cont 162, short 2 pei[130]
variation p:r az:h 12/00E

read the Articles of War & Act of Parliament –[131]

Moderate & fair weather
In company as before

Course	Dis:e	Latitude in	Long. made	MDis:t
SW½W	110	33:*07S	23: 46W	1334W

S:t Jago bore N24:°50'E Distance 1058 leagues

---

[129] "Sounded found no ground with 150 f:s." PL and FC.
[130] Omitted in the PL and FC.
[131] Omitted in the PL and FC.

Remarks Saturday Nov:ʳ 15 – 1766 (49)

H	K	F	Courses	Winds	Remarks
1	4	3	SSW	SE	Moderate & cloudy weather
2	4	4	SWBS	SEBS	
3	4	5			sounded with 140fm: no ground
4	3			19 :00	variation p:ʳ amp:ᵈᵉ 14:00E
5	4	2	SSW½W	SE	
6	3	5	SWBS	SEBS	
7	4	4			
8	4	2			
9	2		SSW½W		
10	2				
11	2				
12	2				
1	1		SW	SSE	
2	1			16:40	calm her head round the compass
3					variation p:ʳ amplitude 14° 22'E
4					medium az:ʰ & ampl:ᵈᵉ 13:30
5					
6					
7	2	5	SSE	SW	
8	3				
9	3	3			Fresh gales & cloudy
10	3				The Swallow & the storeship in company
11	4	4			
12	4		SEBS	SWBS	

Course	Dis:ᵉ	Latitude in	Long. made	M: Distance
SBW¾W	65	34:*08S	24: 11W	1356W

S:ᵗ Jago bore N24:°45'E Distance 1080 leagues

Remarks Sunday Nov:ʳ 16 – 1766 (50)

H	K	F	Courses	Winds	Remarks
1	4	4	SEBS	SWBS	
2	4	4			Fresh gales & cloudy
3	4	6			
4	5	2	East	SWBS	
5	3	4	SEBS	18:20	Bore down to the storeship
6	1	3			
7	4		WBS	South	
8	4		W½S		
9	2	4	SW	SSE	
10	2	5			
11	3				
12	2		WSW	South	
1	4		SW	SBE	Bore down to the storeship[132]
2	3	4	SWBW	16:30	
3	2	4			
4	2				
5	3				Moderate & cloudy –
6	3	4			
7	4		SW	SSE	variation p:ʳ az:ᵗ 14:00E[133]
8	4				
9	3				
10	3				
11	4		SWBW	SBE	
12	3				Light breezes & fair in company as before

Course	Dis	Latitude in	Long. made	M: Distance
S52:°50'W	53	34:*40S	25: 01W	1398W

S:ᵗ Jago bore N25:°37E Distance 1103 leagues

---

132 Omitted in the PL.
133 "Sounded found no ground with 160 f:ˢ." PL and FC.

Remarks Monday Nov.:r 17 – 1766 (51)

H	K	F	Courses	Winds
1	2		NBW	SBE
2	4		SEBW	
3	3		SWS	South
4	3	3		16:00
5	2	3	SWBS	SBE
6	2			
7	2			
8	2			
9	1	5	WSW	South
10	1	4		
11	1	3		
12	1	2		
1	1	4	WBS	SBW
2	1		WBN	SWBS
3	1	2		15:30
4	1	3		
5	1	4	WBN½N	
6	2	4		
7	1			
8	1	4	West	
9	1	4		
10	1		WSW	
11	1			
12	1			Calm

Light airs & fair saw two sails in the NW steering to the NE, bore down to the Swallow & the storeship I ordered them to keep near us –[134]
Sounded with 150 fm: no ground

variation p:r amplitude 15:°00'E

variation p:r amp:de 15:°00'E

found the main topmast cross trees broken got them down & repaired them & got them up again

The Swallow & the storeship in company[135]

Course	Dis:ce	Latitude in	Long. made	MDist:ce
WBS¼S	33	34:*08S	25:°40'W	1430W

S:t Jago bore N25:°37'E Distance 1095 leagues

---

134 Omitted in the PL and in the FC.
135 "Saw large fowl about the ship, brown wings with white bills and their bodies mostly a dull white." Gore.

Remarks Tuesday Nov:ʳ 18:ᵗʰ 1766 (52)

1		4	SW	NBW
2	1		SW	NW
3	1	3	SW	NWBW
4		3		16:30
5		4	SW	WNW
6		5		
7	2	5		
8	4			
9	5	5	SW	NNW
10	4	4		
11	5	3		
12	4	2		
1	4	4		
2	4			16:10
3	5	2		
4	4	3		
5	5	4		
6	4			
7	2			
8	4	3	SWBS	
9	5			
10	6			
11	3			
12	6			

Light airs & fair weather
we being to windward bore down to the Swallow & store ship
& told them to keep near us[136]

variation p:ʳ amplitude 15:°00'E

variation p:ʳ amplitude 15:°08'E

sounded had 54 fm: muddy ground
this is the first sounding we have had since we have been on this coast[137]

saw several grampusses & whales
moderate & hazey in comp:ʸ as before

Course	Dis	Latitude in	Long. made	MDist:ᶜᶜ
SWBW½	86	34:*40S	27:°05'W	1499W

S:ᵗ Jago bore N26:°18'E Distance 1128 leagues

---

136 Omitted in the PL and in the FC.
137 "... of Brazil." PL and FC.

Remarks Wednesday Nov:r 19 1766 (53)

H	K	F	Courses	Winds	Remarks
1	5	5	SWBS	NNW	Moderate & hazey
2	5	4			
3	5				Sounded had 55 fm:s black mud
4	4			16:10	
5	5	5			
6	1				
7	3				Saw a very large meteor which appeared in the NE & went away with great swiftness to the SW about 15:°high and left a vast fiery train behind – he seemed to fly in a horizontal line all the way till he was extinguished – the whole atmosphere was enlightened all the time of the appearance which was better than a minute[138]
8	5			NNE	
9	4	2			
10	5	2			
11	5				
12	4	4			
1	4	4			
2	3	5		16:20	
3	4				
4	4			NBW	
5	5				sounded 55 fm:s fine dark brown sand
6	4	4			saw a seal
7	4	4			
8	3				Punished Jem Field seamen for being insolent & mutinous to the Boatswain & one of the Mates –[140]
9	1				
10	1				Foggy fired a gun every hour which was repeated by the Swallow & the store ship
11	1				
12	1	5		SE	

Course	Dis:t	Latitude in	Long. made	MDistance
SW¼W	94	36:43S	28:30W	1568W

S:t Jago bore N26:52E Distance 1157 leagues
Cape Virgin   S30:30W Dis:ce 405 leagues
CBlanco –   S52:00W Dis – 34

138 "Saw a very large meteor which appeared in the NE and flew with amazing rapidity to the SW about 15 degrees hight in a horizontal line and left a vast train behind; it was near a minute in its progress, and was as light on deck as at noon." PL and FC.
139 "Saw many seals about the ships." PL and FC. Robertson adds: "I suppose we was near some land not yet known, as I never saw seals any considerable distance dist: from the land before." (Carrington, *op. cit.*, p.14).
140 Field receives twelve lashes according to Gore.

REDISCOVERED ACCOUNTS, VOLUME I

Remarks Thursdsay Nov:r 20 1766 (54)

					Remarks
1	1	5	SWBW	ESE	Light airs & foggy – continued to fire a gun every hour till six
2	1	3			when it cleard up – saw both ships a stern –
3	2				sounded 53 fm:dark brown sand
4	3			17:00	bent the best bower cable
5	1	3		SE	saw several seals about the ship
6	1	4			
7	1	5			variation p:r amp:de 15:°00'E
8	1				
9					
10					
11					calm ships head round the compass
12					
1	1		WSW	South	sprung up a breeze made the sig:l for keeping company
2	1			16:10	
3	2				drizzling rain
4	2		SWBS		
5					fine clear weather, sounded 55 fm: fine grey sand
6				Calm	
7	2		SWBS	WNW	variation p:r az:l 16:°00'E
8	1	5			several seals about the ship
9		4			
10		4			foggy fired a gun every hour –
11	2				
12	4		SSW½W	West	clear weather in company as before

Course	Dis:l	Latitude in	Long. made	MD
WSW½S	23	36:*54S	28:55W	1588W

S:l Jago bore N27:°10'E Distance 1161 leagues

97

Remarks Friday Nov:r 21 1766 (55)

H	K	F	Courses	Winds	Remarks
1	4		SBE	SWBW	Fresh gales & fair fill 7 tons with salt water in fore hold
2	5	5	SSE	SW	sounded no ground with 70 fm:[141]
3	4	3	SBE	SWBW	
4	4			SSW	in 2:e reefs topsails
5	6		SE		
6	4		SE½E		variation p:r amp:de 16: 09 E –
7	5	4	SEBE	SBE	
8	5	5	ESE	South	
9	5				
10	4				
11	3	5			
12	3	4			
1	2	3	SEBE	SBW	fresh gales
2	2	5		15:20	
3	3	2			wore ship – variation 15:°00'E
4	3	5			
5	2	4			
6	2	2	WBS		sounded no ground with 150 fm:s
7	2	2	WSW		
8	1	2			
9	1				Light airs & clear weather
10	1		NW	SW	Swallow & P:ce Fredrick in company
11	1				sounded no ground with 150 fathoms
12	1				

Course	Dis:t	Latitude in	Long. made	MDist:
SE½S	59	37:*40S	28:°10'W	1552W

S:t Jago bore N26:°12'E Distance 1172 leagues

---

141 With a 100 fathom line and eight tons of water in the PL and the FC.

Remarks Saturday Nov:r 22 1766 (56)

H	K	Course	Wind	Remarks
1			Calm	
2	1	SWBW	SW	Light airs & fair
3	1	SW		
4	2			
5	4		15:20	Moderate breezes & fair
6	5			
7	6			variation p:r azimuth 16:°24'E
8	6			1st reeft topsails
9	7			
10	7			
11	7			
12	7			Fresh gales & fair in 2:e reefs
1	7			Lightening in the SW quarter
2	8		15:50	
3	8			
4	8		NBW	sounded 70 fm: fine dark brown sand –
5	8			saw many whales about the ship and some threshers on them
6	8			saw a plover & several butterflies many seals & several sorts
7	8			of sea birds –
8	8		NW	Strong gales & heavy squalls, handed the topsails – at 11 set
9	8			m:n tp:s close reeft set the fore topsail
10	6	SWBS	WBN	Sounded 54 fm:s grey sand & shells –
11	5	SSW	West	Little wind & cloudy with a great swell in company as before
12	3	SWBS	NBW	–

Course	Dis	Latitude in	Long. made	MDist:ce
SWBW	135	38:*55S	30:33W	1664W

S:t Jago bore N27:°16'E Distance 1211 leagues

Remarks Sunday Nov:ʳ 23:ʳᵈ 1766 57

1	2	2	SW	
2	3	5		
3	4			
4	5	6		16:20
5	6			
6	7			
7	3	4	SWBS	
8	7			
9	6			
10	6			
11	5	5		
12	6	4		
1	5			
2	5			15:00
3	2		South	West
	5		SE	WSW
4	3		SWBS	NW
5	3			
6	3	5		
7	4	3		
8	5			
9	4			
10	3	2	SSW	
11	4		South	WSW
12	3	4		

Moderate & clear weather

Sounded 48 fm: grey sand shells
From 9 to ½ past lay too for the sloop & transport –
variation – 17:30E
Fresh gales & squally with lightning all round the compass

sounded 46 fm: fine grey sand
very hard squalls with much thunder lightning and large hailstones which continued till past 4
the lightning brighter than any I ever saw in my life furled the topsails – & went under the topsail –

sounded 46 fm: ditto ground –

set the topsails –

Fresh gales & cloudy

Course	Dis:ᶜᵉ	Latitude in	Long. made	MD
S 50:°00 W	95	39:56S	32:08 W	1737W

S:ᵗ Jago bore N28:00E Distance 1241 leagues

Remarks Monday Nov:r 24 1766 58

H	K	F	Course	Winds
1	4	3	South	WSW
2	4	2	SBS	SWBS
3	5		SSE	
4	5	4	SE½E	SW
5	5	4		15:40
6	4	5		
7	3		SSE	
8	4			
9	2			
10	1	4		
11	1	1	SEBS	SWBS
12	1			
1	1	2		
2	1	4		13:10
3	1			
4	1			
5	1	3		
6	1	4	South	WSW
7	1			
8	1			
9	1		SSW	West
10	1		SWBS	WNW
11	2			12:30
12	3			

Course	Dis:ce	Latitude in	Long. made	MDis
S 18:°10W	43	40:*35 S	31:50W	1724E

Fresh gales saw many penguins, some seals & rock weed – A very hollow sea from SW

variation – 17:20E
sounded 58fm: fine brown sand.
set fore topsail
variation p:r amp:de 17:00E

Little wind & a great swell from the SW.

lost a logg & two lines –[142]
sounded no ground with 140 fm:[143]

variation 17:05E.

Moderate & clear –

S:t Jago bore N27:23E Dist:ce 1250 leagues

142 Omitted in the PL and the FC.
143 The PL and the FC note a 160 fathom line.

Remarks Tuesday Nov:^r 25 1766 (59)

H	K	F	Courses	Winds	Remarks
1	3	2	SW	NWBW	Moderate & clear
2	4				
3	4	2			sounded 72 fm: fine brown sand
4	3	4		14 :00	
5	3				variation p:^r az & amp:^{de} ~18:10E
6	3	4			
7	2				
8	5	3		NW	
9	5	4			
10	6	4			Fresh gales & hazey in 3: reefs
11	7				
12	7				
1	7	2			strong gales with a great SW swell
2	7			12:40	close reeft the topsails
3	7				
4	7	5			handed the ftops:^s & struck top gall masts
5	7	2			
6	6				sounded 48 fm: fine brown sand
7	4				
8	4				set fore tops:^s saw some rock weed
9	3	2	SW½S	WBN	penguins & seals –
10	2			West	
11	2	3	SSW		Fresh gales & cloudy –
12	2				

Course	Dis	Latitude in	Long. made	MDis:^{ce}
S56:°30'W	107	41:*35S	33: 56W	1813E

S:^t Jago bore N28:09E Distance 1282 leagues
CBlanco S 54:30W Dis 183 leagues[144]

---

144 Omitted in the PL.

Remarks Wednesday Nov:ʳ 26 1766 (60)

1	2		South	WSW
2	2		SBW	SBW
3	2		SWBS	WBN
4	2			15 :10
5	2			
6	2			
7	1		SWB	variable
8	1		SSW	
9	1		SWBW	
10				Calm
11	1	3	SWBW	
12	2			
1	2		SW	
2	2			13:00
3				
4			Ships head SW	
5				
6	1		SE	SSW
7	3		SEBE	
8	4			
9	4		WSW	South
10	3	5	WBS½S	
11	2			
12	3	4	West	

Remarks:
- Light air
- Sounded 47 fm: fine brown sand
- saw some rock weed
- variation p:ʳ azum:ᵗ 18: 30E
- sounded 50 fm : fine brown sand
- Lightning from NW to NE –
- sounded 52 fm: fine brown sand –
- saw a whale & sea lyon –[145]
- Fresh breezes & variable –

Course	Dis:ᶜᵉ	Latitude in	Long. made	MDis:ᶜᵉ
S47: 30W	30	41:*55S	34: 26W	1835E

S:ᵗ Jago bore N28:°18'E Distance 1290 leagues
CBlanco S22:26W Dis 161 leagues

---

[145] "Saw weeds, whales & seals." PL and FC.

Remarks Thursday 27 Nov.ʳ 1766 (61)

1	3		WSW	South
2	3	4	SWBW	SBE
3	3	4		
4	3	4		13:20
5	2	3	WSW	South
6	2	4		
7	2	3		
8	2			
9	2			
10	2			
11	2			
12	2			
1	1			
2	1			10:40
3	1	2		
4	2	2		
5	2		WBS½S	SBW
6	2	4	WBS	
7	2	4		
8	2	4		
9	2			
10	2			
11	2			
12	2		West	SSW

Fresh gales & cloudy –
close reeft the topsails & got down the top gall mast. Sounded 45 fm brown sand & shells –
squally handed the fore topsail
heavy squalls with hail & a great sea handed the m:ⁿ topsail –

sounded 45 fm: same ground

fresh gales & heavy squalls with a great sea –

sounded 64 fath: same ground
set the m:ⁿ topsail –

sounded 44 fm: same ground

saw several penguins gannets & other kind of birds

fresh gales wth a great sea
The Swallow & the storeship in sight to leeward –

Course	Dis	Latitude in	Long. made	MD
NW	60	41:*12S	35: 21W	1877E

S:ᵗ Jago bore N29:°23'E Dis:ᵗ 1275 leagues

Remarks Friday Nov:ʳ 28 1766 (62)

H	K	F	Courses	Winds	Remarks
1	2		W½N	SSW	Moderate & fair
2	2				set the topsails – sounded 45 fm:
3	3		NNW		bore down to the Swallow[146]
4	4			12:30	
5	2	2	WBN	SWBW	variation – 20:00 –
6	1	5			sounded 39 fm: black sand
7	2				
8	1				
9	1		South	WSW	obser:ᵈ lat:ᵈ by Syrius 41: 12S –
10	3				
11	2	4			
12	2	3	SBE	SWBW	opened a cask of beef N956 – contents 164 – short 8 peices –
1	3		SSE½E	SSW	variation p:ʳ amp:ᵈᵉ & azu: 17:00
2	2	4		11:50	by observation of ☾&☉ – the L observed –
3	2	4	SSE		6:20:49:41
4	2	3			Worked – 6:20:45:15
5	2	2	SEBS	SWBS	4:26
6	2	3			Judge the ship to be about 118 miles to Westward of reckoning[147]
7	2		SE		
8	3				
9	2				
10	2				
11	2				
12	1	5	SEBS		

Course	Dis	Latitude in	Long. made	MD
EBS	20	41:*16	34: 56 W	1858

S:ᵗ Jago bore N29: 30E Dis:ˡ: 1276 leagues

---

146 Omitted in the PL and the FC which (like Gore) though mention the sighting of Egg birds.
147 These observations and calculations do not appear in either the PL or the FC.

					Remarks Saturday Nov:ʳ 29 1766 (63)
1		4	SSE	SW	Light airs & clear
2		3			caught several hake
3				Calm	40 fm: fine brown sand
4				14:30	
5	1		SWBS	WBN	variation – 18:12E
6	2	2	SW	WNW	44 fm: fine grey sand
7	2	2	SWBS		
8	3		SW	NW	40 fm: fine grey sand
9	4	2			moderate breezes & fair
10	4				sounded 40fm: black & brown sand
11	3	3			
12	4				28 fm: the same –
1	5				variation p:ʳ az 18:00
2	6				fresh gales saw penguins & rock weed & gannets –
3	6				opened a cask of pork N 951. Contents 84 – short 18 peices –¹⁴⁸
4	6			13:10	
5	6	3			
6	7				Judged ourselves to be two degrees farther to the Westward
7	7	3			than by reckoning by an observation of the moon at seven in
8	7		---	72:46:51	the morning –
9	7	3	work	72:42:51	L☽ in eclip L observed – 7. 2. 46. 51
10	7	3	West	– 4	by work – 7. 2. 42. 30
11	7				Ship to the Westward 4. 21
12	7	5			

Course	Dis:ᶜᵉ	Latitude in	Long. made	MD
S59:°30'W	100	42:*06	36:51W	1944W

Sːᵗ Jago bore N29:30E Dis:ᵗ 1311 leagues

---

148 These details are omitted in the two other logs (as is now usual), as are all the observations and calculations. The other logs here give the results of only one sounding (40 fathoms).

REDISCOVERED ACCOUNTS, VOLUME I

Remarks Sunday Nov:ʳ 30 1766 (64)

H	K	F	Course	Winds	Remarks
1	3		SW	NBW	Fresh breezes & clear
2	6				43 fm: with brown and black sand with broken shells –
3	7				saw a great number of birds of different kinds as Gannet,
4	6	5		14:45	Sheerwater, Penguins Morits, and many others that I have no
5	6	2	SSW		name for – besides numbers of seals & sea lions –
6	5				variation 19:32E
7	6				
8	2			WBN	
9	2				
10	2		South	WSW	43 fm: black & brown sand mixed
11	1				Lightning from the NE to SW.
12	1				In 3: reefs
1	2	4	SEBS	SWBS	Fresh gales with a great swell
2	2	5		14:00	
3	2	4			
4	2				
5	2				
6	4	3			43 fm:
7	4		SSE		
8	3	2			saw many birds & rockweed
9	4				
10	4				Moderate & cloudy
11	4				In company as before
12	4		SEBS	SWBS	

Course	Dis.	Latitude in	Long. made	MDist:ᵉ
S16:10W	69	43:*14S	37:17W	1963W

S:ᵗ Jago bore N29: 30E Distance 1334 leagues

Remarks Monday Dec:r 1:st 1766 (65)

1	1	4	SSE	SW	Moderate & cloudy
2	1	5			Sounded 52 fm: black sand
3	1	6			
4	2	2	ESE	14:40	Bore down to the storeship
5					
6				Calm	caught several hake –
7	1		SWBS	WNW	variation p:r az: 18:°05'E –
8	1	5			52 fm: ditto
9	2	3			
10	2	3			
11	2				
12	3				
1	4		SBE	SWBW	
2	2		South	WSW	
3	2			13:00	
4	3	3			sounded 53 fm: black sand
5	4		SSE	SW	variation p:r azu:t 18°02'E –
6	3	2	SBE	SWBW	
7	3				
8	3				
9	3	2			Moderate & fair thought we saw land
10	2	5			Swallow & storeship in company –
11	3	3	SSW	SWBS	
12	3	3			

Course	Dis:	Latitude in	Long. made	MDist:e
S½E	50	44:*04S	37:12W	1959W

S:t Jago bore N29: 00E Distance 1349 leagues

Remarks Monday Dec:ʳ 2:ⁿᵈ 1766 (66)

H	K	F	Courses	Winds	
1	3	3	SBE½E	SWBW	
2	2	2			Moderate & fair weather
3	3				
4			up South	off SE	sounded 58 fm:fine brown sand
5					variation p:ʳ az –18:10E –
6	1	4	SSW		
7	1	5	SW	NWBW	unbent the main topsail & bent a new one
8	2	5		NW	
9	4	4			sounded 54 fm: muddy ground
10	4	4			
11	4	4			
12	4	4			
1	4				
2	4			WNW	
3	4				
4	4		SSW	West	59 fm: muddy
5	4		SBW	WBS	
6	4	3			variation p:ʳ az: 18:00E –
7	4		South	WSW	
8	3	5			
9	4				saw rockweed & many small birds
10	3	5	S½E	SWBW	
11	3				sounded 60 fm: brown sand –
12	3	3	SBE		moderate breezes & fair

Course	Dis –	Latitude in	Long. made	MDist:ᵉ
S30:00W	71	44:*05S	38: 02W	1994W

S:ᵗ Jago bore N29: 00E Distance 1371 leagues

Remarks Wednesday Dec:r 3:rd 1766 (67)

H	K	F	Courses	Winds	Remarks
1	3	3	S½E	WSW	Moderate & fair
2	4				
3	3	3			
4	3			13:50	
5	1				
6	1	3	SW	NW	
7	2		SW½W		sounded 59 fm: fine brown sand
8	1	5	SW	WNW	
9	3		SW½W		
10	3				
11	3				fresh gales close reeft topsails
12	4		SWBW	NWBW	
1	3	4			
2	3	2		12:05	sounded 57 fm: grey sand
3	3	3	SW	NNW	
4	3	4	SSW	West	variation p:r Azimuth – 18:°50'E –
5	3	2			
6	3	3			saw great numbers of whales, some seals great numbers of small white gulls & rockweed –[149]
7	4				
8	4		S½W	WSW	
9	4	3	South		sounded 55fm: brown sand wth black specks in it – fresh gales –
10	4	4	SBE	SWBW	
11	5		SSE	SW	cloudy weather. The Swallow & store ship in company
12	5				

Course	Dis:	Latitude in	Long. made	MD
S27:00W	69	46:*06S	38:45W	2024W

S:t Jago bore N29:°00'E Distance 1394 leagues

---

[149] "Saw a great number of whales, some seals and a prodigious number of small white birds call'd Egg birds." PL and FC.

Remarks Thursday Dec:ʳ 4: 1766 (68)

1	2	3	SEBS	SWBS	
2	2	4			Moderate & fair
3	2	3			
4	3	2		13:00	
5	4		SSE	SW	
6	3		SBE		
7	2	4	SSE		
8	2	3	SBE	SWBW	variation p:ʳ amplitude 18:52E
9	1	5	South	WSW	
10	1		SSW	West	
11	1	3	SW	WNW	sounded 50 fm: fine grey sand
12	1	2			variation p:ʳ amplitude & az: 19:40E
1	3	4	SWBW	NWBN	
2	3	5	SW	WNW	
3	3	2		10:56	
4	3	5	SSW	West	
5	4		South		saw several whales
6	4	4			sounded 64 fm: black & brown sand
7	4				
8	3	4			Virgin Mary 40:40 Dis:ᶜᵉ 138 leagues –
9	3	5			or S31: 00 Dis:ᶜᵉ 118 leagues[150]
10	4		S½W		
11	5		SBW	WBS	
12	4	2	SBW½W	West	

Course	Dis:	Latitude in	Longitude	MD
S12 :00W	64	47:*06S	39:03W	2037W

S:ᵗ Jago bore N28:°42'E Distance 1414 leagues
Cape Blanco – West Dis:ᶜᵉ 57 leagues or 30 leag: –

150 Omitted in the PL and FC.

Remarks Friday Dec:ʳ 5: 1766 (69)

H	K	F	Courses	Winds
1	3	2	SBW½W	West
2	3	2	SSW	
3	2	2	SWBS	WBN
4	3		SW½W	12:0
5	4			
6	4	4	SWBW	
7	3	4	SW	
8	3		SSW	West
9	2	3	SBW	WBS
10	3	3		
11	4		South	WSW
12	3			
1	3	4	SEBS	SWBS
2	3		SSE	SW
3	3			10:40
4	3	2	SBE	SWBW
5	3	3	SSE	
6	4			
7	2			
	2			
8	2			
9	3			
10	3			
11	3	4		
12		2		

Moderate & cloudy
saw great numbers of whales –[151]

sounded 65 fm: black & brown sand mud

squally close reeft the topsails
sounded 69 fm: water –

Fresh breezes & cloudy –

Bore down to the store ship –

Little wind & cloudy the Swallow & the store ship in company

Course	Dis	Latitude in	Long: made	MDist:ᶜᵉ
S18 :00W	66 –	48:*08S	39:34W –	2058W

Sːᵗ Jago bore N28:°40'E Distance 1435 leagues

---

151 "Some of our men that was formerly in the Greenland trade, says a ship could soon catch a great number of whales here." Robertson (Corrington, op. cit., p.17).

REDISCOVERED ACCOUNTS, VOLUME I

Remarks Saturday Dec:r 6: 1766 (70)

1	2	2	SBW	West	
2	2	2	S½W		Light airs & cloudy weather
3	1	2			Saw some large grey seals & some penguins
4				WNW	
5				12:00	
6				Calm	sounded 64 fm: black & brown sand
7	4	4	SW		Punished James Triplet[152] for quarrelling
8	5			SEBS	took 2 reefs in
9	3	3	WSW		sounded 64 fm: fine black & brown sand
10	2			South	squally
11	4				
12	3	4	WBS	SBW	squally –
1	2				
2	3		WSW	10:10	
3	3				Sounded 66 fm: ditto
4	3	2	West	SSW	Squally
5	3	3			
6	4		WSW	SW	Strong gales & squally close reeft topsails
7	4		W½N	SWBS	sounded 67 fm: ditto –
8	6		WBN		Long: in by observation – 66:30W[153]
9	4	3			Fresh gales
10	5	4			
11	5	4			Cape Blanco WNW 35 leagues –
12	4	2			C Blanco SWBN – 20 leagues –

Course	Dis:ce	Latitude in	Long: made	MDist:ce
N63:0W	70 –	47:*36S	41:06W –	2120W

S:t Jago bore N   :   E Disan: leagues

---

152 One dozen lashes (Gore).
153 These observations have not been copied into the PL or the FC.

Remarks Sunday Dec.:r 7: 1766 (71)

1	3	5	W½N	SSW	Fresh gales & cloudy –
2	3		West		sounded 52 fm: sand & small stones
3	3			11:25	54 fm: coarse grey sand & black stones
4	4		WBN	SWBS	55 fm: black brown & red sand
5	5		WNW		variation 18:05E –
6	5		NWBW	SWBS	
7	3		West	SSW	56 fm: grey sand
8	2		SE		
9	3		West		
10	2	2	WBN	SWBS	59 fm: grey sand
11	1	4			Little wind
12	1	3	WNW	SW	
1	2		S½E	WSW	60 fm: coarse grey sand & small stones with mud
2	2	4	South	9:30	variation p:r amp:de – 19:20E
3	2	3			at 6 saw the land bearing from SW to WBS ten or twelve
4	2		SBE	SWBW	leagues making like two small islands & sounded 52 fm: mud
5	2				sand & small stones –
6					Tried the current found it set SBE 8:fat:m hour –
7					
8			calm Ships head		Long: judged to be in 65:° 00:' 00"
9			to the S↑ward		Error Westerly 1: 58: 00
10					66: 58: 00
11	2		SW	NNE	Run West + 12: 00
12	5				Penguin Island longitude 67 : 10 W[154]

Course	Dis –	Latitude in	Long: made	MDist:ce
N53:0W	33 –	47:*66S	41:44W	2146W

---

154 "The land bore from WBS to SSW distance 8 leagues it makes in a number of hummocks." PL and FC.

Remarks Monday Dec:ʳ 8: 1766 (72)

H	K	F	Courses	Winds
1	6	4	SW	NW
2	8			
3	6	5	SBW	11:30
4	5	3	South	NNW
5	2			
6	4	3	SBW	
7	6		S½W	
8	6	2	S½E	
9	5	5	SSE½E	
10	6	3		
11	6			NE
12	6	4		
1	6	2	S½E	
2	4		South	9:27
3	2	2	SEBS	SWBS
4	3		SEBE	
5	2	5	SEBS	
6	3	3	SSE	SW
7	4	3		
8	3	5		
9	4	5		
10	4			
11	3	5	SBE	SWBW
12	3	5		
			Lat [...] 56:11 17E	

Fresh breezes saw a number of Penguins

Cape Blanco bore WNW 6 or 7 leagues a remarkable double saddle WS½W 3 leagues 20 fm: water small black stones & shells –
at 8 the Tower Rock at Port Desire bore SWBW½W 4 leagues the extreame of the land from SBE to WBN.
at ½ past 9 Penguin Island bore SWB¼W distance 2 leagues –
                        Long: 41:44

judge Port Desire lat.	17:56 S W –	31
Penguin Island lat:ᵈ	48:06 S	42.15
suppose rather or	48:00 S	29.
		65.15

sounded brown sand & shells 55 fm: the extreams of the land bore from SW to WBN – from the Mast head –
at 1H: 43': 36" Observed the distance from the sun to the Moon & by correcting it was   10:29:57:49
by the ship reckoning –   10:29:54:27
Error ship Westward –   3:22
At 1h: 52m: 53s – L ☽ – ☉ 11:00:4:50
by ship reckoning   11:00:0:00
Error ship West –   4:50
Fresh gales & cloudy   3:22
   8:12
Medium error –   4:06
gives about – 1-58' West –
     Long. Made from Penguin 00° 20'E[155]

Course	Dis	Latitude in	Long: made	MDist:ᶜᶜ
S½W	102	48:*56S	41:50W	2156W

Penguin Island SBE Distance 57 miles

---

[155] All these observations and calculations do not appear in the PL and in the FC.

Remarks Tuesday Dec:r 9: 1766 (73)

H	K	F	Courses	Winds
1	3		EBS	SBE
2	2			
3	3		SWBW	SBW
4	3		WBS	14:30
5	3	3		
6	3	5		
7	2	5	SWBW	
8	2		WSW	
9				
10				Calm
11				
12	1		SSW	WNW
1	2	1		
2	2	3		10:0
3	4			
4	4	2		
5	6	3	SW	NW
6	5	5		
7	5	4	SWBW	
8	4	4		
9	4	3		
10	3	4	SWBW	North
11	4	5	SSW	
12	3			NNE
			Lat […]	Dep. 66.W

Fresh breeze & hazey.
a head sea

sounded 55 fm: coarse grey sand & small stones
variation 23:00

saw vast quantities of red shrimps – that the sea look'd red with them –

Light airs –

55fm: fine grey sand
saw the land from Mast head bearing WBS 8 or 9 leagues –

The extreams of the land from SW to NW½ N & Woods Hill[156] near the entrance of S.t Julians – SWBW½W 3 or 4 leagues

Latitude in 49:*6 –
Course – WBS½ Dis – 69 – Long: made 1:28 MD: 55 miles
Penguin Island bore N37:00E Distance 88 miles –

---

[156] Woods Mount in the PL and in the FC. From the 9th to the 16th December, the PL changes in format numbering two days (as opposed to the usual four) per page, as in the FC.

Remarks Wednesday Dec.:r 10: 1766 (74)

1	5	3	SBW	NE
2	6			
3	5	2		
4				
5				Calm
6	2	3	ESE	NEBN
7	3	4	South	
8	3			North
9	3		S½W	
10	6	2	South	WBS
11	5	3	S½E	WSW
12	4	3	South	
1	3		SBE	WNW
2	4	4		SWBW
3	3	3		
4	4	4		10:20
5	6	3		
6	6	5		
7	6			
8	6			
9	4	3	South	WSW
10	4		SBE	SWBW
11	4	2	South	WSW
12	3	5		
			--- lat	---14
			98 MD	69

Moderate & fair opened a cask of beef
N 1265 contents 174, short 6 peices –
sounded 40 fm: soft mud
at 4 Woods Mount WBN 6 leagues –
47 fm: grey sand & mud
at 6 entrance of S.t Julians harbour SWBW½W, Woods Mount WBN 6 leagues of shoar –[157]
the extreams of the land from SSW½W to NWBN distance of shore 4 or 5 leagues
45 fm: water fine sand

Fresh breezes & squally 45 fm: coarse black sand –

at 4 the land bore from SWBW to WBN of shore 9 or 8 leagues
sounded 45 fm: black sand, mud & small stones

squally with a head sea

fresh gales close reeft the topsails & handed the fore topsail –
In company with the Swallow & Prince Frederick –

Course S8:00W Dis:e 93 Lat in 50:48 Long:e m:de 1:44
Penguin Island bore NNE Dis:ce 58 leagues –
Cape Virgin Mary S28:00W Dis 34 leagues –

---

[157] "This was the harbour where Commodore Anson lay some time to refit before he proceeded round Cape Horn." Robertson (Corrington, op. cit., p. 19).

1	3	5	South	WSW
2	2	5	SBE	SWBW
3	1	4	S½E	WBS
4	1	5		10:30
5	3	4	SSE	SW
6	3	5		
7	3	2	S½E	
8	4		SEBS	WSW
9	4		SBE	SWBW
10	2	5	SEE½E	
11	2		SSE	SW
12	2		WSW½W	South
1	2	2	WBS	
2	2	3	WSW	
3	3	4		9:10
4	3	3	SW	SSE
5	3	5	SWBS	SEBS
6	1			
7				
8				Calm
9				
10	1		SSW	
11	2	2	SWBS	variable
12	2	5	SW	
			MDis – 76	

Remarks Dec:r Wednesday 11: 1766 (75)

Fresh gales with a great head sea handed the topsails

sounded 37 fm: fine grey sand with black specks and small stones –
fresh gales & hazey set the topsail

58 fm: fine grey sand & small stones made the signal & tacked

50 fm: coarse sand & mud –

50 – coarse grey sand & small stones

saw grampusses & sea lioness –
sounded 48 fm: coarse grey sand & small stones –

little wind & hazey thick weather
In company as before

Course S19:°0'W dis: 40. Lat in 51:23 Long. Made 1:°55'W
Penguin Island bore N21:30E Dist:ce 72 leagues –

Remarks Friday Dec:ʳ 12 –1766 (76)

1	3		WBS	SBW
2	2	2		
3	2			
4	1	5		10:56
5	1	2	West	SSW
6	2		NW	
7	3	3	NWBN	
8	2		WBS	
9	5		WBS	
10	3		West	
11	3	3	WBS	
12	3	4	West	
1	3	5		
2	3	5		8:35
3	4		W½N	
4	4		WBSWBN	SWBS
5	4	4		
6	3			
7	3			
8	2	4		
9	2		West	SSW
10	1			
11	2		SSE	SW
12	2			MD 115

Little wind & cloudy –

sounded 50 fm: sand & stones –

50 fm: coarse grey sand & stones –

variation p:ʳ amp:ᵈᵉ 23:00E

fine black sand & stones 49 fm:

48 fm: Ditto –
saw the land from NW to SW
44 fm: Ditto –
40 – fm: muddy
at 8 the extreams of the land bore from SBW to NBE distance off shore 3 leagues – 38 fm: ditto –
tack'd, a Cape bearing NBE½E & the other extream S½W off shore about two leagues – 27 fm: mudd –

Extreams of the land at noon bore from N½E to SSW½W distance off shore about 3 leagues –
Latitude observed – 50:*4S

Cape Beachy Head Lat the N:ᵗʰ Cape is –   50:16S
Cape Fairweather Lat of Southmost is –   50:50S
Cape Penguin Island bore N34:43E Dis 60 leagues.

Remarks Saturday Dec:ʳ 13 – 1766 (77)

1	1	5	SBE	
2		up	SBE off	SSE
3	2		SSE	
4		up	EBS off	NE
5				
6			ESE	
7	2			
8	2			
9	1		SE	
10	1	3	SE½S	
11	1		SEBS	
12				
1				
2				
3		up	SBE	off ESE
4				
5				
6				
7				
8	2	4	WBS	
9	2	4		
10	1			
11	1			
12	1	2	SSE	SW
			∞Lat 10	Dep: 23

Course	Dis:ᶜᵉ	Latitude in	Long: made	MDist:ᶜᵉ
162:00E	26	50:44S	2:34W –	92 W –

Very heavy squalls handed the the topsails & reeft the foresail set the m:ⁿ top:ˡ handed it again –
It continued to be very heavy squall with rain & hail till midnight, then it continued fresh gales with a great SW sea[158]
at 8 in 40 fm: muddy ground
Cape Beachy Head bore N½E distance about 7 or 8 leagues –
The land bore at 9 from NBW to SW distance off shore – 5 or 6 leagues
at 4 the land bore from NWBN to W distance of shore 7 or 8 leagues

made sail under the courses –
the extreams of the land from WBN to NWBN
Fresh gales & squally
In company as before

Penguin Island bore N32:00E Distance 63 leagues –

---

158 The PL and the FC mention it being "very cold".

Remarks Saturday Dec:r 14 – 1766 (78)

1	1		SSE	SW	Moderate & fair – wore –
2	3		WBN		fresh gales & squally with hail & rain
3	2				45 fm: coarse grey sand with small stones & shells
4	1		NWBW	9:40	set the topsails –
5	2		SB½E		variation p:r azum:th 24:00E –[159]
6	4	4	WBS	SBW	45 fm: ditto
7	2		West	SSW	at 10 – 35 fm: Ditto
8	2		WBN		The land from WBS to NWBW –
9	5		West		at 12 30 fm: Ditto
10	3		WBN		at 1 made the signal & tack'd
11	2	5	WNW		
12	2	3			
1	1		SBW	West	The land from SW½W to NWBN – off shore about six
2	1			8:40	leagues –
3	3	4			46 fm: fine sand –
4	5		S½W	WBS	
5	3	3	SBW		
6	2		SBW½W	West	
7	2	2	SBW	WBS	
8	3		SSW	West	
9	2	2			
10	1	5	SBW		Extream of the land from NW to WNW
11	1	4	S½E		Distance off shore about six leagues –
12	3		SSE	SW	In company as before
			∞Lat 8	Dep: 18	

Course	Dis:ce	Latitude in	Long: made	M Distance
WSW¼W	19	50:*52S	3:02W–	110W –

Penguin Island bore N35:°00'E Distance 68 leagues –

Sail'd from the Downs   the 20th Dec.r
Arrived at Batavia   the 18th May
Sailed from D:°   the 1st June
Arrived at Maroa   the 24th D°
Saild D°   the 26 the D°
Made the Ouesan Islands 5th [160]

---

[159] The ML tends in general to include more nautical details than the PL and the FC (distances, depth of water, astronomical observations, weather).

[160] These dates are written on a loose leaf in the ML in seemingly different handwriting if compared to the body of the log.

Remarks Monday Dec:r 15 – 1766 (79)

1	4		SBE	SW
2	2		SE	SSW
3	3		SEBE	SBW
4	2			11:00
5	2		SEBS	variable
6	1	5	West	South
7	9			
8	8			
9	6		WSW	
10	3			
11	5		ESE	
12	3		SEBE	SBW
1	2		SE	SSW
2	2		West	8:30
3	4		WBN	
4	4			
5	2		WNW	SW
6	4		S½W	
7	3			
8	6		SBE	
9	4		SBE½E	
10	4		SSE	
11	4		WBS	
12	3			SWBS

Light breezes & cloudy
fresh gales & squally close reeft top:l
at 7 bore down to the Swallow & storeship
variation 24:11E –
at 8 the extreams of the land bore from NNW to SBW
distance off shore 4 or 5 leagues.
45fm:
at 10 made the sig:l & tack'd
at 1 made the signal & tack'd
at 5 tack'd, the land bore from NBW ro SBE – off shore 4 leagues –
36 fm: 29. 25 fm: mud & clay –
The Swallow not in sight –
at 10 saw the Swallow off the masthead bearing SEBS –
at 8 the extreams of the land from SBE to NBE. Entrance of the River S:t Cruze SW½W off shore about 2 leagues.
had all across the opening 20 fm: water muddy – & then 22 fm: between two & three leagues of the nearest shore –
S:t Cruze from one cape to the other is about South – distance a cross 2 leagues, the land high on the North shore & makes in three capes, the South point low & flat at noon cape Fairweather S½E dis:e 7 leagues – the point of River S:t Croize from on the South side W½N 5 leagues – distance from the nearest shore 3 leagues –[161]
Depth of water 28 fm: oozy ground –
The Swallow in sight a head –

Course	Dis	Lat in	Long: made	MDist:ce
S27:30W	23	51:12	3:18W	120W –

Penguin Island bore N32:°00'E Distance 76 leagues –

---

161 Robertson (Corrington, op. cit., p. 21) remarks on this site as a potential colony: "There is fine low country on each side of this river, that I dare say wants nothing but skilfull hands to cultivate and raise any sort of grain that's produced in England."

Remarks Monday Dec:r 16 – 1766 (80)

1	1	5	SEBS	SWBS	Fresh gales & fair but squally
2	2				30 fm: grey sand –
3	2	3	SSE	SW	The Swallow joined us –
4	2	3		11:00	30 fm:
5	2				32 fm:
6	2	2	SBE	SWBW	at 7 Cape Fairweather bore SW½S dis:e 4 or 5 leagues – a low
7	2		SSE		point running out from it SSW¾W. – 30 fm: black sand
8	1		SBE		35
9	2	5	West	SSW	32
10	2		W½N		at midnight made the sig:l & tack'd
11	2	3			at 1, 30 fm: at 2.30 – at 4 – 26 fm: sand & mud
12	1	5			at same time variation – 19°0'E
1	3	3	SSE	SW	Cape Fairweather SSW 4 leagues –
2	2			9:8	at 6 fresh gales & hazey –
3	3		SSE½E		at 7 shoaled our water to 7 fm: then 6, & continued to shoal it,
4	8	2	SBE		hauled off SEBS 1 mile then last five miles the EBN and
5	1	4	S½E	WBN	deepend gradually into 12 fathom, whe we steered SE again –
6	1	3	SBW	WBS	
7	2				
8	1				NB. Cape Fairweather bore W½N and a lower point WSW
	1		SEBS		about five or six miles
9	3	2	East	NW	made the Swallow signal to come within hail162 – at ½ past 10
	1	5	SBE		having 12 fm: water altered the course, Cape Fairweather then
10	2		SEBN		to the W½S – 4 leagues & the N:°most extream of the land in
11	4		SEBS		sight WNW –
12	1	4	SSE½E		at Noon Cape Fairweather WNW½W, 6 leag:s at same time a
					large hummock bore SW½W – six leagues –
					Extreams bore S½W to NWBW – in 23 fm: fine sand –163

Course	Dis	Lat in	Long: made	MDist:ce
SBE½E	40	51:52	3:00	108W

Penguin Island bore N   E Distance   leagues –

162 "When we first came into shoal water Cape Fairweather bore W½N and a low point without it WSW about 4 miles at the same time made the Swallow's signal to go without it & likewais the store ship –." PL and FC. Gore, like Molineux, points out that the Swallow "not taking notice of it repeated it three times the made her sig:l to come under our stern."

163 Robertson (Corrington, op. cit., p. 21) notes that this is where Magellan "lay some time before he proceeded through the Streights now called by his name. It was in this river, where he first saw the gigantick race of Patagonians."

Remarks Wednesday Dec:r 17 – 1766 (81)

1	4		SSE	North
2	3	2	SEBS	
3	5		SE	
4	4		SE½S	NNW
5	3	4		10:0
6	5		SEBS	
7	6		SE	
8	6		SEBE	NW
9				
10				
11				
12				
1				
2				
3				
4				
5				7:20
6				
7				
8				
9				
10				
11				
12				

Moderate with drizzling rain
The extreams of three remarkable round hills from SWBW to SWS off shore about 2 or three leagues –
at 2 the land bore from SSE to NW
at 4 Cape Virgin Mary SEBS 4 leagues
at 8 was near Cape Virgin Mary saw several people on horseback waving to us –
at ½ past 8 anchord in a bay to the SE of Cape Virgin Mary in 10 fm: water gravelly bottom, the Cape bore NBW½W and a low sandy point very like Dungeness SBW, distance from the shore about one mile
high water at ½ past 11. the tide rose about twenty feet –
At 4 AM, saw great numbers of people on the beach waving & calling to us
Hoisted out the boats, took a party of Marines & another from the Swallow with Capt:n Carteret and went on shoar – the Indians were very docile staid at a distance and sat down by making signs to the, distributed amongst them some ribbons, beads – knives, buttons, scissors, tobacco, bread and several other things – they were a very stout people, few of them if any under six feet, many six feet six inches and one six feet seven inches – for I took a measure onshoar and measured more than twenty –
They had every one a horse, which was about 15 hands high. they had bridles & saddles & stirrups – the spurs were of wood, except one who had a Spanish pair of spurs & simiter the only weapons I saw was stones slung by a string about ten feet asunder of which every one had three or four pair tucked at his girdle & used them very dextrously –[164]

Course	Dis	Lat in	Long: made	MDist:ce
SBE½E	30	52:24	[...]	[...]

[164] "Moderate weather with drizzling rain, at 1 the extreams of those remarkable round hills from SWBW to SW distance from the shore two leagues. At 4 Cape Virgin Mary bore SEBS about four leagues. At 8 we were very neay Cape Virgin Mary saw severall men riding on the pitch of the Cape and waving to us. At half past eight anchored in a bay close under Cape Virgin Mary to the Southward of it in 10 fathom water gavelly bottom. The Cape bearing NBW½W and a low land point like Dungeness SBW distant from the shoar one mile. NB there runs a shoal for near half a league from Cape Virgin Mary & shews it self by the quantities of weeds which are on it. It was high water at half past eleven & the tide rose twenty feet. At four saw a great number of people onshoar who were waving & calling to us, haul'd the boats out & made the signal for the Swallow & Prince Frederick boats all which were mann'd & armed. & took a party of marines at six I landed with the Captain of the Swallow & severall officers before I went from the boat made signs for them to keep at a distance which they did then landed & drew up the marines & brought the boats to a grapnel near the shoar after which made signs for them to come down & sit in a semicircle which they did with great order & cheerfulness I then distributed amongst them severall toys such as knives beads scissors buttons combs looking glasses &:ce with which they seemed greatly pleased and very respectfully received to the women I gave ribbons, I made signs that I wanted meat & seeing some guanicoes near us I pointed to them & some ostriches, I shew'd them some hatchets & bill hooks which I would barter for flesh but they would not understand me, yet were very desirous of the hatchett &:ce. These people had every one his horse with a decent saddle & stirrups & astride the men wore wooden spurs except one who had a large pair of Spanish spurs, brass stirrups and a Spanish scimater without a scabberd he did not seem to be of any greater authority than the rest. Having two measuring rods with me we went round and

measured the tallest amongst them and found one that was six feet and seven inches high, severall that were six feet & six inches but the major part of them were from five feet 10 inches to six feet. They were very well made their hands & feet small yet bony their bodies robust their clothing skins sewed together and tied about their middle the lower part hanging below their knees and the upper part they have above their shoulders they have likewais a sort of a sort of drawers which they pull up very tight over their privites, they all wear a sort of buskins which reaches from the midleg to the instep the toes are not covered nor have they any sole further than the heel evey one had slings tucked to his girdle which was two round stones covered with leather & slung together with a thong about eight foot long. One of these stones they kept in their hand and swung the other round their head & then discharged it at the object they would hit & let go the stone they held at the same time, they were so dextrous at this that they would throw it fiveteen yards & make both stone hit a mark not bigger than a shilling; they had some ostriches tyed to their saddles which they tore to peices and eat raw entrails and all, they offered us some to eat. [They had likewais peices of guanicoes – *FC in free hand*].

After staying about four hours amongst them I made signs to them that I was going onboard & offered to take some of them with me on which eight of them went into the boats as would one hundred more if I could have suffered them when they came onboard they did not seem to be much surprized till they look'd in a glass that diverted them extreamly. We shewed them over the ship, likewais the sheep, pigs & fowles which they admired greatly particularly some turkeys & Guinea hens. They eat beef pork bread and anything that was offered them but would drink nothing but water; to these people I gave each a canvass bag wherein was put needles threaded, a few slips of cloth, knife, scissors, twine, combs, beads, looking glasses, shillings, sixpences & half pence new with a hole drilled in each & a peice of ribbon thro it, some bread, tobacco & some other trifles at about noon the tide being done I made them signs that the ship was going further & that they must go onshoar but they liked their quarters so well that was with great difficulty they could be prevailed on to go into the boat one of them would not go till he got a pair of shoes & buckles & then went away contented. Severall of the men I saw onshoar had their left eye incircled with a red ring painted, many had their faces & arms painted and all the young girls had their eylids painted black. The only word I could understand was Chevow, which I believe is a sort of saluation as they constantly made use of it when they shook hands with any one or wanted anything. They likewais called out Capitaine but being spoken to in Spanish and Portuguise, likewais in French, & Dutch they did not make any reply; speaking to them in English they repeated every sillable as plain as we could which makes me think they would learn our language sonner than any other. [One of them put his hand on his breast & said Capitaine – *FC in free hand*]. I took notice amongst those we saw onshore there were some who had beads similar to those I gave them and two had peices of red baise which makes me think that some among them were seen by Commodore Byron two years ago only their bulk does not answer the description."

Gore describes the encounter thus: "Saw a great number of Indians on shore on horseback and afoot. Captain Wallace went on shore some of the Indians came onboard with him who after staying some little time were put on shore, they seem to be a strong robust people between 6 & 7 feet high."

Molineux also describes the ships arrival in the Straits: "We are now arrivd in the entrance of the Streights of Magellan. Every body on board being in perfect health & spirits two or three excepted who have been sickly ever since we left England. The scurvy nor any other distemper has not yet made its appearance among us. Indeed all human means has been taken to keep the ships company healthy, namely at our first coming out they were put to three watches a thing very uncommon but so sensible were they of the favour that they all to a man exerted themselves to the utmost on every occasion and to do them justice they are I believe as good a ships company as ever sailed in his Majestys service. Since we arrived at Madeira we were serv'd fresh beef and on our leaving that place every man was serv'd 20:^{lb} of onions & as every man on board could not have a chest, there was a chest given amongst a convenient number & the Boatswain receiv'd an order to suply every man with a canvas bag sufficient to contain his necessaries they were also serv'd besides

They were very greedy after food, and tobacco yet what was given to ay one, he freely divided it amongst those nearest to him – they had several ostriches hanging at their saddles – of which they cut of pieces and eat raw – and one of them I saw eating the ostriches (craw or crop) without cleaning – and several eating the raw ostrich after staying with them about three hours I made signs to them that I was going to on board & to know if any would go with me when immediately five came as would one hundred men if I would have suffered them – these I brought on board I shewed every part of the ship^& gave them plenty to eat & some wine but they rather chose water, they seemed to be under no concern when I wanted to send them onshoar again they were very unwilling to go, nay one would not until I had given him a pair of shoes & buckles – I gave each of them a small canvass bag in which I put some bread, tobacco some half pence, & an English shilling and taught them every one to say English man very distinct which they repeated when they went from us.

The whole people seemed the best made of any I had ever seen all straight well limbed very broad over the shoulders and lusty sides but not burthened with more flesh than was necessary – for active people – they were painted of different colour many of the men had red rings painted round one eye – the young girls had their eyelids painted quite black – the word that they made most use of to us was chevow – which was repeated by them all – I saw no sign of religion amongst them – save that one of those who came onboard when he first came into the cabin, touched the glass then his breast and so of most things he saw – I shew'd them the sheep & the hogs at which they did not seem surprised but were wonderfully pleased with the turkeys, fowls & some guinea hens which I thought they they would have never a done admiring – they had many trinkets given them, & shewed a great fancy for any thing red they had a square piece of cloth with a hole in the middle for to put just their head thro' and it hung as low as their waist, I did not see above three of these garments amongst them it seemed to be made of,guanico woole, it was part red part brown & made somewhat like a rug –

---

the things proper allowance of provisions, vinegar & mustard & portable soup boild in the pease every Banyan day.

At St Jago we were again serv'd fresh beef & when we sail'd we carry'd as many live bullocks to sea as could be conveniently be stow'd upon deck. Having heavy rains near the line great care was taken to prevent the peoples wett cloaths lodging between decks & notwithstanding our ship was so much lumber'd with provisions she was always kept sweet & clean thse considerations added to the goodness of Cap:n Wallis whose example was follow'd by every officer of the squadron was doubtless very conducive to preserve the health we enjoy [. . .] we observed the Indians in great numbers on horseback riding along shore, they made a full stand abrest of the ship making signs to us to come on shore these being the people so much talk'd of for their gigantic size we viewed them with great attention but it was now too late to land. At 5 hoisted out the boats arm'd the crews which with the marines went on shore with our Captain & officers in company with those of the Swallow & Prince Frederick storeship. They were amicably received by the Patagonians who seems a harmless inoffensive people. Captain Wallace carried a standard on shore & found them to measure between 6 & ½ feet every way in proportion, their features are regular & their hair is very long stron & black their cloathing is the skin of beasts cheifly that of the Guanacoe, the man & women are so much alike that 'tis difficult to discover one from the other. It is remarkable that these Indians make but little use of paint. The Master of the Prince Frederick is a full lusty man but one of the Indians lifted him from the ground with one hand with pleasure their weapons are two round stones hung in skin in the manner of of a sling with these they are very dextrous in hunting the ostridge & guanaco which I believe to be their principle game. I rather think them to be inhabitants of the [. . .] of the River Galligos the country thereabouts seeming more fertile, pleasant & habitable than here: they have no timber hereabouts to build canoes so consequently have no communication with their opposite neighbours of Terra del Feugo. They face of the country is cover'd with long grass which will burn for several miles when stt on fire. The air is now very sharp & piercing tho this is the middle of summer here which is owing to the Westerly winds blowing over such vast tracts of snow. It might be imagined that we should feel the cold the more sensibly as we lately crossed the line but the Indians themselves shook & trembled as if affected with an aigue this induces me to think that they go to the Northward as their winter approaches. They had many Spanish trinketts among them but it is very uncertain whch way they came by them. As to their government it may be said the oldest & most experienced governs the rest. They seemed to worship the sun as they would sing songs & make many odd gestures whent they pointed towards it. We saw them eat some ostridge raw but I supposed they only do this when they are from home & hunger prompts them. They are not at all jealous for 5 of them came on board with Captain Wallis who she'd them the Cabbin & verey thing that would astonish them after having receiv'd cloathing & trinketts of different kinds they were dismissed but they left the ship with great reluctance. They would pronounce any English word as plain as we could. But the principal word made use of by them in theor own language is Chevoi. Their horses & dogs differ but little from ours & the guanacoa is an animal between a sheep and a goat."

Robertson (Corrington, op. cit., pp. 22–23) praises the inhabitants horsemanship and conjectures about their size: "They appear to manage there horses extreemly well, which made me at first suppose them to be Euopeans [. . .] The strange storys that has been so often talkd of with respect to the size of this people made most of our men suppose, their voices was more like bulls bellowing or lyons roaring nor the common size of men hollowing or talking. This made us all earnestly wish for a new day that we might have the pleasure of seeing with our own eyes. What sort of people this Patagonians is." Robertson (Corrington, op. cit., p. 26) also recounts an incident which is not in any of the Dolphin logs and which Hawkesworth chooses not to relate: "One of them which we supposed to be about eighteen or twenty years of age was mutch fairer and smother faced nor any of the rest and about six foot high. We all susposed this to be a woman but when she showed his breasts and niples which was both very smal for her size and years, we were devided in our opinion, some said she was a maid, oy^{rs} said that was impossible at her time of life espetially as she was in company with so many fine strong healthy broad shoulderd fellows. I moved her cloak and found it mutch finer and better sewed than any of the others. My cureosity led me so farr that I vewed the inside and found it mutch finer hair and not unyke a tiger skinn. She obs^d my cureosity and throw'd one side of of her cloak open to give me a full vew, but carefully wrappt upp what would have soon ended our despute. This modest behaviour of hers immediately put a stop to my cureosity, and made us reflect upon what we had seen in differents countrys, amongst what we call a refined people. This made her laugh very hearty and thro the other side open which I vewed, but still she took great care to cover her self with the oy^r side, which left some of us us still doubtful about this young person." Robertson also gives his divergent opinion on what he writes is often considered a "baren sand desert", he suggests that the country must be fertile if it produces such robust men – "the stoutest and greatest race of mankind" (p. 28).

Hawkesworth's descriptions are more narrativised and include details which are not in any of the Dolphin logs but some of which can be found in Robertson's journal (see Carrington, pp. 22–25): "Their complexion is a dark copper colour, like that of the Indians in North America; their hair is strait, and nearly as harsh as hog's bristles: it is tied back with a cotton string, but neither sex wears any head-dress. They are well made, robust, and boney; but their hands and feet are remarkably small. They are cloathed with the skins of the guanico, sewed together into pieces about six foot long, and five wide: these are wrapped round the body, and fastened with a girdle, with the hairy side inwards; some of them had also what the Spaniards have called a puncho, a square piece of cloth made of the downy hair of the guanico, through which a hole being cut for the head, the reft hangs round them' about as low as the knee [. . .] They jumped into the boats with the joy and alacrity of children going to a fair [. . .] I took them down into the cabbin, where they looked about them with an unaccountable indifference, till one of them happened to cast his eyes upon a looking-glass: this however excited no more astonishment than the prodigies which offer themselves to our

Remarks Thursday Dec:ʳ 18 – 1766 (82)

1			WBS
2			
3			
4			
5			12:10
6			
7			
8			
9			
10			
11			
12			West
1			
2			
3			10:5
4			
5			
6			
7			
8			
9			
10			
11			WBS
11			

Light breezes and cloudy, weighed and made sail – plying to windward, the Swallow sloop a head – the S:°end of its spit NWBS½W one mile Point Possession W½S and Queen Catherine Island SSE.
variation p:ʳ azumuth 24:00E
at ½ past 8 anchord with the best bower in 20 fm: water three miles of C:ᵉ Vigin Mary NEBE½E & P:ᵗ Possession W½S 3 or 4 leagues dis:ᶜᵉ
Tide runs East 1: 8 –
at 4 the tide had fallen 5½ fathoms we having a quarter less 15 fathoms –
at 6 got under sail the Swallow a head – at 9 Point Possession W½S 3 or 4 leag:
at noon the Swallow made the signal for anchoring, anchord with the best bower in 15 fm: clear ground
Point Possession – West & the Asses ears W½S, off shore about three miles –
A prodigious number of Indians came opposite the ship & made fires, they were all on horseback. I sent the Lieu:ᵗ to the shoar but not to land to see if they were the same that we saw yesterday – (as this was the place where Commodore Byron saw his tall men –) and he said they were the same & that he saw two of those I had brought onboard, who called out English man several times to him[165]

1

---

imagination in a dream, when we converse with the dead, fly in the air, and walk upon the sea, without reflecting that the laws of nature are violated; but it afforded them infinite diversion: they advanced, retreated, and played a thousand tricks before it, laughing violently, and talking with great emphasis to each other. After I had carried them through the ship, I ordered the marines to be drawn up, and go through part of their exercise. When the first volley was fired, they were struck with astonishment and terror; the old man in particular, threw himself down upon the deck, pointed to the muskets, and then striking his breast with his hand, lay some time motionless, with his eyes shut: by this we supposed he intended to shew us that he was not unacquainted with fire-arms, and their fatal effect. The rest seeing our people merry, and finding themselves unhurt, soon resumed their cheerfulness and good humour, and heard the second and third volley fired without any such emotion; but the old man continued prostrate upon the deck some time, and never recovered his spirits till the firing was over."

165 "Remarks onboard his Majestys ship Dolphin in the Streights of Magellan.
Light breezes & cloudy at ½ past noon made the signal & weigh'd turning to Westward at ½ past 8 made the signal & anchored in 20 fm: water muddy Cape Virgin Mary NEBE½E Point Possession W½S 4 or 5 leagues distance of shore three miles. The tide runs very fast & West, at 6 PM the tide being done made the sig:ˡ & weigh'd. The tide had fallen thirty feet & its strength is about 3 knotts p:ʳ hour
at noon the Swallow being a head and little wind she made the signal & anchored as did we & the Prince Frederic. Seeing great numbers of on Indians on horseback opposite the ship & Captain Carteret informing me that at this place it was that Comodore Byron had the conference with the tall men I sent the Lieutenant of this ship the Swallow & Prince Frederick to the shoar but not to land the ships having anchord to far off to protect them. On their return they informed me that they were the same people we had seen yesterday with a great number more & abundance of women children and dogs, that all the people who had been onboard waded off to them and would fain have gone with them. They gave them some bread, tobacco & a few toys & pointed to them

REDISCOVERED ACCOUNTS, VOLUME I

Remarks Thursday December 19 –1766 (83)

H			
1			SW
2			
3			
4			10:25
5			
6			
7			WSW
8			
9			
10			
11			
12			
1			
2			10:00
3			SW
4			
5			
6			
7			
8			
9			
10			South
11			
12			

Fresh breezes & clear
NB turned up from Dunguness Point to Point Possession – from 2 miles to six of the shoar & clear ground all the way –

Low water, 9 fathms

High water 15 fathoms. –
at 6 AM weighd & made sail the Swallow a head, – at noon anchord in 12 fathm clear muddy ground with the best bower –
Point Possession East 3 leagues
the entrance of Narrows SW½W & the Asses Ears West. Distance of the bottom of the Bay about 3 miles which is the nearest shoar to us.
The Swallow & the store ship in company[166]

The Indians in great number on Point Possession –
Sandy Point   N21:00E –   N67:00E
P. Possession   N88:55W –   84:55W
Bore NW – three miles –
From Dunguness to Point Possession S81:30W and N81:30E distance 23 miles –
Variation two points Easterly –

2

---

to bring guanicoes ostriches or any thing to make use of but could not make them understand so finding that there was no likelihood of getting any refreshment from them nor could nor could they see any rivulet as they rowed along shore they returned onboard." PL and FC.

166 "Great number of Indians on Point Possession." PL and FC. Molineux notes that "The Indians follow us from place to place & would gladly have us to come on shore they have now their wifes & children with them." The estimate of the numbers on Patagonians on shore at this time is about 400 according to Robertson.

Remarks Saturday December 20 – 1766 (84)

Hour			Wind	Remarks
1			WSW	
2				Fresh breezes & cloudy
3				
4			12:00	veer'd away to a whole cable –
5				at low water 7 fathoms –
6				hove in to half a cable
7				
8			SWBS	veer'd away to a whole cable
9				
10				
11				
12				Fresh gales & clear
1				
2			9:45	
3				
4			SW	hard gales got the sheet anchor over the side –
5				
6				
7				
8				fresh gales & squally with a great sea
9				Depth of water at high water ¼ less twelve fathoms –
10				
11				Very strong gales with a great sea
12			SSW	Struck the yards & topmast. –

The Indians making great fires onshoar at Point Possession – & several others places near the ship – fires likewais made over on the South shoar, on Terra del Fuego –
3

Remarks Sunday December 21 – 1766 – (85)

1			SW	
2				Strong gales & clear weather
3				
4			10:40	
5				A very heavy sea
6				
7				
8				
9				
10				
11				
12			WSW	
1				More moderate –
2				
3				
4			9:00	
5				
6				
7				
8				
9				
10				
11				Strong gales –
12			SW	The Indians still on the shore opposite the ship –

Monday December 22: 1766 – (86)

1	SSW	Strong gales & clear –
2		
3		
4		12:30
5		
6		
7		
8		
9		
10		
11		
12		11:30
1	West	
2		
3		High water ¼ less 14 fathoms –
4		
5		Light breezes & cloudy – got up the topsail:ˢ & yards
6		Sent the boats to sound – hove in to half a cable
7		at 10 low water ship in 8 fathoms. – in weighing the anchor broke the messenger –[167]
8	ESE	
9		weighd & made sail – the Swallow a head
10		
11		
12		at noon the Asses ears WNW½W Point Possession EBN 4 leagues the entrance of the Narrows SW distance of the nearest shoar 2 leagues in 19 fathoms of water – The Indians still going along the shoar –

5

---

167 This detail is omitted in the PL and the FC.

Remarks Tuesday December 23:ᵈ 1766 – (87)

1	West	
2		
3		
4	North	
5	SBE	
6	12:30	
7		
8		
9		
10	variable	
11		
12		
1		
2	10:55	
3		
4	West	
5		
6		
7		
8		
9		
10		
11		
12	SW	
6		

Light airs & cloudy –

at 3 anchord with the best bower in ten fm:
at ½ past 5 anchord in 18 fm: muddy ground
the Asses Ears NWBW½W Point Possession NEBE
the point of the Narrows on the South side SSW distance 3 or 4 leagues –
the tide set SWBS to NEBS about 9 mile an hour[168]

middle squally rainy weather

at 4 high water – 20 fathoms –

opened a cask of port N:°992 cont: 284 short 3 peices
a cask of beef N:°1349 Contents: 172 short 7 peices.[169]

took observations of ☽-☉
Lat:ᵈᵉ 52:34 Long:ᵈ 70:00 […] 8H 1' 38"

Weighd made sail the Swallow & store ship in company –

---

168 "The tide sets here SEBS & NEBN about 3 knots & rises tweny four feet. . . ." PL and FC. Molineux notes "The Indians still follow the ship & make fires onshore."
169 ". . . the whole appeard to be very old repact beef. This gave us all a good deal of concern for fear of finding more of this kind." Robertson (Carrington, op. cit., p. 32).

Remarks Wednesday Dec:r 24 1766 – (88)

			11:30	
12			SW	
1			SW	
2	4	2		
3	4	3		
4	2	4		
5	1	1		
6	1			
7	1	5		
8	Tid	4		knots
9				
10				
11				
12			7	

Fresh breeze – plying to windward the Swallow a head, stood from the Bay over to the middle & never went on either side to less water than twelve fathom[170] we saw the rippling of shoals on the Middle ground but could not send to sound it blowing fresh and a strong wind making to Westward – I judge it best to keep near the North shoar as the Middle is very dangerous & steep too in many places – at ½ past five entered the Narrows – & the tide being done anchord in 40 fm water muddy ground – the extreams of the Narrows SSW½W and S½E – off shore one mile off about two the Swallow at anchor on the North side. The store ship without the entrance on the South shore –& so near a bank that was dry at half ebb – that they were in danger of being on it, as they could not veer more than ½ a cable in 4 fm:[171] water & the tide running six knots with us the tide ran near seven knots but by keeping hands at the helm, she rode tolerable easy, saw several guanicoes on the North shoar & many men came down on horseback to the beach likewais on the S:°shore saw several people who seemed naked but the tide being so rapid would not send a boat from the ship[172] – at midnight weigh'd & towed though the narrows. At 4 a Cape like the N:°fore land SW our depth of water since we left the narrows 91 to 24 fm: S:°foreland SW in 19 fm: muddy ground –
At ½ past 7 light airs anchord in 25 fm: shells & small stones
Cape Gregory W½N, Sweepstakes foreland SW½W of shore 2 leagues

---

170 "The tide was so strong that the Swallow set one way we another and the Prince Frederick another, notwithstanding there was a fresh breeze none would answer the helm, we had various soundings and saw the rippling on the middle ground; in this manner standing on and backing & filling we entered the first narrows and the tide being done at 6 we anchored on the South shore." PL and FC. Robertson (Corrington, op. cit., p. 33) recounts Brine's fears at this time: ". . . he expected every minute that the ship would touch the ground on the side of a shoald bank which was closs by them and very steep. Hade she touchd she would have overset in a few minutes and the ship and cargo must [have] been lost but thank God we had better luck."

171 ". . . and the Prince Frederick not a cable length from a sand bank about 2 miles to the E:wd extreams of the narrow from SSW½W to S½E off shore one mile from the S:°two – Here the tide runs seven knots and at times such [. . .] came down that we expected to be adrift, at midnight slack tide, weigh'd and tow'd the ships thro' soon after sprung up a breeze which continued 'till seven and then it fell calm. We steer'd from the first narrows to the second SW and had 19 f:m water muddy. At 8 anch:d in 24F. Cape Gregory W½N Sweepstakes Foreland SW½W off shore 2 leagues. The Swallow & storeship at anchor a stern." PL and FC.

172 There is no reference to the Indians, naked or otherwise, in the PL and FC entries for this day.

Remarks Thursday Dec:ʳ 25 1766 – (89)

West	Fresh breezes weigh'd & made sail through the second narrows, at 3 Cape Gregory bore NE½N Sweep Stakes Foreland S½W 3 leagues & Elizabeth Island SSW½W had in turning there the 2:ᵈ narrows within half mile of the shore on each side 12fm: in the middle up to 22 fm: a ground – at five S:ᵗ Bartholomews Island S½W 3 or 4 mile & Elizabeth Island SSW½W 5 or 6 miles – the ship shoaled from 17fm: into six & five fathom – bore away to the Main & deepned the water again at 8 having blowing weather anchord under Elizabeth Island in 24 fm: water hard ground gravel & shells – a mile & half off – the extreams of Elizabeth Island bore from SSW to SW½S. Sweepstakes Foreland NE the SW point of Georges Island SE½S & the Middle of Bartholomews SEBE½E –
SW	
SSW	
10:40	
SWBW	
9;00	
South	
	Squally with rain & hail
SSW	Friday December 26:ᵗʰ 1767 between five & six in the morning observed Dis:ᶜ α of ☉-☽ Lat – 53:12. Long:ᵈ 71:00W – α 66:59:20 ☉ ---: 17:02 ☽ al:ᵈ 48:04; declin 23:°23' N.[173]
WSW	

---

[173] "Had an observation of the moon for longitude from London – 71:20 West latitude in 53:12 S – this was near the place where the shoal is that we observed." 26ᵗʰ December. PL and FC. The officers in the boats also shoot sea fowl and collect eggs and other refreshments according to Molineux who adds "This day being Christmas Day every body as merry as prudence & our circumstance would admit of."

Remarks Friday Dec:ʳ 26 1766 – (90)

11			
12			
1			
2			NW
3			
4			
5	8	South	North
6	8	SBE	11:00
7	6		
8	6		
9	4	S½W	NE
10			
11			9:00
12			

Light breeze & variable winds
at 1 AM weigh'd & made sail at 3 abreast of the N end of Elizabeth half a mile distance —[174]
at 5 abreast of the S° end
at ½ past five saw the water very smooth a head & to windward got into 8 & 9 fm: water from 17, bore away to the South shoar & deepened the water.[175] Cape Possession bore WSW½W 3 leagues & the S:°end of Georges Island NE 3 or 4 leagues –
the store ship which was to the windward of us about ¼ of a mile had not above four fathom for several casts of the lead, & for two miles had not above seven fathom – the Swallow who was to windward of her had deep water, I mean to windward she was nearer S:ᵗ Georges Island – I think the safest passage must be running down by Elizabeths Island & so down the North shore –

at 8 a Bluff point with a white patch on it on the NW side of fresh Water Bay six leagues to the N:°ward of cape S:ᵗ Ann SWBW – at the same time Cape S:ᵗ Ann SBE & a low point running from the high land of Terra del Fuego E½N a Fresh Water Bay SW½W 80 fathoms – Little wind & boats a head towing –

174 "Little wind and variable got off from Elizabeth Island a great deal of Sellery and on the representation of the Surgeon gave orders that the people onboard this ship & the Swallow have boiled wheat with portable soup and a large quantity of sellery or other vegetable for their breakfast every morning whilst these things can be got and we can get plenty of water." PL and FC

175 ". . . and made the signal for the other ships to follow us. NB When we were on this shoal Cape Porpus being about half a mile to the S:°ward of us had only four fathoms & for a long while 6 or 7. The Swallow being 3 or 4 m:ˢ to the S:ʷᵈ of her had deep water, for she kept near S:ᵗ Georges Island. I think the safest way is to run down from the NE end of Elizabeth Island about two or 3 miles from the shore, and so on all the way to Port Famine. At noon a low point bore E½N Fresh Water Bay SW½W distance from the N:°shore about 3 m:ˢ no ground with 80 fms – it being calm got all the boats and towed the ship." PL and FC. Molineux adds that "The Swallow & storeship sails so very heavy that without a large wind we can do nothing & even then there is sometimes two knots difference in our sailing."

		Remarks &^{ce} – (91 days)	
variable 1766 Saturday	27	11:00	Light breezes & cloudy with rain at 4 anchord in Port Famine Bay in 13 fm: moord Cape S:^{t} Ann ESE half a mile Sedger River S½W sent the boats out to tow the Swallow & Prince Frederick in, at 8 they both anchord here –[176] sent the boat a fishing, caught very few, AM hard gales struck yards & topmasts – received our men from the store ship – carpenters employed in caulking – Boiled wheat with greens for breakfast every morning ordered the Swallow to do the same
Sunday	28	14:8 SW 8:20	(10) (1) Fresh breezes & squally, unmoor'd the ship & warped her to the S:°ward & then moor'd her the best bower to the S:°& the small to the N:°ward Cape S:^{t} Ann NEBE¾ of a mile, Sedger River S½W – Employed in fixing tents onshoar – in the bottom of the Bay –
Monday	29	12:10 N° SW SSW 10:00	Little wind squally, PM sent the sent the Surgeon with all the sick & came onshoar unbent the sails & sent them with the sailmakers onshoar to repair them stript the topmasts – sent out empty cask up the River Sedger to be washed & trimmed, hauled the Seine a little to the S:°ward of the mouth of Sedger River, & caught plenty of fish – carpenters employed in caulking –[177]

176 "When the ship was moor'd Capt Carteret came aboard of us and tould us we had taken up all the best ground in the harbour, and that it was imposable for them to morr in safety. We then found it was too late to shift our birth. Soon after the store ship anchord within us and moord about a cable length from the rocks. When all the ships were secured, we sent all our boats to hall the seean." Robertson, p. 37.

177 "Little wind the latter part squally rainy weather unbent all the sails & sent them onshoar to be repaired erected tents upon the banks of the Sedger River and sent all the empty cask with the coopers to trim them and a mate with ten men to wash & fill them. Hauld the scene and caught abundance of fish somewhat like mullet but very soft likewais a few smelts some of which was twenty inches long and weigh'd 24 ounces. During our whole stay here we caught fish enough for one meal a day both for the sick and well. We likewais had great plenty of sellery & pea tops which was boiled in the pease and wheat with portable soup and they gathered plenty of berrys which I believe was very anty scorbutick – as well as a leaf we found here that was extremely sower and grew on a bush like a thorn – our people on our arrival began to look very pale & meagre; & severall had the scurvey to a great degree many more had evident simptoms of it coming on them. Yet in a fortnights time by being onshore (having plenty of vegetables making them wash all their things & keeping them very clean & bathing them often in which the officers were indefatigable. They were on any thing that could induce to the health of the company as the success of the voyage there was not a scorbutic on either ship." PL and FC.

Robertson (Corrington, op. cit., p. 38) adds that "This day Capt Walllis gave orders that non of the seamen should be workd hard, but their work to be no more than a moderate exercise for them in order to keep up and recruit their spirets. This was an excellent resolution and for the most part stuck upp to."

In the Hawkesworth account, there is a description of the uprooting of trees for the Falkland Islands (taken from Robertson, p.42): "In the mean time, a considerable quantity of wood was cut, and put on board the store-ship, to be sent to Falkland's island; and as I well knew there was no wood growing there, I caused some thousands of young trees to be carefully taken up with their roots, and a proper quantity of earth; and packing them in the best manner I could, I put them also on boat the store-ship, with orders to deliver them to the commanding officer at Port Egmont. . . ." Robertson continues "If oy^r ships is sent from this Isl^d to bring more young trees from the Streights

Month & Week day		Wind	
December Tuesday	1766 30	12:0 N:° 9:00	(3) Fresh gales & squally people employed in filling water, cutting wood &:[178] Sent the Armourer on shoar & set up the forge – caught plenty of fish – somewhat like mullet & smelt very large – former from ten to twenty inches – the latter 18 & 20 inches long –[179]
Wednesday	31	11:00 N° West 8:40	(4) Little wind employed as before Caught plenty of fish as yesterday
January 1767 Thursday	1	12:20 Variable 10:10	(5) Fresh breezes with showers – gave most of the people leave to go onshoar – this day –[180]
Friday	2	12:12 S:°erly 12:12	(6) Little wind employed in overhauling the rigging & hold & new staving it. Got off some ballast. Sailmaker & smiths onshoar[181]

of Magellan, in a few years this island will be capable of supplying a large fleet with wood and water, and if they carie a few live cattle from the Riojanero and oyther live stock, the place will soon be able to suplay a fleet with all sorts of refreshments. When I saw what sort of pashage we make through the Streights of Magellan, I shall be able to give my oppinion of the necessity of keeping this island, if Great Britain is determined to propagate her discovery in the South Sea, in order to extend her trade and commerce &ce."

The Hawkesworth account also includes description of plants which do not appear in the Wallis accounts: "He reported also, that he had seen a great number of currant bushes full of fruit, though none of it was ripe, and a great variety of beautiful shrubs in full blossom, bearing flowers of different colours, particularly red, purple, yellow, and white, besides great plenty of the winter's bark, a grateful spice which is well known to the botanists of Europe." (See Robertson, p. 46).

178   Gore lists the work being done: filling water, cutting wood, repairing sails which were taken onshore that day, the armourer busy with his forge on both ships, overhauling the rigging, caulking, shortening the cable tins to make room for the provisions, putting nine tons of ballast into the hold to trim the ship. Robertson (Corrington, op. cit., p. 40) notes that here "we saw several stumps of large trees which by their appearance hade been cut down leatly. We suppose thhe have been cutt by some of the French who is now settling on one of the Faclans Islands – where there is no fire wood to be hade."
179   ". . . the carpenter onboard the Swallow in fitting her rudder and caulking her." PL and FC.
180   ". . . & take their dinners with them, and a great deal of fish which we caught." PL and FC. The ship's company are allowed a day's rest as Molineux points out: "This day being the first day of the new year Cap.ᵗ Wallace was pleased to make it a holiday for the people who to a man behaved regular & well."
181   ". . . Besides fish our officers found plenty of salary, cranberries & some wild currants. Our people found some dead bodies in the woods which we suppose to be Indians as they were sew'd up in seals skin." Molineux. Robertson (Corrington, op. cit., p. 40) describes these graves in detail: "The skeletons appeard to be but a moderate size which makes me suppose they are non of the Patagonians; their manner of buering is this, they dogg a sort of round holl, and wraps the body round with a seals skinn, which I suppose is the skin they wear when alive, then they lay the corps on the left side with the head to the Etward, this was the position I saw it in. . . ."

Saturday	3	13:20 Ditto	(7) Fresh breezes, got all the bread up & clean'd the bread room – stored it for to be first expended – caught fish for the people –[182]
Sunday	4	13:00 S:°erly 11:20	(8) Rec:^{d} from the store ship got off brandy & 82 punch. of bread – 1836 pounds.[183] Employed onshoar as before –[184]

Monday Fresh	January 5:th 1767 – (9) Gales & squally employed on the rigging & in the hold – received 4 punch: of beef 15 of pork & 5hh– 1 barrell & 5 half hh of brandy – Carp:^{s} still employed on the Swallow, sailmaker, Armourer &:^{c} employed on shoar the gunner airing the powder –
Tuesday 10:00	January 6 1767 – Wind WSW (10) Fresh gales & cloudy, middle & latter more moderate – employed in getting off wood & water, taking onboard provisions from the Prince Frederick[185] People employed on shoar as before & carpenters on the Swallow
Wednesday 13:00 11:20	January 7 1767 – Wind WNW (11) Fresh gales & cloudy weather – Employed in taking onboard provisions from the store ship, carpenters onboard the Swallow –[186]

182 "... we find the wood here to be excellent [...] & easy to be got. It ressembles white cedar but is not so good. Here is plenty of the wood that produces what is call'd Winters Bark but is hardly of growth enough here to make a bed post." Molineux.

183 "Received from the store ship 82 puncheons of bread which was [...] into the breadroom, & on it we [...] what was taken out two days ago. Received 1400 gallons of brandy."PL and FC. Molineux describes the state of the Swallow: "Cap:^{n} Cartwright of the Swallow having represented to captain Wallace by letter that the ship work'd so bad that there was no depending on her staying or wearing & that it was his opinion as well as the opinion of the carpenters of both ships that by setting a peice on the after part of her rudder she would work the better Cap.t Wallace gave our carpenter orders to repair on board the Swallow & make such alterations as to the best of his judgement should seem proper."

184 "The ships com:^{y} in turns began to go on shore to refresh." Gore.

185 "Ordered a survey on the cask onboard the store ship that had spirits in them the Pursers having represented that they were not full and many deficient severall gallons, the report of which survey was forwarded to the Comissioners of the Victualling." PL and FC.

186 "... many of the sick men recovered and returned to their duty." PL and FC.

Week day	Month Day	Winds	Remarks onboard the his Maj:ˢ Ship Dolphin at Port Famine
January Thursday	1767 8:ᵗʰ	13:20 NW WNW NW 11:48	(12) Fresh gales and cloudy weather, caught plenty of fish for every one – carpenters employed onboard the Swallow people in cutting wood to put onboard the store ship or in gathering greens berry &:ᶜᵉ to exercise themselves the rest in overhauling the rigging & getting out of the store ship provisions. continue to boil wheat portable soup & greens for the peoples breakfasts —[187]
Friday	9	10:45 NWBW 9:00	(13) Moderate & cloudy with showers of rain all the people employed as yesterday
Saturday	10	11:20 NW S:°erly 9:30	(14) Light breezes. clear hawse people employed as before catch but few fish –
Sunday	11	13:00 Westerly 12:0	(15) Fresh breezes the Carpenters finished the Swallow, set them at work onboard here people employed onshoar and onboard as before[188]
Monday	12	12:00 North NW 10:0	(16) Fresh gales & cloudy with rain, PM got off the sails to & bent them. Punished John Clark for quarelling & Benj:ⁿ Ladd for mutinous behavior to the Gunner & midshipman onshoar.[189] Read the Articles of War & Abstract of the Act of Parliament to the ships company
Tuesday	13	14:00 NW 13:00	(17) Fresh gales at night little wind all the boats of the three ships employed in getting of wood onboard the Prince Frederick to carry to Port Egmont.[190]
Wednesday	14	15:00 NW 13:20	(18) Moderate weather with some rain employed in getting the ship ready for sea, got the armourers onboard & sent Will:ᵐ Lewis & Jn:°Williams onboard the storeship they being unfit for the voyage – gave the storeship order to sail.

187 "Fresh gales employed in cutting wood and sending it onboard the store ship to carry to Falklands Island, took coals enough out of her to fill to fill both this ship and the Swallows coal holes, ordered Lieu:ᵗ Brine to shake empty cask to make room to stow away the wood. Carpenters still at work onboard the Swallow." PL and FC.

188 ". . . & sending wood onboard the Prince Fredrick." PL and FC. Molineux notes an accident: "This day Francis Wilkinson (a youth upon duty at my serv.) endeavouring to get the slugs & the small shott out of a musquet the peice went off & shattr'd the inside of his thighs very much."

189 10ᵗʰ January: ". . . punished Jn.ⁿ Clarke, Benj:ⁿ Ladd & Jn:ⁿ Smith for behaving in a contemptuous manner to their superior onshore . . ." FC. In the PL, the behaviour in question is described as being both contemptuous and mutinous.

190 ". . . Besides the fish we catch in the seine there is plenty of clams & mussels the clams are excellent but the mussels are small there is two or 3 differents kinds of beasts inhabit here one of the dog kind another ressembling a fox & another like a wolf. Those of the wolf kind is the most daring as we experienced they having robb'd my party of their provisions more than once so that

Week day	Month Day	Wind	Remarks onboard the his Maj:ˢ Ship Dolphin in the Streights of Magellan
January Thursday	1767 15	15:00 West variable West 13:00	(19) Moderate weather PM got of all our people from the shoar & struck the tents having completed the ship with everything & water to 75 tons – Provisions for upwards of twelve months[191] – at 4 AM un moor'd & I made the signal & weighd the Swallow in company[192] at 11 the wind coming around to the Westward made the signal for anchoring & stood back toward Port famine, ships draught of water Feet inches Forward – 16:9 abaft – 15:1 sent the Master in the Cutter to look out for anchoring places[193]
Friday	16:ᵗʰ	16:00 Nw 14:00	(20) Squally weather, at 2 anchord with the best bower in 11 fm: water, soon after in a squall she drove off the bank hove it up & turn'd in again at 4 anchor'd in Port Famine in 9 fm: water. Point Shut up SBE½E Sedger River S½W & point Sːᵗ Ann NEBN, steadied the ship with the kedge anchor & hawser, completed our water & caught some fish opened a cask of beef N 2697 contents 170 peice short one peice – carpenters employed in caulking the ships sides & decks –[194]
Saturday	17:ᵗʰ	14:00 SSW West Variable 12:00	(21) Fresh breezes & squally with rain, at 5 min after three the Prince Frederick store ship Lieu:ᵗ Brine Commander sailed from hence with a fair wind & a fresh breeze AM completed all our water – Port Famine hath good anchorage from 9 to 6 fm: if you lay in deeper water you are in danger of being driven of the Bank Wooding and watering is easily come at and there is plenty of large fish at the mouth of the River Sedger & small fish about the ship – Cape Sːᵗ Ann is easily known by trees growing on the point and in inland of it it is clear of wood for near a mile & then wood begins again – which is not of Sandy Point or cape Shut up which may be mistaken for Port Famine keep near Cape Sːᵗ Ann[195]

as we lay in a wood we was oblig'd to sleep with our musquetts for bedfellows & our bayonets fixt, they came one night & finding no prey tore a shirt & pair of stockings to peices that lay to dry, they bark like abull dog & mostly are seen two together." Molineux. Robertson also recounts (p. 51) the near encounter with a "large mastiff dog" while camping. Two days later, Robertson's men think they see a "large black beast." Robertson thinks they are wolves but "some of the men said they heard the cry of a tiger, which frightened all the rest so much that none would sleep more until the sun got upp . . ."

191 ". . . completed the ship with all species of provisions at whole allowance and the Swallow near ten having filled my own and all the offciers cabins with dry provisions. Sent the Master in the cutter with a weeks provisions to look out for anchoring places on the N:°shore." PL and FC.
192 ". . . the Prince Fredrick saluted with nine guns, returned 7. . . ." PL and FC.
193 "There was wheat, pease & sundry other things put in the ground during our stay here but it is very uncertain whether they will grow or not." Molineux.
194 The entries in the PL and the FC are reduced to "Squally weather at 2 anchord in Port Famine with the old bearings, sent the boats & caught plenty of fish, carpenters employed in caulking." Robertson sounding the bays, names one Wallis Bay (p. 47).
195 The entries in the PL and the FC are reduced to "Fresh breezes and squally with rain, at 2 PM the Prince Frederick Victualler sailed. AM moderate & fair caught some fish. Carpenter employed as before."

Remarks Sunday Jan:ʸ 18 1767.[196]

H	K	F	Courses	Winds
1				WSW
2				14:00
3				
4				
5				
6				SW
7				
8				
9				
10				
11				
12				
1				
2				20:00
3				NNW
4				
5				
6	3	5	SBE	North
	2	3		
7	2		South	
8	3	3		
9	3		S½W	NEBN
	5	3	---	
10	3		SWBS	
	5		SW½S	
11	3		SW	
12	1		WSW	variable

Cape Froward Lat:ᵈᵉ 54:*03S

Moderate breezes & fair   (22)
The Master returned having found out severall[197] good places to anchor at on this side Cape Froward –

at 5 AM made the signal & weighd in company with the Swallow

at 8 S:ᵗ Anns Point bore SBE½E gull Island & Dolphin Island in one SSW½W 2 leagues. at same time a fire was made on Terra del Fuego –[198]

at 9 Point S:ᵗ Ann NBW, Point Shut up NBW½W, Cape Froward SW distance from Point Shut up 5 miles

at ½ past 10 Staff Point & Cape Holland both in one W½S – close reeft topsails –

at noon light airs. Cape Froward NBE½E Bluff Point NNW and Cape Holland W½S – distance off shore 2 miles – Judge the Streights to be about six miles over at this place –

---

196 The ML takes up the usual hourly format on the 18ᵗʰ January 1767 whereas the PL continues daily reporting in the truncated form.
197 The Master apparently found four anchoring places. PL.
198 This reference to a fire being made is omitted in both the other logs.

Remarks Monday Jan:ʸ 19 1767 (23)

H	K	F	Courses	Winds
1				variable
2				12:09
3				
4				West
5				
6				
7				calm
8				
9				
10				SE
11				East
12				ENE
1				NNE
2				
3				10:00
4				
5				variable
6				
7				West
8				
9				
10				
11				
12				

Light breezes with rain a strong current setting to the SSE round Cape Froward –
at 3 squally turning to windward
at 4 I sent out a boat into Snug Bay to point out anchoring ground to us –
at 8 being close in the wind shifted got the ships head off & towed her out we having 93 fm: to windward of us
at 9 light airs Cape Froward East & cape Holland West –

Cape Holland W½N 3 or 4 leagues

Light airs Cape Holland WBN & cape Froward NE

Plying to windward
Squally – sounded with 140 fm: the ground about 1½ mile from shoar –

at 8 the Swallow made the signal & anchor'd under cape Holland, tack'd and anchor'd at 9 in 10 fm: water clear ground sent a boat to sound all round the ship found from 9 to 4½ fm: at better than a cables length –[199]

Cape Holland WSW½W 2 miles Cape Froward East off the nearest shore about half a mile
Fresh gales & heavy squall – Lat: 53:*58S

---

[199] "... sent the boats to sound found ourselves very near a reef of rock, tript the anchor and drop't further out in twelve fathoms about half a mile from the shore and opposite a large rivulet of water from the mountains for here the land is excessive high –." PL and FC.

143

H	K	F	Course	Winds	Remarks Tuesday Jan:ʸ 20:ᵗʰ 1767 – (24)
2				WBN	Hard gales of wind & rain, let go the small bower under foot, at
4					5 PM – at midnight more moderate took it up again
6				WSW	
8				WNW	The latter part very fresh gales & heavy squalls –
10				11:05	
12					
2				NWBW	carpenter employed in caulking the ship
4					
6					
8					here is water & wood easyly came of & plenty of berrys &
10				WBS	sellery – but no fish except mussels –
12				18:20	
H	K	F	Course	Wind	Remarks Wednesday Jan:ʸ 21:ˢᵗ 1767 – (25)
2					Fresh gales with squalls of rain & hail
4				12:00	sent the boats for water & sellery – and shore sounding – found
6				WSW	there was a shoal a head about a cables length hove up & dropt
8					the ship to the Eastward & anchor'd with near the same bearings
10					there is very good anchorage from the cape to a league below it
12				WNW	about a half a mile from the shoar in 12 to 6 fm: water –²⁰⁰
2					
4					
6					
8				WSW	
10				10:00	
12					
H	K	F	Course	Wind	Remarks Jan:ʸ Thursday 22:ⁿᵈ 1767 – (26)
				WSW	Fresh gales middle & latter cloudy with rain completed our
				11:00	water,
					There is a fresh water river boats may go into in the bite of the
				West	bay & likewais a very good harbor if ships would stay any time
				8:25	here – if not they had best anchor where we are which is about
					half a mile outside from the shoar in 10 fm: water, Cape Froward
				variable	East & Cape Holland WSW½W about two miles opposite to a
					run of water, & to the Westward you see weeds on a shoal not
					half a mile – this is good clean ground²⁰¹

200 "Fresh gales with squalls of rain and hail, sent the boats to sound and found good anchorage from the Cape to four miles below it, about half a mile from the shore: There is a good harbour close by the Cape where a ship may refresh in safety better than at Port Famine, a very large fresh water river & plenty of wood, sellery & berrys but no fish except mussels." PL and FC.

201 The PL and FC entries are reduced to: "Fresh gales & squally, completed our wood & water, brought onboard plenty of seller & mussels for the ships company." Molineux indicates that this bay was called Woods Bay by the *Dolphin* and the land over it Wood's Warren.

Remarks Friday Jan:ʸ 23 – 1767 (27)

1				variable
2				
3			WSW	ENE
4				
5	3		W½s	10:40
6	4	4	West	EBS
7	4			
8	4			
9	2	4		
10		⎡		
11		⎨		calm
12		⎣		
1				
2		⎡		calm
3		⎨		8:55
4		⎣		
5				
6				
7				
8				variable
9				
10				
11				
12				WSW

Light airs

at 3 weigh'd made sail –
at 4 Cape Holland N34:00E distance 2 miles

Cape forward East & Cape Holland EBN

Cape Gallant W½N 2 legues Cape Holland EBN 6 leagues it & Cape Froward near in one a white patch in Charles Island[202] SSW¾W; Monmouths Island WSW, and Ruperts Island WBS, here the Streights is not above four[203] miles wide –

At 10 it fell calm, hoisted the boats out & towed the ships head to the N shore
the tide run very strangely here[204]
at 6 the Swallow made the signal that they had anchorage in 9 fm: water, under Cape Gallant, towed the ship in, and at 9 anchord in a bay to the E:ᵗ of Cape Gallant in 10 fm: water muddy ground
the East Point of Cape Gallant SWBW½W
the Eastern point of the E:tmost land EBS –
A point making the mouth of a river NBW, the white patch on Charles Island SW – our distance off shore about half a mile – sounded all round the ship found very good ground close home to the NE shore & so on to the harbours mouth, & away to the SW – for two cable length & then it deepened into 16 fm:

Corally ground – Lat:ᵈᵉ 53:*50S
This is the bay called Portuguese Bay[205]

---

202 Monmouth Island in PL.
203 Five miles wide in the two other logs.
204 ". . . the ships head could not be kept on any point." PL and FC.
205 Omitted in the PL and the FC.

Remarks Saturday Jan:^y 24 – 1767 (27)

1				
2				
3				
4			WSW	
5			12:20	
6				
7				
8				
9				
10				
11				
12			WSW	
1				
2				
3				
4			10:00	
5				
6				
7				
8				
9				
10				
11				
12			West	

Fresh gales with heavy rain and squalls – sent the Master to examine the harbor within us, who finds it a very commodious one having 4 & 9½ fm: at the entrance & as much in it which is about one mile half long & three quarters wide the entrance about two cables length over and distance from us about one mile[206]

[207]Altho I took the boat with Cap:^n Carteret & a Lieu:^t & examined Cordes Bay which is about two leagues to the Eward of this found it a very bad place tho' a spacious bay it hath very irregular soundings, & the Western side very rocky, & the passage narrow – between the rocks & the shore the side to anchor in is the East about two cables length from the shore in 7 to 9 fm: you may run further up with the same water but it would be right to send boats a head to sound – at the bottom of this bay runs up to the Eastward a lagoon at the entrance of which is only 2 fathom & most half a cable over, and when in it – it hath 10 to 18 fm: for near three miles, & a mile wide

at the head is a fresh water river
in coming down I saw an animal resembling a deer without horns – came pretty near him & fired a volley of musquetry at him but missed look'd at his track & found he had a cloven foot about the size of a large deer – this is the only one of that kind I have seen in these Streights –

206 This bay is described in the PL and the FC as "capable of containing a great number of ships, hath three fresh water rivers and plenty of wood and sellery, here we spoiled a scene and caught but few fish with the wood that lays sunk at the mouth of the rivers, there are great plenty of wild ducks and berries. The mountains here are very high, the Master of the Swallow climbed the highest in hopes of seeing the South sea from thence but was prevented from seeing it by higher mountains on the South shore, he rose a pyramid on the top of it and left a bottle with a shilling and a paper in it on the top of the mountain where I suppose it may remain ages." In the ML, the mountain is called Simpsons Mount.

207 "AM took two boats and examined Cordes Bay which we found to be no way comparable to this, there is a larger lagoon but it is very narrow & hath a hoal bar across it that no vessels of burden can get into it: And the entrance of the bay rocky with much foul ground when you are in; here we saw an animal like an ass but as swift as a deer, we shot at it but could not hit it, it had cloven feet. This is the only animal we have seen since we have been in thse streights except the first entrance where we saw several guanicoes." PL and FC. Hawkesworth ends this description with: ". . . probably it is altogether unknown to the naturalists of Europe [. . .] The country about this place has the most dreary forlorn appearance that can be imagined; the mountains on each side the Streight are of an immense height: about one fourth of the ascent is covered with trees of a considerable size; in the space from thence to the middle of the mountain there is nothing but withered shrubs; above these are patches of snow, and fragments of broken rock; and the summit is altogether rude and naked, towering above the clouds in vast crags that are piled upon each other, and look like the ruins of Nature devoted to everlasting sterility and desolation." Hawkesworth's descriptions of these landscapes seem to be based on Robertson's own "romantick" descriptions of the landscapes' "most dreedfull appearance" (see pp. 54, 74–75)

Remarks Sunday Jan:ʸ 25 – 1767 (29)

1			West
2			
3			
4			12:00
5			
6			
7			
8			
9			
10			
11			
12			SW
1			
2			
3			10:38
4			
5			
6			
7			
8			
9			
10			
11			
12			WSW

Fresh gales & rainy squally weather
AM went with Captain Carteret & one of the Lieu:ᵗˢ over to the south shore to examine. sounded all the passage between the ᴿᵒʸᵃˡˡ islands but found no ground nor any place to anchor in on that shore, found that the current set very strong thro the passage of these islands that we could scarce pull the boat a head the current set near WBS I judge it to be very dangerous for ships to come near these islands (as the draught is so great) – without a fresh breeze of wind, she would be sucked into the openings & having no place to anchor in would be in a dangerous situation –
The N:°shore from one end of these islands to the other is bold too. & no current but what set along the shore therefore you should not go about half a mile fro the North shore – until you get past the Islands –
the narrow place is not a league over
the current here sets to the Eastward allmost the twenty fours through –[208]

Completed our wood & water
handed the small bower 10 fm: from the clinch –
hove up the best bower I look'd at the Cable found all well – let it go again –[209]

---

[208] "Squally weather, went over with the two boats to the Royall Islands and sounded found no ground and a very rapid tide setting thro' where ever there was an opening, and it must be very dangerous for ships yo come near them, therefore they should allways keep the North shore close onboard it being bold to, yet heavy squalls come down from thence, you might not be more than a mile from it till you cross the Royall Isl:ᵈˢ. For the indraught of them is very much to be avoided. The current setts the twenty four hours thro' Easterly. Latitude of Cape Gallant Road 53:°50' S°." PL and FC.

[209] Details omitted in the two other logs.

			Remarks Monday Jan:ʸ 26 – 1767 – (30)
6			Moderate gales – boats employed in gathering mussels & getting brooms –
12		12:00	Sent out a boat to try the current & found it to set 1K 2fmˢ EBS – hauld the
6		West –	scene but caught no fish –²¹⁰
12		16:10	
		Winds	Tuesday January 27 1767 – (31)
		11:00	Fresh gales & cloudy, latter more mod:ᵉ
6		WSW	completed our water, sent to get some fish but found none – the Master of the
		variable	Swallow got on the top of one of the highest mountains here & erected a pillar –
12		WNW	he climbed it to see if could descern the South sea from it but he saw nothing but
		9:10	mountains within mountains – we called it Simpsons Mount²¹¹
6			
		Winds	Wednesday January 28 1767 – (32)
8		WNW	Moderate & cloudy with showers at 8 AM sent a boat into the offin to try the
		12:20	current & see how the wind was, she reported that the current set EBS 1.K 1 F pˢ
12		West	hour that the wind was N:ᵒerly & very squally.²¹² at 11 made the signal &
			weighd – at noon the West point of Cape Gallant WNW½ a mile – the white
6		NW	patch on Charles Island SEBS –
		10:10	
8		NNW	the Swallow in company –
12		NNE	Opened a cask of pork N:°1150 314 short 6 peices

210 ". . . one boat allways out trying the current which set very strong Easterly." PL and FC.
211 See notes for the ML entry for the 24ᵗʰ January 1767.
212 The PL and the FC specify that the crew of the boat "did believe that we could get round to Elizabeth Bay or York Road before night."

Remarks Thursday January 29 1767 – (33)

H	K	F		
1				NNE
2				
3				West
4				
5				
6				
7				
8				
9				
10				
11				WBS
12				
1				
2				10:40
3				
4				
5				
6				
7				
8				WNW
9				
10				
11				
12				

Fresh gales with hard flows of the land
at 2 the West point of Cape Gallant east three leagues York Road Point WSW 5 leagues – at 5 opened York Road, the point bearing NW½ a mile – was taken wih a heavy squall which obliged us to claw all up & the current setting strong to the Eastward was obliged to bear away for Elizabeth Bay – sent the boat in to look for anchorage – she made the signal for ten fathom. Anchord with the small bower – the Swallow at anchor close to Passage Point, sent the barge with an anchor & hawser to assist in warping the Swallow of the shore[213] – at 8 she warped out near us & anchord we steadid the ship with the stream anchor
York Road point bore WBN, a bank of weeds WNW a cables length & half from us
Point Passage SE½E half a mile a rock near the West end of Ruperts Island S½E and a rivulet in the middle of the bay NEBE three cables length –
AM sent the boat for water, several came from the South shoar in canoes, brought of them onboard & gave them beads knives &:[e] – afterward went onshoar to them there were fifteen poor miserable creatures – as ever I saw. all most naked & eating raw seal or porpoise they seemed very inoffensive –[214]

213 "Sent a boat with the kedge and hawser to assist the Swallow she having drove too near the E:[t] part of the bay. This bay has good anchorage but has no cover against the prevailing winds." Gore.
214 The PL and the FC entries for this day take up the remarks made on the 30th in the ML: "AM sent the boats water, at the same time came over three canoes from the South shore, and sixteen of the natives came to our people, they were low in stature were covered with seals skins, the rotten flesh and blubber of which they were eating raw, they seemed as tho' they were perishing with the cold, and kindled in an instant severall fires, they had both men & weomen bows and arrows, and javelines armed with flint made in form of serpents tongues which they threw & shot with great exactness. They eat any thing that was given them but could drink nothing but water –."
Molineux's entry includes supplementary detail: ". . . when the boat returned she brought 3 Indians they were well treated & after a short stay was put on shore. Captain Wallace went on shore & found several families of Indians, they would have gladly treated him with some stinking seal fish & cranberrys which they devoured very greedily. Their canoes are made of bark sew'd together & they use a seals skin for a sail upon occasion. They are of a dark tawny complexion & the tallest do exceed 5 foot. Their legs are crooked mouths wide & feet little. Their cloathing is seals skin which makes a very disagreeable smell. They use bow & arrows the arrow being arm'd with a flint in resemblance of a serpents tongue. They also have pikes or javelins headed with fish bon (bearded like our harpoons they had plenty of whale bone amongst them.")

EXPLORATION OF THE SOUTH SEAS

Remarks Friday January 30 – 1767 (34)

H	Winds	
	12:00 West	Fresh gales & squally rainy weather, rounded the best bower cables ten fathoms from the anchor – compleated our water
		AM the Indians went over to the South there again their canoes – they seem to be the most miserable of the human species I ever beheld, they were covered with a seal skin which loose over their shoulders and tyed round their middle which was all the clothing they had. the women the same; they had bows and arrows points with flint cut like a serpents tongue – they had peirced ears that they struck with any stone they took of the beach – & kindled a fire instantly[215] some of which I got with a bow & arrow
	WBS	I gave them bread which they eat of but they would not taste wine or brandy water they drank of freely – one of them took so great a liking to one of our men that he would give him part of anything he had – and ran to his boat & fetch'd him raw seal & stinking fish which I suppose was a delicacy with them – Sent the Master to look for anchoring places –[216]
	10:10	
	West	
		Wooding & watering easy here, plenty of berrys & sellery. no fish except mussels

215 Hawkesworth: "To kindle a fire they strike a pebble against a piece of mundic, holding under it, to catch the sparks, some moss or down, mixed with a whitish earth, which takes fire like tinder: they then take some dry grass, of which there is every where plenty, and putting the lighted moss into it, wave it to and fro, and in about a minute it blazes."

216 ". . . gave the Indians some knives beads & hatchets, they were the most wretched beings I ever saw being scarce a remove from brutes – soon after I had given them these things they crossed over to the South shore with their wives and children. . . ." PL and FC.

Hawkesworth allows his narrator to reflect upon the miserable state of the inhabitants (reflections drawn from Robertson's journal, p.61): "As this seems to be the most dreary and inhospitable country in the world, not excepting the worst parts of Sweden and Norway, the people seem to be the lowest and most deplorable of all human beings. Their perfect indifference to every thing they saw, which marked the disparity between our state and their own, though it may preserve them from the regret and anguish of unsatisfied desires, seems, notwithstanding, to imply a defect in their nature; for those who are satisfied with the gratifications of a brute, can have little pretension to the prerogatives of men. When they left us and embarked in their canoes, they hoisted a seal skin for a sail, and steered for the southern shore, where we saw many of their hovels; and we remarked that not one of them looked behind, either at us or at the ship, so little impression had the wonders they had seen made upon their minds, and so much did they appear to be absorbed in the present, without any habitual exercise of their power to reflect upon the past."

H	K	Winds	Remarks Saturday January 31 – 1767 (35)
2			Fresh gales & heavy squalls of wind with much rain and sleet, sent the
4		11:20	Master to the South shore to seek for anchoring ground
6		West	at 4 very strong gales struck yards and topmasts – at 8 the Master returned
8			but found only one place called Mussel Bay on the South shore and that but
10			very indifferent anchoring –
12			
2		WSW	
4			
6			opened a cask of pork N 6101 Contents 62 peices short five – and very bad[217]
8		West	
10		9:5	
12			

H	K	Wind	Remarks Sunday Feb:ry 1 1767 – (36)
		8:00	Squally rainy weather – much snow fallen on the mountains –[218]
6		West	
12		SW	
6		WSW	Lat:*3:40 – S
12		7:50	

H	K	Wind	Remarks Monday Feb:ry 2 1767 – (37)
		9:40	Strong gales & squally with much rain & hail, AM more moderate
4		WBN	sent the launch onshoar for wood water and sellery – completed our wood
8		West	and water –
12		WSW	
4		variable	
8			saw several fires over on the Terra de Fuego shore – and great numbers of
12		West	whales spouting between the shore & the Royal Islands –
		7:40	

217 ". . . but as we had plenty of water and greens we made a shift with it." PL and FC.
218 ". . . much snow hath fallen on the mountains whch makes it very cold. People have always a good fire & plenty of sellery & mussels we try the scene & trawl but get very fish not worth the labour & tears our nets to pieces." PL and FC.

H	Winds	Remarks Tuesday February 3:ʳᵈ 1767 (38)
2	West	Strong gales & hazey the middle & latter more moderate but much rain & hail
4	9:30	with heavy showers – AM got up the topmasts & yards & completed our water &
6	WSW	got off sellery which our people eat in great quantities –
8		
10		at 10 made the signal & weigh'd a little before noon the wind had shifted & the
12	variable	ship drove very fast to he Eastward stood in for Elizabeth Bay & anchord in 12
2	7:50	fm: water. the Swallow in company[219]
4	West	
6	SW	
8		
10	South	Lat:ᵈᵉ – 53:*8S –
12	variable	

H	Winds	Remarks Wednesday Feb:ʳʸ 4 1767 – (39)
1	SBE	Moderate & cloudy with frequent squalls & showers of rain & hail – at ½ past
2	variable	noon made the signal & weighd, soon after came on a squall at West which drove
3	South	both us & the Swallow very near a shoal
4	SW	the wind shifted again & we hauled of. at 3 PM the tide being near done the wind
5	9:00	Westing anchor'd in York Road in 8 fm: water, found our selves not far from a
6	WSW	shoal warped her into 11 fm: & moord with the stream cable – Cape Quod W ½S
7		7 leagues. York Point ESE one mile Batchelor River NNW ¾ of a mile
8		the entrance of Jeroms Sound NWBW, a small island on the S:°shore – WBS. the
9	SW	Swallow anch:ᵈ here at six having endeavourd to get further to the Westward but
10		was drove back with the tide[220]
11		
12	WSW	
2	8:30	
4	SW	
6		
8		
10	WSW	
12		sent the boats to sound every way & found very good soundings

219 "... soon after the wind veer's round to the Westward & obliged us to go back to Elizabeth Bay where we anchored at noon." PL and FC.

220 "... the Swallow being got very near Island Bay under Cape Quodd, endeavoured to get there, but the tide obliged her to return to York Road [. . .] we have here very uncertain but rapid tides and for the most part in the stream it sets to the Eastward, we found it sometimes set six hours to the Westward tho' very rarely." PL and FC.

H	Winds	Remarks Thursday Feb:ry 5 1767 – (40)
		[221] Fresh gales & squalls latter more moderate saw several Indians onshoar who all went off early in the morning in three canoes towards S:t Jeroms Island. The Master & another boat out sounding round the Bays – but they could not get over to the South shore or beyong Jeroms Sound it blowing fresh & a rapid tide – they found good anchoring in the bay between this & Elizabeth Bay. Compleated our water and Wood – the tide here runs very uncertain and not above six in the twenty four to the Westward but can give no allowance for some times it ebbs when we expect it to flow & flows when we expect it to ebb –
	9:30	
	WSW	
	8:25 West	There is easy wooding & watering in Batchelors River but you must be carefull in going over the bar; here is likewais great plenty of sellery nettles & scurvy grass of which we daily give the ships company – no fish since we left Port Famine –[222]
	WBN	

	Winds	Remarks Friday Feb:ry 6 1767 – (41)
	9:30	Fresh gales gales & hazey weather with showers of rain – employed in making lats, knotting yarn, & spinning […] yarn
	West	
	9:25	

221 "Fresh gales and squally, saw 5 Indian canoes come out of Batchelors River and go up Jerome Sound. AM moderate weather the boats returned they found good anchorage within Jerome Sound and all the way from hence about half a mile from the shore, likewise between Elizabeth & York point near York point a cable & half from the weeds 16 fath.s muddy ground. On the S:h shore under the islands there was several places that a ship might anchor in, but every one of these places are but very bad roadsteads by reason of the uncertain & rapid tides that runs here, and the heavy gusts that come of the high land which is all round us put fresh hands into the boats and went up Batchelor River here we hauld the scene & should have caught abundance of fish but the net being full of weeds & stumps of trees that we got few and after making severall tryall found that we must not expact any, so gathered mussels, limpets, sea eggs, sellery & nettles which we found great of where had been Indians wigwams and no where else clear water and wood here we had great ease. There is a bar at the entrance of the river that care should be taken at cetain times of tide". PL and FC.

222 "It is a pleasant river & abounds with such game as has been already mentioned, there is a fall of water on the larboard hand going up & the river is some places a mile broad. Here found plenty of cranberries & huckle berries both serve to make tarts & winter bark makes good spice." Molineux.

Winds	Remarks Saturday Feb:ry 7 1767 – (42)
10:20 WNW 9:20	Moderate & cloudy with frequent hard squalls & & thick rainy weather –
Winds	Remarks Sunday Feb:ry 8 1767 – (43)
West 10:40 WNW NNW North West 8:00	Fresh gales with much rain & hail At 4 AM unmoor'd the wind being N:°erly and the Swallow got under way but the wind coming Westerly, she anchor'd again – at 6 moor'd ship with the stream anchor, but first bore up the best bower to look at the cable & split in the same place[223]
Wind	Remarks Monday Feb:ry 9 1767 – (44)
9:00 Westerly 8:00	Moderate & breezes with heavy squalls & much hail & rain[224]
Wind	Remarks Tuesday Feb 10 1767 – (45)
WSW 9:40 WNW variable 8:10	Fresh breezes & squally with rain the latter little wind & variable – completed the wood & water. sent & got off sellery & mussels –
Wind	Remarks Wednesday Feb:ry 11 1767 – (46)
WBS 10:20 WNW variable West 8:00	Fresh gales & squally weather with much rain & lightning, completed our water –

223 This latter detail is omitted in the two other logs.
224 "Moderate breezes at times very heavy squalls with snow and hail. The boats employed in keeping up the wood and water compleat, & in gathering mussels and other refreshments for the people; we saw great quantities of ducks & widgeon, and one day two ostriches on Batchelors river, but so shy that it was with difficulty that we ever got at any of them." PL and FC.

Wind	Remarks Thursday February 12 1767 – (47)
West WSW 11:00 variable WNW West 8:20	Fresh gales & rainy with frequent very heavy squalls of wind – middle latter more moderate, at 1 AM unmoor'd & hove short but the wind coming round to the Westward & blowing fresh veer'd away & moor'd again – dryed the sails –[225]
Winds	Remarks Friday Feb:ry 13 1767 – (48)
WBN variable 9:20 WNW 8:50	Fresh & moderate & cloudy & latter fresh gales & squally with continued heavy rain. Completead our wood & water & gather'd sellery for the people –
Wind	Remarks Saturday Feb:ry 14 1767 – (49)
SWBW 10:20 WSW West WBN 8:20 WBS	Moderate with much rain, latter moder:e & fair. at 9 AM unmoord & weigh'd & made sail in company with the Swallow at 10 the tide set us on toward the point of Batchelor River past put the ship in stays and whilst in stays she being long in coming too – the tide drove us into three fathoms water[226] & as soon as the ship gather'd way we ran about half a cables length and deepened in to 5.10, & […] ground – at noon plying to the Westward Cape Quod bearing W½S 4 leagues. S:t Jeroms Sound NW½N & S:t Davids head WSW½W –

---

225 ". . . sent great part of the ships company onshoar to gather mussels, stretch their legs and air themselves." PL and FC.

226 ". . . and while she was coming about which she was long in doing, we drove over a shoal on which we had little more than 16 feet water rocky ground." PL and FC.

Wind	Remarks Sunday Feb:ry 15 1767 – (50)
SWBW 9:00 WSW West WBN 8:25 WBS	Moderate breezes & fair, from Noon till 4 PM Plying to windward found that we lost ground bore away for York road where we anchor'd at 5 – veer'd away & moor'd in 12 fm: York Point NW½W S:t Davids head WSW Batchelors River NBW½W Cape Quod WBS sent a boat to look out for anchoring places found two between S:t David head & York Road but very indifferent ones – completed our wood & water hauld the scene but caught no fish – opened a cask of pork N 898. Cont: 210 peices over 28 peices – The Swallow with us
Wind	Remarks Monday Feb:ry 16 1767 – (51)
11:30 Westerly 9:20	Moderate & dry weather, dryed all our sails & cleaned ship everywhere and completated wood & water, gathered sellery & mussels – sent the Master away to look out for anchoring places[227] – opened à cask of beef N contents
Wind	Remarks Tuesday Feb:ry 17 1767 – (52)
WSW 12:00 West South SE SEBE SWS 10:00	Light airs & rainy at 5 EM unmoord & got under sail with the Swallow towing with the boats a head. at 9 the ship was drove so near the South shore that we could have jumped to the rocks where we drove in great danger while we opend S:t Davids Sound when we had a little breeze – at noon plying to the windward[228] the boats looking out for an anchoring place Cape Quod bore NNE S:t Davids head SE cape Quod Lat:d 53:*3S.

---

227 Omitted in the two other logs.

228 "Little wind at 5 PM weigh'd and towed out of York Road, at 9 tho' we had a fine breeze the ship was carried away with great violence by a current from the North shore to the South shore, and she was so near notwithstanding all the boats were a head & sails asleep that she drove close to the weed and rocks that the boats were entangled with them and we expecting every moment the ship would be dashed agaist the rocks, in this manner we were hurried along for three quarters of an hour, we hove the lead on both sides up one side that was next the shore we had from 20 to 14 fathoms and on the other side no bottom we were seldom above the ships length from the cliff often nearer so that I believe that we were sometimes not more than her breadth; at last we opened St Davies Sound, & from thence came a current that set us out into the mid channel. The Swallow being all this time on the North shore could know nothing of our danger . . ." PL and FC. Hawkesworth adds to the near tragedy of a wreck with: ". . . as all our efforts were ineffectual, we resigned ourselves to our fate, and waited the event in a state of suspense very little different from despair."

Wind	Remarks Wednesday February 18 1767 – (53)
WSW 10:40	Light airs & hazey weather. at 1 the boats returned having found an anchoring place on the South shore & the Wind Westerly the ship drove fast to leeward. Bore away and anchor'd in 26 fm: water with the best bower veer'd to a whole cable & moor'd with the stream anchor to the SE. The Extreams of the bay from WBN to N½W, a quarter of a mile from each; a small rock in the NE entrance NE½N, a small island S½W two cables length.
West 10:50 SSW	Cape Quod North 4 mile. The Swallow came to anchor in Island Bay under cape Quod – in sight of us bearing NEBN distance about six miles – sent our boats and sounded all round the ship; & in Chance Bay to windward of us – sent the people onshoar to gather sellery & mussels[229] – AM unmoord and hove short – the Swallow underway. the wind shifting to the Westward, moor'd again – sent the Master to sound on the North shore – Lat: 53:55
WBN	

Wind	Remarks Thursday Feb:ry 19 1767 – (54)
10:40 WSW variable 9:00	Light airs with showers, latter fresh gales & squally with continual rain, at 2 PM the Swallow anchord again in Island Bay – not being able to get any ground sent the boats out to try the current & found it to set strong to the Eastward – at least two knots – the Master returned but could not find any place to anchor in[230]

---

229 "Sent all the boats to sound to sound around the ship & the adjoining bays, they report that half a mile to the W:tward is Chance Bay, more open & worse ground than here, and to the Eastward a ¼ of a mile a large bay in which they found no soundings, & that they visited several places Westward until they came to a large open sound but found no ground fit to receive the ship." PL and FC.

230 "Light airs with rain the Swallow got under sail but was obliged to put back again thro' the island in great danger; at noon squally the Master returned from the North shore and sounded in many places but could not find a place proper for the ship and it being very squally and look'd likely to blow hard made him return as he could not get to windward and all the people wet and much fateagued." PL and FC. Robertson (Corrington, op. cit., p. 70) notes for this day that a copy of all the plans of the bays he had explored were sent to the Swallow "in case of her being under the necessity of putting in to any of them."

Wind	Remarks Friday February 20 1767 – (55)
WSW West SW 9:40 9:00	Little wind & rainy – latter squally rainy weather –[231]

Wind	Remarks Saturday Feb:ʳʸ 21 1767 – (56)
10:0 WSW SWNW SW South SW 8:40	Fresh gales with excessive hard squalls of wind & rain – at 8 PM struck yards & topmasts – ran out a hawse & made it fast to the rocks & hove the ship up to the SW let go the small bower and veerd away upon the best until both cables grew taught. the ship rode much easyer a very great sea tumbled in her that broke quite over the ship AM the gale abated hove up the small bower & hove up and down with the best did not find the cables in any way rubbed veer'd away. sent a boat to the Swallow all well –

Wind	Remarks Sunday Feb:ʳʸ 22 1767 – (57)
9:00 Westerly 9:00	Moderate & cloudy with rain, sent the boats to gather seller & mussels – completed our wood & water –[232]

Wind	Remarks Monday Feb:ʳʸ 23 1767 – (58)
10:30 West South To NW 9:00	Light breezes & cloudy with rain, sent the boats to gather seller – tried the current & found it to set strong Easterly – Ships draught of water forward 16 feet 9:ⁱⁿ Boats likewais looking out for anchorage but could find none –[233]

[231] "Squally & rainy weather, the boats out trying the current, found it set at least two hours Easterly." PL and FC.

[232] ". . . at the same time gathered limpets mussels sellery & nettles; here we caught abundance of fine firm red fish some weighing four or five pounds, they are very like gurnetts. Wood & water easily come at." PL and FC. *

[233] "Tried the current constantly found it all way setting to the Eastward dryed the sails, sent great part of the ships company onshoar to wash their cloths gather seller nettles watercresses, mussels limpets & berries and to run about and stretch their legs as it is cold and the bad weather confinded them too much below – ships draught of water 16 feet 9 inches aft 15 feet 1 forward difference." PL and FC.

Wind	Remarks Tuesday Feb:ry 24 1767 – (59)
12:0 West	Moderate & fair & latter fresh gales & squally – at 9 PM struck yards & topm:t warped the ship over to the WSW & let go the small bower & rode betwixt both the Master hath been away sounding in the South shoar about 4 leagues but could find no place to anchor in –[234]
WNW	AM the people employed in making nippers
West	
WSW	
10:35	

Wind	Remarks Wednesday Feb:ry 25 1767 – (60)
Wsw 10:20 West WSW 10:10 West	Fresh gales & squally rainy weather[235] Completed the wood & water & sent the people to gather mussels & sellery –

Wind	Remarks Thursday Feb:ry 26 1767 – (61)
WNW 11:50 WSW 10:10 West	Fresh gales & squally with rain the latter more moderate, sent a boat over to the Swallow hove up the small bower anchor found the cable no way rubbed. got up yards & topmasts – Swallow safe –[236]

Wind	Remarks Friday Feb:ry 27 1767 – (62)
11:00 Westerly 9:25	Moderate & cloudy weather sent the boats out to try the current found it set 1-K 2 F to the Eastwards – and over on the North shore stronger –[237]

234 "The master away with the boat looking for anchoring places: at noon he returned but found scarce any place to anchor in, & none under shelter but close to the shore that could only be used in case of necessity." Hawkesworth's melancholy description of the landscape is as follows: "The country on the south of it was still more dreary and horrid than any he had yet seen: it consisted of craggy mountains, much higher than the clouds, that were altogether naked from the base to the summit, there not being a single shrub, nor even a blade of grass to be seen upon them; nor were the vallies between them less desolate, being intirely covered with deep beds of snow, except here and there where it had been washed away, or converted into ice, by the torrents which were precipitated from the fissures and crags of the mountain above, where the snow had been dissolved; and even these vallies, in the patches that were free from snow, were as destitute of verdure as the rocks between which they lay."
235 Wallis notes here in the PL and in the FC that it was snowing in the mountains.
236 "... shott severall geese." PL and FC.
237 Neither other log notes the speed of the current, describing it as "running strong to the eastwards from one side to the other."

Winds	Remarks Saturday Feb:ʳʸ 28 1767 – (63)
9:20 West variable West 8:20 variable West	Moderate & cloudy AM got up Topmast yards & dryed the sails, completed our wood and water. Opened a cask of pork N: 1135 contents: – 304 pci: Boats out trying the current – still Easterly –[238]

Winds	Remarks Sunday March 1 – 1767 – (64)
10:40 West WSW Calm East ENE Calm West ENE variable West 9:00	Moderate & cloudy, the middle & latter little wind at 4 PM hove up the small bower, at ½ past 4 PM saw the Swallow under sail on the North shore – weigh'd the best bower and at 7 sailed from the bay which I call Butlers Bay[239] – all the boats a head in towing out it being almost calm[240] – at 10 sent the boats to the North shore to look out for for anchoring places – at noon working to windward. Cape Notch bore WBN½N 3 or 4 leagues – Cape Quod E½N 3 leagues the Swallow to windward

Wind	Remarks Monday March 2 – 1767 – (65)
West 9:05 variable 12:00 WBN NW 9:00 variable North	Moderate & cloudy with rain, at 3 PM the Swallow anchord on the N:°shoar, at 4 we anchor'd in the same cove in 40 fm: shelly ground: run out a hawser to the rocks a stern of us to steady the ship to the NNE. sent a boat to the Westward to look out for an anchoring place. she returned after finding two –[241] the extreams of this cove from SBE½E to W½N, the Lyon head (a steep mountain) NE ½ cables length and the West point about the same distance sounded round the ship & found deep water every where close to the rocks & no ground a cables & ½ length of Cape Notch opposite some islands in the mouth of […] Sound. PM the boats trying the current which found to run fast to the Eastward –

238 ". . . the current still setting to the E:ᵗwd near two knots per hour [speed mentioned only the FC] ships company refreshing themselves onshoar." PL and FC.

239 On the 18ᵗʰ January 1767, Molineux notes that this bay was called Butlers Bay as "one of our mates of that name having discovered it."

240 ". . . it falling calm we towed her, but was very near the rocks the passage being narrow." PL and FC.

241 ". . . at midnight they returned & said there was one very indifferent bay about 4 miles off and Good Luck Bay was about three leagues to the Westward. . . .". PL and FC.

Wind	Remarks Tuesday March 3 1767 – (67)
NNE NNW WNW SW 8:55 SSW SW WSW West WNW 8:40	first part little wind & having hazey weather, at 1 PM made sail from Lyons Cove with the Swallow fired three guns for the boats that were looking out for anchoring places – at 5 we anchord in good Luck Bay in 28fm: sand & shells. Moord with the stream anchor to the Eastward – A rocky island at the extream of the bay NWBW a cable a half distance. a low point which makes the E. extream of the Bay ESE about a mile two rocks in the bottom of the bay the largest NEBW the other NBE two cables length from which rocks run off shoals to the SSE on which is weeds – and was little better than a cables length from the ship, & bore about SEBE[242] – at ½ past five sent our launch to assist the Swallow into an anchoring place. at 9 she returned having towed the Swallow into a cove two miles to the Westward of Lyons Cove[243] & about five miles from hence – AM fresh gales & squally with rain. Lowerd the lower yards – Cape Notch bore WBS½S – about one league
Wind	Remarks Wednesday March 4 – 1767 – (64)
9:20 WSW to WNW 8:40	These 2 hours hard gales of wind with very heavy squalls & much rain, at 9 struck the topmasts at 7 let go the small bower anchor & struck miz:^{n} topmasts – and got off the spritsail & the lower yards fore and aft.[244] AM still blowing very hard and terrible gusts of wind from the Westward that we could scarce stand the decks.[245] got up a new messenger the other being much worn –[246] Lat:^{d} Cape Notch – 53:*22S.

242 "... when she swung with her stern inshore then we were in 16f.^{m} corral rock, when we swung off, in 50 f.^{ms} sandy ground. Cape Notch bore from us WBS½W about one league between us and Cape Notch is a long lagoon which we could not sound it blowing so hard all th time so we lay her. After we had moor'd the ship sent two boats to assist the Swallow and one to look for out for anch. The other side of Cape Notch, at 10 ye boats ret.^{d} after finding a good roadstead about 144 m.^{s} of C. Notch the other boats had tow'd the Swallow in to a small bay & as the wind was Southerly & blew fresh they fear'd she must be in great distress the cove being small full of rocks and open to the S:°erly winds –." PL and FC. The drama of the situation is accentuated in the Hawkesworth account "It was a general opinion that the Swallow could not possibly ride it out, and some of the men were so strongly prepossessed with the notion of her being lost, that they fancied they saw some of her people coming over the rocks towards our ship." The source here is Robertson, p. 80.

243 The name of the Cove is not given in the two other logs.

244 Robertson's account of the situation is more alarming than in the *Dolphin* logs: "This was as dangerous a situation as Buttlers Bay. We was obligded to trust to our ground tackeling having no room to cast the ship clear of the reeff of rocks, neather could we with prudence venture to bring her up with less nor a whole cable, if the best bower parted. We hade the greatest reason to bless God, that our ground tackeling was as good as England could affoard, hade this not been the case nothing could have saved our ship here or in Buttlers Bay. A few of our lives might have been saved by getting ashoar on the Barren Rocks but that would have been only spinning them out in longer misery."

245 "... it absolutely brought whole sheets of water all the way from Cape Notch over the ship. The sea was not great the wind blowing off cape Notch but the cables were in a constant strain." PL and FC.

246 Detail omitted in the two other logs.

	Wind	Remarks Thursday March 5:th 1767 – (68)
	11:00 WNW 9:00	Fresh gales & cloudy squally weather with snow hail & rain,[247] at 9 AM completed the water & got some beef & pork out of the hold betwixt decks & put water down in its stead – caught plenty of Red Rock fish weighd the small bower & dropt it again[248]
		Remarks Friday March 6 1767 – (69)
	8:00 Westerly 7:55	Fresh gales & squally with hail snow & rain with frequent hard squalls –[249]
		Remarks Saturday March 7 – 1767 – (70)
	9:40 Westerly Werly 8:30	Fresh gales & squally latter moderate & cloudy AM weighd the small bower & hove short on the best, found no rubs on the cable veerd away got up topmasts & yards & dryed the sails, sent a boat to look for the Swallow –
		Sunday March 8 – 1767 – (71)
	8:55 Westerly 8:40	[250]Moderate & cloudy, latter fresh gales with hard squalls with rain & snow PM sent a boat to look for anchorage on the North shoar, at 4 the boat returned from the Swallow & informed us that she was in great danger being in a small bay full of rocks – at 9 the boat returned from the Westwards & informed us that they had found a road about 3 leagues to the Westward, in 24 to 28 fm: good ground. at 2 PM struck y:ds & topmast & brought both cables a head. the weather being very wet & cold got up eleven pieces of fearnought & cut them into jackets for the ships crew it amoounting to 2 yards & 34in a man – set the taylors to work to make them

247 " Fresh gales & cloudy sent onshore and got of some water and seller with plenty of mussels, sounded likewise all round and found it a very bad bay ..." PL and FC.

248 "... the weather being very unsettled, having very frequent gusts of wind cannot venture to send a boat to enquire how the Swallow hath made it out in this storm – we catch greay plenty of Red Rock fish in this bay with hook & line in 40 & 50 fathom but when the ship swings into 30, 20 & 16, we catch none –." PL and FC.

249 "We have now opened a cask of bad beef which is the second cask of old repact meat that I have yet opened all the oyther provisions that we have opened is good of their kind." Robertson, p. 81.

250 "... at 4 PM the boat returned from the Swallow & informed me that they were safe & well but greatly fateagued. That they had spoiled three cables and were obliged to make fast shrouds and other hawsers and all the large rope they had to the rocks and buoyed them up into cask to keep them from being likewais rubbed to peices that in this manner they have lain ever since they anchor'd and had been heavily in expectation of being dashed to peices. That the moment that the breeze offered they would get out and come here or any other place they can reach – At midnight very hard gales with severe gusts of wind with hail snow sleet and rain, let go the small bower & struck yards and topmasts. The weather being exceeding cold and constant rain or sleet the people never dry got up eleven bales of fearnought and cut them up for jackets for every man in the ship making them as large as possible which they thankfully accepted except M:r Gore Masters Mate who was this voyage before with Commodore Byron who sent me word that he did not want any having brought warm clothes with him. I sent seven bales of the same cloth to the Swallow which made jackets for every man onboard her & they were very thank full for them they being very comfortable, I cut up likewais three bales of the finer cloth and made jackets for the officers of both ships the fearnought being barely sufficient to make every man a use full jacket, there being in each jackett, or rather one with another 28 yards & 94 inches. Set the taylors to work and every one that could sew were employed in making them and to prevent any mistake had every man measured and the jackett cut out large." PL and FC.

Wind	Remarks Monday March 9 1767 – (72)
10:40 Westerly WSW NW NNE 9:00	Fresh gales & squally with hail & rain, latter more moderate with drizzling rain, at 9 PM weighd the small bower got up topm:¹ & yards Completed our water.
	Tuesday March 10 1767 – (73)
variable Wsw 11:00 9:10	Very hard gales & squally with rain and hail – at 1 PM let go the small bower & struck yards & topmasts. AM more moderate completed our water, this day put the ships company to two thirds allowance of all species of provisions except spirits.²⁵¹ gave the Cap:ᵗⁿ of the Swallow orders to do the same
	Wednesday March 11 1767 – (74)
11:20 West 9:05	Fresh gales & squally with rain AM sent a Man from every mess to the rocks to gather mussels²⁵²
	Thursday March 12 1767 – (75)
WNW 10:40 Sw 9:15 South	first & middle fresh gales & squally with rain latter very hard gales – with heavy squalls & much rain & hail the wind shifting from West to SW & South²⁵³ – at 9 AM veerd away to a whole cable on the small bower at noon hove in to half a cable –²⁵⁴
	Friday March 13 1767 – (76)
10:00 West SW South 8:30	Fresh gales with hard squalls, snow hail & rain & lightning in the SE, AM sent our boats & completed the ship with water – Taylors employed still in making jackets for the ships company who are in great need of them they having very little thick cloaths²⁵⁵

251 "... except brandy continued their breakfasts to them by the Surgeons advice whilst greens and water can be had in plenty." PL and FC. "This day the ships company were called upon the quarter deck where Captain Wallis acquainted them that our being detain'd longer in the Streights than he expected he was under the necessity of putting every body to 2/3 allowance of provisions grogg excepted & that they should have a wheat breakfast as susual every morning. Captain Wallice's goodness hiether to has so endear'd him to the people that they receiv'd this declaration with thye greatest cheerfulness." Molineux.
252 Also limpets and greens in the two other logs.
253 "... which brought in a heavy sea and strained the cables much, as the ship was on a constant sheer." PL and FC.
254 Omitted in the two other logs.
255 The PL and FC entry is shorter: "Fresh gales with heavy squalls at times, compleated our wood & water and brought off mussells and greens for the ships company."

Winds	Saturday March 14 – 1767 (77)	
11:00	First & middle fresh gales & cloudy latter more moderate with drizzling rain sent the boats & got of mussels for the ships comp:	
SW	AM hove up the small bower then hove up the best & dropt the small in its place found the best bower cable very much rubbed and unfit for service so 'twas condemned unbent it & cut it up into junk, bent the second cable of the best bower & rounded ten fathom from the clinch[256] at noon saw the Swallow under sail sent the launch to assist her in getting in here	
NW		
9:00		
	Sunday March 15 – 1767 (78)	
9:00	Moderate & cloudy, the launch returned from the Swallow & informed us that they had towed her into a good harbor on the South shore	
Westerly	[257]at 8 AM unmoor'd at 10 weighd & made sail for the Swallow, at noon the Master of the Swallow came onboard (having fired many guns) & piloted us into Swallow Harbour a moord us a cable each each way in 26 fm: Entrance NNW & the E:ⁿ side N:°this is a very excellent harbor & sheltered from all winds plenty of wood and water, the entrance in is not above three quarters of	
8:05	a cables length – from weeds to weed, but the Easternmost channel is wider –	

256 "... being in great want of nippers & plats, rounded the new best bower cable 15 fathoms from the clinch, for to do which was obliged to unreeve much running rigging & reeve new in the stead, at noon saw the Swallow under sail, sent our launch to assist her it being calm." PL and FC. Robertson's journal entry (p.84) is rather more alarming concerning the best bower cable: "In several places it was so bade that we were surprized to see it bring the anchor up – hade not providence allowed us this few moderate hours, our best bower must certainly have parted soon, which would have put us in the greatest danger hade we not totally lost the ship."

257 "At 8 AM got up yards & topm.tˢ and sailed from Good Luck Bay & steered over to the Bay where the Swallow was at anchor, fired several guns for their boats to come to assist us in, and moor'd ship with the bower a cable each way in 28 fathoms muddy ground, this is a very excellent harbour and sheltered from all winds, the passage in is but narrow however the dangers are seen by the weeds growing on the rocks; there are two channels. Wood and water is plenty as for greens &c.ᵉ we can but judge little of as our stay here was so short, sent the Masters of the Dolphin & Swallow with a weeks provision to the Westward to seek for anchoring places." PL and FC.

Winds		
		Monday March 16 – 1767 (79)
11:00	variable	Moderate & cloudy latter fair, at 8 PM sent the Masters of the Dolphin & Swallow for four days to the Westward to look out for anchor places, at 9 they returned having found the wind Easterly without, made the signal & weighd immediately to make sail, at noon Cape Notch bore EBN 3 leagues took the Swallow in tow[258]
9:00	ENE	
		Tuesday March 17 – 1767 (80)
NE		Moderate weather, at 5 it falling a little wind sent the boat inshoar to find out an anchoring place, at 7 she returned and informed us that the place was very indifferent, at 8 fresh breezes, got down top gallant yards, at midnight Cape Upright SSW½W 4 or 5 miles, at 7 AM got up top gall:[1] yards & took the Swallow in tow – [259] soon after it came on very thick weather saw the land under our lee tack'd & cast of the Swallow, sent the boat to look for anchorage but could find none bore away for Upright Bay, at eleven the Swallow made the sig:[1] of distress, sent our boats to her assistance & towed her out from amongst the rocks are in great perplexity not knowing where we are, sent the boats inshoar of us we sailing to the Eastward so foggy can scarce see a cables length. at noon by the number of islands about us we suppose ourselves in Island Bay two leagues from Cape Upright, very foggy weather.
9:00		
N°		
NNE		
NBW		
NW		
WSW		
WNW		
9:00		

258 ". . . I was sent onboard the Swallow with cloth to make jackets for the people where the Lieutenan:[1] told me that the place they lately left had near put an end to their voyage they being in the most imminent danger of going upon the rocks indeed upon the whole the Swallow is not calculated for a voyage of this kind as in all probability we should have been through the Streights before this time had we had a consort capable of keeping way with us. This is still worse if we consider that she cannot store a sufficient quantity of provisions for their people more than 12 months & then for a long run they would be short of water she not stowing so much by the 20 Jan of water as the [. . .]." Molineux.

259 ". . . Captain Carteret advised me to bear away for Cape Upright which I agreed to, he went a head the boats inshoar of him and we followed, at eleven it falling little wind and a large lagoon open the current set through into it, the Swallow being near the shoar it being very thick was carried away by the current close on the lee shore amongst the breakers where she made the signal of distress there being no anchorage and the surf running very high hoisted out our launch and other boats (boat in the PL) & sent to her assistance and towed her off by the help of a breeze that came seasonable down from the mountain. At noon it being very thick and foggy with a great swell we hauld over for the N° shore, we knew not where we were nor which way to steer being surrounded with islands and very close to them, the boats sounding amongst them but could find no anchorage, we conjectured that we must be in the Bay of Islands so had no chance but to haul directly out whch we did, frequently tacking to weather some island or rock." PL and FC.

	Wind	Remarks Wednesday March 18 – 1767 (81)
	10:05	[260]Foggy with drizzling rain at 5 PM the Swallow told me that we were entering Upright Bay a half past two both anch there in 24 fm: sandy ground, the Swallow soon after drove a great way to leeward with two anchors a head, we veerd to a whole cable & had 45 fm: the extreams of the Bay from NW to NEBE½E a high bluff on the North shore NW½W 5 leagues a small island within us SBE½E 3 cables leng the weeds to the Westward about half a cables length from where we dropt our anchor – struck yards and topmasts at 11 PM squally dropt the small bower in 47 fm: at 4 AM sent the launch & cutter with a number of men to assist the Swallow hung her with the stream cable to our ship her bower anchors having entangled with each other, at noon she cleared her anchors & warp in shore & moord. This bay is called Upright bay it is about 2 miles ESE from Cape Upright, the Cape is a high steep rock with a small island laying of it, then runs in a bay or sound & when you are passed by it you enter Upright Bay where you run close to the weeds & anchor. sent our boats & sounded & found from 20 to 188 fm: a half mile from the ship & then no ground until you come close to the Eastern shoar a very dismal situation to be in –
	NW	
	SSW	
	9:55	

260 "Foggy weather with drizzling rain, at 4 it cleared for a minute, saw Cape Uright and steered directly in for it, and at half past 5, we with the Swallow anchored in Upright Bay in 24 fath & when we had veer'd away to a whole cable was in 46 fathoms muddy ground. Soon after we were anchored a squall came on & the Swallow drove to Leeward notwithstanding she had two anchors ahead, she at last brought up in 70 fms water about a cables length astern of us. Squally w.r struck the yards and topmasts and let go the smallb.r in 45 fathom water. AM at 4 sent the boats with with a number of men, anchors & hawsers onb.d the Swallow, to weigh her anchor & warp her up to windward when they hove up her best b.r they found it entangled with the small. Sent the stream cable onboard her and swung the shift by it, it took up the whole day to clear the anchors and warp her up into a proper birth. Where we lay, a high bluff on the N.º shore bore SW½N 5 lg⁵ – a small island within us SBE½E where we let go our anchor about half a cables length from the weeds." PL and FC.

Wind	Remarks Thursday March 19 – 1767
11:30 WNW 10:00	Fresh breezes, at 3 PM hove up the small bower & moord with the stream in 78 fm PM got off some wood & water, a canoe with Indians came onboard, who were almost naked having only a seals skin over their shoulder nothing to cover their privities. gave them some beads & other toys likewais some bread & fish which they eat raw immediately. they seemed more surprised at seeing themselves in a looking glass than any thing else. they looking behind & often putting their head behind it. their furniture in the canoe was only some seals flesh & penguins stinking & rotten & few pieces of wood with a tip of sharp iron in it to serve them instead of hatchets at noon they went to the Swallow —[261]
	Friday March 20 – 1767 – (83)
11:00 Nw 10:40	Fresh gales & cloudy weighd the stream anchor – & let it go again in 57 fm: spliced a shroud hawser to it & moord the ship again.[262] Employed in making plats points gaskets & nippers. at 6 AM sent the Master of the Swallow & a Mate from this ship to the Westward to see for harbours for four or five days having provisions & a double proportion of brandy with sails & tarpaulins to make tents at night. —[263]
	Saturday 21 March– 1767 – (84)
11:20 9:20	Lat observed 53:00 S – Fresh gales & cloudy squally weather[264]

261 "Fresh breezes sent the boats to sound and found from the ship to either shore 40, 45, 50, 70 to 100 fathoms, half a mile then no ground till within a cables length of the lee shore, where was 90 fathoms. Moor'd the ship with the stream anchor in 78 fathoms. AM got off some wood & water, sellery and mussels; came alongside two canoes with Indians they were very like those that we saw at Elizabeth Bay, they had seals flesh blubber & penguins in their boats which they eat raw, here we caught plenty of fish with hook and line some of which the people gave the Indians who greedily eat them raw as soon as they had them beginning at the head and then set on without minding bones, scales, or finns, they eat any thing that was given them but drink nothing but water they had javelins with which they struck fish seals & penguins. They had no instrument of iron except a peice about the size of a common chizzle fastened to a peice of wood which served them to hew with their canoes are very badly made nor did I see anything that they had that shewed the least ingenuity among them, they were naked having nothing even tho cover their privities, but when they were out of the boat or not rowing they covered their backs with a seals skin they were excessive chilly had most of them sore eyes which is owing to to their allway hudling over a smoky fire and they smell most intolerable I suppose from living wholly of fish or flesh and that raw gave them some beads hatchets and toys, soon after they went away to the S:°ward and we saw no more of them." PL and FC. The architecture of the canoes is described in detail in the Hawkesworth account (taken from Robertson's journal, p. 88): "Their canoes were about fifteen foot long, three broad, and nearly three deep: they were made of the bark of trees, sewn together, either with the sinews of some beast, or thongs cut out of a hide. Some kind of rush was laid into the seams, and the outside was smeared with a resin, or gum, which prevented the water from soaking into the bark. Fifteen slender branches, bent into an arch, were sewed transversely to the bottom and sides, and some strait pieces were placed cross the top, from gunwale to gunwale, and securely lashed at each end: upon the whole, however, it was poorly made, nor had these people any thing among them in which there was the least appearance of ingenuity."

262 This detail is omitted and the boats were also well stocked with provisions for a week according to the PL and the FC.

263 "[. . .] 4 Indians came on board in a canoe after being kindly entertained they went on board the Swallow." Molineux.

264 "Fresh gales & cloudy squally weather, put on shoar great part of the ships company on some islands near the ship to gather sellery there being but little to be met with here, they likewais employed themselves in gathering limpets, & mussles & washing their cloathes." PL and FC.

	Wind	Remarks Sunday March 22 – 1767 (85)
	11:20 Westerly 9:20	Cloudy squally weather sent the people onshoar & gathered mussels & dryed two sails. Employed as before[265]
		Monday March 23 – 1767
	11:40 West NW 9:00 North	Fresh gales with rain weighd the small bower & hove in to the service of the best Completed our water & filled the empty bread puncheons with water
		Tuesday March 24 – 1767 (86)
	10:40 NW 9:00 WNW	Fresh gales, at 4 PM let go the small bower at the same time the boat returned & informed me that they had been about 10 Leagues to the Westward where they found a very good bay called Dolphin Bay but between this & that bay there is no place for a ship to anchor in with any kind of safety, nay not without the risque of loosing her that they had in their way down met with six canoes of Indians who were very surly & if they had not been well armed & shewed a resolution believes (the Indians being 27, ours 16) they would have attacked them for they took several things up that were in the boat, & because the people took them from them they drew up in a body & around themselves with their lances which they shook at our people, but did no more and some time after they were better recociled to each other[266] Compleated our wood & water caught many fish here –

265 ". . . people onshoar gathering mussels and greens and stretching their legs it being very cold onboard and we judge that shore exercise most usefull to help them from the scurvey and that every man will be able to pick a few greens for his mess beside what is boiled in the wheat & pease – many of the people have colds but soon get the better of it by running about on the islands." PL and FC.

266 ". . . at the same time the boats returned, they had been to the Westward about ten leagues and found but two places to anchor at, one to the W.'ward of Cape Upright in the Bay of Islands, but very bad to get out of or go into, and the other ten leagues off called Dolphin Bay, a good bay & even ground all over, there were some small coves but very dangerous as you must let go your anchor half a cables length from a sea shore and steady the ship with hawsers to the rocks. They slept one night on an island where there came to them six canoes full of Indians, they making free with all the things that were in the boat but our people preventing them, they immediately flew to their canoes and armed themselves with long poles with javelines of fish bones and stood threatening our people who, likewais stood on the defensive but by giving them a few trifles they became friends however they kept on guard all the time they were among them they were about thirty, ours twenty two." PL and FC. Robertson (Corrington, op. cit., p. 90) adds "I was afterwards tould the Indians hade their wives allong with them which occasioned the differences between our men and the Indians."

Wind –	Remarks Wednesday 25 March – 1767 – (88)
10:40 WNW 9:00	Fresh gales & squally weather employed in making plats, nippers, spun yarn &:^{ce} reev'd new fore topsail braces used the old ones tho' not half worn for rounding for the cables. at 11 AM let go the small bower it blowing excessive hard with heavy rain & hail —[267]
	Thursday March 26 – 1767 – (89)
10:40 WNW 10:20	Hard gales with hail & lightning[268] AM got off some wood and water
	Friday March 27 – 1767 – (90)
10:50 WNW WSW 10:20	[269] Fresh gales the middle & latter excessive hard gales at 6 AM got the topsail yards fore & aft in the tops & spritsail yard & jib boom in & veerd away to two cables on the best bower – at noon more moderate low'd our main sail to dry found it very much mildewed & fear that most of our sails were rotten and the yards not having a dry hour to air them. at noon it blew so hard was obliged to furl the main sail again. weigh'd the stream anchor
	Saturday March 28 – 1767 – (91)
12:40 West WNW 10:00	Hard gales & squally rainy weather the middle & latter fresh gales & squally AM got off some wood & water, let go the stream anchor – found our fire place very bad got up the forge & set the armourers at work to make an iron back to the grate.[270]

267 "... insomuch that I thought it impossible for this ship to hold tho' she had two anchors a head & two cables an end." PL.

268 "... the sails much mildew'd and cannot losse them for fear of setting the ship adrift." PL and FC.

269 " Fresh gales & middle & latter, as severe a storm as ever I felt with fresh gales of wind (with such gusts of wind – PL) & used suddenly to strike the ship that the shocks that it gave was incredibl. Got the lower & t.s yards, fore & aft." PL and FC.

270 "... and made a back of iron & burnt shells and made lime of it and fitted up the fireplace anew." PL and FC.

Wind	Remarks Sunday March 29 – 1767 – (92)
West NW 10:20 North NE 10:30	Fresh gales & squally middle & latter moderate & fair – at 7 AM weigh'd the small bower then weigh'd the best, found the cable very much rubbed. Cut off twelve fathom & spliced it again.[271] at noon let the best bower go in 33 fm: & moor'd with the stream anchor in 59 fm: the bearings the same as before, sent the Master of the Swallow & the Master from this ship to the North shore for three days to look out for anchoring places. Armourers employed as before –[272] Lat:^{d} of Cape Uright – 53:*5 S –
	Monday March 30 – 1767 – (93)
N 12:10 NW West 10:40	Moderate & fair, got up topmast & yards & dryed all the sails. got of wood & water. got up the spair sails & found that the rats had cut them very much set the sailmakers at work to repair them the armourers at work for the Swallow[273]
	Tuesday March 31 – 1767 – (94)
West 12:00 WNW 11:5	Fresh gales & squally at 6 PM struck yards & topmasts & let go the small bower anchor – sent the people & gatherd mussels – completed the water – several Indians came onboard[274] gave them knives hatchetts scissors beads & many other things they were almost naked & eat raw fish entrails or any sort of garbage but very excessively fond of tallow they brought none of their women with them

271 "... found the b.^{t} b.^{r} rubb'd in many places for upwards of 30 fathoms cut off the bad and new bent it, unreeve'd the braces, yard tackle falls &c:^{e} tho' not half worn & rounded the cable near twenty fathoms, at noon dropt the ship into 34 fathoms and there let go the best bower & steadied with the stream anchor in 58 f:m Cape Upright in the latitude 53.°55' South –." PL and FC. Molineux provides more technical details: "... found the cable very much rubb'd so much that it was thought unserviceable in consequence of which cut 12 f.m of the rub'd part off when upon examination it was found much worse than it appear'd to be the strand in particular having only 3 whole yarns in it." See also Robertson (Corrington, op. cit., p. 91).

272 This detail appears in the 30th March entry of the two other logs.

273 The *Swallow's* fireplace "being all in peices." PL and FC. These two logs also record the arrival of Indians: "saw severall canoes full of Indians land on the East side of the bay."

274 "... they were just such people as the former we had seen, these were the Indians our boat met with the other day." PL and FC.

Wind –	Remarks Wednesday April 1 – 1767 – (95)
11:40 NW 11:20	Moderate & cloudy weather, sent the people to gather mussels. Cleard hawsers hauld up the small bower anchor. the Master of the Swallow returned & informed me that he had found three good anchoring places one about 4 miles within to the E:ward of Cape Providence another under Cape Tamar & a third about for miles to the Eastwards of cape Tamar that under Cape Providence there in no anchorage it being quite rocky until you get up the bay –²⁷⁵
12:00	Remarks Thursday April 2 – 1767 – (96)
NNW N:º NW West 10:20	Little wind & cloudy, latter fresh gales & squally with much rain struck yards & topmasts²⁷⁶
	Remarks Friday April 3 – 1767 – (97)
12:10 WNW NW 11:00	These 24 hours fresh gales & rainy squally weather, got of wood & water –
	Remarks Saturday April 4 – 1767 – (98)

275 ". . . severall Indians came off and brought birds called Race Horses which our people purchased of them for trifles they are some what larger than a goose and very fishy I gave the Indians a few hatchets beads, knives and other trinkets –." PL and FC. Molineux indicates that they live on shell & other fish & shelter in wigwams or huts.

276 "PM the boats returned & the Master of the Dolphin informed that he had found three good anchoring places on the North shore about four miles to the Eastward of Cape Providence (about 4 m.ˢ to the E½S of Cape Providence – FC), another under the East side of Cape Tamar and a third about four miles to the Eastward of Cape Tamar – that he had found no place to anchor in under Cape Providence it being very rocky. Got some mussels & greens." PL and FC. In the Hawkesworth account, the entry for the 4ᵗʰ April is as follows: "This day two canoes came on board, with four men and three young children in each. The men were somewhat more decently dressed than those that we had seen before, but the children were stark naked. They were somewhat fairer than the men, who seemed to pay a very tender attention to them, especially in lifting them in and out of the canoes. To these young visitors I gave necklaces and bracelets, with which they seemed mightily pleased. It happened that while some of these people were on board, and the rest waiting in their canoes by the ship's side, the boat was sent on shore for wood and water. The Indians who were in the canoes, kept their eyes fixed upon the boat while she was manning, and the moment she put off from the ship, they called out with great vociferation to those that were on board, who seemed to be much alarmed, and hastily handing down the children, leaped into their canoes, without uttering a word. None of us could guess at the cause of this sudden emotion, but we saw the men in the canoes pull after the boat with all their might, hallooing and shouting with great appearance of perturbation and distress. The boat outrowed them, and when she came near the shore, the people on board discovered some women gathering muscles among the rocks. This at once explained the mystery; the poor Indians were afraid that the strangers, either by force or favour, should violate the prerogative of a husband, of which they seemed to be more jealous

		Squally at 2 PM let go the small bower anchor
		AM moderate driyed the sails –
	12:10	several Indians came onboard to whom I gave knives & hatchets beads &:.^{c my cook} ^{understood an} Old man that was amongst them he spoke the Malayan tongue this I did
	NW	not know till they left the ship sent after them & brought them onboard again but the old man was gone from them & we could never see him after[277]
	11:00	

than the natives of some other countries, who in their appearance are less savage and sordid. Our people, to make them easy, immediately lay upon their oars, and suffered the canoes to pass them. The Indians, however, still continued to call out to their women, till they took the alarm and ran out of sight, and as soon as they got to land, drew their canoes upon the beach, and followed them with the utmost expedition." This report is taken from Robertson (2nd April, pp. 92–93) but not all the details are noted, thus Robertson notes less meritorious conduct: "When the boats crew them making so noise and padling at so great a rate and hollowing, we supposed they lay on their oars untill they came near them, but one of our men observed a very great smock, which he supposed was the Indian wives dressing diner, this he toald the rest in the boat, and to get a little fun they puld at a great rate towards the smock, this made the pooor Indians almost distracted, they puld like mad men and roard out more lyke wild beasts nor any of the human race. When our boats got near where the smock was they saw two Indian women gathering mussels amongst the rocks, then they lay on their oars untill the Indians came up with them, then made signs they wanted wives, but the poor mad creatures padeld on and hallowed untill the two women went out of sight, they they shaked their padels at our boats and lookd very fierce, but our men laughd at them and rowed in towards the watering place, having alwys strick orders not to hurt any of the Indians."

[277] Carrington in a footnote indicates that Wallis does not mention this incident (p. 96) (and there is no mention of this encounter in the PL and FC) but of course Wallis does in the ML as shown here. The entries in the PL and FC are brief: "Squally rainy weather let go the small bower. AM moderate and fair dry'd sails, completed our wood & water & sent a man from each mess to gather mussels and to seek greens which are now very scarce but abundance of mussels and limpetts." Robertson (entry for the 6th April) describes the encounter at length (pp. 94–96).

Winds	Remarks Sunday April 5:th 1767 – (99)
10:55 NW 10:30	Little wind & hazey, latter fresh gales with much hail rain & snow. PM got off some wood & water[278]
	Remarks Monday April 6:th 1767 – (100)
12:10 variable West WNW NW 9:00	Moderate & fair middle & latter fresh gales & squally with much rain & hail
	Remarks Tuesday April 7 – 1767 – (101)
10:00 Varia NNW 8:15	All these 24 hours very hard gales with squalls & much rain hail & snow lightning in the SE – the whole of the country covered with snow & very cold
	Remarks Wednesday April 8 – 1767 – (102)
NW WSW SW S WSW WNW West	All these 24 hours very unsettled weather as lightning, calm, squalls, snow, hail, rain & little wind –[279] 8:55 7:00
	Remarks Thursday April 9:th – 1767 (103)
W Calm SSE South To WSW 6:00 6:50	First part moderate breezes, intermixed with squalls with rain hail & snow, the latter mod but variable having much hail & snow at 4 PM hove up the small bower, AM got up topmast and yards and completed our wood & water, sent the Master to try the current, to see how the wind was without[280]

278 "... many of the people taken ill with colds and fluxes the Doctor desired that no more mussels might be brought into the ship." PL and FC.

Robertson (Corrington, op. cit., pp. 94) describes another incident which is not mentioned in the *Dolphin* logs: "This day two canoes came off full of men and young children but non of the women except one young girl about twelve or thirteen years old, all came in but her and an old man who set closs by her in one of the canoes. The Capt. Gave all the young children some beeds and oyther toys, and the men got some hatchets old cloaths &c. – but hade nothing to give in return – I lookt several times over the side but never saw the young girls face, untill they were all in their canoes and pulling of to go onb^d the Swallow. The old fellow then allowed her to turn around and look to us but not before, the young creatur seemd mutch fairer and was decenter drest nor any of the rest. We all though it was a young girl and made signs that if she came back she should get some presents, but the old man made her turn round and padeld away to the Swallow which left us in dout about this young creature, not knowing for certain what sex she was of untill a gentleman from the Swallow informd us afterwards, that he seeing the young creature mutch fairer nor the rest, and not permited to come onb^d by the old man who still keept by her – he stept into the canoe and gave her some trinkets. After he saw it was a girl he tryd to get her onb^d but the old man would not permit her to go out of the canoe and set off for the shoar."

279 Robertson (Corrington, op. cit., pp. 96–97) notes the arrival of four Indians one of which "our people cloathd in sailors dress and a marine cape." Robertson describes how this Indian "did everything which this young man

Wind –	Remarks Friday April 10 1767 – (104)
7:90	PM squally with rain hail & snow lowered the lower yards AM moderate breezes with some squalls & hail. got up the lower yards, at 10 AM weigh'd in company with the Swallow & sailed out of Upright Bay at noon Cape Providence bore NNW distance 4 or 5 miles[281]
6:55	
	The Dolphin of Cape Pillar 11:th April 1767 Observed –
	The 11:th at noon observed lmatitude 52:* 38 S
	Cape Pillar correct ENE WSW, 6 leag: 0 7 S Dep:^{e} 16':6"
	The latitude if Cape Pillar 52: 45 s
M:^{r} Byron's	Cape Pillar – Lat:^{d} 52:54 S Long from London - 77:°00'W
	By another - 52:52, - 78:00 W
	Another - 52:53, - 76:00 W
Ap:^{l} 10 1767	Cape Pillar lat:^{d} 52:*8s. Long: 75:45 West Bellin

---

[Boatswain's mate – Richard Jones] did and I do believe he would have soon learnd the duty of a seaman. When the oyr three Indians went in to the canoe he run down below amongst our men, and seemd very unwilling to go ashoar. When the rest calld too him he took no notice of them untill they returnd onb^d and caried him off – very much against his will." The next day (April 9th), the Indian comes onboard and hides but is taken away by force, Robertson notes: "When this too was parted it ws hard to say which of them was most affected. Jones declared he would willingly spear him half his allowance for the voyage if he was permitted to go along with the ship."

280 The Master finds it very "unsettled". PL and FC.
281 None of the observations appears in the PL and in the FC.

Remarks Saturday April 11: 1767 (105)

1				
2				7:00
3			W½S	SBE
4				SBW
5	3	2		South
6	3			SE
7	3		West	
8	3	4		
9	3			SSE
10	3	2	W½N	ESE
11	3		WBN	
12	2	5	W½N	
1	2	3	West	
2	3	2	WBN	
3	2	4	WBN	5:55
4	2	2	WBN½N	
5	2	3		
6	2			
7	2		WBS	SSE
8	2			
9	2	3		
10	3	3		South
11	3	3	W½S	SSW
12	3	2	West	

Light airs

Cape Tamar^{At 4 o'clock} NWBW½N 3 leagues Dolphin Bay WBS½S 6 leagues. Cape Providence NNE½E 3 leagues Cape Upright ESE½S 2 leagues Cape Pillar West 10 leagues, Westminster Island WNW 8 leagues – Cape Tamar NW½N 3 leagues – Dis:^{c} from S:°shore – three miles at six o'clock

Light airs Swallow a stern Cape Pillar W½S, Westminster island NWBN –

Latitude observed at noon off Cape Pillar was 52:*8S.

Westminster Island NNE Cape Pillar WBS 3 miles, saw a large fire on the North shore

Cape Pillar SW half a mile, the Swallow about six miles a stern – Little wind was obliged to make all the sail I could to get without the Streights mouth as I found the current set the ship over to the North shore –[282]

At 10 would have shortened sail for the Swallow but was obliged to carry to weather the Islands of Direction & we could not fetch into the Streights again this was the opinion of myself & the officers.[283]

At noon the Swallow bore EBN. The Islands of Direction N21°00 W3 leagues, S:^{t} Pauls Cupula & Cape Victory in one North 7 leagues Westminsiter Island N67:°00E 10 leag. Cape Pillar East 6 leagues Cape Dessiada S65:00E dis:^{t} 11 or 12 leagues –

282 "... it is 2 year yesterday since the Dophin & Tamar pass'd Cape Pillar into the South Sea." Molineux.

283 " Light airs, at 4 sprung up a breeze Cape Tamar NWBW½W, 3 leagues, Dolphin Bay WBS½S 6 leagues, Cape Providence NNE½E 3 leagues, Cape Upright ESE½S 3 leagues and Cape Pillar West ten leagues, we steerd about W½N all night and ran by the log 38 miles to six o'clock in the morning, at which time Cape Pillar bore SW half a mile, the Swallow about three mile a stern of us, it falling little wind was obliged to make all the sail we could to get without the Streights mouth. At 11 would have shortned sail for the Swallow but could not and was obliged to carry to clear the isles of Direction the current setting us strong down upon them and the wind Westing we soon after lost sight of the Swallow and never saw or heard of her after, I would have gone back into the Streights but the weather coming on thick and dirty we were all of the opinion that we had nothing to do but but get an offin as soon as possible for the sea raising fast and the weather greasy that the ship could not weather Terra del Fuego on one tack nor the Land off Cape Victory on the other uless we pressed her with sail before the sea rose to a great height – At noon the Islands of Direction bore N.° 21:°00' West." PL and FC.

The Hawkesworth account concludes this day's entry with: "Thus we quitted a dreary and inhospitable region, where we were in almost perpetual danger of shipwreck for near four months, having entered the Streight on the 17th of December 1766, and quitted it on the 11th of April 1767; a region where, in the midst of summer, the weather was cold, gloomy, and tempestuous, where the prospects had more the appearance of a chaos than of Nature, and where, for the most part, the vallies were without herbage, and the hills without wood." Hawkesworth's publication then offers "A particular Account of the Places in which we anchored during our Passage through the Streight, and of the Shoals and Rocks that lie near them." Hawkesworth's

Remarks Sunday April 12: 1767 (1)[284]

H	K	F	Course	Wind	Remarks
1	5		WBN	SWBS	Moderate & cloudy lost sight of the Swallow & the wind coming on to the Westward was obliged to carry all the sail we could to get an offin is possible, stowed the boats & anchors & made the ship clear
2	5				
3	4	4	WNW½N	SWBS	
4	5		NWBN	7:30	
5	5				Cape Pillar bore EBS¼S 10 or 12 leagues the Islands of Direction NE 7 or 8 mile –
6	4		South		
7	6	4	W½N	SSW	at 4 it came on to be thick hazey weather
8	5	2			at 5 tack'd, the N:°most land bearing NNW½W 7 or 8 leagues
9	5		West		the N:°most Isle of direction ENE½E 7 or 8 miles –
10	5		W½N		at 6 o'clock hazey squally weather tack'd the wind shifting that we could make a good slant off the shore – carried all the sail the ship would bear which was trebble reeft topsails
11	6				
12	6		West		
1	5	3	W½N		
2	5	4		7:20	squally with rain –
3	6	4	WBN	SWBS	Latt:ᵈ of cape Pillar 52:°*8 South –
4	6	3			
5	4	5	W½N	SSW	variation suppose to be 22:00 Easterly
6	4	2			
7	5	5	WBN	SWBS	
8	5	4			
9	6		W½N		
10	6				
11	6				Fresh gales & thick squally weather
12	7				

Course	Dis:ᵉ	Latitude in	Long. made	M: Distance
N53:°10'W	142	51:°23'S	3: 3West	113W

Cape Pillar bore S53:°10'E Distance 47 leagues

---

source here is the PL at the end of which Robertson first lists thirteen pages of calculations related to the "Observations of the longitudes taken after Doctor Maskelines method onboard his Majestys Ship Dolphin on her voyage in the years 1766, 1767 & 1768. These pages are followed by descriptions of the places and ports visited, of the marks for anchoring, of the wooding and watering facilities, of the provisions available, of the fortifications and landing places and of the shipping. Robertson also includes tables of distances from point to point which Hawkesworth reproduces. This part of the journal written by Robertson is specific to the PL and does not appear in the earlier ML or in the later FC.

284 Here the PL and the FC take up the hourly format of the log as the *Dophin* sails into the Pacific Ocean.

Remarks Monday April 13: 1767 (2)

H	K	F	Course	Winds	Remarks
1	6	3	W½N	SSW	
2	6	4			Fresh gales & close clear weather
3	6	3			Unbent the cables, out 3:ᵈ reefs topsails
4	6			8:50	
5	6	2	West	SBW	saw several whales
6	7				
7	7				
8	7				Ditto weather
9	7				
10	7				
11	7				
12	7				Out 2:ᵈ reefs topsails –
1	5	5	W½N	SSW	
2	6	5			
3	6	5			Great numbers of gannets sheerwaters gulls pestadores[285] &
4	6	4			other sorts of birds about the ship
5	6	2	West		kill'd one that measured 7 feet 4 inches from the tip of one
6	7				wing to the the tip of the other –[286]
7	6				Fresh gales & close hazey weather –
8	6				Cape Pillar bore S54:°50'E Distance 97 leagues[287]
9	6				
10	5	4	WNW	SWBS	
11	5	3			
12	5	5			

Course	Dis:ᶜ	Latitude in	Long. made	M: Distance
N53:°30'W	153	49:°55'S	6: 21West	239W

---

285 Pintado Birds in the PL and FC.
286 Not noted in the PL and FC.
287 Robertson records in his journal (p.100) that "Our Capt. now intimate to the principle officers that the intention of our voyage was to make new descoverys, this was known to the most of us before, but he now repeated it in order to put us all on our gard, that we might always keep a strick look out both night and day, as we was now going intirely on a new track that no ship hade ever been in before, our books and charts of course could be no manner of service too us, therefore a good look out was the only thing we hade to depend on, with the assistance of the almight which is neaver wanting to those who sincearly applys for it. . . ."

Remarks Tuesday April 14: 1767 (3)

1	6	4	WNW	SWBS	Fresh gales & cloudy hazey weather
2	7	2			
3	7	5			
4	7	5		9:00	
5	7				
6	7	2			
7	7	3			
8	7	4			
9	6	3			
10	6	3			
11	6	5			
12	7	2			
1	7	4			
2	7	5			
3	8	2			
4	8				
5	8				
6	7	4			
7	7				
8	6			7:55	
9	6				Read the Articles of War & the Abstract of the Act of Parliament
10	7	3			
11	6	4			
12	6	3			
		172			Fresh gales and thick hazey weather

Course	Dis:ᵉ	Latitude in	Long. made	M: Distance
NW	170	47:°54'S	9:25West	360W

Cape Pillar bore S51:°50'E Distance 155 – leagues –

Remarks Wednesday April 15: 1767 – (4)

H	K	F	Course	Winds	Remarks
1	6			SBW	Fresh breezes & close hazey weather –
2	6				
3	6	4			
4	7	4	W½N	8:00	
5	5	3	West		
6	5	4			
7	5			SE	
8	5	4		ESE	
9	8				
10	6				
11	6	4			
12	7				
1	7				
2	6			EBS	
3	6			7:30	
4	5	5			
5	6				Got up top gall:¹ masts & yards –
6	5	3		East	Reeved a new tiller rope
7	6				variation by the mediums of four azumuths between 8 & 10
8	7	2	125		o'clock – 16:°40' Easterly
9	8		WBN		this is the first we have taken –
10	8				
11	8	4			Fresh gales & cloudy employed in working up junk into points
12	9				gaskets robins spun yarn &:ᶜᵉ
			158		Cape Pillar bore S54:°55'E Distance 205 leagues –²⁸⁸

Course	Dis:ᵉ	Latitude in	Long. made	M: Distance
WNW	158	46:°54'S	13:52West	506W

Cape Pillar bore S54:°55'E Distance 205 leagues –

---

288 The PL and the FC entries are more succint during this period: "Fresh gales & hazey weather. Got up top gallant masts and yards. Variation 16:°40' Easterly. Fresh gales. People employed in working up junk."

Remarks Thursday April 16: 1767 – (4)

1	9		WBN	NNE	Fresh gales & hazey –
2	9				In 2:^d reefs topsails – got down top gall:^t yards –
3	9	3			
4	9	4		9:30	
5	9	4			Hard gales with a great sea
6	9	2			
7	8				haul'd up the mainsail & handed the fore topsail –
8	9				
9	9				
10	7				
11	6	3			Lowerd down the Mizen yard –[289]
12	6	4			
1	7				
2	6	5		9:00	
3	6	4			
4	6	4			
5	6	3			Set the fore topsail with 4 reefs in it
6	7	4			
7	7	4			at 10 the ship laboured so much was obliged to haul her to the
8	7				W:°ward to make her go easyer –
9	8				
10	4 2		NWBW	NEBN	at noon strong gales with drizzling rain and a very heavy sea – [290]got down the togall:^t masts mz:ⁿ topmast & cross jackyard
11	6	4			& spritsail yard in –[291]
12	6	3			

Course	Dis:^e	Latitude in	Long. made	M: Distance
WNW	186	45:°40'S	17:03W	676W

Cape Pillar bore S57:°25'E Distance 205 leagues

---

289 "A very heavy sea & the ship labours much and makes a great deal of water." PL and FC.

290 ". . . ship strains much, the rain & sea find way thro' every seam, that there is not a dry place in her."

291 "Handed the main topsail." PL and FC.

Remarks Friday April 17: 1767 – (6)

Strong gales & rainy weather –

very hard gales with a great sea
brought the ship under the main & mizen staysail – reeft & furled the fore sail
ship works much and makes a great deal of water & the decks are so leaky that there is not a dry place in the ship –[292]

made sail under the foresail & main staysail

broke the main staysail & hallyards & reeved new ones –
Fresh gales & a very heavy sea –

1	4		NWBN	NE
2	4			
3	4			
4				11:00
5		up	NBW off	WNW
6				
7				
8				
9				
10				
11				
12		up	NNW off	WNW
1				
2				
3				
4				
5				
6				
7		up	NBW off	WNBW
8				
9	6			
10	6		WBN	NBE
11	5			
12	4			

Course	Dis:ᵉ	Latitude in	Long. made	M: Distance
W9:00N	50 –	45:°32'S	18:08W	725W

Cape Pillar bore S58:°39'E Distance 279 leagues

---

[292] "A very heavy sea, ship makes much water every way many things washed overboard by the frequent seas that broke over us." PL and FC.

Remarks Saturday April 18: 1767 – (7)

1	5	4	WBN	NNE
2	5	3		
3	4	4		
4	3	5		12/30
5	3	2		
6	3	5		
7	5	5		
8	4		WNW	
9	2	5	WBN	NBW
10	2	2	WSW	NW
11	1	3	NNW	West
12	1	4		
1				
2				Calm
3				12:00
4	3		SSW	West
5	2	4	NWBN	WBS
6				
7				Calm
8				
9	1		North	WNW
10	1		NNE	
11	1		NBE	
12	1	4	NNE½E	NW

Fresh gales with a very heavy sea & much rain set the m:ⁿ topsails

set the fore top:ˡˢ & let the reef out foresail

Light airs with a great swell got the mz:ⁿ topm:ᵗ & yard up – & out 2:ᵈ reefs tops:ˢ

Little wind & foggy

ships head NNE

Light airs & hazey foggy weather with a very great swell – got the spritsail yard across –
Light airs & hazey weather

Course	Dis:ᵉ	Latitude in	Long. made	M: Distance
NW	45	45:°00'S	19:03W	757W

Cape Pillar bore S 58:°28' E Distance 293 leagues

Remarks Sunday April 19: 1767 – (8)

			Head from	N:° to ENE	
1		} her			Light airs & hazey weather with drizly rain & a great swell from the NE
2					
3	1	3	ENE	North	Saw several gannets and sheerwaters with some small white gulls –
4	1			12:10	
5	1		NE	NNW	
6	1		NEBN		
7	1		NE		
8	1		NEBE	NBW	
9	4		WNW	North	
10	5	5			
11	6	2	West	NNW	
12	7				Fresh gales & rainy close reeft topsails
1	6	2	WBN	NBW	
2	5	4		11:20	
3	4	2	WNW	North	
4	4	2	West	NNW	
5	4		WSW		Split the jib – repaired it –
6	3	5	NNW½W	W½S	Moderate gales with a great sea out 2:ᵈ reefs
7	1	4	NNW	West	Handed f top:ˢ – set the f topsail
8	2				
9	5				
10	4				
11	3				moderate gales with a great NE swell
12	4		NBW		

Course	Dis	Latitude in	Long. made	M: Distance
NWBW	51	44:°32'S	20:02W	799W

Cape Pillar bore S57:°50'E Distance 310 leagues

EXPLORATION OF THE SOUTH SEAS

Remarks Monday April 20: 1767 – (9)

H	Knots	F	Winds	Course
1	4		NNW	WBS
2	4	5		
3	4	2		
4	4	3		
5	5	4	NWBN	WSW
6	6			11:20
7	7			
8	7			
9	5	5		
10	6			
11	5	5	NW	SWBW
12	5			
1	5			
2	6	2		10:45
3	5	4		
4	5	4	NWBW	SW
5	5	4		
6	4	5		
7	3	4	NWBW	
8	3	5		
9	3	2	NNW	West
10	3		North	WNW
11	3	3		
12	1	4	NBE	

Fresh gales & squally with a great swell – ship takes in so much water on deck which runs thro' that there is scarce a dry bed in the ship –[293]

fresh breezes & clear weather set the f. topsail

out 2:^{d} reefs of the topsails –

Light breezes & hazey[294]

Course	Dis	Latitude in	Long. made	M: Distance
NBW	119	42:°36'S	20:36W	823W

Cape Pillar bore S53:°30'E Distance 342 leagues –

---

293 "The people begin to fall down with colds." PL and FC.
294 "Several large birds about the ship some all brown and others white bodies & brown wings with black tips." Gore.

Remarks Tuesday April 21: 1767 – (10)

H	K	F	Courses	Winds	Remarks
1	1		NBW½W	West	
2	1		North	WNW	Light airs & cloudy with a great swell
3	1	4	NNE	NW	
4	2	3		12:00	Fresh gales close reeft the topsails
5	4		NEBE	NWSW	
6	2		WSW	NW	
7	3				
8	3	3	WBS	NWBN	
9	4		West	NNW	Rainy with a very great sea from the Southward –
10	4	5			
11	4				
12	4		W½N		
1	3	4	WBS	NWBN	Handed the topsail
2	2	4		12:35	
3	2	5	SWBW	NWBW	
4	2	4	SW	WNW	Moderate & cloudy reeft the F topsail out 2:ᵈ reefs
5	1		SWBW	SWBN	
6	1		SW	WNW	Cape Pillar – longᵈ – 79:24:00
7	2		SWBW	NWBW	Long. made from C. Pillar 20:36:00
8	2	4			Ship supposed in – 100:00:00:
9	3		SW		& long. observed – East – 4:14:00
10	3	3	NE	WNW	Long:ᵈ observed the ship in – 95:46:00 W²⁹⁵
11	4				Tuesday April 21: at 8 AM –
12	4				

Course	Dis:ᵗ	Latitude in	Long. made	M: Distance
North	12	42:*4S	20:36W	823W

Cape Pillar bore S53:00E Distance 346 leagues –

---

295 The result of the observation is given in the PL and the FC but not the calculations.

Remarks Wednesday April 22: 1767 – (11)

1	4	4	NBE	NWBW	Fresh gales & hazey with a SW swell
2	5		NNE	NW	
3	5				
4	5			14:00	
5	5		NBE	NWBW	variation – ^{azumeth} 11:06 – Easterly
6	4	5			
7	3	5			
8	3		N½E	WNW	
9	3		North		
10	3	2			
11	3	4	NNE	NW	Fresh gales
12	4	2	NBE	NWBW	On the 21:st Tuesday
1	3	3		13:00	At 8 in the morning had observation of the ☉ from the ☽
2	4		NBE½ E		(long supposed 100:°00' […])
				Time	H. M. S ☉. al:^{e} ☽. Alt:^{d} cor – χ dis ☉-☽
3	3		Add	Time	7.44.23 – 10 :°14' 10:18 – 45:41' 40"
4	3	5	The 21st	Apparent	6.10.00
5	4	4			2^H 24^M 23^S – M:^{m} time 21^{Day}. 2:^{H} 29:^{M} 00^S
6	4				
7	3	4	North	WNW	☽ Long: in eliptic – 5:00:14:59
8	3				☽ true long by observation 9:29:55:38
9	3		NNE	NW	Difference ship to the East – 9:11^{296}
10	4		NEBN	NWBN	
11	5		NE	NNW	Fresh gales & hazey with a great swell from the SWS
12	3		WBS	NWBN	

Course	Dis:^{t}	Latitude in	Long. made	M: Distance
N24:°18E	90	41:*02S	19:48W	788W

Cape Pillar bore S49:00E Distance 259 leagues –

---

296 None of these calculations appear in the PL and in the FC.

Remarks Thursday April 23: 1767 – (12)

1	5	5	West	NNW	Fresh gales & squally with a great sea brought too & set up the topm:ᵗ rigging
2		up	W½N	off WSW	
3	3		West		
4	3		W		made sail close reeft the topsails and handed the fore topsail
5	3		WBS		handed main topsail –
6					
7		up	NEBN	of East	at 5 a very heavy squall the fore top mast staysail split to pieces – unbent it –
8					
9					at 6 wore & brought too under the main & mizen sails, it blowing
10		up	North	of NE	
11					very hard and a heavy sea from the WSW –
12	1		North	WNW	made sail
1	2		NBE	NWBW	fresh gales with lightning in the SW and rain
2	2	5			
3	2	5		14:05	
4	3				
5	3				
6	4				fresh gales set the fore topsail –
7	4		NNE	NW	saw some Pintado birds sheerwaters & Gannets –²⁹⁷
8	4	4			
9	3		NBE	NWBW	
10	2	4			
11	3	3			
12	4				fresh gales & hazey with a great SW swell

Course	Dis:ᵗ	Latitude in	Long. made	MDistance
N28:°00E	30	40:*34S	19:32W	776W

Cape Pillar bore S47:°00'E Distance 361 leagues –

---

297 "Several birds about the ship two kinds one small spotted black and white, the other the bigness of a gull all black with white bills." Gore.

Remarks Friday April 24: 1767 (13)

1	3	4	NBE	NWBW
2	3			
3	1	4		
4	2			15:20
5	3	4		
6	3		NNE	NW
7	3	2	NNE½E	
8	2			
9	2	4	NEBN	NWBN
10	3			
11	3			
12	3			
1	3			15:10
2	2	4		
3	2			
4	1	4		
5	1		NNE	NW
6	1	2		
7	1	3	NEBN	
8	1	3	SWBW	NWBW
9	2		WSW	NW
10	1	4		
11	2	4	W½N	NBW
12	4		WBN	

Moderate & fairweather with a very great swell from the Westward

many of the people taken ill every day of violent colds owing to the quantity of water the ships & runs thro' the decks & upper works, that there is not a dry hammock in the ship –

Fresh breezes & hazey rainy weather with a very great SW swell –[298]

Course	Dis	Latitude in	Long. made	MDistance
NE½N	44	40:°00'S	18:55W	748W

Cape Pillar bore S45:°19'E Distance 365 leagues

---

[298] "Some small white birds about the ship such are seen in great numbers on the East side of the continent." Gore.

Remarks Saturday April 25 1767 (14)

H					Remarks
1	5		WNW	North	Fresh gales & rainy weather with a great sea
2	6				
3	3		NW	ENE	Close reeft the topsails
4	3		WNW	variable	
	4		West		
5	3		WBS	NWBN	
6	3	2	West	NNW	
7	5	5		15:40	fresh gales with a very heavy head sea
8	5	4			
9	4	3			
10	4	4			
11	4				handed the fore topsail –
12	5		WBN	NBW	
1	3	2			
2	3		WNW	15:25	
3	3				
4	2	5	NNW½W	North	Hard gales handed the main topsail
5	3	3			
6	3	4			set the main topsail
7	5	1	WBN		
8	5				
9	5	4	W½N		
10	5	3			hard gales with a great sea with rain & hazey weather –
11	5				
12	5		WBN		

Course	Dis	Latitude in	Long. made	MDistance
WBN	193	39:40S	21:07W	849W

Cape Pillar bore S47:°51'E Distance 392 leagues

Remarks Sunday April 26 1767 (15)

H	K	F	Courses	Winds	
1	4		WNW	NBE	Fresh gales & squally hazey weather with a very great Western swell
2	3	5			
3	3	3	WBN	North	
4	4		WBN½N		
5	4	3		16:00	
6	4	5			set the fore topsail –
7	4				
8	5	5			
9	6	2	WNW		fresh gales & squally with a great sea –
10	5	4			
11	5	2			
12	5				
1	4	6			
2	4		SWBW	variable	wore ship
3	2		NNE	WNW	
4	1	4	North	15:30	set the fore topsail & our 3:ᵈ reefs –
5	1		NBE		
6	1		North		Moderate & cloudy with a great swell
7	2		NBW		
8	3		North		
9	2	5	SBW		
10	3	4	NNW	West	
11	3	5	SWBS	WSW	Fresh breezes & hazey[299]
12	5				

Course	Dis	Latitude in	Long. made	MDistance
N55:°30'W	71	39:*00S	22:19W	907W

Cape Pillar bore S48:°12'E Distance 415 leagues

---

[299] "Some of the aforementioned & large birds about the ship some brown and others white bodies with brown wings." Gore.

Remarks Monday April 27: 1767 (16)

H	K	F	Courses	Winds		
1	6		NW	WSW		Fresh gales & fair weather
2	7					
3	7	5				variation p:ʳ az:ᵗʰ 11:°00'E
4	7			15:00		
5	7					2:ᵈ reefs topsails
6	6					
7	7		SWBW	SW		
8	6	3				
9	6	4				
10	6					
11	6					
12	6	3				
1	7					
2	6	4		14:00		
3	2	NW	WSW			
	3					
4	6					
5	6	2				
6	5	4				
7	5					variation p:ʳ az:ᵗʰ 8:°50'E —³⁰⁰
8	5	3				
9	5		NWBN			
10	4	2	NNW			
11	4	2				
12	4		North	WBN		moderate breezes & fair weather

Course	Disᵗ	Latitude in	Long. made	MDistance
N30:°30'W	145	36:54S	23:54W	982W –

Cape Pillar bore S46:°40'E Distance 459 leagues

300 "Moderate & fair, dryed all the peoples cloths & got all the sick upon deck – they have saloup – and wheat boiled with portable soup every morning for breakfast – and all the ships company as much vinegar and mustard as they can use: and portable soup boiled in their pease & oatmeal constantly." PL and FC. "The large white and brown birds about the ship." Gore.

Remarks Tuesday April 28: 1767 (17)

H	K	F	Course	Wind	Remarks
1	5		NBE½E	NWBW	Fresh gales & cloudy
2	6				In 2:ᵈ reefs topsails
3	6			15:00	
4	6				
5	6	2	NNE	NW	
6	5	2	NEBN	NWBN	Tack'd in 3:ᵈ reefs topsails –
7	6	4	NE	NNW	Fresh gales with a heavy head sea
8	1		West		
9	4	3	WBS	NWBN	Squally close reeft topsails
10	4	2	SWBW		
11	3	3	SW	WNW	Tack'd – the ship pitching very heavy –³⁰¹
12	3	4	SW½W		
1	3	4			Out 3 reefs topsails
2	4	4	NBW	WBN	
3	5			15:20	
4	4				
5	4				
6	4	2			
7	5	4	NBE	NWBW	
8	6				
9	5				
10	4				
11	4		NBE½E		Fresh gales close reeft topsails and handed the fore topsail –
12	5	4			Fresh gales with a heavy sea from the WSW –

Course	Disᵗ	Latitude in	Long. made	MDistance
N26:°00'W	72	35:50S	23:20W	951W –

Cape Pillar bore S44:°26'E Distance 476 leagues

---

301 ". . . the ship pitched so much was afraid of carrying the mast away." PL and FC. Roberston (p.105) notes the change in course to North ". . . being afraid to stand farther to the Westward the weather being so dark and thick, and the ship by account to the Westward of all knowen tracks. . . ."

Remarks Wednesday April 29 1767 (18)

H	K	F	Course	Wind	Remarks
1	5		NBE	NWBW	Fresh gales & hazey weather with a very heavy sea from the WSW –
2	4		NBW	West	
3	3	5			
4	4			17:05	
5	3	5	N½W	WBN	hard squalls with rain handed the main topsail –
6	5		North		
7	5		NBW		
8	5		NNW	West	hard gales & a great sea –
9	4	5			
10	4	4			
11	4	2	NNW½W		
12	4	2			
1	5		NNW		
2	5			16:05	
3	5	4			fresh gales & fair set M:ⁿ topsail
4	6		NWBN		
5	5	3			set the fore topsail
6	5	4			
7	6		NNW½W		out 3:ᵈ reefs of topsails –
8	6				
9	5				fresh gales & cloudy
10	3	2			
11	2				
12	3		North		Moderate & cloudy weather

Course	Disᵗ	Latitude in	Long. made	MDistance
North	117	33:53S	23:20W	951

Cape Pillar bore S41:°44'E Distance 507 leagues

Remarks Thursday April 30 1767 (18)

1	2	3	North	WNW	
2	2		NBE	NWBW	Light breezes & hazey with a SW swell –
3	1	4	NNE	NW	
4	3	5	West	NNW	fresh breezes with drizzling rain
5	3	5	WBE	NWBN	in 3:ᵈ reefs – people still very wet between decks & recover
6	5		WSW	17:30	slowly –
7	4		SWBW	NWBW	
8	4		NNW	West	
9	4	5			
10	4		NBW	WBN	
11	4				
12	3				
1	2	4			
2	2	4	N½W	17:20	
3	2	3	NBW		
4	2				
5	2	3			out 3:ᵈ reefs –
6	3				variation p:ʳ azum:ᵗʰ 8:°30' Easterly
7	3	5	N½E	WNW	lost a log & two lines overboard
8	4	4	NBE	NWBW	
9	5	3			
10	4	4			fresh gales & fair hazey weather very like a trade wind –
11	4				saw a turtle –
12	4	3			

Course	Dis:ᵗ	Latitude in	Long. made	MDistance
N7:°10'E	64	32:50S	23:11W	944W

Cape Pillar bore S40:°03'E Distance 523 leagues

H	K	F	Courses	Winds	Remarks Friday May 1: 1767 (20)
1	5	4	NBE½E	NW	
2	5	3			Fresh gales & hazey in the horison
3	6	2	NNE½E		Saw a turtle
4	6	4			
5	5	2		19:30	
6	4	3	NNE		close reeft the topsails, handed f. top:¹ & hall mizen –
7	4		NBE		furled the mainsail
8	3	4			
9	2	3	N½E	NNW	
10	2	4			
11	2	3	North		
12	2				
1	3	5	N½W		
2	4		WNW	SSW	very heavy squalls with rain, the wind shifted to the SSW –
3	4			18:50	
4					
5					set the topsails –
6			ships	head NW	
7					
8	1	5	WNW		calm³⁰²
9					
10			ship head	calm	hazey with drizzling rain and a great swell from the SW –
11			WSW		
12					calm with thick dirty weather & a SW swell –

Course	Dis.ᵗ	Latitude in	Long. made	MDistance
N29:00E	58	32:°38'S	22:°38'W	916W

Cape Pillar bore S38:°30'E Distance 531 leagues

---

[302] "People still fall down the ships always wet, as is all the ships companys bed –." PL and FC. Robertson (Corrington, op. cit., p. 106): "I am almost certain that we hade some land to the windward of us from noon to 8 P.M. by the smoothness of the water and the variableness of the wind [. . .] weather – I am pursuaded most seamen will be of my opinion."

Remarks Saturday May 2:nd 1767 (21)

H	K	F	Courses	Winds	Remarks
1					Calm & rainy weather with a great swell from the WSW –
2					
3					
4			ships	head to the NW	
5				18:00	
6					
7		4			
8		5			
9		2	NNW	WBS	Fresh gales & squally with rain close reeft the topsails & handed the fore topsail –
10	3				
11	2	5			
12	2	5			
1	2	5			
2	3				
3	4	3	NBW	West	
4	4	4			
5	4		NNW	WSW	
6	4	3			
7	4	4			Fresh gales & cloudy –
8	5				Set fore topsail & 4:th reefs topsails
9	5	5			Fresh gales & hazey, the main topsail being much worn – unbent it and bent another
10	5	3			sailmakers employed in repairing it –[303]
11	5	3			
12	5	3			

Course	Dis.^t	Latitude in	Long. made	MDistance
NBW	67	30:54S	22:°55'W	930W

Cape Pillar bore S37:°30'E Distance 552 leagues –

303 "People sickly still as so much water runs thro' the sides & decks –." PL and FC. In the FC there is an additional comment in freehand: "that there is not a dry birth or hammock."

Remarks Sunday May 3:rd 1767 (22)

H	K	F	Courses	Winds	Remarks
1	6	2	NBW	SW	Fresh breezes & cloudy with a great swell from the WSW —[304]
2	6	6			
3	5	4			
4	6			17:20	
5	5				
6	4	5			
7	3	4			
8	3	5		SSW	Moderate & hazey with a great swell –
9	3	5			
10	3	5			
11	3				
12	3	2			
1	2	4			
2	2	3		16:40	
3	3				
4	2	3			Light breezes with a great swell
5	2				got the top gallant masts up and the yards across –
6	2				
7	2	2			saw a pitterell –
8	2	4			saw a sea swallow – a bird about the size of a woodcock with
9	2				a forked tail colour of a gull
10	2	3			light breezes & fair weather
11	3		North	SE	saw four more of the above birds
12	3	5			

Course	Dis.t	Latitude in	Long. made	MDistance
N½W	90	29:*24S	23:°07'W	940W

Cape Pillar bore S36:°00'E Distance 581 leagues

---

[304] "Fresh gales & cloudy with a great Western sea kept the ship away to the N°ward as there is no chance of getting Westing where we now are and it is the Surgeons and all the officers opinion that we shall soon be very sickly unless we can get into with better weather that the people may recover themselves." PL and FC. There are few " anticipatory" remarks such as these (and those in Roberston's narrative) in the ML.

Remarks Monday May 4:th 1767 (23)

H	K	F	Courses	Winds
1	3	4	NNE	EBS
2	3			
3	3			
4	3	2		18:5
5	3			
6	3	2		
7	2	5		
8	2	3		ESE
9	2	4		
10	3	4		
11	3	5		
12	4			
1	3	4		
2	2	5		17:05
3	2			SE
4	1	4		
5	2			
6	2			
7	2	3		
8	2	3		SSE
9	2			
10	2	3		
11	2			
12	2			ESE

Little wind & fair –
At four this afternoon had an observation between the sun & moon – and on working it found the ship supposing her to be in longitude of from London   100:00:00
Error of reckoning – Easterly   3:33:33
Ship in the long: of   W 96:26:27

variation p:r az: – 5:44:E

variation p:r az: – 6:24: East[305]

Light breezes

Course	Dist	Latitude in	Long. made	MDistance
NNE½E	74	28:*20S	22:°28'W	906W

Cape Pillar bore S34:°25'E Distance 593 leagues

---

305 5°58' in both other logs. Robertson (Corrington, op. cit., p. 107): "As Capt. Wallis was positive to touch at this land if any such their be [Davis Land or Easter Island] – I think it will not be amiss to mention the course we steerd and the distance run every day we was in search for it with latt^{de} and long^{de} every noon . . ." (which he proceeds to do though Wallis is keeping such a record).

Remarks Tuesday May 5:th 1767 (24)

1	1		NNE	NW
2	1			
3	1	3		
4	1	2		19:00
5	2			
6	2			
7	2	4		
8	2	5		
9	3	4		
10	4			
11	4			
12	3	5		
1	3	2		
2	4			17:55
3	4	4	NNE½E	NWBN
4	4	3	NNE	NNW
5	4	5		
6	5		NEBN	
7	5	4		
8	5	5		
9	5	2	NE½E	
10	5	2		
11	5	2	NE	NNW
12	5	2		

At 4 had sevrall observation of dist:^{ce} between sun & moon and at that time supposed the ship to be in the longitude from London of –   96:00:00
Error of reckoning Westerly   21:00
Longitude ship is in West   96:21:00

variation p:^{r} az: – 6:°46':E

saw a Tropic bird –
variation p:^{r} amp:^{de} – 5:°42:E
saw some pilot fish near the rudder –[306]

moderate breezes & fair –

Course	Dis^t	Latitude in	Long. made	MDistance
N42:°10'E	85	27:*18S	21:°24'West	950W

Cape Pillar bore S32:°11'E Distance 604 leagues

---

[306] "... keep all the ailing men on deck picking oakham –." PL and FC.

Remarks Wednesday May 6 1767 (25)

1	2	3	NEBN	NWBN
2	6	2	WSW	NW
3	5			
4	4	5		19:00
5	4		WBS	
6	3		West	NNW
7	4		SWBW	
8	4		SW	
9	4	4	SWBW	NWBW
10	4			
11	4			
12	3	2		
1	3	5	SW	WNW
2	2			19:40
3	2	5	SWBS	West
4	4		WSW	NW
5	4	2	WSW½S	
6	4	5		
7	4	4	WSW	
8	4	4		
9	4	3		
10	3	4	WBS	
11	3	6	WBS½S	
12	4	4		

Moderate weather punished F. Pinkney for pissing on the sails and behaving with insolence afterward to the Boatswains Mate[307]

variation p:^{r} amplitude 8:°00'E

opened a cask of pork N:°1014 cont: 370 short six peices.

Squally with small rain in 2:^{d} reefs

Course	Dis^t	Latitude in	Long. made	MDistance
WSW½S	96	28:*50S	23:°00' West	934W

Cape Pillar bore S34:°42'E Distance 603 leagues

307 One dozen lashes (Gore).

Thursday May 7 1767 (26)

H	K	F	Course	Winds	Remarks
1	6	5	SW½W	NWBW	Fresh gales with a great swell from the SW – wore ship –
2	5		NBE	2	
3	5				
4	4	2	N½E	20:30	Saimakers employed in repairing the main topsail
5	4	3	NNE		
6	4	2			Squally weather
7	4	2	North	WNW	
8	4	2	NBW		
9	3	2	North		
10	3	5			
11	4	3			
12	5	5	NNE	NWBW	
1	4	3			Squally with small razin
2	4			20:00	In 3:ᵈ reefs –
3	3	5			
4	3	5			moderate & hazey thick weather
5	2	3	N½E	WNW	
6	3				
7	4		NBE½E		
8	5				
9	5	4			
10	6		N½E		
11	5		North		Moderate gales with a great SW swell fair weather
12	4	4	NNE		

Course	Dis:ᵗ	Latitude in	Long. made	MDistance
N27:°10'E	97	26:*34S	22:°13' West	890W

Cape Pillar bore S32:°32'E Distance 623 leagues

Remarks Friday May 8 1767 (27)

H	K	F	Courses	Winds	Remarks
1	4		NE	NNW	Fresh breezes & fair tack'd
2	4	2	SWBW	SWBW	
3	4	4			got up the small bower cables and cleaned under them[308]
4	4	2		21:00	moderate & hazey
5	6	2			
6	2	5			
7	2				
8	2				
9	2	3			
10	2	3			
11	3		WSW	NW	Fresh breezes & squally –
12	4	4			
1	4	5	WSW½W		
2	4	2	WSW	20:00	
3	3	5			fresh breezes & fair
4	4	3			out 2:^{d} reefs topsails
5	3	5	WBS	NWBN	variation p:^{r} amp:^{de} 7:11 East:^{y}
6	4				
7	4	5	WSW		
8	5				opened a cask of beef n:°1445. Contents 190 pieces – short
9	4				three pieces –[309]
10	3	2			moderate gales & hazey
11	4				
12	4				

Course	Dis^t	Latitude in	Long. made	MDistance
WSW¼S	85	27:*10S	23:40 West	966W –

Cape Pillar bore S 34: 43E Distance 624 leagues

---

308 "Likewais washed between decks with vinegar –." PL and FC.
309 This type of detail is often omitted in the two other logs which gives an uneven idea of the provisions remaining onboard in the FC.

Remarks Saturday May 9:ᵗʰ 1767 (28)

1	4		WSW	NW	Fresh breezes & fair
2	4	2			Employed³¹⁰ in working up junk –
3	3				saw severall sea swallows and some sheerwaters –
4	2	5	---	20:00	variation by medium azumeth and an amplitude – 7:00E
5	2	5			
6	2	5			
7	3	2	WBW		moderate and fair
8	3	2	WBS½S	WBN	
9	3	4			
10	3				
11	3	2			
12	3				
1	3	2	WSW	NNW	
2	2			19:45	
3	2			NNW	
4	3	5`	West		
5	3				
6	3	3			variation – 6-23 Easterly
7	4				
8	3	2	WBS	NWBN	Squally
9	2	4			
10	3				
11	3	4	West	NNW	Moderate & cloudy
12	4				

Course	Dis.ᵗ	Latitude in	Long. made	MDistance
S7:°00WW	76	27:*33S	25:02 West	1038W –

Cape Pillar bore S36:°36'E Distance 630 leagues

---

310 The PL and FC specify that the "ailing" people were here employed in the picking of oakham.

Remarks Sunday May 10:th 1767 (29)

1	4		West	NBW
2	2			
3	4			NNW
4	4	5		19:50
5	4	5		
6	5	5		
7	5	2		
8	4		WSW	NW
9	3		West	NBW
10	3			North
11	5	4		NBW
12	6			
1	5	3		
2	5			North
3	5			19:30
4	5	3		NBE
5	7			North
6	6	4		
7	5			
8	5	2	WBS	NWBN
9	7		West	
10	6			
11	5	2		
12	8			North

Moderate gales with a SW swell – set up the topmast & rigging

var:n p:r az: 7:07E

Squally with rain in 3:d reefs top:s
Saw severall porposies –

Fresh gales & cloudy

Fresh gales & squally rainy weather –
variation p:r amp:de – 6:09E
out third reefs –

fresh gales with a great sea & cloudy hazey weather –

Course	Dis:t	Latitude in	Long. made	MDistance
West	126	27:*33S	27:25 West	1164W –

Cape Pillar bore S39:°07'E Distance 651 leagues

Remarks Monday May 11:ᵗʰ 1767 (29)

1	8		West	NBW	
2	7				
3	6	3			
4	6	4		19:20	Fresh gales and cloudy weather –
5	6	5			Squally in 3:ᵈ reefs of topsails
6	5				
7	6				
8	5	3			saw a large flock of sheerwaters
9	5	4			
10	6	4		North	Fresh gales & cloudy with a great sea
11	6				
12	6				
1	6	4			
2	5	3		19:40	
3	5			NBW	
4	4	3			Out third reefs this morning began to take water out of the
5	4	4			hold all that was stored on deck being expended –
6	4	4			variation p:ʳ amp:ᵈᵉ
7	5	5			& azumeth 4 :00E
8	5	3			
9	5	4			Saw two Tropic birds
10	5	3			
11	6	3			Squally weather
12	5				Punished W Field for mutinous behavior to the Boatswain

Course	Dis:ᵗ	Latitude in	Long. made	MDistance
W¼N	140	27:*28S	30:05West	1303W –

Cape Pillar bore S41:°34'E Distance 680 leagues

Remarks Tuesday May 12 1767 (31)

					Remarks
1	5	4	NWBW	variable	Moderate gales
2	4	5	WBS	NWBN	squally with rain – & a great sea
3	3			20:10	shifted a futtock shroud
4	4		W½S	NNW	variation p:^{r} azum:th 6:00E
5	4		West		in 3 reefs –
6	4	3		variable	squally weather, saw a Petterell and some sea swallows &
7	4	4			sheerwaters –
8	4	3			squally & wind uncertain –
9	4		WSW	NW	
10	4		WBS	NWBN	
11	3	4			moderate out 3:^{d} reefs –
12	3	4	W½S		
1	4	4			moderate
2	5	3	SWBW½S	NW	
3	6	4	SWBW	20/5	
4	6	4			
5	7	2			squally tack'd –
6	2	3	SWBS	WBN	
7	2		NNW	West	lost a log and two lines –[311]
8	3		NBE		
9	3		NNE		
10	4		NBE		moderate breezes
11	4	4	NNE	NW	
12	4				

Course	Dis:^{t}	Latitude in	Long. made	MDistance
West	73	27:*30S	31:47 West	1376W

Cape Pillar bore S43:°40'E Distance 698 leagues

---

311 This is not mentioned in the two other logs.

Remarks Wednesday May 13 1767 (32)

H	K	F	Courses	Winds	
1	1	2	NNE		
2	1	3			
3	2	4			
4	3			20:00	
5	2				
6	1	3			
7		5			
8		4			
9					
10					
11			ships	Head	
12			to	NNE	
1				calm	
2			head SSW	19:55	
3	1		NEBN		
4	1	2			
5	2	4			
6	2	3			
7	3				
8	4				
9	4	3			
10	4	5	NEBN	NWBN	
11	5	3	NNE½E	NW	
12	5				

Course	Dis.ᵗ	Latitude in	Long. made	MDistance
NBE½E	64	26:*28S	31:31West	1362W –

Moderate & cloudy weather –
punished John Smith for throwing his shipmates dinners overboard –[312]

saw sixteen sea swallows and four Tropic birds near the ship –

variation p:ʳ az:ᵗʰ 6.29E
saw many porpoises about the ship –
squally with small rain

[313]Serve mustard & vinegar to the people every week & boil portable soup every day with the pease & oatmeal –

Light airs & variable –

Cape Pillar bore S42:°03'E Distance 710 leagues

312 "Punished John Smith for throwing his provisions overboard." PL and FC. Robertson (Corrington, op. cit., p. 109): ". . . for which rascally action he was tyed up and got a dozen lashes from each of his mess mates on the bare back, as he justly deserved they paid him well and keept without meat till nixt day at noon. . . ."
313 "The sick and ailing people kept on deck when the weather is fair – serve mustard & vinegar to all hands as oft as they want it & boil portable soup in the pease & oatmeal." PL and FC.

Remarks Thursday May 14 1767 – (33)

1	3	4	NNE	NW	Light airs and fair weather
2	3		NBE		
3	3		N½E		
4	3			20:20	
5	4		NBE	NWBW	
6	3	2			variation p:ʳ az:ᵗʰ & amp: 5:00E
7	3	5	N½E		
8	3	4	NBE	West	
9	2		NBW	WBN	
10	2				
11	2				Light airs
12	2	2			
1	3		North	NWBW	
2	3	2	NBE	NWBW	
3	3			19:55	
4	3				
5	3	4			saw a dolphin[314]
6	2	5			
7	2		WBS		
8	3	4	North		variation p:ʳ az:ᵗʰ – 2:00E
9	2	5	NBE		
10	1		NE		
11	1	2	NEBE	variable	moderate breezes & fair –[315]
12	1				

Course	Disᵗ	Latitude in	Long. made	MDistance
N32:°00'E	47	25:48S	31:°02'W	1337W

Cape Pillar bore S41:°01'E Distance 716 leagues

---

314 "Saw some fish call'd dolphins." Gore.
315 "... we now gave over all hopes of seeing Davis Land and concluded that there was no such place." Robertson, p. 109.

Remarks Friday May 15 1767 (34)

H	K	F	Course		Remarks
1	5	4	NE½N		Fresh breezes & clear –
2	6		NNE		
3	6				
4	3	3	ENE	20:30	Saw something like land to the ENE – bore away for it, saw a
5	6	2			flock of brownish birds it having still the appearance of land
6	4	2			continued to standing toward it –[316]
7	5	5			
8	5				
9	4				
10	4	4			
11	5	2			
12	6	3		NBW	
1	6			19:55	
2	6			NW	having run 18 leagues and seen nothing – haul'd the wind
3	4		NE½N		
4	4	2			
5	4		NNE½E		
6	3	5	NNE		
7	3				fine clear weather –
8	3		NBE		variation 3:51 E
9	1	4			employed in repairing all the boats –
10	1	4			
11	1	4			
12	2		NBE½E		

Course	Dis.ᵗ	Latitude in	Long. made	MDistance
N52:°50'E	96	24:50S	29:15W	1258W

Cape Pillar bore S38:°30'E Distance 715 leagues

---

316 "Fresh breezes and clear weather. Saw a very large flock of brownish birds flying to the E:ᵗward. At four saw something to the E:ᵗward that looked like high land bore away for it. At sun set it still having the same appearance, kept in the same course – at two in the morning having run 18 leagues & can see nothing hauled the wind – at daylight fine clear weather, could not see any land. Set the carpenters at work to repair the boats; the sailmakers the sails. Variation p azimuth 3:°51'E. The ailing people mend apace." PL and FC. Hawkesworth's version indicates that they were all this time "looking out for the Swallow."

Remarks Saturday May 16 1767 (35)

1	3	3	NNE	NW
2	3	4	NBE	NWBW
3	3	3		
4	3	2		20:50
5	2	5	NNE½E	
6	3			
7	3	3	NBE	
8	3	4	N½E	
9	2	3	NNW	West
10	2		NW	
11	1	2	NBE	NWBW
12	1	3		
1	1	4	NNE½E	
2	2	2		
3	2	4		19:55
4	2	4	NE	
5	2	5		
6	2	5		
7	3		NBE	
8	3			
9	3	4	NNE	
10	3		NBE	
11	3	4		
12	3	3		

Moderate & fair – the people recover apace having very few but what do duty –

variation p:^{r} az: –   3:55E
    amp:^{de} –   4.04 – E

Light airs & clear weather

Sailmakers in repairing several sails eaten by the rats –[317]

Saw a Man of War bird[318]

Light airs with a great swell

Course	Dis^t	Latitude in	Long. made	MDistance
N23:°0'E	63	23:56S	28:52W	1237W

Cape Pillar bore S27:°23'E Distance 723 leagues

---

[317] "Got up all the sails and aired them, found them very much eaten by the rats. Carpenters employed in repairing the boats and stopping rat holes with the portable soup cannisters." PL and FC.

[318] Gore seems unfamiliar with maritime fauna (see note on the dolphin): "Saw a bird called a Man of War."

Sunday May 17 1767 (36)

H	K	F	Courses	Winds	Remarks
1	4		North	WNW	Light airs and clear weather
2	3	4			
3	4	4	NBW		
4	5	3	NNW	West	variation p:ʳ az: – } 6:10E
5	5	4		19:40	amp:ᵈᵉ –
6	5	5			
7	5	2			
8	5	5	NWBW		Light breezes & fine clear weather
9	5	2	NW½W		
10	4	4	WNW	SW	
11	4		WNW½N	SWBW	
12	4				
1	4		NWBW		
2	4	4	NW½W	19:55	
3	5				
4	6		NWBW		
5	7		WBN	SSW	variation by four az – 3:°12'E
6	6	5			
7	6	4			
8	7				still employed about the boats and sails –
9	4	5		SSE	Light airs & clear
10	2	5			
11	2	5			
12	3			SE	
Course	Disᵗ		Latitude in	Long. made	MDistance
NW	108		22:40S	30:15W	1313W

Cape Pillar bore S37:°44'E Distance 762 leagues

319 "Most of the sick people recovered." PL and FC.

Remarks Monday 18:th 1767 (37)

H	K	F	Courses	Winds	Remarks
1	2	5	WBN	SBW	Light breezes & clear weather
2	2	3			
3	4	3			
4	5	4		20:30	fine breezes & clear pleasant weather –
5	6	4			
6	7				
7	7	2			
8	6	2			
9	4	4			
10	5	4			
11	7				
12	6			South	small showers
1	6	4			
2	6	5			clear
3	7			20:20	
4	7			SSE	
5	6	4			
6	5				
7	6				
8	5	5		SE	variation amp:de 4:00
9	5				
10	4	5			exercised small arms
11	4	4			people picking oakham
12	5 3	3			carpenters caulking upper works & forward

Course	Dis:t	Latitude in	Long. made	MDistance
W20:°00'N	136	21:52S	32:15W	1313W

212

Tuesday May 19 1767 (38)

1	6		WBN	South	Moderate breezes & carpenters employed in overhauling and repairing the boats –
2	5				exercised the people at great guns and small arms –
3	5				
4	4			20:30	
5	5	5		SE	
6	5	3			
7	5	5			moderate breezes & clear weather
8	5				
9	4	5			
10	4	4			
11	4	3			
12	4	4			
1	5				
2	5				painted the boats –
3	5			19:55	killed a sheep and gave it to the sick and recovering people –
4	5				
5	5				
6	4	4			
7	4				
8	4				
9	5				
10	4				moderate breezes & fair weather
11	4				
12	4			SSE	

Course	Dis⁻	Latitude in	Long. made	MDistance
WBN½N	116	21:*18S	34:31W	1540W

Cape Pillar bore S40:20E Distance 827 leagues

Wednesday May 20 1767 (39)

1	4		WBN	SSE
2	4	4		
3	6	3		
4	4	2		South
5	5			20:50
6	4			
7	4			
8	3			
9	3			
10	3	2		
11	3			
12	3	2		SE
1	3			
2	3	3		
3	3			20:10
4	2	4		SSW
5	2	4		
6	2	3		
7	2		WNW	
8	2			
9	2	3		
10				
11				Calm
12				

Light breezes & fair
Employed in repairing the boats
Sailmakers overhauling and repairing sails —[320]

Longitude supposed to be in – 110-00W

☉ al:	☽ al:	∞ dis:^{t} of ☉ & ☽	Declination
28:38	47:22	93:21:00	20:2N
Hour 20^H: min 54: second – 18 –			

variation p:^{r} amp: – 4:°32'E

Took severall observations of the Dis:^{ce} between the sun & moon –
and found
the long dis eclipitical
reckoning – supposing the ship   10^s:2 26°; 1':10"
in long 100:00 from London West
found the long in ecliptic by the   10:25:54:0
observation being observed –
                                      0.0:7:10E
which makes 3:°13':0" E –   3:13:0
from long:^{d} supposed –   110:00:0
remains long ship is in –   106:47 W[321]

Course	Dis	Latitude in	Long. made	MDistance
WNW	69	20:*52S	35:39W	1603W

Cape Pillar bore S41:00E Distance 847 leagues

---

320 "Saw some Tropic birds. At noon the Isle of Disappointment N78° 32'W 612 leagues." Gore.
321 None of the calculations appear in the two other logs.

Remarks Thursday May 21 1767 (40)

1		Calm	ships	Calm weather & fair set up all the topmasts & lower rigging worked two more observations of distance between the ☽ & ☉ & found the ship by each to be nearly in the long:de of 107:°00'W from London –
2		head	to the	
3		North	ward	
4			20:50	
5				
6	2	WNW	SW	
7	2			light breezes with drizzling rain
8	1 5	NNW	West	
9	1	NWBN	WBS	
10	3	WBN	SWBS	
11	3			light breezes & cloudy
12	3 4		SBE	
1	3			
2	3 2			
3	3 3		20:25	
4	3 4			
5	5 1			Found the fore topmast cross trees & trassle trees broke – struck the mast & got up new ones.
6	6		South	
7	5 5			saw a flying fish these being the first we have seen since we have been in the South seas –
8	5 5			
9	5			
10	5			
11	5			
12	5			

Course	Dis⁻	Latitude in	Long. made	MDis:ce
NWBW	65	20:*18S	36: 39W –	1657W

Cape Pillar bore S41:°21'E Distance 866 leagues

Friday May 22 1767 (41)

1	6		W½S	SE	Fresh breezes & fine clear pleasant weather –
2	6				Severall tropic birds about the ship
3	5	5		21:00	
4	5	5			variation p:r azumeth – 5:°20'
5	5	5			
6	5	5			
7	5	5			
8	6				
9	5	4			
10	5	2			
11	6				
12	5	2			
1	5				Long:d supposed from London – 110:°00'W
2	5	2		20:25	At 9 in the morning took two observations of the distance of
3	5				the sun from the moon
4	4	5			
5	5	3			
6	5	2			
7	4	5			
8	5				Saw some bonettos and Dolphins
9	4	3			
10	4	2			
11	4				
12	3	4		East	

	☉ al:	☽ al:	x dis:t of ☉ & ☽	Declinat
	38:°17'	51:01	66:6:12	20:6: N

Hour 21: min 50: sec:d 49

☽ long. Eclipticly work –   11:24:57:20
☽ long. by observed […]   11:24:59:40
To sup long: add – 1:°3':4'W   West 2:20
Longitude in from London at 10 o'clock 111:03:00 West[322]

Course	Dis	Latitude in	Long. made	MDis:ce
West	125	20:*18S	38:°52'W –	1782W

Cape Pillar bore S43:°00'E Distance 890 leagues

---

[322] The PL and FC often recapitulate the results of these observations and calculations in a summary entry, here for example: "At 9 AM observed for the longitude found the true longitude that the ship was in to the 111:00 W of London at ten AM."

Saturday May 23 1767 (42)

H	K	F	Course	Winds
1	4		W½S	EBS
2	3	5		
3	4			
4	4	2		21:00
5	4			
6	4	5		
7	4	5		
8	4	5		
9	4	5		
10	5			
11	5			
12	4	5		East
1	5			
2	5	3		20:30
3	4	4		
4	4	4		SE
5	4	4		
6	5	2		East
7	3	1		
8	4			
9	4			
10	6			
11	6	5		
12	6	4		NE

Course	Dis	Latitude in	Long. made	MDis:ᶜᵉ
West	114	20:*18S	40:°54'W –	1896W

Light breezes & clear pleasant weather
got up the cables on deck and cleaned under them
saw severall Tropic birds and some flying fish –

Longitude supposed from London 114:°00'W
Observed distance between ☉ & ☽

☉ al:	☽ al:	Dis of ☉ & ☽	Declinat
26:43	61:8:30	53:1:44	20:34 N

Twenty Hour : forty three mins: twenty seconds
execrcised small arms –
☽ in exclipticly work –   8:42:21
☽ in eclipticly by observed – --- 8:38:10
Subtract from supposed long   4:11 E

Moderate breezes fine pleasant weather
Longitude in at 8 – 112:°6': 30 W[323]

Cape Pillar bore S43:°45'E Distance 896 leagues

323 See previous note.

Remarks Sunday May 24 1767 (43)

1	6		W½S	NE
2	4	5		
3	3	5		23:30
4	3			
5	3	4		
6	5			
7	4	6		
8	4	2		
9	3	4		
10	4			
11	3	4		
12	3			NNE
1	2	4		
2	3			
3	5			21:15
4	5			ˎENE
5	4			
6	3	5		
7	3	4		
8	3	3		
9	3	5		
10	4			
11	3			
12	2		WBN	SWBS

Moderate breezes & fair clear weather

variation p:ʳ amplitude 5:°1'E

light breezes & cloudy

got up a cask of pickled cabbage and gave the surgeons to distribute amongst the sick & recovering people as such times as he shall think of necessary —³²⁴

Light breezes & close weather with drizzling rain

Course	Dis:ᵗ	Latitude in	Long. made	MDis:ᶜᵉ
West	92 –	20:*18S	42: 32' W –	1988W

Cape Pillar bore S45:°35'E Distance 929 leagues

---

324 "Severall of the people who have been lately recovered from sickness are falling down in the scurvy, got up a cask of pickled cabbage and served half a pint a man every day whilst it lasted the Surgeon makes wort of malt for all those in scorbutic complaints." PL and FC. "At noon, the Isle of Dispapointment N 76° W 514 leag:ˢ" Gore.

Monday May 25 1767 (44)

H	K	F	Courses	Winds	Remarks
1	1		W½S	variable	
2	1		SWBS		Light airs & cloudy weather
3	1		W½S		Got up the forge & set the armourer to work in repairing the
4	2			East	ironwork which was broke in many places –
5	3	1		20:30	variation p:^{r} amplitude – 4:°18'E
6	3	3			
7	2	5			
8	2	3		EBE	
9	2				
10	1	4			
11	1	4			
12	1	3		EBN	
1	1				Light airs –
2	1				
3	1			20:40	
4	1			SE	
5	1				
6	1				
7	1	3		South	Employed in repairing & painting the boats –
8	2				Light airs & clear weather
9	2				variation p:^{r} amplitude – 4:°38'E
10	3				
11	3	5			
12	3	2		SSE	Light breezes & fair weather[325]

Course	Dis:^{t}	Latitude in	Long. made	MDis:^{ce}
WBS	46	20:*25S	43:20W	2033W

Cape Pillar bore S46:°13'E Distance 937 leagues

---

[325] "Surgeon desired wine to be served the sick." PL and FC.

Tuesday May 26 1767 (45)

1	4		W½S	SE
2	3	5		
3	4			22:00
4	1	2		
5	5			
6	6			
7	6			
8	5			SSE
9	5			
10	4	4		
11	4	2		
12	4	4		
1	4	5		
2	5			
3	5			26:10
4	5			SE
5	5			
6	5			ESE
7	5	3		
8	5	4		
9	6			
10	5	3		
11	5			
12	5	4		ESE

Light breezes & pleasant weather

sailmakers repairing the sails

variation p:^{r} amp:^{de} 4:°20'E

saw two grampusses

Course	Dis:^{t}	Latitude in	Long. made	MDis:^{ce}
West	118	20:*26S	45:26W	2151W

Cape Pillar bore S47:°36'E Distance 962 leagues

Wednesday May 27 1767 – (46)

H	K	F	Courses	Winds	Remarks
1	6	3	W½S	ENE	Fresh breezes & cloudy in the horison –[326]
2	7				employed in working up junk
3	7			22:00	sail makers repairing sails & armourer the ironwork –
4	5	5		NNE	
5	5	3			
6	5				
7	5	2			
8	5	1		ENE	
9	6				
10	5				
11	5				
12	5			SE	
1	5	4			Cloudy with lightning in the SE
2	6	4			
3	6			21:05	squally with rain
4	5			EBS	little wind & fair
5	4				
6	2	3			
7	2	4			
8	3	4			
9	7				fresh breezes & squally cloudy weather
10	5	4			
11	4				
12	6				fresh breezes & cloudy

Course	Dis.t	Latitude in	Long. made	MDis:ce
W¼S	127	20:*32S	47:42W	2278W

Cape Pillar bore S49:°13'E Distance 987 leagues

---

326 "Saw a grampus." FC.

Thursday May 28 1767 – (47)

H	K	F	Course	Winds	Remarks
1	4		W½S	ENE	Moderate breezes with a large SW swell –
2	5				
3	5			22:00	saw a large grampuss –
4	4	5			variation p:^{r} azu:th & amp:^{de} 5:20E
5	5	3			4:54
6	5	5			
7	5	2			
8	4	4			
9	5				
10	5	3			
11	5	3			
12	5	4		NEBE	Moderate & cloudy
1	5	5			
2	5	3		21:18	
3	5				
4	5			NNE	Moderate & fair
5	4	4			
6	4	4			variation 4:00E
7	4	4			saw an alcatross, severall Tropic birds, & flying fish –^{327}
8	4	4			
9	5	4			Exercised small arms
10	5	5			
11	5	3			fine breeze & pleasant weather
12	5	4		NE	

Course	Dis^t	Latitude in	Long. made	MDis:^{ce}
W½S	123	20:*43S	49:54W	2401W

Cape Pillar bore S50:°27'E Distance 1008 leagues

327 "Saw some Tropick birds, many flying fish and a large bird with black eyes and the tips of the wings black, the rest white." Gore. Robertson (Corrington, op. cit., p. 112) describes the state of the provisions and the men's health at this point: ". . . our seamen was now falling doun in the scurvey fast, the Capt and us spears as mutch of our fresh stock as posable to the sick, but it now begins to run short, our hay which we made in the Streights of Magellan for our sheep in now near done and we can afoard but vey few peas to keep them upp – as for the poor hogs there is so little given to them they could not walk on the deck without falling since the people has been at 2/3 allowance they have left no bargo nor peas for the poor pigs [. . .] the greatest blessing we enjoyed all this time was fine weather and plenty of water. . . ."

Friday May 29 1767 – (48)

1	5		W½S	NEBE
2	5	3		
3	5			21 :55
4	5	2		
5	6	4		
6	7			
7	5	4		
8	6			
9	6			
10	6			
11	5	2		
12	5	2		NE
1	6			
2	6			NNE
3	1	4		variable
4	2			21:55
5	3			
6	3	4		
7	3	3		
8	2			
9	2			
10	2	3		NE
11	2	2		
12	2	3		

Moderate breezes & fine pleasant weather –
Exercised the small arms –
Saw several birds, and one small one about the bigness of a swallow[328]
cleard the aft hold to get at some provisions –[329]

Fixed new bowling bridles to mtop:ˡˢ

variation – 4:40E

Light breezes employed on knotting yarns, & working up junk for severall uses[330]

Course	Disᵗ	Latitude in	Long. made	MDis:ᶜᵉ
West	105 –	20:*46S	51:47W	2506

Cape Pillar bore S50:°29'E Distance 129[331] leagues

---

328 "Cannot say if it is a land or a sea bird." PL. Gore identifies these birds as Mother Carys "black ones, birds seen all over the world."
329 This remark and the next in the ML are omitted in the two other logs.
330 Robertson points out on this day that all the boats (barge, launch, cutter, jolly boat) had been prepared for potential landing and that the boat crews had been adequately trained in handling various arms (p. 113).
331 Error in the ML (1029 in the PL and FC).

Remarks Saturday May 30 1767 – (49)

1	2	4	West	variable
2	2	3		
3	2			
4	2			22:30
5	2			EBN
6	2			
7	2			
8	1	2		variable
9	1			
10	2	2		South
11	2			
12	2	2		
1	1			22:00
2	2			SSE
3	2	3		
4	2	3		
5	2	2		
6	2			variable
7	2	2		
8	2	3		
9	2	2		
10	2			
11	3			
12	3			East

Light airs & cloudy

saw a bird about the size of a gull with a forked tail – white belly & breast – black back & wings –[332]

Light airs

Light airs

variation p:ʳ az:– 4:°20'E

served pickled cabbage –

Light breezes & clear weather

Course	Dis:ᵗ	Latitude in	Long. made	MDis:ᶜᵉ
West	51 –	20:*44S	52:42W	2107

Cape Pillar bore S52:°37'E Distance 1041 leagues

---

332 "Sasw a Man of War bird." PL and FC.

Sunday May 31 1767 – (50)

1	2		West	ESE	Light airs –
2	2				Opened a cask of pork N1409 Contents 310 – one peice over –
3	2			22:00	saw two grampusses
4	2	2		SE	
5	2	2			variation p:^{r} amp:^{de} – 56:°00'E
6	2	2			
7	2				saw a very large dolphin
8	2	4			
9	3				NB the people are served vinegar and mustard as often as they
10	3				have occasion for it, portable soup is boiled every day there is
11	3	2			pease or oatmeal – Saloup is given to such men as are sick and
12	3	2		ESE	weak and cabbage served every meat day to each mess a
1	3				proper portion –^{333}
2	3				
3	3	2		20:25	
4	3	2			
5	3	4			
6	3	4			saw a Man of War bird this bird is black all over except the
7	3	4			belly & that is white, its tail is seperated in the middle which
8	4				looks as tho' half of the feathers of the tail were plucked out
9	4	2			of the middle and those on each side left. this bird soars much
10	4	2			like a kite or hawk^{334}
11	4	2			saw dolphins & flying fish –
12	5			variable	Taken aback –
Course	Dis^t		Latitude in	Long. made	MDis:^{ce}
W¼N	76 –		20:*38S	54:03W	2183W

Cape Pillar bore S53:°51'E Distance 1160 leagues

---

333 "The people begin to look very pale & meagre, and fall down fast in the scurvy. They have vinegar & mustard whenever they want it, the ailing men have wine instead of spirits have likewais wort and saloup – Portable soup boiled constantly in the pease and oatmeal – their birth and cloths kept very clean and all that come on deck are kept up in the air; the hamacoes are constanly brought up at 8 in the morning and down at 4 in the afternoon and some beds aired & hammock washed every day. The water made quite wholesome by ventilating it and the between decks washed with vinegar as aften as the Surgeon requires it." PL and FC.

334 This description does not appear in the two other logs.

Monday June 1:st 1767 – (51)

1	5		West	North	
2	4	6		North	
3	5				
4	6		W½S	NNW	
5	6	5		22:30	
6	7	6			
7	7	6	WBS		
8	7	6	W½S		
9	7	2	West		
10	7	4			
11	7				
12	5	2	WBS		
1	3			21:20	
2		up	NBE off	NEBE	
3					
4	2		WBS½S	NWBN	
5	2				
6	2				
7	3	2	WBS		
8	4	2			
9	4	4			
10	4		SW	WNW	
11	1	4			
12	2	4	SW½S		

Course	Dis	Latitude in	Long. made	MDis:ce
WBS	107 –	21:*00S	55:57W	2289 W

Cape Pillar bore S 53:°51' E Distance 1878 leagues

Moderate & cloudy
Observed for longitude & found the Ship to be in
– 127:°45:09' W

a swell from the SSW
variation p:r az –   5:09E
            amp –   5:00E
got down top gallant yards
fresh gales with lightning in the SW
in 1:st & 2:nd reefs
at midnight, squally with heavy rain & lightning wind all
round the compass & blowing hard, cleard all the sails up &
close reeft tops:s
Employed in catching rainwater[335]
at 3 made sail out 3:rd reefs –
moderate gales & cloudy –
variation amp:de – 5:45
             azmth – 5:42E   }

very squally rainy weather
in 3:rd reefs –
Fresh gales & squally with a NW swell the ship makes a great
deal of water owing to her upper works being very open I
believe…

---

335 "... it raining very heavy, every man of the watch employed catching water, at 3 it cleared away we saved better than two tuns." PL and FC. Robertson (Corrington, op. cit., p.114): "... we now began ro reflect serious for the want of our poor, dull consort the Swallow, hade she been in com- panywe could have run without feat by making her go a head, and if she did not meet with danger or run ashoar our boats with her own could easily saved the men, and the loss of such a ship would be be but of very little consequence when compared to mens lives - another thing our ship was sufficient to care [for] her ships company and our own without distressing us a great deal – but in our present situation, the loss of our ship, is the loss of our lives to our King and country – besides the loss of any discovery that we may make."

Remarks Tuesday June 2 1767 – (52)

H	K	F	Courses	Winds
1	4		N½W	WBN
2	4			WNW
3	5	6	North	21:20
4	5	1		
5	6		N½E	
6	5		North	
7	2	2	NBW½W	West
8	3	2		
9	3	3		
10	3	4	NNW	WSW
11	3	2	NWBN	
12	4		NW	
1	3	5		
2	3	2	NWBW	SWBW
3	3	4	WNW	SW
4	3	4		2:05
5	2	5	WBN	SWBS
6	3			
7	3	2	WNW½W	
8	4		NW	
9	4	5	NWBW	
10	4	4	WNW	
11	4	2		
12	4			

Fresh gales & very squally weather
served mustard & vinegar –
Observed the longitude – 129:°15:'11"W
Squally weather furld the mainsail & close reeft the topsails
observed for longitude and found the ship in long:$^{d-}$ 1

squally with showers
got down to gall:^{t} yards –

dry squally weather with much lightning in the SSE –

saw some Men of War birds
Fresh gales & cloudy – with a SW swell –

Course	Dis	Latitude in	Long. made	M: Distance
NBW½W	90	19:*34S	56:24W	2315W

Cape Pillar bore S53:°53'E Dis:^{c} 1106 leagues

Wednesday June 3 1767 – (53)

H	K	F	Courses	Winds
1	4	3	WBN½N	SWBS
2	4	2	WBN	
3	4			
4	4	3		22:00
5	5	4	W½N	SSW
6	5	2		
7	4	3		
8	4	2		
9	4	2	West	
10	4	4	WBN	
11	4	2	West	
12	5		W½S	SBW
1	5			
2	5			21:55
3	4	2		
4	4			
5	4	4		
6	5	4		
7	5	5		
8	5			
9	5	4		
10	5	2		
11	5	4		
12	5			

Fresh gales & squally with a SW swell –

Observed longitude in 129:°49:12"W
got top gallant yards across –
People begin to fall down of the scurvy fast they look sallow & unhealthy –[336]

Fresh breezes & clear but cloudy in the horizon –

variation – am 5:45E
az – 5:42

Moderate & fair weather, with a Western swell –[337]

Course	Dis:ᵉ	Latitude in	Long. made	M: Distance
WBN –	112 –	19:*12S	58:21W	2432W

Cape Pillar bore S53:°43'E Distance 1136 leagues

[336] "People fall daily down in the scurvy & look very unhealthy, yet have very good spirits in hope of getting sight of some place to refresh in –." PL and FC.
[337] "Saw a Man of War bird." Gore.

Thursday June 4. 1767 (54)

H	K	F	Wind	Course	Remarks
1	4		W½S	SBW	Moderate breezes interrupted with squalls –
2	4	3			
3	4			22:55	Saw three Gannets –[338]
4	4	2		variable	Light airs variation amp – 5:°04E
5	2				
6	2	4		SBW	Light breezes & cloudy with drizzling rain –
7	2				
8	4			South	Cloudy
9	4	2			
10	4	3			
11	4	2			
12	3	4			
1	3	5			
2	3	5		21:58	
3	4				Moderate breezes & fair cloudy horizon
4	4			SSE	
5	4	2			variation p:ʳ am: 4:43E
6	4	3			azu: 4:38
7	6	2			
8	5				exercised great guns & small arms
9	4				sailmakers repairing sails –
10	3			WBS	
11	4	5			Light breezes & fair weather
12	3				

Course	Dist:ᶜ	Latitude in	Long. made	M: Distance
W5:°00'W	94 –	19:*06S	60:00–W	2526W

Cape Pillar bore S54:°25'E Distance 1159 leagues

---

338 ". . . which with the uncertain weather we have makes us hope we are not far from land –." PL and FC.

Remarks Friday June 5. 1767 (55)

1	3	5	WBS	SSE	Light breezes & clear weather
2	3				
3	2	2			saw severall birds of a darkish colour a little bigger than
4	2	4			pigeons and two large gannets —[339]
5	3				
6	3	2			fine weather –
7	3	2			
8	4				
9	4				
10	5	3			
11	6				
12	6				
1	6	4			
2	6	4			
3	6	5		21:50	Fine clear weather cloudy in the horizon –
4	6	4		SE	
5	6	2			variation p:r amp:d – 5:°48'E –
6	5	5			a turtle pass'd by the ship –
7	5	3			
8	6	2			
9	7				
10	7				moderate gales & fine clear weather
11	6	5			saw a turtle to windward —[340]
12	6	2			

Course	Dist:e	Latitude in	Long. made	M: Distance
W½S	124	19:*18S	62:10 – W	2644W

Cape Pillar bore S55:°30'E Distance 1183 leagues

339 "Saw severall brown birds at a distance; they were smaller than gulls; saw likewise some Gannets." PL and FC. ". . . saw some Egg birds. They fly mostly in small flocks are of a lush white smaller than a [. . .] bird and most seen near land." Gore.
340 "Saw a turtle close by the ship and another to windward likewais saw some birds of different sizes." PL and FC.

Remarks Saturday June 6. 1767 (56)

					Remarks
1	6		WBS	SE	Moderate weather
2	6				saw some birds to windward but could not tell what they were
3	6				one Man of War bird near the ship
4	6			22:50	sailmakers employed in repairing the sails –
5	6	3			a swell from the SW –
6	6	4			
7	6	5			
8	7				
9	6				variation p:^{r} amp:^{de} 6:°08'E
10	6				cloudy in first reefs –
11	6				
12	6				Cloudy weather
1	5	2			
2	5			22:40	
3	4	2			
4	5	2			
5	6	5			cloudy & hazey all round the horison
6	6	3			
7	6	4			
8	7				saw some birds which look'd like land birds –
9	6				at ½ past 11 saw land from the mast head[341] to the WNW –
10	6	4			at noon saw it off the deck bearing WNW 5 or 6 leagues low
11	7				land into two hummocks in the middle –
12	7	4			moderate breezes & hazey

Course	Dist:^{e}	Latitude in	Long. made	M Distance
W½S –	148	19:*30S	64:47W	2797W

Cape Pillar bore S56:°45'E Distance 1242 leagues

---

341 "... at half past noon Jonathon Puller (seaman) called out land from the mast head in the WNW – at noon saw it plainly off the deck it was a low island bearing WNW distance about 5 or 6 leagues – fine pleasant gale & hazey, all the sick overjoyed at our discovery as were likewais the well –." PL and FC. According to Gore's log the Isle of Disappointment lay N 37° 37' 137 leagues.

Robertson (Corrington, op. cit., p. 116) reports that "at this time" Captain Wallis and the First Lieutenant were taken ill with a "bilious disorder." "The joy which every one on board felt at this discovery, can be conceived by those only who have experienced the danger, sickness, and fatigue of such a voyage as we had performed." Hawkesworth.

Remarks Sunday June 7. 1767 (57)

1	5	4	WNW½W	South	at ½ past noon the island bore from NBW¾W to NW¾N
2	4		NBE	SE	dist:ᶜᵉ from the middle of it about 4 or 5 miles
3	1	4	N½W		at 3 saw two other islands one bore from NW to WNW & the
4				23:00	other West hoisted the boats out and sent them with an Officer
5					and armed to see what refreshment was to be had – saw two
6					canoes put of the island & stand Westward
7					at 9 the boats returned and brought some scurvy grass & few
8	3	5	NNW	NE	cocoanuts. Stood off & on all night in the morning at day light
9	1		ESE		sent all the boats from the ship to endeavor to get
10	4	2			resfreshments but the surf was so great they could not land, so
11	4	2	ESE½E		they returned to the ship at eleven o'clock
12	4				at 7 the island bore SBW three miles second WNW – nine
1	3		NNW	NEBN	miles³⁴²
2	4			NE	
3	1	4	ESE	22:30	
4	2				at 11 bore away for the other island
5	2	2			
6	2	4	NNW		at noon the body of the Westermost island S60:00W distance
7					1½ miles
8					
9					
10					The body of the first island which I call Whitsun Island bore S
11	3		NBW½W		32:°10'E distance about four leagues –
12	4	5	SWBW		

Course	Dist:ᵉ	Latitude in	Long. made	M Distance
		19:18 –	64:47W	2797W

at noon the Westermost island bore South 60:°00' W Distance about 1 mile & half
Lat: Whitsun Island – 19:25S long from Cape Pillar 64:50'W

342 At half past noon the island bore from NBW¾W to NW¾N distance from the middle of it four or five miles, at same time saw another island bearing NWBW. At same time saw another is:ᵈ bearing NWBW. At 3 brought too hoisted out the boats man'd & armed them and sent them with Lieut:ᵗ Furneaux to the shore, on his coming near the island two canoes put off and ran away for the lewardmost island, at 7 the boats returned and brought with them severall cocoa nutts and three bags of scurvey grass, they report that there are only three huts on this island and there were some canoes building, that twas with great difficulty they landed that there was no place to anchor nor fresh water on the island, only few cocoa nutt trees and no other kind of fruit; scurvy grass in great plenty got all the sick up and gave them cocoa nutts and scurvey grass likewais all the ships company had as much scurvey grass as they could use – stood off and on all night. AM sent the boats again to sound and use their endeavors to find out a place to anchor in, at 11 the boats returned empty the surf running so high that they could not find any place in the whole island where a boat could land with safety that every part thereof was surrounded with a platform rock & that on the weather side there was an opening into a large bason which ran into the middle of the island this made them hope they had found a harbor but coming near it they found it full of breakers that they could not venture near it with the boats; hoisted the boats in and bore away for the leeward most island, the first island being discovered on Whitsunday I called it Whitsun (Whitsunday Island in the FC) Island, at noon it bore S22:00E distance about four leagues – the island not visited S60:00W distance 1½ miles. Latitude observed 19:°18' South. Whitsunday Island in lat:ᵈ 19:°26'S.° Longitude 137:°56' West from London. Observed by ? & ?." PL and FC.

In Gore's log for the 7ᵗʰ : "Both cutters were hoisted out and sent to seek an anchoring place for the ship, at the same time saw another island bearing W about 3 leag:ˢ distance at 7 the boats returned having found no anchoring place. They brought off some cocoa nutts, scurvey grass and

Remarks made at the first of the Whitsun Isles —[343]

at 2 PM hoisted all the boats out & sent Lieu:^{t} Furneaux with Proper Petty Officers & men armed to make a landing on the 2 Islands which they with much difficulty effected on account of the Surf which runs very high every where – at 7 they returned and made me the following report : that the Island was of a circular form with a large lagoon in the middle but both ends were guarded with large reefs of rocks that they found it impossible to get a passage thro' them; that there was ten or a dozen neat little habitations and one canoe built and more on the stocks that the habitants had but just gone he supposed by seeing their tools laying in confusion the tools consisted chiefly of shells and fish bones, he saw no kind of metal, the canoes were neatly sew'd together & their hutts very decent & clean he left every thing in the same manner he found it — and gathered scurvy grass of which there was great plants and a few cocoa nutts. At day light in the morning sent him with the boats to get off more refreshments but after trying in every part that seemed practible he returned at eleven o clock without landing the surf running so high that the boats could not venture near the shore.

	Lat: in	from Ca. Pillar	course	Distance from each other
Whitsun Island	19:°26*S	64:°52'W		
Queen Charlotte	19:18	65:00		
Prince Wm Henry	19:20	65:27		
Duke of Gloucester	19:11	67:8		
Pr. Brunswick	19:18	67:40		
P:^{r} Henry	19:00	68:04		
Bishop of Osnaburg	17:51	74:27		
K. Georges	17:48	75:32		

---

purslane. Hoisted the boats in and made sail off and on [. . .] The boats were hoisted out and sent away to the first Is:^{d} for refreshments. At 10 they return'd empty there being too much surf to land with safety. At 11 made sail for the 2 Is Wmost." Hawkesworth's version takes up the idea of the inhabitants fleeing: "As he approached it, we saw two canoes put off, and paddle away with great expedition towards the island that lay to leeward." Roberston in his journal writes a long detailed account (pp.116–117) of this landing and the canoes leaving the island "set out paddling from this island towards the oyther with three or four men in each." He also highlights the fact that Furneaux was commanded to take possession of the island that day and that on leaving the island "the men brought off several pearl oyster shells and several pices of tortoiseshell." These details are not recorded in the *Dolphin* logs.

343 There are no remarks as of yet in the PL and the FC. These remarks are in the ML on the usual third of a page. In Gore's log for the 7th : "The boats were hoisted out and sent away to the first Is:^{d} for refreshments. At 10 they return'd empty there being too much surf to land with safety."

Remarks Monday June 8. 1767 (58)

1		EBS
2		
3		
4		23:40
5		
6		
7		
8		
9		
10		
11		
12		
1		
2		22:40
3		
4		
5		
6		
7		
8		
9		
10		
11		
12		

Little wind & fair standing off & on near the second island, the boats inshore great many inhabitants on the beach at 1 the boats returned having purchased from the inhabitants about sixty cocoanuts for which gave them nails, bill hooks, hatchetts &:^{ce} – they would not suffer the people to land – except two who they soon put into the boat again – stood off and on all night at daylight sent the boats with an Officer to endeavour to get more cocoa nutts & scurvy grass. the natives had launched for double canoes and were embarked on board of them, on our approach they landed, but on the boats going to windward of them they all embarked & set sail and steer'd away WSW until we lost sight of them we then landed and found that they had taken everything with them except two or three canoes – at noon the Lieu:^{t} W. Furneaux sent off the barge loaded with cocoa nutts & greens – which was distributed amongst the ships company he took possession of this & the other island in name of the King George the third & at noon the island bore from SWBS to SEBS off shore about three miles – observed the latitude by Arcturas at 9 PM and found it 19°:06' S at the same time observed the distance of Arcturas from the moon for the longitude

variation p:^{r} amplitude : 3°:38' E
Lat:^{d} observed 19 :*14 island South four miles –[344]

[344] "Moderate breezes hoisted out all the boats man'd and armed them and sent them under the command of Lieu:^{t} Furneaux to the shore (where I saw about fifty people drawn up with long pikes & running about with firebrands) ordering him to where these people were and endeavour to traffic with them for fruit water or anything that might be usefull to us at the same time not to give them any offence but endeavor by civil means to get refreshments from them at the same time to employ the boats in sounding for anchorage, at 7 he returned and told me that he had sounded but could find no ground further than half a cable from the shoar that very deep & sharp rocks, that he had got only a few cocoa nutts and a little water from the natives who waded of to them with it for which they gave them some nails beads and a few hatchets that they stood on their guard with long pikes & would not suffer our people to land and that after staying till dusk sounding and endeavouring to persuade them to bring down some scurvy grass which they would not do he came off.

Stood off and on all night, sent the boats at daylight with orders to make a landing but act so as not to offend the inhabitants if possible to be avoided when our boats came near the shoar they were surpized to see seven large double canoes with two stout masts in each laying just in the surf, the inhabitants close down by them and beckoning to our people to go higher up, which they did and landed where immediately these people embarked and sailed away and at the West end were joined by two more, they all steer'd away WSW till we lost sight of them. At noon Lieu:^{t} Furneau returned with the boats laden with cocoa nutts, palm nutts and scurvy grass, he said that every soul had left the island and taken every thing with them except four or five canoes that he had found a well with very good water that the island was sandy & level, full of trees no underwood nor many cocoa nutt trees but plenty of scurvy grass." PL and FC.

Gore's log recounts the landing thus: "... the boats returned having got a few cocoanuts from the natives in exchange for other things. Hoisted in the boats and made sail off and on [...] Hove too and hoisted out the boats ½ past they put of well armd and the commander our Second Lieutenant, the ship plying off and on near the shore at 10 our boats landed and the natives embarked in 4 sail of double prow making sail to the WBS." Molineux describes the natives as "abandoning" the islands in four large canoes.

The account which Hawkesworth gives varies somewhat (based on Robertson's account (pp. 118–122): "As the boat approached the shore, the Indians thronged down towards the beach, and put themselves upon their guard with their long pikes, as if to dispute the landing. Our men then lay upon their oars, and made signs of friendship, shewing at the same time several strings of beads, ribands, knives, and other trinkets. The Indians still made signs to our people that they should depart, but at the same time eyed the trinkets with a kind of wishful curiosity. Soon after some of them advanced a few steps into the sea, and our people making signs that they wanted cocoa nuts and water, some of them brought down a small quantity of both, and ventured to hand them into the boat: the water was in cocoa nut-shells, and the fruit was stripped of its outward covering, which is probably used for various purposes. For this supply they were paid with the trinkets that had been shewed them, and some nails, upon which they seemed to set a much greater value. During this traffick, one of the Indians found means to steal a silk handkerchief, in which some of our small merchandize was wrapped up, and carried it clear off, with its contents, so dexterously, that no body observed him. Our people made signs that a handkerchief had been stolen, but they either could not, or would not understand them. The boat continued about the beach, sounding for anchorage, till it was dark; and having many times endeavoured to persuade the natives to bring down some scurvy-grass, without success, she returned on board."

Robertson's account (p. 119–121) makes note of men and women lighting fires in different places to prevent the boats from landing. This made "our people suppose they worship fire." Importantly, the *Dolphin* logs make no mention of the firing of a nine-pounder (or the theft of the handkerchief) which startles the people and according to Robertson induces friendlier relations and allows three of the company to land and trade. The next morning, Robertson's account is again entirely different to that in the *Dolphin* logs: "... our boats got closs in abreast of the Indian town where they found four large double canoes all loaded, with their wives and children all onb^d, when our boats rowd near the canoes all the young women jumpt overboard and swimd ashoar to the men, who was all drawen up on the shoar side with their picks in their hands, but the men immediately orderd them back to the canoes and made signs for our boats to keep away from their canoes, this the Lieu^t complyed with rowd closs to the shoar in order to land, but the Indian men drawd up in a line along shore and seemd resolved to prevent our people landing, upon seing this the Lieu^t made signs of friendship and let them know that he wanted more cocoa nuts and water, but they still keept shaking their picks and pointing to the ship, meaning that our people should go onb^d and not land but the Lieu^t orderd the men to row closser in, which the Indians observed and advanced some steps in to the water looking very fierce and shaked there picks as if they were resolvd to run the first man that lands throw with their picks, by this time the poor women was got into the canoes with their children and seemd greatly afraid – our boats lay some time on their oars thinking the men would go off to their wives and children, but finding they still persisted on our boats going off, the Lieu^t orderd a musket to be fired along shoar that they might see the ball take the water in order to frighten them but this hade not the desired effect untill he orderd a musquetoon to be fired near them, then they all seemed greatly afraid, and made signes that they were all to imbark with their famelys and to desert the island, if our boats would go a little to leeward and land there, this our people complyed with and the Indians immediately imbarkt and made sail to the westward steering about W.S.W. or W.B.S. – their was four double canoes went from this little town and one from the West end of the island joind them –."

Remarks Tuesday June 9:th 1767 (59)[345]

[346]Moderate & clear –

at two I went on shoar being told there were some pitts of water which found to be very good tho' scarce – got some palm nutts, cocoa nutts – purcelane & scurvy grass –

at six returned onboard again

stood off & on all night

at day light hoisted all the boats & sent them onshoar with empty casks to fill the water

at noon the boats came for more casks but could not get no water fil'd untill a rolling way was made sent a Mate with 14 men and ten marines to get water & clear a way thro' the wood land the Surgeon with the scorbutick men to take a walk & come onboard again at four o'clock.

The extreams of the island from S¾W to SWBS½W – standing off and on

Latitude observed 19:°12*S

1		ESE	
2			
3			
4		22:30	
5			
6			
7			
8			
9			
10			
11			
12			
1			
2			
3		22:10	
4			
5			
6			
7			
8			
9			
10			
12			

Latitude in: Island	Long. From Cape Pillar	MDis: from Cape Pillar
19:18 – S	65:00W	2798W

variation – 4:°40' Easterly

345 In Gore's log the 9th and 10th of June are titled "Transactions off Queen Charlotte's Islands". Molineux writes in a NB "Captain Wallace order'd this island to be call'd Queen Charlottes Island."

346 "Afternoon sent Lieu:t Furneaux with all the boats onshoar and a mate & twenty men to make rolling way for to get the water cask up and down from the well. At the same time ordered the Lieu:t to take possession of the island in his Majesty's name and call it Queen Charlotte's island in honour of her Majesty. The boats returned with cocoa nutts & scurvy grass and informed me they had found two more wells the water very good and not far from the beach – I tho' much out of order went onshoar the Surgeon and many of the scorbuticks to take a walk and seeing these wells so commodious ordered a weeks provisions to be sent onshoar to the Mate and twenty men who I left to fill water; these men had arms and ammunition left with them. The boats and all returned at night except the waterers, and we stood off and on not being able to find any anchorage – at daylight sent the boats with empty cask – the surgeon & number of the scorbutick men to walk on shore but to keep near the waterside and in the shade, with strict orders not to pull down any of the houses or destroy the canoes or cocoa nutt trees there being but few, had people to climb and take them down and not cut the trees down for the sake of the fruit. At noon a rolling way being made received a cutter load of water, tho' getting it off the beach is very troublesome as it is all a platform rock and at times a great surf tumbles in upon it found the variation here to be 4:46 Easterly – ship standing off and on. The inhabitants were of a reddish colour were naked except a mat about their middle, they were well made, & the weomen hansome; we saw no kind of mettal, the tools they make use of for building their canoes are shells sharpened & fixed on sticks and made like adzes, chizles and awls they sew the boards together, and lash two canoes in which they will carry twenty people – we know nothing more of these people –." PL and FC.

The Hawkesworth account (based on Robertson's detailed description of the island) makes mention of ". . . several repositories of the dead, in which the body was left to putrefy under

Remarks Wednesday June 10:th 1767 (60)

1				ESE
2				
3				
4				23:08
5				
6				
7	3	4	NEBE	SEBE
8	4			
9	5		SBW	
10	2		NE	
11	4	4	South	
12	3	4	NE	
1	5	2	South	
2	4		NE	
3	4		South	22:10
4	3			
5	4			ESE
6				
7				
8				
9				
10				
11				
12				ESE

[347]Moderate breezes & pleasant weather, standing off and on

received a cutter load of water, left a Mate & 24 Men on shoar at the island –

at 7 the extreams of the island from SE to SW off shore three miles

fresh gales & squally, standing of & on all night
a great swell –
at day light sent the boats onshoar to get of the people & what water was filed – received in all about three tons –

At noon all the boats returned loaded with scurvy grass and palm nutts – the red cutter was ^{near} filled with water in her passage off which spoiled all the bread & much other provisions – and they were obliged to throw much overboard to save her fom sinking and to … to bale
Latitude observed 19:*5 South

---

a canopy, and not put into the ground." Robertson (Corrington, op. cit., pp. 123–125) describes the "town" and the houses, the canoes, the "turtle backs", their fishing nets, the carpenters' workshops, the tools and the two burying places which Hawkesworth mentions.

347 "Moderate & fine pleasant weather, received a boat load of water, another of cocoa nutts, palm nutts & scurvy grass, at 4 all the ailing men with the Surgeon returned much recruited by their walk – stood off and on all night, at midnight it came on very squally, dirty weather with a great sea at day light stood in shore and ordered the mate to send of all the water that was filled and be ready to come off with his people when the boats returned again at the same to gather as many cocoa nutts and scurvy grass as he could. At 8 the boats returned with all the casks filled and reported that the surf was very high that they feared twould be difficult bringing of the people as it was tide of flood and made the landing worse cleard the boats, stood well up to the windward, and sent but a few hands in the boats to bring those people who were on the shore, they returned on board with all the men, – in coming off the cutter shipped a sea that near filled her the barge being by good part of the people got into her, the rest clear'd her of the provisions, cocoa nutts & bag of greens, & free'd her without any other loss than the provisions. At noon hoisted the boats in; there being a very great sea, here the surf running very high on the shore, and no anchorage I thought it most prudent with the refreshments we had to leave this place and bore away – we left a union jack flying, some hatchetts, nails, glass bottles, beads and shillings six pences & halfpences; together with the ship name time of our calling here and taking possession of this and Whitsun island – this island is in latitude 19:18, longitude 138:°04' West of London." PL and FC. The gifts are described as an "atonement for the disturbance we had given them" in Hawkesworth. The ML log at this point accounts for only two days instead of the usual three.

Remarks Wednesday June 11:ᵗʰ 1767 (60)

1	6		WBS	
2	7	2	WSW	
3	6	4	WSW	
4	7		WBS	
5	6			
6	5	4		
7				
8				
9				
10				
11				
12			Up NE off	North
1				
2				
3				
4				
5		up	ENE of	NNE
6				
7	5		West	EBS
8	7	3		
9	6			
10	8			
11	8			
12	7	4		East

Course	Dist:ᵉ	Latitude in	Longitude made	MDistance
W¼NW	64	19:*06 South	01:17W	2803W
			65:26	
			66:46 West from Cape Pillar	

³⁴⁸Moderate gales with a great sea under sail saw an island to leeward – lost my little cat
at 2 Charlott Island bore EBN 15 miles –
at ½ past 3 the new island bore from the East end of it SE about one mile at this time we were abreast of seven sail of double canoes that were hauled up on to the beach and were the same people that left Charlott Island, the people all sitting on the beach & their things just taken out of their canoes³⁴⁹ – could see no place to anchor in and a very great surf running on the shoar very few huts on the island and no cocoa nutt trees – & the island quite narrow & rocky under the trees not sandy like the last island – the wind likewais blowing fresh I stood from the island and brought to at six –
with the ships head to the NE –
at six PM observed the Long: in by the moon & Virgin spike to be 138:°48 W from London –
Lat:ᵈ of 3:ʳᵈ island – 19:°20'S Long from Cape Pillar 65:26W
Saw severall Tropic birds & Man of War birds flying fish & bonettos lost two log & four lines these 24 hours – unbent the fore topsail & bent another the sailmakers employed in repairing sails –
NB: at 6 at night the island bore EBN by compass distance about four leagues –
Dis: from second to third * lat: 7:ˢ Dep:ʳ 24 West
third latitude of the island 19:20S long:ᵈ 64:26 W

Egmont Island bore EBS¼S Distance 21 leagues – Longitude from Whitsun Island to Charlotte 00:7W to next island 0:66W – Long: from Cape Pillar 65:26W

348 "Moderate gales and hazey weather at 1 saw an island bearing WBS - Charlotte Island bore EBN 15 miles – at ½ past three we were close to the island it bearing SE about ¾ a mile the East end of it ran close along the shore had no soundings, the whole island or rather islands being surrounded with a platform rock, the islands were full of trees but not one coca nutt on any part there of – on the Westermost, we saw the canoes with all the inhabitants by them that had fled from Charlotte Island, there were not any hutts but the people had hauled up their canoes upon the beach and placed their weomen & children under them and they came down close to the waterside with big pickes in their hands, & some with firebrands making a great noise and dancing in strange manner. There were 7 or eight double canoes with about four score men weomen and children. These islands were sandy and not grass under the trees as Charlotte Island was they're likewais so narrow that we could see thro' from one side to the other, the shore rocky & no anchorage nor any likelihood of refreshment to be met with on it. Made sail till six o'clock & then brought too, her head to the NE – Egmont Island bearing EBN by compass distance about 12 miles at 6 PM had an observation for longitude and found Egmont Island (which name I gave it in honour of the Rt Honorable the Earl of Egmont) to lye in the latitude of 19:20S longitude observed 138:30 west from London. Longitude made by dead reckoning from Cape Pillar to E of Egmont Isle 65:26 West. At six am made sail cloudy rainy weather with a great southern swell – at noon fresh gales & cloudy with some rain." PL and FC.

349 Gore describes the "natives walking along the shore arm'd with their long wooden lances." Robertson (Carrington, op. cit., p. 126) indicates that Captain Wallis fires on the people (again omitted in the *Dolphin* logs and in the Hawkesworth account): "...when abreast of the middle of the island we saw seven

Remarks Friday June 12, 1767 (62)

1	7	2	West	ESE	
2	3	3			
3	4	4	SW	South	
4	4		WSW		
	3		SWBW		
5	3		W½N		
	2		WBS		
6	7		W½S		
	3	4			
7					
8	⎫	up	NEB off	NNW	
9	⎬				
10	⎭				
11	⎫				
12	⎬				
1	⎭				
2		up	NE off	North	
3					
4				25:55	
5			made sail		
6	4		W½S	NE	
7	7		SWBS		
8	3		WNW		
9	1		NW		
10					
11			Calm her	head	
12			to the N°	ward	

Course	Dist:ᵉ	Latitude in	Longitude made	Distance
W¼N		19:02	67:52	2955 – W –

[350] Fresh gales & cloudy with showers & great swell from the Southward – saw an island bearing WSW – stood for it at 4 ran past it twas not a quarter of a mile broad and four or five mile long and the back of it was made a circle by a reef of rocks that went round it, where the sea beat very high – we saw here about sixteen inhabitants the island seem'd full of wood & stones – low with the waters edge – not one cocoa nut tree on it – ran within musquett shot of the shoar, no soundings nor any place to anchor in there being a very great surf on every part of the beach –
I saw no canoes & very few hutts on the shore – the people seem to be the same in manner & complexion as those in the other islands – came down to the waterside with fine & long pikes – the weather looking dirty made sail from it and at six brought too –
at 4 PM – the SW end of the island bore SSE two miles – caught a King fish being the first fish ʷᵉ caught in the South seas
squally dirty rainy weather all night –
squally with heavy rain at 7 saw the land bearing ⁴ ᵐⁱˡᵉˢ SSW stood for it but it blowing very fresh and coming on our fourth island latitude 19:10S Long: from Cape Pillar 67:1W
Light airs & cloudy saw the island bearing SSE about three leagues distance –
at noon the middle of the ᶠⁱᶠᵗʰ island bore SSE½E dist:ᵉ four leagues
This island lyes in lat:ᵈ of 19:*6 S longitude 67°48'W from Cape Pillar

---

double canoes halld up on the shore with their masts up – and about fifty men all armd with picks walking allong shore, and weaving to us to keep off from their shore, this we complied with, when we was abreast of the small fleet the Capt. Orderd a nine pounder to be fired over the Indians heads, which terefied them greatly the ball went whistling over their heads and lodged in a lagoon in the middle of the island – they all stard at the ball when the heard it go over their heads, and seemd greatly terefied and stood still not one of them moved while we could see them. . . ."

350 "Fresh gales & rainy weather with a great Southern swell at one saw an island in the WSW stood for it at 4 were within a quarter of a mile of it ran along the shore sounding but could get no ground these islands are somewhat like Egmont Islands only much narrower full of trees but not one cocoa nutt tree and surrounded on every side with rocks on which the sea breaks very high. On the West end amgost the rocks we saw about sixteen inhabitants they had no canoes but carried long poles in their hands were much such people as we had seen before; it blowing very hard and staing here would be only loosing time made sail from it till eight o'clock and then brought too. This Island I called Gloucester Island in honour of his Royal Highness the Duke of Gloucester it lyeth in the latitude of 19:11S & long:ᵗ observed West from London 140:04 – by reckoning longitude West from Cape Pillar 67:08 – Served cocoa nutts to the people who had every day as much scurvy grass as they could make use of which hath been of inifinite service to them. At 5 AM made sail. Dirty squally weather saw an island made sail for it at 10 very squally & rainy saw a long reef with breakers on each side of the island brought too with her head off shore. At noon light airs we judge this island to be in lat: 19:18S and long:ᵈ West from London 140: 36 from Cape Pillar by computation 67: 40 West." PL and FC. Gore mentions that on seeing the Indians,

Remarks Saturday June 13, 1767 (62)

1	1	2	W½S		Light airs & cloudy
2	2				
3	2				at two the island bore SE —[351]
4	2	3			Light breezes & fair weather
5	2	4			variation p:r amp:de –
6	2				azum – 7:10 Easterly –
7	2	2			
8	1	4			
9	2	4			
10	3	2			treble reeft the topsails & brought too –
11					
12			up NNE of	NWBN	
1					
2					
3				22:00	
4					
5			up North	of NW	Light breezes & pleasant weather saw the land in the NE from
6			W½S	NEBE	the masthead – it made in low flatt keys –
7	3				it was about five leagues distance
8	4				The middle of fifth island latitude 18:°58'S long 68:°12'W
9	2	4			served cocoa nutts to every man in the ship –
10	2	5			
11	3				Light breezes & fair, a SSW swell –
12	3	2		NNE	

Course	Dist:e	Latitude in	Longitude made	Distance
W¼N	46	19:*00S	68:41W	3081W –

onboard the *Dolphin*, they fix a gun and shew their colours. But Robertson (Corrington, op. cit., p. 128) makes it clear that the guns are fired: ". . . at 3 PM we was abreast of the East end of another island, where we saw no inhabitance but a great smock near the middle of the island when we got up abreast of the smock we fir'd a nine pounder, Soon after we saw about sixteen or eighteen indians runing allong shore arm'd with long picks lyke those of the oy'r islands, every thirty or forty yards that they run allong one of them lighted a fire and made a great smock, when we got near the West end of this island the Capt order'd a nine pounder to be shoted, and fired near where the Indians stood, that they might see the ball take the water, this was done and the Indians observ'd the ball take the water, a great way from the shore, then saw it rise again and lodge near where they stood, this made them all stand the same as those on Lord Egmonts island, where they stopt they soon after made a great fire. . . ."

[351] " Little wind & cloudy with a SW swell – the island bore SE was low and had many breakers around it therefore had no hope of finding any refreshments on it stood on to the Westward. This island I called Cumberland Island in Honour of his Royal Highness the Duke of Cumberland – it is about the size of Queen Charlottes Island. Variation p:r azumeth 7:10 Easterly. At daylight saw another island bearing in the NE it making in small flay keys & right to windward kept on to the Westward in hope of finding higher land where in all probability we might find both anchorage and refreshments – This island I called Prince William Henrys Island after his Majestys third Son. It lays in latitude of 19:°00' S and longitude observed 141:°06' West from London and longitude by observation West from Cape Pillar 68:°04' At noon light breezes and fair." PL and FC.

Long:^{de} Made from Cape Pillar[352]
To the First Isl^d - - - - - - - 65:°56' W

Bearings
of the Isl^{ds} from
each other

$\left.\begin{array}{c}1\\ \&\\ 2\end{array}\right\}$ NW and SE dist 10:^{gs} Latt:^{de} : 19:°25'
                                                                                                   19:°10'

$\left.\begin{array}{c}2\\ \&\\ 3\end{array}\right\}$ W¾S and E¾N dist 25:^{s} 19:21

$\left.\begin{array}{c}3\\ \&\\ 4\end{array}\right\}$ W½N and E½S dist ---:^{s} 19:12

$\left.\begin{array}{c}4\\ \&\\ 5\end{array}\right\}$ WBS½S and EBN¼ N dist ---:^{s} 19:19

Long:^{de} the 5th is in from Cape Pillar 68:°28'11"
B. Butler

---

352 These coordinates are noted on a small sheet of paper sewn into the ML (and they are not copied into the two other logs).

Remarks Sunday June 14 1767 – (64)

H	K	F	Winds	Courses
1	3		WS	North
2	2	5		
3	2		NW	
4	2		WBN	22:20
5	2		WNW	variable
6	1		NNW	
7			calm her round the	head all compass
8				
9		4	West	Nnw
10	4	3	W½S	South
11	6			
12		up	EBS off	EBN
1				
2				
3				21:50
4		up	WSW off	WNW
5				
6				
7	5		W½S	South
8	6			
9	6	2		
10	6	3		
11	7		West	SBW
12	7	2		

Light airs & cloudy dark weather with a great SW swell

variation – 4:°30'E –

dark cloudy weather with squalls all round us –

much lightning in the SSW –
at 9 sprung up a breeze

brought too – close reeft topsails –

Fresh gales & squally with drizzling rain & a great SW sea

wore a great sea from the SW –

made sail

unbent the main topsail & bent another.
out 4:th reefs –
Fresh gales a great sea – clear overhead cloudy in the horizon

saw large brownish birds with white bellies –

Course	Dist:e	Latitude in	Longitude made	MDistance
N60:00W	60	18:35 South	69:38W	3054W –

Remarks Monday June 15 1767 – (65)

1	7			South
2	7			
3	8			SBE
4	8			20:10
5	8			
6	8			SSE
7				
8				
9				
10				
11				
12		up SWBS	off WBS	
1				
2				
3				19:50
4				
5				
6	5	W½S		
7	8	W½S		SSE
8	8			
9	7			
10	7			
11	7			
12	5			

Fresh gales with a great sea saw some large grey birds their heads & tails white –
Severall albacores about the ship –
close reeft top:^{s} & got down the top gallant yards –
at night brought too dark cloudy weather in the horizon –

a great sea – the ship labours much –

made sail out 3:rd reefs fresh gales with a very great sea from the SSW –
saw some Noddies, Boobies & Man of War birds –

Squally weather with a great sea –

Little wind & variable towards the SW quarter
a great swell from the SSW –[353]

Course	Dis:^{e}	Latitude in	Longitude made	MDistance
WBN	102	18:*10 South	71:24W	3154 West –

---

[353] "The people served cocoa nutts every day which hopes keeps the scurvy from gaining ground." PL and FC.

Remarks Tuesday June 16 1767 – (66)

1	6		WBS½S	SSE
2	6	4		
3	7	2		
4	8	2		21:00
5	9			
6	7			
7			up WBS	off WSW
8				
9				
10				
11				
12			up SSW	off WSW
1				
2				20:00
3				
4				
5			ships head	WSW
6				
7	1	4	WSW½W	SSE
8	5			
9	6			
10	7			
11	6	4		
12	6			SSE

Course	Distance	Latitude in	Longitude made	Merid: Distance
W½S	87	18:*74S	72:°56'W	3241 West –

Fresh gales & cloudy with a great SSW swell – makes the ship labour much –[354]

Brought too close reeft topsails & bunted the courses –
Fresh gales clear overhead dark & cloudy in the horizon

squally dark & cloudy with a great swell from the SSE –
Little wind & cloudy
made sail, clear overhead dark all round the horizon caught a large Bonneto & Albacore –

Saw some Tropic birds & one Man of War Bird –
Fresh gales & squally – suppose the SW swell hath set the ship so much to the Northward as we have not above half a point variation

---

354 "The scorbutick people rather worse & many more complaining yet few lay bye but struggle against it, they have vinegar & mustard as much as they can use. Malt made into wort every day and every other thing that can be got for them, put every one at whole allowance, & the Pursor having a quantity of sugar and rasins he purchased at Madeira, he paid them for the time thay had been at short allowance with it and rice at a respectable price so as all were content there with and judge it to be of great use to them and as we catch rain water, we can afford them a good deal having never stinted them yet of as much as they choose to drink. And the sick always had plenty our daily expence being about somewhat more than half a ton –." PL and FC.

H	K	F	Courses	Winds	Remarks Wednesday June 17 1767 – (67)
1	6		WSW½W	SBE	Squally dirty rainy weather with a great SSW sea caught some rainwater –[355]
2	4	5	WNW	variable	
3	3				Little wind & close weather
4	3		WSW½W	SSE	
5	6			20:00	
6	6				Fresh gales & hazey at six close reeft topsails and brought too
7					
8		up	South off	SW	
9					
10					
11		up	S½W off	WSW	Fresh gales & cloudy
12					
1					
2		up	SW off	WBS	Little wind
3				20:20	
4					Made sail out reefs –
5					
6	4	2	WBS½S	SEBS	Saw some land from off the deck – bearing WBN making in a small round hummock –
7	4	5			
8	4				Squally with rain –
9	3	4	WBS		at noon the above island bore N64:°00W distance 5 leagues it looks like the Mew Stone in Plymouth Sound only somewhat larger – the ship twenty miles at least to the N:°ward of our reckoning –
10	7				
11	5			variable	
12	4	4			

Course	Dist:^ce	Latitude in	Longitude made	MDistance
W10:°00'N	67	18:*02S	74:°05'W –	3307 West

---

355 "Saved about four hogsheads of rain water." PL and FC.

Remarks Thursday June 18 1767 – (68)

1	2	5	WBN½N		
2	4				
3	4		WNW		
4	4		WNW½N		
5	2		SBE		
6	2				
7	1	4	SBW		
8	1	5	SBW½W		
9	2				
10	2		South		
11	1		SBE		
12	1				
1	1				
2	1	2			
3	2	2	NE		
4	3	2	NNE		
5	2	5	NEBN		
6	3		NNE		
7	3				
8			standing	off and	
9			on -	about	
10			two miles	from the	
11			island -		

^{356}Light shuffling breezes & cloudy with rain and at times very thick & hazey at 4 haul'd the wind in 2 reefs topsails S:º part of the island NWBN½W – 2 or 3 leagues –
at 6 the body of the island North distance 9 or 10 miles at 8 bore N¾E –
at 12 it bore NBE
at 2 it bore NBE½E
at 6 it bore NBE – light airs –
at 8 brought too & hoisted the boats out sent the second Lieu:^{t} with the boats mann'd and armed to seek for an anchring place or what refreshments could be had, he went very near three or four canoes – who all pulled for the shore the island shore bore NBW – variation p:^{r} amp:^{de} & azimuth – 7:º00'E –
at 9 the body of the island North about 1 mile distance
opened a cask of pork N:º955 cont: 314 short 2 peices
the boats landed on the island but in so bad a place that it was with great difficulty the inhabitants were standing off about two hundred men weomen & children – all well look'd stout people – the women handsome & dress'd in white, on the boats coming to a grapnell the weomen the island on showing some beads & trinketts were in a great haste to come to the boats but the men prevented them & sent up the cliff. they made signs that they would bring fowles cocoa nutts hogs &:^{ce} but after waiting several hours not one came & the woods inaccessible the boats returned and we sailed from the island –
at noon the boats laying at a grapnell under a rock close in shore – on the SW side of the island – the island in the middle bore NEBE distance two miles – the island I named the Bishop of Osnaburgs Island

Course	Dist:^{ce}	Latitude in	Longitude made	MDistance	
		17:*52 South	74:27W –	3325W	

356 "Light breezes & very unsettled weather with rain at times. At 5 the S:º part of the island bore NW½N 6 or 8 leagues, haul'd the wind and continued of and on all night, at 10 saw a light on the shore which tho' very small island gave us spirits that it was inhabited and we might possibly get anchorage and refreshments, the land being very high and full of cocoa nutt trees which is a certain sign of water –

AM hoisted the boats and mann'd and armed them and sent Lieu:^{t} Furneaux putting all kinds of trinkets into the boats to go onshoar and endeavor to get refreshments at the same time endeavor to find a place to anchor in, severall canoes coming off put back on seeing our boats – at noon the boats returned and brought with them a pig and a cock a few plaintains and cocoanuts, he reported that he saw at least 100 inhabitants and believes that there were many more that he had sounded all round but could find no place to anchor in and scarce a landing place for the boats, that he came to a grapnel and threw a warp on shore which the natives held fast, and then conversed with them by signs he saw no weapons among them save some white sticks which those in authority wave and kept the people back that on them giving him the pig cock &:^{ce} he gave some beads a hatchett, looking glass and several trinkets and combs which the weomen seeing they all ran down to the waterside but the men drove them back soon after a man came round a rock and dived down and weigh the boats grapnel at the same time the people onshore made an effort to draw the boat into the surf, they immediately fired a musket over the man who weigh'd the grapnel he let it go as did the people their rope on shoar, after which our people lay on their oars and finding they could not get any thing more, they returned onboard." PL and FC. Gore compares the inhabitants of this island to those of King Georges Island which shows that the daily entries were

Remarks Friday June 19:ᵗʰ 1767 – (69)

1				
2				
3	3		WSW½W	ENE
4	3			22:00
5	3	2		
6	3	4		
7	3	4		
8	4			
9	4			
10	2			
11	⎫			
12	⎪	up	SSE off	SSW
1	⎬			
2	⎪			
3	4	4	WSW½W	23:00
4	5			
5	4	4		
6	4			
7	6		WNW	ENE
8	5			
9	4			
	2			
10				
11	1		SE	
				ENE
12	2			

Course	Dist:ᶜᵉ	Latitude in	Longitude made	MDistance
West	66	17:*53 – S –	75:37W –	3391W

Light airs & fair weather at ½ past one the boats returned hoisted them in & made sail toward land we discovered in the WSW
at 9 AM observed the longitude the ship was then in which was – 149:°42':00" West from London
variation p:ʳ amp:ᵈᵉ & az: 7: 10 E – the land bore from WNW¾W to W½S Oznaburg Isle ENE –
at 8 AM it came on dirty squally weather, at 9 it cleard up and we had near one hundred canoes great & small about the ship some had only one man in others there four five & six – and some double canoes a dozen they had no sails were not above 18 inches wide & two feet deep each canoe having an outlicker –
several of the people came on board but brought nothing with them we shewd them fowles and hogs which they shewd signs of having onshoar – but turkey & sheep they did not know – they had severall things given them & signs made for them to go onshoar & get stock & we would give iron in exchange –
which they seem to be excessively greedy of they are so thievish that if they lay hand on anything they take it & jump over board with it immediately – one of the Midshipmen having a new hat on with a gold button & loop leaning on the fore boom – one of them snatched it off his head & jumped off the toprail & swam away with it –at noon the East end of the island bore NBE distance 2 leagues[357]

---

modified or adjusted during or after the voyage (this section is typical of the adjustment process because there are insertions and crossings-out. Robertson (Corrington, op. cit., p. 133) indicates the presence of an authority figure on shore: ". . . there was one middle aged man in this island, that appeard to have the command over all the rest, he was frequently seen chastiseing several of the oyʳ Indians, and the whole appeard to pay respect to what he said, he was a stout well made man and cloathed better not the rest, and wore a large white turbin on his head – all the women hade some sort of white stuff about the loins, but several of the men was naked."

357 "M:ʳ Furneaux told me that bothe men and weomen were cloathed, a peice of the cloth he brought with him, that the inhabitants seem'd to be more in number than he could think the island could support that there were some large canoes there & he thought that there might be places not far off where we might get refreshments for this being but a small place no anchorage and very difficult of access and if the natives would not supply us we could not get anything as one man could keep of a hundred having considered of this I resolved to run further to the Westward hoisted the boats & named this island Osnaburg Island in honour of Prince Frederick – This island lies in lattitude 71:51 South and longitude West from London 147:30; and from Cape Pillar 74:27 West variation 7:10 Easterly –." (Molineux describes the island thus: "The shore has a delightful appearance & the inhabitants very numerous.") At two bore away at ½ past discovered very high land in the WSW this cheer'd all our spirits as we were in hopes of getting a place to secure the ship in & recruit. At 7 Osnaburg Island bore ENE and the new discovered land from WNW to WBS. It being squally & dirty brought to 'till daylight or rather till it clear'd away & then made sail. At 8 AM we got in close under the land when it clear'd away & we were much surprized to find that we were surrounded by some hundred of canoes which had from one man to ten in them

who made such hallowing and shouting that we could scarce hear each other speak. The land very high in peaks but the sides of the hills look'd cultivated and the shoar full of houses and people, it was level by the waterside and that full of cocoa nutt and fruit trees – and from the sides of the mountains we saw large rivers falling down into the sea. Or near it. We made signs for some of them to come onboard which they did and on our shewing them fowles & hogs they made signs that they had those things but when we shewed them goats and sheep they ran away and jumped overboard with fear but recovering themselves they came onboard again gave them some nails & other things and made signs to them to go onshoar and bring off some hogs fowles fruit &:^{ce} they did not seem to understand but were watching their time being the veriest thieves I ever met, they saw nothing that they did not endeavor to make their own, at last one of the Midshipmen came off with a new laced hat and was talking by signs to one of them these people, he took his time snatched his hat of leaped of the toprail and swam away with it. Latitude 17:*3 Longitude 75:37." PL and FC. Gore's only comment on the inhabitants is: "they proved very thievish."

The account in Hawkesworth specifies some hundreds of canoes with eight hundred people, instead of a hundred or canoes specified in the *Dolphin* logs. More detail based on Robertson's account (unrecorded in the *Dolphin* logs) is given, for example as to why the Tahitians jump overboard: "As one of these Indians was standing near the gang-way, on the larboard side of the quarter-deck, one of our goats butted him upon the haunches: being surprised at the blow, he turned hastily about, and saw the goat raised upon his hind-legs, ready to repeat the blow. The appearance of this animal, so different from any he had ever seen, struck him with such terror, that he instantly leaped over board; and all the rest, upon seeing what had happened, followed his example with the utmost precipitation: they recovered however, in a short time, from their fright, and returned on board."

Robertson on sighting Tahiti supposes that it is the "long wishd for Southern continent." He also describes the first contact between the Tahitians and the English: ". . . in a short time the fogg cleard up, and we saw the E'most point of this land bearing N° two leag^s, at same time saw breakers betwixt us and the shoar – and upward of a hundred canoes betwixt us and the brakers all padling off towards the ship, when they came within pistol shot they lay by for some time – and lookt at our ship with great astonishment, holding a sort of counsel of war amongst them mean time we made all the friendly signs that we could think of, and showd them several trinkets in order to get some of them onb^d after their counsel was over they padled all round the ship and made signs of friendship to us, by holding up branches of plantain trees, and making a long speech of near fifteen minutes, when the speech was over he that made it throwd the plantain branch in to the sea, then they came nearer the ship, and all of them appeard cheerful and talkt a great dale but non of us could understand them, but to pleas them we all seemd merry and said something to them. . . ." Robertson again indicates that a nine pound shot is fired over their heads (not mentioned in the *Dolphin* logs) when they become a little "surly."

Remarks Saturday June 20 1767 – (70)

1			standing	off & on
2	5		WBN½N	East
3	2	4		
4			standing	off & on
5	2		SEBS	EBN
6	3			22:50
7	2	4	SE	
8	2	5	SEBS	
9	3			
10	3	4		
11	3			
12	3			
1	6	3	NBE	
2	6	3		
3	6			22:50
4	4		SEBS	
5	6			
6	2		NBE½E	East
7	5			
8	5		NBE	
9	5	4		
10	5	5		
11	6		N½E	
12	6		NBW	

Course	Dist:t	Latitude in	Longitude made	MDistance
NE	14 –	17:*44S	75:26W –	3381 West –

Fresh breezes & cloudy made sail a long shore sent the boat in to sound at 4 saw a vast number of canoes full of people surround the boats – made the signal to come on board standing off & on at half past came on board, informed me that they had no soundings within a cables length of the breakers that there is a platform reef runs off a quarter of a mile the shore everywhere that there was a fine bay to leward but full of breakers & that they could not get ground with 70fm: line – the inhabitants came off in their canoes & was beginning to pillage them & throw stones there being near one hundred canoes about them so they fired a musquet clear of them to let them see on which they set up a great hallow & came close to the boat on which they shot at one & wounded him for they were quite surrounded & expected they would board them in a moment on which they pulled off at a distance & never came near them again & they got safe onboard at the same time we had some hundreds of canoes about the ship – to whom I gave nails & some trifles but they brought nothing in exchange & so thievish that they were clambering up the side & taking everything they could lay hand on –
at 5 made sail the extreams of the land from NWBW 18 leagues & there seemed to be land beyond it to NE 5 leagues – a remarkable sugar loaf peek NNE off shore two leagues variation p:r amp:de & azum:th 5:°00'
the shore pleasant beyond imagination full of inhabitants a million of cocoa nut trees fine cascades running of the mountains – saw a large canoe under sail in shore. Breakers all along as we go – a great way of shore the land very mountaineous –[358]

---

[358] "Hoisted the boats out and sent them in shoar to sound we running on & sounding without them had no ground being about half a mile from the breakers, at two brought to and sent the boats into a bay hoping to find anchorage there but they found not close to the breakers, they then stood round to an opening when they were surrounded by a vast number of boats bore down to them and at the same time made the signal for them to come onboard the boats then did attempt to board ours and threw stones at them on which I ordered a shot to be fired over them and the Mate that was in one of the boats found that if he suffered them to come nearer he should not be able to defend him self fired musquett with buck shott and wounded a man (who was then standing up ready to jump onboard) in the shoulder, on which they all moved off and suffered the boats to return to the ship without any molestation – the officer sent on this duty informed me that there was a platform rock that lay half a mile from the shore everywhere they sounded & close to it twas as steep as at any of the other islands we had been at however we had hope left still as we were now on the weather side of the island that in all reason we might expect anchorage in running to leeward but on finding breakers running off the sound end a great way off we hauld the wind and was all night turning to windward in order to run down the East side of the island –
At 5 made sail the land bearing from NWSW 10 leagues and there seemed to be land beyond it to NE 5 leagues – a remarkable peak like a sugar loaf NNE we were about two leagues of the shore which seemed delightful & pleasant full of houses & inhabitants saw some large canoes in shoar under sail but not coming towards us –
At noon running along by the shoar the land bearing from SW to NWBW distance of the shore two or three miles – latitude in 17:*4S, Long:d made 75:26W merid dis:ce 5381W –." PL and FC.

Remarks Sunday June 21 1767 – (71)

1	6	3	NWBN	ESE	
2	5	5	NW½W		
3	3	2	NW		
4	3		NWBN		
5	7	3	West	22:50	
6	2	4	SBE		
7	3		NEBN		
8	3	4			
9	3	2			
10	2			23:05	
11	2				
12	2	3		East	
1	2		SBE½E		
2	2				
3	2	3			Observed the longitude & found the ship to be in – 149:30 West from London
4	2	2	SSE		
5	2	4			
6	2	5			
7	2				
8					
9					
10					
11					
12					
Course	Distance		Latitude in	Longitude made	MDistance
N55:0WE	25		17:*30S	75:47W –	3391W

Fresh gales & pleasant weather sailing along the shore four miles off – and sometimes half a mile no soundings haul'd in to most places where we saw likelyhood of anchoring, at six haul'd the wind & plyed off & on all night as it look'd likely for anchoring –
at 6 am sent the boats inshore we standing after them at 9 they made the signal for 20 fm: bore down to them and at half past anchored in 17 fm: – fine clear bottom dark sand – the extreams of the land from ESE to SWBW off shore about one mile – AM at 9 ordered the Master with the boats mann'd and arm'd to sound along the shore to the Westward and look for a watering place there were at this time severall hundred canoes about the ship and between the shore, & when the boats came near the shore severall boats that were very large laid the barge onboard & threw stones at them and the other boats were coming up with them fast that they could by no signs make them keep of not even by firing musquets over them, & two more large sailing double canoes full of men coming [...] – for the boats side and would have certainly sunk her he fired & wounded two which made them all shoar off and they made no more attempts so the boats continued sounding in shoar and looking out for a good watering place The canoes about the ship brought off cocoanuts, plaintains, a few fowls and small hogs & other refreshments which they bartered for nails beads &:ce –The extream of the land from ESE to NWBW – At noon at anchor off a pleasant valley & lay at two miles distance[359]

Molineux indicates that the whole of the country exceeds description or any thing I ever saw but neither Gore nor Molineux make mention of this attack (Gore was in one of the boats and fired the shot which wounded the Tahitian – see Robertson, p. 139). The account in Hawkesworth describes a peace ceremony (based on Robertson's account) which none of the *Dolphin* logs mentions: "As soon as the boats reached the ship, they were hoisted on board, and just as she was about to stand on, we observed a large canoe, under sail, making after us. As I thought she might have some Chief on board, or might have been dispatched to bring me a message from some Chief, I determined to wait for her. She sailed very fast, and was soon along side of the ship, but we did not observe among those on board, any one that seemed to have an authority over the rest. One of them, however, stood up, and having made a speech, which continued about five minutes, threw on board a branch of the plantain tree. We understood this to be a token of peace, and we returned it, by handing over one of the branches of plantain that had been left on board by our first visitors: with this and some toys, that were afterwards presented to him, he appeared to be much gratified, and after a short time, went away."

359 "Fresh gales and very pleasant weather, sailing along the shore sometimes not above a half a mile and at others four or five miles off. I had no soundings & having got opposite a river at six o'clock, & the shore looking better than any we had yet seen determined to stand of and on all night and try for anchorage in the morning hauld the wind and stood off and on constantly sounding saw great numbers of lights all along the shore –
At day break sent the boats in shore to sound, soon after they made the signal for 20 fathoms, ran in immediately and anchored immediately in 17 fathom clean sandy ground the extreams of thee land from ESE to NWBW about one mile off shore and opposite to a large run of water as soon as we had secured the ship sent the boats to sound all along the shore and to look at the place

Week Day	Month Day	Wind	Remarks Onboard his Maj:ˢ Ship Dolphin at King Georges Isle 72
June	1767	East	Moderate cloudy with rain, the canoes still about the ship did not suffer them to come onboard as they stole every thing they could lay their hand on, the boats having found a fall of water sent them with some breakers to endeavour to get them filled. the inhabitants some thousands came down to the watering place &
		24:00	swam of with a few bamboos full of water on which our people sent two breakers which they filled & brought off. they then gave them four more to fill but they did not choose to return
Monday	22		them: after waiting a considerable time the Mate Mːʳ Gore who I sent on this service (I and the First Lieutenant being very ill & the Master had been for a long while in the boats) made signs to them to them that he could use force to recover the breakers &
		23:00	fired a musquett along the shore on which they ran back a little & then came back again & made signals for them to land & they would haul the boat up there being a very great surf on the shore –
22	1767	SEBE	& when they found that would not they sent their young girls down with their coats pulled up who made a thousand antick tricks to entice them to land, but on finding that none of their

where we saw the water at this time a great number of boats came of from the shoar to the ship and brought with them hogs fowles and plenty of fruit which we bought of them for nails and such like things; but when our boats pulled toward the shore most of the natives went after them keeping at a distance but as the boats drew nigher, the natives grew bolder and on a suddain three large sailing boats ran at the cutter and carried away her outlicker and stove her quarter, more coming down they fired two musquetts over them, which they only laught at and attempted the barge who fired at the boat that was lagging her onboard and much wounded a man on which they desisted and went away to leeward and others returned to the ship again and traded. The boats continued sounding until noon – when they returned and said that the ground was very clear & that there was five fathom within a quarter of a mile of the shoar, that there was a very great surf at the place where the water was, and a vast number of inhabitants on the beach that they swam off to them with bamboos filled with water and brought fruit likewais off & invited them onshoar, the women particularly came down and stript themselves naked and made all the alluring gestures they could to invite them onshoar. Gave the people a meal of fresh pork –." PL and FC. In the Hawkesworth account (based on Robertson, pp. 141–146), the death of the one of the Tahitians is described: "Our people being thus pressed, were obliged to fire, by which one of the assailants was killed, and another much wounded. Upon receiving the shot, they both fell overboard, and all the people who were in the same canoe, instantly leaped into the sea after them: the other two canoes dropped a-stern, and our boats went on without any farther interruption. As soon as the Indians, who were in the water, saw that the boats stood on without attempting to do them any farther hurt, they recovered their canoe, and hauled in their wounded companions. They set them both upon their feet to see if they could stand, and finding they could not, they tried whether they could sit upright: one of them could, and him they supported in that posture, but perceiving that the other was quite dead, they laid the body along at the bottom of the canoe. After this some of the canoes went ashore, and others returned again to the ship to traffick, which is a proof that our conduct had convinced them that while they behaved peaceably they had nothing to fear, and that they were conscious they had brought the mischief which had just happened upon themselves." Again, Gore (commanding one of the boats) restricts his account to nautical details.

Robertson (Corrington, op. cit., p.145) is critical of Wallis' as concerns this battle with the Tahitians: "...when I found them so very resolute, I orderd one of the marins to fire his musquet right across their canoe, in hopes of frightening them, without dowing them any more hurt, but this hade not the desired effect it only startled them a little and when they found non of them was hurt, they all gave

			schemes would take they threw apples & bananoes & some stones at the boats on which he returned onbaord.
			at 8AM sent the boats with some water casks & all kind of trinketts to endeavour to get water &:ce from the shoar, where the number of people increased and there came off more boats with refreshments to the ship nor did they attempt to go near the boats but rather avoided them – the soundings between the ship and the shore regular & clear, 6 fm: within a third of a mile from the shore – the wind blows here a long shore & raises a pretty great swell.[360]

a shout and run directly for our boats starn again, and the oyther two came right for the middle of our boat, fully resolved to board us, which if they hade their prows would have sertainly sunk our boat, and all of us must have inevitablely pereshd at same time they were attempting to board the cutter, I then found it was too leat to treat them with tenderness espetially as the ship took no manner of notice of us, altho they saw the whole transaction very plain, hade their been a nine pound shot fired over their heads, perhaps it may have frightend them from hurting us - but that not being done I thought myself under a necessity of using violent means, I therefor orderd the serjent and one of the marins, to wound the two most resolute like fellows, that was in the boat which first bearded us, this orders was complyed with and the one was killd which the serjent fired at, and the oyther was wounded in the thigh, and both fell overboard, when the oyther fellows in the canoe saw this they all jumpt overboard, and the oyther two canoes immediately steerd of, when we pointed the musquets to them they hield up their paddles before their faces and dropt astarn clear of us – and when they saw we gave them no more trouble, the crew of the canoe that first boarded us all jumpt in to their canoe and halld in the two men that was wounded, the one appeard quite dead, they tryd to make him stand, and when they found he could not, they endeavourd to make him sit, but found he was quite dead – then they laid him doun in the bottom of the canoe, and one of them suported the oyther, and the rest made sail and stood in for the land. After this non of them attempted to come near our boats . . ." Later (23rd June, p. 148) Robertson writes that some of the company suggest that the natives are enraged because he (Robertson) had now "killd two of them." Robertson justifies himself: "I gave a very concise answer by telling this two men, that what I hade done I was ready to do again if necessity required it."

360 "Remarks onboard his Majestys ship Dolphin at anchor. 22 June

Moderate and cloudy weather sent the boats with some breakers & small cask to the shoar to get water, the canoes still about the ship suffer none of the natives to come on board for they are so thievish that they steal all they can lay their hands on. At five the boats returned with only two breakers of water which the natives filled for them, and for their trouble kept all the rest, nor could they be persuaded to return them but made signs for our people to come onshoar there were gathered at the watering place some thousands of people when the boats came away.

AM sent the boats again for water and gave them nails hatchets &:ce to gain the friendship of the inhabitants, the canoes came of to our ship ass yesterday with bread fruit, plaintains, fowles, hogs, & fruit somewhat like apples only much better; for which I ordered nails knives beads &:ce to be given, and procured fresh pork enough for the ships company for two days at one pound a man – the boats returned and only brought a few calibashes of water. The numbers of people that were assembled on the beach prevented their landing, the young weomen acting every lewd action they could think of to entice them to land, and brought down fruit and meat to the water side and pointed for to come and partake thereof. Our people shewed them the breakers in the boat and made signs to bring of those they kept yesterday and when they could not prevail on them they weigh their grapnells and sounded all round to see how near the ship might come in and cover the waterers. At their putting off they were pelted with [sic] the weomen threw apples and bananas at them and made great hallowing –. On sounding they found that the ship might ride within two cables length of the shoar, sandy. The wind blows here right along the shore and raises

Week Day	M:th Day	Wind	Remarks (73)
June	1767	Easterly	Moderate & cloudy with some rain, at 4 the boats returned but could get only a few calabashes of water but they kept the breakers, they made use of the same arts as they did yesterday to entice them to land.
Tuesday	23	23:40	At 9 AM weigh'd sent the ^(Master with) the boats down to a Point of a Reef about four or five miles to the Westward & ship following half a mile a stern. when the boats came to the reef close to, they had from 12 to 2 fathoms & further had 12 fm:. a cable length and a half from it on which they made the signal for anchorage, the ship standing in, ran on a shoal to leeward which we did not find again but she ^(in about half an hour) of wore round and after a few thumps got into deep water; sounded the leewardmost reef and
		23:55	found it ran along shore from five to two fm: coral rock about one mile & then deepened into twelve, the boats then sounded
		Easterly	within the reef & found from 12 to 4 fm: and an excellent harbour almost land locked with a fine sandy bottom & an appearance of a fresh water river, was obliged to fire some shot over a multitude of canoes that were standing after our boats, which made them keep at a distance. at 11 the Master after placing two boats on the end of the reef came aboard and & took charge of the ship & piloted her safely within the reef and
		Calm	anchored her in 17 fathom water; fine black sand, it being calm got ready small anchor and warps to warp the ship up the harbour near the river.
			The place we were onshoar on was hard coral rock but luckily there was no great sea or she must soon have thumped her bottom on it but we got out the longboat & clear'd the decks. the boat was hurt by it and some glass and loose things broke likewais the main topmast trussle trees. we don't find that the bottom is any way damaged nor does she make more water than usual —[361]

a great sea alongside and a pretty high surf on the shore –." PL and FC. Gore's account is very succinct and makes no official mention of the details which are recorded here even though he was in command of the expedition sent ashore. Molineux is also brief: "Their number was very great & their women endeavou'd by every allurement to induce our men to land."

361 "Moderate and cloudy with some rain, boats employed in sounding, at daylight weigh'd with an intent of anchoring off –

the watering place, stood of to get further to windward when we discovered a bay about six or eight miles to leeward; bore away for it sounding the boats a head, at 9 hauld round a reef the boats making the signal for 12 fathoms and stood in with an intent to anchor, when we came near the boats there being one on each bow the ship stuck on a shoal from 17 fm: to two and a half clew'd all up as fast as possible and clear'd the ship of what lumber was on deck got the longboat out & stream & kedge anchor & stream cable & hawsers ready to carry out but had no ground without the reef, the ship beating at times pretty hard, at the same time there were some hundred of canoes full of men close by the ship – but did not attempt to come near us, after laying in this situation about three quarters of an hour the wind coming off from the shoar luckily the ships head swung off and we pressed all the sail immediately on her and stove some water in the fore hold thee ship being by the head & hung there the stern being free, she began to move of and very soon after she ran into deep water; stood of and on the boat sounding to leeward found that the reef ran down to the Westward one mile and after that you might haul into a very good harbour, and that when we were aground that there was a passage of near a cables length to windward the

Week Day	M:th Day	Wind	Remarks in Port Royal Harbour at King Georges Island –
June	1767		(1)
Wednesday	24	24:00 / 22:40	Moderate & fine weather, PM warped the ship up the harbour & anchored in 15 fm: & moord with the stream. The boats employed in sounding in order to warp the ship up to the head of the bay. – many canoes about the ship from whom we purchased fruit hogs & fowles which is given to the sick – and other people – put the ships company at <u>four</u> watches. Loaded all the guns & small arms & kept thirty men constantly around, the rest of the people had arms ready at a moments warning – at six AM there came of about three hundred canoes & before nine they were near double the number with multitudes of people near the shoar. these canoes had from eight to three men in each. some few had sixteen or eighteen. they brought of plenty of hogs, fowls & fruit, which we got in exchange for nails beads &:^{ce} at ½ past nine a boat with a large canopy over the middle & brought a large plaintain tree with a bunch of various coloured feathers & a pig & a man who sat on the top of the canopy made motions of peace & pointed to himself and then to the ship <u>is</u> tho' twas to be given to the superior. I being very ill came & looked out of the gallery window & was preparing some presents to give him in lieu & he seemed to be very attentive to all the boats that were round the ship in many of <u>which they had placed</u> three or well-looking girls^{in a row onboard severall large canoes}, who were making all the lascivious motions & playing all the wanton tricks imaginable, during this time likewais the boats drew nearer the ship & I perceived they had vast quantities of pebble stones of a pound to two or three weight

Master after placing a boat on the end of the reef & the longboat with anchor and hawsers with a guard for fear of being attacked, he came onboard and piloted the ship safely round the reef and anchord her 17 fathoms water fine black sand – this was about noon –

The place the ship ran onshoar at was a reef of sharp coral rocks, the soundings very uneven from two to 5 and six fathoms and unluckily where the boats were, the weather most in twelve and the leewardmost in nine fathoms with the reef between them – luckily we got of when we did for the wind freshening only a little after we got of and now fallen calm again, yet the surf runs very high on the reef and breaks much which had not the least appearance before so I believe the ship would have been soon wreck'd, our boats lost their grapnels on the reef we have look'd at the ships bottom as far as we can see and find nothing amiss except a small peice beat of the bottom of the rudder nor do we find that the ship makes any water, the trusssle trees at both fore mast and mizzen mast heads are broke short which suppose was done when the ship thumped so hard on the rocks; however we hope that her bottom is sound and that we shall be able to repair all our damages here for this bay appears to be a very snug one if it is clear of rock and shoals.

Sent the Master with all the boats armed to sound the upper part of the bay that if he found good anchorage we might warp thee ship up within the reef and anchor her in safety; a great number of boats on the reef and crowds of people on thee shoar." PL and FC.

Gore's account is again very succinct: "Fresh breezes and squally weath. Heavy showers of rain. PM the boats return'd having having attempted to get water without success the natives having kept two barkes as there being too much surf the natives numerous and the ship too far off to force a landing and get water our selves. We the next morning weigh'd with an intention to go nearer onshore to cover the boats and force a landing. But on second thoughts we made sail to the Westward to gain a more convenient place round the aforementioned low point. The boats going ahead sounding, in hauling round a low rocky point which runs from the aforementioned

Week Day	M:th Day	Wind	Remarks –
June			which we supposed they had for ballast, however keept the people constantly on their guard. just as I had prepared my present there was a silence amongst the canoes and two more covered canoes ^{came off who} were mounted with a man on the top ^{of each} and in an instant after he that was on the first canoe lifted up a plaintain leaf & threw a stained red cloth over his shoulders, on which every canoe set up a halloo & threw such a shower of stones at all parts of the ship that was astonishing, on which I ordered the people to fire on them, they persisted sometime but some of our great guns breaking a few of their large canoes & the quarter deckguns fired loaded with musquett that made them sheer off however they kept hovering at a distance & throwing stones – with slings things they did with great judgement and hurt many of our people they on our ceasing fire after a pause made a second effort and came on with a great resolution but on their coming near & slinging stones we fired a few ^{loaded with} great guns and grape at them and they all pulled for the shore so that at noon there was not a canoe to be seen –
Got up the six guns that were in the hold and mounted them, put two of them out at the stern & two forward –
at noon warped the ship to the upper part of the bay about two cables length from the river and as much from the reef and about four from the upper end of the bay and moord a cable each way. the small bower to the Eastward and carried out the stream for a spring.³⁶²
Wednesday	24	Sea	
		Land	
		Breezes	

point and not being aware of a shoal und:^r water fell upon it. But by the help of the sails shott off and running a little further to the Westward hauld round and anchor'd in 18 fathom water. Good ground and veer'd half a cable, the natives in abundance round the ship in canoes binging with them fruit, hogs & fowls for which we bartered nails."

The Hawkesworth account of the ship running aground is rather more dramatic: ". . . but when we came near the boats, one of which was on each bow, the ship struck. Her head continued immoveable, but her stern was free; and, upon casting the lead, we found the depth of water, upon the reef or shoal, to be from 17 fathom to two and a half: we clewed all up as fast as possible, and cleared the ship of what lumber there happened to be upon the deck, at the same time getting out the long-boat, with the stream and kedge anchors, the stream cable and hauser, in order to carry them without the reef, that when they had taken ground, the ship might be drawn off towards them, by applying a great force to the capstern, but unhappily without the reef we had no bottom. Our condition was now very alarming, the ship continued beating against the rock with great force, and we were surrounded by many hundred canoes, full of men: they did not, however, attempt to come on board us, but seemed to wait in expectation of our shipwreck. In the anxiety and terror of such a situation we continued near an hour, without being able to do any thing for our deliverance, except staving some water casks in the fore-hold, when a breeze happily springing up from the shore, the ship's head swung off. We immediately pressed her with all the sail we could make; upon which she began to move, and was very soon once more in deep water."

Robertson's account at this point is extremely interesting and is indicative of the tensions on board ship between Clarke and Robertson (see Robertson, pp. 147–153).

362 "The weather very pleasant, the Master returned and said that it was good anchorage every where, turn'd to and began to warp the ship up the bay and at four the people being much fateagued secured the ship, and laid out the stream cable and anchor with hawsers ready to warp up the bay early in the morning, at the same time put the people at four watches, one watch always under

arms loaded & primed all the guns, and fixed musquetoons in all the boats and ordered all the rest of the people in case of an alarm to be at the quarters assigned them in a moment, there being at this time great numbers of boats some very large and full of men, very few came near the ship and these only small ones we got from them fruit some hogs and fowles –

At sunset they all rowed for the shore –

At six AM began to warp the ship up the harbour, soon after came of many canoes and went under the stern where I ordered the Gunner and two Mid:^{m} to barter with them for their hogs fowles fruit &:^{ce} and gave them beads knives nails and trinkettts forbidding any person but them to have any commerce with the natives, about 8 the number of canoes increased much and those that came off last were large double canoes with a dozen or more of stout men in each – that they had very little in them to dispose of and that they were balasted with round pebble stones; on seeing this I sent for the Second Lieu:^{t} and bid him to keep the fourth watch constantly at their arms for fear of any attempt whilst the others were warping the ship, soon after came of more canoes who had placed a number of weomen in a row onboard them; who made all the gestures and wanton tricks they could invent at the same time the boats at a distance drew nearer to the ship and blew concks, & played on flutes, and severall men with hoarse voices sung. At last a man sitting on a canopy that was fixed on a large double canoe, made signs to let him come near the ship which I allowed him to do when he gave a bunch of red and yellow feathers to one of our people to bring to me, and then put of. I then got some trinketts in lieu to give him but in a moment there was a strang kind of hallow on this mans throwing up the branch of a cocoa nutt tree and a shower of stones was poured on the ship from every side and all the canoes in motion at once toward the ship, the guard I ordered to fire and the two quarter deck guns which I had loaded with small shot were fired likewais, this put them in some confusion, however after a minutes pause they began again, our people by this time having all got to their quarters, I gave orders for the great guns to be fired, some to fire constantly at a place on the shore where there was a great number of canoes who were taking in men and putting of toward the ship as fast as possible – I beleive there were not less than three hundred boats about the ship and on an average two thousand men beside some thousands on the shore and boats coming from every quarter, however on hearing our guns and seeing their boats pulling off from the ship they lay quiet, and we left of firing. On their seeing that a great number of canoes came together again and lay sometime looking at the ship about a quarter of a mile off, and then on a suddain hoisted up white streamers pulled toward the ships stern and began again to throw stones which they threw dextrously and at a great distance and at a great distance with slings, the stones weighing two pounds; having run out two guns abaft and pointing them well, as we did some forward at a number of canoes that were coming toward the bow of the ship from whence I beleive they had taken notice no shot had been fired, I ordered them to be fired on and one of the shott hit the canoe that had called the others to him and cut it asunder, on seeing which they immediately dispersed that in half an hour there was not canoe to be seen, the inhabitants that had been looking on from the shore all retreated over the hills up into the country. We then set at work and warped the ship up the harbour, that at noon we were near the upper end of it opposite a fine river, and not above a cables length and half and better than two from the reef and a half a mile from the upper part of the bay in 9 fathom water and had five close to the shore. Moor'd the ship and carried out ye stream anchor with the two shroud hawsers for a spring to keep the ships broad side opposite the river at the same time got up the eight guns that were put into the hold and mounted them. Gave what fruit and pork was onboard amongst the sick." PL and FC.

Gore's account is once again brief: "Fresh breezes without, within light breezes varying being influenced by the hig land over us. The W fair all day. PM weigh'd and warped into 15 fathom water and steadied with best bower & stream. Early in the morning the natives men and weomen came round the ship some in double others in single canoes bringing with them fruit hogs & fowles some as presents the rest to barter, the weomen most of them diverting our people in pulling up their colaths, and other tricks, as appears from what follows to draw off our defensive attention, for whilst we were busy, some trading, some giggling laughing and gaping at the

Week Day	M:th Day	Wind	Remarks at Port Royal Harbour in King Georges Island –
June	1767		(2)
		23:00 variable	Moderate sea & land breezes & pleasant weather punished M. Welch for cheating one of the inhabitants of a cock & ordered that no man shall trade with them but with an officers leave a few boats having come off with green boughs and some hogs & fowles which we bought of them, boats employed in sounding on the reef and all along the shore, very few canoes to be seen any where but great numbers of the inhabitants all along the shore particularly at the place that appeared to be a river; at noon the boats returned & the Master informed that it was clear ground from the reef all the way to the upper end of the bay and close to the shore several miles to the West ward – gave what fruit & pork we had amongst the sick –[363]
Thursday	25	20:40	

wanton positions of the weomen, others looking out on the watch, in the midst of all things a sig:[1] being given by one of the natives who wav'd a staff around the top of which was [...] a white cloath they began to shower stones by hand & sling to from all the canoes as thick as hail. But by the help of a few of our small arms and great guns they were dispers'd with the loss of several of their lives."

Molineux's account of the conquest of Tahiti is rather less dramatic: "A.M. A great number of canoes & Indians about the ship to trade, ½ past 8 they hove some stones into the ship at our people upon which orders was given to fire some shott to frighten them and it had the desir'd effect they immediately disapersin & went on shore."

Robertson typically provides a detailed description of the battle and alludes to a high death toll (p. 153–156)

363 "Pleasant weather the boats employed in sounding all round the bay and looking at the shore where there were many inhabitants, & if they seemed inclined to disturb us, he was employed with the boats on this service all the afternoon and morning, & at noon returned with a tolerable survey of the place, reported that there were no canoes in sight, the beach every where fit to land on & the whole bay clear of danger except the reef and some rocks at the upper end that shew'd themselves – that he was certain the river that we were opposite was fresh water, tho' it emptied itself on the other side of the Point of this bay.

At noon ordered Lieu:t Furneaux to take all the boats with the marines and other men properly armed, and land opposite the ship, and secure himself under the cover of the boats and the ship in the clearest ground he could find which seem'd to be opposite where the ship lay. It may seem strange that I constantly sent the Second Lieutenant on service, but the reason was the First Lieutenant hath been so ill for near six weeks and still continued so; I likewais have been so ill for these ten days past that it hath been with the utmost difficulty I have been able to crawl about, and am so much worn down at this time that with the fateague & hurry of being onshoar, & the attack, I find myself much worse – many of our men are likewais very low and weak –." PL and FC.

Gore here clarifies his position concerning the descriptions of the places discovered: "PM from what happened yesterday got all our guns out of the hold and made all clear for and aft, we likewise weigh'd & warp'd further to the E.w.d more into the bay and moor'd a cable each way inland WSW with the stream to the SW for a spring to bring our broadside to bear on the shore occasionally and cover our boats in landing should the natives oppose. This is a commodious and safe bay and good clear black ground regular soundings and good landing, you are cover'd from the NNW ground Eastward to the SW [...] Here is plenty of good refreshment such as good water hogs fowles breaf fruit yams plaintains sweet potatoes coco nutts and a sort of apple very plesant to the taste and makes good pudding. All is bought at very cheap rates, limes oranges they [...]. The women are very easy of access both men and weomen have black backsides artificially dyed

Friday	26	21:00 Sea & Land Breezes 20	Fine pleasant weather at 3 PM sent Lieu^t Furneaux with sixty men armed to the shoar to find out a watering place and take possession by right of conquest in the name & for the use of his most sacred Majesty King George the 3: and of the other islands to the Westward in the name of his Royal Highness the Duke of York – a little after three he landed about three cables length from the ship where he found a fine fresh water river running about ten yards within the beach – the inhabitants to a very great number were assembled about half musquett shot on the other side of the river, but came no nearer he made signs for one of them to come over when three set out but on making motions for one only two stayed behind – and one came with a pig and laid it at his feet & gave him some beads, nails &:^{ce} shewed him that he wanted water & refreshments and filled two casks & put them onto the boat he then read a paper I gave him & took possession for his Majesty & he cut a turf & plantted a pendant

their natural colour some of a deep copper colour others almost white and some quite black their hair black some tying it in on the tops of their heads others wairing it loose about their shoulders, they are in general strong well limbed people. Their features of the men manly and humane some cheerful others serious, the weomen [. . .] and wanton. A more particular account of this island, its bays, harbours, soil produce, inhabitants &:^{ce} I leave to those who are better qualified and whose province it is to treat of our voyage in every particular and so of the rest." Gore inserts a paragraph here giving a geographical description of King Georges Island estimating its length to be 13 leagues from East to West and from 20 to 30 leagues circumference. He gives directions to the anchoring places to future naviagtors.

Robertson recounts the nature of the contact between Tahitians and the ship after the previous day's battle (p. 158): ". . . notwithstanding the skirmish, that we hade yesterday a few canoes venterd off about noon, with the tops of plantain trees set up in the bows of their canoes, and smal branches in their hands, as emblems of peace and freindship. We this day behaved very haughty to them and only sufferd two or three to come along side at one time, when they disposed of what they hade we orderd them off, and let two or three more come along side – the poor creatures used a great deal of ceremony this day – before they came within a hundred yards of the ship, they all stood up and lookd hard at us and heald up the plantain boughs in their hands and one of them made a long talk, and all the rest seemd very atentive untill he hade done, then they all throwd their boughs to the sea, and began to paddle nearer the ship still keeping their eyes fixt on us, and if any of us lookt surly they immediately heald up the tope of the plantain tree, and forced a sort of smile, then laid doun the plantain tree top and showd us what they hade got to sell – if we wanted what they brou^t off, we made signes for them to come along side.

Then they began another part of their ceremony by pointing to the green plantain tree top, then made a long talk and put their bodys in several postures, some times he who made the talk would look up to the heavens seemingly very serious – then look at us and hold up the tree tope for some time, then turn round and point to the shore – and to all his partners in the canoe, after that they again lookt at us and talkt a little, then threw the tree top onboard the ship – then pointed to their hogs, pigs, fowls and fruit and began to trade very fair and honestly . . ."

Week Day	M:th Day	Wind	(3)
June			
			on a high pole & then came off when the boats put off the natives ventured over the river and two old men advanced toward the pendant and threw green boughs with many antick tricks multitudes behind them crawling on their hands & knees & when the pendant blew out they would start back in great confusion about five they ventured to touch the pole & they brought two hogs & lay at the foot of it after which they came of with them to the ship & made signs for us to accept it, and then returned to the shore again they would take nothing in return for their hogs but pointed to the pendant –
Friday			at 6 am sent Lieu.t Furneaux with sixty men to fill water & endeavor to get a trade for provision and fruit with the natives in exchange for hatchetts knives &:ce at ½ past 7 got off three tons of water. at 8 a great number of the inhabitants appeared from amongst the trees on each side of the river, and approached our people that were on the beach who made them signs to keep at a distance at the same time we saw from the ship vast crowds of people coming over the hills from every way seeming in great haste and severall hundred canoes came round a point about a mile from the ship, being full of men; and from a creek to the Eastward a great number more and they all pull'd close along shore & made directly for our boats On this I made the signal for the boats to come off which they did immediately leaving the cask behind them
			The inhabitants had by this time gained the beach where the cask were and beckoned to our people to return again who beckoned them to keep at a distance the canoes still advancing and more people coming from over the hills on which and seeing them roll the cask away, I ordered a shot to be fired at them and a few more

Week Day	M:th Day	Wind	
June Friday			at the canoes who made the best of their way when they found that they were so near us about fifty ran their canoes on the beach the rest pull'd off, I fired several shott in to different parts of the woods, and some at a tree I believe a mile and a half distance on a very high hill where there were some thousands assembled who had ran from the watering place & from the woods two shot fell a little beyond a tree and they all marched off I then mann'd the boats & sent Lieu.ᵗ Furneaux with eighty men to destroy the canoes they being furnished with axes for that purpose – & which he performed with expedition – he reported that many of them were double & many in the skirts of the woods ready for launching that we could not see that they had great quantities of large pebbles of two or three pounds weight several of the canoes were fifty & sixty feet long. they had no stock in & from the preparations they had made and their actions this morning I am firmly of opinion that they were bent on a second attack – had we not prevented them – those that came near our people had long poles in their hands & those that were at a distance had the like with them which none of them had yesterday. at noon the boats returned having destroyed upward of sixty canoes – gave the hogs that were got yesterday to the ships company which came to more than a pound a man made broth of it which was very good, gave leave to the people to take as many cocoa nutts that we brought from Q:ⁿ Charlotts island, & get of here the first day of anchoring at this island as they could make use of without waste – ³⁶⁴

364 "Fine pleasant weather with sea & land breezes & refreshing showers, at 3 PM the boats landed without any opposition. The Lieutenant stuck up a staff and on it hoisted a pendant turned a turf and took possession of this land in his Majestys name, and called it on honour of his most sacred Majesty King George the thirds island, then went to the river and tasted the water which he found to be exceeding good, of which he made some grogg and gave every man a drink [corrected to a "pint" in the FC], to drink his Majesties health after which he seeing two old men in a suppliant posture he beckoned them to come over the river which one did creeping on his hand and knees, when he came over, he shewed him what he wanted by filling two cask of water, and at the same time, made signs for hogs & fruit, produced some hatchetts & other things which he would give in exchange, then shewed him the stones that were thrown at the ship, and endeavoured to make him sensible that we did not mean any harm to them, that we came only for water & provisions and would trade very peaceably with them – after which he gave him a hatchett some nails beads and other trifles, then embarked onboard the boats leaving the pendant flying and came onboard. Soon after the old man danced round the pendant for a considerable time then retired and came again with some green boughs and threw them down then he retired and came again with about a dozen of inhabitants all in a suppliant posture who would sometimes come up close to it but when the wind moved they would retreat with great precipitation – soon after they all came up dancing with two large hogs which they laid down at the foot of the pendant staff after staying there a while, they brought the hogs down to the water side launched a canoe and the old man, who had a large white beard came down and off to the ship with them, when he came alongside he made a speech, handed in several green plaintain leafs [and "boughs" in the FC] and said …

Week Day	M:th Day	Wind	Remarks at Port Royall – (4)
June	1767		Pleasant weather at 2 PM about ten of the natives came down to the beach with green boughs & stuck them up and then went back and returned with severall hogs & dogs tyed by the feet and laid them on the beach & then they brought a quantity of the cloth that they cloth themselves with & hallowed to us to come and receive it; mann'd the boats & sent Lieu.^t Furneaux to them on which they retired & left the offering of peace; he took the hoggs & turned the dogs loose & left the cloth and in return for nine hogs he gave them hatchetts bill hooks nails &:^{ce}. but they would not take it unless they took the cloth which we did & they went away rejoicing – the boat then went to the watering place and sent of six tons of water, an old man who seemed to have some sway amongst them and who came over first to our people when they landed came & made a speech and then cross the river, when the officer shewed him the stones with which they had assaulted the ship and those in the canoes – was the reason of our attacking them that we would not molest them unless they began & that we would give them in exchange what we had for fruit & provision – the old man turned round to his people & shewed the stones & spoke to them & shook his head, pointing at the ship many of the people went away & returned with yams plaintains & bread fruit a few fowles & roasting pigs – they brought them over one by one to the old man who gave them to the Lieu.^t in lieu of nails and beads. at sun down he returned onboard with fresh provisions enough for the ships company and the surgeon being of opinion that giving the company a breakfast of wheat, bread fruit, bananoes & apples would be of
		Easterly	
		22:00	
Saturday	27		
		21:00	
		Westerly	

every one he gave in, then he sent in the two hogs, he then pointed to the shore, I ordered some presents to be given him but he would take nothing and went onshoar, at night we heard the noise of many concks, drums and wind instruments and great numbers of light all along the coast, at six in the morning seeing no people on the shoar and the pendant taken away ordered he Lieu:^t to take guard onshoar and if all was well to send of and we would begin watering he soon sent of four empty cask and at eight o'clock he sent off four tons of water, some of the inhabitants had brought a little fruit and a few fowls which he likewais sent of. The old man being with them they kept on the opposide of the river, at half past eight saw a great number of natives coming over a hill about a mile of and at the same time a vast number of canoes came round the point & kept close to the shore, looking at the watering place I saw at the back of it where it was clear a great number of people creeping along behind the bushes and at the East point of the bay canoes in great plenty coming round the point and in the woods thousands of the inhabitants pushing along toward the watering place with great speed sent a boat to acquaint the officer therof and to embark his men and come onboard without the cask. Before the boats reached them they were embarked having spyed them creeping thro' the wood towards them he immediately dispatched the old man and beckoned for them to keep at a distance and pointed that he only wanted water, they finding they were discovered set up a hallow and crossed the river and took possession of the cask and made great rejoicing at the same time the canoes pulled up the shore briskly the people on land keeping pace with them except a multitude of weomen and children who seated themselves on a hill that overlookd the bay and beach; and as they drew nearer the ship they put to the shore and took in more men – who seemed to have great bags in their hands, the canoes still coming round each point both to the Eastward and Westward and all along accompanied with numbers

| | | | great assistance to them in clearing them of scorbutic complaints, we having few or none in the ship we had more or less of it; ordered the Purser to issue it to them as long as the Surgeon should think it necessary AM employed in clearing the ship & painting her upper work, clearing the hold and overhauling rigging – [365] |

on the shore especially as some of them had taken men onboard and come of toward the ship. I thought it no longer a doubt that their intentions were to try their luck with us a second time and that it was necessary to conquer them in the beginning therefore every man being at quarters I ordered them to fire first in the group of canoes which was done so effectually that those to the Westward pushed onshore as fast as possible those to the Eastward got round the reef & soon out of our reach I then directed the fire into the woods in different parts which made them soon quit the wood and they got to the hill where the weomen & children were, where they assembled to a multitude of some thousands I really believe, ordered some of the guns to let down as low as possible and fired four shot toward them, they thinking themselves in great security when two of the shot fell close by a tree where a great many were sitting, that so afrighted them that in two minutes time there was not one to be seen – I immediately mann'd and armed the boats and sent a strong guard with all the carpenters with their axes with orders to destroy all the canoes that were ran on shore which they performed before noon, many of the canoes were sixty feet long and three broad two lashed together would carry a number of men the boats had vast quantities of stones and slings in them and nothing else except a few small canoes which had some fruit and a few fowles. They destroyed upwards of fifty of these canoes – the few fowls and hogs that were found in the canoes, with the two that we had last night I ordered to be distributed amongst the ships company which was more than a pound a man." PL and FC.

In Gore's log: "Severall canoes came round the ship with peace offering which are plaintain trees but were kept off. Our boats sounding about ship. Punished William Welsh seamen with a dozen lashes for defrauding the natives and disobeying orders. AM our boats man'd and arm'd went ashore unde:^{er} the command of the Second Lieutenant to fill water and trade with the natives, at 10 great numbers of the natives some on shore others in canoes appearing our boars were order'd off, we fir'd several shot from ship which soon dispersed them, we on all quarters endeavour'd to avoid hurting the natives and bring them to friendly correspondence . . ."

In the Hawkesworth edition, when Furneaux notes that the staff has disappeared, there is a reference to one of Aesop's fables which is not to be found in the ship's logs: ". . . observing that the pendant was taken away, which probably they had learnt to despise, as the frogs in the fable did King Log . . ."

Molineux gives no description of this expedition though he had the command of the three boats.

365 "Fine pleasant weather at 2 PM about ten of the natives came out of the wood with green boughs in their hands which the stuck up near the waterside and retired; soon after they came again and brought with them severall hogs with their legs tyed and placed them by the boughs & went away, then returned with more hogs and severall dogs with their legs tyed over their heads and after that they brought down severall bundles of cloth where with they are clothed it is exactly like paper. these they left on the beach and called to us onboard to come and take it, sent the boats to the shore and brought of the offering which consisted of nine good hogs, cast the dogs loose and left the cloth on the beach and in lieu of the hogs left some nails hatchetts and other things and pointing to them to take their cloth and the things we had sent on shore, the boats came off, the people brought two more hogs down to the beach and called to the ship, sent the boat again, they pointed for to take the hogs & cloth, they took the hogs but left the cloth, the natives would not touch the hatchetts &:^{ce} that I sent them on the return of the boats they said that they believed the reason the natives would not receive our present was because we would not receive of their cloth,

on which I sent for it, which as soon as we had taken up they came down rejoicing and took up all the things I had sent them. Our boats then went to the watering place and filled and brought off all the cask about six tons – they were not hurt, but some leather bucketts and funnells that were left behind were taken away. PM sent onshoar a guard and the boats to get water, soon after the old man who came over to them first came again and made a long speech and then crossed the river, when he was come over the Officer shewed him the stones that were brought there since his first landing and likewais some of the bags which were taken out of the canoes we had destroyed and endeavoured to make him sensible that we had acted as we did thro necessity after which the old man made a speech to the people and shewed them the stones slings and bags and seemed rather furious in his speech to them after which we shew'd him that we wished to be in friendship, shook hands and embraced him and gave him a few trifles and pointed to him that we would traffic with them for provisions, they to keep on one side of the river and we the other and not any number to come down – this they came into and by noon, a traffick was begun and provisions of fowl and hogs with vast quantities of fruit was brought onboard so that both the sick and the well had as much as they could make use of – I likewais at the request of the Surgeon ordered wheat and portable soup and bread fruit to be boiled every morning for the people's breakfast. – having settled matters so well ordered the second Lieu:[1] and Surgeon to look round and fix on some place to send the sick, they returned saying that everywhere seemed very proper, but that it would be very imprudent for them to be sent at any other place than the watering place as they would allways be under the protection of the ship and the guard and prevent their stragling and could be constantly with the others be brought of to the meals, that we had so many ailing and employed we could not separate them knowing the treachery of the inhabitants." PL and FC.

Gore describes the encounter thus: "PM our boats went and distroy'd some canoes on shore as a means not to be disturb'd with numbers about the ship after which our boats went to the watering place for water, the natives prov'd humble being in great consternation concerning all the consequences of our firing, in the evening our boats return'd with water, pigs fruit and fowls."

Robertson's account includes details which none of the *Dolphin* logs relates: ". . . when the cloath was put in the boats our people made signs for the natives to take the thing which we laid doun, this they complyed with and brought doun some more hogs, pigs and fruit, this our men received and paid them with nails and toys. But our young men seeing several very handsome young girls, they could not help feasting their eyes with so agreable a sight this was observed by some of the elderly men, and several of the young girls was drawen out, some a light coper colour others a mullato and some almost white. the old men made them stand in rank, and made signs for our people to take which they lyked best, and as many as they lyked and for fear our men hade been ignorant and not known how to use the poor young girls, the old men made signs how we should behave to the young women, this all the boats crew seemd to understand perfectly well, and begd the officer would receive a few of the young women onboard, at same time they made signs to the young girls, that they were no so ignorant as the old men supposed them, this seemd to please the old men greatly when they saw our people merry, but the poor young girls seemd a little afraid, but soon after turnd better aquanted. The officer in the boat having no orders to bring off any of the natives, would not receive the young girls but made signs that he would see them afterwards, and orderd all our men onb[d] the boats, and returnd onbd the ship, when our boats returnd to the ship all the sailors swore they neaver saw handsomer made women in their lives, and declard they would all to a man, live on two thirds allowance, rather not lose so fine an opportunity of getting a girl apiece – this piece of news made all our men madly fond of the shore, even the sick which hade been on the doctors list for some weeks before, now declard they would be happy if they were permited to go ashore, at same time said a young girl would make an excelent nurse, and they were certain of recovering faster under a young girls care nor all the doctor would do for them, we past this night very merry supposing all hostilitys was now over and to our great joy it so happend."

Week Day	M:th Day	Wind	Remarks on Board his Majestys Ship Dolphin – (5)
June Sunday	1767 28	23:00 Sea & Land Breezes 21:00	Moderate & fair weather got off some water, and an old man who had been over before at the watering place, came from the side where the natives were to our people & exchanged hogs, apples &:^{ce} for knives, beads, nails & other things – so that we have plenty of fresh provisions & fruit; this old man is of service to us in keeping the natives in order at noon served fresh pork & fruit – employed about the ship, carpenters, painting & caulking armourers with the forges – sailmakers in over hauling & mending the sails –[366]

[366] "Moderate and fair weather, appointed the Gunner to command the party that was sent onshoar every day to protect both the people filling water and the sick who were sent onshoar with the surgeon and had a hut [tent" in the FC] erected for them where they kept them themselves out of the sun and rain; I likewais directed the Gunner not to suffer any trade to be carried on between our people and the natives but all to come thro' him to prevent any disturbances and to endeavour to attach the old man to his interest, which service from the beginning to the end he performed with great diligence and care much to my satisfaction and ease, nor did he neglect complaining of any one that transgressed these orders, which I severely punished and by making a few examples in the beginning hindered a growing evil, the old man was likewais greatly usefull to us and by signs would caution our straglers to get back for fear of being assaulted, which kept them always on their guard – employed in the ship in caulking & painting the weather work, overhauling the rigging and stowing the hold and doing sundry other things this day I was obliged to take to my bed and continued dangerously ill of a bilious cholic for near a fortnight the first Lieu:^t & Purser likewise very ill, and some of the seamen, others recover very fast from their scurvy. Ordered the Second Lieutenant to be particularly carefull that the people that were sent onshore kept themselves orderly that they did not straggle nor by any means insult the natives; to procure fruit and fresh provision for the ships's company as long as possible he could, & always to keep a proper guard to prevent being surprised and never let the boats be from the ship after sun set; all these things he very punctually obeyed and gave me no kind of trouble in my sickness – the people being daily served with pork fowles and great quantities of fruit, that on my getting up I could scarce believe it was the same ships company that I arrived here with – they were looking so healthy and well –." PL and FC.

Gore: "Employ'd watering cleaning the ship and trading. The natives begin to understand us. Our people on shore having orders to be allways on their guard nor to take any thing forcibly from the natives or hurt them in any respect whatsoever."

			(6)
Monday	29	22:50 Easterly 21:00	Fine pleasant weather sent the Gunner with a strong guard to the watering place & the coopers with stores to set up & the repair water casks the Surgeon with all the sick who were to keep in the shade amongst the trees or under the tents on the side of the river by the watering place – the Gunner had orders not to suffer any to straggle for trade with the natives but himself[367] to whom I gave cloth, beads knives buttons scissors nails and many other things he returned at night with twenty small hogs some fowls bread fruit, bananoes & apples served fresh pork – people employd as before the Master out sounding the reef and taking a survey with one of his Mates – no canoes except small fishing ones, the natives begin to be very courteous and behave very quietly, the weomen particularly fond of prostituting themselves. gave orders that the people were constant on their guard and not suffer themselves to be surprised[368]

367 Robertson may have been slightly put out by Wallis' choice of the Gunner as the principal trading intermediary and reports in his journal (p. 170): "... it was supposed the Gunner was the man that persuaded the Capt to give this orders, out of a privet vew, that he might have it in his power to carry on all the trade, as we hade now resolved to let no canoe trade along side the ship but to send every day, the Gunner with forteen or sixteen armd men, besides four of the young gentlemen and the serjent of marines to assist him." A few days later on the 1st July he levels implicit criticism at the Gunner's trading policy accusing him of treating the women like slaves "(the women were not allowed to come across the river to trade their pearls and the Gunner had asked the old man to act an intermediary but the women refused to give up their pearls to him)." See also Robertson, p. 175.

368 "Fine pleasant weather, employed in watering and other services, sent the boats to haul the scene but caught no fish, likewais trawled but without success, indeed it was no great loss as the people fared sumptuously every day – my being ill with the first Lieu:t & Purser prevented us from making observations on the satellites of Jupiter as duty fell so hard on the 2:nd Lieu and Master, and the great guard that was constantly onshoar every day and as large a one onboard at night, where as if we had observed the satellites we must have had a guard onshoar at night and left no officers onboard – as the Master and M:r Furneaux were the only ones that could make any observation of them, and they not expert at it. M:r Harison the Purser being very ill was a great misfortune to us as he is very expert in every branch of the mathematics, however we had many sights of the sun and moon for setling the longitude which we have since worked and hope that we have it nearly by the agreement of the different observations –." PL and FC.

Week Day	M:th Day	Wind	Remarks &:ce –
June Sunday	1767 30	Sea & Land 23:00 Breezes 21:50	(7) Fine weather with refreshing showers employed as before the guard with the Gunner onshoar who sent of hogs fowles & fruit served fresh pork – & fruit[369]
July Wednesday	1	24:00 Ditto 22:30	(8) Fine weather boats & people employed as before served fresh pork fruit – the old man was not at the watering place –[370]
Thursday	2	23:20 variable 21:00	(9) Cloudy with rain & lightning. got the sheet anchor over the side hauld the scene several times in all parts but caught no fish Gunner had very little trade to day[371] only enough for the sick – punished Rich Cann for disobedience of orders onshoar[372]
Friday	3	22:00 variable 21:00	(10) First and middle squally rainy weather latter fair Little trade this day served fresh pork & fish to about thirty men – & fruit enough for the breakfast – scrubbed between wind and water, when heeld we did not perceive that the bottom was any way hurt & was as clean as when she came out of the dock –[373]
Saturday	4	23:00 21:00 variable Observed the Long. At 7 PM 150°26′ West from London	(11) [374]Light airs employed as before the Gunner sent off hogs and fruit enough to serve (part of) the ships company at 10 we caught a shark that was 13 feet long and nine in circumferance towd it on shoar to the beach & when they put off made signs to the natives to take it when some hundreds came over and in a quarter of an hour had cut up & carried it all away.
Sunday	5	22:10 Sea & Land	(12) Cloudy weather employed as before, the Gunner sent of the Gunner [sic] sent of 12 small hogs some fowles & plenty of fruit, served fresh pork – the sick recovered of the scurvey fast

369 ". . . one of our men found a peice of salt petre onshoar, the Surgeon made enquiry if any one had brought such a peice with them but all declared they had none and on enquiring onboard had the same answer he shewed it to the natives but could not know from them if they had any such thing or not, and during our whole stay we saw no more than this one piece . . . Gunner supplies the ship with hogs & fruit in plenty." PL and FC.

370 ". . . engaged in wooding and watering the ship the Surgeon with the sick daily onshoar, the Master with one of his Mates sounding all along the shore for four miles down, none of the natives came near our boats with their canoes, not within a mile or two of the ship. Gunner with his guard on shore. PL and FC.

371 ". . . Gunner hath not such quantities of pork, fowls & fruit as before, the old man being absent, yet enough to serve most of the messes, reserving plenty for the sick and recovering." PL and FC.

372 Robertson reports in his journal that the Surgeon began to fear for Wallis' life (p.172).

373 "On the 3d, we heeled the ship, and looked at her bottom, which we found as clean as when she came out of dock, and to our great satisfaction, as sound." Hawkesworth.

374 "Light airs had tolerable success at markett, sent off hogs and fowls enough to serve every mess with plenty of fruit, at noon caught a very large shark, sent it onshore when the boats went for the people to come of to dinner, when the boats put of the gunner made signals to the natives to cross the river, which they did and he gave them the shark which they soon cut in pieces and carried away greatly pleased –." PL and FC.

Week Day	M.ᵗʰ Day	Wind	Remarks – (13)
		Breezes 20:50	but some have fallen down of a billious fever however they soon get over it having plenty of fruit and wheat & vegetables, with portable soup for breakfast and fresh pork & broth of vegetables for dinner every day –³⁷⁵
July Monday	1767 6	22:00 Sea & Land Breezes 20:40	Fine pleasant weather. carpenters, smiths sailmakers &:ᶜᵉ employed about repairing the ships sails & iron work which was very much wanting. The Gunner with his guard the Surgeon with the sick onshoar with him; & the coopers setting up casks. The old man returned & trade comes in pretty well, he made signs that he had been up the country & carried with him his hatchett nails &:ᶜᵉ and a coat that was given him, served fresh pork and fruit – I went with the Master about three leagues to the Westward & sounded the coast and found excellent anchoring all along but where was reefs which shew them selves the country very populace & vast numbers of large double canoes – they have great plenty of hog, fowles & fruit and fish they catch on the reefs – we got very little from them being employed in sounding – they did not attempt to molest us but brought down green boughs as tokens of peace & swam of with some fruit – we returned in the evening, this is the first time I have been out of the ship having been kept to my cabbin & bed these few weeks the First Lieu:ᵗ still very ill³⁷⁶
Tuesday	7	23:00 Ditto 21:00	(14) Employed as before, sent a Mate with thirty men to a village to get fresh stock &:ᶜᵉ but they asked more for it than they sold it for at the watering place. Served fresh pork to the ships company to the sick & petty officers – fowles – with great plenty of fruit.³⁷⁷

---

375 "Cloudy weather had plenty of fowls and ten small hogs from the Masters tent, the scorbutic men recover very fast, severall compkaints of bilious fevers and cholicks but they soon get over it except myself & the First Lieu:ᵗ who remain very ill, the Purser better took an observation for finding the longitude, together with M:ʳ Furneaux and the Master." PL and FC.

376 "Fine pleasant weather, the old man returned to the Gunner and made signs to him that he had been up the country to get the people to come in with trade: soon after came down several people with larger hogs than we had yet seen severall of which were sent onboard the old man likewais came of and brought a roasted hog with him as a present gave him an iron pot looking glass drinking glass and severall other things ["which no man was in possession but himself" Hawkesworth]. PL and FC. Wallis does not mention seeing a *marae* on the short trip out in the boat with the Master (Robertson gives a detailed description in his journal, pp. 178–179).

377 "Sent a mate with 30 men to a village to purchase stock but they gave more for it there than at the waterside, where they had advanced the price of things greatly by some of our peoples stealing iron from the ship and exchanging it with the natives, so that instead of small nails for midling hogs they shew'd large spikes and would not part with them as before, made a search severall cleats being drawn, but could not discover the agressors, offered a good reward but to no purpose I being able to get up and weather being pleasant rowed down the coast about four miles it was exceeding populous and pleasant they had great numbers of boats, but none came of to us, nor did they take any notice of the boat as she passed along the shore. at noon came onboard, this is the first time of my being out of the ship, the first lieu still dangerously ill –." PL and FC.

Week Day	M:th Day		Remarks – (15)
Wednesday	8	22:20 Ditto 19:30	Employed as before. served fresh pork to the ships company. gave the old man a goose & gander, a turkey cock & hen & three Galleaneas an iron pot, many sorts of garden seeds & shewed him how to plant them, set in different places plumb, peach, cherry apples, mellon and pumpkin, lime, lemon & orange seeds – I was taken very ill again –[378]

Week Day	M:th Day	Wind	Remarks – (16)
July Thursday	1767 9	22:30 Sea & Land Breezes 20:00	Pleasant weather with refreshing showers. Employed in wooding and otherwais as before, the natives seemed much displeased at our cutting their breadfruit tree down but on giving a nail for a tree they were well satisfied and for a small nail & man carried it down to the boats. got but very little trade, just enough for the sick, two of the inhabitants came of with the wooders one seemed to be a chief. he dined with the Officers, he tasted of everything that was given to him but eat yam plaintain & apples. showed him silver gold & brass but he knew nothing of it & preferred iron before them all. shewd him many pictures & one of a ladys portrait in minature at which he was in raptures. made him some presents & set him onshoar This man we called Jonathan.[379]
Friday	10	22:00 Easterly 21:00	(17) Cloudy. employed as before. got very little trade few inhabitants came down – served fowles to the sick people read the Articles of War & Act of Parliament, punished Jms Proctor for drunkeness & mutiny[380]
Saturday	11	22:20 ESE	(18) Fresh breezes & rainy. employed as before. got only two fowles & a little fruit which with the fowles we have onboard served to the sick who are much recovered & all the peoples complextion

378 "Employed in compleating our wood and water gunner with his guard as usual is obliged to give more than formerly for what he gets, yet have enough for the daily expence and great plenty of fruit." PL and FC. Robertson informs Wallis that he has seen a fleet of some very large and small small canoes coming round the reef and going into a harbour out of view of the ship (p.182). Wallis decides it is imprudent to investigate which annoys Robertson somewhat.

379 "Pleasant weather, employed as before, trade for hogs & poultry very bad fruit in great plenty. read the Articles of War and punished some of the people who had been disobedient to orders that were given them onshoar particularly James Proctor the Corporall of Marines who not only left his station but insulted the officer & when he came onboard and was ordered into confinement, he knocked the Master at Arms down." PL and FC.

The Hawkesworth account provides further details: "The commerce which our men had found means to establish with the women of the island, rendered them much less obedient to the orders that had been given for the regulation of their conduct on shore, than they were at first. I found it necessary therefore, to read the articles of war, and I punished James Proctor, the corporal of marines, who had not only quitted his station, and insulted the officer, but struck the Master at Arms such a blow as brought him to the ground."

380 "Moderate weather, some of the inhabitants came onboard in our boat who had been very kind to the wooders. They seemed both by their dress and actions to be above the common sort, gave them some presents and put them onshore again – but little trade, just enough to supply the sick –." PL and FC.

Robertson (p. 187) recounts an incident onshoar which indicates that the young gentlemen in question had met the "queen": "At sun rise we sent the traders ashore to the usuall place, and the

		22:10	are altered from a thin & pale visage to a healthy countenance at 10 AM the man that dined with the officers Thursday came onboard with two roasted hogs & some fruit. punished James Proctor for knocking down the Master at Arms —[381]
Sunday	12	22:30 ESE 21:00	(19) Fresh breezes & clear employed as before. got some hogs, fowles & fruit and served fresh pork to all the ships company got of some water found several of the large belaying cleats drawn & the nail taken away and many nails in places drawn — searched but could find none of them. offered a reward but no discovery[382]

wooders to the n°ward.of the river as their appeard to be several old trees their, they purchasd the trees here for a large spike nail the same as the oyther place, the method was this, our people stuck in the nail to the tree and desired the owner to take it out, if he took out the nail and keept it, they cut doun the tree, but if returnd the nail or pointed to another tree then the first tree was let stand and the oyther cut doun, one of the young gentlemen tould me that their was a great dispute hapend this day between two of the natives where he stick in the nail to pay for the tree, and old man took it out who it seems was the owner of the tree and hade his house closs by it, but another stout well lookt man who seemd to be one of their cheifs took the nail from the old man and kept it, he says their was a good many ill naturd words past betwixt them, and the old man gave up the point, and went in to his house. A few minutes after their came doun a fine well lookt woman of the dark mustee colour, with a great many men allong with her, who seemd to pay her a great deal of respect some of these was standing by when the dispute happend betwixt the two men, tould her what hade happend and she spoke to one that stood by her, who calld to the old man, who immediately appeard before her trembling, she spoke to him a few words, but the old man scarce made any answer, she then talkd to him that hade the nail, and he immediately gave up the nail to the old man, and walkt of seemingly in great fear and this woman spok to him very angery lyke, and soon after walkt in to the woods with the man who came doun with her: this in my oppinion plainly demonstrats, that their is both justice, and property in this happy island."

381 "Fresh breezes and rainy. got only two fowls, the inhabitants all making signs for large nails in looking round the ship the Carpenter found that all the belaying cleats were ripped off and most of the hammock nails drawn – ordered all hands up and endeavoured to find out who had been the thieves, then told them that if they would not discover I would put a stop to their going onshoar, could make no discovery, the Corporal James Proctor Corporal of Marines behaving in a mutinous manner – punished him immediately." PL and FC. Two women come onboard with "Jonathon" (see Robertson, p. 190). Wallis makes little mention of the quite considerable role "Jonathon" plays in maintaining trade and relations onboard ship (see Robertson, p.193).

The Hawkesworth account puts forward the reasons for these thefts: "While our people were on shore, several young women were permitted to cross the river, who, though they were not averse to the granting of personal favours, knew the value of them too well not to stipulate for a consideration: the price, indeed, was not great, yet it was such as our men were not always able to pay, and under this temptation they stole nails and other iron from the ship. The nails that we brought for traffick, were not always in their reach, and therefore they drew several out of different parts of the vessel, particularly those that fastened the cleats to the ship's side. This was productive of a double mischief; damage to the ship, and a considerable rise at market. When the gunner offered, as usual, small nails for hogs of a middling size, the natives refused to take them, and produced large spikes, intimating that they expected such nails as these."

382 "Fresh breezes, Gunner sent off hogs & fowls enough for the ships company." PL and FC.

Week Day	M:th Day	Wind	Remarks Onboard his Maj Ship Dolphin at Port Royall
July	1767	East	(20)
			Fresh breezes & clear middle & latter fresh gales & heavy rain –
			at ½ past noon the Gunner brought of a weoman of between
			forty & fifty of a very comely presence and with her three
		22:00	people who seem'd to pay her great respect he said she came
			down about three days ago and seemd to attach herself to the
			Sargeant of Marines, to whom she brought hogs & fowles &
			gave some of her country dress to, & would take nothing in
			return – that trade being dull near the waterside he took a party
			with him and went back about a mile from the river the
			inhabitants very peaceable & quiet, that he then came to a
Monday	1767		village where the houses were better than any he had yet seen
	13		and one amongst them was 380 feet long 37 broad & supported
			with pillars from one end to the other, that here this weomen was
			and had with her near 1000 people whom she was giving
			portions of provisions to & then she was fed by two weomen,
			she gave them fruit & came with the Gunner & people to the
			water side & on his shewing her the ship she came of with him
		20:00	as mentioned. I was very ill however I had her into the cabbin
			and gave her some cloth ribbons & other things with which she
		SE	seemed greatly pleased; when she landed she sent off hogs
			enough for one day for the ships company – who from this day
			never wanted a fresh meal all the while we staied here – AM –
			the weather so bad could send no boat onshoar. the natives came
			down to the watering place and cut the bank of the river and
			made a new channell as the water had risen very much on the
			flat ground – this forenoon came came of two cheifs & brought
			with them some roasted pigs & fruit, gave them presents in
			return –[383]

383 "Fresh breezes and fair, at PM the Gunner came onboard with a tall well looking weomen about forty five years old, she had a very majestic mein and he seeing her paid great respect by the inhabitants, she being just come there he made her some presents, she in return invited him to her house about two miles up the valley and gave him large hogs & showd an inclination to go onboard the ship. she was quite free & easy on her coming onboard and all the time she was there, I gave her a large blue mantle that reached from head to her heels and tyed it with ribbons, and gave her severall sorts of beads a looking glass and many other things, she taking notice that I had been ill pointed to the shore, I made signs that I would be there tomorrow morning, she soon after went onshoar and the Gunner with her, who saw her habitation, he said it was a prodigious large house and that it was extremely well built that her guards and domesticks lived in it and that she had one close by it that was very large but it was closed with lattice work in the morning I went onshoar for the first time where the queen I may call her soon came [Hawkesworth notes "my Princess, or rather queen"] and made some of her people to take me and all that went with me that were ailing up in their arms and carry me a cross the river and so on to her house & ordering a guard to follow, tho there was a multitude of people, she only waving with her hand, or

Week Day	M:th Day	Wind	Remarks&:ce (21)
July	1767	ESE 21:00 20:00 SSE	Fresh gales & rainy, the boats went on shoar & returned again immediately with four hogs, two dozen of fowles & plenty of fruit, it rained very hard. served fresh pork &:ce384
Tuesday	14		

speaking a word they immediately withdrew – and left us a free passage. When we came near her house a great number of men and weomen came out to meet her, and she brought them to me and after shewing me by signs they were her relations she took hold of my hand and made them kiss it – after this we went into the large house (a plan of which I have here inserted) – [this remark is missing in the FC] she made us all sit down then she called four young girls who took down my stockings and shoes and pulled of my coat, and they smoothed down the skin gently chafing it, she likewais had the same operation performed on the first Lieu:t and Purser who were both ailing but those who were in health she did not trouble, after a certain time I beleive near half an hour they left of and dressed me again at which they were very awkward, however I found that it had done me much service and the others declared the same she then ordered some bundles to be brought and took from these some country cloth which is like paper, and clothed me and all that were with me after their manner, I seemed unwilling but at last not choosing to offend her accepted it, at my going away she ordered a very large sow big with young to be taken down to the boat, she accompanied us and I choosing to walk she took me by the arm and lifted me over every slough with as much ease as I could (when in health) a child – in the morning I sent her by the Gunner six hatchets, six bill hooks & some other things – the Gunner said that when he came there she was giving an entertainment to he believed neare a thousand people – that there were severall people making up messes and brought to her and the guests being seated in rows round the great house she gave to every one a mess from her own hands after which she sat down by her self in a high place and two weomen placed themselves on each side and fed her she opening her mouth as they brought their hands up with food, she ordered a mess for the Gunner, he said he beleived it was fowl pick'd small and apples cut up with it and seasoned with salt water that it was very well tasted – she accepted the things that was sent her and seemd much pleased with them and they came away. after this the trade went on very well peole came in daily with fowles and hogs many very large one only we were obliged to pay much for them that we did at first by the people spoiling the market yet everything was as cheap as dirt – served fresh pork –." PL and FC.

Gore makes no mention of the Queen in his log. Robertson does not note the visit either. In the Hawkesworth account, an instance of comic relief is inserted: "our Surgeon, who had walked till he was very warm, took off his wig to cool and refresh himself: a sudden exclamation of one of the Indians who saw it, drew the attention of the rest, and in a moment every eye was fixed upon the prodigy, and every operation was suspended: the whole assembly stood some time motionless, in silent astonishment, which could not have been more strongly expressed if they had discovered that our friend's limbs had been screwed on to the trunk; in a short time, however, the young women who were chafing us, resumed their employment."

384 "On the 14th, the gunner being on shore to trade, perceived an old woman on the other side of the river, weeping bitterly: when she saw that she had drawn his attention upon her, she sent a young man, who stood by her, over the river to him, with a branch of the plantain tree in his hand. When he came up, he made a long speech, and then laid down his bough at the gunner's feet: after this he went back and brought over the old woman, another man at the same time bringing over two large fat hogs. The woman looked round upon our people with great attention, fixing her eyes sometimes upon one, and sometimes upon another, and at last burst into tears. The young man who brought her over the river, perceiving the gunner's concern and astonishment, made another speech, longer than the first: still, however, the woman's distress was a mystery, but at length she made him understand that her husband, and three of her sons, had been killed in the attack of the ship. During this explanation, she was so affected that at last she sunk down unable to speak, and

			(22)
Wednesday	15	21:00 variable 20:10	Mod:ᵉ & cloudy got eight hogs & ten fowles with plenty of fruit. paid them as usuall tho' they have advanced the price much upon us – owing to some of our people stealing large nails & giving them by stealth for trifles so that we were surprised to find them come down with nails so large the Gunner never having had any of that size. put a stop to the people going on shoar the sick with the doctor, I put on a point of a beach where there was a long […] & placed a centenal to keep off the inhabitants and prevent any of our people from stragling. Served fresh pork & fruit.³⁸⁵
Thursday	16	21:40 Easterly 21:00	(23) Fair weather, sent the Second Lieu:ᵗ with sixty men at day break down to the Westermost point to endeavour to get a trade there at half past noon he returned having landed about three leagues below the ship with fifty men & walked along shoar & got nine hogs & three dozen of fowles – that they had great plenty of things but were rather shy. they were no way troublesome nor did our people molest them but paid them for what they got, that he believed a few days would bring about a trade with them, but as I intended to go away soon & the fateague was so great it was best continue on our old trade tho' it cost a little more – served fresh pork³⁸⁶

the two young men, who endeavoured to support her, appeared to be nearly in the same condition: they were probably two more of her sons, or some very near relations. The gunner did all in his power to sooth and comfort her, and when she had in some measure recovered her recollection, she ordered the two hogs to be delivered to him, and gave him her hand in token of friendship, but would accept nothing in return, though he offered her ten times as much as would have purchased the hogs at market." Hawkesworth (based on Robertson, p. 194).

385 "Moderate and cloudy employed in gathering fresh stock, the Gunner complains that the trade is greatly spoiled by the large spikes that are stole from the ship and brought onshoar which the people give the weomen – that they will now part with nothing but for twice as much as they did yesterday. Gave orders that every man that goes onshoar should be searched before he lands and not to suffer the weomen to cross the river –." PL and FC.

386 "Fair weather sent the Second Lieutenant with all the boats and sixty men down to the Westward to look at the country and try what was to be got, at noon he returned having marched along shore about six miles, he sais the country is very pleasant, very numerous of inhabitants, had great plenty of fowles hogs and vegetables, that they were not fond of parting with any thing nor did they anyway molest them, gave them cocoa nutts and plaintains, they purchased nine hogs and a few fowles, that he beleives they would soon come in to trade but it is too far off as it would take so many men for a guard, they have abundance of large canoes & many buildings they have no kind of metal, their tools being all made of stone with which they work very well and fast, they have no kind of animals except hogs and dogs, their houses large and well built they have no earthen vessels but eat everything roasted or broiled – that a ship may anchor on the way down in 20 to 10 fathom less than a mile from the shore." PL and FC.

Gore mentions the purchase of trees: "Began to cut wood (the bread fruit trees) giving for each tree in proportion from a single spike nail downwards. This tree is great plenty of which the natives make their canoes. The apple tree [. . .] and numbers is a large high strong tree, the coco nut and palm together with the plaintain and banan trees are present growing most near the sea and in the valleys, among the native inhabitants at the heads of the valleys there are other large strong trees bearing a black berry, near the heads of the mountains these trees are to be found. The natives value their fruit trees much particularly the bread fruit, it affording both food and cannoes for them. There is a great deal of ground on this island without trees or inhabitants. The seaward valleys of which there are many well water'd and rich in soil and near the mountain tops is the most cloathed with trees, the South side of the Island is more woody. Trade beginning to slack

Week Day	M:th Day	Wind	Remarks &:ce (24)
Friday	17	23:30 Easterly 21:10	Light airs, sent the boats with the Gunner to trade as usuall & set up more empty cask for water got plenty of fruit and six hogs – served fresh pork & fruit. Second Lieu:^{l} taken very ill & Purser – read Articles of War & punished J. Proctor for drunkeness & mutiny –^{387}

Week Day	M:th Day	Wind	Remarks &:ce (25)
July Saturday	1767 18	23:20 ESE 21:20	Moderate & fair. employed as before got fourteen small hogs & a dozen of fowles & as many bananas plaintains apples and bread fruit as will last for two days, for eating and boiling Served fresh pork – this day the Queen showed herself again she having been absent some days –^{388}
Sunday	19	22:00 Sea & Land Breezes 20:40	(26) Fair weather, sent the boats as before, at four the Queen came onboard and was shown the ship & at five I was going to take the air with the sick officers invited her to go in the boat. giving her some glass bottles a looking glass & a few trifles, after rowing round the bay landed her at the watering place where she was received with great respect by the natives who all retired back on her landing we landed on the beach & she harangued the people taking me & the Officers in her arms & shaking us by the hand & pointing to the ship – it growing late, we went onboard. next mor: the Gunner sent of more stock than any day before no less than forty eight hogs, & pigs with four doz:^{n} of fowles & plenty of fruit – served fresh pork &:^{ce389}

here, our boats man'd and arm'd und:^{r} the command of Lieutenant Furneaux went trading along shore to the Westward at noon they came back with some success but not agreeable to expectation. The traders therefore return'd to their station the watering place."

387 "Fine Pleasant weather, Gunner onshoar trading the Surgeon with the ailing cooper setting up more water cask, the Second Lieutenant taken very ill, the first and myself very low and weak can scarce crawl, punished James Proctor marine for being mutinous – got off plenty of hogs & fowles. The queen hath been absent severall days but by signs of the people will be here tomorrow." PL and FC.

388 "Moderate and fair the queen came down to the beach and soon after a number of new people came with trade – the Gunner sent off fourteen hogs and plenty of fruit." PL and FC. James Proctor is punished with twelve lashes for disobedience and drunkenness (Gore).

389 "Afternoon the queen came onboard and gave a present of two large hogs, in the evening she went onshoar sent the Master with her and a present she on landing took him by the hand made a long speech to the natives and then led him up to her house where she cloathed him in her country manner. AM the Gunner sent of more stock than any day yet; viz: forty eight hogs and pigs, four dozen of fowls, great plenty of bread fruit, bananas, apples and cocoanutts –." PL and FC. According to Robertson's account (p. 205), Wallis does not actually meet the queen that day ("Soon after the Queen came onb^d with six of her chief men, which we entertain'd in the gun room the Capt. Being very poorly at the time she came on board, we could not carry her Majesty to the Great Cabin. . . ."

Week Day	M.th Day	Wind	Remarks – (27)
Monday	20		Moderate & fair employed as before. Completed our water and wood, got off twenty seven hogs & pigs, six fowles & some fruit but pay dearer than usuall on acc:t of some thieves onboard who hath stolen iron & nails and thereby advanced the price of things very much – tho' all is cheap enough God knows Served fresh pork to the ships company –[390]

Week Day	M.th Day	Wind	Remarks – (28)
July Tuesday	1767 21	21:50 Sea & Land Breezes 19:50	Pleasant weather. boats employed as before got eighteen hogs & pigs a doz:en of fowles & plenty of fruit. Three of the ships company: W:m Welch, Taylor & Hugh Howard said that Pinckney Seaman two nights ago drew of with a crow the belaying cleat of the main sheet under the half deck, and on their detecting him he begged them not to tell & he would nail it up again, however it was gone in the morning – this he could not deny but said he immediately nailed it in its place and that some one else must have stole it & that as for the other cleats that were ripped off he knew nothing of – however as he was detected in drawing it off and on searching his chest found a great number of the country fish hooks and a collection of large shells which the inhabitants don't part with without nails or iron from which am certain he could not come of honestly – therefore by way of example made him run the gauntlett three times round the deck – as a proper reward for his crime – served fresh pork and fruit[391]
Wednesday	22	21:40 Easterly 20:00	(29) This day the Queen came onboard again & insisted on my going to her house. She brought with her severall hogs & would take nothing in return – I shewed I would go onshoar in the morning which I did with severall officers & was carried up to the house. I brought a handsome present of hatchets billhooks knives buttons thread needles scissors – a shirt a peice of broad cloth and many other things – she made me the two Lieu:ts & Pursor who had been all ill sit down & called a number of her attendants & they chafed our legs thighs sides & necks for near half an hour, after which she tyed breds of hair round our hats, & a bunch of cock feathers which I saw none wear but herself & sent after us a large Hog & a Sow big with Pigs – fruit of all sorts.

390 "Moderate & fair. People all hearty & well the officers sick & weak Gunner with his guard still trading with good success." PL and FC. Gore indicates that Proctor punished the day before "deservedly got the other dozen and was releas'd."

391 "Pleasant weather found that Francis Pinckney had drawn the cleats that the main sheet was belayed to, and stole the spikes & threw the cleats overboard, turned the people up shewed them what a wanton crime he had been guilty of that many more must have been concerned in the like theft that they had as much fresh meat every day as they could make use of, & that the price there of was risen above twice its value since we came here, occasioned by the theft of these large nails. then ordered them to prepare nettles and him to run the gauntlet [the "gantlope" in the FC] three times round the deck which he did but was so tenderly handled that I told the people that they rather encouraged thieves than punished them when one was given over to them who had committed so great a crime to the whole community, therefore put a stop to any person except the guard from going onshoar again. We get of plenty of stock –." PL and FC.

Week Day	M:th Day	Wind	Remarks at Port Royall – (29)
July Wednesday	1767 22	22:30 Easterly 21:20	Fruits of all sorts in great abundance, & then came down to the beach – I then made signs that we should leave this place in four days. She understood me well, & pointed to the country, & shewed she was going there & made signs for us to stay twenty or 15 days but on my showing her that four days was the time she sat down & cryed very much – and we went onboard – The Master finished the draught of the bay he having been kept constantly onboard by reason of my self & all the officers being sick – got twenty hogs & plenty of fruit – served fresh pork & fruit.[392]
Thursday	23	21:30 Easterly 20:40	30 Fresh gales & cloudy with rain – it seemd to blow very hard without and in the wood there were many trees blown down – however we felt but very little where the ship lay. got six hogs & some fruit. served fresh pork to the ships company.
Thursday	24	22:30 ESE	31 Cloudy & squally with rain; the Gunner onshoar with the Sargeant: trading got off eighteen small & large hogs, some fowles & fruit – give more for them than we used to do,

[392] "Moderate and fair, the queen came onboard and brought severall large hogs as a present would take nothing for them pointed for us to go onshoar with her which I did with severall of the officers. She made us sit down took our hats and tyed bunches of feathers on them, and tyed round our necks wreaths of hair knotted together which was knotted and worked like sinnet and she made signs it was her hair and her work she like wais gave us some matts very well wrought and accompanied us back to the beach, when we went into the boat to go onboard she put in a very large fine sow big with pig and a quantity of fruit, in the mean time I endeavoured to make her understand that we should go from this place in seven days, she immediately understood what I meant and made signs to stay twenty days, to go two days into the country stay there a few days, bring down plenty of hogs and fowles and then go – I shewed that I must go at that time, on which she sat down and cryed bitterly – am the Gunner sent of no less than twenty hogs with great plenty of fruit, our decks quite full of hogs and fowles, kill the small & keep the large for sea, they nor the fowles will eat nothing but fruit. The Gunner desired a present for the old man who hath been very usefull to him, gave him an iron pott some hatchetts & bills and a peice of cloth. The Gunner hopes that the old man will let his son go with us as he seeming inclined so to do, & the boy very willing." PL and FC.

Robertson describes in detail the meeting between the queen and Wallis (p. 210): "Eight AM the queen paid us another visit and brought of a very good present of live stock, for which the Capt. gave her another present in return, I convoyed her and one of her princaple attendance in to the Great Cabin, where the Capt. orderd brakfast to be got immediately and made her and the chef both sit doun to tea and bread and butter but before the chief toutched the bread and butter he rose up and made a long speech looking all round the cabin, then went to the Quarter Gallrey and lookt out towards the sun and kept still talking which makes me supose they worship the sun, when his talk or speech was over he sit doun on the qeens left hand and took up a pece of soft bread and smelt it, then began to eate hearty. We gave him a knife and showd him how to spread the butter on the bread, but he mistook our meaning and laid doun the knife, and took up a little of the butter, with the nails of his two formest fingers and smelt to it, then throwd it down I suppose according to the custom of his country, as they were always observed to throw away a little of every thing they eate, this put one that was present out of humor and was so rude that he snatched the butter away, and orderd the Capt[s] servant to bring clean butter this behaviour surprized the chief and prevented him from eating any more, it likeways made the queen very grave, who was

		21:20	however we shall soon leave the place we are getting as much off as we can – served fresh pork to the ships company[393]
			Variation p:ʳ amplitude – 5:20 azumeth – 5:36 Easterly – amplitude – 5:30

very merry before, this made the Capt very unease, but he said nothing to old groul, and soon after made the queen a present which made her good humord, but she neather eate nor drank while she was onbᵈ." There is also a reference to a treaty which does not appear in the *Dolphin* logs. Robertson, after breakfast, takes the queen on a tour of the ship and then he : "... convoyed her to the Captᵘ cabin, where I left her in great spirits and the Capt showd her all his cureosetys, but the queen looking upon him as our king wanted him to signe a treaty of peace in order to settle all differences betwixt Majˢ people and ours, but the Capt. at that time being very poorly and having a little paralytick disorder in his hand could not hold the pen, therefor excused him selfe untill another opportunity." Robertson was not present so the source of this information is unclear.

The Hawkesworth account indicates that two animals were brought back to England: "Our decks were now quite full of hogs and poultry, of which we killed only the small ones, and kept the others for sea stores; we found, however, to our great mortification, that neither the fowls nor the hogs could, without great difficulty, be brought to eat any thing but fruit, which made it necessary to kill them faster than we should otherwise have done: two, however, a boar and a sow, were brought alive to England, of which I made a present to Mr. Stephens, Secretary to the Admiralty; the sow afterwards died in pigging, but the boar is still alive."

[393] "Squally with rain the latter fair, sent the queen two turkeys, two geese five guniea hens, a cat big with kittens, come china glass bottles, shirts, needles thread, cloth, ribbons, pease, and about sixteen different sorts of garden seeds, as cabbages, turnips &:ᶜᵉ the Gunner took up two Marines with shovells and made a large bed and planted a little of all sorts in it, and gave her the seeds and a shovel. severall of the garden seeds and pease we knew would grow as he planted some in many places that were very flourishing. I like wais sent her two iron potts, knives scissors & spoons the Gunner brought off eighteen hogs and some fruit." PL and FC.

Week Day	M:th Day	Wind	Remarks –
July	1767	23:00	Fresh breezes & clear weather, got from the shore twenty four hogs & pigs, some fowles & fruit; at daylight sent M:r Gore Mate of this ship with a party of forty men to go up the valley by the river & examine by the falls & what other places he could if there were any metals or mineralls & get up in the mountains, plains, & woods and examine them and take notice of anything that came in his way such as metalls, soil, birds beast fruit, trees &:ce and make me a report, at his return and bring with him samples of any thing he met with that was worth notice
Saturday	25	Easterly	at the same time I sent the Master Purser & some Midshipmen with a guard to a point of land with the telescope quadrant &:ce – to make an observation of an eclipse of the sun which was to happen this morning. before they could fix the reflecting telescope the eclipse was begun but the Purser M. Harrison had a twelve foot telescope, saw it almost as it did begin – which they reckoned the immersion began about 6^H 51^M 50^S nearly & ended exact at 8^H 1^M $00"$.
		21:40	In that duration of the eclipse was one hour nine minutes and 10 seconds –
			served fresh pork[394]

To work the time			
M:r Harrisons watch	7^H :03':20"	⊙:s Al:de	8:°43'} true time 7^H :05':20"
M:r Atkinson watch	7:06:00	}	Morning
M:r Hutchinson	8:10:12		
M:r Roberston	8:13:00	⊙: Al:de	22° :52'} true time 8 :12 :12

Immersion by true time nearly – 6^H:51':50"
Emmersion by true time –   8: 1: 00

---

[394] "Fine pleasant weather and the air cool after so much rain, am ordered M:r Gore with all the Marines and forty six men forward to go up the valley by the river as high as he could and make his remarks on the soil and what kind of trees plants &:ce he saw in his way up, to examine where he saw any stream from the mountains if he could find any mineral or oar, likewais at the head of the river from thence to get up as high as he could on the hills and take notice of the soil and produce then taking care allway to be on his guard and to secure himself and make a fire if he should be attacked. – at the same time took a Gunner onshaor at a point of land erected a tent, and with M:r Harrison the Purser to observe an eclipse of the sun which they luckily saw the morning being very clear, and it was as expected underneath ["& on the other side the Queen with many hundred being present at the observation." This latter remark has been inserted in free hand in the FC.]

   Latitude of the point we stood on – 17:°30' South
   Sims Declination at that time 19:°40'
   Saturday July 25:th 1767 an eclipse of the sun happened nearly about six hours & fifty two minutes in the morning (or AM by the log)." PL and FC.

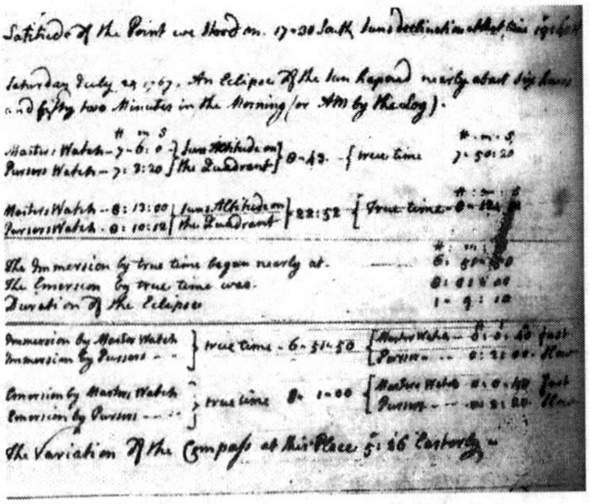

Figure 19 Wallis's calculations as they appear in the PL[395]

395 The 25th July entry continues after the calculations: "After the Observation was taken went to the the queens house and shewed her the telescope, she lookd thro' it and was all astonishment then made many of her attendants look thro' it after this I invited her and many of her court to come onboard which they accepted. I thought by securing her and some of her principall people there could be no danger to the party that I sent off, entertained them with a good dinner, she eat nothing nor would she drink all the others eat very heartily but drank only plain water." PL and FC.

Week Day	M:th Day	Wind	Remarks &:ce (33)
July Sunday	1767 26th	23:00 Sea & Land 22:00 Breezes	Fresh breezes & clear, the Queen our friend came onboard & brought a present of some hogs & fruit & the Gunner had great trade on shoar. he sent of about thirty hoggs & pigs with some fowles & much fruit, at night M:r Gore with his party returned whose account (I shall with those of the others sent at different times) insert in the next leaf – served fresh pork & greens; &:ce 396

396 "Fresh breezes and fair weather. In the morning when our people returned from the excursion they had made into the country and came down to the beach, I took the Queen and her attendants & put them into the Boats and sent them onshoar the Queen expressed great sorrow when she found that we persisted in leaving this place and made signs that she would be here again tomorrow morning – The Mate when he came onboard made me this written account.

Sir, I landed at four in the morning on the 20 fifth ["twenty fifth" in the FC] of July by your orders with four Midshipmen, a Serjeant and twelve Marines, twenty-four seamen all armed, four that carried hatchets, and traffick and four loaded with ammunition and provisions, every man had his days allowance of brandy, the hatchett man two small kegs to give when I should think proper.

After I landed immediately followed the track of the river first calling on the old man who went with me we marched by the river a party on each side until it narrowed so much that we were obliged to keep on one side, the river winding much and mountains hanging over our heads we found it difficult travelling; for the first two miles we found it very well inhabited with gardens walled in with plenty of fowles hogs and fruit, the soil look'd to be a rich fat [at this point, on the next page in the FC, Wallis notes in freehand "The Queen on the day of the eclipse brought severall weomen who she made signs to me were her realtions, by drawing them near to her & then pointing that they came from the same weomen, & by their resemblance of her I believe they were her sisters, after this she took my hand and made them all kiss it. She look'd long thro' the telescope at the distant parts of the island and when she had done she felt about with her hands as one does in a dark room which I suppose was occasioned but her missing those objects she had seen thro' the telescope she shew'd signs that her friends might look thro's the telescope which I granted them, she gave me severall pearles & bunches of feathers which she fixed to the braided hair she wore on her head – all which I delivered into the hands of the S:r Edw:d Hawke for her Majesty when we arrived in England -."] blackish earth, there were canalls cut in the sides of the hills for to lead the water from the high parts of the river into their gardens and to their fruit trees they had a herb in their gardens which they eat of raw, some of which they had ever brought down to the water side. I tasted it and found it pleasant and think it is in taste like callelor in the West Indies but the leaf unlike it, the ground was fenced off very prettily and the bread fruit and apple trees planted in rows on the side of the hills the cocoa nut and plaintain in the level requiring more moisture, it made it pleasant and cool, here was very good grass and no underwood –

When we were four miles up being weary'd with last miles bad road we sat down to breakfast, the people pleasantly seated under a large apple tree when of a suddain we heard a confusion of voices and a great hallowing and soon saw a number of men weomen and children above us, the old man beaconed to us to sit still and he went to these people who immediately were silent and went away in a few minutes after they returned with a large roasted hog, roasted bread fruit, yams, and fruit and gave it to the old man who gave it to the people – I in return gave them some nails, buttons and such things as I had with which they seemed much pleased, after this we went up the valley as far as we could searching all the runs of water and places where the water had run down but could find no kind of metal or aor except the peices I have brought with me, I likewais showed them the salt petre they did take no notice of it, the old man being weary he pointed to us to go up the side of the mountain & made these people take the baggage with fruit cocoa nutts

			(34)
July	1767	23:00	Moderate & cloudy weather, afternoon our friend the Queen came onboard, & wept prodigiously on my informing her that I should sail in the morning she by signs endeavoured to make us stay ten days or a week longer pointing to the country & made shew if we would many hogs, poultry & much fruit should be sent down – when night came, she with much difficulty was persuaded to go onshore, and made signs that she & her attendants might stay till morning at day break we unmoord & hove short, at the same time sent the boats to fill the few empty water cask we had. there were some thousands of people on the beach that had slept there all night amongst the rest ^{the Queen} who on the approach of our boat seemed to rejoice greatly. She made every person ashore to the other side of the river before our boat landed, she herself being only on the side where the boat was when the boat was
		ENE	
		Calm	
Monday	27		
		23:00	

filled with water and follow us he going away home; the people first brought green boughs then took small berrys and painted themselves red and some bark of a tree which had a yellow juice & rubbed some of it on their cloaths after which we began to climb the mountain which was very steep. The old man seeing that it was with much difficulty that we forced our way through the woods and brush which grew very thick he turned back & called to the natives who to the number of twenty or thirty went before us and cleared a very good path and all the way gave us water and fruit and helped us up in the most difficult places, for without this assistance we could never have got up this way I believe this hill was near a mile from top of it to the water side, I mean the river we came from and six mile from where we landed in the morning being arrived at the top of the hill we set down to refresh and rest our selves; this was a very high hill yet there were many at the back of it so high that we seemed to be in a valley, but on our looking toward the ship it was delightfully pleasant, the side of the hills being full of trees and villages, and the valleys still thicker inhabited – we saw very few habitations higher than where we were but saw smoaks ascending from between the high hills which makes me think that there must be many inhabitants there – in coming up the hill we found severall springs and when on the hill saw a number of houses that we had passed by undiscerned, all even the highest mountains were covered with trees that but what sort I know not, those that were the height of this we were on was clear on the tops and plain past the side woody, the top rocky with fern, the lower and flat parts a sedgy grass and weeds the soil seems to be rich – we saw several bushes of very good sugar cane and large it seems to grow wild. I likewais found ginger and turmerick every where samples of which I have brought; seeds I could find none the trees being in blossom. When we were in a very difficult part of the hill found a tree really like a fearn only 14 or 15 feet high, this I cut down and the inside was exactly like a fearn likewais, would have brought a peice of it with me but found it cumbersome and knew not what the difficulties we meet with before we could reach the ship which we judged must now be a great way from us; after having sufficiently recruited ourselves, proceeded from the hill towards the plains & valley keeping our line toward the ship only straying a little when we saw any houses pleasantly situated, where we found the people ready to us any thing they had; we saw no wild beast except a few hogs, nor fowl except parrots, peroquetts, green doves by the river plenty ducks every place that was planted & cultivated seemed to thrive extremely well tho' it was in the midst of what seem'd barren ground, therefore beleive that if the whole was cultivated it would produce abundance of every thing –

I planted peach stones, cherry, plum & other seeds you gave me, with all the garden seeds in such places as I thought they were most likely to thrive and the limes lemons and oranges in such places as they generally are found in the West Indies – afternoon we got at a pleasant place about three mile from the ship where we procured two [three in the FC] hogs and some fowles, which the natives dressed for us very expeditiously and well with breadfruit, we staid here till the cool of

Week Day	M:ᵗʰ Day	Wind	Remarks &:ᶜᵉ (33)
July	1767	Calm	which as soon as they had taken in the water she beckoned to some of her people who brought over three very large fat hogs – enough to serve the ships company a day & half & had them put in our boat, then she got into a large double canoe of her own & put of for the ship all the people on the shoar as soon as our boats put off came over & made signs of sorrow at our leaving them & beckoning them back again –
Monday		Calm	at 8 we weighed, the Queen kept in her canoe, at the gunroom port, & wept very much – I gave her severall usefull presents & the Officers all did the like but she seemed to take little notice of them, she seemed to be wholly taken up with sorrow and was unhappy unless some of us sat in the gunroom port, she made signs for us to come back again soon & when we shewed her signs for 150 days she expressed it to 50 but finding we still made the same signs she made the same to us & seemed better satisfied – she was about five feet eight inches high, very lusty & had a majestic look and spoke with authority & dignity to the islanders who seem'd to be very submissive to her. I judged she was at least forty five years of age she did not seem to have had
	Lat:observed 17:*2 S	ESE	any children – as her breasts were not large like others of her age. I did not find that any of our people had anything to do with her so our wonder was the greater that she should have so great a regard for us all. at ten a breeze sprang up & we took leave of the Queen & all our worthy friends – there were thousands on the hills looking after us – at noon Port Royal bore SE½E 4 leagues —³⁹⁷

the evening then marched for the ship having first handsomely rewarded our guides, and people who provided us so good a dinner, we parted in great friendship with each other, the men with me behaving themselves the whole day thro' with great order and decency; this is all the account I can give of the country. John Gore." PL and FC. The entry continues in format: "26ᵗʰ continued Fine pleasant weather the queen came onboard about 10 o' clock and brought some fowls and hogs as a present and went onshoar again soon after, the Gunner sent of this day near thirty hogs and great plenty of fowls and fruit completed all our water and wood and got all ready for sea more inhabitants came from the country than we had seen before many seem to be cheif men by the respect paid them by the others –." PL and FC.

397 "Light breezes and fair weather, at 3 in the afternoon our friend the queen came down with a great number of the inhabitants, crossed the river with her attendants and came onboard with the old man – she brought some very fine fruit, made signs for us to stay ten days longer and she would go into the country and bring us plenty of hogs, poultry and fruit on shewing her that we should sail in the morning she wept bitterly, then she made signs when should we return again, shew'd her fifty days, she made signs for thirty, but finding fifty always made to her she seemd satisfied the Gunner and guard came of having completed our markett, the decks full of hogs and prodigious quantities of fowls and fruit; at night the queen could be scarce prevailed upon to go onshoar she lay down upon the arm chest and cryed a long time, at last she with her retenue went onshoar the old man I believe had hid his son away for two evenings ago he took the boy from the watering place and hath not been seen since, the old man seemed to show that he was gone with the country to see his friend and would be back to go with us, but we never saw him after; at daybreak unmoored and hove short at the same time sent the barge and cutter to fill all the empty casks, on their coming near the shore they were surprised at seeing such a number of

Remarks made at King George the 3:ʳᵈ Island in Latitude 17:30' S and Longitude from London of 152:°00' W by Observation at Port Royal.

The whole time we have been at this Island the Master or Mates have whenever a boat could be spared been sounding & making remarks. like Lieu:ᵗ Furneaux with a guard of as many men as could be spared hath been along shore three or four leagues both to the Eastward & Westward of the ship untill he was taken ill and then M:ʳ Gore, the Mate was sent to look into the rivers & falls of water, the plains mountains valleys and woods directly back. their reports to me were as follows –

Lieu:ᵗ Furneaux sais that all the way along the shore and in many places a mile or a mile and a half back that the country is exactly the same as it is here at the landing place – that between every mountain runs a river or rivulets but none navigable, the plain is full of breadfruit, cocoa nutt, plaintain & apple trees, cotton shrubs very coarse which they make no use of their houses neat & plantations of trees for cloth neatly fenced of as it is here, the country full of inhabitants, that they had hogs & cocks in plenty but he saw neither hens chickens or eggs (nor did any of our people that have been in the mountains, yet we have had both hens & chickens brought onboard but not one egg) they saw no other animal except dogs & ratts the latter of which are innumerable but they don't trouble themselves about them, the grass seemed to be very good and in great plenty. Fish were small mullet, crawfish of two pound, abundance of shell fish and some Parret fish and others we have no name for but all kinds of fish are scarce here for tho we tried with scenes trall, line and every other method I don't remember any but one shark that was caught all the time we lay here. M:ʳ Furneaux sais that they had abundance of boats built, & building many sixty feet long. that the people were very civil and no way molested them except their numbers which novelty had made follow him, that they gave the cocoa nutts breadfruit ready dresst & roasted hogs, that as there was a market established at our watering place

---

inhabitants as covered the whole beach that they were going to pull of again for the ship when the queen came forward and called to them and made the inhabitants retire to the other side of the river and let them fill the casks, she brought some fruit and hogs and put into the boat and would have come of in our boat but the officer had directions not to bring any the people of, she presently launched a double canoe and came of to the ship, on which about fourteen or sixteen more were launched and followed when she came off she cried a great deal she came in and staid about an hour, there springing up a breeze weighed the anchor and made sail we then sent her into her boat, she greived extreamly at it, embraced us all in the most affectionate manner as did all her attendants who seemed to be very sorrowful at our leaving them, soon after it fell calm, sent the boats a head, the canoes returned to the ship again and the one which the queen was in made fast to the gunroom port, and she came into the bow of it where she sat crying we gave her many usefull things which she accepted yet made little account of she being under so much affliction at – am sprang up a fresh breeze the ship being now without the reef and apoling sea she shook us all by the hand and then put of the canoe all the rest following her –

at noon, Port Royal Harbour being the name I gave the port we sailed from bore SE½E distance about twelve miles –

The extreams of King George 3:ʳᵈ Island from ESE six leagues to SBW five leagues

The Duke of Yorks island from WBS five leagues to SW six or 7 leagues

Ship in latitude observed 17:22* south –

Served fresh pork to the ships company who thank god we are all healthy and well, myself and two Lieutenants being the only invalids and we in a recovering way tho' excessive low and weak." PL and FC.

the natives seemed rather inclined to carry their hogs & poultry there than sell them of their own houses. in his way back he went up the sides of severall hills & found what was cultivated was very fertile, the soil appearing to be fine rich reddish & brownish earth. that they had very large well tasted yams, but he saw none growing. the people made the signal that they were not in season. some of the seamen told him they saw some large pearls in the ears of the natives but he could not find them. he got six small ones but sadly mangled in boreing holes thro' them. this was all his report except that he saw ducks herons parrets and green doves & some small birds. their burying places were walled in with stone and had at one end tall trunks of trees with ten or dozen men badly carved on them one over the other; the same we find opposite the ship – he sais the plantations further to the Westward appear to be better cultivated than those nearer the ship as the country is leveler & goes back with an easy ascent some miles whereas it is more mountaneous here; besides the reefs that run of here affords subsistance for multitudes of inhabitants for they go out on the reef with a little bread at low water and catch small fish & shellfish which they break and eat immediately & so much time is lost every day which would otherwais be employed in cultivating the ground. They saw no kind of metal amongst them, their knives are mussel shells which they cut up their meat with, their apples bread fruit &:^{ce} & kill hogs & fowls with. for axes & adzes they grind stones into the shape of an adze, & work extremely well with them. they build canoes very neat & sew the plank together with cocoa bark and make holes with bone ground sharp –

Their mast steps in the middle & the sail is made of a mat, the riggin of cocoanut bark they steer with a paddle & row laikwise with paddles they have outlickers made of two spars & boards laid on them where to windward one or more sit to ballance the boat. The double canoes are very large and are lashed together about three or four feet asunder forward abaft & a midships. they have two masts which they step between the two canoes & one forward & one abaft & their shrouds are fixed to the outer gunwale of each canoe they have large sails & are very stiff – and go swift and [. . .] in a great sea, they are about two feet and a half broad within board and the plank of some of them at the whale is above three inches, and at the gun wall about two. they are covered both forward & abaft for eight or ten feet with plank and curved at each end so no water can come in but a midships they have laikwais many of them large square rooms or awnings fixed over ^{both} boats that will hold a dozen people besides two or three on the top – this awning is generally fixed near the boats bows so it no way incommodes those who row – but if they sail then the awning is fixed between the two masts; we saw no kind of earthern ware amongst them the utensills were cocoa nutt shells, calibashes, wooden trays neatly dug out, & basketts of different kinds in which they hung up their victualls of the boughs of trees to keep the rats from carrying it away. the way they dress their meat is thus they get a heap of round stones that are hard, (it is sort of iron stone) and make a pavement of a few feet square then they make a large fire of cocoanutt shells & wood and leaves thrown over it to keep it from blazing. when they think that the stones are thoroughly heated they take of the fire and brush the stones very clear then they take a small hog wraped in plaintain leaves or a larger cut in quartors and lay on the stones and yams wraped in plaintain leaves & fowles & as much as they want to dress, on these they lay bread fruit & bananoes & plaintains & other things that they mix up for eating all wraped up as the former, and on them they lay plaintain leaves all round these cocoanutt leaves & after that the embers and coals of fire that was raked of on it they place cocoa leaves & close it well in and over with earth at least six inches & let it remain 'till it is dressed & then they take all of it as well dressed as anything I ever tasted without being in the least burnt or dirty and full of gravy. they eat no kind of sauce neither did I see any salt or vinegar among them. but on M:ʳ Furneauxes first landing he found a small peice of salt peter but never saw any since. Sugar cane grows plenty & some large but the natives make no other use of it than to chew sometimes. there is great plenty of sorrel like – clover in the woods which our people eat of & had put in their broth both for breakfast & dinner with bread fruit or plaintains. – [398]

398 "Remarks made at Georges Islands

The inhabitants of this island are a stout clean-tinted active peple, they are from five feet 7 to five feet 10 high, some few taller & some shorter. The weomen most of them from five feet to five feet six. Men of a tawny colour those that go on the water much redder than those who live onshoar they have strong black hair which they tye on the top the head in the middle other in two bunches one on each side and some few dont tye it up, these generally have curled hair of different colours, black, brown, red and whitish or flaxen, especially the young boys and girls – they all are cloathed very decently in white and appear very gracefull. their cloth is made of the inner rind of a shrub somewhat like hazle, this they beat by a brook on a flat board with a notched peice of wood until all but the fibres are washed away and after that they lay these peices length ways close to each other throw some cocoa nutt oil on it when dry and beat it with a fluted stick every way and then lifting it up and where it is thin they add some of the cleansed bark and beet it in so that it looks exactly like China paper, they make it of different finess and sizes, and with this they cover themselves, having first a peice that reaches from their shoulders to their mid leg on both sides their being a hole in the middle to put their head thro' and after this they have a finer peice of four or five yards long and one broad which they wrap themselves up in a very easy manner, the weomen in general are very handsome some really great beauties yet their virtue was not proof against the nail for they would prostitute themselves for a nail the lower sort for a small one & the nail must be larger in proportion to the ladys beauty, even the fathers and brothers brought them to the people and shew'd sticks proportioned to the nail they were to give and would then send them a cross the river it was some time before the officers found out this for the men never crossed the river and our people used to stragle but a little way, whilst the other kept a look out and it was this that increased the stealing all the nails they could come at, and drew the belaying cleats for none of them attempted to trade, as they found that they dayly had as much fruits provisions & fruit as they could make use of –

The boats made use of here were of three sort, canoes made out of single trees capable of carrying from two to six men these were cheifly for fishermen and were generally of fishing on the reef the second sort were of different sizes made of severall plank dexterously sewed together and would carry from ten to forty men. these generally consisted of two lashed together and two masts step't between them or a large single canoe with an outlicker on each side and only one mast, with these boats they go to sea quite out of sight and sail to different parts of the of the islands, bring plaintains, bananas, and yams which were not so plenty here as they seem to be windward, the other boats are made cheifly for shew & procession they being very large and made in shape like the venetian gondola and have large awning rose over the middle of them and people sit both on the awning and under it, we saw none of these except the first and second day near the main, but three or four times a week we saw a procession of eight or ten with streamers flying and thousands of people running along the shore and numbers of small canoes attending them, when they rowed out to the outer point of a reef that was about four mile to the westward of us, where they stayed about one hour and then returned ; they never went in but in very fine weather and all the people that attended these canoes were dressed which at other time they were not wont to be when in their boats the rowers in the large canoes & those that steer'd them were dressed in white the others that sat on and under the canopy had white and red clothing and two were mounted on the prowe of each boat were dressed in red, they were constantly opening and folding up certain pieces of cloth of white, red and spotted – we did not go nearer to them than a mile as it was far from the ship and they very numerous, we stood on the outer part of a reef and with spying glasses saw as plain as if we had been amongst them –

I found in going to the queens house severall places walled in like sheds, within the walls and without severall uncouth figures of man, weomen, hogs, carved on posts drove into the ground, when I was told that everywhere that our parties had been they saw such places, particularly at the west end where they were much larger that they frequently saw the people go into these places with dejected looks and from these beleived them to be places where their dead were buried, the greatest part was very handsomely paved with large round stones and some of these places seemed to be quite paved over and grass growing up between as tho' it had not been used for a long while I endeavour'd to find out if they had any sort of worship but could not perceive they had [remark added in freehand in the FC "except offering up some prayers when they pass'd by their burying places –"].

The food they cheifly live on is breadfruit, bananas, plaintains, yams, apples and a sour fruit not good of itself but beat up with the roasted bread fruit is pleasant enough. Flesh is hogs and fowles. they have abundance of rats but they don't seem to trouble themselves about them only hang their baskets with their meat and fruit at the beams of their houses or on the boughs of trees to prevent them from eating it, they have very good mullet in the river tho' not large nor plenty – conchs mussels and other shellfish on the reefs which they gather at low water and eat raw with their bread fruit on the reef they likewais have very fine crawfish, the fishing boats have both hooks & lines and very large long nets with small meshes with which they catch abundance of small fish about the size of sardines and with their hooks they catch parrot fish, groupers and many others, yet they are so fond of them that they were loth to part with any, their hooks are made of mother of pearle, we tried to catch fish both with nets and lines but could not with no success we likewais tried with their hooks but to as little purpose – we found among the weomen a few real pearls of which I got two dozen small and spoiled in boring the sum to be of a good colour. M:^{r} Furneaux saw severall when he was down at the West end but they would not part with them and some of the people said they saw some as big as large pease but as none of the officers saw them and seamen allway exaggerate things I cannot say wither this be not the present case, for if they were so plenty undoubtedly they could bring them to market in exchange for them – I put down a Johannes a guinea, a crown piece a Spanish dollar some shillings and new half pence and two large nails and pointed for them to take what they liked but the nails were immediately seized on and a few of the half pence whilst the silver and gold lay neglected some of the people that had no nails I suppose had cut up lead and made it like peices of iron which many of the natives got from them and to their sorrow brought them to the Gunner in hopes of his giving them real nails for it – they having no use for it, the nails they fixed in stick sand sharpened the points with which they bored holes in the plank to sew the canoes together as that was done before with pieces of bone, the plank is made by splitting a tree with the grain into as many thin pieces as they can and then with their tools made like shipwrights adzes they rub it level every man having by him a stone and a cocoa nutt shell filled with water with which he sharpens his adz every minute, six or eight will work on one of those peices of wood and in a short space will bring it into a plank of ten, fiveteen or twelve feet long and an inch through more or less according to the part of the boat it is to be placed in, and will after fitt it to the boat with the exactness of an expert joiner, they cutt the tree down with large hatchetts and after into planks of such size as they have occasion for then they heat the end of it till it begins to crack and split after which they make use of wedges made of hard wood and soon split them into peices the breadth of the tree so that some of their plank is near two feet broad but the generality is about one foot, the tree they use mostly is the apple tree, it being tall and straight, many of which I had measured and they were about eight feet in girth and from twenty to forty to the branches and diminished very little in size from the bottom to the branches – the Carpenter sais it is not a very good wood being light; the small canoes are made of the bread fruit tree hollowed out, it being a light spongy wood – they have some ebony as appears from the clubs they beat their cloth, and staffs that some of the people who seemed to have authority, yet we saw none growing, indeed we could not make so many discoveries as we wished being so few in number and the great guard we were obliged to keep both onboard and onshore that we had as much as we could possibly undertake without running the risque of being all cut of, for not withstanding all their civility, I doubt not but it was more thro' fear than love that they respected us so much one thing I cannot help remarking because it was a happy means I believe of keeping them in proper order and keeping their distance, the first day the Surgeon went onshore with the sick people after placing them in some sheds on the beach and out of the sun he walked a little way by the river side the natives on the other side when a wild duck flew over his head which he fired at and it fell dead amongst the natives who were all affrighted and ran away, he made signs for one of them to bring it over with fear and trembling, at which time severall more flew over his head and he luckily brought down three more, (they seeing this and many other times that he shot ducks) that a man approaching them with a musquett could make a thousand run away so that it was easy to keep them at a distance, and the Gunner as so well managed matters that with the old man's assistance he kept them in exceedin good order and when at any time they pilfered he would make them bring back what was stolen, a fellow one day had crossed the river and stole a hatchett on which he got his party ready as tho' he would go after him and brought back the hatchet and other things he had stole, the gunner made him lay it down and insisted on their bringing the thief and at last they went out again and brought him (he knowing the man) he sent him onboard and after much intreaty had him onshore again and gave him his liberty at which there was general rejoicing & next day he brought the gunner and his party a large roasted hog & bread fruit. –

The manner in which they dress their meat is as follows, they dig a pit about half a foot deep and two or three yards in circumference, this they pave with large pebbles laid down very smooth and even then they make a fire with leaves and wood & cocoa nutt husk and burn them to ashes and make the stones as hot as they think is necessary for what they have to dress then they rake back the ashes on every side after which they lay on the stones a layer of green cocoa nut tress leaves stript of, then they wrap up their hog (if small whole, if larger split) in plaintain leaves in the same manner, than they cover all with the hot embers, on this they put bread fruit, yams &:^{ce} wrapped in plaintain leaves but first well scraped they throw the remainder of the hot embers on this after which they cover the embers with cocoanut leaves and over that throw a quantity of earth so that all the heat is kept in, and after continuing covered for half an hour or more according to the size of what is dressing they take it out and I think it is the finest way of dressing I ever met met with for the meat is quite tender and full of gravy, the fruit is excellent quite unlike any we could dress they have no sauce but salt water, nor knives but shells with which they carve dextorously all ways cutting from them; they have the use of – as appeared from one of our men running a large splinter into his foot. The surgeon not being there some of the people endeavoured with their knife to take it out, but after putting the man to a good deal of pain they were obliged to give it over, the old man then called to a man who crossed the river and looked at the seaman's foot then went down to the beach took up a shell and broke it to a point with his teeth and in an instant laid open the place and took out the splinter the old man who had gone over to the other side returned with some gum and placed it in the wound tore of a piece of his wrapper tyed up the wound and in two days his foot was whole, the surgeon got some of this gum of the tree – many of the trees produce a gummy juice, particularly – that they make use of a pitch for closing the seams and rents in their canoes, they use cocoa nut oil for burning in lamps for making their cloth and anointing their hair for the latter they scrape a root which smells like roses into it where it lays in steep and hath a fragrant smell, they have many flowering shrubs the flowers they stick likewais into their hair they have no combs yet they dress up their hair very neatly, however these that had combs from us used them very well and did their hair up much neater than those who had none, I did not see one tortoise or turtle whilst here, yet on showing them some small turtle we brought from Charlotte Island, they made signs that they had large ones: I was unlucky in loosing a he goat soon after I left S:^{t} Jago, having two she ones which would have left at this place if the he one had lived or the others with kid, as I doubt not but in a few years they would have greatly increased – the SE end of the island seem to be better cultivated and inhabited than this end for boats daily came round from thence laden with plaintains but keep allwais at a distance from the shore until they are past the ship and then land at the West end from thence they bring up the things to market and on the arrival of their boats we find greater plenty and cheaper than at other times –

The climate here seems to be very good by the health full look of the natives and the greenes of the trees and valleys, no fogs and vapours arising out of rivers or from the low ground that being everywhere well drained and what is more surprising though it so warm a climate our meat kept very well two days the fish one, we were not troubled with muskettoes in the low ground, nor flyes as half so much as you are in the summer in england nor did our people during our whole stay there in all the excursions they made ever see a frog, toad, viper or snake, scorpion or centpieds, and very few ants which is the only place I ever saw without most of the above mentioned noxious reptiles.

These people I believe have wars with each other having seen severall with large scars, which they shew was done with stones and bludgeons and point to the mountains, they have bows and arrows but the arrows are all blunt with peice of round hard stone in the end and with these they knock down parrots & doves – I saw none that had anything sharp in the end. – The tide rises and falls very little and that quite uncertain – being wholly governed by the winds which blows generally from the East to SSE – a pleasant gale at most times.

Tho' there is much sugar cane and pretty large in some places the natives made very little use of it, only taking a small piece to chew when they come past a patch of it nor did I find they made any kind of liquor but drank clear water allwais – they were much astonished to see the Gunner drop fowls and pork in a pot onshoar as they have no kind of vessel but wooden ones they are quite ignorant of what boiling water is, but the old man now boils the pot I gave him every day. But for flesh or fish and hath numbers of friends to partake thereof always with himself meal times – I gave the queen and many of the principal people iron potts of which they make much use –

I forgot to remark that all the men & women have their backsides marked black with stricking a thing with teeth like a comb into their flesh & rubbing it with a paste made of sutt & oyle – those who are under twelve are not marked – some people I saw had their leggs marked in chequers. They seemed to be of greater note than the others." PL and FC. In the FC, this entry is followed by five blank pages. The account in Hawkesworth integrates supplementary details: "One of the principal attendants upon the queen, appeared much more disposed to imitate our manners than the rest; and our people, with whom he soon became a favourite, distinguished him by the name of Jonathan. This man, Mr. Furneaux clothed completely in an English dress, and it sat very easy upon him. Our officers were always carried on shore, it being shoal water where we landed, and Jonathan, assuming new state with his new finery, made some of his people carry him on shore in the same manner. He very soon attempted to use a knife and fork at his meals, but at first, when he had stuck a morsel upon his fork, and tried to feed himself with that instrument, he could not guide it, but by the mere force of habit his hand came to his mouth, and the victuals at the end of the fork went away to his ear." There is also a remark on veneral disease which is obviously retrospective: "It is certain that none of our people contracted the venereal disease here, and therefore, as they had free commerce with great numbers of the women, there is the greatest probability that it was not then known in the country. It was, however, found here by Captain Cook, in the Endeavour, and as no European vessel is known to have visited this island before Captain Cook's arrival, but the Dolphin, and the Boudeuse and Etoil, commanded by M. Bougainville, the reproach of having contaminated with that dreadful pest, a race of happy people, to whom its miseries had till then been unknown, must be due either to him or to me, to England or to France; and I think myself happy to be able to exculpate myself and my country beyond the possibility of doubt. It is well known, that the Surgeon on board his Majesty's ships keeps a list of the persons who are sick on board, specifying their diseases, and the times when they came under his care, and when they were discharged. It happened that I was once at the pay-table on board a ship, when several sailors objected to the payment of the Surgeon, alleging, that although he

[399]July 25:th 1767 Sent Mr Gore Mate of the Dolphin with two Midshipmen Sergeant & all the Marines & twenty seamen armed, with four unarmed to carry provisions up the river to search for minerals and explore the hills valleys &:ce a bring me an account of what he had seen or found at his return sais as follows:

When we landed we went up to the Queens Great House to get the old man to go with us which he did. we then marched in two partys one on each side of the river. but the mountains were so steep that we were frequently obliged to turn again & the river winding so much from the foot of one mountain & the other that it made it very difficult travelling, the first two miles was well inhabited the soil seemed very rich but in many places stoney they had many gardens fenced in with stonewalls & canalls to turn the water into the gardens from the river, the chief things that were in their gardens were rows of apple, bread fruit & plaintain trees, and between them a plant with a broad dark coloured leaf which they eat of tastes like – in the West Indies. after we left them the valley still grew narrower & only a house was to be seen in a quarter of a mile – about three mile up they sat down to breakfast but had not sat long before they heard a a number of people hallowing & making a great noise. sent the old man to them, who soon made them quiet and soon after they brought green boughs, with a pig ready roasted, bread fruit, cocoa nutts & apples. made them presents in return. we then proceeded up the valley about five miles in our way saw on each side of the hills many plantations. several of the people followed us – they gathered some red berrys of a tree & squeezed them and expressed a yellow juice with which they stained their cloth we gathered severall of them, but they were so watery they would not keep laikwais cut of the rind of a tree & painted themselves red with it. This tree had no fruit on it. we saw severall large canoes building & plank preparing on both sides of the river, we were now five miles up the valley here we found a very large fall of water and having searched the river all the way up without finding anything, hoped that here we might meet with something but were disappointed having found only two mineral stones which we brought to the Captain. here we were obliged to climb the hills or rather mountains. the old man made signs to the natives and they cleared away a path and carried the peoples baggage helped them in the difficult places, & supplied them with cocoanutts, apples, & water all the way up which

---

had discharged them from the list, and reported them to be cured, yet their cure was incomplete. From this time, it has been my constant practice when the Surgeon reported a man to be cured, who had been upon the sick list, to call the man before me, and ask him whether the report was true: if he alleged that any symptoms of his complaint remained, I continued him upon the list; if not, I required him, as a confirmation of the Surgeon's report, to sign the book, which was always done in my presence. A copy of the sick list on board the Dolphin, during this voyage, signed by every man in my presence, when he was discharged well, in confirmation of the Surgeon's report, written in my own hand, and confirmed by my affidavit, I have deposited in the Admiralty; by which it appears, that the last man on board the ship, in her voyage outward, who was upon the sick list for the venereal disease, except one who was sent to England in the Store ship, was discharged cured, and signed the book on the 27th of December 1766, near six months before our arrival at Otaheite, which was on the 19th of June 1767; and that the first man who was upon the list for that disease, in our return home, was entered on the 26th of February 1768, six months after we left the island, which was on the 26th of July 1767, so that the ship's company was intirely free fourteen months within one day, the very middle of which time we spent at Otaheite; and the man who was first entered as a venereal patient, on our return home, was known to have contracted the disease at the Cape of Good Hope, where we then lay."

399 The profiles of Cape Blanco and the sketches of the fish are placed here in the ML.

was near a mile and very fateaguing, when they came to the top they rested themselves and it being very high they overlookd many valleys which they say were delightfully pleasant full of houses & plantations and gardens well fenced in – they judged themselves to be about six miles from the watering place. the tops of the hills are very rocky & full of fern, above them I call mountains which are full of trees, what sort I cannot tell but many very large, they gathered the fruit of severall on the sides of the hills, but none were ripe & they all rotted. the nut with a tree or a weed that was about 14 inches diameter and fifteen or sixteen feet high exactly like a fern, they cut it down & found it striped black & white they would have brought it with them but the roads they had to pass made it impossible –

After resting sometime on the top of the hill, we walked round it and observed the country which we found had much the same appearance as before mentioned viz – the valleys very fertile and the sides of the hills if not too steep were full of bread fruit apple & cocoa nutt trees & good plantations the plain or easyest ascent of the hill very rich good soil but not cultivated the inhabitants choosing to live in valleys or on the side of the hills above the rivers – high up the hill very rocky and full of ferns – the mountains cloathed with large trees to the very top – They saw no kind of wild animal – except rats which are plenty in the valley but more in the hills – here were abundance of wild duck on the river and on the hills numbers of parrets & peroquetts of different kinds – and green doves & a sort of heron – white and white & black – at the plantations they had only hogs & cocks for they scarce saw & hen & never saw an egg or young chicken – The inhabitants all the way they went behaved with great kindness to them and gave them to eat & drink of what they had & followed them with more in case they wanted – at night they returned to the ship. I gave to the Queen & the old man a cock & hen turkey, three guinea fowles a cock & two hens – a goose & gander; – some iron potts & bottles, glasses, hatchetts saws chizzles, nails with a number of other things besides all kinds of garden seeds & shewed them how to plant them I planted lime, lemon, orange, cherry, peach, plumb & appricott in a great number of places some of which I hope will come to perfection – I had two she goats, but had lost the hee goat in the Streights of Magellan which I was very sorry for as from their being left amongst them in a few years the whole country would be stocked – I gave them a cat big with kitten of which they were fond – and surprized to see her attack the rats so eagerly. They have a sort of cur dog amongst them that they keep by way of pet for they allway carry them in their arms especially if they come to a brook – we had three dogs which used to go onshoar with the sick and the natives were so much afraid of them that one of them would make five hundred run away. they having vast dread of them as the dog had at first bit several of them who had come too near the tent –

[400]Given me on the passage from S:ᵗ Helena to England – A Poetical Essay on the Dolphin Sailing Eound the Globe in the years 1766,1767, & 1768 – by R. Richardson. Barber of the Said Ship

Let Holland France or Haughty Spain
Boast their Discoveries o'er the Main
and Sing their Heroes Mighty Fame
which now with time Decays.
Brittannia's Isle at length hath found
A Man who Saild the Globe around
Discovering Isles 'till now unfound
And well deserves the ....

Wallis I sing the Hero Brave
who to his Country like a Slave
undaunted Plough'd the Southern Wave
In search of Land unfound:
His ship the Dolphin, and his Crew
all young & healthy, tho' but few
get with him Dauntless, Bold and True
they sailed the Globe around.

A wellcome Breeze fills every Sail
No more the Maidens tears avail
for Honour o'er their Tears prevail
   Adieu to Plymouth Sound
ye Virgins fair forbear to Weep
for you sincere our hearts will keep
for you will plough th'extensive Deep
and Sail the Globe around –

Madeira first supplyd our need
S:ᵗ Jago next; from thence with speed
whilst Oxen for us daily Bleed
   S:°West; our Course we steer.
The Well known Streights we enter then
so famed for its Gigantic Men
whose Height from Six feet, reach'd to ten*
   and safely Anchor'd there –

* Six feet Ten Inches.

as farther thro the Streights we go
where lofty Cliffs are tip't with Snow
And rapid Cataracts swiftly flow
   adown their Craggy Sides
Where Winter too incessent Reigns
and AEolus mighty God, disdains
to curb the Wind, who free from Chains
   Our Allmost derides.

Some Natives here, the few we find
a Savage Race of human kind
scarce blest with Sense, to reason Blind
   In Ignorance rudely bred
nought to defend their Swarthy lives
but Beasts, or Fishes nauseous hides
more Nauseous Food, and nought besides
   Morassy Ground their Bed.

Into the Wide Paciffic sea,
from such unpleasing sights as these
Waft as some fair auspicious Breeze
   and be our constant Guide

The Mighty God the Prayer received
our Sails we loos'd, our Ship relieved
the Streight we clear, & undeceived
   Our Toils he well rewards

No longer now our greif he mocks
no more Our ship in Streights he locks
from Dangers freed we see those Rocks
   At Distance far behind

Pleased with the Change those Danger O'er
with Joy we View the Distant Shore
and Bless the God whose awfull Pow'r
   is ever unconfin'd

---

400 This poem does not appear in the two other logs.

(next page)

Now fraught with Wind our Canvass Swell
tho' some rude squalls our Ship assail
yet all in vain, they nought avail
    Wide from the Dangerous Coast
For Neptune kind with Pleasant Gales
for some few Weeks repleats our sails
and on his Son such Fame entails
    as Europe nee'r could Boast.

Swiftly he wafts us o'er his Waves
grants every Boon our Hero craves
Scarce in the Southern Seas he leaves
    an Isle to him unknown

Respecting every Son of Fame
Great Wallis gives to each a Name
with titles free from others claim
    But trusts to Fate his Own.

On Whitsunday the first was seen
which bore the Name with due esteem
the next to Brittains Royall Queen
    Charlotte's Name he fixed

some few we pass'd in Number Four
whose names are still reserved in Store
tho next the Royal Bishops Bore
    And George great George the next

Here wait my must awhile to View
a Beauteous Scene to Brittains New
whose Climate equall'd is by few
    The British Monarch's Isle.
And Or my Muse thou Heavenly Maid
an Artless Bard Invokes your aid
let all his skill be here display'd
    and O'er this Essay smile.
Our Anchors well secured in ground
sails furled, yards Topmasts Lower'd down
well pleased we view the Fertile ground
    well worth a Monarchs care
Safe in Port Royal Bay we Ride
Where's no rude Wind, no rapid Tide
Or Rugged Rocks unseen abide
but all's Serene and fair

The Swarthy Indians round us flock
with each a pittance from their stock
which they for various trifles truck
    Content with what we spare
Oft on our Ship they fix their Eyes
as oft on us with Deep Surprize
and deem our Floating world a prize
    for them next Morn to share

Prepar'd next Morn with Stones they came
which well they Hurled with Dextrous Aim
but soon were all repulsed with Shame
    and some Canoes unmann'd,
Fatal attempt, Ambitious thought:
poor simple men, to late you're taught
that Brittons ne'er are easy Caught
    with Schemes so badly plann'd

No safe Retreat they now can finde
for dire Distruction unrestrain'd
With Balls swift Whistling thro' the Wind
    O'ertakes the Insulting Band

but O! to paint their Vast Surprize
the Terror sparkling in their Eyes
Or their confused & hideous Cries
    Requires an Abler Hand.

Then cease my Muse the Cannons Roar
is ceased: the Vanquish'd make for Shore
their Comrades fate with Tears deplore
    and seek a speedy flight.

A gentler theme demands your care
to paint the Beauteous Isle prepare
whilst we fatigue'd tho' void of fear
    In slumbers pass the Night
The Morning Dawns the well known Call
from gentle Sleep awakes us all
our Boats well mann'd and arm'd withal
    The Conquer'd Isle we claim
soon as the Sea Beach Side we make
the Indians all their Hutts forsake
And we in form Possession take
    In Georges Royal Name

(next page)
Now free to Range we find with Fruits
Pigs, Fowles and most salubrious Rootts
Refreshments such as aptly Suits
    the Seamens Briny food
Than all of these an Iron Bar
or Rusty Nail's more precious far
to them, ee'n Gold or Diamonds are
    less valued, less ....
The Natives yet more polished are
than other Savage Indians are
The girls well featur'd passing fair
    and kind in all respects,
The Men well made, Robust and Tall,
Subject to none, by none enthrall'd
thoughtless of every future call
    They live as life directs.

In Tillage quite a useless Band
but Nature kindly tills their Land
whose fertile soil at her Command
    Yeilds all the Sweets of Life
at least such necessary Store
that pleased with it they seek no more
nor Covet gold or Silver Oar
    the Common Source of Strife
The Slender Garb their Bodies hide
is far too Curious to Discribe
In this Invention's well supply'd
    with Nicest Art their Wants
attend ye Anticks of the Trade
whom here I seek not so degrade
It's neither wove, nor Spun but made
    from Wild & simple plants.

I scorn with Lyes your thoughts to Bilk
but know its' neither Flax no Silk.
Cotton nor Wool tho' white as Milk
    and wrought with Matchless pains
some coarse, some fine, and Painted O'er,
some Plain; In Breadth two yards or more
and Oft in length full seven Score
    each Curious peice Contains

Thro' every Grove a Silver Stream
clear as the Brightest Christal Gem
which Banks of Beauteaus flowers hemm
    unnumberd Vales Adorn
whilst unmolested Birds unite
To form the Rural Sweet Delight
closing with Various Notes each Night
    and ushering in the Morn –

A Thousand Beauties more's too few
to give this Royall its due
but here I cease, least these tho' true
Should seem romantic talk

Yet let me not in Silence pass.
What well in this deserves a Place
an Island Sacred to his Grace
    The Royal Duke of York –

Which here in View with grandeur rears
Proud of the Royal Name it Bears
High as the lofty Glittering Stars
    Its ever Verdant Head.
Beneath whose ^{Shades} Pleasant Lawn
Which Various Fragrant shrubs adorn
and Beauteous flowers daily born
    around the borders spread.

But hark! the Boatswains call, how shrill
up Anchor Boys your Topsails fill
and staysails hoist with free good Will
    Each Jovial Tar Obeys.
and now we dare the wave once more
neer Plow'd by Europe Keels before
discovering Still a long hid Store
of Isles within those Seas

For daily now fresh Land we make
and all in course their titles take
Saunders & How the first partake
    Next Scylly, dagerous Isles we Spy
A Beauteous Island then we made
be that Boscawen's; Wallis said
tho' low in Dust the Hero's laid
his Name shall never Dye

(next page)

The next we made was Keppels Isle
where Nature kindly seem'd to Smile
Fertile in fruits as Rich in Soill
    Inferior to none
Then Several Days (with Gentle Gales
smooth seas, nor more than half fill'd sails
Elaps'd.) But Neptune scorn'd to fail
a Work so well begun.
Pleasd with his Noble Generous Soul
who rather chose the fame to Enroll
of Absent friends, than keep the whole
    to Immortalize his own.

An Island soon the God prepared
which just at Dawn of Day appeard
and thus the friendly Monarch's heard
    to address his Darling Son
Wallis be this your own he said
Rearing above the Waves his head
whilst Narieds round the God head spread
    And all approved the same
From me Your Sire my Son receive
with Laurells such as I shall give,
this Isle, which time shall n'eer outlive
    But ever Crown your Fame
Pursue your Voyage with utmost Speed
may every future Wish succeed
Long may you Wear what Fate's decreed
    Should only Crown your Brow
my Self will o'er the Dangerous Seas
Escort you safe where'er you please
Then disappeard. a gentle Breeze
    confirm'd The Monarch's Vow.

The Breeze Increas'd and freshning Gales
Repleat the Bosoms of our Sails
Swift O'er the Boundless deep She Steals
    Our Course for Tinian steer
But nothing notice worth Occars
no Isles Except the Piscadores
we make, and those described before
Need no discription here

of Wind or Weather Good or Bad
or weather $^{calms\ or}$ storm we had
or whereabouts these Lands were Made
    Some may Conjecture well
Let home bred Travellers as they Please
Whose Book's their Helm, their Ships &
Seas
perplex their thoughts. To such as these
    O! Muse forbear to tell.
Why Starts my muse, what Sudden Cry
proclaims the wish'd for Island Nigh
from topmast head Tinian she Spies.
    at least some Neighbouring Cliffs
Wellcome thrice Wellcome happy Isle
whose much reputed fertile soil
so well rewards the Seamens Toil
    with Natures Bounteous Gifts
With Crowded sails we make the Shore
Our Anchors Drop not long before
Our Boats we Mann & ply each Oar
    the friendly beach to gain

With some few Spanish Huts we found
Our Tents we Pitch and form a Town
and groves with Various fruits around
    compleats a Rural Scene
Domestic Fowles Around us fly
Wild as the Birds that Climb the sky
of these each Day a Number Dye
    each Day as many's hatch'd

Reptiles of many Various forms
tho' few from which we fear much harm
yet Flyes innumurable swarm
    unmissed tho' Millions catch'd

And now O'er Hills with Swiftest pace
young steers or feircer Bulls we Chace
who Stranger to all Human Race
    gaze at this unusual form
In numerous Herds they daily feed
Undaunted all, yet Fate's decreed
One of their Milk white Herd shall bleed
    For us each coming Morn.

(next page)

And Once in Chace we kill'd a Boar
Thick as the Sheild Great Ajax wore
his Brisley Hide, with hideous roar
    The Aged Monster falls
His Burnished Tusks of Wondrous size
Ploughs up the Ground the savage Dies
Triumphant home we bear the Prize
    Astonishing to all.

Minute details I here forbear
In Ansons' Voyage they're better far
Described in Prose than here I dare
    attempt to Write in Verse
may it suffice that whilst we staid
Refreshment Various ways we had;
Our Ship repair'd our Anchors Weigh'd
    and Steer'd our Destind Course

For Javas famous Belgick Isle
the Pride of Holland Seamans Toil
Batavias ever fertile soil
    Which all their States Obey
Here Grandeur Luxury and Pride
and all the Pomp of Wealth beside
O'er all their Indian States Preside
    with Arbitrary Sway

Hither in some few weeks we came
but all remarks I cease to Name
The Indian Seas so well has Fame

    Described in every Realm
Let Infant Bards such Themes decline
at least an artless pen like mine
wholly unformed for such design
    shall n'eer attempt the Helm

We Anchor here tho' short our stay
and soon refresh'd our Anchors Weigh
Wing'd with success we skim the Way
    and Princes Island made
Which Water, Wood, & fowl affords
and Turtle too a feast for Lords
Of these our Ship's not slightly stor'd
    when we our Anchor Weighd.

Homeward our Voyage we now pursued
but Long before the Cape's in View
a Dreadfull Flux seized half our Crew
    and Gastly Death Appear'd

Yet scarce th'Almighty's aid implored
ee'r heaven all kind our health restore
and Only Two of all Onboard
    the Dire Effects has shar'd

Now O! my Muse aloud proclaim
Once our much Loved Captains Name
nor leave Exempt from Circling Fame
    One Officer apart
To Heaven and them our Lives we owe
as fuller Journalls best can their
by them their Daily care you'll know
    unmixed with Flattring text.

Stiff Gales now Waft us O'er the Sea
The Cape we make in Table Bay
Amidst the Belgian Fleet we lay
    and safe at Anchor Ride

But Ah why faints my friendly Muse
or why your former Aid refuse
O speak what'ers the fatal News
    with me your Grief divide

Then know thy Muse was n'eer thy Foe
then Cease to ask what when you know
will Damp you joys with Deepest Woe
    and quite enerve your hand
I n'eer denied a Boon before
and must I then the case Explore.
Know then thy Prince Great York's no more
    The Pride of all your Land
At this the Sailors all confest
their loss & Tears their greif Exprest
and hope & fear in every Breast
    Their various thought divide
we then our Rigging overhaul
Repair our Ship but best of all
repair our Health, for Natures call
    is finely here Supplyed –

(next page)

With fresh Provisions every day
and greens & fruit: a Month we Stay
then Cheerfully our Anchor Weigh
    for St Helena Bound
but needless 'tis to observe that here
Refreshment Scarce & very Dear
our Stay's as short, then straight we steer
    our Course for British Ground

Bless'd with a fair and Pleasant trade
we soon Assension Island made
But Anchor'd not no ee'n delayd
An hours time to Wait
For Turtle which for Size or Store
it yields the Best but nothing more
from such a Wretched Barren Shore
    Kind Heaven Avert our Fate

Be kind ye Gales & waft us O'er
The Briny Waves to Brittanias Shore
Let us with joy behold once more
    Our much loved Native Sand
Then Shall our Voyage on lists of Fame
Immortalize the Dolphins Name
wrote in a more aspiring Strain
    by some more able hand –

Between the Island of S.ᵗ Helena, and the Island Ascension, the SE trade blows all the year long, fine, steady, pleasant gales and mostly fair weather. The variation decreases very gradually between them. In the latitude of Ascension, and 1½ deg. To the Eastward thereof we had 10½ deg.; and about one degree to the E:ᵗ ward of it, had 9 deg. 52 min. W & at Ascension had 9 deg. 40 min. W –

This is a high barren, rocky island about 20 miles in circumference and may be seen 10 leagues in clear weather. It is so intirely barren, that there is not the least appearance of any kind of vegetation nor is there any fresh water on it: these are sufficient reasons for it being unhabited. Yet there are many goats on this island, of which our people shot several; they were very meagre, as might reasonably be expected: and it abounds in sea turtle, the largest and finest perhaps in the world. A ship bound to this island must sail down along the North side of it, and may keep it close aboard it being bold and steep to; and when you come to haul up for the road you must still keep the shoreclose aboard: you may sail within two cables length or less of it (there being no danger) till you bring Cross Hill in the middle of the sandy bay.

This Bay is about a large quarter of a mile deep, and about ¾ of a mile wide. The Westernmost point of this bay is dangerous, a reef of rocks running out from it about a mile from the shore, on which, in bad weather, the sea breaks, therefore care must be taken not ot go too near it. The anchoring place is on the NW side of the island off the above-mentioned sandy bay, opposite which inland, there is a high hill by itself, with a flag staff a cross upon it which give it the name of Cross Hill. A good mark for anchoring is to bring Cross Hill on the middle of the sandy bay when it still bear SSE½E and the extreams of the island from NE½E to SW½S when you will be in 10 fathom water, and about ½ a mile of shore. The bottom is sand and gravel, clear ground. This is as good a birth as any in the road.

The latitude, observed in Ascension road is 7 deg. 57 min: S. and Long:ᵈ made from S:ᵗ Helena, 7 deg. 41 mins W. according to Mʳ Maskeylyne's table of the longitude of places determined by astronomical observations, the true difference of long:ᵈ between these islands is 8 deg. 10 min: which shews that we have been about ½ a deg. to the E:ᵗward, in our run from S:ᵗ Helena hence. But we were not sensible of any curr.ᵗ by our observ:ⁿ of the lat:ᵈ. I am the rather inclined to allow the differences to a current, as I find Mʳ Maskeylyne, in the Warwick, made the ships reckoning but 6:°50'W from S:ᵗ Helena to Ascension – [401]

The 25 July 1767 – [402]

After we left the great house we march'd in two partys one on each side the river, but we had not gone far before we found the hills so steep as to oblige us to join the valley being very stoney, and the rivers running from one side to the other made it very difficult marching; for the first two miles we passed a good many houses and the inhabitants seemed prety numerous, but afterwards we saw only

---

401 This entry in the ML log is in different handwriting which may be Robertson's.
402 The handwriting in this entry may be that of Gore's as it differs from that in the ML.

a house now & then, there is a very rich soil all the way we went in the valley but exceeding stoney, we saw a great many fruit trees and gardings full of plants which a broad pale green colour'd leaf, and grows in bunches like the callalo in the West Indies; the gardings were pil'd round with stones and there was piles of stones run a cross the river for to turn the wtaer into ye plants the ^{roots} of which were under water; They pull'd up one and shewd us they eat the roots, but I have seen them eat the ye leaves by way of greens; The hills one each side grows very steep & rockey as ye valleys grow narrower, and we saw several sm:^{l} drains of water falling down them: we laikwais saw a tree which bears a little red berry which the Indians took & squeezd and got a ya!low juice out of them which they us'd for paint. When we had got about three miles up ye valley we stopt to breakfast where we saw a number of Indians sitting under some trees, at first seeing us they the made a great hallowing but the old man sent one of the Indians that followd us to them where upon they left of and came to us with a green bow & a small pig, they brought ye people cocoa nutts and appells as much as they wanted for which we gave them some small nails. here the valley begins to be very narrow and the hills allmost perpendicular being cloathed very thick with wood some of which we took to be mangrove like-wise saw a cannows building on the ye side of the river and a large fall of water which we found to fall from one rock to another with such rapidity as has wore a round bason in the solid rock at least 5 foot deep and so has wore a spout from which it falls to another rock; over this fall hangs a high precipice where we saw four or five people looking over at us but M:^{r} Gore made sines with his piece that he could bring them down where upon those below waved their hands for them above to go back which they did we afterwards saw from ye hill, that behind there is valley which lies between this precipice and a hill further back where we saw houses & very pleasant plantations & gardings. After we left this fall, the hill allmost joins and opposite to where the Indians shewd us a path up the hills, which is a bout 5 M^s from ye house right perpendicular for at least a quarter of a mile and is nothing but a hard rock, seeing no end to ye vally we ventured up ye hill to t^e left hand being piloted by some of ye Indians who carried water and fruits all our baggage when we came half way up we saw a place not so steep as the rest, where there was houses and people, here we saw several frut trees we stopt and refreshed and then set out again, at last with a great deal of difficulty, and assistance of ye Indians, we arrived at the top, having found nothing in the woods worth remark, except a tree bearing a frut in the inside of which was a shell resembling a wallnutt, the tree is as large as the appel tree and spreads out in branches very much. the soil is prety good in some places but for the ye most part rockey and the hills so steep as to oblige us to walk allong the edges and clamber up by the roots of trees which tir'd us so as to oblige us to rest seven times in going up ye top, which we found overgrown with fern a great deal of which had been lately burnt up, as we march'd down we found the soil very dry & shallow and in some places rockey we found in one of ye valleys a fern tree about 13 or 14 foot high, and about 4 inches diameter, being clear of branches all the way up to ye top, and then spread like a common fern we cut the wood and found it stripd black & white, we likewise saw another tree in the same valley which was prety large and full of little black berreys the leaves was like the leaves of a cherry tree, the wood of a soft white nature, and the bark very thick, and red, out of which we squees'd a juce that stain'd red; in the valley we observed vast quantitys ^{of} blew parrakeets, and green doves, all y^e valleys we saw as we march'd down seem'd very frutfull and inhabited having runs of water in the middle $^{\text{with many ducks that were very easely shot being no way shy}}$. but we saw no water nor trees upon y^e plains, nor very little grass being mostly overgrown with fern the inhabitants of y^e country seem'd of a very civil disposition and very ready to serve us –

NB we found ginger and termerack roots in the valleys

[403] An Account of the Provisions that was Onboard his Maj:ʸ Ship Dolphin (under my Command). On the 21st day of August 1766 – being the Day she sailed from Plymouth.

Bread –	28.000	⎤ Pounds
Ditto by flour –	16.151	⎦
Beer –	Six	Tons
Brandy –	2239	Gallons
Beef –	5750	⎤ Pieces
Pork –	6400	⎦
Flour –	2956	⎤
Suet –	2440	⎬ Pounds
Raisins –	5000	⎦
Pease –	200	⎤
Oatmeal –	60	⎬ Bushells
Wheat –	105	⎦
Butter –	700	⎤
Cheese –	1000	⎬ Pounds
Sugar –	1522	⎦
Oil –	312	⎤ Gallons
Vinegar –	513	⎦
Mustard –	260	Pounds
Malt –	20	H: Hdd:ˢ –
Cabbage –	2	H:dd:ˢ
Portable soup	3000	Pounds –
Salloup	4 bottles 9^{lb}½ each – in all 36 pounds	

Water Sixty Eight Tons.

---

403 This list is not reproduced in the two other logs and does not seem to be in the same handwriting as the rest of the ML. The first volume of the ML ends here.

Names of the Places Discovered	Times when	Latitude in	From Cape Pillar Long: Made	from London Long: Observed	variation of the compass
Whitsun Island	June 7:th 1767	19:*6S	65:42 W	137:°56'W	6:00E
Queen Charlotts Isle	June 7: 1767	19:*8	65:00	138:04	5:00E
E: of Egmont	June 11: 1767	19:*0	65:27	138:30	6:00E
Duke of Westminister	June 12: 1767	19:*1	67:08	140:04	
Duke of Cumberland P: William Henry	June 13: 1767	19:*8	67:40	140:36	7:10E
Prince W Henry	June 13: 1767	19:*0	68:04	141:06	
Bishop of Oznaburg	June 17: 1767	17:*1	74:27	147:30	7:10E
King George 3	June 19: 1767	17:*8	75:32	149:15	
Port Royal	June 24: 1767	17:*0	76:00	149:30W 150:26	5:30
Duke of York	July 27: 1767	17:*0	76:16	150:16	
S:r Cha:s Saunders	July 28: 1767	17:*8	77:02	151:04	
Lord Howes –	July 30: 1767	16:*6	80:38	154:13	7:52
Scilly Islands	July 31: 1767	16:*8	81:22	155:30	9:00 10:00
Boscawens Isle	Agus:t 13 1767	15:*0	101:20	175:09	11:44
L:e Keppels Is	Aug:t 13 1767	15:*4	101:24	175:12	11:30
Wallis Island	Aug:t 17 1767	13:*8 11:*0 North	104:00 119:35	177:00W 192:30W	10:00
Piscadores	Sept:r 3: 1767	11:*0 North	119:35	192:58W	11:40E
Tinian	Sept:r 30: 1767 Otob:r 17: 1767	14:*8 North	119:40	214:10W	6:20E
Grafton Island	Otob:r 29: 1767	21:*4 North	163:12 78 15:00	239:00 W	0:25W
Pulo Condore	Nov:r 8 1767	8:44 North	256:10	253:°38'W	0:00

Names of the Places Discovered	Times when	Latitude in	From Cape Pillar Long: Made	from London Long: Observed	variation of the compass
Island of Pulo Tinian	Nov:r 15: 1767	2:*44N	258:°05'W	255:°33'W	0:32W
Pulo Aro	Nov:r 15: 1767	2:*28N	258:00W	255:11	1:00W
Lucipara	Nov:r 26: 1767	4:*10		254:46W	0:00
Batavia	Dec:r 01: 1767	6:*8		254:30W	1:25W
Princess Island	Dec:r 15: 1767	6:*41N	256:00W	256:30W	1:00W
at sea	Jan:y 26: 1768	34:*24 South	325:00W	323:30W	24:40W
at sea	Jan:y 27: 1768	34:*14S	324:00W	323:13W	23:46W
Table Bay & Good Hope	Febr:y 11: 1768	34:*00S	345:00W	342:04W	19:30W
Table Bay Onshoar	Feb:y 12: 1768	34:*00S	345:00W	342:00W	19:30W
at sea	March 15: 1768	16:*44S	From London 3:00W	2:00W	13:00W
at sea	March 15: 1768	16:*36S	2:00W	2:05W	12:50W
Ascension NW end bore SEBS 14 leagues	March 24: 1768	7:*28S	14:30W	14:38 West	9:48W
S:t Helena	March 19: 1768	15:*27S	3:49W	5:40W	12:47W
Ascension	March 23: 1768	7:*58S	14:18W	14:04W	9:53W

Long:de of Ascension   5:40:00
Long: of Ascension Mask.   13:59:06
Long; of A:n p:r Observation   14:05:00

Names of the Places	Times	Longitude	Longitude	Latitude	variation
		By account from London	By Observ:ⁿ from London		
Port Desire	Dec:ʳ 8: 1766	07:20W	66:24W	47:*56S	23:15E
Cape Virg: Mary	Dec:ʳ 17: 1766	70:04W	69:06W	52:*24S	23:00 East
Point Possession	Dec:ʳ 23: 1766	70:11W	69:58W	52:*30S	22:56E
Point Porpuss	Dec:ʳ 26: 1766	71:00W	71:36W	53:*12S	23:00E
Port Famine	Dec:ʳ 27: 1766		71:32W	53:*42S	22:30E
Cape Froward	Jan:ʸ 19 1767			54:*03S	22:40E
Cape Holland	Jan:ʸ 20 1767			53:*58S	22:40E
Cape Gallant	Jan:ʸ 23 1767			53:*50S	22:58E
York Road	Feb:ʸ 4:ᵗʰ 1767			53:*40S	22:30E
Cape Quod	Feb:ʸ 17: 1767			53:*33S	22:30E
Cape Notch	March 4: 1767			53:*22S	23:00E
Cape Upright	March 18: 1767			53:*05S	22:40E
Cape Pillar	April 8: 1767	76:°00'W		52:*46S	23:40E
at sea	April 21: 1767	97:12W	95:46W	42:*30S	11:15E
at sea	May 4: 1767	100:80W	96:30W	28:*12S	6:00E
at sea	May 20: 1767	110:00W	106:47W	21:*00S	4:32E
at sea	May 23:1767	116:54W	112:06W	20:*20S	5:00E
at sea	June 1: 1767	131:00W	127: 50W	20:*38S	6:00E
at sea	June 3 1767	134:00W	129: 50W	19:*30S	5:40E

Remarks Onboard his Maj:ˢ Ship Dolphin July 27 1767
(1)[404]

1			
2			
3		Port Royal Lat:ᵈᵉ	
4			
5			17:*0S
6		Long:ᵈ	76:00
7			
8			
9			
10		K G Isle, Port Royal	
11		Latitude - 17:*0 S	
12		Longitude –	76:00W
1		Long: Observed Merdien	3400 miles
2		Middle D; Yorks Isle	
3		Latitude –	17:*0S
4		Long:ᵈ –	76:16
5		Long: Obser;ᵈ	
6		S:ʳ Charles Saunders Isles	
7		Latitude –	17:*8S
8		Longitude –	77:02W
9		Long: Observed	
10		Lord Howes Isle	ESE
11		Lat:ᵈ	16:*6S
12		Long:ᵈ –	80:38 –
		Observed Long:ᵈ	

Little wind and fair weather employed in compleating the ship with wood & water & getting ready for sea –

When we sailed from hence we had onboard 78 tons of water

at 5 AM unmoor'd & weigh'd at six towed out of the bay of Port royal – at 8 we got with out the reef and we took our leave of the inhabitants who parted with us with much seeming regret.
particularly the better sort amongst them, the Queen followed us longer than any and cryed much as she had done for three days before on my first making signs to her of my departure (when onshaor observing an eclipse of the sun) –
at 11 a fresh breeze

at noon, the bay we sailed from called Port Royal bore SE½E four leagues, the extreams of King George the 3:ʳᵈ Island bore from ESE six leagues to SBW five lagues – The Duke of yorks Island being the Westermost land in sight from WBS five leagues to SW six leagues –
 Latitude Observed – 17:*2 South
served fresh pork to the ships company

---

[404] This is a second 27ᵗʰ July entry in the ML log.

Tuesday July 28:th 1767 –   (2)

1	5		NWBW	East
2	3	4	WNW	
3	3	3	WSW	
	4	3		
4	4	3	SW	
5	5		SW½S	SE
6	4	4	SWBW	
7	8		West	
8		]		
9				
10			up SWBW	off SWBW
11				
12		]		
1				
2			up SSW	off SW
3		]		
4				20:10
5	5		West	
6	3		SBW	
7	5			
8				
9	8		West	SE
10	9			
11	9			
12	9			

Course	Dist^{ce}	Latitude in	Long. made	MDistance
W¼N	100	17:*27 South	77:44 – W –	3500 West

Fresh breezes & cloudy with rain & squalls of the land
Running along shore of the Duke of Yorks Island about one &
a half miles distance from it & anchorage all along the W side
but it being squally rainy weather, and this island three
leagues from King Georges, I examined no further
it is more mountaineous than the other but the valleys and all
the shore is very full of plantations and the inhabitants the
women as same as at the other island who they have a
constant intercourse with –[405]
at 4 the N end of KGeo Isle East, extreams of D: Yorks Isle
from SEBE½E to SBW½W dis:^e off shore 3 leagues –
at six the SW end of York Isle SE½E, 6 or 7 leagues, the NE
end of it is in a line with Port Royal on K Georges Island E¼S
– distance 7 or 8 leagues – Brought too – a great swell from
the South ward –
[406]at ½ past 5 saw land, haul'd up for it, at 8 being within half
a mile of it ran along shore found it inhabited. it is low land
about five or six miles long near squatt in the middle a
mountain that is about one mile long & of a tolerable height,
there are reefs of rocks all round it, we found no anchorage
but believe there may be some of the reefs. it is full of cocoa
nutt trees, those that are to the South ward seem terribly torn
with a gale of wind. – at 9 bore away – This Island I named
Saunders Islands – it bore ESE three miles
at 11 it bore EBS from G. Isle   long; made – 104:00W –
at noon squally with rain   M Dis: 100:08W

Port royal on King Georges Island bore East ½ South Distance 33 leagues –
The middle of Duke of Yorks Island – W½S Distance 29: Leag:^s Long:^d 0:°14' W M Dis – 13:°00
The middle of Adm: S:^t Charles Saunders Island – East Dis: 10 leagues, lat:^d 01:°02'
Served fresh pork to the ships company –

405 "Fresh gales and cloudy with rain & squalls of the land, running along the shore of his Royal Highness the Duke of York's Island about one and a half miles or two distance from the shore – there seems to be very good bays all along & in the middle a fine harbour but it being so very near Georges Island and boats passing from one to the other, the inhabitants being the same and as numerous, the weather looking very dirty and greasy did not send onhoar. This island is very moutaineous in the middle and the West end and lower at the East end, is full of trees and exactly like Georges Island near the waterside being cocoa nut, breadfruit, apple and plaintain trees . . .". PL and FC. Robertson in his journal bitterly complains of Wallis' lack of curiosity and his refusal to fully explore Tahiti and York's Island as he considers the discovery of these places as being of great strategic importance (see Robertson, pp. 213–235).

406 "At daylight made sail saw land hauled up to it and ran along the lee side of it the weather many great breakers & less rocky but in many places clear spots to anchor in, here were but few inhabitants & these lived in a different manner than those at Georges Island, they having only small huts, here were abundance of cocoa nutt trees but had all their heads blown away as had most of the other trees which I suppose must have been by a hurricane. This island is about six miles long, it hath a tolerable high mountain in the middle which seems to be fertile; we being in want of nothing made sail from this Isle. –Which lays in the latitude of 17:°*8' S Longitude West from London by last observation 151:°04' – and from Cape Pillar by account 77:02 West. This island I called Sir Charles Saunders Island." PL and FC.

Remarks Wednesday July 29 1767 – (3)

H	K	F	Courses	Winds	Remarks
1	8		West		Fresh gales & squally thick & rainy weather – with a great Southern sea
2	8				
3	8				saw severall birds –
4	8				
5	8				
6	8				close reeft the topsails & brought too
7					
8					
9					
10					
11					
12			up NEBE	of NBE	Fresh gales & squally
1					
2					
3				20:00	
4					Made sail
5					variation p:^{r} azumeth 8:°00' Easterly
6	3		West	ESE	
7	9				fresh gales & fair weather with a great Southern swell
8	8				found that the ship much much water than she did before we
9	7	4			went into Port Royal & ran aground –
10	8				
11	7	4			fine pleasant weather
12	7	3		East	served fresh pork to ships company[407]

Course	Dis:^{ce}	Latitude in	Long. made	MDis:^{ce}
W12:00N	110 –	17:*04S	79:20W –	3606 West

King Georges Island[408] bore E¾S Dis: 72 leagues

---

407 "... at night brought too find that the ship makes much more water than she did before she ran aground and the rudder is very losse & shakes the stern of the ship very much [...] served fresh pork to the ships company one pound a man with fruit and bananas, &:^{ce} boiled in their pork broth which is very good the pork being wholly fed on fruit eats finer than mutton or veal –." PL and FC.

408 In the PL and the FC, Port Royall is used as the reference point (St Geroges Island in the ML) until August 13th.

Remarks Thursday July 30 1767 –   (4)

1	6	3	West	East	Moderate & pleasant weather
2	6	2			
3	6			ESE	
4	7				variation p:ʳ azum:ᵗʰ – 7:°52' E
5	7			22:00	saw a flock of birds about the ship the size of gulls flyin high
6	7			SE	– and some larger birds near the ship with white bodys &
7	6	4			brown wings head & tail – close reeft topsails.
8	6				
9					
10					Fresh gales with a Southern swell
11			up SEBE	off SSW	
12					at daylight saw the land from NBE to NNW – the NW end 4
1					leagues the NE about 3 low land like broken islands & a reef
2				20:40	all the length of them
3			up South	off SW	stood in for the island & sent the Master in the boats to sound
4					at 10 he returned having sounded the whole length of the lee
5					side of the island & found no ground nor saw any inhabitants
6	2		West		but saw some smoaks. he took possession for his Majesty &
	3		NBW		called it Lord Howes Island –⁴⁰⁹
7	3	4	NWBN		
8	6	4			served fresh pork
9	2		NEBN		at noon Lord Howes Island bore from ESE½E to E½S
10			up NE	off NW	distance 5 or 6 leagues
11	5		West	EBS	
12	5	4			

Course	Disᵗ	Latitude in	Long. made	MDis:ᶜᵉ
W14:30N	83 –	16:*44:S	81:°00'W –	3686 West

King Georges Island bore S81:00E Dis:ᵗ 96 leagues –

---

409 "... made sail at day light made sail saw the land bearing from NBE to NW stood in for it and sounded all round could find no anchorage it being quite surrounded with breakers, saw no inhabitants but saw two smoaks to the windward, a few cocoa nutt trees grew on the lee part of the island – This island or Island, I called Lord Howes Island." PL and FC.

Remarks Friday July 31 1767 –   (5)

1	5	4	West	East	
2	5	4			
3	5	4			
4	5	2	WNW	22:00	
5	5		WNW		
6	6		SW		
7	4		SBE½E		
8	4	3	South	ESE	
9	3		NE½E	ESE	
10	2	5	NE		
11	2	4			
12	2	3	NE½N		
1	2	3	SBE	EBS	
2	2		SSE	East	
3	3			21:00	
4	2				
5	4		NE½N		
6	4		NE		
7	3		NNE	East	
8	8		NNW	EBN	
9	7		NW		
10	5	4	West		
11	5				
12	5				

Moderate & fair –
saw the land bearing WNW at 4
stood for it
at 5 saw breakers to the S° ward and soon after saw low land in the SW and reefs from SW½NNE – hauled of to the Southward. at 6 the Eastermost Island bore NNE½E two leagues, the breakers to the S:°ward of it NW about 4 miles, and low land to the S:°ward of it SW½W about 4 leagues – squally dirty weather –
turning to windward all night, having dreadfull shoals to leeward and a head for eight leagues we could see before night how much further cannot guess –[410]

at 3 PM observed the longitude & found the ship to be in 15:°49' W from London –

Served fresh pork
Scilly Islands bore EBS – 5 leagues –
Lat – 16:*8S – Long:ᵈ from London 81:°22W

Course	Disᵗ	Latitude in	Long. made	MDistance
N61:0W	46 –	16:*22S	81:°40'W –	2728 West

King Georges Island bore EBS Distance 108 leagues –

---

[410] ". . . at six the Eastermost land NEBN 3 leagues breakers to the S:°ward of it NW four or five leagues and breakers every where about it. Very squally dirty weather, kept turning to windward all night. At daylight crowded sail to get round these sholes and at nine got round them named them Scilly Islands, it being a group of islands and shoals that are very dangerous as the shoals are so far of every way that a clear night or hazey weather one might run on them without seeing land. . . ." PL and FC.

Remarks Saturday August 1:ᵗ 1767 –   (6)

H	K			Remarks
1	5	WSW	ESE	Moderate breezes and fine pleasant weather –
2	5			
3	5			Observed the longitude found the ship in – 156:°00 West
4	4		22:10	from
5	5			London
6	5			
7				
8				
9				Moderate & fair weather –
10				
11				
12		up SSE	off SSW	
1			21:00	
2				
3				made sail – William Welch seaman fell of the main yard on
4				the ships gunwell & broke himself to pieces, & dyed at ten in
5				the morn:ᵍ
6	9	West	EBS	
7	8			
8	8			Fresh gales & fair weather –
9	8	SWS	EBN	served fresh pork
10	8			
11	8			
12	8			

Course	Disᵗ	Latitude in	Long. made	MDistance
W12:00S	90	16:*43S	83:°12'W –	3816 West

King Georges Island bore 83:°30' E Distance 138 leag:ˢ

Remarks Sunday August 2:^{d} 1767 –   (7)

H	K	F	Winds	Course
1	6	3	WSW	ESE
2	7			
3	6	5		
4	7	2		22:10
5	7			
6	6			
7				
8				
9				
10				
11				
12			up SE	off SBW
1				
2				21:20
3				
4				
5				
6	4		West	EBS
7	8	2		
8	9			
9	8	4		
10	9			
11	8	4		
12	9	3		

Moderate & fine pleasant weather

variation p:^{r} azm:^{h}: 8:40E

Brought too –

Fresh gales made sail
variation p:^{r} azm:th: 9:°00'E –

Fresh gales & pleasant weather –
Served fresh pork

Course	Dis	Latitude in	Long. made	MDistance
WBS½S	108	17:*14S	85:°00'W –	3916 West

King Georges Island bore E½S. Distance 172 leagues

Remarks Monday August 3:ᵈ 1767 – (8)

1	8	2	WBS	ESE	Fresh gales & clear
2	8	2			
3	8	3			
4	8	4		22:10	variation p:ʳ azum:ᵗʰ: 9:°30'E
5	8	4			at 6 brought too –
6	9				
7					NB ever since we have been with fine weather, we pump
8					every watch, but if it blows fresh every two hours or oftener at
9					17 or 18 inches and such at 8 or 9 but, in bad weather, have 20
10					or 22 inches & such at the same. the water comes up so clear
11					up that we wash the decks with it –⁴¹¹
12			up SE	off S:°	
1					
2				21:50	
3					
4					
5					
6	3		WBS	East	
7	6	4			
8	7				
9	7				
10	8	3			Moderate gales & hazey –
11	8	2			served fresh pork
12	7			EBN	

Course	Dis:ᵉ	Latitude in	Long. made	MDistance
W¾S	108	17:*30 – S	86:°50'W –	4120 West

King Georges Island bore East Moderate gales & hazey – Distance 207 leagues

---

411 "We make much water when it blows fresh & carry sail – when little wind the ship makes no more water than she did before ran aground –.". PL and FC.

Remarks Tuesday August 4:th 1767 –   (8)

1	5		WBS	ENE
2	5			
3	5	4		
4	5	3		23:00
5	6			
6	4	3		
7				
8				
9				
10				
11				
12			up NNW	off NNW
1				
2				21:30
3				
4				
5				
6	3		WBS	NE
7	6	4		
8	6			
9	6			
10	5	4		
11	5			
12	4	3		

Moderate breezes & hazey weather

Variation p:r azm:th & amp:de – 10:°00'E
hazey brought too –

Hazey cloudy wearther & great dew or dampness in the air –

Variation p:r amp:de – 9:°20'E

saw a flock of large birds at a distance –

moderate breezes & cloudy served fresh pork

Course	Dis:ce	Latitude in	Long. made	MDistance
W¼S	74	17:*34S	88:°07'W –	4694 West

King Georges Island bore East Distance 251 leagues

Remarks Wednesday August 5 1767 – (10)

1	3		WBS	NNE
2	2	5		
3	2	5		ENE
4	3			
5	3			22:10
6	2			
7				
8				
9				
10				
11				
12			up NNE	off NWBS
1				
2				
3				21:10
4				
5				
6	1	4	WBS	East
7	3	4		
8	3	5		
9	4			
10	3	5		
11	4			
12	3	2		EBN

Lights airs with a SE swell –

saw severall Tropic birds and some sheerwaters –[412]

Brought too

Light breezes & fair weather
Variation p:^{r} amp:^{de} – 9:°30'E

Light airs & fair Served fresh pork

Course	Dis:^{ce}	Latitude in	Long. made	MDis:^{ce}
W5:°00'S	46	17:*39S	88:°57'W –	4140 West

King Georges Island bore E¼N Distance 247 leagues

---

412 The PL and the FC do not specify which birds were sighted.

Remarks August 6 1767 –   (11)

H	K	F	Courses	Winds	Remarks
1	3		WBS	EBN	Light airs & clear
2	3				
3	2				
4	2	5		22:10	variation p:ʳ Azumuth – 9:°17'E
5	3	3			and amplitude –
6	4	4			
7					Brought too
8					
9					
10					
11					
12			up NNE	off NW	
1					
2				21:30	
3					
4					
5					
6	3		WBS	ENE	
7	3				Light airs & fine pleasant weather
8	3	4			served fresh pork this being the last day.[413]
9	4	3			Read the articles of War to the Ships comp:ʸ
10	4	5			Saw some flocks of Egg birds –
11	5				Fine pleasant weather
12	5	3		NE	

Course	Dis:ᶜᶜ	Latitude in	Long. made	MDis:ᶜᶜ
West –	56	17:*38S	89:°55'W –	4190 –

King Georges Island bore E¼N Distance 266 leagues

---

413 "Served pork to the ships company this being the last day it being allowed except for the sick – They have had at least a pound of pork a man every day since we left Port Royall Harbour and as much, or more, the thirty four days that we lay in Port Royall Harbour –." PL and FC. Robertson (Corrington, op. cit., p. 247) notes on this day that the Captain and the two Lieutenants were "recoverd greatly." On the 14ᵗʰ though he writes that the Captain "is sick in bed."

Remarks Friday August 7:^th 1767   (12)

1	7	4	WBS	NBE	Fresh breezes & fair
2	7	2		North	saw severall gulls, & large brown birds
3	7	3		NBW	
4	7	4		NNW	variation p:^r az:^t − 10:°39'E
5	7	4		23:00	amp :^de 10:°30'
6	6	2			great number of Egg birds about the ship –
7	4				
8			up WBN	of SW	brought too
9					
10					
11					great numbers of Egg birds about the ship all the night –
12					
1					
2			up SBS	off SSW	
3				21:40	
4					fresh breezes – made sail –
5					opened a cask of pork ^{N:°1239} – short 10 pieces
6	2		WSW½S	NWBW	
7	4		SWBW		Squally with rain –
8	4				
9	3	2	NW	WSW	Great numbers of birds about the ship –
10	6				Squally thick weather, great numbers of Egg birds about the ship
11	4		NW½N		
12	6		NNW	variable	

Course	Dis	Latitude in	Long. made	MDistance
W½S	69	17:*44S	91:°07'W –	4264W

King Georges Island bore E4:00N Dist:^ce 288 leagues

Remarks Saturday Aug:ᵗ 8 1767   (13)

H	K	F	Winds	Courses	Remarks
1	5		NW	WSW	Moderate & hazey cloudy weather & rain
2	3	4	NWBW	NWBW	
3	5		West	SSW	
4	6	3		21:00	moderate with small rain
5	8				
6	6				brought too
7					
8			up SW	of WBS	
9					
10					
11			up WBS	off SSW	
12					
1				20:08	hazey weather
2					
3			up SW	off West	
4					
5					made sail
6	5		West	SBW	
7	7	4			
8	7	4			
9	6	2			
10	6	4			
11	6	4			Fresh breezes & fair hazey in the horizon –
12	7				

Course	Dis:ᶜ	Latitude in	Long. made	MDistance
WNW½N	90	17:*06'S	92:°34'W –	4344W

King Georges Island bore E¼S Distance 316 leagues

Remarks Sunday Aug:t 9:th 1767   (14)

H	K	F	Courses	Winds	
1	6	5	West	SBW	
2	5	4			
3	6				
4	6			21:00	
5	5				
6	4				
7					
8					
9					
10					
11			up SSW	of WBS	
12					
1					
2					
3				20:00	
4					
5	4		West	SBE	
6	5				
7	4	2			
8	5				
9	5	2			
10	5	5			
11	6	5			
12	6	5		SE	

Course	Dis:e	Latitude in		Long. made	MDistance
WBN½N	89 –	16:*42S		94:00W –	4426

Fine pleasant gales hazey in the horizon –

saw a flock of Egg birds

Will:am Lochlan fell overboard and with much difficulty was saved –
threw cork jacketts & gratings &:ce overboard – it being near dark he got hold of one my chairs & was saved – the things thrown overboard were lost –

two grampusses near the ship.

made sail
saw some Tropic birds & Men of War birds –
cloudy weather –

Moderate & fine pleasant weather

King Georges Island bore E ¼ S Distance 344 leagues

Remarks Monday August 10:th 1767   (15)

1	6	4	West		SE
2	6	5			
3	7	2			
4	7	3			21:40
5	6	4			
6	6	4			
7	6	4			
8	6	2			ESE
9	6				
10	6				
11	6				
12	6				
1	6				
2	5	3			
3	5				
4	5	2			East
5	5	5			
6	5	5			
7	5	5			20:30
8	6				
9	7	3			
10	8	4			
11	8	3			
12	8		1552		

Moderate & cloudy –

variation p:r azumeth ⌉10:35E
               amplitude ⌋10:50

Double reeft the topsails & hauld up the fore sail & sailed under them all night, it being a fine clear moon light –

porpoises or albacores & bonettos about the ship –

At five made sail saw some Men of War birds and one Egg bird –

Variation   p:r amplitude –⌉ 9:54
               azumeth –   ⌋ 9:42E

saw severall flying fish and many birds

fresh gales & fine pleasant weather.

Course	Dis:e	Latitude in	Long. made	MDistance
W½N	156	16:*10S	100:39W –	4578W

King Georges Island bore E¼S Distance 393 leag:s

Remarks Tuesday August 11:th 1767   (16)

H	K	F	Courses	Winds	Remarks
1	8		West	NBE	Moderate gales & pleasant weather
2	8				
3	7	5			
4	6			23:00	
5	7	2			
6	6	3			shortned sail saw some Boobies & Men of War birds about
7	5	5			the ship –
8			up NBW	off NNW	Richard Conway fell of the main yard on deck and bruised
9	5		West	ENE	himself much.
10	5				
11	4	5			
12	4	2			
1	4				
2	5	5		21:10	Light airs with rain & lightning
3			Variable		
4					Ships head all round the compass –
5	6		West	ENE	Made sail –
6	4				
7	6			EBN	fresh gales & hazey –
8	6	2			
9	7				fresh gales & squally. judged we saw the land in the SBE –
10	8				hauled the Wind
11	4	3	SSE		
12	4			ENE	saw some large Pitterells –
					squally with small rain

Course	Dis:t	Latitude in	Long. made	MDistance
W7:°00N	112	15:*50S	98:34W –	4689W

King Georges Island bore E 86:00 S Dis:e 430 leagues

Remarks August 12 1767   (17)

H	K	F	Courses	Winds	Remarks
1	5		SSE½E	East	Moderate gales & cloudy. at 1 it being very clear & we having stood near five leagues toward what we took for land at eleven – & now could not see the appearance of any. Bore away – West – Variation – p:^{r} az:th 11:47E
2	6	2	West	NEBE	
3	7			23:00	
4	4	2			
5	7		W½S	NNW	
6	5				
7	3	2	West	North	Shortned sail
8	3	5			fine moonlight –
9	5	5			
10	5	5			
11	6				
12	6				fresh gales & fair
1	6	4		NBW	
2	5	3			
3	4	3		NNW	
4	1		NE	variable	
5	2		NW		light airs & showery –
6					
7				21:55	variation p:^{r} amp:^{de} – 10:°00'E
8			Calm		
9					
10					
11					fresh breezes & cloudy –
12	5		West	NBW	

Course	Dis:^{t}	Latitude in	Long. made	MDistance
West –	79	15:*56S –	99:50W –	4767W

King Georges Island bore E86:50S Distance 456 leagues –

Remarks Thursday August 13 1767   (18)

1	2		WBS	variable
2	2		SW	
3	1	3		24:00
4	1			
5	1	3	West	
6	1		WBN	variable
7	1	2	WNW	
8	1	3		
9	1	1	West	
10	1			
11				
12			[…] the	all round compass
1				
2				
3				22:00 South
4	3	4	WNW	
5	5			
6	7			
7	7			
8	6		W½W	
9	6			
10	6			
11	7	4		
12	7	3		

Light airs & variable –

variation p:ʳ azum:ᵗʰ   11:°30'E –
saw a bird somewhat like a Snipe
shortned sail

at 10 wind varying all round the compass with heavy shower of rain

cloudy heard severall birds about the ship –

at 4 made sail cloudy & the wind variable –

at 7 saw the land in a high hummock bearing about WBS –
haul'd the wind & stood for it, variation p:ʳ az:ᵗʰ 11:°44'E
at 8 fresh gales and cloudy weather
at 10 saw another island bearing WSW
at noon the middle of the first island which makes like a sugar loaf W¾S distance, distances 4 or 5 leagues –
at the same time the second island⁴¹⁴ in the middle bore WSW
the first of these I named Boscawens Isle
The second – Keppels island –

Course	Dis:ᵗ	Latitude in	Long. made	MDist:ᶜᵉ
W½N	65	15:*50S –	101:4W –	4832W

King Georges Island bore E4:10S Dis: 478 leagues

---

414 The second island is described as having a peak likewise but flat all round.

Remarks Friday August 14 1767   (19)

1	7		SWBW½W	SBE	
2	8	4	SW	SEBS	
3	2	5	EBN	SEBS	
4	5	3	ENE½E		
5	8	3	SWBS	22:00	
6	3		East	SSE	
7	3	5			
8	4				
9	3	4			
10	3	3			
11	3	4			
12	4	4			
1	3		SW	SE	
2	4			21:40	
3	3	4			
4	2	5	SSW		
5					
6			Standing of &		
7			On		
8	2		Between the two		
9	3		islands		
10			Saw many whales &		
11			Grampusses which		
12			we at first took for		
			reefs –		

Fresh gales & fair –
At ½ past 2 Boscawens Isle NNW 3 miles
Keppels isles the extreams fm SWBW to WBW about two miles, saw severall inhabitants
at six shortned sail –
at 5 AM sent the Master with two boats in shore to look for anchorage
Keppels Isle bore ENE –
Boscawens isle NW½W –
The ship standing off & on between the two islands –
at noon the Master returned with the following report:
that he stood close in shore & sailed all along the side of the Island as near as he could go could get no ground, that he then ran round a reef which lay of from the shore & went into a large deep bay where he hoped to meet with anchorage but found it every where so full of rocks that the boat could scarce find a refuge, that he rowed up to the shore where he found a rivulet of good fresh water that he took possession in the Kings name that sixty of the inhabitants came down & brought some coco nuts plaintains & bananas, he saw few fowls but no hogs but in all they probably have plenty, as the ship kept out to windward of the Island he did not care to venture into the country but went out again with the boats and sounded all along the reef where he found in severall places pretty good anchorage only corally bottom – the water smooth and near half a mile from the reef – carried on –*415

---

415 "Fresh gales and fair weather at two being two miles from Boscawens Isle saw severall inhabitants but Keppels Island being to windward and more likely to find anchorage we hauled up for it – At six Keppels Isle the extreams from WBS to SWBS, a bout a mile and half distance saw many inhabitants, and breakers a long way off the shore stood of and on all night. At four in the morning sent the boats to sound and visit the island. We ran down at daylight and lay of the middle of the island, at noon the boats returned and reported that they ran down close by the island within a cables length & could not get any ground that severall rocks lays of it but no anchorage, he then hauld round the reef and came to a large deep bay which was full of rocks – he sounded without it and found anchorage in 14 to 20 fathom sand and coral after that he went into the bay and found a rivulet of good water but the place being rocky he went to a place about half a mile further and landed and found from there to the water a good rolling way might be made and supply a ship with plenty of water but it would require a strong guard for fear the inhabitants should be troublesome – he saw no hogs but believe there may be such things in the country, he got two fowles, some cocoa nuts plaintains and bananoes, there came two canoes with six men in them who seemed peaceably inclined they had the first joints of their little fingers taken off, they had only mats for clothing but in make were the same sort of people as at Georges Isle there were about fifty people came down and stood at a distance from them but come not nearer than a hundred yards after making what observations they could they then put of when three of the people went into one of the boats and when they were about half a mile from the shore they all three suddainly jumpd overboard." PL and FC. Gore also indicates that there is plenty of fruit trees some of which were plaintain and banana trees, and notes concerning the inhabitants that they did not seem to be numerous. Gore also indicates the "loss of the little finger" and their very neatly made canoes.

Course	Dis	Latitude in	Long. made	MDist:^{ce}
NW½W		15:*52S –	101:20W –	4842W

At Noon Keepels Island bore –   SWBS Dis:^{ce} six miles –
         Boscawens Island bore –   NWBW – three miles –[416]

---

[416] Here the PL and the FC also give the latitudes and the longitudes of the two islands: Boscawens Island latitude 15:50 South, longitude observed 175:00 from London, Keppels Island latitude 15:54 South, longitude observed 175:12 from London.

Remarks Saturday August 15 1767 (20)

1	3		North	SE
2	3		WBN	
3	8		WNW	
4	8	5		
5	8			21:40
6	8	2		
7				
8				
9				
10				
11				
12			up ENE	off NNE
1				
2				
3				
4				
5				
6	6		WNW	ESE
7	7	4		21:20
8	8			
9	8	3		SEBE
10	8	4		
11	8	2		
12	8			

The inhabitants are rather darker than at Georges Island but had their backsides marked as they had with some variation but the most remarkable is that half the people had the second joints of their left little fingers taken off –

At noon we bore away and finding only a small bay at Boscawens Island we did not send out boats, as the island to windward is so much better

so we kept on our course –

Friday noon Kepels Island SW BS, the middle distance two leagues –

Boscawens Island NWBW three miles

At 4 PM Boscawens island SEBE 8 leagues

Keppels Island SE¼E distance ten leagues

At 6 Boscawens Island bore ESE Distance sixteen leagues shortned sails & brought too

Fresh gales & cloudy all night –

At 5 AM made sail out 2:nd reefs –

variation – Az:th 12:00 East –

Fresh gales & cloudy[417]

Course	Dis	Latitude in	Long. made	MDist:^{ce}
NW½W	118	14:*36S	102:53W	4922W
			1:33W	

Boscawens Island bore SE½ E Distance 39 leagues.

---

[417] "The boat being returned with the before mentioned account, the ship leaking & the the rudder shaking the stern much, and not knowing what damage she may have received in her bottom and it being the depth of winter, and must expect very bad weather to go round Cape Horn, or to gain the Streights of Magellan, and if her leak should prove worse (which it had hitherto done when it blows hard) we should have no where to push to and if we should luckily get well round the Cape yet we must refresh somewhere and in all probability we shall sooner be home by way of the Cape of Good Hope, as we may recruit at Tinian & Batavia, whereas our watering here would take up a considerable time and much fateague. Therefore having considered all these things and many more and having so good an account of the refreshments that may be had for any future expedition that may be made to this part of the world, I thought it most prudent and more for the benefit of his Majestys service to make the best of my way to Tinian, Batavia & to Europe and if we found the ship not in a condition to proceed we had in a manner a certainty of saving our selves & perhaps of getting refitted as from hence to Batavia is a calm sea. We have made longitude by account from Cape Pillar 104:70 West, Cape pillar from Cape Horn 6:00W, longitude from Cape Horn 110:00 West. Variation p:^{r} azumeth 12:°00' Easterly. At noon we bore away and passed to Boscawens island we did not visit it it is a high island & is full of wood & hath many inhabitants but Keppels is by far the largest and best." PL and FC.

Remarks Sunday August 16 1767   (21)

H	K	F	Courses	Winds	Remarks
1	8		WNW	ESE	Fresh gales & cloudy –
2	8				saw a large flock of Egg birds
3	8				
4	8			22:20	at 6 fresh gales & squally thick weather
5	8				close reeft the topsails & brough too –
6	6				
7					
8					
9					
10					
11					
12			up NEBE	off NBE	Fresh gales and a great sea –
1					
2					
3					had an observation of ☽ and ☉
4					made sail variation p:r amp: 10:°20' E
5				21:50	at 9 squally rainy weather in 3:d reefs
6	4		WNW	SSE	at 10 saw the land bearing NBE
7	8	2			hauld the wind for it –
8	8	4			at noon the extreams of the land bore from ENE½E 5 or 6
9	8				leagues, to NNE about three leagues – the land seems pretty
10	4		NWBN		high & hilly and in many places double, the coast seems full
	2		NNW		of rocks & shoals – vast reefs running off miles on every side–[418]
11	7	2	N½E	EBN	
12	7		NNE	East	

Course	Dis	Latitude in	Long. made	MDist:ce
NW	106	13:*26S	104:07W –	4994W

Boscawens Island bore SE¼E Dist:ce 73 leagues.

[418] "... The land pretty high but low at the waterside and where we are now running along full of cocoa nut trees, see a few huts, no clear land but smoaks in the country. At noon hoisted out the boats and sent them inshore while we sailed along the coast and hauld without a parcel of breakers and a reef of rocks to get round to the lee side of the land – This land looks extremely pleasant." PL and FC. Gore: "This island is nam'd after our Captain."

Remarks Monday August 17 1767 (22)

1	3		North	EBS
	4		NNW½W	
2	4		NBE½E	
	3		NNE	
3				
4			Standing off and on	
5			without the reef –	
6			Variation – 9:°15' E	
7				
8				25:20
9				
10				
11				
12			up NE	off NBW
1				
2				
3				22:10
4				
5				
6	4		NW	EBE
7	8			
8	8			
9	8	3		
10	7	5		
11	7			
12	7			

Course	Dis:ᵉ	Latitude in	Long. made	M Distance

from Cape Pillar

Wallis Island Latitude 13:*8S Long : 104:°00'W

Fresh gales & cloudy
at 1 the extreams of the land bore from N25:°00'E to S44:°00'E Dis: off shore 3 or 4 miles
at 2 it bore from N62:00E to S14:00E of NW point Miles
at 6 the Island bore from SBE to NE distance off shore 4 miles – a breach in the reef where the boats sounded SE two miles – stood of shore NW three miles & then brought too –
The Master returned with all the boats having sounded all along the back of this reef about ½ of a mile from it & half way between the SBE & NE points, there was a good spot to anchor in, from 18 to 12 fathom and coral there are some more places, but not so good –
within the reef at this place there there is a breach in the reef of half a cables length wide, 14 fathom but no anchorage within it being from one end to the other full of sunken rocks for upward of two mile, the boat pulled to the shore which they could not come nearer too than a cables length there was no clear ground & very thick of underwood about forty inhabitants came to them in canoes but could get nothing from them, saw no fruit but cocoa nutts the other trees are very large but could not tell what sort they were the inhabitants much the same at the last island – carried on.

EXPLORATION OF THE SOUTH SEAS

Remarks Monday August 17[419] 1767 (22)

1				Mr Clarke & the rest of the officers of the ship did me the honour to call this Island after my name –
2				
3		Observed the longitude at ½ past 8 AM, found the ship to be in	177:°00' West from London	The Anchoring place bring the extream of the main island to bear NNE½E & SE½E and the opening in the reef S½E distance from it about a quarter of a mile in case of necessity you may warp the ship within the reef & moor her in safety in 8 to 12 fathoms waters only take care to sound all round the for fear of sunken rocks as the greatest part of the way between the reef & shore are full of them.
4				
5				
6				
7				
8				
9				
10				
11				This whole island is guarded by a reef of rocks and severall small islands & keys it looks very pleasant the SE side is full of cocoa nutt trees which is the weather side the NW is full of other trees, very large but don't know what sort they are, we saw no watering place and it growing dark & a strong tide running to the NW – the boats came off they believed that in severall places where they saw cocoa nutt trees growing it being in valleys, there was water but it was so rocky they could not land over it and the time so short they could not examine further – so came off.
12				
1				
2				
3				
4				
5				
6				
7				
8				
9				fine pleasant gales & fair weather
10				
11				
12				

Course	Dis:ᵉ	Latitude in	Long. made	M Distance
NW¼N	75	12:*18S	104:46W –	5039

Wallis Island SE¾S distance 25 leagues –[420]

---

419 This page is also dated 17 August.
420 "Fresh gales and cloudy weather, the boats in shore & on the reef sounding the ship standing of and on. At six the boats returned, the island bore SBE to NE.

The Master sais that all within the reef it is so rocky but without it he found two or three pleaces to anchor in about two cables length from the reef, and at the place he found a break in the reef of about sixty fathom a road wherein in case of necessity a ship might anchor, or more in 8 fathom but she must not more with more than a cable – the places without is in 18, 14 & 12 sand and coral –

That he rowed close along the shore and found it rocky with trees growing close down to the waterside, the trees were of different sorts but had no fruit on them, they were many of them very large, that there were on the leeside very fine cocoa nutts and not one house, that he saw several small rills of water which by clearing away would run in a longer stream he beleives, that there came to him severall canoes with six and eight men in each the people robust and strong had only a mat about their middle, he gave them some trinkets and had in return two heavy clubs (". . . they were armed with large maces or clubs, such as Hercules is represented with . . ." Hawkesworth), he saw no kind of animal or fowls except sea fowl nor could he make them understand if they had any or no, they seem to be very designing for while he was parlying with them they took hold of the boats painter and hauld the boat upon the rocks, and with difficulty they made them desist (". . . Our people endeavoured, in vain, to make them desist, till they fired a musket cross the nose of the man that was most active in the mischief. No hurt was done . . ." Hawkesworth), and then finding the water had ebbed of a suddain our boats put off and had much trouble in getting off to the ship, for the water had fallen so much that where they came in in deep water they found the points of rocks standing up so that they were at least half an hour getting from thence to the

Remarks Tuesday August 18:th 1767   (23)

1	7	4	NW	
2	7			
3	7			
4	7	2		
5	8			
6	7			
7				
8				
9				
10				
11				
12			up NEBE	of
1			NBW	
2				
3				
4				
5				23:07
6	6		NW	EBS
7	7	2		
8	7	2		
9	6	3		
10	6			
11	6	3		
12	7			

Fresh gales & clear pleasant weather –

variation p:r   azumeth   ⎤   11:00E
                amplitude ⎦   10:00

shortned sail & brought too, a very great swell from the ENE

variation p:r azum:th 9:05E

Took an observation of the ☽ dist ☉
Longitude in 178:°37' West of London

Moderate gales & fair weather

Course	Dis	Latitude in	Long. made	M Distance
NW¾N	100	10:*58S	105:47W –	5099W

Wallis Island SEBS¼E distance 58 leagues –

---

enterance in the reef all the rest that was covered when they went in being now dry, and the sea breaking much over." (August the 17th continued): "The canoes followed them as far as the reef and then turned back it being then near six o'clock they came onboard; and I having this report hoisted the boats in and ran down four miles to leeward where we lay till morning and seeing nothing of the island made sail.

A plan of this and the other islands are delivered in with this; and as we have had opportunities of observing the true latitude of them all and likewais by frequent observations of distance of the sun from the moon of getting the true longitude nearly between these islands and London – I hope that it will be no very difficult matter to hit any of them in order to refresh or make further discoveries of their produce – One thing is very remarkable that we have not found any kind of metal amongst the number of islands and yet these people the moment they get a bit of iron they immediately sharpen it, which they do not do with either brass or copper. –

We found the variation here to be 9:15 Easterly.

The latitude of Wallis Island – 13:18S, longitude observed West from London 177:00, longitude made by reckoning from Cape Pillar 184:00 West –

The officers of the [ship] did me the honour of calling this island after my name – at 6 PM the Island bore from SBE to NE distance of shore about one league the breack in the reef where a ship may anchor SE one and half miles from hence ran off shore NW four miles and brought too. At 6 AM made sail, Wallis Island then bore SE½E nine leagues –." PL and FC.

Gore's description of the island and the inhabitants is as follows: ". . . this island is closely cover'd with trees of what kind we know not it is inhabited by a people in every respect like those on Keppel I.d that is of a deep copper colour strongly built their hair of a mixt rusty colour, some

Remarks Wednesday August 19 1767   (24)

H	K	F	Courses	Winds	Remarks
1	7	5	NW	ESE	Fresh gales & fair weather
2	7	5			Saw a Man of War bird & some Egg birds
3	8				Punished James Field seaman for steering the ship very
4	7	5		24:00	negligently & behaving in an insolent manner to the Quarter
5	7	5			Master and the Gunner[421]
6	6	3			variation – p:r azumeth – 10:°30'E
7					an Eastern swell –
8					
9					
10					
11					
12			up NEBE	of North	Fresh gales & fair with an ESE swell
1					
2					
3					
4				23:25	made sail
5					variation p:r amp:de – 10:30E
6	5		NW	East	azum:th – 10:20E
7	7	5			
8	9				saw a flock of Egg birds & some Men of War birds & Tropic
9	9				birds –
10	9				Opened a cask of pork N954 contents 302 – short five peices
11	8	5			Fresh gales & fair weather
12	9			EBN	

Course	Dis:e	Latitude in	Long. made	M Distance
NWBN	118	9:*20S –	106:54W	5165W

Wallis Island bore S35:°15'E distance 97 leagues

---

having it ty'd on the tops of their heads others loose about their shoulders waring matts about their lower parts which are dyed black from their hips half down their thighs having clubbs as offensive or defensive weapons, all thievish and sly yet timorous. This much we saw of those that go in cannoes and in all. Probably the landmen if any there are differ but little from the canoe men some of them have black hair. The inhabitants on the above donn't seem to be numerous both from few we saw and closeness of the country there being but here and there . . ."

Robertson gives Wallis the things he has acquired from the islanders (clubs of iron wood and two necklaces). In the list of objects handed in to Admiralty, in the FC, only one club from Wallis Island is mentioned and none of the necklaces. Robertson's journal ends here.

421 The PL and the FC specify that Field was punished "for mutinous behaviour & ill steering the ship." He received a dozen lashes (Gore). Gore also distinguishes between two types of Egg birds in these seas, one species dark and the other white. The former larger than the latter, both flying like Tropic birds and the white Egg bird being often seen among the reefs and shoals.

Remarks Thursday August 20 1767   (25)

H	K	F	Courses	Winds	Remarks
1	8	3	NW	EBS	Moderate gales & pleasant weather
2	8				
3	8				
4	8			24:40	
5	8	2			squally with small rain
6	6				saw some birds at a distance
7					variation p:ʳ azumeth – 10:30E –
8					
9					
10					
11					
12			up NEBE	of NBW	squally with small rain
1					
2					
3					
4				24:00	
5			NW	EBS	made sail
6	5				variation p:ʳ amp – 10:°20'E
7	8			EBN	saw a bird somewhat like a Snipe
8	9				fresh gales & squally at times –
9	9				
10	8	2			
11	8			NEBN	Fresh gales & cloudy
12	7	5		NNE	

Course	Dis:ᶜ	Latitude in	Long. made	M Distance
NW½N	110 –	7:*56S	108:04W	5235W

Wallis Island bore S36:40E dis:ᵗ 134 leagues

Remarks Friday August 21 1767   (26)

H	K	F	Course	Wind	
1	6	2	NWBW	NBE	Moderate & cloudy
2	6	3			Saw a bird like a Snipe some Men of War birds & Tropic
3	6	4			birds
4	5	2		24:30	variation p:r azumeth 10:°07E
5	4		WNW	North	
6	6		NWBW	NBE	
7			⎫		
8			⎬ up NNE	of NW	
9			⎭		
10			⊢ up EBS	off N	
11					
12			⎫		
1			⎬ up NBE	off N	Light airs with small rain heard many Tropic birds & Egg
2			⎭		birds about the ship –
3			⎫		
4			⎬ up NNW	off NW	
5			⎭	24:00	variation p:r amp:de – 10:50E
6	4		NW		azumeth – 10:32E
7	4				
8	2	4	NW½W		Light airs caught a shark –
9	2				saw severall porpoisses –
10	1	5	NW		
11	2				Light airs & clear weather
12	1	2			

Course	Dis:e	Latitude in	Long. made	M Distance
N49:°00'W	61	7:*16S	108:50W	5281W

Wallis Island bore S38:10E distance 154 leagues

Remarks Saturday August 22: 1767 (27)

H	K	F	Courses	Winds	Remarks
1	1	3	NW	NNE	Little wind and fair weather.
2	2				
3	3			NE	
4	3	2			
5	3	4		ENE	variation p:ʳ azumeth – 10:32E
6	3	3		24:20	amplitude – 10:20E
7	2	4			
8	3				
9					Little wind brought too –
10			up NEBN	off North	
11					
12					Cloudy squally with rain
1				24:20	
2					
3			up NBE	off North	
4					
5					Light breezes –
6	2		NW	ESE	
7	5			NEBN	Moderate & cloudy variation 10:°32'E
8	7			NNE	
9	6				saw a bird like a Plover
10	6				
11	6				Fresh breezes & fair weather –
12	5	4		NNE	

Course	Dis:ᵉ	Latitude in	Long. made	M Dist:ᶜᵉ
NWBN	67	6:*20 South	109:27W	5318

Wallis Island bore S38:°50'E distance 176 leagues

Remarks Sunday August 23 1767 (28)

H	K	F	Course	Winds	Remarks
1	5		NW	NEBN	Moderate & fine pleasant weather
2	5				
3	6			24:20	variation p:r azum:th 11:°54'E
4	6	4		NE	
5	6				
6	6	4			Shortned sails & brought to.
7	3				
8					
9					
10			up NNE	off NWBN	squally with rain –
11					
12					
1					
2					
3				23:10	moderate and fair –
4					
5					fresh gales & squally with rain
6	5		NW½W	NNE	
7	7				
8	2	4	NW	ENE	squally with rain –
9	6	3		NE	fresh gales & fair
10	8	3			
11	8	3		NEBN	Fresh gales & clear weather
12	8				

Course	Dis:e	Latitude in	Long. made	M Dist:ce
NW½N	94	5:*37 South	110:26W –	5378W

Wallis Island bore S38:°10'E distance 207 leagues

Remarks Monday August 24 1767   (29)

H	K	F	Wind	Wind2	Remarks
1	7		NW		Fresh gales & cloudy
2	8				
3	8				variation p:r amp:de 10:°49'E
4	7	2			
5	7	5			brought too
6		1			
7					
8					
9					
10			up NBE	off NW	moderate gales & fair
11					
12					
1					
2					
3					
4					
5					
6	6	5	SW	NEBN	variation p:r amp : ⎤ 10 :56E
7	8				azu : ⎦ 11:15
8	5	5			got up all the cables & stowed them away again after they
9	6	5			were well cleaned –
10	7	2			
11	7	5			Fresh gales & squally –
12	7		NWBW		

Course	Dis:e	Latitude in	Long. made	M Dist:ce
N40:°40'W	99 –	3:*54S	111:31W –	5443W

Wallis Island bore S38:°10'E distance 207 leagues

Remarks Tuesday August 25 1767   (30)

H	K	F	Courses	Winds	Remarks
1	6		NW	NE	Moderate & hazey –
2	5				
3	4	4			Saw some birds employed in rounding the cables –[422]
4	4				
5	4	2		23:40	variation p:r az:t 10:°30'E
6	4				
7					
8					
9					
10			up NNE	off NWBN	
11				variable	squally with rain –
12					
1					
2					
3			up NNE	off NNW	
4				23:10	
5					variation p:r az 11:°22'E
6	3	4	NW	NE	
7	3	5			
8	3	5			
9	3	4			
10	3	3			
11	4				Little wind & cloudy
12	4				

Course	Dis:e	Latitude in	Long. made	M Dist:ce
NW½N	60	3:*08S	112:10W	5481W

Wallis Island bore S39:°08'E distance 260 leagues

---

422 "Employed in rounding the small and best bower cables twenty fathoms from the clinch." PL and FC.

Remarks Wednesday August 26 1767 (31)

H	K	F	Courses	Winds	Remarks
1	4		NW	East	Moderate & cloudy with squalls
2	3	5			
3	3	4			
4	3			SEBE	caught a bird somewat like a dove both in colour & size but it
5	4	2		24:10	had web feet —[423]
6	4				Brought too
7					
8					
9					
10					
11					
12			up NNE	off North	
1					
2					
3				23:50	
4					
5	3		NW	ENE	squally saw some Egg birds –
6	3	5			variation p:^{r} azum:th 11:°19'E
7	4	4		NEBN	
8	4		WNW	North	
9	3	4	NW	NE	
10	5	2			
11	6				squally with rain at times
12	5	5		variable	

Course	Dis:^{e}	Latitude in	Long. made	M Dist:^{ce}
N41:°00'W	66	2:*20 S	112:54W –	5524W

Wallis Island bore S39:°00'E distance 282 leagues

---

423 The bird in question has red legs (PL and FC).

Remarks Thursday August 27 1767 (32)

1	5		NW	NEBN	Moderate & cloudy sometimes squally with showers –		
2	5		NW½W				
3	5		NW	variable			
4	4	5		24:10			
5	3	4	WNW		Fresh gales & very squally		
6	3		NWBW				
7			up NNW	off NW	squally dirty weather –		
8					brought too –		
9							
10			up N:°	off NNW			
11							
12							
1					moderate & hazey with an Eastern swell –		
2							
3			up NBW	off NW	variation	amp:^{de} –	10 :34E
4				23:55		azu: –	11 :20E
5	5		NW	NE			
6	7	2					
7	8						
8	8	2					
9	8						
10	7	5					
11	7	5			Fresh breezes & fair		
12	7	4					

Course	Dis:^{e}	Latitude in	Long. made	M Dist:^{ce}
NW¼N	90	1:*14S	113:56W –	5580W

Wallis Island bore S39:°50'E distance 313 leagues

Remarks Friday Aug:t 28 1767 (33)

H	K	F	Courses	Winds	Remarks
1	6	4	NW	NE	
2	6	3	NNW		Fresh breezes & fair weather
3	6			24:00	
4	6				
5	7				variation p:r azum:th – 9:44E
6	7				apml:de – 10:4E –
7	3			ENE	shortned sail[424]
8	3				
9	4				
10	4				
11	4				
12	4				
1	4				
2	3	5		23:50	
3	3	4			
4	3				At this time reckon we crossed the line into North latitude
5	3	2		NEBE	after being 310 days in South latitude
6	3	3			saw some plaintain leaves & cocoa nut husk drive past the
7	3	5			ship variation p:r amp –
8	5				az – 11:°00'E
9	5	4			Observed the longitude the ship was in – 187:°24' West of
10	5	3			London
11	4				Moderate & fine pleasant weather
12	4			NE	

Course	Dis:e	Latitude in	Long. made	M Dist:ce
N13:°00W	109	00:*31 N	114:22W	5612W

Wallis Island bore S37:°20'E dist:ce 342 leagues

---

424 "Shortned sail but it being fine clear weather continued our courses." PL and FC.

Remarks Saturday August 29 1767   (34)

H	K	F	Winds	Courses	Remarks
1	5	2	NNW	NEBE	Fine pleasant weather –
2	5	2			
3	6				
4	6	3		EBN	
5	7			24:20	Shortned sail
6	7	5			
7	5	4			Caught a large porpoise –[425]
8	5	3			
9	4				
10	4				
11	4	2			
12	4	4		NEBE	Fine breeze & fair weather
1	5				
2	4	4			
3	4	3			
4	4	5		23:45	
5	4	4			
6	5	2		ESE	
7	7				saw some birds swimming –
8	6				squally with rain
9	5				
10	4	2			moderate & fair
11	4	3		East	squally with rain
12	5	3			

Course	Dis:^{e}	Latitude in	Long. made	M Dist:^{ce}
NBW	125	2:°33'N	114:49W	5638W

Wallis Island bore S34:°15'E dist:^{ce} 382 leagues

---

425 "Struck a large porpoise which served all the ships company." PL.

Remarks Sunday August 30 1767   (35)

H	K	F	Wind	Course	
1	7		NNW	ESE	
2	5	5			
3	6	2			
4	5	5			
5	5	3		24:00	
6	5	4			
7	4	3			
8	4	4		ENE	
9	4				
10	4				
11	4				
12	4	2			
1	5	4			
2	5	3			
3	4	5		24:00	
4	4	5			
5	5				
6	5				
7	6				
8	6				
9	5				
10	4	4			
11	4	4			
12	6				

Fresh breezes & cloudy with squalls –
Crossed a great rippling of a current stretching from NE to SW as far as we could see from the masthead[426]
shortned sail –

variation   p:^r   amplitude –   9:°00'E
                        azumeth –   1:°30'E

Fresh breezes & clear weather

Course	Dis:^e	Latitude in	Long. made	M Dist:^{ce}
NBW	131	4:*42W	115:°15'W	5653W

Wallis Island bore S32:°00'E distance 418 leag:^s

---

426 "... sounded but had no ground with 200 fathoms of line." PL and FC.

Remarks Monday August 31 1767   (36)

H	K	F	Winds	Course	Remarks
1	6		NNW	ESE	Moderate & fair weather –
2	6	3			
3	6				
4	5	4		ENE	variation p:ʳ amplitude – 11:00E
5	4	2		25:00	azumeth – 11:00
6	4				
7	4	4			
8	5			NEBE	
9	6				Showery
10	6	3			
11	5	4			
12	5				Cloudy
1	5				Squally with some rain –
2	4	3		24:10	
3	4				
4	3	5	NNW½W	NE	
5	4	4	NNW	ENE	
6	5				
7	5	4			
8	7	4	NWBN	NE	
9	7	4			variation – 11:°30'E
10	7	3			
11	7	2			Fresh gales & fair weather
12	7				

Course	Dis:ᵉ	Latitude in	Long. made	M Dist:ᶜᶜ
NNW	128	6:*40 W	116:°04'W	5702W

Wallis Island bore S30:°50'E dist:ᶜᶜ 466 leagues

Remarks September 1:ˢᵗ 1767   (37)

H	K	F	Courses	Winds	Remarks
1	7		NWBN	NE	Fresh gales & cloudy
2	8				
3	7				
4	6			25:00	fair weather
5	6				variation p:ʳ azu:ᵗ & amp:ᵈᵉ 11:°18'E
6	6	2			
7	5	5			
8	5	5			
9	7				
10	6	3			
11	5	4			
12	5	4			
1	5				
2	4	4		24:10	
3	5				
4	4				
5	4		NW½N	NNE	
6	5	4	NW		variation p:ʳ az:ᵗ – 12:00ᴱ
7	5	4			
8	6	3			
9	6				
10	5	4	NWBN	NE	
11	5				Fine pleasant weather
12	5				

Course	Dis:ᶜ	Latitude in	Long. made	M Dist:ᶜᵉ
N35:°00W	138	8:*33N	117:°24'W	5781W

Wallis Island bore S31:°30'E distance 510 leagues

Remarks Wednesday September 2:nd 1767   (38)

H	K	F	Courses	Winds	Remarks
1	3	5	NWBN	NEBN	Moderate & fine clear weather
2	4	2	NWBW	NBE	
3	4	5	NW	NNE	
4	5		NW½N		variation p:^{r} azum:th – 10:00E
5	5	4	NWBN	NEBN	ampl:^{de} – 10:34E
6	5	3		25:00	
7	4				
8	5	2			
9	4	4			
10	5	4			
11	4	4			
12	5	5		NE	fine pleasant weather
1	6				
2	6			24:20	
3	6				
4	6				
5	6	2			variation p:^{r} am – 12:00E
6	6	4			az – 11:51E
7	6	2			
8	5	4			Read the Articles of War &:^{ce}
9	6				
10	5	5			
11	5	5			Fine pleasant weather
12	5			NE	

Course	Dis	Latitude in	Long. made	M Dist:^{ce}
NWBN½N	136	10:*32N	118:°28'W	5845W

Wallis Island bore S29:°30'E distance 556 leagues

Remarks Thursday Sep:ʳ 3:ᵈ 1767   (39)

H	K	F	Courses	Winds	
1	4	3	WNW	NE	fine pleasant weather
2	5				
3	5	4			
4	5			25:00	
5	5				
6	4	2			
7	4				at 5 AM saw land bearing ENE about 2 or 3 leagues distance
8	3	4			at half past five saw more land bearing NW. saw a boat in the
9	4	3			NE. She stood toward us sometime and then made sail from
10	4	4			us, as she was to windward & sailed fast we could not come
11	5				up with her. She was exactly the make of the Indian proa that
12	4	3			is described in Lord Ansons Voyage —⁴²⁷
1	3	2			at 7 PM the land bore from SWBW to West – & to windward
2	3			24:00	NE —⁴²⁸
3	2	5			
4	3	3			
5	3	4			
6	4				
7	5		NNW		
8	4				
9	4				variation p:ʳ amp:ᵈᵉ 11:40E —⁴²⁹
10	3	4			
11	3				Light breezes & pleasant weather
12	2	3			

Course	Dist:ᶜᵉ	Latitude in	Long. made	M Dist:ᶜᵉ
NWBW	98	11:*42N	119:35W –	5911W

Wallis Island bore S29:50E distance 590 leagues

427 In the account of Anson's voyage (*A voyage round the world, in the years MDCCXL, I, II, III, IV by Richard Walter, 1716-1785*, published in 1797), the *proa* is described in detail (with figures): "The construcion of this proa is a direct contradiction to the practice of all the rest: of mankind. For as the rest: of the world make the head of their vessels different from the stern, but the two sides alike; the proa, on the contrary, has her head and stern exactly alike, but her two sides very different; the side, intended to be always the lee-side, being flat; and the windward-side made rounding, in the manner of other vessels: And, to prevent her oversetting, which from her small breadth, and the straight run of her lee-ward side, would, without this precaution, infallibly happen, there is a frame laid out from her to windward, to the end of which is fastened a log, fashioned into the shape of a small boat, and made hollow: The weight of the frame is intended to ballance the proa, and the small boat is by its buoyancy (as it is always in the water) to prevent her oversetting to windward; and this frame is usually called an outrigger."

428 "At 5 AM saw land bearing ENE dis:ᶜᵉ about four or five miles – at half past five saw more land in the NW – at six saw an Indian Prow (such as described in my Lord Anson's voyage) – in the NE she stood towards us, we hoisted Spanish colours, when she came within two miles of us to windward she tack'd & stood from us away to the NNW, but she soons left us – at 8 the islands which I take to be the Piscadores bore from SWBW to West and to wind ward from NBE to NE, making small flatt keys full of cocoa nutt trees, they being about three leagues from us the nearest both to wind ward and to lee ward, but others were seen a great way off." PL and FC.

429 "Lat Piscadores   11:00   Long   192:30
                      11:20 North   192:58 W
     Long. Made from Cape Pillar   119:00 W
                                             119:35." PL and FC.

Remarks Friday Sep:ʳ 4:ᵗʰ 1767 (40)

H	K	F	Wind	Course	Remarks
1	2	3	NNW	NEBE	Light airs & pleasant weather
2	2	5			
3	2	5		24:40	
4	2	5			variation p:ʳ azumeth – 10:°40'E
5	3		NWBN	NEBN	amplitude –
6	4				found my legs much swollen[430]
7	3	2	NNW	NE	
8	3				
9	4				
10	4	2			
11	4	5			
12	5	2			
1	5				
2	4			24:10	cloudy with much lightning in the ESE –
3	3	4			
4	3	5			
5	4		NNW½W		
6	5		NW	NNE	
7	4	3	NWBW		
8	4	4			variation – 11:20E
9	5			NEBN	
10	4	5			
11	5	2			Moderate breezes
12	5	4		NE	

Course	Dist	Latitude in	Long. made	MDist:ᶜᵉ
N25:°00'W	96	13:*10N	120:°16W –	5951W

Wallis Island bore S29:°50'E distance 620 leagues

---

[430] "Severall of the people and among the rest I and the two Lieutenants find great weakness and swollen legs." PL and FC.

Remarks Saturday Sep:ʳ 5 1767 (41)

H	K	F	Courses	Winds	Remarks
1	4		WBN	ENE	Moderate & cloudy.
2	3	5			saw severall birds
3	4				
4	5	2		25:0	a great swell from the Eastward
5	4	5			
6	4	5			
7	4				
8	4				
9	5				
10	5				
11	4	4			
12	3	3		EBN	
1	3	4			
2	4			24:15	
3	4				
4	4				
5	4				
6	4	2	East		squally weather
7	4	2			variation – p:ʳ azum:ᵗʰ 12:30
8	5		EBS		opened a cask of pork N1134 contents 324 short 2 peices
9	3	4			
10	5		SE		
11	6	4	SBW		Fresh gales & squally
12	7				

Course	Dis:ᵗ	Latitude in	Long. made	MDist:ᶜᶜ
WNW¼N	106	13:*58N	121:°52W –	6046W

Wallis Island bore S35:°30'E dist:ᶜᶜ 653 leag:ˢ

Remarks Sunday Sep:ʳ 6:ᵗʰ 1767   (42)

H	K	F	Courses	Winds	Remarks
1	6	3	W½N	SSW	Fresh breezes & cloudy with a swell from the Westward.
2	6	4			
3	4		WBN	SWBS	
4	2				Light breezes & cloudy with some drizzling rain
5	2		West	SSW	
6	3			24:00	
7	3	3	WSW½W	South	
8	3				Light airs
9	2	3			
10	2	4		SE	
11	2	3			
12	2	4			
1	2	3			
2	2	5		23:42	
3	2	2			
4	2	3			
5	3	2			
6	4				
7	4	4			
8	4	5			variation – 12:19E
9	5				
10	4				
11	4				Moderate & cloudy –
12	4	3			

Course	Dis:ᵗ	Latitude in	Long. made	MDist:ᶜᵉ
WBN	85	14:*12N	123:14W –	6127W

Wallis Island bore S35:°00'E distance 675 leagues

Remarks Monday Sep:ʳ 7:ᵗʰ 1767   (43)

H	K	F	Courses	Winds	Remarks
1	2		WBS½E	East	
2	2				Light airs
3	2	4			
4	3				
5	4			24:40	
6	3	5			variation p:ʳ amp:ᵈᵉ – 11:°00'E
7	3	3			
8	3	4			
9	3	4			
10	3			SSE	
11	3	4			
12	1	4			Cloudy with rain
1	1			ESE	Squally –
2	4	4		23:30	
3	3				Lightning from the SW
4	2			NE	opened a cask of beef N:°1328, contents 160 peices –
5	2	3			variation p:ʳ amplitude 10:°20'E
6	3	4			
7	3	4			saw a Curlew & Pewit –
8	4				
9	4				
10	4				Fresh breezes & squally
11	4	4			
12	6	2		NE	

Course	Dis:ᵗ	Latitude in	Long. made	MDistance
W½S	80	14:*05N	124:04W –	6206W

Wallis Island bore S36:°50'E dist:ᶜᶜ 692 leagues

Remarks Tuesday Sep:r 8:th 1767   (44)

H	K	F	Winds	Course	Remarks
1	5	3	WBS½S	ENE	Moderate & fair
2	5	4			
3	5	4			
4	5	3		25:00	
5	4	4			
6	4	5		NE	
7	5	2			
8	5	4			
9	5	4			
10	5				
11	4	1			
12	3	5		ENE	Squally
1	6			24:20	Little wind
2	1	4			
3	3	2			
4	3				
5	4	4			
6	4				
7	4	4			
8	4				
9	4				
10	4				
11	4	3			Moderate & breezes & fair weather
12	4	4			

Course	Dis:t	Latitude in	Long. made	MDis:e
W½S	109	13:*56N	126:24W –	6315W

Wallis Island bore S39:°28'E dist:ce 706 leagues

Remarks Wednesday September 9 1767 (45)

1	4	2	WSW½W	EBN
2	4	2		
3	4			
4	4	2		25:00
5	5	4		
6	3	5		SEBE
7	1	3		
8	2	4		ENE
9	4			
10	4	2		
11	4	3		
12	4			
1	4			
2	5			23:45
3	5			SE
4	7			
5	4	4		ENE
6	4			
7	4	4		
8	5			
9	4			
10	4			
11	4			
12	4			

Moderate & fair

caught a land bird about the size of a Snipe, but it was speckled with white & brown[431]

Squally with some rain –

Little wind & fair

Course	Dis:¹	Latitude in	Long. made	MDis:ᵉ
W5:°0'S	101	13:°*50'N –	128:08W –	6346W

Wallis Island bore S42:°30'E distance 727 leagues

---

431 "Caught a land bird very like a stirling." PL.

Thursday September 10:ᵗʰ 1767   (46)

H	K	F	Courses	Winds	Remarks
1	4	3	West	ENE	Light breezes & fair
2	4				
3	4				variation – p:ʳ azum:ᵗʰ 8:30
4	4			25:20	
5	5			NE	
6	5				
7	4	3			
8	4	5			
9	4	5			
10	5				
11	4	5			
12	3	4			
1	4			24:40	
2	4	3			
3	4	4			
4	5				
5	4	4			
6	5				
7	4	4			variation p:ʳ amp:ᵈᵉ 9:08
8	3	3			
9	3				
10	2	4			
11	1	5			Light airs & fair
12	1	5			

Course	Dis:ᵗ	Latitude in	Long. made	MDis:ᵉ
W9:°0'S	98	14:*05N	129:49W –	6514W

Wallis Island bore S49:°30'E distance 753 leagues

Remarks Friday Sept.ʳ 11 1767   (47)

1	1	3	West	NE	
2	1	4			
3	1	3			
4	1	4		25:20	
5	2				
6	2				
7	1	4			
8	2			NNE	
9	2	4			
10	2	4			
11	2	4			
12	3	5		North	
1	3				
2	3				
3	3			24:40	
4	3				
5	2	3			
6	2	3			
7	3	2			
8	3				
9	2	3			
10	2	3			
11	2	4			
12	3	4			

Light airs & pleasant wea:ʳ
Employed in overhauling the hold –
found two casks of beef with their heads burst –[432]

variation   amp – 9:20E
            az – 8:47E

Light airs & fair

Course	Dis:ᵗ	Latitude in	Long. made	MDis:ᵉ
W¾N	58	14:12 –	130:50W	6572W

Wallis Island bore S44:°15'E dist:ᶜᶜ 768 leagues

---

432 "Overhauled the hold and cleaned it of all the filth and dirt made new pickle for them and repaired the cask meat tolerable good." PL and FC.

Remarks Saturday Sept:r 12 1767   (48)

H	K	F	Courses	Winds	Remarks
1	2	2	WBN	East	Light airs & pleasant weather
2	2	2			
3	2	2			
4	2	3		25:05	
5	2	2			
6	2	2			
7	3	2			
8	2			SE	
9	2	3			
10	2				
11	1	3			
12	5			South	Squally with rain
1	5	3			
2	2	4		23:40	
3	3				
4	2		NWBW	SWBW	Light airs & clear weather
5				Calm	
6	1		SW	Variable	variation 9:22
7	1	4	WBS		
8	1	3	WBN		
9	2			NE	
10	2	3			
11	3				Light breezes & fair
12	4				

Course	Dis	Latitude in	Long. made	MDistance
WNW	63	14:*36N	130:51W	6630W

Wallis Island bore S45p:00E dist:ce 788 leagues

Remarks Sunday Sept:ʳ 13 1767   (49)

1	3	2	WBN	East
2	3	4		
3	4			
4	5	2		25:00
5	5			
6	4	4		SE
7	5			
8	4	2		
9	4			
10	4			
11	4	2		
12	4			
1	4			SBE
2	3			
3	2			24:55
4	4	3		
5	4	4		
6	4	3		SE
7	4	4		
8	2			EBS
9	2			
10	3			
11	3			
12	3	5		

Light breezes & fair –

variation p:ʳ medium of four   azumeths   7:42
                                   amplitude – 8:00

Little wind & pleasant weather

Course	Dis:ᵉ	Latitude in	Long. made	MDistance
WNW	80	15:07	133:°08'W	6707W

Wallis Island bore S45:°40'E distance 810 leag:ˢ

Remarks Monday September 14 1767   (50)

H	K	F	Winds	Courses	Remarks
1	4		WBS	EBN	Moderate breezes & fair.
2	5				
3	5				
4	4				
5	4	4			
6	4	3		25:30	
7	6	2			
8	3	7		SEBS	fresh breezes & squally
9	3	4			
10	3	4		EBN	
11	3	4			
12	3	4			light breezes & cloudy with lightning in the NNW
1	4	3			
2	4			25:0	
3	4				
4	4	4		East	
5	3	4			variation p:r azum:th 7:35E
6	2	2			open'd a cask of beef No: 1237 Cont: 176 pieces short two –
7	2	3			squally with rain
8	2	2		South	
9	3				
10	4	4			
11	4				Light airs & looks squally all round –
12	3				

Course	Dis	Latitude in	Long. made	MDis:ce
West	95	15:08N	134:46W	6802W

Wallis Island bore S47:11E dist:c 836 leagues

Remarks Tuesday Sept:r 15 1767   (51)

H	K	F	Courses	Winds	Remarks
1	1		West	SWBS	Light airs & cloudy sultry wea:r
2	1	4	WBS	NE	
3	2				
4	2	3		25:30	
5	2				
6	2				
7	3				
8	3	4		ENE	Observed by Lyra lat:d in 15:°05'N
9	3				
10	6			East	squally with much thunder
11	2			NE	Lightning all round the compass
12	3				
1	2				
2	2			24:00	
3	1	5			
4	2			NNE	
5	3				
6	3	3		NEBE	variation p:r amplitude 7:48
7	4				
8	4	4		EBN	reeved new main braces —[433]
9	3	4			
10	3	3			
11	3	3			moderate breezes with a Southern swell
12	3	2			

Course	Dis	Latitude in	Long. made	MDis:ce
W2:00S	68	15:*08N	135:56W	6869W

Wallis Island bore S48:00E dist:e 853 leagues

---

[433] "Reeved new main braces tacklefalls and other rigging – the old to round the cables." PL and FC.

Remarks Wednesday Sept:r 16 1767   (52)

1	5	4	WBS	NBE	Squally weather
2	4			
3	3				moderate & cloudy
4	3			
5	3	4		25:0
6	2	4		
7	6				squally with heavy rain
8				
9				Calm
10	2	3	WBS	ESE	cloudy
11	3			
12	3	2		
1	3	5		
2	3	2		24:40	squally with rain
3	3				Moderate & cloudy
4	2			ENE
5	3			
6	2	2			variation p:r azumeth 8:52 East
7	2	3		
8	2	2		
9	3			
10	3	5		
11	2	5			Light airs & fair
12	3			

Course	Dis:e	Latitude in	Long. made	MDistance
W2:00S	70	15:*00N	137:°08'W	6939W

Wallis Island bore S49:21E distance 870 leagues

Remarks Thursday Sept:ʳ 17 1767   (53)

H	K	F	Courses	Winds	Remarks
1	3	4	West	EBN	Moderate & hazey –
2	3	4			
3	4				
4	3				25:0
5	3				
6	3	2			
7	3	2			
8	3	5		NBE	
9	6				Squally with rain
10	4	5		East	
11	4	5			
12	3	4			
1	3				Light airs –
2	3				24:10
3	2				
4	2				saw two Gannets –
5	1	2			
6	1	2			
7	1	5			
8	2	3			
9	2				
10	2				Light airs – Tinian West 31 leagues
11	1	2			
12	1	2			

Course	Dis:ᶜ	Latitude in	Long. made	MDistance
West	64	15:*00N	138:18W	7007W

Wallis Island bore S50:30E distance 890 lea:ˢ

Remarks Friday Sept.ʳ 18 1767 (54)

1	1		W½S	ENE	Light airs and pleasant weather but sultry –
2	1				
3	1	3		NE	
4	1	5			
5	2			25:40	variation p:ʳ azumeth – 7:40E
6	2	2			amplitude – 6:41E
7	2	5			
8	3				
9	3	2			Light breezes & cloudy
10	4	2			
11	4	4			Rounded the small bower 18 fm: from the anchor – & bent the
12	5				best bower cable & did the same to it –
1	5				
2	4	4			
3	4	3		25:0	At six saw the island of Saypan bearing WBN 9 or 10 leagues
4	4				
5	4				
6	4				variation p:ʳ azumeth – 6:10E
7	3	3			
8	3				
9	3		WBN		at noon the extreams of Saypen bore from N35:°20'N to
10	2				N78:00W
11	2		West		Distance of shore three leagues
12	3		WSW	East	

Course	Dis:ᵉ	Latitude in	Long. made	MDistance
West –	77–	15:*00N	139:38W	7084W

Tinian bore from S66:50W to West dis:ᵉ of S:°end five leagues
The middle of the Agugan S59:00W dis:ᵉ 6 leagues

Remarks Saturday Sept:ʳ 19 1767   (59)

					Light airs with squalls & rain
1	2		SWBW	East	at eight the South end of Tinian SWBW –
2	1	2			
3	1		SWBW		
4	1				
5	1			24:50	most part of the night calm with lightning and rain & very close & sultry –
6					
7				Calm	
8					at 5 AM the South part of Tinian bore WBS, distance 3 leagues –
9	1	3			
10	1	3			
11					
12					
1				Calm	at 5 AM made sail – cloudy with flying showers
2				24:30	at half past 9 anchord in Tinian Road in 23 fm: sandy ground with coral rocks – veerd to a whole cable – the N:°side of the bay bearing N39:00W Cocoa point NW
3					
4					
5	1	4	EBS	NEBN	Landing place NEBN & the S:°end of the island S38:00E off shore a mile & three quarters of a mile from the reef –
6	3	4	WSW	ENE	
7					The extreams of the Aguigan S24:0W to S29:00W distance six miles –⁴³⁴
8					
9					
10					
11					
12					

Course	Dis:ᵉ	Latitude in	Long. made	MDistance
		15:00N	139:40W	7086W

---

434 ". . . sent the boats onshoar to erect tents and bring off some refreshments immediately at noon they returned with some cocoa nutts, limes and oranges." PL and FC. There is a small, rough sketch of the bay on this page of the PL.

Week day	Mo Day	Wind	Remarks at Tinian onboard the his Maj.ˢ Ship Dolphin
September Sunday	1767 20	24:35 ESE 24:00	Moderate & cloudy employed in getting the tents onshoar for the sick, wooders, waterers & hunters with the forge and provisions & sundry stores in the evening I & the first Lieu:ᵗ with the sick landed, and in the morning more people with the empty cask were sent on shore – On board the Master with two boats sounding for a good anchoring place, the surgeon came onshoar to attend the sick – the Master reported that the ground to the S:°ward of where the ship lay was fine white sand, but to the N:°ward rocky – Sent a party out to hunt[435] (1)
Monday	21	24:00 NE to 24:50 SE	Squally rainy weather latter fair at 6 PM the hunters returned with a bull about 400lb served it to the ships company at 6 AM weigh'd the small bower & warped the ship to the SE into fine sandy ground by the soundings anchor'd in moor'd the bewt bower in 22 fm: and small in 32 fine white sand, sounded all round & dragged the lead all clear ground. Carpenter employed in caulking sailmakers in repairing sails – coopers in trimming cask and boats carrying empty bringing of full cask – sick & well from the ship onshoar fifty three men.[436] (2)

[435] "Moderate & cloudy weather, the tents being erected sent the sent the Surgeon and all the sick and ailing people onshoar a quantity of all sorts for at least two months for forty men the forge and a chest of carpenters tools then I went onshoar with the First Lieu:ᵗ we being both much out of order. Took likewais a Mate and twelve men to go out and hunt for cattle. The Master sounded all round the bay and though there was better lying to the Southward of where the ship is, warped the ship a little way up and moored with a cable each way, the best bower to the SE in 22 fathoms sandy the small bower in 32 sandy clear ground having dragged the lead and sounded the ground every way round where the anchors are placed." PL and FC.

[436] "At six PM the hunters brought in a fine young bull near four hundred weight kept part of it and sent the rest onboard with breadfruit limes and oranges. Set the carpenters at work to caulk the ship all over and repair every thing as well as possible got all the sails onshoar and set the sailmakers and others at work and others to repair them, the armourers to repair all the iron work and make new rudder chains & many other jobs. Have onshoar from the ship sick and well fifty three men." PL and FC.

Week day	Mo Day	Wind	Remarks onboard the his Maj:^{s} Ship Dolphin at Tinian
September Tuesday	1767 22	25:10 NE to SE 25:0	Moderate & cloudy with rain – at ½ past noon moord the ship the best bower to the SE – Employed in clearing the ship carpenters sailmaking armourer &:^{cc} employed as yesterday. Served fresh beef to the ships company^{437} (3)
Wednesday	23	24:20 SE 24:30	Fine pleasant weather people onboard employed in drying sails & clearing the hold, onshoar in cutting wood & filling water, hunting & getting refreshments for themselves & those onboard. – no beef this day sent of some water & & hog – with severall cocks, hens & limes – breadfruit & oranges & papaw apples:^{438} (4)
Thursday	24	25:00 East to South 24:10	Light airs & cloudy with flying showers, employed in overhauling the rigging, & stowing the hold the people on shore as before, served fresh beef – ^{439} (5)
Friday	25	25:30 East to SSE 24:30	Ditto weather struck the topmast overhauled the rigging & fixed new cross trees & got it up again served fresh beef^{440} (6)
Saturday	26	25:0 SE 24:05	Fresh breezes & cloudy employed in drying sails clearing the ship, and carpenters in caulking & refitting it served 4 lb of beef a man – as it will not keep two days – severall cocks & hens sent from the shoar Punished Will:^{m} Oman on shoar for stealing six pound of sugar from the store tent. –^{441} (7)

437 "Moderate and cloudy employed in clearing the ship and sending empty casks and stores onshoar, served fresh beef to the ships company, the Surgeon desired that the people might be allowed boiled wheat for breakfast every morning to be boiled with paw paw apples, breadfruit and mountain cabbage as the best antyscorbutic that can be made use of by them. Sailmakers armourers & carpenters at work as before." PL and FC.

438 ". . . had no luck this day with hunting, except the hogg, which with breadfruit, limes and oranges & paw paw apples sent onboard killed many cock and hens which made into soup for those onshoar, don't suffer any one to catch fish either onboard or onshoar, the sick keep in the cool shade all the day but in the evenings the Surgeon takes them out to walk two or three miles and they all seem in a mending way." PL and FC.

439 ". . . the people that go a hunting return terribly jaded picked out a fresh party, so that they go out only every other day. Employed overhauling and setting the rigging to rights struck the topmasts fixed new cross trees & got up the topmasts again." PL and FC.

440 "Fresh breezes, began to send of wood and water, all the people employed in different ways, work only in the mornings and evenings, served fresh beef – the weather so warm the meat will scarce keep good twenty hours the beef excellent and as much as the people can eat, but very difficult to come at. Cocoa nutts scarce any within three miles, the trees near the watering place all being cut down and none growing up in their stead breadfruit scarce likewais so are oranges but limes in great plenty and paw paw apples and cabbage trees in plenty about three miles of, for gathering of which allway employ a party of eight men –". PL and FC

441 The PL and FC specify that Oman was "centinel" there at the time and Gore indicates that he received twelve lashes.

Week day	Mo Day	Wind	Remarks onboard the his Maj:s Ship Dolphin at Tinian
September Sunday	1767 27	25:0 ESE 25:40	Fresh breezes & cloudy – received 80 lb of pork – kill'd no beef this day – [442] (8)
Monday	28	25:00 ESE to ENE 24:40	Fresh gales & squally with much thunder & light & rain. exchanged many of the people that were onshoar, & sent others in their stead. no luck this in hunting [443] – people both onboard & onshoar employed as before – (9)
Tuesday	29	24:10 ESE 24:50	Ditto weather with much rain employed as before. – kill'd a wild boar – but got no beef [444] (10)
Wednesday	30	25:30 East ESE SE 25:30	Moderate & cloudy, employed as before, clear hawser. Received wood & water, served fresh beef [445] (11)
October Thursday	1767 1	NE 25:45 SE 24:30	Moderate & clear, employed as before, no beef. Some fowles, wood & water (12)
Friday	2	NE 25:50 East SE	Moderate & cloudy looked at both anchors found all very well – moor'd again received fresh beef [446] wood & water – people employed as before – (13)
Saturday	3	25:40 ENE 24:50	Fresh gales & cloudy received wood & water sent a party of 14 men to the N:°end of the island to hunt as we have great difficulty in getting any cattle here – under the direction of M:r Gore Mate of this ship who was here before – [447] (14)

442 ". . . hunters very much fateagued, many give up – as they go ten or a dozen miles thro' a constant thickett and if they have luck have a heavy load back." PL and FC.

443 ". . . the cattle so wild they cannot come near them." PL and FC.

444 ". . . the hunters brought in a wild boar, killed no beef, they report that cattle are plenty at the other end of the island but they are so much fateagued that when they get there, they are quite spent." PL and FC.

445 "Got the ship by the stern to come at some copper that was much torn, in repairing of which, the carpenter found a large leak under the lining of the knee of the head which they set about and repaired and he hopes that much of the water the ship hath made latterly in bad weather was occasioned by this leak." PL and FC.

446 ". . . the hunters so much jaded ordered M:r Gore one of the mates with fourteen men to go to the other end of the island and kill cattle, where I would send a boat every morning at daylight for what they should kill." PL and FC.

447 John Gore having sailed with Byron: ". . . sent the party to hunt at the the other end of the island and fix themselves, at the same time sent a party to hunt near hand for this day as we cannot expect anything from the new party till they have fixed themselves – the hunters brought in a fine bull." PL and FC.

Week day	Mo Day	Wind	Remarks at Tinian –
October Sunday	1767 4	25:30 ENE East 25:0	Fresh breezes & clear sent the cutter to the N:°end of the island who returned with fresh beef. Received wood & water and recovered men likewais excepting those who had been a week on shoar, & sent others in lieu. Served to the ships company beef 360lb[448] (15)
Monday	5	25:35 NE East SE 25:0	Moderate & fair compleating the ship with wood & water, carpenters, sailmakers & armourers emp:^{d} as before. – served fresh beef – received beef 570 (16)
Tuesday	6	26:10 ENE East 25:00	Moderate & cloudy weather. Employed as before, served fresh beef. received wood & water. received beef 410lb[449] (17)
Wednesday	7	26:20 East to ESE 26:00	Moderate & cloudy, the Master finished the survey of the Bay of Tinian – employed as before – served fresh beef – limes breadfruit & oranges – beef 430lb. (18)
Thursday	8	25:00 East ESE SE 24:0	Light airs & cloudy finished over hauling the riggin, and parsled the rigging with bullocks hides[450] – served fresh beef &:^{ce} – 100lb fresh beef[451] (19)
Friday	9	ENE 24:40 East SE	Fresh breezes with much lightning & rain received 322 fresh beef & some bread fruit[452] (20)
Saturday	10	North 25:30 NE 24:00 East	Fresh gales with thunder lightning & rain, received water wood bread fruit & 396lb of fresh beef – Lieu:^{t} Clerke went onboard & Lieu:^{t} Furneaux onshoar[453] (21)

448 "Fine breezes, sent the cutter to the North end of the Island (this boats crew being kept for no other use) she returned with fresh beef. Exchanged the men onshoar, they having been each party one week onshoar, and this party compleats every mans turn, every one now having been onshoar, exclusive of the sick, the scorbuticks the doctor has kept constantly onshoar. Served fresh beef." PL and FC.

449 "The Master employed with the boats in taking a survey of this road and sounding every where." PL and FC.

450 The PL and the FC specify on the 7th that this was because they had expended all their canvas and hamocks.

451 "The Master finished sounding this bay, employed in getting of wood & water, coopers setting up more water cask – others in getting breadfruit and other vegitables, carpenters & sailmakers still busy on the ship and the sails." PL and FC.

452 "Fresh gales with much thunder or lightning and rain and a great sea alongside – served fresh beef – carpenters near finished caulking and repairing the ship sailmakers the sails and armourers the iron work – The ship almost completed with wood and water, all things kept in constant readiness for putting to sea at a moments warning." PLand FC.

453 "... sent of all the recovered men, and kept only the wooders, waterers and ailing people on shore." PL and FC.

Week day	Month Day	Wind	Remarks –
October Sunday	1767 11	25:00 NE East ESE 24:30	Fresh gales with lightning thunder & rain, this day the Master finished sounding Tinian Bay rec:^{d} 226lb of fresh beef. (22)
Monday	12	26:00 NE East 25:00	Fresh gales with rain, employed as before in caulking sailmakers repairing sails, & armourers repairing the iron work – this day exchanged the people onshoar for a like number from the ship which completed the whole crew being onshoar a week man – received 326 pounds of fresh beef –[454] (23)
Tuesday	13	26:10 East 24:50	Fresh gales, at 3 PM found the small bower parted hove in the cable, found it cut above twenty two fm: from the anchor by a sharp rock – the anchor being in 32 fm: & being sunk, twas impossible to get it again. hove up & down with the best bower, found all well – bent a new cable to the spare anchor & got it over the side. the ground where we lost the anchor & where the best bower lies had been sounded above 1000 times, besides crossing & dragging the lead & we found it all clear[455] – served beef to the ships company (24)
Wednesday	14	ESE NE ESE	Fresh breezes & squally, dryed sails, stranded the messenger in endeavouring to weigh the best bower veerd away, shifted the spare anchor to the larboard bow[456] – served fresh beef – (25)

454 "... employed in getting the ship compleat with water and wood, the cooper having set up severall tons of cask which we have seasoned and now sent on board, have between seventy and eighty tons of water and at the same time the betwixt decks pretty clear, the people every day bringing of a few cocoa nutts. Have daily plenty of cabbage, pawpaw apples and breadfruit for breakfast and dinner." PL and FC.

455 "Reev'd a new messenger the old one being broke and quite worn out." PL and FC.

456 "... people employed in gathering limes, oranges, cocoanuts & vegetables, oboard in getting the spare anchor for a small bower, compleating the ship for sea. Bent a new fore topsail." PL and FC.

Week Day	M:ʰ Day	Wind	Remarks –
October Thursday	1767 15	25:20 East 24:50	Fresh gales with rain, employed in getting of all the wood & water. Provisions &:ᶜ & getting ready for sea –[457] (26)
Friday	16[458]	24:56 East ESE at 4	(27) Fresh breezes & squally with rain, at 4 PM I came onboard with all the people tents &:ᶜ – the ship being compleat with every thing that could be got here. at 6 AM weigh'd and stood to the North end of the Island, sent the boats onshaor and brought of M:ʳ Gore & his party, with a bullock – they lost a grapline, & rope – at noon Tinian bore from 36:00 East to N74:00E distance from shoar 3 leagues – Aguigan – S16:°00'E – Saypan – N56:00 served fresh beef. [459]Whilst we lay here ᵀⁱⁿⁱᵃⁿ ᴿᵒᵃᵈ observed the latitude and longitude by severall observations of the distance between the sun and moon, and found it in –

Latitude of the ship at Noon p:ʳ observation	Latitude Tinian Road where ship lay	14:*8 North
	Latitude of watering place –	14:*9 North
Friday Sep:ʳ 18:ᵗʰ 1767 off Tinian	Long: of the body of Tinian from London –	214:°00': 00" West
Monday 25 Sep:ʳ 1767 at anchor	in Tinian Road, long:ᵈ of ship was then in –	214:08:1 W
Wednesday Sep:ʳ 30:ᵗʰ 1767 at anch:ʳ	long. Ship –	214:15:0 W
Saturday Oct:ʳ 17:ᵗʰ 1767, at sea	long by observation	216:25:0 W
		2:17:0 W
Sat. Oct:ʳ 17 1767 at sea in in latitude 16:*00N & 2:°25' West from Tinian Road – lon.ⁿ		2:10:0 W
Table 214:08 from 216:25 – or from 214:°15		long. 2:17:0 W

---

457 "Fresh breezes & squally weather, all the boats employed in getting every thing from the shore and people in gathering refreshments as limes and other vegetables. At noon having got provisions forge, tents and all things onboard, embarked with all the people, they having I believe five hundred limes a man at least and several half tubs full on the quarter deck to squeeze into their water when they please. Served fresh beef." PL and FC.

458 John Gore's log ends here and is signed Jn: Gore Master Hunter.

459 The calculations in the PL and the FC differ slightly but the final result for the longitude by observation is the same in all three logs: 216:°25:'0"W.

Remarks Onboard his Majesties ship at Tinian between the 20:th of September 1767 and the 16:th Day of October 1767 –
BLANK PAGE

Remarks Saturday Oct:r 17 1767   (1)

H	K	F	Courses	Winds	Remarks
1				East	Moderate & pleasant wea:r
2				EBN	at 4 o'clock, the extreams of Saypan from ENE to East of
3	5	4	WNW		Tinian from S74:E to S55:E distance 6 or 7 leagues –
4	5			25:0	from Anigan – S34:E distance nine leagues
5	6				squally
6	6				
7	6				with
8	8				
9	7				much
10	6				
11	6				rain
12	7			East	
1	7				Tinian latitude 15:*00 North
2	6			25:00	
3	6				
4	6				served fresh beef to ships company
5	7				bent new topsails
6	7				had onboard 76 tons of water
7	6				
8	7				
9	6				
10	6				fresh gales & hazey weather
11	7				
12	6			ENE	

Course	Dis	Lat in	Long. made	M Dis.
N6:0W	154	16:°*10'N	2:18W	133W

Tinian bore S62:00E distance 52 leagues –

Remarks Sunday Oct:ʳ 18 1767 (2)

H	K	F	Courses	Winds	Remarks
1	6	4	WNW	ENE	Moderate gales & cloudy with some squalls –
2	6				
3	7	3			
4	7			25:00	
5	7	3			
6	6	4			
7	6				
8	7				Fresh gales & squally rainy weather
9	7				
10	9				
11	6	5			
12	7			NE	
1	7				
2	7	2		24:45	
3	7				
4	7			East	
5	7				
6	7				
7	7	4			variation p:ʳ azumeth 5:°15'E
8	9				
9	8			ENE	
10	7	3			
11	6	5			Fresh gales & squally
12	6	4		East	

Course	Dis:ᶜᶜ	Latitude in	Long. made	M Dist.ᶜᶜ
NWBW¾W	171	17:*37 Nor:ᵗʰ	4:51W	279W

Tinian bore S60:°30'E distance 106 leagues

Remarks Monday October 19 1767   (3)

1	6		WNW	ENE
2	6	2	W½N	
3	6	4		
4	7			25:00
5	8			
6	8			
7	7	4		
8	7	3		
9	7	5		
10	7	4		
11	7			
12	7	2		
1	6	5		
2	6	2		25:10
3	6	1		
4	6	5		
5	7			
6	7	3		
7	7	5		
8	7			
9	8			
10	7	5		
11	6			
12	7			

Fresh gales & squally weather

Squally showery weather –

Fresh gales & squally with rain

Course	Dis:^{ce}	Latitude in	Long. made	M Dist.^{ce}
WBN	171	18:14N	7:49W	446W

Tinian bore S67:12E distance 161 leagues

Remarks Tuesday October 20 1767   (4)

H	K	F	Courses	Winds	Remarks
1	6	5	W½N	ENE	Fresh gales & squally with rain
2	6	2			
3	7	2			
4	7	2		25:20	Fresh gales & cloudy –
5	7				variation p:ʳ azumeth – 3:°28'E
6	7				
7	6	5			
8	7	2			
9	7	4			fresh gales & cloudy –
10	7				
11	6				
12	6				
1	6	4			
2	6	3			
3	6	5		24:00	
4	7				
5	7	3			
6	7	2			
7	7	3			unbent the small bower cable & took of the rounding from the end of it, carpenters employed in repairing the boats which are much shattered –
8	7				
9	8				
10	9	5			fresh gales & hazey –
11	8				
12	8	2			

Course	Dis:ᶜᵉ	Latitude in	Long. made	M Distance
W76:°00'N	170	18:*14N	10:45W	612W

Tinian bore S70:00E distance 218 leagues

Remarks Wednesday October 21 1767 (5)

H	K	F	Course	Winds	Remarks
1	7	4	W½N	ENE	a fine brisk gale clear over head & hazey in the horizon –
2	7	3			
3	7	4			
4	7	3		24:10	
5	7				variation by medium of ⎤ 2:°10' East
6	7				three azumeths ⎦
7	7	2			
8	7	5			squally with rain –
9	8				
10	7				
11	7				
12	7			EBN	fresh gales & cloudy –
1	6	5			
2	7				
3	6	4		25:0	
4	7				
5	6	4			
6	7	5			
7	7	5			
8	7				
9	7				a brisk gale with a following sea – some squalls with rain
10	7				a few Tropic birds & Sheerwaters about the ship –
11	7	2			
12	8				

Course	Dis	Latitude in	Long. made	M Distance
W¾N	177	19:*20N	13:51W	788W

Tinian bore S71:°40'E distance 277 leagues

Remarks Thursday October 22 1767   (6)

H	K	F	Course	Wind	Remarks
1	7	5	W½N	East	Fresh gales & hazey with a large following sea –
2	7				
3	8				
4	7	5		25:40	
5	7				
6	7				
7	7				squally with rain
8	6				
9	5	4		ESE	squally with thunder lightning and rain –
10	6	2		ENE	
11	5				
12	5			variable	
1	6			East	fresh gales & squally with much thunder lightning & rain –
2	6	4		25:00	
3	7			ESE	
4	6	5			got down the top gall:¹ yards –
5	6	5			
6	7				saw three birds whose bodys white & feet bill & tips of wings black the same sort we saw thirty leagues before we saw Tinian –
7	7				
8	7	5			
9	7				
10	6	2			fresh gales & squally weather –
11	6	5			
12	5			SEBE	

Course	Dis	Latitude in	Long. made	M Distance
W12:00N	164	19:*54N	16:38W	946W

Tinian bore S72:°40'E distance 333 leagues

Remarks Friday October 23 1767   (7)

H	K	F	Wind	Course	Remarks
1	6	3	W½N	SEBE	Fresh gales & squally with thunder lightning & rain
2	4	5			
3	5				
4	8			24:40	
5	6				squally with very heavy rain & a great sea which makes the
6	5				ship labour much –[460]
7	5	4			
8	5	5			moderate & cloudy
9	5	5			
10	6				
11	6	2			
12	6				
1	7				
2	6			South	
3	6			24:0	
4	7				very hard squall & heavy rain –
5	7	3		SSE	
6	7	5			
7	7				moderate gales & cloudy –
8	7	5			
9	8	2			
10	8				
11	8	5			Fresh gales & hazey –
12	9	2		South	

Course	Dis:ce	Latitude in	Long. made	M Distance
W12:19N	162	20:*30N	19:28 West	1104 West

Tinian bore S73:°15'E distance 387 leagues

---

460 "... the ship labours much, the rudder very loose which shakes the stern very much –." PL and FC.

Remarks Saturday October 24 1767   (8)

H	K	F	Courses	Winds	Remarks
1	7	5	W½S	SEBE	Fresh gales and hazey with a great swell from the South ward unbent the main topsail & bent a new one
2	8				
3	7				
4	8			24:40	
5	7	5			
6	7				
7	6	2			
8	6	3			
9	7				
10	7				
11	7				
12	6				
1	6	3		South	
2	7			24:0	Fresh gales & hazey
3	7	4			variation p:r azm:th 0:°47' West –
4	7	2			in a heavy swell split the jibb & main topsail & staysails
5	6	4		SSE	repair'd them
6	7				cut of 20 fm: of the best bower cable where 'twas much rubbed –
7	7				
8	7				saw some small land birds –
9	5				moderate & hazey with a very great swell from the South ward –
10	5				
11	5				
12	6			South	

Course	Dis:ce	Latitude in	Long. made	M Distance
WBN	161	21:*02N	22:18West	1262W

Tinian bore S74:°15'E distance 441 leagues

Remarks Sunday October 25 1767   (9)

H	K	F	Courses	Winds	Remarks
1	5		W½N	South	Moderate and hazey with a very great swell –
2	3	5			
3	3	5			
4	5	2		25:30	
5	4				
6	3				
7	1	4			
8					
9			up	SSE	off SW
10					
11					
12			up NW	off West	Strong gales & heavy rain close reeft topsails & handed the Brought too under the mizen –
1					
2			NWBW	off NWBN	
3				22:20	
4					At six wore & made sail at this time split the fore sail to pieces &
5					blew away & Miz:^{n}
6					unbent them & bent new ones
7	4		WBN		made sail under fore sail & main
8	1		EBS	NEBN	Ballanced the Mizen
9	2	2			
10	3				Very hard gales with a great sea & much rain got spritsail
11	3	2			top:^{ls} in & top gall: masts down on the deck –[461]
12	3				

Course	Dis:^{ce}	Latitude in	Long. made	M Distance
WBS¼S	36	20:54N	22:54W	1296W

Tinian bore S   E distance   leagues

[461] "... it still blowing very hard and a heavy sea, got the top gallant masts down on deck & jib boom in, as the ship labours much and makes more water than usuall." PLand FC.

Remarks Monday October 26 1767   (10)

H	K	F	Courses	Winds	
1	3	5	ESE	NE	Strong gales with constant rain and a very heavy sea from the NE –
2	3	3			
3	3	5			
4	3	4		22:00	a sea washed away the round houses forward and blew up the rails of the head & washed severall things off the fore castle –[462]
5	3		EBS	NEBE	
6	3				
7	3	4			
8	3	2			a very heavy gale of wind with continual rain & severe squalls
9	3	4			
10	3				obliged to carry sail as we are on a sea shore & by Lord Ansons account very near[463], but by M:r Byrons, better than thirty leagues off –
11	2	5			
12	2	5			
1	3		EBS½S		
2	3			22:20	
3	3	3	ESE	NE	a very heavy sea which frequently breaks over us, many small land birds about us & some Shaggs & Ducks sounded no ground with 160 fm:
4	3	4			
5	3				
6	2	4			
7	2				many horse flys about the ship –
8	2				
9	2		NWBN	NEBN	strong gales with a very great sea which frequently breaks over the ship – very heavy rain –
10	3		NW½N		
11	3				
12	3				

Course	Dis	Latitude in	Long. made	M Distance
SEBS	53	20:10N	22:23W	1267W

Tinian bore S EBS E distance   leagues

---

462 Wallis again notes that the ship labours greatly and makes much water (PL and FC) and "not a man dry for these two days past."
463 The Bashee Islands (PL and FC).

Remarks Tuesday October 27 1767   (11)

1	3	4	NWBN	NEBN
2	3	3		
3	3	4		
4	3	3		
5	4	5	NNW½W	NE
6	1	4	ESE	23:0
7	2		ESE½E	
8	2		ESE	
9	2	2		
10	3			
11	3		ESE½S	
12	2	5		
1	2	4	ESE	
2	2	3		22:15
3	2			
4	2	4		
5	1	5		
6	1	4		
7	1	5	NNW	
8	2			
9	4		NWBN	NEBN
10	4			
11	3	5		
12	3	5		

Very strong gales & a heavy sea with much rain –

a great sea broke on the ship and stove in all the half ports on the starboard side, broke severall iron stanchions & did much more damage & washed many things over board –

saw a shag – a small bird and flocks of Boobies

had observation of sun as follows –

H:M:S $\odot:^s$ altitude corrected –
9:41:30 – 36:°01' $\odot$ dec:^{n} 13:03
9:58:58 – 39:°19'
11:13:30 – 50:°58' lat:^{de} in 20:00
11:15:40 – 51:°13'
On working them several times we found the ship to be at ¾ after 10 PM to be near latt:^{de} of :   20:50N
Supposed lat:^{de} at noon   20:10[464]
Ship to be Nor:° of reckoning   :40 N

Strong gales with rainy hazey weather –

Course	Distan	Latitude in	Long. made	M Distance
West	8	20:18N	22:32 W	1275 W

Tinian bore   distance   leagues

---

464 20° 00 in the PL and the FC.

Wednesday October 28 1767   (12)

H	K	F	Courses	Winds	Remarks
1	4		NNW	NE	Strong gales & squally with rain
2	4	3			
3	4				
4	3	2		23:0	
5	3				
6	2	5			
7	2	2	SE½E	NEBE	
8	2	2			Observed lat:^{d} by …
9	2	2	SEBE		lat:^{de} – 21:05 North
10	2				
11	1	4			moderate with some squalls –
12	1	2	SE	ENE	
1	1	3			
2	1	4		23:00	
3	1	3	NBE	EBN	
4	1	2			Observed by Syrius 21:03N
5	2				set the topsails & made sail
6	3		NW		
7	6			ENE	
8	5	4			find the ship 30[465] miles Northward of her reckoning at noon
9	5	2	West		
10	6	2			moderate gales altered the course
11	6	5			Long.made to Bashee isles – 23:30 West
12	6	2			

Course	Dis:^{ce}	Latitude in	Long. made	M Distance
WNW¼W	61	21:30S	23:20W	1350W

Tinian bore   distance   leagues

---

465 40 miles in the PL and FC.

Remarks Thursday Oct:r 29 1767   (13)

1	4		SBW	ENE	
	2	4			
2	2	3	South	ESE	
	2				
3	2		WSW	NE	
4	5				
5	4	4		23:00	
6	5	2			
7	1				
8	3	2		NEBE	
9	4				
10	4	4			
11	6			NBE	
12	6	8			
1	6	3			
2	7				
3	7	5		NE	
4	7				
5	7	2			
6	7	5		22:25	
7	8	3			
8	8	4			
9	8	2			
10	8	3			
11	8				
12	8				

at ½ past 1 saw the Bashee Isles bearing from SBE to SSE in two isles & & rock near the Eastermost they were 5 or 6 leagues distance
at 5 the N:°most of the Bashees bore SE¾E distance six leag:s
Three islands, the two N:°most are high islands – the S:°most low –

Latitude Graftons Isle	21:* N°
Longitude from Tinian	23:30 W
by an observation of sun & ☽	
found ship in long. of	239:°07' W

Graftons Isle bore SSE dis: twenty miles		7' E
Graftons Isle in lat:de 21:04 N, long:d		239:07W

at midnight fresh gales & squally
Edward Morgan Marine had the misfortune to fall overboard and was drowned –466

Long: Georges Isle 150:00 W	
Long: Tinian	214:10S
Difference of Long.	64:10W
Long: Tinian	214:10W
Long Graftons Isle	239:00 W
Difference of Long.d	24: 50W
Long: Cape Pillar	78:00W
Long. Of Grafton Isle	239: 00W
Difference of Long.d	161:00W

Fine pleasant weather

Course	Dis	Latitude in	Long. made	M: Dis:ce
W13:°30S	142	20:*33N	2:23W	134W

The Bashee Island bore N76:30E distance 47leag:s

---

466 "Edward Morgan was missing who we supposed fell overboard and was drowned, he was a marine taylor and I fear had drank more than his allowance –." PL and FC.

Remarks Friday Oct:ʳ 30 1767 (14)

1	7	5	WSW	NNW	Moderately fresh gales with fine pleasant weather –
2	7	5	SWBW		Long. from London by observation – 241:°32'W
3	8				Sounded no ground with 160 fm:
4	7			22:50	
5	7	4			variation p:ʳ amp:ᵈᵉ 1:00W
6	8				
7	6	4			
8	6			NWBN	fresh gales & cloudy
9	6				
10	5	4		North	
11	5				
12	5			NNE	
1	6		SSW	North	
2	6			21:50	
3	5	4			
4	6				
5	5	5			
6	6	3			
7	6	4			variation p:ʳ azumeth 00:37W
8	6	5			
9	6				
10	6			NNW	
11	6				The ship 17 miles Southw:ᵈ of reckoning by observation
12	5	2			

Course	Dis:	Latitude in	Long. made	M Dis:ᶜᶜ
S35:10W	156	18:*5N	4:°5' West	228W

The Bashee Islands bore N34:00E dist:ᶜᶜ 92 leagues

Remarks Saturday October 31 1767   (15)

H	K	F	Courses	Winds	
1	5	3	SSW	NBE	
2	5	5			
3	5	5			
4	5	4			22:20
5	5	3			
6	5				
7	5	4			
8	5	3		NNE	
9	5				
10	5	2			
11	5	4			
12	5	4			
1	5	4			
2	5	6			21:55
3	6				
4	5				
5	5				
6	6				
7	6	4			
8	5	6		NEBN	
9	5	2			
10	6				
11	6				
12	6				

Fine pleasant weather with a moderate gale –

variation by a medium of azum:th and amplitude 1:18W –

unbent the m:^{n} topsail to repair it and bent a new one

The ship 10 miles to the N:°of her $^{reckoning\ by}$ observation

Moderate gales & pleasant weather

Course	Dis:^{ce}	Latitude in	Long. made	M Dis:^{ce}
SSW –	124	16:30N	5:00W –	279

The Bashee Islands bore N44:°50'E dist:^{ce} 130 leagues

Remarks Sunday November 1 1767   (16)

H	K	F	Courses	Winds	
1	6		SSW	NNE	
2	6				
3	6				24:00
4	6				
5	5	5			
6	5	5			
7	5	2			
8	5	3			
9	7				
10	6	5			
11	7	2			
12	7				
1	6				
2	6				
3	6				23:55
4	6				
5	5	5			
6	6	4			
7	7				
8	6	2			
9	6				
10	5	5			
11	5				
12	4	4	145		

Course	Dis:^{ce}	Latitude in	Long. made	M Dis:^{ce}
S26:30W	123	14:*37N	5:58W –	383W

Moderate gales & pleasant weather[467]
sailmakers employed in repairing the sails & carpenters on the boats in painting them –

no variation

Light breezes –
The ship was 20 miles to the Northward of her reckoning by observation

Grafton Island bore N40°50'E distance 172 leagues

---

[467] ". . . saw sevrall birds like gannets." PL and FC.

EXPLORATION OF THE SOUTH SEAS

Remarks Monday Novemb:^{r} 2 1767   (17)

1	3		SSW	NEBN	Moderate breezes & cloudy weather
2	3	4			
3	4	4		East	
4	5	5		ESE	variation p:^{r} azumeth 00:°12'W
5	4	2		NE	
6	3	5		23:50	
7	4	3		EBN	
8	5				
9	5	5			
10	5	4			
11	5	5			
12	5				
1	6				
2	6			NE	
3	6			23:50	
4	6	2			
5	7				variation p:^{r} azum:th 00:°25'E
6	7	2		EBN	
7	8				
8	9				
9	8				The ship was 14 miles to the Norward of her reckoning by observation
10	7	5			
11	8				
12	8		143.4		

Course	Dis:^{ce}	Latitude in	Long. made	M Dis:^{ce}
W24:40W	135	12:38	6:55W	390W

Grafton Island bore N37:°30' E distance 215 leagues

Remarks Tuesday November 3:^{d} 1767 (18)

1	8	2	SSW	NEBE	
2	8	3			
3	8			24:50	
4	8	3			
5	7	5			
6	7	5			
7	6				
8	6	4		ENE	
9	6	4	SW		
10	6	4		NEBE	
11	6	4			
12	6	3			
1	6				
2	6	2			
3	6			24:00	
4	3				
5	5				
6	5	5			
7	6				
8	5		SBE	EBN	
9	5		SW	EBS	
	2		SSW		
10	6	5	SSW		
11	6	2			
12	4 2		SWBW		

Moderate & fair –
saw severall birds such as we met with before we fell in with Tinian & Graftons Islands, their bodys white & tips of wings feet & bill black – they are very like a Gannet but not near so large these birds we remark all way to be within 20 or thirty leagues of land –
and the nearer you come to land the more you see for at any distance one seldom sees above two where as when near land you see them in flocks –[468]
Rainy

heavy squalls with lightning and thunder & much rain
sounded with 140 fm: no ground –
in 3:^{d} reefs – little wind out reefs
at 7 saw a ledge bearing SWBS¾W about 3 miles distances hauld off from it
variation 00:20W –
at 11 saw another ledge off breaker bearing SWBS 5 o 6 leagues miles of them –
Lat of first shoal – 11:*8W
Long of first shoal – 8:00W

Lat of E:end of second –   18:46
Long. of NE end of second –   8:13
Ship 16 miles North of reckoning by an observation

Course	Dis:^{ce}	Latitude in	Long. made	M Dist:^{ce}
S35:00W	136	10:*40N	8:13 W –	468W

Grafton Island bore N37:°30'E distance 256 leagues

---

468 These details are omitted in the PL and the FC.

Remarks Wednesday Novem:r 4 1767   (19)

1	1 4		NNE	S½E	East
2	4			S½W	bore to N½E dis 2 miles
3	4	3		SW	
4	5				
5	5	4			24:40
6	5				
7	}		up NNE		off NBE
8					
9					
10	}		up EBS		off SEBS
11					
12					
1	}		up North		off NW 24:20
2					
3	2	4	NBW		NEBE
4	4		SEBE		
5	1		NWBS		
6	1	3	SSW		
	2	3			
7	2	2	SSW		NE
	2	2	SW		
8	5				
9	6				
10	6				
11	6		NWBW		NNE
12	6	3	West		

Moderate & clear at ½ past noon saw shoal water on the larboard bow, tack'd stood to the SE. at two the ledge from North … miles to West two miles, the South end of the ledge had sand bank above water about two cables length long to the Southward of it saw a low small island
at five the small island NBE six or seven miles, another low island larger than the former – bearing SBW three or four leag:s* at six brought too, the long low island bearing from South to SBE 2 or 3 leag:
NB: we have frequently sounded with 140 fm: line – but could get no ground –
at 2 the island EBS 5 or 6 miles –
at 6 made sail the island E½N 8 miles
at ½ past six saw island bearing SEBS & a ledge of breakers S½W 6 iles
at 7 the island bore SE 4 leagues – & the island that we lay too by all night ENE – the breakers SE½E 4 miles
at ten saw breakers bearing SSW about 2 leagues – half past saw breakers from WSW to W½N, hauld the wind –
at noon the N end of the great reef bore SEBE two leagues
at same time saw another bearing WNW

Sandy Island - lat.	10:°40' — lon:de	8:17
Small Key —	10:37 —	8:16
Long Island —	10:20	8:24
New Island	10:10	8:40
Shoal	10:14	8:36
2 shoal	10:04	8:45
3 shoal	10:4	8:50[469]

Fine weather carpenters & sailmakers employed on boats & sails

Course	Dis	Latitude in	Long. made	M: Dist:ce
S48:00W	54	10:*10N	8:53W	508W

Grafton Island bore N37:°50'E distance 276 leagues

---

469 These islands were named by Wallis according to the Hawkesworth account.

Remarks Thursday Novemb:ʳ 5:ᵗʰ 1767 (20)

H	K	F	Courses	Winds
1	5	4	NWBN	NEBN
2	5			
3	5	5	West	
4	4	5	SW	
5	4	5		24:30
6				
7				
8				
9				
10				
11				
12			up NWBN	
1			of WBN	
2				24:00
3				
4				
5				
6	3		WBS	NEBN
7	7	5		
8	7			
9	6	4		
10	6	3		
11	6	2		
12	6	4		

Course	Dis:ᶜᵉ	Latitude in	Long. made	M: Distance
W18:°00'S	72	9:45	10:04W	580W

Moderate gales & fair weather the reef we saw at noon SW dis:ᶜᵉ 3 miles end of reef – 10:15 long – 9:°00'W variation p:ʳ azumeth – 0:24W.

brought to & reeft the topsails
sounded no ground with 140 fm:

variation p:ʳ azumeth – 0:44W

fine pleasant weather employed in repairing sails, boats & covering the poop –[470]

Graftons Islands bore N40:°00'E distance 296 leagues
found a current that set to the S:°ward about a mile –

---

[470] "The ship eight miles to the S:°ward of her reckoning." PL and FC.

Remarks Friday Nov:r 6:th 1767   (21)

H	K	F	Winds	
1	7		WBS	NE
2	6	3		
3	6	3		
4	5	5		24:30
5	6	5		
6	6	3		
7	5	4		
8	5	5		
9	5	4		
10	6			
11	6	2		North
12	6			
1	6	4		
2	6			
3	6	4		24:00
4	6			NE
5	6			
6	6			
7	7			
8	8			
9	7	3		
10	6	4		
11	6	2		
12	6	4	156	

Moderate & fair

opened a cask of beef N 1250 con:t 194 short six peices —[471]

The ship ten miles to the N of her reckoning by observation

Course	Dis:ce	Latitude in	Long. made	M: Distance
W7:00S	152	9:*28S	12:26W	730W

Graftons Island bore N46:°20'E distance 336 leag:s

---

[471] "Employed in new covering the poop awning it being quite rotten." PL and FC.

Remarks Saturday November 7 1767   (22)

H	K	F	Courses	Winds	Remarks
1	5	4	SW	NE	Fresh breezes & cloudy –
2	6				served mustard & vinegar
3	6	4			
4	6			NNE	no variation
5	6			24:00	
6	5			NE	sounded had 90 fm: water brown sand
7	5	2			
8	5	4			
9	5	4			
10	5	4			sounded 65 fm: brown sand
11	4	4	West		severall rippling currents and we now pass'd thro' these last three hours –
12	5				52 fm: brown sand
1	6	4			49 fm: ditto –
2	5			North	
3	4			23:10	
4	3				48 fm:
5	4			NE	
6	4				saw from 8 to 10 much wood and things like cones of fir trees which swam in a stream NE to SW –[472]
7	5				
8	5				
9	5				at noon moderate gales with light squalls and rain – sounded 25 fm: brown sand with small shells & stones –
10	6				
11	6				
12	5	5		NE	The ship ten miles to the Southward of obser:[n]

Course	Dis:[ce]	Latitude in	Long. made	M: Dis:[e]
WSW¼S	128	8:*56N	14:14W	830W

Graftons Isle bore N48:°00'E distance 369 leagues

---

[472] "Saw a great deal of driftwood cocoa nutt leaves & much weed which swam in a stream NE & SW." PL and FC.

Remarks Sunday November 8 1767   (23)

H	K	F	Course	Wind	Remarks
1	5	5	West	NNE	Fresh breezes & pleasant weather
2	5	4			at two saw the island of Pulo Condore from the mast head
3	6	5			bearing W½N
4	6	6	SSW	ENE	sounded 25fm: fine brown sand –
5	6	2			at four sounded 20 fathoms, bore away
6	5	5		23:30	The extreams of the land bearing from West to NWBW high
7	7				hummocks distance about 12 or 14 leagues –
8	6	4			M Distance
9	5	4			Lat:^{d} of Condore 8:40 890W
10	5	2			to 8:44 }
11	5	3			Longitude made from Bashees 15:14W
12	4	5			at 4 altered the course sounded every to hours had from
1	5				twenty to twenty four fathoms brown sand –
2	5			23:20	This forenoon searched all the hamicoes & chests in the ship
3	4	5			and took from the seamen & petty officers all the logs journals
4	4			ESE	& other papers relating to the voyage since our arrival in the
5	4				South seas and secured them in a box & directed the officers
6	4				to keep theirs from sight of every one but themselves.
7					M:^{r} Gore mate of this ship was the only person that took any
8					umbrage at it, and asked me on quarter deck if it was my
9					orders that he should deliver his log & journal to the First
10					Lieutenant.[473]
11					
12					

Course	Dis:^{ce}	Latitude in	Long. made	M: Dis:^{e}
S3:°00'W	99	7:*03N	0:5W –	5W

Pulo Condore bore N¼E distance 33 leagues –

---

473 This entry is reduced to "At AM got up all the hamacoes chest &:^{ce} on the quarter deck and took from the seamen, & petty officers, all the log and journal books they had relative to the voyage [added in freehand in the FC "to give to the admiralty."]." PL and FC. Molineux also mentions Wallis' requiring "every body" to deliver their journals & logs & every paper relative to the voyage. The fact that Molineux's journal continues may indicate that he did not give up his papers.

Remarks Monday November 9 1767   (24)

H	K	F	Courses	Winds	Remarks
1	3		SSW	NEBE	Moderate breezes & pleasant weathr
2	4				at 1 grey sand 24fm:
3	4	3			at 4 brown sand & mud 24 fm:
4	4	5		24:00	at 6 – 30$^{fm:}$, at 10, at 12, 30 fm:
5	4				at 2 – 23 fm: at 4 – 30 fm: at 6 32 fm:
6	4				at four observed by Syrius, lat – 6:13S
7	3	4			
8	3	3		ESE	
9	3	2			
10	3				
11	3	2			
12	3	5			
1	3	3			
2	3			SE	
3	3			23:45	
4	2	5			
5	2				
6	2				variation – 00°49' Easterly
7	3				
8	2	3			32 fathom muddy –
9	2				
10	2		SWBW	SBE	33 fm:
11	1	4			Light airs –
12	1	3	WSW	South	32 fathom muddy –

Course	Dis	Latitude in	Long. made	M: Dis
SSW –	72	5:*56N	00:34W –	33W

Pulo Condore bore NBE distance 57 leagues –
P Timoan – S35:15W distance 65 leagues –[474]

---

[474] The PL and the FC do not specify the coordinates of Pulo Timoan.

Remarks Tuesday November 10 1767   (25)

1	1		SSW	SE
2	1	3		
3	1			ENE
4	1			
5	1			25:00
6	1			
7	1			
8	1			
9	1			
10	1			
11	1			
12	1			
1		4		
2		3		
3				24:00
4				NNE
5	1		SSW	
6	1			
7	1	3		
8	1	3		
9	2			
10	1			
11	2			
12	2			

Light airs & clear –
sounded 33 fm: soft mud
33fm:

33

33

38

37

37
calm her head to the SSW –
38

unbent the main top:^{s} & bent an old one
variation p:^{r} azu:th – 00:°10'W
Light airs with heavy rain
39fm:
Light airs
40 fm: muddy ground
the ship ten miles South by observation

Course	Dis:	Latitude in	Long. made	M: Dis:^{ce}
S15:20W	37	5:20*N –	00:44W –	43W

Pulo Condore bore N12:°10'E distance 70 leagues
P Timoan – N17:°50'W distance 50 leagues

Remarks Wednesday November 11, 1767   (26)

1	2		SSW	NEBN
2	2			
3	2			
4	2			24:40
5	1			
6	1	4		
7	1	4		
8	1			
9	1			
10	1			
11	1			
12	1			
1				
2			her head	SSW
3				24:15
4	1		SSW	
5	1			
6				
7				Calm
8				
9	1		ESE	
10				
11				Calm
12	1		SSW	NE

Light airs,
tryed the current found it set to the SBW half a knot p:ʳ hour –
sounded 41 fathoms soft blue mud.
variation p:ʳ azumeth – 0:61W –
42:fm

42 fm:

Calm

42 fm:

had an azumeth found no variation

opened a cask of pork N1146 cont: 300 short 5 peices –[475]

Light airs – 42 fathom water; mud
ship to

Course	Dis	Latitude in	Long. made	MDistance
S17:00W	25	4:°56'N –	0:50W –	49 W

Pulo Condore bore N12 :°50'E distance 77 leagues
P Timoan – S29:30W distance 43 leagues

---

[475] "Ship ten miles to the S:°ward by observation." PL and FC.

Remarks Thursday November 12, 1767 (27)

H	K	F	Courses	Winds	Remarks
1				Calm	
2	1	4	NW	SSW	Light airs & calm –
3					sounded 40 fathom soft mudd
4				Calm	41 fm:
5	1		EBS	SBE	
6	1	3		24:00	42 fathom
7	1				
8					ship head to the Eastward
9					
10				Calm	
11					rain
12					
1					observed by the * Casopus Lat 4:°39'N
2				24:50	ships head all round the compass –
3				Calm	sounded 43 fm: muddy –
4					
5					
6					light airs no variation
7	2		SSW	NEBN	
8	3				
9	3				light airs 43 fathom Muddy ground
10	2	3			
11	2				ship by observation ten miles south of her reckoning –
12	1	4			

Course	Dis	Latitude in	Long. made	MDis:ᵗ
SBW½W	27	4:*30N –	00:56W –	57 W

Pulo Condore bore N13:20E distance 87 leagues
P Timoan – S37:°00W distance 33 leagues

Remarks Friday November 13, 1767 (28)

H	K	F	Courses	Winds	Remarks
1	1	4	SSW	ENE	
2	1	3			Light airs & cloudy –
3	2				sounded 43 fathoms muddy
4	2			25:0	
5	1				43 fm: rainy weather
6				Calm	
7					
8					
9	1		SSW	North	
10	2		SWBW	SEBE	15 fm
11	2				
12	2	3			
1	1			23:38	42 fm: light airs & rainy
2				Calm	
3					43 fm:
4					Ships head all round the compass
5					
6	1		SWBS	ENE	sounded 40 fm:
7	2	3			
8	2	5			29 fm:
9	2			SE	
10	2	4			Light airs, 38 fm: muddy –
11	1	4	SW	SSE	
12	2				Ship by obersv:^{n} 10 miles South of reckoning

Course	Dis:^{ce}	Latitude in	Long. made	MDistance
S36:30W	36	3:*58N –	1:14W –	73W

Pulo Condore bore N14:30E distance 98 leagues
P Timoan bore S37:°30W distance 24 leagues

Remarks Saturday November 14, 1767 (29)

1	2		SWBS	variable	
2	2		SEBE		Light airs with rain
3	3		SWBW		Sounded 38 fathoms muddy
4	3		SSW	24:30	
5	3		SSE		
6	3	5	SE		at six saw three islands bearing from SSW½W to SBW
7	3	5	SSE		distance 15 or 16 leagues which I take to be Pulo Timoan, P:
8	2		SBW		Aroe & Pesang
9	1		SBE		sounded 39 fm: blue mud
10	1				
11	1	4	South		
12	2				
1					39 fm:
2				Calm	
3				24:00	39 fm:, ships head from South to ESE
4					
5	1		SWBS	variable	41 fm:
6			39 fm:		
7	1				Pulo Timoan SW Distance 10 or 12 leag:^{s}
8	1				
9	2		SSW	NNW	39 fm:
10	3				
11	2	3			40 fm:
12	3				Rainy weather – 38 fathom

At noon Pulo Timoan bore WSW Dist: 8 or 10 leagues
ship 15 miles Southward of reckoning

Course	Dis:^{ce}	Latitude in	Long. made	MDistance
S¾W	52 –	3:07N* –	01:20W –	79W

Latitude in –   3:7   long made   1:20 ⎤ Meridien 104
Pulo Timoan WSW, 27 –0:9   25 ⎦
P Tin:^{n} latitude in   2:58   long of Tin:^{n} 1:45

Remarks Sunday November 15, 1767 (30)

H	K	F	Courses	Winds
1	3	2	SSW	NNE
2	2	2		
3	2			
4	3	5	South	23:00
5	4			
6	4			
7	4	3		34 fm:
8	4			
	1	5		
9	1	3	SSE	NBE
10	2	5		
11	3	5		
12	3	5		NW
1	3	5		35 fm:
2	3			
3	3			24:00
4	3			
5	2			35 fm:
6	2	4		NNW
7	4			
8	4	2		
9	4			
10	4	2		
11	4	4		
12	4	2		

Fresh breezes with rain –

at 4 Timoan bore from S83:00W to S60:00W, Pulo Pesang SW and Pulo Aroe SSW¼W, 38 fm: muddy
at 6 P: Aroe S36:00W – Pulo Penang S63:00W and Pulo Timoan from N83:00W to S31:30W distance about ten leagues –
34 fm: muddy –
41 fm: fine sand & mudd –

Pulo Aroe bore West –

Observed by Capella – lat 2:23N –
little wind with heavy rain

Pulo Aroe NWBW 7 or 8 leagues –

30 fathoms black & brown sand
Moderate breezes – 27 fm: same
Ship 20 miles South by observation, of reckoning

Course	Dis	Latitude in	Long. made	MDistance
S12:°00E	97	1:*32N –	01:00W	59W

P Tioan bore N23:30W distance 33 leagues –
Dep:ᵉ from P Aroe – 34 E – Long 00:34E
From Timoan – Long 00:48E –[476]

---

[476] No coordinates for this day (except the latitude) and until the 26th November in the PL and the FC.

Remarks Monday November 16 – 1767   (31)

H	K	F	Courses	Winds		Remarks
1	5	4	SSE	NNW		
2	4					Squally with rain
3	3	5	SEBS			25 fm: coarse grey sand with black specks
4	4	5		25:00		
5	7					
6	5	5		NW		25 fm: same ground –
7	4	2			25	
8	4				27	25 fm: fine white & grey sand with black specks
9	4		SBE		27	
10	4				26	Fine brown sand & mud
11	4	4			25	
12	3	3		24:05	25	
1	4			variable	25	
2	4	3	SSE		24	
3	4	5	SEBS		24	grey sand with black specks –
4	4	4	SBE		24	mud
5	3	2	South		25	
6	4		SWBS		24	grey sand
7	4	5				
8	4	5	SSW		24	
9	4		SBW			
10	4		South	WSW	22	
11	4	5				Fresh gales & hazey rainy weather
12	6		SBE½E	SW	25	Soundings 25 fm: brown sand with black specks

Course	Dis:ᶜᵉ	Latitude in	Long. made	MDis:ᶜᵉ
S12:°00E	102	1:10N –	01:37W	36W

Long from P Aroe –   0:57E Mer. Dis –   56 E
Long from Timoan –   1:10E – M Dis –   70 E

Remarks Tuesday November 17 – 1767   (32)

1	6		NWBN	variable		Squally with rain
2	6		SBW½W		22	Grey sand with broken shells –
3	4		SSW	West	20	Saw the Peak of Lingin WBN 17 leag:ˢ & an island SBW,
4	4			23:40		distance 7 or leagues
5	3	2	SWBS	WBN		At six the Peak of P: Taya WBN½N, one island SBE – 5
6	3	2			20	leagues and another SBW about 7 leagues distance
7	2	5	SW		20	
8	1	4	N½E		19	
9	1	5	NNW	West	19	grey sand with black specks –
10	2	5			19	fine clear weather with light airs & lightning in the
11	4				19	horizon in the SW –
12	4				19	at five very dark & dismal with heavy squalls and much
1	4		NBW	24:50	20	rain clew'd up every thing & brought too till day light –
2	4	3	NWBN	WBS	21	split the fore topmast staysail bent a new one –⁴⁷⁷
3	3		SSW	West	20	… watch
4	3	2	SBW		20	
5	1	4	NBW		20	at 9 saw the two islands we saw last night –
6		up	SW off	WBN	20	at ½ 10 past the NEmost bore SSE, 6 or 7 leagues (called
7						Pulo Tote)
8					19	The other bore South –
9	3		SSW	West	19	
10	4		SBW½W		19	
11	4	3			19	Heavy squalls & rainy weather –
12	4					Pulo Tote bore – SEBS –
						the other island – S½E –
						Lat 16: Depar 30 West –

Course	Dis:ᶜᵉ	Latitude in	Long. made	MDis:ᶜᵉ
		00:30S	1:07West	66

Pulo Aroe – Long –26 – East –
From Timoan – Long – 4 – East –

---

477 ". . . split and blew to peices the fore and main topmast stay sails & severall other sails split – unbent them at daylight and bent others." PL.

Remarks November 18 – 1767 (33)

				fm:	
1	4	3	SSW		Fresh gales & dirty squally weather
2	5	4		17	saw the islands –
3	3	4	NNW	16	
4	3	2	24:40	16	
5	3			18	at six Pulo Toty SE 5 leagues –
6	2		SSW	15	and other island S¼E 4 leagues the 7 isles SW dis:^{ce} 8 leagues
7	3		NBW	16	
8	3		NNW	WBN	17 coarse sand and shells
9	3		NBW		At 2 AM: a very heavy squall with rain clewd all up & lay too
10	2	5	SBW½W	18	till five – in the squall discovered by the flashes of lightning a
11	2	4	SWBS	19	sail allmost onboard of us haild her and shew'd lights and
12	2	3	SSW½W	19	soon past each other, we know nothing of what she was, nor
1	2		N½E	18	could we see her at daylight –[478]
2		4	23:00	18	
3		up	NWSW	off North	
4				17	
5	3		NWBN	WBS	Pulo Toty bore SSE 5 leagues
6	3	2		20	
7	3			18	
8	2	4		18	at 8 saw a sail at anchor in the ESE
9	2	5		18	
10	2		NNW	17	at noon Pulo Toty S33:00E long:
11	2	2	NW½N	15	the other island S13:00E long:
12	3		NW½W	16	at same time saw the land bearing WNW –
					ship twenty miles south of the observation

Course	Dis:^{ce}	Latitude in	Long. made	MDistance
		00:*34S	1:27 West	86W

Long from Aroe –   00:°6 East –
Long from Timoan –   0:28 East –

478 "... by the flashes of lightning we saw a large vessel close onboard of us our ship sprung her luff & we just cleared each other, it blew so hard we could not understand what was said or of what nation she was. This is the first vessel we have seen since we parted with the Swallow." PL and FC.

1	1		SSW	West
2	3		SBW	
3	4		SBW½W	
4	4	2	SSW	24:50
5	3			
6	3			
7				
8			Drifting current	& wind
9				
10		3	SSE	NW
11				
12	1			WNW
1				
2				24:00
3				
4				
5				
6				
7	3		NNW	West
8	3	2	SSW	17
9	4	3	SSW	15
10	4	4	SW½W	16
			SWBS	WBN
11	4	5		7
12	4	3		16

Remarks Thursday Nov:r 19 –1767   (34)

Fresh breezes & squally.
16 fm: sand & shells.
15 saw the 7 Islands bearing SWBS & the Peak of Lingin NWBW½W about 18 leagues distance –
at six anchor'd in 15 fm: water with the best bower, sandy ground –
the middle of the 7 islands SW½S
the Peak of Lingin NWBW¼W
Pulo Taya about West –
Pulo Tote ESE five leagues –
another island SE½S –
tried the current, found it set ENE about three fathoms p:r hour

at 5 AM weigh & made sail, squally with thunder lightning & rain –
at 8 Pulo Toty SEBE & the other SSE

saw two sail a head further to leeward

at noon Peak of Lingin N49:00W
Pulo Taya – N71:00W
Middle of Seven Islands – SSW
West Isle – S04:00E
Pulo Toty – N85:50E –
Latitude observed – 00:*56S –

Remarks Friday Nov:r 20 –1767   (35)

1	4	3	SWBS		
2	4	3			15
3	4		SSW		15
4	4	3	NNW		15
5			25:10		
6			current		
7	1	5	EBN	WNW	
8					
9					
10	1		EBN		
11					
12	1		SEBS		
1					
2	1		SEBS		
3					
4			24:00		
5		5	SBE		
6					
7	4		NBW½W	WBN	
8	5	4			16
9	4	5			16
10	4	2	SW		
11	4				15
12	4	2			15

Moderate & cloudy. saw a great deal of wood cocoanutts and other things floating on the water –
at six finding that the ship drove fast to the Eastward, anch in 15 fathom – sandy ground –
Lingin double peek – N54:00W
Puo Tay – WBN
Middle of 7 islands – S32:00W
Polly West – S60:00E
Pulo Toty S82:00E
Found the current set EBN 1^K:5^F p:r hour
at 5 AM began to heave on the small bower
at ½ past the cable parted & it blowing very fresh, made sail in order to tack and anchor again near the buoy when we examined the cable found it cut thro with the rocks, so twas in a manner impossible to recover to anchor again it blowing so hard that if we came too with another anchor we might possibly loose it like wais – as the ground was foul and had but two anchors left[479] –

Pulo Toty –	S85:00E lat:	0:56S
Polly West –	S69:30S –	58S
Seven Islands	S19:00W –	1:12S
Pulo Taya –	N80:00W –	0:46S
Lingin –	N52:00W	15 or 16 leag:s

Fresh gales & cloudy with a swell
Latitude observed 0:*53S

worked the distance of the middle of the 7 islands & judge it to lay in lat:de 1:*14S
at ½ past 2 Saturday it bore S½E dis:ce about four miles – the ship had sailed from noon about SSW½West – 18 miles which is near the latitude

---

479 "At 6 AM the current being slack hove in the small bower which soon after parted at a third from the clinch, hove in the cable and found it cut thro' with the rocks tho' we had taken great care in sounding before we anchored and found all clear ground – The current being strong and it blowing fresh the ship a great way to leeward made sail in hopes to get up and recover the anchor but it was impossible unless we anchored and was very fear full of letting go in foul ground so was necessitated to stand on it being squally." PL and FC.

Remarks Saturday Nov:ʳ 21 – 1767   (36)

H	K	F	Courses	Winds
1	4		SW½W	NWBW
2	5	4		14
3	5	3		13
4	2	3	SW	WNW
	2		North	
5	4	3		13
6			25:10	
7	1	4	East	
8			Current	
9	1	4		
10	1		SEBS	
11	1	2		
12			SSE½E	24:00
1				
2	1	4	SSE	
3				
4	2	3	SSE	
5				
6	1		SE	WSW
7	4		North	
8	5			
9	5	5	SW	14
10	6	2	SW½S	15
11	5			
12	6		SSW	NW

Fresh gales & cloudy – saw severall small vessels to windward, and amongst the islands –

at ½ past 3 P: Taya N55:00W
extreams of 7 isles from SW to S½E dis 5 ᵐⁱˡᵉˢ
Pulo West N32:00E
Pulo Toty N50:00E
Pulo Lingin N30:40W –
At half past five anchord with the best bower in 15 fm: sandy

Pulo Taya N66:00W
Middle of 7 isle S16:00W–
A small round isle S96:00W
Pulo West – East –
Lingin – NW
at 10 a very heavy squall with much thunder lightning and rain –
at 6 AM hove up & made sail

Moderate & fair

The Northermost of the 7 isles –   N73:00E
a high rock without it –   N43:00E
a low craggy rock without it –   NEBN –
the S:°most of Seven Isle –   SE –
The extreams of land to the South:ᵈ from SSE to SSE½E[480]

---

[480] Latitude 1°12' South in the PL and the FC.

Remarks Sunday November 22 –1767   (37)

1	7		SBW½W	NWBW	12
2	6		SSW½W		11
3	5				12
4	5	3		NW	13
5	5				14
6	5			25:00	15
7					
8					
9					
10					
11					
12					
1				23:40	
2					
3					
4					
5				WNW	17
6					19
7	4	2	SSW		21
8	4	4			16
	2				15
9	1	3	SBW		14
10	2	4	SBE½E		14
11	3		SBE		12
12	2	5	SBE½E		11

Moderate & clear – saw & pass'd by three sail of sloops, or doggers[481] –
at 3 Monopin Hill bore S34E –
the N:°most of 7 isles – S62:00E
the S:°most – SE –
the islands between NW to NWBW
at 4 Monopin – S14:30
middle of 7 isles – NEBN –
the isles between – S70:°00'E to S60:°00'E
current
at 6 the extreams of the land in sight, SBE½E to E½N
and the Hill of Monopin S27:00S 8 leag:^{s}
at ½ past 6 anchor'd in 15 fm: muddy
a very heavy squall with thunder lightning and rain –
at 6 AM the tide making … knot
weigh'd & made sail
at ½ past six saw the Sumatra shore
at 8 Monopin Hill S59:00E 5 leagues
extrems of Sumatra from W to SBW –
at 9 Monopin Hill EBS 5 leagues –
Batacarang WBS 7 miles –
at noon Monopin Hill N6:45E distance five leagues –
The extreams of Banca from S¼E to EBN –
Batairang Point on Sumatra N50:00W
the S :°most point of Sumatra insight SE½E
Latitude observed 2:*08S

---

481 See Falconer's dictionary: "DOGGER, (dogre-boat, Dut.) a Dutch fishing-vessel navigated in the German ocean. It is generally employed in the herring-fishery, being equipped with two masts, viz. a main-mast and a mizen-mast, and somewhat resembling a ketch."

Monday November 23 –1767   (38)

1	3		EBE	NE	9
2	1				7
3			current		9
4	1	4		ENE	
5				25:10	
6			current		
7		5	NNE	North	
8					
9				West	
10			no	current	10
11					
12					
1	1		SSE		
2					
3	1			23:50	
4	1	2	SEBS		
5	1				
6		3	SSE	variable	
7					
8					10¾
9					
10		5			
11					1
12					2

Light airs & anchord in 9 fathom muddy ground –
Monopin Hill NE½E[482]
The extreams of Sumatra from NW to SEBE – distance from the Sumatra shore about six or seven miles –
spoke a Dutch sloop from Batavia for Malacca, no news from him –[483]
scrubb'd ship between wind water
at 6 the water was deepend to 10 fm:
at midnight to daylight much thunder lightning & rain –
at 7 AM two Duch vessels at anchor near the Sumatra shore –
Draught of water forward   15 feet 9 inches
                    abaft   14 feet 3 inches
Difference   1 foot 6 inches

At Noon a light breeze weigh'd and made sail

Latitude observed 2:*10 S

---

482 "Spoke with a Dutch sloop of the mouth of Palambam River, she was a guard coast had no news –." PL and FC.

483 "Sent the cutter on board a Dutch sloop that came out of Balampan river this morning. Her crew was very ill of the scurvy she belongs to the Dutch East India Company & is employed bringing the produce of Sumatra from the several Dutch factories to Bataviathey had some excellent accurate drafts of the coast [. . .] but no money could purchase them so jealous are the Dutch that it would be death for the Master of a trader to part with them. They informed that 44 Malays embark'd in canoes last night to go in pursuit of a young Malay prince who had fled from the King his father." Molineux.

1	2		SBE	North	12	
2	3	4			14	
3	4	4	ESE		13	
4	4	3	EBS		10	
5	4	4		25:10	9	
6	3	4	E½S		11	
7			current		13	
8					14	
9					13	
10				none	11	
11					10	
12						
1						
2	1	5	EBN			
3				22:40		
4	1	2				
5	2	5				
6					11	
7					12	
8	2		EBS		13	
9			SEBE½E		11	
10			from S½E	to SE	12	
11					12	
					13	
12					14	
					14	

Remarks Tuesday Nov:r 24 –1767 (39)

Light airs
at 2 Monopin Hill NNE –
at 3 Monopin – N7:00E
at 4 Monopin Hill N5:00W
Quedo Banka N65:00E & Sumatra from S55:00E to S68:00W –
Sable rocks NNE –
at six anchord with small bower in 10 fm: muddy –
Monopin Hill NNW
Quedo Banca – N57:00E
extreams Sumatra S53:0E to S63:00W
Sable Rocks – N8:00W –
hard squall with thunder light: & rain–
at ½ past 5 AM weigh'd & towed the ship in the tide with the boats –
at 8 Monopin Hill N45:00W
Quedo Banca N42:00E
and 3:d point of Sumatra S55:00E
at noon anchord in 14 fm: water it being calm & the current setting the ship over on the Nanca Islands –
Third point of Sumatra S7:00W 5 or 6 miles –
Monopin Hill N54:00W
Quedo Banca – N25:00E
Nanka Islands SE –
Latitude observed 2:*24S

Remarks Wednesday Nov:r 25 – 1767   40

1			NW		14
2					
3				NW	13
4	1		S¾W		14
	1		S½E		13
5	2		South	25:0	15
6	2		SBE		14
7					13
8					10
9					
10					
11					
12					
1					
2					
3				24:35	10
4					9
5					8
6				North	12
7	2	3	SE		8
8	6	5	SE¼E		10
9	4		SEBS		14
10	3	4	SBE		14
11	3				10
					18
12	4	3	SE		19
					18
					18
					18
					17
					14
					13
					13

Current set EBS 2½ knots p:r hour
at 3 it set EBS 1 knot – weighd & made sail

at 4 Monopin Hill – N50:00W
Quedo Banca – NNE –
Nanka Isles Middle S
Mount Parmesang – SEBE
Extreams of Sulatra West to S½E

At six anchord in 10 fm: water
Monopin Hill & 3 point of Sumatra in one bore – NW (third point, 8 miles)
Quedo Banca NBE½E –
Mount Parmissang – SEBE½E
2 point Sumatra 118 leagues –
the N:°most of Nanka Isles NEBN½E

at ½ past six weighd & came to sail
opened a cask of pork N:°935 contents 292 – short 3 peices –
at 7 AM pass'd by a shoal not above a quarter of a mile from the ship
the N:°most isle of Nanca – N3:00E
The second point of Sumatra in one with the end of the Bank S14:00E
The N:°most high land – N47:E
The middle of the S°most East
A small island under the high land of Banca – near East.
The ship about mile from Sumatra.
At 10 3:d point sumatra   N72:00W –
Mount Parmissang –   N51:00E –
SW end Banca –   S47:00E –

at noon ⎧ second point of Sumatra –   N38:00W – four leagues
⎪ Mount Parmisang –   N51:00E
⎨ first point of Sumatra –   SE – five leagues
⎩ extreams of Banca – from N¼W to S77:00 East
latitude observed – 2:52S –

Remarks Thursday November 26 – 1767 (41)

1	5		SE¾E	NNE	18
2	5		SE		
3	3	5	S½W	Sounding 13,17,15 11,10,9	14 10
4	4		South	9.9.7	10
5	3	5		7,7½, 8	
6	3	3	S½E	25:40	9
7	2	5	SSE		
8	3				
9			no	current	
10				NNW	
11					
12					
1					
2					
3				23:55	
4					
5					
6					
7					6½
8	2		SSE		5
9	2 1		SBE	NW	5 5¼ 5½
10	3				6
11	5				6½ 6½
12	5			NNW	7 7½ 8 8½ 9

Lucipara by account bore North 29 miles

Fresh breezes & cloudy Island Lucipara in one with the first point of Sumatra bearing S35:00E
at 4 Lucipara S75:00E, first point of Sumatra & Parmissang bore N13:00W
the Southmost point of Sumatra S53:00W –

from four to five 5¼, 5, 5, 4¼ 4, Lucipara bore from East to ENE –
at six the sounding between 5 & 6, was as under 4, 4, 3¼, 3, 3¼
Lucipara bore from ENE to NE, 3 or 4 leagues
at ½ six Lucipara NE½N
from six to seven 3¼, ¾, ¾ – 3½, ½, 3¾, 3¾ 3¾ 4
from seven to eight 4, 4, 4, 4½, 4, 4, 4½
at 8 anchord in 4¼ water muddy –
at midnight very heavy squalls with much thunder lightning & rain –[484]
at 7 AM weigh'd & sent the boats a head of the ship sounding –
Lucypara bearing NBE½E about 5 leagues
at 8 Lucipara N13:00E about 17 miles
Extreams of Sumatra – NNW to WBN –
a hill on Banca NE½N –
at 10 a fresh breeze hoisted the boats in

at Noon saw land bearing WSW about 6 or 7 leagues distance
Latitude observed 3:°*41S

484 "At midnight heavy squalls with rain thunder & lightning and the sea all round us looking like fire which in our situation was very horable to behold." PL.

Remarks Friday November 27 – 1767   (42)

Moderate brezes & cloudy
saw much drift wood & trees –

H	K	F	Courses	Winds	
1	5	5	SBE to	NBW	9
					7
2	2	5	SEBE	7½ 7	½
3	3	4	SSE	9, 10	6
4	3	5	SBE		½
					10
5	3		SBE	SWBW	10
6	2			24:0	9
7	1	}	drift	calm	10
8					9
9					9
10				calm	9
11					9
12					½
1		4	NNE		10
2		5	SSE	24:10	10
3		4			10
4		4			9
5					½
6		4			9
7	1				½
8	1		SBE	variable	9
9					¾
10	1				10
11	1	2	SSE		9
					¾
					9
					½
					10
12					10
					10
					10
					10
					¼

light airs & calm
variation 1:20W p:ʳ amplitude

Light airs & calm –

Light airs & calm
    Master
course SBE½E dis:ᶜᵉ 29 miles, lat: 4:09S
Long: 0:8E, Lucipara N¾W, dis:ᶜᵉ 58 miles
    Gore
course S17:00E dis:ᶜᵉ 33 miles – Lat 4:74S lon: 0:8E
Lucipara N7:00W Distance 22 leagues –

Remarks Saturday Novem:ʳ 28 – 1767   (43)

1	1		SBE		10
2	1	3	SBE		9½
3	1	3			9½
4	1		SBE		10
5	1		South		11
6					
7					
8					
9					
10					
11					
12					
1					
2					
3					
4					
5					
6					
7					
8					
9					
10			Ships head	from	
11			North to	East	12
12					

Light airs & cloudy –
Saw much drift wood

Anchor'd in 11 fm: water muddy
current set SSE about 4 fm: –

squally with thunder lightning and rain

the current set NBW – 4 fathoms

weigh'd & made sail
squally with very heavy rain & thunder – light airs

at noon dark rainy weather –
No variation

course S12:°45' Dis:ᶜᵉ 9 miles, lat: in 4:°17'S
longitude made – 0:°14'E
Lucipara bore N11:°38'W distance 21 leg:ˢ

Remarks Sunday Novem:r 29 – 1767   (44)

1	1		SBE	NNW	12
2	1				13
3	1		SSW	25:10	12
4	1				13
5					12½
6					
7			SSE	NBW	12
8					13
9	1		SEBS		12
10	1				13
11	2				12
12	2				13
1	2				13
2	2			24:0	
3	2			NW	
4	1	4		SW	
5					12½
6					12
7	3		SBE	NW	12
8	3				12
9	4	2			12
10	4	4	SBW		12
11	3	4			12
12	2	1	SSW	West	12
	2	2	SBE		12
					12

Saw three sail a stern of us

Light airs & cloudy –
Spoke a Dutch sloop from Balamban for Batavia – who told us the North Watcher bore SEBS½S about twelve leag:s Dutch vessel supposed to be in lat: 4:°30'S had some talerins & a dozen of fowles from the sloop –[485]
at 4 AM rainy & calm anchord in 12½ fm: muddy ground

at

at 9 AM saw the North Watcher bearing SW about 4 leagues –

at noon, the North Watcher WBS about 3 leagues – a shoal on our lee beam bearing EBS – distance about 3 or four miles –
The Thousand Islands from the mast head bearing SBW

Saw much drift wood every day which at a distance look like vessels
Latitude observed 5:*11 South

at noon the North Watcher West – 4 leag:s
a sand bank – East – 4 miles –
Thousand Islands – SSW –

---

[485] "... he sent a dozen of fowles & some tamarinds onboard and would not be paid for them." PL and FC.

Remarks Monday November 30 – 1767   (45)

1	3	3	SBE	West	12
2	3	2			13
3	3	3	SBW½W		16
4	4	5	S½E	24:10	17
5	1	4	NW		20
6					22
7					
8					
9					
10					
11					
12					
1					
2				24:00	
3					
4					
5					
6					
7	2	4	NW		
8	2	5	South		
	5	4	SBE		
9	6		South		
10	5				
11	4	4	NBW		
12	5	4			

Moderate & fair –
the N:°Watcher N60:00W 5 or 6 leagues
the high land of Bantam S40:00E

at 6 anchor'd in 22 fm: muddy
The South Watcher S13W Dis: 3 leag:^{s}
Bantam Hill SW –
Extreams of 1000 Islands from S54:00W to N62:00W
dis:^{ce} from middle 3 leagues
at 6 AM weigh'd & made sail –
at 8 the South Watcher WBS & miles
Bantam Hill SW¼W
at noon Onrust bore S 40:00W
Batavia South dis:^{e} 10 or 11 miles
Edam E¾S one mile –

at this time saw the ships mast at Onrust & in Batavia Road

Latitude 5:58

Week day	Month Day	Wind	Remarks on board his Maj:ˢ Ship Dolphin at Batavia
December	1767	24:30 ESE	Moderate & cloudy, running in South to Batavia Road the steeple or domes right a head – soundings from 15fm: to 5½ where we anchor'd. Onrust bearing N51:00W One tree Island N63:00E, the dome South and the the fort S9:10W distance from the shore about two miles, found riding here a Dutch commodore with about twelve sail of India ships and as many at Onrust; his Majestys ship Falmouth laying on the mud in a wretched condition – sent an officer to the Governor to acquaint him of the arrival of his Britannick Maj:ˢ ship Dolphin & that we might be permitted to furnish the ship with such necessaries as we would, that we would salute if he returned an equal number of guns from the fort onshoar, that being agreed to, at sunrise saluted with 13 guns, the fort returned 13 guns – scraped and tared the sides, & served fresh beef –[486]
Tuesday	1	SW	
		WSW 22:15	
Wednesday	2	25:00 SW 23:20	Moderate weather with some rain served fresh beef Purser onshoar getting of rack & necessaries – the Surgeon likewais procuring for the sick –[487]
Thursday	3	24:50 D:º 22:30	Rainy weather employed in overhauling rigging & the hold sent the Boatswain & carpenter to Onrust to see the condition of the Falmouth stores and if any were fit for our use, she returned a pair of main jacks & reported to me that every thing there was spoiled the mast rotten and all the stores decayed they likewais went to view the Falmouth and say they think she cannot last long but will be in peices the first gale of wind –[488]

486 "The Purser sent off fresh beef and plenty of vegitables which I ordered to be served immediately – turned all hands up and acquainted them that I would not suffer any liquor to come onboard & would punish severely any who disobeyed these orders and endeavoured to shew them that by temperance we might go from hence as healthy as we arrived here – scraped and tarrd the Dolphin." PL and FC.

487 ". . . thank God we have but few at present and every means taken for their recovery never suffer the people to straggle into the town not any to go onshoar but on duty – served fresh beef." PL and FC.

488 ". . . that the mast yards cables &:ᶜᶜ were all rotten and even the iron work was so rusty that it was scarce worth looking after, they likewais went onboard the Falmouth to look at her, and report that she is all to peices and think that she cannot last out the next monsoon as many ports are washed into one, that the stern port is quite decayed and no place in her that a man can keep himself from the weather, and that the few people belonging to her are almost worn out and do expect to be drownded in the ensuing monsoons – served fresh beef." PL and FC.

Week day	Month Day	Wind	Remarks &:ce
Friday	4	24:20 SSW 23:00 West	Moderate weather with rain – served fresh beef employ'd in the hold and on the rigging
Saturday	5	24:00 D:o 23:0	Little wind with some rain, received rice & arac & stowed it away – served fresh beef[489]
Sunday	6	22:45 NNW West 24:30	Little wind & rainy [490] the carpenter found all the leather of the chain pumps eat of by the rats which are so plenty in the ship that they destroy sails rigging provision & the peoples clothes – served fresh beef
Monday	7	25:00 WSW 23:30	Rainy at time received all our stores of Arack &:ce and got all ready for sea, served fresh beef.
			The Warrant Officers of the Falmouth petitioned me to take them home and appoint others in their stead the carpenter says that he would gladly go in the meanest capacity for his health is so bad that he is sure he cannot live the cook likewais is in a low way & the Boatswain is now crazy in the hospital the Gunner died about three years ago – & the Surgeons Mate sailed for England soon after, their petition was this, that as I could not take them home I would make their miserable case known tho the Lords of the Admiralty and pray their Lordships would be pleased to order them home as the stores they had under charge are all spoiled by laying in bad warehouses and that what remains is not worth looking after –[491]

489 "Employed in overhauling the rigging rapairing of sails taking coals out of the fish room and putting them into the cole hole – got of greens and fresh beef which the people have every day – all health – and sober –." PL and FC.

490 ". . . the ship being in want of 3 & 3½ inch rope, and one anchor having lost two, and had expended all the rope of the before-mentioned size, for rounding the cables, and the officers that I had sent to seek these supplies brought word that the price of all these things were so intolerable that they had not bargained for any, on which I went onshoar for the first time and went around the diferent stores and arsenals and found their report true that I determined to make any shift rather than be imposed upon – for I beleive they thought we could not do without their assistance and the season being now very sultry and constant rain that I gave them till tomorrow to come to any price for that I would sail on Tuesday mor:ng therefore it must come tomorrow or not at all they came down a trifle and said if I would stay a week they beleived they could serve us near my own terms. Onboard the carpenter found that the rats had eat the leather off the pumps and have done great mischief the ship swarming with them." PL and FC.

491 "The warrant officers of the Falmouth petitioned me to let them go home and that I would appoint others in their stead, or let them to go without it as there was nothing to look after, the Gunner hath been long dead, his stores all spoiled, the powder being spoiled was by order of the Dutch thrown into the sea – the Boatswain mad and in the hospital and his stores rotten and spoiled the roof of the store house fallen in the beginning of a wet monsoon and remained so for many months untill they could get another place to put them in, the carpenter in a very low weak condition and I think cannot live long the Cook a wounded cripple –. I told them that as they had charge of the stores that it was not in my power to releive them and they must wait orders from home, they said that they never had a single order from England since they were left here and therefore

Remarks Tuesday 8:th Dec:^r 1767 (1)

1			West	
2				
3				
4			24:00	
5				
6				
7				
8				
9				
10				
11				
12				
1				
2			22:00	
3				
4				
5				
6				
7	5	NNW		
8	5	NW½N		
9	5	NWBN		
10	5			
11	2			
12	1	South	WBS	

Squally rainy weather –

Completed our provisions and made the ship clear for sea^{492} –

Ship draught of water   15:8 forward
14:4 aft –

at 6 AM, weigh'd & made sail
at 8 Onrust S19:°30'W Edam S88:°06'

at noon it falling calm with much rain anchor'd in 25 fm:
Pulo Pare SWBW 2 miles
South Watcher NNE 4 leagues –
N:°most of 1000 Isles NWBW¼W
S:°most of 1000 Isles NWBW¼W – 3 leag:^s

---

humbly prayed that I would make their deplorable case known, that there may be some releif given them, that they have ten years pay due, are grown old men, and would be happy to go home sweepers and forfeit even their ship nor hope to be employed again if they could only be relieved from the miseries they suffer here, for they cannot stay onshoar at night if ever so ailing nor any one come onboard to them if them sick – that they are robbed by the Malayes – and in danger of being destroyed by them as they did Siam prize by burning her – I assured them that I would make their case known and they left me with tears in their eyes –

Got all ready for sea served fresh beef to the ships company every day since we have been here and carry some beef & an ox with us – all the people in good health." PL and FC. Carrington (op. cit., p. xxv) specifies that it was two years later that the *Falmouth* fiasco came to an end thanks to the help of the Dutch East India Company. Colledge (*Ships of the Royal Navy*, Casemate, 2010 (1987), p. 138) lists the ship (Captain William Brererton) as having been damaged and then abandoned in Batavia after action in Manila in 1765. Brereton was rather a contested figure and was court-martialed for another episode in his career, leading to the publication of the case (see *Case of William Brereton, Esq; late Commander of his Majesty's ship Duke*, 1779) in an attempt at vindication. In 1784, in a petition to the government, for compensation of expences incurred in Manila and Batavia, Brereton explains this abandonment of the ship, after a six-month stay in Batavia arguing that he was unable to repair the vessel and was forced to leave her there. The men though were "disposed of" and sent on to Madras, which was evidently not the case.

492 "... we have only one man on the sick list except one who had had rheumatic pains ever since we left the Streights of Magellan." PL and FC.

Remarks Wednesday 9 Dec:ʳ 1767   (2)

1			West	
2			Calm	
3				
4			24:00	
5				
6				
7				
8				
9				
10				
11				
12				
1			23:00	
2				
3				
4				
5				
6			Sw	
7			Calm	
8			WSW	
9				
10				29
11				30
				36
12			West	45
				35
				30

Light airs

Punished Jm:ˢ Woolridge for drunkeness[493]

at 5 AM weigh'd
moderate breezes & fair sometime
Light airs – boats ahead –
at 8 a fresh breeze turning thro between the 1000 Islands and Wapon Van Horens islands –

at noon Bedro Isle SSW 2 miles
middle of Wapon Isle WBS 2 mile
Emost of 1000 Isles from N 14:00 W to N55:°00E – the S:°Watcher N58:10E

---

[493] "Punished John Woolridge one of the bargemen for being drunk last night." PL and FC (8ᵗʰ December).

1			
2			
3			
4		25:00	
5			
6			
7			
8			
9			
10			
11			
12			
1			
2		23:00	
3			
4			
5			
6			
7			
8			
9			
10			
11			
12			

Latitude – 5:*51 S.

Remarks Thursday Dec:^{r} 10 1767 (3)

Fresh breezes, plying to windward –

At Pulo Baby & Bantam Point in one bearing WNW Wapin Isle SSE½E about 3 or four miles Distance

at six anchord in 15 fm: muddy
Men Eaters Isle SE 5 or 6 mile
Wapen Isle – NNE – 6 mile
Pulo Baby WNW 3 or 4 leagues
Bantam Hill SW½W –
Gaffers Isle – South

at 6 AM weighd & plyed to windward

at eight, Pulo Baby NWBW½W 7 mile
Bantam Hill SW¼S –
middle of Wapen Isle – NEBE¼E –
stood off to 25 & in to 15 fathoms

at noon the West end of Pulo Baby NWBN distance 2 leagues –
Plying to Windward with a large Dutch ship which sailed five days ago from Batavia calld

Remarks Friday Dec:ʳ 11 – 1767 (4)

1			WSW	31
2				31
3			WNW	29
4				
5			WSW	28
6				
7			25:00	25
8				
9				
10				
11				
12				
1				
2			24:00	
3				
4				
5				
6				
7				
8			NW	
9				
10				
11			WBN	
12			SW	

Lat:ᵈ 5:*51 S.

Fresh breezes & cloudy plying to wind ward

Pulo Baby ESE 3 or 4 leagues
Bantam Point SWBS 5 or 6 leag:ˢ

At 7 fresh gales & squally rainy weath:ʳ
Anchord in 25 fm: water sandy –
Bantam Point SW¾S – 7 miles
Pulo Baby – E¾N
Button Isle WSW – the current set NW near two knots –

at 9 slack tide
at 2 AM the stream WSW 1-3 p:ʳ hour
at 5 ESE – 1 knot
at 6 made sail
at 8 Bantam Point S½E 2 miles
Button isle –WSW
Cap Isle

at noon the Capp & Small isle bore S 15:00 W about 3 leagues –
Button Isle one with the S:°end of Middle Isle – SW½W
Bantam Point East[494]

---

494 "Several people fall down with colds and some few fluxes." PL and FC.

Remarks Saturday Dec:ʳ 12 – 1767   (5)

Fresh breezes – had no ground when near Button Isle or Middle Island with 40 fm: – but on the Java shore 20, plying to windward –
at six anchored in 28 fm: sandy
Middle Isle N½E –
Cap Island – NE
Button Isle – N27E
Anger Point N60:00E
North Point of Pepper Bay S¾W of shore two miles –
variation – 1:25W –

at 4 stream set NE 1:4 p:ʳ hour –

at 8 weighed & made sail – we had only 25 fm: – lost the buoy & buoy rope –

at noon the S:°Point of Pepper Bay SSW
Anger Point NEBE½E 3 leag –
the S:°most high land on Sumatra W¼S
had from 20 to 30 fm: water –

turning to windward with the current –
came onboard a Dutch boat with turtle lost a logg & 3 lines in trying the current –

1		SW	
2			47
3			28
4		25:00	30
5			
6			
7			
8			
9			
10			
11			
12			
1			
2			
3		24:00	
4			
5			
6			
7			
8			22
9			21
10			
11			16
12			13

Lat:ᵈ 6:*09S

Remarks Sunday Dec:ʳ 13 – 1767 (6)

1		NBE	SW	
2		South	WSW	
3		SBW	West	
4				47
5			24:20	28
6				30
7				
8				
9				
10				
11				
12				
1				
2			24:00	
3				
4				
5				
6				
7				
8				
9				
10				16
11				22
12				26
				25

Lat:ᵈ 6:*57S

Moderate breezes & fair plying to windward

The high land of Princess Island WSW the N:° Point of Wellcome Bay SBW½W –

at 7 anchord in 12 fm: water, muddy –
South point of Pepper Bay SSW 12 miles
the high part of Hunger Point WNW E½E
Caracatora Island WNW¾W –
Distance from Java shore 3 or 4 miles
at 8 saw a prodigious number of lights on the shoar which we took to be made by the natives to draw the fish near the shoar & then to catch them, the same as done at Georges Island –[495]
Moderate & fair
at ½ past five wiegh'd and made sail

at noon the S:° part of Sumatra NWBW South point of Pepper Bay S½W 4 leagues
Princess Island SW¼W –

Served turtle to the ships company[496]

---

495 The PL and FC specify that this was done almost every night at King Georges Island.
496 Turtle is served every day until the 19ᵗʰ of December.

1			WSW	26
2				23
3				20
4			25:20	25
5				41
6				40
7				38
8				32
9				
10				
11				
12				
1				
2			24:20	
3				
4			South	
5				
6				
7				
8			SBW	
9				
10				
11			no ground with	
12			45 fm: –	

Latitude 6:*34S

Remarks Monday Dec:^{r} 14 – 1767 (7)

Moderate breezes

At 7 anchord in 32 fm: water muddy
S point of Pepper Bay SE½S 2 miles
Princess Isle WSW½W
Caracatora sle NNW¾N –

at six AM got under sail
at 8 Princess Isle from SW to SBW
N:° Point Wellcome Bay S¼E

at noon extreams of P:^{s} Isle from SW to W½S –
N:° Point of Wcome Bay S¼West

EXPLORATION OF THE SOUTH SEAS

Remarks Tuesday Dec:ʳ 15 – 1767   (8)

1				
2				
3				
4			25:00	
5				
6				
7				
8				
9				
10				
11				
12				
1				
2			24:10	
3				
4				
5				
6				
7				
8				
9				
10				
11				
12				

Moderate breezes –

hoisted a boat out & sent her to sound for anchorage under Priss Isle –

at six we ran in and anchored in 40 fm: muddy ground about 3 cables length from the shore –
Java Head S20:00W
Extreams of Pris:ˢ Isle S48:00W 1 mile to N20:00E about two miles –
a reef bearing N21:00E, three cables length –
Watering place N3:00E ☒ of a mile
the highest peak of land N20:00W –
steadied with the kedge anchor

AM sent people onshoar to cut wood & fill water –
served turtle –
fired a gun to alarm the inhabitants who soon after came with turtle & fowles –[497]

employed in clearing the hold –

Lat:ᵈ 6:*41S

---

[497] There is no mention of the warning shot in the PL/FC but the inhabitants bring down "fowles & hog dear, fish & fruit and sold them pretty reasonable." Molineux provides a description of the inhabitants at this point.

Week day	Month Day	Wind	Remarks Onboard his Maj:ˢ Ship Dophin at Princess Island (1) 9
December Wednesday	1767 16		Light airs with some rain employed in getting off wood and water and stowing the hold & over hauling the rigging[498]
Thursday	17	23:40 South 23:40	2 (10) Light airs with some rain employed as before AM Bejamin Lad fell from the main yard into a boat alongside and hurt himself terribly, & bruised two other men in the boat that he fell partly on –[499] fetching wood & water; served turtle –
Friday	18	24:20 South SSW 24:00	3 (11) Moderate breezes with thunder lightning & rain in the night, the latter part fine pleasant weather. People employed in wooding & watering & boats in bringing it onboard –[500]
Saturday	19		4 (12) Fresh breezes and cloudy with thunder lightning and rain latter pleasant weather, employed as before – gave many of the people leave to go onshoar to wash their & their messmates cloaths – served turtle to the ships company – Latitude observed – 6:*40S[501] sent & haul'd the scene, it got foul of the rocks & was torn all to peices – with it they lost some ... –

498 "... the island seems very unwholesome, many complain of an aguish sort the people that had colds recover apace. Served turtle." PL and FC.
499 "... in his fall he struck John Woolridge who I beleive cannot recover; John Clarke was much bruised and broke Jonathon Pullers great toe." PLand FC.
500 "... hauled the scene caught very few fish and had the bad luck to taer the nett all to peices. Served turtle." PL and FC.
501 "The natives have not brought any thing but a few fowles these two days but say they will bring plenty of turtle in the afternoon – however they did not keep their word – served turtle." PL and FC.

Remarks Onboard his Maj:ˢ Ship Dophin Sunday Dec:ᵉʳ 20:ᵗʰ 1767
(5) 13

1				NW
2				
3				
4				25:00
5				
6				
7				
8				
9				
10				
11				
12				
1				
2				
3				23:40
4				
5				
6				West
7				
8				NW –
9				
10				
11			SSW	WBN
12				

Moderate & cloudy – at 4 compeated all our wood and water to – 76 tons –
Ships draught of water –   16: feet 4: inches – forwards
                          14: feet 4 inches – abaft –
weigh'd the kedge & made all ready for sea –

squally with much thunder lightning & rain
at 6 AM weigh'd & made sail & steer'd out close by the wind SSW, SW & WSW, and at 9 the West end of Java bore SBE 1½ miles –
at 10 the West end of Java EBN 3 miles, Java Head SE½S 3 leagues
The extreams of Princess Island from NBW½W to NE½N – the nearest part distance about six miles –

unbent the cables – & stowed the anchors –
served turtle to the ships company –

squally with rain
at noon Java Head bore N43:°00'E distance six leagues
Latitude observed 7:*00 South –⁵⁰²

---

502 "When we sailed from Princess Island we had a larger sick list than we have had for many months – there being sixteen on it – yet five of them were accidents and many hath been in a low week way for near twelve months – by the 1:ᵗ of January our sickness increased to that degree being fevers & fluxes we had no less than forty men down and had buryed three, those that were down in a very low weak condition and quite disponding as the ship hath been so very healthy during the voyage the Surgeons mate very ill and the nurses taken ill a day or two after attending in the sick birth made a very large birth for the sick by removing a number of people from below to the half-deck – hung the sick birth with painted canvas keep it constantly clean wash it with vinegar and fumigate it once or twice a day – yet the sickness increases –

The water we have is well tasted, is constantly ventilated and a loggerhead and red hot quenched in it, the ailing have every assistance that can be given them – not a sick man but hath wine instead of grogg they have saloup every morning for break fast or sago (the Surgeon having laid in a great quantity) and have two days in a weak mutton broth – and others have between a fowle or two given them they have rice sugar and wine and other malt mashed so that at sea I never knew seamen have such refreshment in a sickly ship – indeed I should do the Surgeon

Remarks Monday December 21:ˢᵗ 1767 (14)

1	6	5	SSW	WBN	
2	6	4			Fresh gales & cloudy
3	6	2			At ½ past two Java Head bore NBE½E
4	7			24:00	Java Head in latitude – 6:*46 S
5	7				from London longitude –
6	6				
7	5				
8	4				
9	3	5			
10	3	5	SBW	varia	
11	3	3			In first reefs –
12	2	5			Dark cloudy weather
1	3		SSE		Rain thunder & lightning
2	3	3	SE	SSW	
3	3	2		23:00	
4	3	2			
5	2	5	SBE½E	SWBW	Squally rainy weather –
6	5	4			
7	4	4	South	variable	saw many birds amongst which was a sort of gulls that were
8	4	2			very prettily mottled –
9	4		S½W		
10	3		S½W		
11	3		SEBE	variable	very squally & rainy weather –
12	3		ESE		

Course	Dis:ᵗ	Latitude in	Long. made	MDist:ᵉ
S½W	110	8:35S	01:10W	10W

Java Head bore N½E distance 33 – leagues

---

great injustice if I did not say that he is indefatigable in procuring them necessarys as well as giving them due attendance.

Sick list on the 20:ᵗʰ December	Disease	When and how discharged
May 30:ᵗʰ Fre: Murphy	Rheumatic	
Dec : 11 – Sam: Laurence	Cold	Dec:ʳ 25:ᵗʰ rec:ᵈ
15 Jn: Bowden	Flux	Dec:ʳ 27 DD
Sam Law	Fever	Dec:ʳ 21 rec:
17 – Ben Ladd	Hurt	
Jn: Woolridge	Hurt	Dec:ʳ 22 DD
Jon:ⁿ Pullar	Hurt	
Jn: Clarke	Hurt	
Jer:ʰ Neal	Bill Fever	Dec:ʳ 22:ⁿᵈ rec:ᵈ
M:ʳ Cole	Cold	Dec:ʳ 22:ⁿᵈ rec:ᵈ
Fra: Whitney	Hurt	Dec:ʳ 30: rec:ᵈ
Jn: McCarty	Fever	
Mat: Patisson	Fever	Dec:ʳ 23:ʳᵈ rec:ᵈ
Rob: Johnson	Fever	
Fra: Davies	Fever	Dec:ʳ 29:ᵗʰ rec:ᵈ
Geo: Lewis	Bi: Vomit	Dec:ʳ 28 DD

Remarks Tuesday December 22 1767   (15)

H	K	F	Courses	Winds	Remarks
1	1	3	West	SSW	
2			⎫		Light airs with much rain
3			⎬	Calm	
4	1	2	S½W	WBS	
5			⎫	23:0	Calm with rain & a Southern swell
6			⎬		
7			⎭	Calm	
8					
9	1		SSW	WNW	Thick dirty weather –
10	1				
11	1				
12	1				
1	1	2			Light airs &rainy
2	1	5		23:10	
3	1	5			
4	1	2	SBW	WBS	
5	2		SSW	West	rainy weather
6	3		S½E	WSW	
7	4	4	SEBS		
8	4	4	SE	variable	moderate breezes & rainy weather –
9	2		SEBE		
10				Calm	Read the Articles of War to ships company
11					Light airs & cloudy –
12	1	5	SSE	SW	

Course	Dis:ᵗ	Latitude in	Long. made	M:Dist.
S18:00E	34	9:*07S	00:00W	0

Java Head bore North distance 47 leagues

Remarks Wednesday December 23:ʳᵈ 1767   (16)

1	2		SE	SSW
2	3		ESE	South
3	1		WSW	
	2			
4	4		SWBW	24:00
5	5			
6	5	2	SW	SEBS
7	5	5		
8	6			
9	6			
10	5	4		
11	5			
12	4			
1	4	5		
2	5			
3	4	3		23:45
4	4	3		
5	4	3		
6	4	3	SW½W	
7	6		SWBW	SSE
8	5	5		
9	6			
10	6			
11	6			
12	5			

Light breezes, with a Southern swell

Drizzling rain –

George Lewis Quarter Master departed this life he was taken with the ague and that in so violent a manner that the second cold fit killed him –[503]

lost a log & two lines[504]

squally rainy weather

Fresh gales & cloudy weather –

carpenters repainting the boats –

moderate & cloudy –

Course	Dis	Latitude in	Long. made	M:Dist:ᵉ
S51:00W	104	10:*12 E	1:12West	80

Java Head bore N21:°15'E distance 74 – leagues

---

503 "George Lewis Quarter Master departed this life he was very well two days ago, and seemed not an hour ago to be tolerable but being seized with an ague fit he expired; A very good and usefull man, he being sober and carefull, he spoke both Spanish & Porteguise." PL and FC.
504 "We lose many logs by reason that the lines are rotten." PL and FC.

Remarks Thursday Dec:r 24 1767   (17)

H	K	F	Courses	Winds	Remarks
1	3		SW	SSE	Light breezes and cloudy
2	3	5	SWBW	SBE	
3	2	5	SEBS	SWBS	
4	2	5	SE½S	SSW	squally rainy weather with a swell from the SE –
5	2		SEBE	SBW	
6	4		West	24:08	
7	2		NNW	variable	
8	2		NW		
9	2	3	ESE	South	
10	3	2	WSW		John Woodridge seamen departed this life – he was much bruised on the 17 instant by Benh:n Ladd falling on him from the main yard into the barge[505]
11	4	4			
12	5	3	SWBW	SBE	
1	5	3	SW½W		
2	5	5	WSW½S	23:50	fresh gales & squally with very heavy rain
3	4		WSW	South	
4	2	4			squally dirty rainy weather
5	3		SWBW	SBE	
6	5				
7	4				squally rainy weather
8	5				
9	6				
10	6				
11	5	3			fresh gales & squally –
12	5			SEBS	

Course	Dis	Latitude in	Long. made	M:Dist.ce
S59:°30'W	88	10:°52'S	2:28W	147W –

Java Head bore N31:°30'E distance 96 – leagues

---

505 "... and hath never spoke since." PL and FC.

Remarks Friday December 25 1767 (18)

H	K	F	Courses	Remarks
1	4	3	SW	Fresh gales & hazey cloudy weather
2	5			
3	5		23:20	
4	5			
5	5			
6	5	4		
7	6			
8	6		Ditto	
9	6			
10	6	3		weather
11	6			
12	5		Ditto	
1	5			
2	6			weather with some rain
3	6		2300	
4	6			
5	5	5		
6	5	4		Ditto weather & cloudy –
7	6			
8	8			
9	8	4	SWBW	
10	8			
11	8			fresh gales with a pretty great sea –
12	8	4		

Course	Dis:ᵗ	Latitude in	Long. made	M:Distance
SW	153	12:40 South	4:20 West	255 West

Java Head bore N35:°45'E distance 146 – leagues

Remarks Saturday Decem:ʳ 26 1767   (19)

H	K	F	Courses	Winds	Remarks
1	8		SWBW	SEBS	Fresh gales & cloudy –
2	8				
3	8				
4	8			23:40	
5	8	2			
6	8				
7	7	5			
8	7	2			
9	7				
10	7				
11	7	2			
12	7	2			Fresh gales & cloudy –
1	7				
2	6			23:00	
3	6				
4	6	5			
5	6	4			
6	7	3			
7	8			SSE	The ship makes near three feet water in a watch –
8	8				got four of the foremost guns into the waist –[506]
9	7	3			
10	7				
11	7				Fresh gales & cloudy –
12	7				

Course	Dis:ᵗ	Latitude in	Long. made	M:Dist:ᶜᵉ
SWBW	172	14:12S	6:46 West	398W

Java Head bore N42:°30'E distance 281 – leagues

---

[506] "... the ship makes more than three feet water in a watch, the upper works very open and loose." PL and FC.

Remarks Sunday Dec:ʳ 27 1767   (20)

H	K	F	Courses	Winds	Remarks
1	6		SWBW	SEBS	Fresh gales & cloudy –
2	7	3			
3	8	3	WSW		Opened a cask of pork N 1148, short of 310, 3 peices –
4	7	4		22:10	
5	6	4			
6	7				Fresh gales with a following sea
7	7	2			
8	7			SSE	
9	7	5			
10	8				
11	8	2			
12	7				Fresh gales
1	8				
2	6				
3	7			22:20	Fresh gales
4	7				
5	8				John Bowden seamen departed this life he had been ill for a
6	8				long while of a fever & then of a flux –
7	8				
8	7	2			severall people taken ill of fevers & fluxes and they seem
9	7				much cast down which I believe is owing to the damp air, for
10	7				the ship is very clean & the sick have everything they could
11	7				wish to make use of [507]
12	7	3			

Course	Dis	Latitude in	Long. made	MDist:ᶜᶜ
WBS½S	177	15:*04 South	9:40	566W

Java Head bore N48:50E distance 252 – leagues

---

507 "... & every possible assistance given to the sick yet the number increases." PL and FC.

Remarks Monday Dec:ʳ 28 1767   (21)

H	K	F	Course	Wind	Remarks
1	7		WSW	SSE	Fresh gales & hazey –
2	6				many men taken down daily with fevers and fluxes –[508]
3	6	5			
4	7			21:20	
5	7				variation p:ʳ azumeth 3:57 West
6	7				
7	6	5			Fresh gales & cloudy weather
8	6	3			
9	7				
10	7	4			
11	7	4			
12	7				Fresh gales & cloudy weather
1	7				
2	7			21:20	
3	7				
4	7				Fresh gales & cloudy weather –
5	6	4			
6	6	3			No variation p:ʳ three azumeths –
7	6				
8	7				
9	7				
10	7				
11	7				Fresh gales and hazey weather –
12	8				

Course	Dis	Latitude in	Long. made	MDist:ᶜᵉ
WBS½S	166	15:*56 South	12:24W	722W

Java Head bore N52:°30'E distance 301 leagues

[508] "... cleared away a large birth forward for the sick and removed the people that were well under the quarter deck the sick birth is enclosed with painted canvas, washed once or twice a day with vinager and fumigated to prevent the infection from spreading if possible –." PL and FC.

Remarks Tuesday December 29 1767   (22)

H	K	F			Remarks
1	8				Fresh gales with a great sea[509]
2	8	3			cleared a very large birth for the sick and separated them from
3	8	4			the rest of the ships crew – this birth is kept exceeding clean
4	8	3			and washed every morning with vinegar and fumigated with
5	8	3			pitch &:ce every evening –
6	8	2			Fresh gales with a great sea –
7	7	5			
8	7				
9	6	5			
10	7				
11	6				
12	5				Fresh gales & rainy
1	6				
2	6	3			
3	8				
4	8				Fresh gales & cloudy
5	8				
6	8	3			
7	9				variation p:r azum:th 0:45W
8	8	4			
9	7				
10	7				
11	8				Fresh gales & hazey –
12	8				

Course	Dis:ce	Latitude in	Long. made	MDist:ce
WSW	182	17:*03 South	15:24 West	894W

Java Head bore N55:°30'E distance 363 leagues

---

509 ". . . the ship makes much water." PL and FC.

Remarks Wednesday Dec:ʳ 30 1767   (23)

1	9		WSW		Fresh gales & rainy weather –
2	5				
3	7	2	WBS		Ditto with a great sea –
4	7			21:50	
5	7				
6	7	5			
7	7				Moderate gales & cloudy
8	6				
9	7	2			
10	7	2			
11	7				
12	7				
1	7				
2	6	5		21:5	
3	6	3			
4	6	2			
5	7				
6	8				
7	8				variation p:ʳ amp:ᵈᵉ 1:°00'W
8	8	3			opened a cask of beef N 1338, contents 160 short three peices
9	9	4			
10	9	2			
11	8	3			fresh gales & hazey weather –
12	8				

Course	Dis	Latitude in	Long. made	MDis
WBS	183	17:*40S	18:33 West	1074

Java Head bore N59:°00'E distance 423 leagues

Remarks Thursday December 31 1767   (24)

1	7		WBS	SSE
2	7			
3	7	3		
4	7	4		21:50
5	7	3		
6	7	4		
7	7			
8	6	3		
9	6			
10	6			SE
11	5	3		
12	5			
1	6			
2	6			21:40
3	6			
4	6			
5	6	4		
6	6	5		
7	6	5		
8	7	4		
9	8			
10	8	4		
11	8			
12	8			

Moderate & fine plesant weat:^{r}

variation p:^{r} amplitude 1:45W.

fine pleasant weather –

variation p:^{r} azumeth 1:26 W –
Fresh gales and hazey
bent a new mizen topsail the old being split
washed the ship with vinegar –

fresh gales and hazey with a following sea –

Course	Dis	Latitude in	Long. made	M: Distance
WBS	164	18:*12S	21:33W	1235W

Java Head bore N61:°11'E distance 475 leagues

Remarks Friday January 1:ˢᵗ 1768   (25)

H	K	F	Winds	Course	Remarks
1	6	4	WBS	ESE	Fresh gales & pleasant weather with a following sea
2	6	3			
3	6	4			People still very weak and low & more falling down daily, we
4	6			22:00	have now thirty ill of fevers & fluxes amongst whom is the
5	6	3			Surgeons mate, which makes it very heavy on the Surgeon,
6	7	5			who spared no pains to serve the sick –⁵¹⁰
7	7				
8	7				
9	7	4			
10	7	3			
11	7	4			
12	7				
1	6				
2	6	4		21:50	
3	7	5			
4	7				
5	7				
6	7				
7	7				variation p:ʳ amp:ᵈᵉ & azu:ᵗʰ 2:40W –
8	7				
9	6	3			
10	7				fine pleasant gale and clear weather
11	7	3			
12	7	4		East	

Course	Dis:ᵉ	Latitude in	Long. made	M:Dist
S76:15W	167	18:°*51'S	24:14W	1397

Java Head bore N62:°58'E distance 530 leagues

510 "Washed the ship thro'out with vinegar & fumigated her we are dreadfully pulled down, having now forty sick men in fluxes & fevers and a great many more who are just recovered & can scarcely crawl, the Surgeons mate & all the nurses that attend the sick likewais ill that the Surgeons hath a slavish time of it yet for his credit he gives them great attendance and spares no pains or cost to serve them he gives them saloup or sago (of which he got a great quantity at Batavia) rice sugar & wine malt mash every morning for breakfast & twice a week they have mutton and those that require more nourishment, we give fowles to in that there is nothing that I and the officers have that the sick have not a great share of." PL and FC.

Remarks January 2:ᵈ 1769   (26)

H					Remarks
1	6	5	WBS	ESE	Moderate gales & pleasant weather with a following sea –
2	7				the sick much the same, some few are recovered but more
3	6	5			taken ill than what are recovered, those are very weak and low
4	7			22:00	—
5	7				fresh gales
6	7	3			
7	7				
8	7	2			
9	7	2			
10	8				
11	8				
12	8	2			squally –
1	7				
2	6	4		21:45	
3	6	2			
4	6	5			fresh gales & cloudy –
5	7				variation p:ʳ amplitude 3:10W
6	8				
7	7				
8	7	4			
9	6				
10	7	5			
11	7				
12	7				moderate gales & cloudy –

Course	Dis	Latitude in	Long. made	M:Dist
WBS¼S	170	19:*30S	27:14W	1567 –

Java Head bore N64:15E distance 588 leagues

Remarks Sunday January 3, 1768   (27)

1	6	5	WBS	East
2	6	3		
3	6	4		
4	7			22:10
5	7	4		
6	7	4		
7	7			
8	7	2		
9	7	3		
10	6			
11	7	4		
12	8			EBN
1	7			
2	6			21:55
3	5	4		
4	5	3		ESE
5	6			
6	5	5		
7	5			
8	5			
9	5			
10	5	5		
11	4	5		
12	4	5		ENE

Moderate gales and hazey with a SE swell –[511]

squally with showers

unbent the fore topsail to repair it and bent a new one –

Course	Dis:ᵉ	Latitude in	Long. made	M:Dist
WBS¼S	153	20:*22S	29:48W	1721W

Java Head bore N64:50E distance 640 leagues

---

[511] "Some few of the sick recover but many more fall sick." PL and FC.

Remarks Monday January 4:th 1768   (28)

Light breezes and hazey with a swell from the SE –

variation p:r amplitude 4:00W

variation p:r amplitude 4:00W

H	K	F	Winds	Course
1	4	4	WBS	ENE
2	4	3		
3	4	4		
4	4	3		22:30
5	4	3		
6	4			
7	4	5		
8	3			
9	3	4		
10	3			
11	3			
12	3			
1	3	4		
2	3	4		22:30
3	3	2		
4	2	5		
5	4			
6	4			
7	5			
8	5	4		
9	4	4		
10	4	4		
11	4			
12	4			

Course	Dis:e	Latitude in	Long. made	M:Dist
WBS¼S	95	20:*45S	29:48W	1721W

Java Head bore N65:E distance 672 – leagues

Remarks Tuesday January 5:th 1768   (29)

H	K	F	Course	Wind	
1	5	2	W½S	East	
2	5	5			Moderate breezes and pleasant weather
3	4	2	West		
4	5	4		22:0	
5	5	4			
6	4	3			
7	5	3			
8	5				
9	5				
10	5	1			
11	5	3			
12	5				
1	5				
2	6			21:50	
3	6	2			
4	5	4			
5	5	4			
6	5				
7	6				variation p:r azumeth 5:°39' West
8	6	2			sailmakers and others employed in repairing the sails –
9	7	2			
10	7				read the Articles of War &:ce to the ships company –
11	7	2			fine pleasant weather
12	6	4			

Course	Dis	Latitude in	Long. made	MDis
W¾S	140	21:*36 West	33:55W –	1951W

Java Head bore N66E distance 718 leagues

Remarks Wednesday January 6 1768   (30)

			West	ENE	
1	5				Moderate and pleasant weather –
2	5				
3	5				
4	5				
5	5				Lost between four in the afternoon and midnight four log and
6	5			23:20	seven lines – the lines being all rotten
7	5				killed a sheep for the sick to make them broth – there are now
8	5	2			forty on the list, most of them in a weak low way having been
9	5				torn to peices with fluxes and fevers – the Surgeons Mate still
10	5	3			very ill, makes it fall heavy on the Surgeon whose humanity
11	6				will scarce allow him scarce a single moments rest –[512]
12	6			21:55	
1	6				
2	6				
3	6				
4	6				
5	5	5			
6	6				
7	7	3			variation p:r 3 azumeths – 5:°30'W
8	7	2			reeved a new tiller rope
9	7				
10	6	5			people employed in working up junk
11	6				
12	6	4			fine pleasant weather –

Course	Dis:e	Latitude in	Long. made	MDistance
W¼S	140	21:*11S	36:22 – W	2098W

Java Head bore N67:20E distance 762 leagues

---

[512] "The sick list increased to forty two, and I suppose there are twenty who are recovered from the flux & fevers, who take watch yet who are very weak & low – the Surgeon hath hard work his mate still very ill and his nurses are not above two or three days before they are taken ill – we use all precautions to prevent it spreading but to no purpose – it runs like wild fire having gone thro' half the ships company allready. Lost this night no less than seven log lines they being so rotten." PL and FC.

Remarks Thursday January 7:ᵗʰ 1768   (31)

H	K	F	Wind	Course	Remarks
1	5	4	West	East	Moderate breezes and pleasant weather
2	5	3			
3	5	4			
4	5	3		22:55	
5	5	5			
6	5	5			
7	6	3			
8	6	4		EBN	
9	6	4			
10	6	2			
11	6				
12	6	3			
1	6	5			
2	7			21:55	
3	6	5			
4	7				
5	6	4			variation p:ʳ amplitude – 6:30 West
6	6	3			
7	7				
8	7				
9	6	4			
10	6	3			
11	6	3			moderate gales & hazey, pleasant weather –
12	6	4			

Course	Dis	Latitude in	Long. made	MDistance
W9:0S	150	21:*35S	39:02 – W	2246W

Java Head bore N68:30E distance 811 leagues

Remarks Friday January 8 1768   32

H	K	F			
1	5	5	West	ENE	Moderate and pleasant weather
2	5	3			
3	4	5			
4	4	4		East	
5	4	5		22:45	
6	5				
7	4	4			
8	4				
9	4	2			
10	4				
11	3	4			
12	3	2			
1	2				
2	2	2		22:10	
3	3				
4	3				
5	3	3			
6	3	4		ENE	
7	4				variation p:^{r} amp:^{de} azum:th 9:00W
8	4			NE	
9	4	4			
10	4	2			washed between decks with vinegar
11	5	5			
12	5	2		NNE	

Course	Dis:^{e}	Latitude in	Long. made	MDistance
W½S	98	23:*43S	40:46W	2341W

Java Head bore N 29:°0'E distance 844 leagues

Remarks January 9:th 1768   33

1	5	2	West	North
2	4	5		
3	4			NBW
4	3	5		
5	2			23:0
6	2	2		
7	2	2		
8	2	2		
9	3	4		
10	4	5		
11	4			
12	4	3		
1	5			
2	5			
3	5			23:0
4	5			
5	4	5		
6	5			
7	4	5		
8	5			North
9	6			
10	5	4		
11	6			
12	6	5		

Moderate and pleasant weather
people employed in working up junk –

variation p:^r amplitude 8:46 West:^d

Moderate and cloudy weather

Course	Dis:^e	Latitude in	Long. made	MDis:^e
WBS	106	23:03S	42:36W	2341W

Java Head bore N69:50E distance 879 leagues

Remarks Sunday January 10:th 1768   34

H	K	F	Courses	Winds	Remarks
1	5	3	West	North	Moderate & cloudy –
2	5	4			
3	5				
4	4	4		23:0	Rainy
5	5	5			
6	4	4		NE	Cloudy
7	5				
8	5	3			fresh gales & cloudy
9	6				
10	5				
11	6	3			
12	7			NBE	squally rainy weather
1	6	4			
2	6	2		North	
3	5	5		23:00	
4	5	3			
5	3	5			
6	4	4		NNW	
7	2,2	2,5	WBS	NBW	
8	5				
9	4	3			a great many Tropic birds about the ship
10	5				
11	5				moderate with squalls –
12	3	3		NWBN	

Course	Dis:e	Latitude in	Long. made	MDistance
W74:00S	126	22:*41S	44:47W	2568W

Java Head bore N69:46E distance 921 leagues

Remarks Monday January 11 1768   35

H	K	F	Courses	Winds	
1	1	2	WBS	North	Light airs and cloudy
2	2	2			
3	3				
4	4	3	WSW	NW	
5	4	5	SWBW	NWBW	variation p:ʳ amplitude – 11:00W
6	3			23:0	
7	1		variable		
8			WBS		
9	3			NE	
10	3	5			
11	4	4			
12	4	4			
1	4	2		NNE	
2	4				
3	3	5		22:50	
4	3	5			
5	3				variation p:ʳ amp:ᵈᵉ & azumeth 11:54W
6	3	4			
7	3				opened a cask of beef N
8	2				contents 180 short 13 peices –
9	2			NNW	
10	1	4			Light airs –
11	1	5			
12	1	2			

Course	Dis:ᵉ	Latitude in	Long. made	MDistance
W28:0S	70	23:*14S	45:55W	2630W

Java Head bore N69:40E distance 945 leagues

Remarks Tuesday January 12 1768   36

H	K	F	Course		Remarks
1	1		SW		Light airs and fair weather
2	1				
3	1				
4	1			variable	variation p:ʳ amp:ᵈᵉ 12:46W
5	1		South		
6	1			24:40	
7	1		WBS		
8	1				
9	1	3			
10	1				
11	1				Light breezes and clear weather.
12	2				Joseph Gilson Marine departed this life[513]
1	2	2	NE		
2	3				
3	4	4		24:00	
4	4	3			variation p:ʳ azumeth 12:40W
5	2	5			
6	4	2			moderate breezes with a SW swell
7	4				
8	4				
9	5				
10	5				
11	4	4			moderate breezes –
12	4	3			

Course	Dis:ᵉ	Latitude in	Long. made	MDistance
WSW¼S	63	23:*44S	46:57W	2687W

Java Head bore N69:°27'E distance 966 leagues

---

513 "At midnight Joseph Gilson Marine departed this life, he dyed of a flux we have still a sickly ships company there being thirty people than can scarce crawl and many that are recovering but so weak and low that they cannot do any duty but pick oakham – Gave the Surgeon twenty pounds of soap to wash the sick mens cloaths." PL and FC.

Remarks Wednesday January 13 1768   37

H	K	F	Winds	Course	Remarks
1	3		WBS	North	Light airs and fair weather
2	3				
3	1		WSW		
4	1				
5	1	2	WBS	23:45	
6	1	2			
7	1				
8	1	2			showery
9	2				
10	1				
11	2				
12	1	4			Light airs and fair
1	2			23:40	
2	2	4			
3	4			ENE	
4	4				
5	4				
6	4				variation p:^{r} amplitude 14:00W:^{d}
7	3				
8	3	3			
9	3				employed in fixing new topmost shrouds & back stays –
10	2	4			
11	2	5	SWBW		
12	2		SW	WNW	

Course	Dis:^{e}	Latitude in	Long. made	MDistance
WSW½S	63	24:*06S	48:00W	2744W

Java Head bore N69:32E distance 985 leagues

Remarks Thursday Jan: 14 1768   38

H	K	F	Courses	Winds
1				Calm
2				NE
3	4		WBS	variable
4	3			23:50
5	1	2		
6	1			
7	6		West	SSW
8	6	4	WBS	SBW
9	6			
10	6			
11	5			
12	4	5		
1	4	4		
2	4	2		22:05
3	4	5		
4	4	5		
5	4	3		
6	5	4		
7	5	5		
8	6			
9	4			
10	4	2		
11	3	3		
12	2	2		SBE

Light airs and coudy

opened a cask of pork N 958 – contents 284, short 3 peices

fresh breezes and cloudy weath:^{r}

variation p:^{r} azumeth 14:00

light airs and cloudy

Course	Dis	Latitude in	Long. made	MDis
WSW	100	24:*46S	49:40	2834W

Java Head bore N69:15E distance 1017 leagues

Remarks Friday Jan:ʸ 15 1768   39

H				
1	2		WBS	SBE
2	2	3		
3	2	4		
4	3		SBW	
5	4		24:25	
6	4	2		
7	5	5		
8	5			
9	5	5		South
10	4	5		
11	4	2		
12	5			SSE
1	4			
2	4			23:0
3	4	4		
4	4	4		SE
5	4	2		
6	4			
7	4	3		
8	4	2		
9	4	4		
10	4	4		
11	5			
12	4	4		

Light airs & pleasant weather

variation p:ʳ amplitude 15:30W

Moderate & cloudy weather –

Course	Dis:ᶜ	Latitude in	Long. made	MDistance
S61:0W	100	25:33S	51:17W	2922W

Java Head bore N69:2E distance 1051 leagues

Remarks Saturday Jan:ʸ 16 1768   40

1	3		WBS	East	Rainy dirty weather
2	2	4			
3	3	4			
4	2	4			
5	5	4			
6	4			22:00	
7	2				light airs & heavy rain
8				variable	
9	2		WBS	ESE	
10	1				
11	1				
12	2				
1	6	2			Rainy all night
2	6	4		21:20	
3	4	5			
4	5				
5	6	4		East	fresh gales & cloudy dark weather
6	7				
7	8				
8	9				
9	8				
10	8				
11	8	3			fresh gales & cloudy –
12	8	3		ENE	

Course	Dis:ᵉ	Latitude in	Long. made	MDis:ᶜᶜ
S60:0W	115	26:*30S	53:06 West	3020W

Java Head bore N68:40E distance 1087 leagues

Remarks Sunday January 17 1768   41

1	5	4	WBS	NE	Fresh gales & squally dirty weather
2	7		WSW		
3	6		WBS	NBW	
4	5	4			
5	3				
6	3			22:00	variation p:ʳ amplitude 17:06W
7	3			NE	
8	2	4			moderate and fair
9	5			ENE	
10	4	5			
11	5				
12	4	5		NE	moderate and hazey
1	4				
2	4			22:0	
3	2				
4	3			NWBN	
5	3				
6	3	4	WSW		variation p:ʳ azumeth 17:°44'W
7	3				
8	3	4	SWBW	NWBW	saw an Alcatross —[514]
9	3	3			
10	3	3			Little wind and fair with a swell
11	3				ship ten miles to the Southward
12	2				

Course	Dis:ᵉ	Latitude in	Long. made	MDis:ᶜᵉ
S52:00W	101	27:*32S	54:36 West	3100W

Java Head bore N68:20E distance 1118 leagues–

514 "... and caught some bonettos." PL and FC.

Remarks Monday Jan:ʸ 18 1768   42

H	K	F	Courses	Winds
1	1	3	SWBW	variable
2	1			
3	1		WBS	
4	1			
5	1			23:00
6	1	4		NE
7	1	5		
8	1			EBS
9	1			
10	1			
11	1			
12	1			
1	1	4		
2	1	5		
3	2			SE
4	3			23:00
5	4	5		
6	6			
7	5	3		
8	5			
9	6			
10	6	5		
11	5			
12	6			

Light airs & hot sultry weather –

Pleasant weather –
variation p:ʳ amp:ᵈᵉ – 19:14W

variation p:ʳ azumeth 10:17W

fine breezes & pleasant weather

Course	Dis:ᶜ	Latitude in	Long. made	MDis:ᶜᶜ
S58:0W	68	28*01S	55:32 West	3149W

Java Head bore N68:04E distance 1139 leagues –

Remarks Saturday Jan:ʸ 19 1768   40

1	6		WBS	SE
2	6			
3	6			
4	6		23:0	23:0
5	5			
6	6	4		
7	6			
8	6	3		
9	6	5		
10	6	2		
11	6	2		
12	7			ESE
1	6	5		
2	6	5	22:0	
3	6	5		
4	6	4		
5	6	2		
6	6	8		
7	6	2		
8	6	2		
9	6	2		
10	6	3		
11	8			
12	5	4		

Moderate gales & pleasant weather

saw a great ripling –
variation p:ʳ amp:ᵈᵉ – 20:17W

lost a log & two lines –

variation p:ʳ amp:ᵈᵉ 20:°46'W

Moderate & pleasant weather

Course	Dis	Latitude in	Long. made	MDistance
WSW½S	151	29:*13S	57:50 West	3269

Java Head bore N67:40E distance 1180 leagues –

Remarks Wednesday Jan: 20 1768 (44)

H	K	F	Courses	Winds	
1	6	3	WBS	SE	
2	6			ESE	Moderate and pleasant weather
3	6				
4	6	4			
5	6	5		22:20	
6	7				
7	7	4			hazey
8	7	3			
9	7				
10	7	3			
11	6	5			
12	6	4			
1	5	4			hazey
2	6				
3	5	5		22:10	
4	5	5			
5	5	5			
6	5	5			variation p:r azumeth 21:06W
7	5	4			
8	5	5		East	
9	5	5			
10	5	5			saw an alcatross
11	5				
12	4	4		EBN	

Course	Dis:t	Latitude in	Long. made	MDistance
SWBW	150	30:*32S	60:16W	3396W

Java Head bore N67:10E distance 1227 leagues

Remarks Thursday Jan:ʸ 21 1768   (45)

1	4	WBS	EBN	
2	4			Moderate breezes and pleasant wea:ʳ
3	4			employed in working up yards
4	5			variation p:ʳ azum – 21:40W }
5	4		22:20	amplit – 23:30
6	5			
7	5			
8	5			
9	5			
10	5			
11	5			
12	6		EBS	
1	5			
2	6		22:10	Fresh gales & cloudy –
3	6			
4	6			
5	6			
6	7		ESE	variation p:ʳ amp:ᵈᵉ – 23:30
7	7			variat:ⁿ p:ʳ azumeth – 23:16
8	6			by another compass – 23:33
9	6			
10	6			
11	6			
12	6			moderate gales & cloudy –

Course	Dis:ᵗ	Latitude in	Long. made	MDistance
NWBW	148	31:*51S	62:36W	3516W

Java Head bore N66:°10'E distance 1271 leagues –

Remarks Friday Jan:ʸ 22 1768   46

H	K	F	Courses	Winds
1	5	4	WBS	ESE
2	5	3	WBN	
3	5	4		
4	5	3		23:0
5	6	5		
6	6	5		
7	6	4		
8	6	5		
9	6	3		
10	6			
11	5	4		
12	5	2		
1	5	4		22:20
2	6	2		
3	6			
4	5	4		
5	5	5		
6	5	4		
7	5	4		
8	6			
9	6	5		
10	6	4		
11	6			
12	6			EBS

Moderate and cloudy weather.

showery & hazey weather

Course	Dis:ᵗ	Latitude in	Long. made	MDistance
W76:0S	144	32:*26S	65:20W –	3656

Java Head bore N67:24E distance 1320 leagues

Remarks Saturday January 23 1768   47

1	6	6	WBN	EBS	Moderate gales & cloudy
2	6	5			
3	6	4			
4	7	2			fresh gales & hazey, with a pretty great sea following us
5	7			22:00	
6	7	4			
7	7	3			
8	7				
9	7	4			
10	7	3			
11	7	5			
12	7	4			Fresh gales carried away the main top gallant yard in the
1	7	3			slings by the strap of the main topsail tye block giving way –
2	7				
3	7	4		21:00	
4	7	3		East	
5	7				
6	7	4			got up the spritsail topsail yard for a main top gallant yard
7	7				carpenters making a new one & the sailmakers repairing the
8	7				sail
9	7	2			
10	7	3			
11	7	3			a fresh gale & hazey weather –
12	7	5			

Course	Dis	Latitude in	Long. made	MDis
WBS	174	33:00S	68:44W –	3826W

Java Head bore N67:°45'E distance 1379 leag:[s]

Remarks Sunday January 24 1768   48

H	K	F	Winds	Remarks
1	8		East	fresh gales & dirty weather
2	8			
3	8	4		Alcatrosses about the ship –
4	8	5		
5	8	4	20:40	
6	8			
7	8	3		
8	6	3		
9	9			Strong gales with a great sea
10	9	5		
11	10			
12	10			
1	9			
2	8	4		
3	8	4	20:50	
4	9		ENE	
5	10	2		Blows very hard got down the top gallant mast split the main topsail all to peices.
6	9	2		
7	7			very heavy gale of wind, brought the ship too under the lower stay sails and mizen –[515]
8	7			
9	7			
10	4	up	WBN off	very hard gales & a dismal sea the ship makes much water and no one place dry in her which makes it bad for the sick –
11			SWBW	
12				

Course	Dis	Latitude in	Long. made	M:Dist:
WBS	180	33:°40'S –	72:17W	4003W

Java Head bore N68:00E distance 1442 leag:ˢ

---

[515] "... the sea broke much over the ship the starboard rudder chain broke and severall links were lost; brought the ship too under the lower stay sails – many of the booms washed away from the larboard chains." PL and FC.

Remarks Monday January 25 1768   49

1		up West	off SW	Hard gales with a very great sea from the NW –
2		WSW	NW	
3	2			more moderate made sails of topsails
4	2	1	21:00	saw severall butterflys –
5	4		NWBW	
6	4	3	SWBW	West
7	4	4	SSW	
8	3	2		
9	3		SBW	WBS
10	3	3		
11	3			
12	2	4	South	WSW
1	2	4			fine clear weather, got up top gall:^{t} masts – a NW swell –
2	2				a great number of Alcatrosses & Sheerwaters about the ship –
3	2		SBW		
4	2	5	NWBN	WBS	opened a cask of beef – N1329: con:^{t} 160, short 2
5	1		NNW	West	
6	1				bent a new main topmast stay sail
7					sailmakers employed in repairing sails
8				20:00	severall alcatrosses about the ship –
9					aired all the sails, cleaned the ship below & washed with
10				Calm	vinegar^{516}
11					ships head all round the compass
12					a great swell from the WNW –^{517}

Course	Dis	Latitude in	Long. made	MDis:^{t}
S¾W	45	34:*24S –	72:24 W –	4009 –

Java Head bore N67:34E distance 1452 leagues

516 ". . . dryed all the sick mens bedding" PL and FC.
517 ". . . everyone that handle a needle employed in repairing sails which are now in a very tattered condition." PL and FC.

Remarks Tuesday January 26 1768   50

1				calm and clear weather a NW swell
2				
3				ships head all round the compass
4		ships	head	variation p:^{r} az & amp:^{de} 24:00W
5				from WNW to West
6				
7				
8				
9				
10		ships	head	West
11				
12				
1				
2		ships	head	from WSW to WNW
3				
4			20:00	
5				
6				variation p:^{r} amp:^{de} — 25:15W
7				p:^{r} 3 azum:th 25:10W
8				
9				
10				
11				calm & cloudy
12				

Course	Dis	Latitude in	Long. made	MDis:^{t}
WNW	20	34:*16S –	72:40W –	4027W

Java Head bore N67:°38'E distance 1456 leagues

Remarks Wednesday January 27 1768   51

H	K	F	Course	Dis:ᵉ	
1		3	WBN		
2		4			
3	1	3			
4	1	3		20:20	
5	2				
6	2				
7	1	3			
8	2	3			
9	2				
10	1	3			
11	1				
12					
1					
2				20:00	
3				calm	
4					
5	1		WBN	SBW	
6	1	3			
7	1				
8	1				
9	1				
10	1	5			
11	2	2			
12	2				

Light airs and fair weather –
sailmakers employed in repairing the sails[519]

variation   p:ʳ azumeth – 23:36W
            amplitude   – 24:00

at 5 had an observation of the dis of ☽ from sun & found the ship in the longitude of 323:13 West from London

ships head from West to WNW

variation p:ʳ amp:ᵈᵉ 23:30 Westerly

Light airs & fair –

Course	Dis:ᵉ	Latitude in	Long. made	MDis:ᵉ
WBN	15	34:*13S –	73:00W –	4044

Java Head bore N67E distance 1462 leagues

Remarks Thursday January 28 1768 –   52

H	K	F	Courses	Winds	Remarks
1	2		WBN	NE	Light breezes sailmakers employed in repairing sails
2	2				
3	2	4			Opened a cask of beef N 1147 contents 304 –
4	2	2			variation p:^{r} azumeth – 23:26W –
5	2	4			amplitude – 23:43
6	3	2			
7	3	5		19:00	
8	4			ENE	
9	5	3			
10	6				
11	6	3			
12	6	4		NE	fresh gales & hazey weather –
1	6	5			
2	7	2			
3	8	2		19:10	
4	8	3			
5	8	4		NBE	
6	8	4			
7	5 4		WNW		variation p:^{r} 4 azum:th – 25:15W –
8	9	3			
9	10				got down the top gallant yards –
10	9	3			
11	9				fresh gales with a pretty great sea
12	9				

Course	Dis	Latitude in	Long. made	MDistance
W10:0S	150	34:*38S –	76:00W –	4192W

Java Head bore N68:21E distance 1511 leagues

Remarks Friday January 29 1768 –   52

H	K	F	Courses	Winds	Remarks
1	8	5	WNW	NNE	very fresh gales with a sea and hazey weather
2	8	3			
3	8				reeved a new tiler rope
4	7	5			sounded twice with 140 fm: of line no ground –
5	7	2			variation p:r amp:de 23:19W –
6	7	4			
7	6			21:30	
8	5				
9	5	2		North	
10	5				
11	4	3	WSW		
12	3	4		NW	
1	2		SWBS		
2	6		NWBW		
3	7		WNW	SSW	Fresh gales & hazey with a very great head sea –
4	6	4	SWBS	21:30	
5	5				
6	5		WNW ½W	SBW	
7	6				
8	7		WBN		
9	6	4			
10	6	5			fresh gales & cloudy weather
11	6				
12	6				

Course	Dis:e	Latitude in	Long. made	M:Distance
W½S	148	34:*50S –	78:56W –	4336W

Java Head bore N68:53E distance 1559 leag:s

Remarks Saturday January 30 1768   53

H	K	F	Courses	Winds	Remarks
1	6	4	WBW	South	fresh gales got up top gallant yards
2	6				sailmakers employed in repairing the sails[518]
3	6				
4	7			SE	variation p:ʳ azumeth 24:20W
5	7	3			amplitude 25:10
6	7			19:0	
7	6	2			sounded no ground with 14 fathoms
8	7	5		ESE	
9	5				
10	7				
11	7				
12	7			East	sounded with 140 fm: no ground –
1	7				
2	7				
3	7				
4	8			ENE	variation p:ʳ azumeth 24:14 Westerly
5	8	5			amplitude 22:57
6	8			17:55	
7	8				
8	8	5	NW		fresh gales with a pretty great sea
9	9	3			carryed away the jib stay –
10	9	3			bent the bower cables –
11	10				
12	11				

Course	Dis	Latitude in	Long. made	MDistance
W3:04S	180	34:*40S –	82:36W –	4516W

Java Head bore N69:°20'E distance 1620 leagues

---

518 "Sailmakers still employed in repairing the sails which are almost worn out, as is all our running rigging." PL and FC.

Remarks Sunday January 31 1768 –   54

1	9	4	NW	NE
2	9			
3	9	5		
4	10			
5	9	2		20
6	9	2		
7	8		WNW	
8	6			
9	6	5		
10	2			
11				
12				
1			up SSE	of SSW
2				
3				19:10
4				
5	3			
6	4		NWBW	NBE
7	3		SW	WNW
8	6		NNE½E	NWBN
9	2		NEBN	
10	6		SW½S	
11	5			
12	5		SW	WNW

Course	Dist:ce	Latitude in	Long. made	MDis:
West	80	34:*40S –	84:16W –	4596W

fresh gales & hazey, at one the water changed colour so believe we are in soundings –
many Gannets Sheerwaters, Pittorells, Alcatrosses & other birds about the ship
variat:^{n} 23:59W
at six saw the land bearing from NBW to NBE 7 or 8 leagues – close reeft topsails, sounded 50 fathoms coarse grey sand & shells –
at 10 o clock saw two lights in the NNE – brought too –
sounded 60 fathoms coarse gravell

60 fm: […] a midships –

62 fm: –
at 4 sounded 64 fm: made sail

crossed a great ripling
saw great flocks of Gannetts & Sheerwaters with abundance of seals & porpoises –
variation – by 5 az:th – 20:54W
moderate & hazey weather –

Java Head bore N70:°16'E distance 1654 leagues –

Remarks Monday Febr:ʸ 1 1768 – 55

H	K	F	Courses	Winds
1	3	4	SW½W	NWBW
2	3	2	SWBW	
3	3		SW½S	
4	4		NEBN	NWBN
5	5		NNE	
6	4		NNW	20:30
7	2		SSW	
8	2			
9	1	5	WBS	NWBN
10	1	5		
11	2	2	West	NBW
12	2	3	WSW½W	
1	3	3	SWBW	
2	5		SW½S	
3	5		SWBS	
4	3			19:40
5	2		SBW	
6	2		NW	WSW
7	3			
8	3			
9	3	3		
10	3	4		
11	4		NW	
12	4		NW½N	

Course	Dis	Latitude in	Long. made	MDist
S27:00W	32	35:*08S –	84:30	4612W

Moderate & hazey sounded no ground with 140 fathoms of line

fresh gales & squally close reeft the topsails & down the top gallant yards –
sounded 65 fathoms fine grey sand –

at midnight fresh gales with dirty weather and a great Western sea –
at 9 it blew very hard & the ship labours much[519] sounded with 100 no ground – handed the fore topsail –

fresh gales lightning in the NE

moderate

moderate gales & cloudy
The ship by observation 20 miles to the Southward of her dead reckoning –

---

519 ". . . and makes more water than usual." PL and FC.

Remarks Tuesday Febr:ʸ 2 1768 –   (56)

H	K	F	Courses	
1	1	3	NNW	
2	4		NNE	
3	6	4		
4	6	3		
5	6			18:00
6	4			
7	3			
8				
9	2		WNW	SWBW
10	2	2		
11	2		West	
12	1	4		SBW
1	2			
2	2			SE
3	1			
4	1			17:30
5	2			East
6	2		WBN	
7	3			
8	3	4		
9	3			
10	2			
11	3			
12	3			

moderate & cloudy
variation p:ʳ amplitude 22:30W
at ½ past six sounded 63 fm: sand & shells saw the land in the WNW –
at midnight & at 4 AM sounded 62 fm: grey sand with shells –
at daylight saw the land from NEBN to NWBW distance from the nearest shore eight or nine leagues

sounded 64 fm: fine bright sand

The extreams of the land from the mast head from NWBN to NEBE distance of shore 9 or ten leagues –

Course	Dis	Latitude in	Long. made	MDis:ᵗ
NW½W	49	34:*38S –	85:°17'W	4650W

Remarks Wednesday Febr:ʸ 3 1768 –   (57)

H	K	F	Courses	Winds
1	4		NWBW	ESE
2	5	4		SEBE
3	6			
4	6			18:00
5	5	5		
6	6	3	NWBN	EBS
7	6	5		
8	6			
9				
10			up SSE	of SSW
11				
12			up SSE	of SSW
1				
2			up NE	of NBW
3				
4				
5	2		NW	SE
6	3			
7	3		NW½W	
8	3			18:00
9	3	3	WNW	
10	4	2		
11	5	4	WBN½N	
12	6	5	W½S	

Course	Dis	Latitude in	Long. made	MDistance
W2:0S	86	34:*40S	87:02W –	4736W

fine breezes & pleasnt weather –
The extreams of the land off the deck from NW½W (a low point) to NNE
a low point at the same time some remarkable hills in land NNW – & further in land mountainous –
at 4 tho the extreams of the land from NWBW to NE –

at 8 brought to had all night 38 to 40 fm: water fine grey sand

at 8 AM the land bore from East to WBW½W distance from the nearest shore – four miles –
variation – p:ʳ az & amp:ᵈᵉ 21:45W

at noon the land bore from E½S to NWBW – distance from the nearest shore – four miles –

Remarks Thursday Feb:ʸ 4:ᵗʰ 1768 (58)

1	9		W½S	SEBS	
2	8	4	WBS		finr gale & pleasant weather –
3	8	4	WSW		at 4 Cape Legullas bore EBN 5 or 6 leagues – the Westermost
4	8				land in sight NNW½W distance ten leagues – of shore about
5	7		West	18:00	two leagues –
6	3	4	WNW		variation p:ʳ azum:ᵗʰ 20:10W
	2	3			amp 21:0
7	3	4			at midnight sounded 60 fathoms coarse rocky ground –
8	3	3			
9	3	2			
10	3	4			Cape Falso NBE 5 leagues
11	3	3			variation 21:00W
12	3				at 8 Cape Falso NNE½E 4 leagues –
1	2				
2	1				
3	1				
4				17:00	
5	5		NW		
6	5		NW½W	SW	
7	3	3			
8	3				
	2				at noon Cape Falso N76:0E dis 3 leagues
9	1		NW		Pitch of Cape of Good Hope N19:00E 3 lea:ˢ
10	3				Westermost land of the Cape North[520]
11	2	5			
12	3	2			

Course	Dis	Latitude in	Long. made	MDis
W2:00N		102 34:*38 South	89:04W	4836W

---

520 "The current here sets about NWBW about 1 knot." PL and FC.

Remarks Friday February 5 1768[47] (59)

1	3		NNW	SWBW	
2	3	3			
3	4	3			
4	4	5			
5	5	2	N½W	South	
6	5	5	NBE	SBE	
7	5		NBE½E		
8			up SW	of WBN	
9	1		ESE	17:00	
10	2				
11	1	5	EBS		
12	1	2			
1					
2		up	ESE	off EBN	
3					
4					
5				19:40	
6					
7					
8					
9					
10					
11					
12					

Moderate, at two a rock to the Southward of the Cape Land in one with a bluff head in False Bay N76:00E, the extreams of the Cape Land from N9:00E to N72:00E

at six the extreams of the Cape Land from SSE to NE½E the Sugar Loaf Peek NE½N distance off shore three miles –

at 8 brought too, sounded 60 fm: shells & sand – kept the ship off & on till day light when the Sugar Loaf bore SEBE½E distance six or seven miles – 63 fm: water

made sail light airs – hoisted the boats out and towed the ship in between Penguin Island & the South shore, at 8 in 31 fm: rocky Penguin Island NE½N 3 miles, there is a great reef runs off the S:°side of this island, the chanell from the islands to the main about 3 miles broad in towing into Table Bay had soundings 22 fathoms, to 15, 10 & 7 – where we anchored at ten o'clock and moord Windy Hill S141:00W the extreams of the Table Hill from S25:°W to SW, Sugar Loaf Hill S71:°00W Green Point, N50:00W Penguin N10:00W distance from the shore one mile, sent to the Governor to let him know of our arrival & desire leave to get refreshments that I would salute him if he returned an equal number of guns which he agreed to.[521] found riding here a Commodore with fifteen sail of East India ships belonging to the Dutch a French India ship and the Adm: Watson Capt:ⁿ Griffin English East Indiaman[522]

---

[521] "... the officer returned & told me that the Governor received him very civilly that we were welcome to every refreshment and assistance the Cape afforded and that he would return the salute with the same number he was saluted with." PL and FC.

[522] "... East India packett bound for Bengall." PL and FC.

469

Week day	Month Day	Wind	Remarks Onboard His Majestys Ship Dophin –
Febr:y Saturday	1768 6	19:00 variable 17:00	Fresh gales & hazey latter moderate and clear Saluted the Governor with 13 guns, he returned 13 guns The Adm:l Watson saluted with 9 Guns we returned 7[523] AM served fresh mutton & greens to the ships company which we continued to do every day either mutton or beef all the time we lay here –
Sunday	7	21:35 Ditto 22:00	Sent the Surgeon to hire quarters for the sick but could get none under two shillings a day, and if any of them got the small pox there would be an extraordinary price according to the degree of the disease (the small pox was all over the town) finding that to be the case and half the ships company never had them I applied to the Governor for leave to erect tents on the point under the Lyons Rump, to take observations and for our people to walk on shore there & the Governor permitted it to be so – Sent the Surgeon onshoar with the sick & two Midshipmen to look after them nor suffer them to go the town and to bring the sick off between four and six at night.[524] Unbent the sails struck yards & topmast & began to overhaul the rigging. Sailmakers mending sails armourer repairing iron work carpenters caulking boats in filling & bringing of water

[523] The *Dolphin* returned nine guns to the Admiral Watson's salute of 11 guns according to the PL and the FC then "at two the French India ship saluted with 9 guns, returned 7. Got of mutton for the ships company with plenty of greens. Served mutton or beef and greens to the ships company at one pound a man in broth every day whilst we lay here. I being very ill was put onshoar and carried up the country about eight miles where I continued all the time we lay there and went of rather worse than I came onshoar." PL and FC.

[524] "Here I ordered tents to be erected and the Surgeon or his mate to attend with proper officers and not suffer any to straggle to the town, nor any kind of liquor to be brought there, they went from the ship early with their provisions & fixing returned between four and six for many that were low and weak, I directed the Surgeon to purchase such extra provisions as he judged was proper for them, particularly milk tho' tis excessive dear, there was only two that did not go onshoar the first day; the men seemed greatly refreshed only by being onshoar a few hours: we did likewais take severall observations of the longitude of the tent." PL and FC.

W:day	Day	Wind	Remarks –
Fbr: 1768 Monday	8	22:00 S:°erly 21:00	Little wind & clear, punished Michael Kann[525] seaman for drunkenness. Employed as before –
Tuesday	9	21:40 Variable 21:00	Fine pleasant weather, sailed hence the Adm:^{l} Watson Indiaman who saluted with 9 guns returned 7. Employed as before
Wednesday	10	22:55 D° 21:30	Ditto weather, black the yards, mast head & rigging carpenters, sailmakers smiths, &:^{ce} employed as before having filled great part of our water, and got the heavy work under, gave twenty men leave to go onshore in the morning, & to come of again at night, exclusive of the sick with order not to go into any house where the small pox was and whilst they kept to their time & behaved well they should have that liberty continued to them whilst we lay here.[526]
Thursday	11		Ditto weather, employed as before, our sick people recover fast and have kept themselves very orderly, the Midshipmen prevent any of the inhabitants coming to them it being two miles from the town & an open pleasant spot –

---

525 Richard Kann according to the PL and FC.

526 "Gave twenty men leave to go onshore at the town that were past the smallpox those that were not were landed at a distance with orders not to go into the country and return to the boat in the evening which they very punctually obeyed, for which reason I ordered the liberty to be continued to them while we stayed by which means our people look (and are) healthyer than they did when we left England, except two or three who seem to be in a decline –." PL and FC.

W:day	M: Day	Wind	Remarks –
February 1768 Friday	12	20:00 SSE 19:00 SSW	Fine pleasant weather, every one employed as yesterday carpenters, smiths, sailmakers, armourer &:ᶜᵉ the sick & liberty men, all the company begin to look wholesome, to what they did on our arrival
Saturday	13	20:10 South	Pleasant weather, employed as before
Sunday	14	20:00 SSE 20:50 SSW 19:10	Fresh gales & clear weather, employed as before
Monday	15	20:00 South 19:0	Fresh gales & hazey latter strong gales & clear, the French ship parted her best bower & drove near a mile before she brought up – people employ'd as usuall –[527]
Tuesday	16	19:50 SSE SW 19:15	fresh gales & clear latter moderate & pleasant at 3 PM anchor'd here & saluted with 9 guns, returned 7 the Norfolk India ship from Bengall for Europe employed as before
Wednesday	17	20:0 SE 19:20	Fresh gales and hazey. Employed as before.
Thursday	18	19:30 Variable 19:00	Moderate & clear weather scraped the masts and sides & paid them with varnish of pine, got up the still & cleaned it, to make fresh water – The artificers employed as before, sick and liberty men onshoar as usuall –

[527] "... sick & liberty men keep their time well & behave likewais so." PL and FC.

W:day	M: Day	Wind	Remarks –
February 1768 Friday	19	20:00 Variable 18:55	Moderate & thick hazey weather, at 5 AM charged the still with 56 gallons of salt water and lighted the fire under it at 7 it ran and so continued for five hours and thirteen minutes; when we put out the fire drew of thirty six gallons wine measures good & wholesome fresh water – NB after 42 gallons Pursers measure was drawn off there remained salt water in the still thirteen gallons & two quarts – 4⊠ gallons 55 quarts – Expended in the experiment wood nine pound coles sixty nine pounds –[528] People employed as before
Saturday	20	19:40 Ditto 19:00	Moderate hazey employed as yesterday[529]
Sunday	21	19:30 NW West 18:40	Clear weather employed in compleating the ship and getting ready for sea. got of part of our bread – Liberty men & sick as before – the people recover fast only a few that have been long ill do not mend so fast as we could wish
Monday	22	19:50 NW West South 18:42	Foggy weather employed as before
Tuesday	23	19:35 Variable 18:00	Mod:^{e} weather PM anchor'd here Osterly Indiaman from China she saluted with 9 returned 7 guns, a Dutch ship from Holland anchor'd here, employed as before
Wednesday	24	19:50 South SSE 19:00	Got up yards & topmast, bent the fore sail topsails & stay sails, sailed hence the Norfolk India Man for Europe – employed variously – She saluted with 9 guns returned –

[528] "The water was perfectly sweet and free from any ill taste whatever and from our former tryalls we are certain that it is very wholesome, we made this tryall to show the India captains and officers that it was possible to procure good and wholesome water at sea and that if they begin in season it would perhaps be the means of saving many lives; for I think by being able to allow plenty of water not only for drink but for boiling chouder, lobs scouse or any other provisions they have or even tea or coffee; to seamen who go long voyages and that cheifly in warm climates is conducive to their health, I speak this from experience that during the voyage I never put the people to an allowance of water, however did not allow it to be taken away but by order of the Officer of the Watch who gave to such as brought their tea fish or other provisions a propoer quantity for dressing it we saved at all times rain water and used it with the same frugality we did the other and did not use the still but when we were reduced to forty five tons (but for experiment) which hapned seldom during the voyage." PL and FC.

[529] "Employed in reeving new rigging and fixing all new the old braces lifts &:^{ce} being totally unfit for any service scarce fit for rounding, this rigging, with some canvass & some other stores we purchased onshoar – at a much less price than at Batavia." PL and FC.

W:day	M: Day	Wind	Remarks –
February 1768 Thursday	25	18:40 South SE 19:30	Fresh gales & cloudy later moderate & clear – people employed in different manner, half on shoar on liberty which hath perfectly recovered them except two who seem to be consumptive – they have had beef mutton and greens as much as they could eat every day –
Friday	26	20:00 SSE 19:30	Moderate & fine pleasant weather, the carpenters finished the caulking the ships, employed as before
Saturday	27	19:40 Variable 19:00	Compleated our water bread and most other things Employed in receiving new running of all kinds the old being quite worn out we purchased new here as we did canvass and other stores: received a number of live sheep & some straw – Read the Articles of War &:^{ce} –[530]
Sunday	28	18:40 Variable 18:40	Light airs & clear got the ship ready for the sea draught of water forward 16 feet; aft 14 feet 4 inches, sailed from hence a large Dutch ship –
Monday	29	20:10 Variable 19:00	Moderate & cloudy foggy rainy weather the Dutch fleet weigh'd and ran out into the middle of the bay in readiness for a fair wind – we unmoord and lay at single anchor in readiness for sailing as soon as we can get a wind – put an end to going on shoar –
March 1768 Tuesday	1	20:00 Variable 19:00	Light airs & foggy latter clear – got of a tun of water to keep the ship compleat stowed the sheet anchor & unbent the cable –

[530] ". . . at the same time I came onboard and got all ready for sailing, unmoord and lay at single anchor in readiness." PL and FC.

W:day	M: Day	Wind	Remarks –
March Wednesday	1768 2	19:30 Variable 18:57	Most part of these 24 hours calm & foggy – Kept our water compleat
Thursday	3	19:55 NW Calm SW Calm	Moderate breezes & foggy at 5 it clear'd away and sprung up a light breeze, weigh'd & saluted the governor with 13 guns, who returned the same number, the Osterly Indiaman saluted us with 9 guns we returned 7 guns, at 6 it fell calm anchord At noon anchor'd here a French Indiaman –[531]
Friday	4	20:00 Variable 19:10	Light airs and clear weather found the variation here to be by many observations 19:30 Westerly The latitude – 34:*04S & 34:*02 – South The longitude by severall observations both onshoar & onboard by Doctor Masculins method – 342:°04 West from London – onboard 360 17:54 East from London – Onshoar under a small fort near the Lyons Rump Observed – 342:00 West from London 360 True long:^{de} in 18:00 East from London[532]

---

531 From "Mauritias." PL and FC.
532 "Longitude of Table Bay observed – 34:°02'S°
    Longitude of Table Bay East from Greenwich observed – 18:08E
    Variation of the compass 19:30W." PL and FC.

Remarks Saturday March 5:th 1768   1

H	K	F	Wind	Course
1				Variable
2				
3				
4			NNW	SSE
5	3			
6	2			
7				20:20
8			Variable	
9				
10	6	4	NWBN	SW
11	6	5		SSW
12	6	5		
1	6	3		
2	6	4		
3	6	4		
4	7			19:00
5	7			
6	6	4		
7	5			
8	5			
9	4	5		
10	4			
11	4			
12	5	3		SW

Light airs –
variation p:r amp:de 19:°20' Westerly
at 4 weigh'd and made sail the Osterly Indiaman with us
at ½ past 7 the middle of Penguin Island in one with the middle of the Table Mountain South –

the NW point of Cape Land WSW½W about four leagues –
Coney island N½W
the Dutch fleet got under sail for Europe
at midnight the light on the middle of Penguin Island SSE three mile

variation p:r ampl:de 20:°00'W
the best bower cable much rubbed four fathom from the anchor, cut it off

The Osterly Indiaman a stern –
Moderate & clear weather –
had onboard 79 tons of Water –

Course	Dis:e	Latitude in	Long. made	M: Distance
N46:0W	68	32:*55S	1:27 West	

The Cape of Good hope bore S46:0E Dis:ce 39 leag:s

Remarks Sunday March 6:th 1768 2

1	6		NWBN	SWBW
2	6	3		
3	6	5		
4	7			
5	7			
6	6	5		19:30
7	6	3		
8	6	3		
9	5	4		
10	4	5		
11	5			
12	5	3		
1	4			
2	3	5		
3	4	3		
4	5	2		19:00
5	5	4		
6	7			
7	7			
8	6	4		
9	5	4		
10	5			
11	4	2		
12	4			SSW

Moderate & clear

variation p:^r   azu –   18:09
                amp:^{de} 18:33W

variation p:^r   amp:^{de} 19:02
                azum   18:54W

The Osterly near us –
fine pleasant weather

Course	Dis:^e	Latitude in	Long. made	M: Dis:^e
N51:W	136	31:*26S	3:32W	

The Cape bore S49:0E Distance 79 leagues

Remarks Monday March 7   1768   3

1	5		NWBN	SW
2	4			
3	5			
4	6		NNW½W	
5	6	4		20:00
6	6	3		
7	6	4		
8	6	5		
9	7	2		
10	7	4		
11	6	4		
12	7	4		SSW
1	7			
2	7			
3	6	4		SSE
4	6			19:90
5	5	4		
6	5	5		
7	5			
8	7	3		
9	6			
10	7			
11	6	4		
12	7			

Moderate &pleasant weather lost company with the Osterly

variation p:ʳ az: – 17:56 West

hazey –

drizling rain

by observation found the ship eight miles to the North of dead reckoning

fresh gales & hazey

Course	Dis:ᵉ	Latitude in	Long. made	M: Dis:ᵉ
N43:00W	154	29:*33S	5:34W	

The Cape bore S46:36E Distance 130 leagues

478

Remarks Tuesday March 8 1768   4

H	K	F	Courses	Winds	
1	7	4	NNW½W	SSE	
2	7	2			
3	7	4			
4	8				
5	8	2			
6	9			19:0	
7	8	4			
8	8	5			
9	8	5			
10	8	4			
11	8	2			
12	8	4			
1	9				
2	9	2			
3	8	3			
4	8	5		20:00	
5	8	3			
6	7	5			
7	7	4			
8	8				
9	8	4			
10	8				
11	8				
12	7	4			

Fresh gales & hazey with a great sea,
Got the two foremost guns aft to ease the ship –
Split the fore topmast & top gallant steering sails, sailmakers employed in repairing them –

fresh gales & hazey –

Course	Dis:ᵉ	Latitude in	Long. made	M: Dis:ᵉ
N47:00W	193	27:*21S	8:41W	

The Cape bore S46:40E Distance 194 leagues

Remarks Wednesday March 9 1768   5

1	6				Moderate gales & pleasant weather –
2	6	3	NNW½W	SSE	Read the Articles of War &:^{ce}
3	6	5			variation p:^r azumeth 16:24W
4	6	3			
5	6	5		20:00	
6	6	5			
7	7	4			
8	6				
9	6	5			
10	7	5			
11	7				
12	7				Fresh gales & close hazey weather
1	7	2			
2	7	3			
3	8	3			
4	7			19:10	opened a cask of beef N 1264 – contents 170 pieces –⁵³³
5	8	5			variation by 3 azumeth 16:34W
6	7				
7	7	5			
8	6			SE	
9	6	3			
10	7	5			
11	7	2			fresh gales & cloudy –
12	7			SBW	

Course	Dis:^e	Latitude in	Long. made	M: Dis:^e
N46:00W	162	25:*29S	10:23W	

The Cape bore S46:31E Distance 248 leagues

---

533 Noted in the PL and the FC on the 11th March 1768.

Remarks Thursday March 10 – 1768 6

H	K	F	Courses	Winds	Remarks
1	7		NNWW	South	Moderate gales & cloudy –
2	7				
3	7				
4	7				variation p:r az: 15:54W
5	7	3	NWBN		
6	6	2		20:10	
7	6	2			
8	7				
9	7				
10	7				
11	7				
12	7				
1	7				
2	7				
3	7				
4	7			South	
5				19:10	
6					variation p: azu:h 16:00W
7					
8				SSE	
9					
10					
11				SEBE	fresh gales & hazey –
12				SE	

Course	Dis:c	Latitude in	Long. made	M: Dis:c
N47:00W	170	23:*38S	12:40W	

The Cape bore S46:35E Distance 305 leagues

Remarks Friday March 11 – 1768   7

1	6	3	WBW	SBE	Moderate gales & cloudy
2	6	5			
3	6	3			variation by four azum: 15:24W
4	6	5			
5	6	5			
6	6	4		2000	
7	7				
8	6	5		SE	
9	6	2			
10	7				
11	7				
12	7	2			Moderate gales & cloudy –
1	7	3			
2	7	3			
3	8				
4	7	5		19:00	
5	8				
6	7	5			
7	7				
8	6	3			
9	6	5			
10	7	2			
11	.7				Moderate and fair[534]
12		7		SEBE	

Course	Dis:^{e}	Latitude in	Long. made	M: Dis:^{e}
N49:00W	167	21:*44 S	14:56W	

The Cape bore S47:00E Distance 359 leag:^{s}

---

[534] "This day finished serving fresh mutton; opened a cask of beef N:°1264 contents 170 peices." PL and FC.

Remarks Saturday March 12 – 1768 8

H	K	F	Courses	Winds	
1	7		NWBN	SEBS	Moderate gales & fine weather
2	7				
3	7	5			
4	7	4		20:30	
5	7				
6	7	2			
7	7	4			
8	7	5			
9	7	2			
10	7	5			
11	7	5			
12	8			SE	
1	7	5			
2	7	5			
3	8			19:40	
4	8				
5	7	3			variation p:ʳ azumeth 14:28W
6	7				
7	7	5			
8	7	2			
9	7				
10	7	4			
11	7				Moderate & cloudy –
12	7	4			

Course	Dis:ᶜ	Latitude in	Long. made	M: Dis:ᶜ
N50:00W	180	19:48S	17:24W	

The Cape bore S47:22E Distance 359 leag:ˢ

Remarks Sunday March 13 – 1768   8

Having sailed Westward 360:°00' from the Medium of London; by which means we have lost one day compleat Therefore I ordrerd this day to be added and called it Monday the 14th of March – 1768 –

H	K	F	Course	Wind	Remarks Monday March 14 1768 9
1	7		NWBN	SE	Moderate gales & cloudy –
2	7				
3	7	2			
4	7				
5	7	5			21:00
6	7				
7	7	4			Close hazey weather
8	7				
9	6	5			
10	7				
11	7				
12	7	5			
1	7	5			
2	7				
3	6	5			
4	6				
5	7				19:55
6	7				
7	7	4			
8	6	4			
9	6				
10	6				
11	5				moderate breezes & close hazey weather
12	4		SEBS		

Course	Dis:ᵉ	Latitude in	Long. made	M: Dis:ᵉ
NW½W	160	18:*07S	17:24W	

The Cape bore S47:40E Distance 473 leagues

Remarks Tuesday March 15 – 1768

H	K	F	Courses	Winds	
1	6		NWBN	SE	
2	6				
3	5				
4	4	4			23:10
5	4	4			
6	5				
7	6				
8	5				
9	5	2			
10	5				
11	4				
12	5				
1	5	4			
2	5	5			
3	5	4			
4	6				
5	6	5			20:00
6		3			
7	6				
8	6	4			
9	5	3			
10	5	3			
11	5	3			
12	4				

Remarks:

Moderate & cloudy

variation p:r azumeth 13:°30'W, the only opportunity since we have been out took an observation of the sun & moon

moderate & pleasant weather

Course	Dis:e	Latitude in	Long. made	M: Dis:e
NW	133	16:*33S	21:13W –	

The Cape bore S47:30E Distance 517 leagues

Remarks Wednesday March 16 – 1768

H	K	F	Courses	Winds	Remarks
1	3	5	NWBN	SWBS	Moderate & clear –
2	4				
3	4	3			
4	5				
5	5		WBN½N	23:00	variation p:r azumeth – 12:40W
6	5			SSE	amplitude – 13:17W
7	5	2			
8	5	4			
9	5	5			Latitude observed by Hydra's Heart 16:11S
10	5	4			by Regulus 16:09S
11	6				
12	7				
1	6	5			
2	6	3			
3	5			20:30	
4	5	3		South	Light breezes & cloudy
5	5				
6	5	3			
7	5				variation p:r amp:de – 12:41W
8	5	2			azumeth – 13:02
9	5				saw severall S:t Helena Pigeons
10	5			SSE	
11	5				fine pleasant weather
12	4				

Course	Dis:e	Latitude in	Long. made	M: Dis:e
N76:W	123	16:*03S	23:16W –	

The Cape bore S49:23E Distance 552 leagues –

Remarks Thursday March 17 – 1768

1	4		WBN½N	SEBS
2	5	3		
3	5	3		
4	5	3	22:20	
5	5			
6	5	3		
7	5			
8	5			
9	5			
10	4	5		
11	4	3		
12	5			SSE
1	3			
2				
3				
4			up E of	NE
5			up SW of	WBN
6	1	4	West	21:00
7	5	3		
8	4			
9	3		WSW	SSE
10				
11				
12				

Course	Dis:ᵉ	Latitude in	Long. made	M: Dis:ᵉ
W½N	76	15:*56S	24:35W –	

Moderate & fine pleasant weather
at 6 PM variation 12:47W – at the same time saw the Island of S:ᵗ Helena bearing from N76:0W to N85:00W distance about 14 leagues –
at midnight the Island bore WBN two leagues brought too –

at day break made sail and ran into S:ᵗ Helena Road where we at noon anchor'd in 13 fat: water, sandy ground veer'd away & moor'd the flagstaf bearing S½E & Mundens fort SEBS the extreams of the Island bore ENE to S½W – distance from the nearest shore which is the watering crane two cables length –

found riding here the Northumberland Indiaman[535] who saluted with eleven guns, returned nine –
soon after the Fort saluted with 13 guns returned 13 –

got the boats and sent them to the watering place with out empty casks – and people to fill them[536]
Light breezes and fine pleasant weather.

The Cape bore S50:46E Distance 570 leagues –

---

535 Captain Mitford according to the PL and the FC.
536 "... and some people onshoar to gather purslane which grows here in plenty." PL and FC.

Remarks Friday March 18 1768   13

1			SE	
2				
3				
4			22:39	
5				
6				
7				
8				
9				
10				
11				
12				

Fine pleasant weather went on shoar was saluted by the Garrison with 12 guns, the ship returned the same number – the Governor and all the principal officers waited on me and did me all the honours that they had in their power, I staid at the Governors house,[537] at 2 PM began to get of water and at night had near completed – at 8 AM the Osterly Indiaman anchord & saluted us with 11 guns, returned 9. at noon completed all our water, got everything ready for sailing as soon as a breeze shall spring up –[538]

1				sent the boats crews onshoar to gather purslane for the ships company –[539]	
2			21:20		
3	S:t Helena			Latitude -by Masculine	15:°57'*S
				Longitude –	5:°49'W
4	Ascension			Latitude –	by Masculine 7:°51'*S
5				Longitude –	13:°59'W
6					
7	S:t Helena by an observation			Latitude –	15:58*S
8				Longitude –	5:40
9	Dolphin 16 March 1768			by dead reckoning –	
10	Ascension 23:d March 1768			Latitude –	7:58*S
11				Longitude –	14:05W
12				dead reckoning –	14:18W –

Course	Dis:e	Latitude in	Long. made	M: Dis:e
		15:*56S –		

---

537 "I went on shore and was saluted with 13 guns which I returned. The Governor and all the principal people of the island met me at the waterside and conducted me to the fort and told me I was expected to make that my home during my stay." PL and FC.

538 "Ships draught of water   forward –   16 ^{Fat} – 0 ^{Inches}
                                Abaft –   14   2"." PL and FC.

539 The ensuing calculations do not appear in the PL and the FC.

Saturday March 19:ᵗʰ 1768   14

H	K	F	Courses	Winds	Remarks
1					Light airs & fair –
2					
3			22:40		
4					At five unmoord & hove short, soon after came off, the
5					Governor and all the principal people of the island came to the
6					waterside and as soon as the boat put off saluted me with 13
7	4		NWBN		guns which was returned from the ship at six got under sail
8	5	2			when the first of the two India ships saluted with 12 guns each
9	5	2			– which we returned –⁵⁴⁰
10	5	2			at 8 the Island bore from SEBE to S ½ East distance 4 leagues
11	5	2			
12	4	3			
1	4				
2	5				
3	3	3	21:50		
4	4	5	SE		AM the rudder works pretty much, put four foremost & four
5	5	4			aftermost guns into the hold in order to ease the ship –
6	5	5			
7	5	3			
8	5	5	South		
9	5	3			had at noon 78 tons of fresh water
10	5	3			
11	4				fine pleasant weather –
12	4		SE		

Course	Dis:ᵉ	Latitude in	Long. made	M: Dis:ᵉ
N47:0W	87	14:57S	1:06W –	

S:ᵗ Helena bore S47:00E Distance 30 leag:ˢ

---

540 "At five I came onboard, at leaving the shore I was saluted with 13 guns and soon after got under way the fort saluted with 13 more guns which we returned – then the India ships saluted with 13 guns each I returned 13 – made sail." PL and FC.

Remarks Sunday March 20 1768   15

1	5	4	NWBN	SE	Moderate & pleasant weather –
2	6				
3	5	3			
4	5				variation p:^{r} amp 11:°49'W
5	5	4			
6	5	4		22:50	
7	5	5			
8	5				
9	6				
10	7	4			
11	6				
12	7	5		SEBE	fresh breezes –
1	7				
2	6				
3	5				
4	5	5			
5	5	5			Lost a log & three lines
6	5	4			
7	6				variation p:^{r} azumeth 11:°18'W
8	6			22:00	
9	7				
10	7				lost a log & 3 lines[541]
11	7	5			fresh gale & pleasant weather –
12	7				

Course	Dis:^{e}	Latitude in	Long. made	M: Dis:^{e}
N46:0W	140	13:20*S	3:50W –	

S:^{t} Helena bore S46:°30'E Distance 76 leagues

---

541 "... all the log lines quite rotten." PL and FC.

Remarks Monday March 21 1768   16

H	K	F	Courses	Winds	
1	7	4	NWBN	SEBE	Fresh gales & pleasant weather
2	7	4			
3	7	2			
4	7				variation p:ʳ ampli:ᵈᵉ — 11 :30W
5	7			22:55	
6	7	3			
7	7	2			
8	7	4			
9	7	5			
10	7	2			
11	7	4			
12	7	5			
1	7	5			
2	7	2			
3	7	5			
4	7			23:00	
5	6				
6	7				variation p :ʳ amplitude 11:00W —[542]
7	6	4			
8	7	2			
9	7	2			
10	7	4			fine pleasant weather –
11	7	5			ship twelve miles to S:°ward of observation
12	7	2			

Course	Dis	Lat:ᵈ in	Long. made	M: Dis:ᵉ
NW¼W	165	11:*290S –	4:55W –	

S:ᵗ Helena bore S47:°00'E Distance 131 leagues

---

[542] "Lost another log and three lines examined the log lines and find them pretty strong – but wet them and they are quite rotten that they will not lift a weight of six pound of the deck." PL and FC.

Remarks Tuesday March 22 – 1768   17

1	7	2	NWBN	EBN	Moderate gales & pleasant weather
2	7	5			
3	8				variation p:ʳ amplitude – 10:00W
4	8			22:45	
5	8				
6	7	5			
7	7	3			
8	7	3			
9	8				
10	8	2			
11	8	3			
12	8			SE	
1	8				Lost a logg & two lines
2	7	5			
3	7	4			variation p:ʳ amplitude – 10:30W
4	7	4		21:10	
5	7	4			
6	7	4			
7	6	2			
8	7			SEBS	
9	7	3			
10	7	4			Moderate gales & cloudy –
11	7	5			Ship 20 miles to the S:°ward of observation
12	7	4			

Course	Dis:ᵗ	Lat:ᵈ in	Long. made	M: Dis:ᵉ
N47:0W	163	11:*29S –	6:56W –	

S:ᵗ Helena bore S24:00E Distance 185 leagues

Remarks Wednesday March 23:ʳᵈ – 1768

1	7	4	NWBN	SE	
2	7	3			Fresh gales & pleasant weather –
3	7	4			
4	7	3			Saw severall Men of War birds
5	7	4		23:10	
6	7	2			variation p:ʳ medium of nine azumeths – 11:°43 Westerly
7	7				
8	7	2			
9	7				heard the cry of many birds about the ship –
10	7				
11	7				lost a log & line
12	6	5			saw severall sorts of birds –
1	6				saw the Island of Ascension bearing NWBN distance
2	6				variation by a med:ᵐ of azum:ᵗʰ 9:°53' West
3	6	2			saw a ship who brought too & made a sig:ˡ we shew'd her
4	6			23:00	our colours, he hauld down his signal and stood in for the
5	6	4			Island –⁵⁴³
6	6				the difference of long: by my reckoning between S:ᵗ Helena
7	7		NNW½W	SEBS	& Ascension is 8:°30' West & the course by compass
8	7	5			NWBN dis: 233 leg:ˢ
9	7	5	NW	sailing	at noon Island of Ascension bore S18:°00'E distance seven
10	8	2	NNW½W	two miles of shore	leagues
11	7	5			
12	8				

Course	Dis:ᵗ	Lat:ᵈ in	Long. made	M: Dis:ᵉ
N27:0W	21	7:*40S –	0:10W –	

S:ᵗ Helena bore S27:0E Distance 7 leagues

---

543 "Run down close enough to the NE side of the island and look'd into the bay but saw no ship there and it blowing a stiff gale made the best of my way –." PL and FC.

Remarks Thursday March 24 — 1768   19

H	K	F	Wind	Course	Remarks
1	8		NNW½W	SE	Fresh breezes and fair weather
2	8				
3	7				
4	8	3		23:50	reeved a new tiller rope –
5	7				variation p:r azumeth 9:48W
6	8	4			
7	7				
8	7	4			
9	8	5			
10	8				
11	6	2			
12	6	2		ESE	
1	8	2			variation p:r amplitude 9:30W
2	8				exercised great guns & small arms
3	8				
4	7			23:45	
5	7	3			
6	7	3			
7	5	4			
8	6	4			
9	6				
10	7				
11	7				fresh breezes & hazey –
12	7	3	176 –	SE	

Course	Dis	Latitude in	Long. made	M: Dis:e
N39:0W	174	5:*25S –	2:00W –	

Ascension bore S39:00E Distance 65 leagues

Remarks Friday March 25 – 1768   20

H	K	F	Courses	Winds	Remarks
1	7		NNW½W	EBS	Moderate & fair
2	6	4			Exercised great guns & small arms
3	6	4			
4	6	2			
5	7			24:00	
6	6	5		SE	variation p:ʳ azumeth 10:00W
7	7				
8	7	2			
9	7				
10	6	2			
11	6	4			
12	6				variation p:ʳ medium of azuth: 10:09W
1	6				Fresh gales & cloudy –
2	6				Exercised great guns & small arms
3	5	3			
4	4			24:00	Ship 14 miles to S:°ward by her observation
5	4	4		SEBS	Moderate gales & cloudy hazey weather –
6	5	3			
7	6				
8	6	4			
9	6				
10	6	3			
11	6	5			
12	6		148 –		

Course	Dis	Latitude in	Long. made	MDis
N40:0W	129	3:*46S	3:23W –	

Ascension bore S67:59E Distance 320 ᵐⁱˡᵉˢ leagues

Remarks Saturday March 26 – 1768 21

H	K	F	Courses	Winds		Remarks
1	5	4	NNW½W	SEBS		Light winds and cloudy –
2	5	3				Lost a log and three lines
3	5					exercised great guns and small arms –
4	5					variation p:ʳ azumeth – 9:9W
5	5	4		24:00		amplitude 8:30
6	5	3				
7	5	4				
8	6					
9	6					
10	6					
11	6					
12	6					
1	6					
2	6					
3	6			24:20		
4	5	3				Squally with small rain –
5	6					
6	7	5				variation by many az: 10:16W
7	8					
8	8					
9	7					got the still up
10	7	3				ship 8 miles to S:°of her observation
11	7					fine pleasant gales – caught some Bonnettos –
12	6					

Course	Dis	Latitude in	Long. made	M:Dis:ᶜᵉ
N40:W	132	2:*04S	4:48W –	

Ascension bore S39:10E Distance 151 leagues –

Remarks Sunday March 27 – 1768 22

1	4	3	NNW½W	SEBS	Latter wind and fair
2	5				
3	5	3			variation p:ʳ azumeth – 7:51W
4	5			25:10	
5	4	5			
6	4	3			little wind & cloudy
7	4	4			
8	5				
9	4	5			
10	5	2			
11	5				
12	5				
1	5	3			
2	5	4			
3	5	3		21:40	
4	5				
5	5	3			variation p:ʳ amplitude – 9:10W
6	5	4			azumeth 8:6
7	5				
8	4	5			
9	5	2			
10	5				
11	5				Little wind & cloudy –
12	4	2			

Course	Dis:ᵗ	Latitude in	Long. made	M:Dis:ᶜᵉ
N37:00W	114	00:°34'S	5:57W –	

Ascension bore S38:41E Distance 189 leagues –

Remarks Monday March 28 – 1768   23

1	4	3	NNW½W	SE	Little wind and fair weather
2	4	5			
3	4	3			
4	4	5			variation p:^{r} azumeth – 7:29W
5	3	5		24:40	amplitude – 7:31
6	3	5			
7	3	5			
8	3	2			variable weather, sometimes rain cloudy & fair –
9	4				
10	4				
11	3				
12	2	4			crossed the Equinoxe –^{544}
1	3			SE	
2	3	5			
3	4				
4	3	4			ditto weather
5	4			24:00	squally rainy weather
6	4				opened a cask of beef N 1234 contents 186 – short 3 peices –
7	3	4			
8	3	3			
9	2	4			
10	2	4			
11	3	4			Moderate breezes a swell from the Eastward –
12	4	5			Squally rainy and fair
	89				

Course	Dis:^{t}	Latitude in	Long. made	M:Dis:^{ce}
N37:00W	89	00:°37' – North	6:51W –	

Ascension bore S38:30E Distance 220 leagues

544 The equinoctial line in the PL and the FC.

Remarks Tuesday March 29 – 1768   24

H	K	F	Courses	Winds	Remarks
1	4	3	NNW½W	EBS	Light airs & cloudy –
2	4	2			
3	3	5			variation p:ʳ azumeth – 8:20W
4	3	2			amplitude – 8:50
5	3	3			
6	3	3		24:30	
7	4				
8	4		NBW		
9	4				
10	4	3			Lost a log and one line
11	4	4			
12	4	2			
1	4	3			
2	4				Lightning to the Northward –
3	3	2			
4	3	2		24:00	Little wind and dark cloudy weather
5	3	4			
6	3	4			a Northerly swell
7	3	4			
8	4			East	
9	4	3		ENE	
10	4				
11	5		NW	NNE	squally with thunder lightning and rain
12	3	4	NWBW	NBE	
	81				

Course	Dis:ᵗ	Latitude in	Long. made	M:Dis:ᶜᶜ
N29:0W	92	1:°57'N –	7:36W	

Ascension bore S27:22E Distance   749 leagues
                                    250

Remarks Wednesday March 30 1768   25

H	K	F	Courses	Winds / Remarks
1			Calm	Calm & cloudy, caught a shark –
2			ships head from North	
3	1	4	to NW	
4		4	23:50	
5		}		
6				ships head Northwards
7	2	1		
8				Ditto weather –
9		]		
10				
11				
12			Calm	ships head NBW
1				
2				
3		]	23:00	
4	4			fresh breezes & rainy squally weather[545]
5	1	4		
6			Calm	
7	1	3	NNE	
8	2	1		
9	1	5	NE	
10	2	4		
11	3	3		Light airs & small rain
12		5	NEBE	

Course	Dis:ᵗ	Latitude in	Long. made	M:Dis:ᶜᵉ
N34W	26	2 18 N	7:50W	

Ascension bore S37:°15'E Distance 258 leagues

---

545 "Served mustard and vinegar." PL and FC.

Remarks Thursday March 31 – 1768 26

1				Calm & cloudy	
2			ships head	caught two sharks –	
3					
4				variation p:r azumeth – 8:17W	
5			23:00		
6		from	NWBN	to WBS	
7					
8					
9					
10			ships head NW		
11					
12				Light airs	
1	1	NW	NNE		
2	1	NNW	NE		
3	2	NBW	ENE	squally with rain	
4	4				
5	1		23:25		
6	1				
7	2				
8	2		EBN		
9	3		WBS		
10	2				
11	1			Light airs & cloudy –	
12	2		East		

Course	Dis:t	Latitude in	Long. made	M:Dis:cc
NBW	43	3:00N –	7:58W	

Ascension bore S36:00E Distance 271 – leagues

Remarks Friday April 1 1768 27

1	3		North	EBN	Light breezes & cloudy weather
2	2	5	N½W		
3	2	4			Lost a log & line
4	2		North		
5	1	2		25:00	Rainy
6	1		NNW		
7					Calm her head to the Northward
8	1		NBE		Light airs
9	1		North		
10	1				
11	2	3			
12	1				Light squalls & rainy
1	1	2	NW	NNE	
2	1	3	NNW	NE	
3					
4				Calm	ship head NBW
5	1		NNW	East	
6	1			24:00	
7	3		NW		
8	2	4		NNE	Light squalls & rainy –
9	1		NWBW		
10	3	4			
11	4				Squally rainy weather
12	5	3	NW½W	NBE	

Course	Dis	Latitude in	Long. made	M:Dis:ᶜᶜ
NNW	62	3:*57 North	8:22W	

Ascension bore S35:°00'E Distance 291 leagues

Remarks Saturday April 2 1768   28

H	K	F	Courses	Winds	Remarks
1	1	5	NNW		Light airs and rainy
2			⎤		
3			⎟		
4			⎟		Calm the ships head from North to WBS –
5			⎟	24:00	
6			⎦		Dark cloudy rainy weather
7	5		North	ESE	a very hard squall clew'd all up, carri'd away the fore top:^{s}
8	5				sheet & main and fore topmast stay sail hallyards and sheets,
9	3		NBW	ENE	split the sails bent new ones double reeft the topsails and
10	4				made sail
11	4				
12	4				
1	3	4			fresh breezes & cloudy –
2	2	5			
3	3	3			
4	4			25:00	
5	5				fresh breezes & cloudy –
6	5	5		EBN	
7	5	5	North		found the main top:^{s} split, sailmaker employed in repairing the
8	5			ENE	sails
9	5		NW½N	NEBN	
10	4		NWBN		
11	4		NNW	NE	fresh breezes & cloudy weather –
12	5		NW	NNE	

Course	Dis:^{ce}	Latitude in	Long. made	M:D
NNW½W	101	5:*28 North	9:°06'W	

Ascension bore S34:°04'E Distance 324 leagues

Remarks Sunday April 3 1768 29

1	4		NW	NNE	Moderate gales & cloudy with a head sea –
2	5				
3	5	3			variation by azumeth – 5:30W
4	6	2		24:00	amplitude – 4:10W
5	5	5	NWBW		
6	5	5	NW½W		
7	6		NW½N	NEBN	
8	6				
9	5	5			
10	6				
11	6	2			
12	6	3			fine pleasant gale & cloudy –
1	5	4			
2	5	4			
3	5	3			
4	5	3		23:00	
5	5	4			variation by amplitude – 5:30 West
6	5	3			azumeth – 5:26
7	5	5			
8	6				
9	5	4			
10	6				
11	5	3			Moderate gales & cloudy.
12	6		NW	NNE	

Course	Dis:^{ce}	Latitude in	Long. made	M:D
N36:0W	136	6:*44 North	11:°00'W –	

Ascension bore S36:°43'E Distance 367 leagues

Remarks Monday April 4 1768 30

1	6		NWBW	NBE	Moderate gales & hazey with a pretty great Northern swell – variation p:ʳ az: – 3:45 West[546]
2	6		NW		
3	6	4	NWBW		
4	6	4		23:50	
5	6		NW½N		
6	6	2	NW	NNE	
7	5	5	NW½W		
8	6				
9	5	4	NW	NNE	
10	5	3			
11	5	4			
12	6				
1	5	5			
2	5	4	NW½N	NEBN	
3	5			22:30	variation p:ʳ azumeth – 5:20W
4	5	2		NNE	
5	5	3	NW		exercised great guns & small arms
6	6				
7	6				
8	5	2			
9	6				
10	6				
11	6				
12	6				

Course	Dis	Latitude in	Long. made	M:D
N59:0W	139	7:*53N	13:°00'W –	

Ascension bore S39:°09'E Distance 410 leagues

---

546 "Carpenters employed in repairing the boats and painting." PL and FC.

Remarks Tuesday April 5 1768 31

H	K	F	Course	Wind	
1	3	2	NWBN	NEBN	Moderate gales & cloudy weather
2	4				
3	3	4			variation p:r amplitude 5:°20'W
4	4	3	NW½N		
5	5			23:00	
6	5	3			
7	5	2	NWBW	NBE	
8	4	3			
9	5	4	NW	NNE	
10	5	2			
11	5	4	NW½W		Fresh gales and hazey weather –
12	5		NW		
1	5	3			
2	5	2			
3	5				
4	5	3		22:10	
5	5	3			variation p:r az:th 4:°10'W
6	6				
7	7		NW½W		fresh gales & cloudy
8	7				
9	5	4			exercised great guns & small arms –
10	4	5	NW½W	NEBN	
11	5	4			fresh gales & cloudy –
12	5	2	NNW½W	NE	
		123			

Course	Dist:ce	Latitude in	Long. made	M:D
N55:W	135	9:*13N –	14:53W –	

Ascension bore S40:47E Distance 454 leagues

Remarks Wednesday April 6 1768

H	K	F	Course	Wind
1	4	3	NNW	NE
2	4	5		
3	5	4		
4	4		NNW½W	
5	5	4	NWBN	NE
6	5	4	NNW½W	
7	5	4	NNW	23:30
8	5	3		
9	6			
10	6	4		
11	5	4		
12	4	5		
1	5		NNW½W	
2	5	3		
3	5		NNW	
4	5	4		21:45
5	5			
6	5	3		
7	5	5		
8	6			
9	6	4		
10	7	2		
11	6	5	NNW½W	
12	6	3	NNW	
		133		

Fresh gales & cloudy with a pretty great sea
Carpenters employed in repairing & painting the boats –

Fresh gales with a head sea –

got down top gallant yard and took in two reefs –
fresh gales & hazey –

Course	Dist:^{ce}	Latitude in	Long. made	
N38:W	138	11:*04N –	16:12W	

Ascension bore S40°15'E Distance 499 leagues

Remarks Thursday April 7 1768   33

1	6		NBW	NE
2	5	3	NBW½W	NEBE
3	5	2		
4	5	2		
5	5		NBW	22:35
6	5	2	NBW½W	
7	5	4	NB	
8	5	5		
9	5	3		
10	5	4		
11	6			
12	5	4		
1	5			
2	5			
3	5	4		
4	5	4		21:30
5	6			
6	6	5		
7	6	3		
8	6	4		
9	6	5	NBW½W	
10	6	3		
11	6	4		
12	6		NBW	

Fresh gales with a great head sea

variation by azumeth –   4:48 West
        amplitude –   4:14

Fresh gales with a pretty great sea
M:r Edward Lambert Midshipman departed this life – he was a martyr to the bottle –

fresh gales & a great sea –

Course	Dist:ce	Latitude in	Long. made	
NNW	140	13:*12	17:06W	

Ascension bore S40°15'E Distance 499 leagues

Remarks Friday April 8 1768   34

H	K	F	Courses	Winds	Time	Remarks
1	5		NBW½W	NEBE		Fresh gales with a great sea –
2	6					
3	6					
4	6					
5	5	4				
6	6				21:30	
7	6		NBW			
8	6		N¼W	ENE		
9	6			NEBE		
10	6	4				
11	6	2				
12	6	4				reeved a new tiller rope
1	6					
2	5					
3	5					
4	5				21:00	
5	6					
6	7					variation p:ʳ amplitude 4:14W –
7	7					
8	7		NBW½W			employed in painting the ship & the boats –
9	7		NBW			had an observation for longitude
10	6	5	N½W			ship long:ᵈ observed – 36:00W –
11	6	4	NBW			fresh gales & cloudy
12	6					

Course	Dis	Latitude in	Long. made	
NNW	143	15:*23N	18:°04W	

Ascension bore S37°30'E Distance 589 leagues

Remarks Saturday April 9 1768

1	6		N½W	NEBE	Fresh gales and hazey weather
2	5	5			
3	5	3			
4	5	4			
5	6	3	NW	21:25	
6	6				
7	7	4	NNW	NE	
8	7	2			
9	6	3	NBW		
10	6		N½W	ENE	
11	6	5			
12	5	4			squally with some rain –
1	6	4	North		
2	6	3			
3	5	5			
4	5		N½W		
5	6			20:30	
6	6				
7	6	3			
8	6				
9	7	4	North	ENE	
10	6				
11	6	5			Fresh gales & cloudy –
12	6	3	NBE	EBN	

Course	Dis	Latitude in	Long. made	
NNW	150	17:*42N	19:02W	

Ascension bore S36:00E Distance 634 leagues

Remarks Sunday April 10 1768   36

H	K	F	Courses	Winds	Remarks
1	6		NBE	EBN	Fresh gales & clear made more sail
2	5	5	N½		
3	5	3	North		variation p:ʳ az : 4 :30W
4	5	4			
5	5	5		21:20	
6	5	4	N½W	ENE	
7	5	5			
8	6				
9	6	4			
10	6	3			fine weather
11	6				
12	5	5			
1	6	4			
2	7				
3	7	2			
4	7		N½E	EBN	
5	6		NBE	20:45	variation by amplitude 5:00W
6	5	3			split the main top gallant sail repaired it –
7	4	4			
8	6	3	NBE½E	East	Pleasant weather with a NNW swell –
9	6				
10	6	3	NNE	EBS	
11	7				Fresh gales with a NNW swell
12	7	4			

Course	Dis:ᵗ	Latitude in	Long. made	
N40:W	146	20:*07N –	19:07W	

Ascension bore S33:40E Distance 676 leagues

Remarks Monday April 11 1768   37

H	K	F	Courses	Winds	Remarks
1	5	5	NNE	East	Moderate breezes & pleasant weather
2	5	4			
3	4		NBE	EBN	
4	3	3			variation p:^r azu:th & amp:^{de} 4:°30'W
5	4				
6	4	4	N½E	21:00	
7	4	5	NBE		
8	4	5	NBE½E	East	Little wind and fair
9	5	4			
10	5				
11	3	4	North	ENE	
12	2	3	NBW		Light airs and small rain, cloudy all round –
1	2		NW	variable	
2	1	5	NWBN		
3	2		NNW		
4	1	4	NNE		
5	1		NBW	00:45	
6	3		North		saw some gulph weed
7	5		NBW		caught a dolphin
8	5				NB: the first weed we have seen –
9	4				saw a white turtle –[547]
10	3	5	NBW½W	NE	
11	4	3	NW	NNE	Light breezes & fair
12	4		NWBN	NEBN	

Course	Dis:^t	Latitude in	Long. made	
N9:00W	90	21:*36N –	19:22W –	

Ascension bore S32:44E Distance 703 leag

---

547 This note is omitted in the PL and the FC.

Remarks Tuesday April 12 1768   38

1	3	5	NBW	NEBE	Light breezes & fairweather
2	3	4			
3	2	4	NBW½W		variation by amplitude 5:°26'W
4	2	3			
5	3		NNW	21:0	
6	3		NWBN		
7	2	5	NW	NNE	
8	3	2	NW½N		
9	3	2	NW		
10	3	5	NWBN		
11	4				
12	3				Light airs with a great swell
1	3	3	NW		
2	3	2	NW½W		
3	3	3	WNW	North	
4	3	2		20:45	
5	3		NWBW		
6	3	2	NW	NBE	variation by amplitude 6:00W
7	3				by three azumeths – 6:40W
8	3	2			
9	2	4			by observation found the ship 10 miles to the Northward of
10	2		NNW	NE	her reckoning
11	3				fine pleasant weather
12	2				

Course	Dis:ᵗ	Latitude in	Long. made	
N49:0W	75	22:*30N –	20:18W –	

Ascension bore S33:°0'E Distance 728 leag

Remarks Wednesday April 13 1768   39

H	K	F	Courses	Winds	Remarks
1	1	4	NBW½W		Light airs with a great swell from the NW
2	1	3		NEBE	
3	1	3			
4	1	4		21:00	variation p:ʳ azum:ᵗʰ 4:°30'W
5			⎫	Calm	her head NBW
6			⎬		
7	1		North ⎭		
8	1				
9	1		NBW	variable	
10	1				
11	1				
12	1				
1			⎫	20:00	calm her head North
2			⎬		
3			⎭		
4					set up the main topmast rigging
5	1	4	NNE	East	variation p:ʳ azumeth – 6:10W
6	1				
7	1	2		ESE	saw a sail in the NW, steering West ward
8	3				
9	3				pass by much Gulph weed –
10	3				
11	4				fine pleasant weather
12	3				

Course	Dis:ᵗ	Latitude in	Long. made	
North 39	39	23:*11N –	20:18W –	

Ascension bore S32:31E Distance 739 leagues

Remarks Thursday April 14 1768   40

H	K	F	Courses	Winds	Remarks
1	3		NNE	SE	Moderate breezes & pleasant weather
2	3	3			
3	4			SSE	
4	4	4			
5	4				
6	4			South	
7	3	5		20:40	
8	3	4			
9	3	2			
10	4	2			
11	5	2			
12	5	5		SW	
1	5	4			cloudy weather
2	6	4		WNW	
3	7				squally with drislin rain –
4	5				
5	5	3		20:35	fresh gales
6	6				
7	5		NNE½E	NW	variation p:ʳ amplitude 7:00W
8	5		NE	NNW	
9	3	2	EBN	NBE	showery
10	3	3			
11	3	3			fresh breezes and hazey
12	4				

Course	Dis	Latitude in	Long. made	
N30:0E	98	24:36N –	19:21W –	

Ascension bore S38:09E Distance 753 leagues

Remarks Friday April 15 1768 41

H	K	F	Courses	Winds	Remarks
1		5	EBN	NBE	Fresh gales and hazey with a very great head sea
2	4	5	East	NNE	
3	4	5	NW½N		
4	4				variation 7:40 West
5	4	2	NWBW	NBE	
6	4	2		19:00	Fresh gales & a great sea from the NW
7	4		NW½W	NNE	
8	3	4			variation by azumeth 7:51W
9	3	4	NW½N		
10	3				
11	4		NW	NE	
12	3	4	NW½W		
1	3		NNW½W	NEBE	opened a cask of beef N 1241 –
2	3				contents 172 – short one peice
3	3			18:40	
4	3			NE	
5	3		NNW		
6	3	3	NNW½W		
7	3	3	NNW		
8	3	3	North	NEBE	
9	3	3	NBW		
10	2	4			
11	2	3			Light breezes and hazey
12	2				

Course	Dis	Latitude in	Long. made	
N46:W	61	25:*18N –	20:12W –	

Ascension bore S30:°34'E Distance 773 leagues

Remarks Saturday April 16 1768   42

H	K	F	Course	Wind	Remarks
1	2	2	NBE	EBN	Light breezes and fair weather with a NW swell
2	3				
3	2	4			
4	2	2	N½W	ENE	
5	3	4	NNW		
6	3	4	NBW	19:10	variation by severall azum:th 7:23W
7	3	4			
8	4		North		
9	3		NBE		
10	4	3	NBE½E		
11	4				
12	3		North	ENE	
1	2	5			
2	2	5	N½E		
3	3		NBE	EBN	
4	3	4	NNE		
5	3	4		19:00	
6	3				variation p:^{r} azumeth 8:°48'W
7	4		NBE	East	
8	4	3	N½E		fresh breezes & cloudy
9	5		NNE		
10	5				
11	4	4			moderate & hazey weather
12	4	2			

Course	Dis	Latitude in	Long. made	
North	81	26:*30N	20:12W	

Ascension bore S29:40E Distance 797 leagues.

Remarks Sunday April 17 1768   43

1	5		NNE	ESE	Moderate & pleasant weather
2	5				
3	5	2			
4	3	3			
5	4			21:30	
6	5	4		South	
7	2	2			
	2	4	NEBN		
8	4				Light breezes –
9	3				
10	3	2		SSE	
11	3	3			
12	3				
1	3				
2	4				
3	4	4		19:45	
4	4	3		South	Ditto weather
5	5				
6	5			SSE	
7	6				
8	6			ESE	
9	5				
10	4	2		South	Scrape & payed the masts with varnish of pine –
11	6				Moderate brezes & cloudy –
12	5			SSW	

Course	Dis	Latitude in	Long. made	
NNE	110	28:*20N	19:33W	

Ascension bore S27:30E Distance 819 leag:[s]

Remarks Monday April 18 1768   (44)

H	K	F	Courses	Winds
1	4	2	NEBN	SSW
2	4	1		
3	5			
4	5			
5	4			
6	3	5		19:15
7	4	2		
8	4			South
9	4	5		
10	4	2		
11	3	5		
12	4	4		SSW
1	4	3		
2	5			
3	5			19:0
4	4			
5	4			SW
6	5			
7	5			
8	5			
9	5	2		
10	5	4		
11	5	4		
12	5			

Moderate & cloudyweather

variation by a medium of azumeths –   9:40W
variation p:^{r} amplitude –   9:40W

variation p:^{r}
azumeth 11:00W

Bent a new fore sail and miz:^{n} top:^{s}
moderate breezes & fair weather

Course	Dis:^{e}	Latitude in	Long. made	
N25:0E	108	29:*56N	18:43W	

Ascension bore S25:°24'E Distan 839 leag:

Remarks Tuesday April 19 1768   (45)

1	5	2	NEBN	SSW	Moderate fair sailmakers employed in repairing the sails
2	5	2			
3	4	4			a swell from the NNW
4	4				
5	5			20:00	variation p:r azumeth 10:28W
6	5	5			
7	6				
8	6	5		South	
9	6	5			
10	7	3			
11	7	4			
12	7			SSW	
1	5	4			a heavy dew which I never heard of so far from land –
2	5	4		18:20	
3	4	2			
4	3	3		SBW	saw two flocks of birds thought we saw the water discoloured,
5	3	4			but got no ground
6	4				
7	4	4			no Gulph weed seen this day –
8	4	4			read the Articles of War –
9	3	4			Bent a new fore topsail
10	4	4			
11	4	5			fine pleasant weather
12	5				

Course	Dis	Latitude in	Long. made	
N24:°00'E	118	31:*44N	17:47W	

Ascension bore S23:12E Distance 864 – 2591 leagues

Remarks Wednesday April 20 1768   (46)

H	K	F	Courses	Winds	Remarks
1	4		NEBN	SSW	Fresh breezes & pleasant weather
2	4	2			
3	4	3			variation by azumeth 10:18W
4	4	5			
5	5				
6	5				
7	6	4		19:30	
8	6	4			
9	6	2			
10	6	4			
11	6	3			
12	6	2			a heavy sea
1	6	2			
2	5	5			
3	5	4		17:50	
4	5	4			
5	5				variation bu azumeth 11:°32'W
6	5	2			
7	5	2			
8	5	2			saw some rock weed, but no Gulph –
9	5	3			
10	5	3			
11	5	2			fresh breezes & hazey weather –
12	5	5			

Course	Dis	Latitude in	Long. made	
N25:00E	130	33:*38N	16:40W	

Ascension bore S21:00E Distance 891 leagues –

Remarks Thursday April 21 1768   (46)

H	K	F	Courses	Winds	Remarks
1	6	5	NE	South	Moderate and cloudy sailmakers employed repairing the sails
2	5	5			
3	4	4			opened a cask of pork N 919 content 286 – short two pieces –
4	2	4			
5	4	4		SW	saw a flock of birds at a distance flying like pigeons –
6	2	4		19:17	
7	2	3			a great swell from the SW –
8	3				
9	3	5			observed for long:^{de} 35:55 – lat:^{d} in supposed long:^{de} in 00:06
10	3	2			– true long in – 33:00 West from Lon:^{d}
11	4	3		South	hazey weather, a heavy dew fell
12	4	5			
1	4	3			
2	5				
3	5			SW	
4	5	2		17:40	variation azumeth – 11:34W
5	5	5			
6	5	5			
7	5				
8	5	2			
9	5				broke the m:^{n} top gallant tye fixed a new one –
10	6				
11	7				fresh gales & hazey with a NNW sea
12	7	4		SWBS	

Course	Dis	Latitude in	Long. made	
N36:10E	105	35:*00N	15:26W	

Ascension bore S18:00E Distance 908 leagues –

Remarks Friday April 22 1768 (48)

1	6		NE	SW	Moderate & cloudy with a WNW swell
2	7	5	NEBE		
3	7				
4	5	4			
5	6	2	EBN		Squally hazey weather
	2		EBS	variable	
6	2				
	2		ENE	17:20	
7	5		NEBE	NBW	Light breezes –
8	5				
9	5				
10	5				
11	4	4			
12	4	2			fresh gales
1	3	3			
2	4	2			
3	4			NNW	
4	3	5		16:20	
5	6	4	ENE	NBW	
6	6			North	
7	6	4	EBN		
8	7		ENE		
9	5	4			
10	6				fresh gales & clear weather –
11	6				
12	5	4			

Course	Dis:ᶜᵉ	Latitude in	Long. made	
N59:0E	130	26:*06N –	13:10W	

Ascension bore S15:58E Distance 917 leagues

Remarks Saturday April 23 1768 (49)

H	K	F	Courses	Winds	
1	6		NEBE½E	NBW	Moderate gales & squally
2	6		NEBE	NNW	observed longitude 29:31W
3	6	5			
4	6	2			
5	5				variation p:r az – 11:30W –
6	5	5	ENE	16:45	
7	6				
8	6				
9	4	2	EBN		
10	4				
11	5				
12	4	4			
1	4	4	East	NNE	
2	4	3			
3	4		E½S	14:45	
4	4				
5	2		ESE	NE	
6	4		NNW		variation p:r azumeth – 16:33W
7	2		NBW		
8	2				ships head to the Northward –
9			}		
10				calm	
11					light airs and hazey with a swell from the NW
12					

Course	Dis	Latitude in	Long. made	M
N62:0E	80	36:*44N –	11:54W	

Ascension bore S14:00E Dist:ce 921 leagues

Remarks Sunday April 24 1768 (50)

H	K	F	Course	Winds
1			NNE	calm
2				
3				
4	1			
5	2			16:45
6	2			
7	2	2		
8	2	2		
9	4			
10	5	3	NEBN	
11	5	4		
12	6		NE	
1	3			
2				
3		up		15:00
4				
5	3		NE	ESE
6	6	3		
7	4			
8	4	4		
9	4	4	NE½N	
10	4		NEBN	
11	4	5		
12	5		NNE½E	EBS

cloudy weather, sounded with 200 fathoms no ground
Little wind
at 8 fresh gales
at midnight brought to sounded no ground with 20 fathoms –
sounded every hour 'till daylight no ground very dark squally rainy weather –

at 4 made sail at 5 saw of the Western islands bearing NNE I suppose sixteen leagues off –
it made a high peak –[548]
The steering sail boom broke & the sail was lost, not being able to get it in in a heavy squall of wind –[549]

at noon the extreams of the land from N½W to NEBE and a high peek on the Westermost end of the Eastermost island NNE, distance about ten leagues
Lat in 38:40 28:30 lon.

Course	Dis:^ce	Latitude in	Long. made	
N10:30E	68 –	38:00	11:30W	

Ascension 3:00
           14:00
           28:30

---

[548] Identified as the Pike of Pico in the PL and the FC (Peak).
[549] Detail omitted in the the two other logs.

Remarks Monday April 25 1768   (51)

1	4	3	NE	ESE	moderate & fair at 4 the extreams of the land bore from ENE 7 or 8 leagues to NE 5 or 6 leagues –
2	4	4	ENE	SE	the extreams of Fyal N¾E six leagues to NBW 7 or 8 leagues,
3	4		NNE		the extreams of both low, the middle mountaneous
4	3		NW	SSE	at six Pico bore from N250E to East
5	4				the Peek N49:00E, distance from the nearest shore 5 leagues –
6	3	4		16:00	variation p:ʳ amp: 19:30W
7	3	2			at 7 Fiall N10:00W to N25:00E
8	3				Pico bore N29:00E to S82:00E
9	3	3			The Peek N69:00E – of the rock betwixt the two isles, N 41:00E
10	5				
11	4				
12	3				
1	3	2	NBW½W		at midnight the NW end of Fyall bore NE 3 or 4 leagues. The Pike ESE
2	3	2			at 4 the West ed of Fyall EBS.
3	2				saw two sail to the Westward
4	3		NNW		saw a turtle –
5	3	5			variation p:ʳ amp:ᵈ 19:19
6	4	2			variation p:ʳ azum: 17:52
7	4	3	NNW½W		
8	3	5			at noon the body of Fyall bore S37:05E distance 12 or 13 leagues
9	3	5	NNW		Fyal in Long:ᵈ 28:30 West
10	3	5	NBW		Latitude – 38:30 North
11	3	5			
12	3		North		

Course	Dis	Latitude in	Long. made	
N27:0E	86	39:*05N	12:24W	

Ascension S13:47E – 969 leagues –

Remarks Tuesday April 26 1768 (52)

H	K	F	Courses	Winds		
1	2		NBE	EBN	Light airs and fair	
2	3	2	NBW		at two the middle of Fyall bore SEBS –	
3	2					
4	3				variation p:^{r} amplitude 20:00W	
5	3					
6	3	4		16:00		
7	1					
8	2					
9	1					
10	1	1				
11						
12						
1						
2					calm	
3				15:00	light airs –	
4	1					
5	1				variation	by amplitude – 18:49
6						by azumeth – 18:52
7					scraped the ships sides & pay'd them with varnish of pine –	
8						
9				calm	calm & fair weather ships head all round the compass –	
10					Lat:^{d} of Fyall N	
11					Long: of Fyal W of London	
12						

Course	Dis	Latitude in	Long. made	
N23:53W	23	39:*26N	00:40W	Fyall 28:15W

Fyall bore S05:00E distance 17 leagues   Long. in 29:06

Remarks Wednesday April 27 1768   (53)

H	K	F	Courses	Winds	Remarks
1				⎤	Calm & pleasant weather –
2					
3					
4				calm	with a swell from the Northward
5					
6				18:00	
7					
8	2	1	ENE	SSE	
9	1				
10	1	4			
11	2	3			
12	2	2			
1	3		SW		
2	4				
3	4	4		15:00	
4	5				
5	5	4			
6	5	4	WSW		variation p:^{r} amplitude 17:30W –
7	5	4			
8	5	4			
9	5	4			28:30W[550]
10	5	4			Moderate gales & hazey 1:21E
11	5	5			27:10W
12	6	5			

Course	Dis:^{e}	Latitude in	Long. made	
NEBE	65	40:*02N	00:°21'E	

Fyall bore S12:00W distance 30 leagues –

---

550 "Fyall in latitude 38:°20' North longitude of 28:30 West from London by an observation of longitude two days ago." PL and FC.

Remarks Thursday April 28 1768 (54)

H	K	F	Course	
1	6		ENE	
2	6			
3	6			
4	6	4		
5	6			
6	6			18:00
7	5	5		
8	6			
9	6	3		
10	6	4		
11	6	4		
12	6	5		
1	6	2		
2	7			15:00
3	6	4		
4	6	4		
5	7	2		
6	8			
7	8			
8	8	2		
9	2 4	3	EBN	NBE
10	2			
11	5			
12	4	4		

Remarks:

Fresh gales & hazey

variation p:r amplitude 14:00W
saw a sail in the NE –

Fresh gales & hazey –

squally rainy weather –

moderate & hazey

Course	Dis:e	Latitude in	Long. made	
N57:0E	152	41:*25N	3:08 East	

Fyall bore S42:°0'W distance 72 leagues

529

Remarks Friday April 29 1768 (55)

1	6		ENE½E	North	Fresh gales & cloudy –
2	6	2	ENE		
3	6	5			
4	7	2			
5	8			17:00	variation p:ʳ azumeth 16:49W
6	7	5			
7	6				
8	5	4	EBN		
9	6				
10	6				
11	5	5	E½N		
12	5				Moderate & cloudy
1	5		East		
2	5	4		14:30	
3	4	4			
4	2				Light breezes & cloudy
5	1				
6	3				
7	4	4			fresh gales saw a sail in the SE –
8	5		E½S	NNE	spoke a brig from Liverpool for S:°Carolina – all peace at home[551]
	3		SEBE		
9	3	3	SEBS		
10	5		SSE		moderate weather –
11	3		SEBE		28:30
12	5		S		

Course	Dis:ᵉ	Latitude in	Long. made	5:36
N72:0E	117	42:*01N	5:36E –	22:54

Fyall bore S 52:20W distance 108 legues

---

551 In Europe in the PL and FC.

Remarks Saturday April 30 1768

H	K	F	Courses	Winds	
1			ESE	NE	Moderate & cloudy with a swell from the NW –
2	4				
3	3	5			
4	3				
5	2				
6	2	2			16:00
7	2	2			
8	1	5	East	NNE	
9	2		EBS		
10	2				
11	2				
12	2	5			Showery –
1	2				
2	3				14:06
3	2		ESE	NE	
4	2		East		
5	2	2		NNE	
6	3		ESE		variation by azumeth – 16:°47'W
7	4	4		NE	
8	4	4	E½S		
9	3			NNE	
10	4				
11	3	4			Little wind & hazey
12	3		ESE	NE	

Course	Dis.ᵉ	Latitude in	Long. made		5:36
E5:00N	66	41:*57N	7:05E		22:54

Fyall bore S59:06W distance 130 leagues

Remarks Sunday May 1 1768   57

1	2		EBS	NEBW
2	2			
3	3			
4	3		ESE	
5	2	4	SEBE	
6	2		SE½E	16:10
7	3			
8	2		SE½S	
9	3	3	N½E	EBN
10	3			
11	3	2	NBW	
12	2			
1	4	4	N½E	
2	4	4		
3	4	2		13:45
4	4	2	N½W	ENE
5	3	3	North	
6	5	5	NBW	
7	1	4	ESE	NEBE
8	4	4		
9	2		SE	
10	2			
11	2		North	
12	4		NBW	

Light breezes with a Northern swell

Lost a log and two lines

pass'd by a schooner who was steering NW –

unbent the main topsail and bent a new one
Fresh gales & hazey

Course	Dis:ᵉ	Latitude in	Long. made	5:36
North	23	42:*20N	7:05E	22:54

Fyall bore S57:00W distance 130 leagues

Remarks Monday May 2 1768 58

H	K	F	Courses	Winds	Remarks
1	5		NNW½W	NE	fresh breezes and fair
2	5	2			pass'd by a turtle
3	6		NWBN		
4	5	5			a great NE swell
5	6				
6	5	2		14:00	variation p:^{r} azumeth – 23:°55'W
7	7	5			
8	2		EBS½S	NEBN	
9	4	3			
10	4		EBS		
11	4		EBS½S		
12	3	5			Rainy squally weather, broke the jibb hall yards, reeved new ones –
1	5		E½S	NNE	
2	4				
3	4	3			
4	3		E½N	12:50	fresh gales with a great sea, the ship pitches very heavy –
5	2		E½S		
6	4				
7	4	3			
8	4				
9	4	2	East		
10	4	5			Fresh gales & squally with a great sea sailmakers repairing sails
11	4	2			
12	4	5		NNE	

Course	Dis:^{e}	Latitude in	Long. made	5:36
N55:50E	56	42:*38N	7:45E	22:54

Fyall bore S57:00W distance 141 leagues

Remarks Tuesday May 3 1768   59

1	5	5	E½S	NNE	hard gales with a great sea
2	3	4			got down the top gall:ᵗ yard & close reeft the topsails –
3	3	6	East		
4	5			14:20	
5	5	3			carryed the main topsail sheet block away fixed a new one[552]
6	3	4			
7	5				
8	5				
9	6				
10	6	4			
11	5	4			
12	5			12:20	
1	4	4			
2	4	3			
3	4	3			Fresh gales & squally with rain and a great sea –
4	4	4			
5	5		E½S		
6	5	3			
7	5	4			
8	5	3	EBS½S	NEBN	
9	5				
10	5	3			reeved a new tiller rope –
11	5		EBS		
12	6				

Course	Dis:ᵉ	Latitude in	Long. made	10:35 28:30
E¼N	124	42:*43N	10:35E	17:55 5:24

Fyall bore S63:25W distance 141 leagues   11:31

---

[552] "Sailmakers are employed with as many more as can work with a needle in repairing our sails which are much worn and are tearing every hour." PL and FC.

Remarks Wednesday May 4 1768

H	K	F	Courses	Winds	Remarks
1	4	3	EBS	NEBN	hard gales and squally with a very heavy sea
2	4	5			
3	4	5			
4	4	4	ESE½S		
5	5			13:0	handed the fore topsail
6	5	4	ESE		
7	5		ESE½E		
8	5				
9	4				
10	4		ESE		
11	4				
12	4		EBS		
1	4	2			
2	3	4	EBS		
3	3	5		12:10	
4	4			NNE	handed the main topsail
5	4		E½S		
6	3	4			
7	4				
8	4	3			
9	4				
10	3	5			
11	3	4			Fresh gales & hazey –
12	3	2			

Course	Dis:ᶜ	Latitude in	Long. made	
S76:0E	99	42:*20N	12:51E	

Fyall bore S69:54W distance 208 leagues

Remarks Thursday May 5 1768

1	2	5	East	NNE	Strong gales with a great sea
2	3				Broke the topmast stay sail stay fixed a new one
3	2	3			
4	8		EBN		more moderate
5	2	5	ENE	12:13	
6	3	5			
7	2				
8	1	4			
9	2	3	NEBE		set the topsails
10	3			NBW	
11	2				
12	3	2			
1	3			12:10	
2	2				
3	4	4			Squally with hail & rain
4	3		NE		
5				NW	
6	2			calm	Little wind got top gallant yards across, saw a sail in the NE –
7	4		NEBE½E		
8	5				Squally with rain and hail a great sea –
9	2	3	NE		
10	4	2		WNW	
11	4	2			Fresh gales & squally
12	5	5		SW	

Course	Dis:ᵉ	Latitude in	Long. made	
ENE¼N	70	42:*54N	14:12E	

Fyall bore S68:30W distance 227

Remarks Friday May 6 1768   62

H	K	F	Courses	Winds	Remarks
1	6	4	NE	WNW	Fresh gales & squally cloudy weather – a great sea –
2	7				
3	6				variation p:ʳ azumeth 17:00W
4	8	4		SW	
5	7	3			
6	7	2		12:20	
7	7				
8	7				
9	7				
10	8				fresh gales & hazey –
11	8	5			
12	7	4		WSW	
1	7				
2	6	4			variation p:ʳ azumeth 16:40
3	6	4		12:10	
4	7				
5	6	3			
6	6				
7	5	5			
8	5				
9	5	4			
10	6	4			
11	6	5			fresh gales & hazey –[553]
12	6	5		SWBW	

Course	Dis	Latitude in	Long. made	
NNE½E	160	45:*10N	16:00E	

Fyall bore S61:12W distance 267 leagues

---

553 "Spoke to an English snow who told us the Lizard bore NEBN 180 leagues." PL and FC.

Remarks Saturday May 7 1768 63

H	K	F	Courses	Winds	Remarks
1	5	5	NE	WSW	fresh gales & hazey
2	7				
3	5	4			
4	5	4			
5	5				
6	4	4		14:40	variation by azumeth – 16:52
7	4	4			amplitude – 19:00W
8	4	5			
9	4	5			
10	5				
11	8				
12	7				
1	5				
2	5				
3	4	4		10:45	at 6 AM spoke with a snow from London – Lizard bore
4	7			SSE	NEBN 100 league:^{s}
5	6				saw two brigs steering Westward
6	6	4			
7	7				
8	7	3		SE	
9	8				
10	8				
11	8				fresh gales and hazey –
12	8				

Course	Dis:^{e}	Latitude in	Long. made	
NNE½E	142	47:*18N	17:36E	

Fyall bore S55:56W distance 305 leag:^{s}
Lizard NE½E dis:^{ce} 93 leagues

Remarks Sunday May 8 1768

H	K	F	Courses	Winds	Remarks
1	9		NEBE	SE	
2	6	2			Fresh gales and cloudy weather
3	8	3	ENE		saw severall ships & vessels
4	6	3			pass'd by two who were standing to the Eastward under
5	8		ENE½N		English colours
6	9	5		14:30	
7	8		ENE½E		
8	7				
9	7	3		SEBS	fresh gales sounded with 200 fm: no ground –
10	6	5			
11	6	4	ENE		
12	6				
1	7	4			
2	7				
3	7	3			
4	7	3		13;00	variation p:r amplitude 18:00W
5	7	4	NEBE	SEBE	saw a sail in the SE –
6	7	4			
7	7		ENE½N		severall strange ships in sight
8	7				
9	6				Scilly NE distance 22 leagues –
10	7				fresh gales & hazey
11	7				Bent the cables –
12	6		NEBE	SE	

Course	Dis:e	Latitude in	Long. made	
NE	142	49:*35N	20:08E	

Fyall bore S53:00W dis:t 360 leag:s
Lizard N77 :07E dis : 98 miles

Remarks May 9 1768   65

H	K	F	Courses	Winds	Remarks
1	7	3	NE	SEBE	Fresh gales[554]
2	7	4			
3	7	2			variation p:r azumeth – 16:°40'W
4	6	4			
5	6	4		14:0	sounded had 75 fathoms waters oozey ground –
6	6	4		SEBS	
7	3	2	SSW	SSE	
8	3	2			
9	4		SWBS		hazey with rain
10	3		SW		
11	3	4			
12	3	4	SWBW		
1	3				
2	3				variation p:r ampitude 17:°27'W
3	5		E½S	SBE	
4	5				sounded 60 fm: sand and shells
5	5		EBN	12:30	
6	5				
7	4		East	SSE	
8	4				sounded 64 fathoms fine sand
9	4		EBN		hazey with small rain
10	3		SW		
11	4		SSW½W		
12	2	4	SSW	SE	

Course	Dis	Latitude in	Long. made	
NEBE¼N	38	50:*01N	21:10E	

The Lizard bore East 23 leagues –

---

554 "... several ships about us saw some gannets and gulls." PL and FC.

Remarks Tuesday May 10 1768   66

H	K	F	Courses	Winds
1	3	2	SSW½W	SE
2	4			
3	3	5	SW	SSE
4	4			
5	4		SSW½W	SE
6	4	5	SBW½W	
7	4	4		
8	4	3	SSW	13:20
9	4	3		
10	4	3		
11	4	4		
12	3	5	ENE½E	
1	3	5		
2	4		ENE	
3	4	3		
4	4	2		12
5	4		EBN½N	
6	5		ENE	
7	5	5		
8	5	3	NE	ESE
9	5	4		
10	5	4		
11	5	3		
12	6			

Course	Dis:^{e}	Latitude in	Long. made	
East	21	50:02N	21:28E	

Scilly bears East   long. Out forty miles East
The Lizard bears East

Moderate gales –

Lost a log & line

variation p:^{r} azumeth –   23:06
                     amplitude – 23:00

                     amplitude – 20:32
variation p:^{r} azumeth –   19:51W
fresh gales and clear weather

had an observation for longitude found the true longitude that the ship was in to be 8:00 West from London
Silly eleven leag:^{s} 7:06
                        52 East

sounded 63 fathoms sand & shells
Fresh breezes & fair –

Remarks Wednesday May 11 1768 (67)

H	K	F	Courses	Winds
1	4		South	ESE
2	4		S½E	
3	4			
4	3		SW	
5			up SBW	of SW
6	4		SBE	1230
7	3	4		
8	4		SBE	EBS
9	4			
10	3			
11	4			
12	3	2		
1	3	4	SSE	
2	3	3		
3	3			12:50
4	4			
5	3	3	SEBS	
6	4	2	South	
7	3			
8	3			
9	4	2		
10	4			
11	4	2		
12	3	4	SE½S	ENE

Course	Dis:ᵉ	Latitude in	Long. made	6:20
SSE	84	48:44 –	22:08E	

The Lizard bore NNE Dist: 26 leagues –

Moderate and fair weather
at ½ past Noon saw two sail to windward steering SW, we soon perceived that they were a ship and a sloop. the ship fired severall guns at the sloop we seein this edged away fired a shot at her and brought her too. the ship to windward being nearest her sent a boat and took possession of her
came onboard Captain Hammond of his Maj:^{s} sloop Savage, who reported that the chace was the Jenny of Liverpool, Robert Christian Master from Roscoe in the Isle of Bass bound for Bergen. When the Savage fell in with her there was in company an Irish wherry, on their finding her to be a Man of W they seperated and hauld the wind the other bore away he first chaced the wherry but finding she went from him they then chaced the above named cutter. She being laden with tea, brandy & such goods, we detained her –[555]
Long: in by observat:^{n} 8:00W
                                         :50 E
                                         7:10W

Fresh gales the Savage & sloop in company –
                                 28:30
                                 22

555 "Fresh gales and cloudy, at ½ past saw a ship in chace of a sloop & fired severall guns at her, we bore away & at 3 fired a shott at the chace & br:^{t} her to. The ship to windward being near to the chace sent her boat onboard & soon after came on board Capt: Hammond of his Majestys sloop Savage & told me that the vessel was in company with an Irish wherry but on his coming near them they on discovering him to ba a man of war, took different ways, the wherry hauld the wind & this bore away, he heuld the wind but found that he could not gain ground bore away, and luckily I came in the way & stopt her as he found he scarce gained any of her. She was laden with tea brandy and other goods from Bascoe in France a bound to Bergen in Norway if a SW course would carry him there. She belongs to Liverpool, called the Jenny, Robert Christian Master. She having the before named goods on board in small bags, detained her to send to England – Fresh gales – both ships in company." PL and FC.

Remarks Thursday May 12 1768 (68)

H	K	F	Courses	Winds
1	3		NNE	East
2	3	4		
3	4	3		
4	4			
5	5		NBE½E	
6	4	4		12:20
7	4	4		
8	4	2		
9	5			
10	6		NBE	
11	4	5		
12	3	4	NNE	
1	4		SSE	
2	5 2		NBE½E	EBN
3	3			
4	6		NBE	12:0
5	5	2		
6	4	5		
7	5			
8	4	5		
9	5			
10	6		N½E	
11	4	4	SE	
12	5			

Course	Dis.ᵉ	Latitude in	Long. made
N17:0W	75	49:*56N	21:34

Fresh breezes & hazey

In sight of the Savage[556]

sounded 64 fathoms fine grey sand and shells –

variation p:ʳ azum: 21:06W –

Fresh gales & clear weather

---

556 "Lost sight of the Savage & cutter." PL and FC.

Remarks Friday May 13 1768   (69)

H	K	F	Courses	Winds	Remarks
1	5		SE	ENE	Moderate & fair
2	3		SSE	East	
3	3				sounded 62 fathoms brown sand & shells –
4	2				
5	1	3			60 fathom grey sand
6	1	4	ESE		severall vessels in sight.
7	1		SEBS		
8	2		SE		variation p:r az – 19:52W
9	2	3	ESE	14:00	amp – 19:12
10	2	4			
11	3				60 fathom grey sand
12	3	5			at ½ past five saw Scilly Islands bearing NBE –
1	3		SEBE		at Scilly bore from N42:00E to N7:0W
2	3		SBE		The Lighthouse NNE 2 leagues –
3	3	2	NBE		The Lands End EBN 9 or 10 leagues –
4	4	4	NEBN	13:5	The lat:d yesterday – 49:56 –
5	5		NNE		& lat at 8 AM – 0:00
6	5				Latitude in 49:00
7	5	5	SSE		Long in yesterday 7:50W
8	4	5			& long:e at 8 AM 0:46E
9	3	4			Long in at 8 7:04W
10	3	3			Scilly bearing North two leagues –[557]
11	4		NEBN		at Noon Scilly bore from NW to NEBN
12	3		NNE		Lighthouse N½West 2 leagues –
					saw river all vessels at anchor –

Latitude
49:40 –

557 The two other logs include an additional table detailing the course

Course	Lat.N	S	E $^{Dep:r}$	W
SEBE – 5		2.5	4.3	
SEBS – 9		7.5	5	
EBS – 4		1	4.9	
SE – 15		3.5	3.5	
ESE – 16		6.4	14.0	
SSE – 4		3.7	1.5	
NBW – 22	21.6	21.6	34.0	4.3
		21.6	4.0	
			30 E	

Latitude of yesterday	49:°56'N	Long. In	7:°50'W
+ Latitude -	00:00 –	Long –	.46E
Long. Ship at 8 AM			7.04W
Scilly North two leagues." PL and FC.			

Remarks Saturday May 14 1768 (70)

H	K	F	Courses	Winds
1				
2				
3				
4				
5				
6				15:0
7				
8				
9	1	3	ESE	NE
10	2	2		
11	2			
12	7	5		
1	2	4		
2	3	4		
3	3	4	NE	13:0
4	4			
5	3	4		
6	3	2		
7	2		North	ENE
8	1	3	SE	
9	1	3		
10	1	4		
11		4		
12	1	1	SBE	EBS

Light airs and calm –

Variation by azumeth 21:33

The Lighthouse bore North Dis:ᵉ 6 or 7 leagues –

Sounded 53 fathom brown sand & shells

at 8 the Lands End bore NE
the Golf Rock NENE 2 leagues
Scilly Lighthouse NW –
Depth of water 44 fm: brown sand and shells –

Light breezes in 44 fathom

The Lands End N40E Dis:ᵉ 5 leag
Latitude in 49:*45N

H	K	F	Winds		Remarks Sunday May 15 1768 (71)
1	1			Calm	calm 50 fathoms coarse shelly ground
2	1				
3	1	5	South		
4	1	1			
5	2	3	EBS		many ships & vessels in sight –
6					
7				15:0	variation p:r amp:de 20:00W
8					
9					The Lizard bore N71 :30 East –
10					
11				Calm	and clear
12					
1					
2					
3					
4	1		EBS	NEBN	variation p:r azumeth – 20:00W
5	2			South	amplitude – 20:20
6	2	2	SEBE	NEBE	The Lizard at 8 bore NEBN –
7	2	2			
8	2	2	SE	ENE	
9	1		NNE	East	
	1				
10	3	4			
11	3	3			
12	2	4			The Lizard Light House N64:00E

Distance about 3 leagues –
Latitude observed 49:°*51N

Remarks Monday May 16 1768 (72)

1			
2			
3			
4			
5			
6			13:0
7			
8			
9			
10			
11			calm
12			
1			
2			
3	2		ESE
4	3		
5	1		12:40
6	2	5	
7	3		
8	2	5	
9	2	3	
10	2	4	
11	2	2	
12	2		EBN

Calm and clear –

In 40 fathoms rocky ground –
Lizard bore NE½E –

Lizard Lighthouse North 45 fm: shelly –
variation – 19:35W

at midnight Lizard Light NBE

45 fathom shelly

Lizard Light house NWBN
45 fm: coarse sand, shells & small stones –
at 8 the Dodman N½E 6 or 7 leagues –
NE

The Ram Head N54:0E distance 9 leagues
Light breezes and fair – a great number of vessels in sight –
Latitude observed 49:52N

Remarks Tuesday May 17 1768   73

1	1		EBN	North	Light airs –
2	1				
3	3	5			
4	3	5	E½N		
5	5			10:40	
6	4		East		
7					The Start NEBN 2 leagues
8	1	3			
9	1	4			
10	3				
11		3			
12	1	4			
1	1	4			
2	2	3			
3	2	2			
4	2				at 4 the Start bore n 9:00E about four miles –
5	1	3			
6	2				at 8 Berry Head NBW distance 4 or 5 leagues –
7	2				
8	2				
9	2				
10	2				
11	2				light airs and rainy
12	3			NW	

off the Berry Head –[558]

---

[558] The PL ends here on the 17th May, 1768. Samuel Wallis' signature appears at the end of this page. The next three pages – 18th, 19th and 20th May are blank except the HOUR column. There follows a page of notes (brief questions and annotations with page numbers). Pages 86–94 are blank and then follows a detailed catalogue by George Robertson of nearly 35 pages describing discoveries, specifying the coordinates of each, noting the anchoring places and briefly descrbing the encounters with the islander peoples (not transcribed here).

Remarks Wednesday May 18 1768   74

1	1		E½N	WNW
2	1	5	E½S	
3	2			
4	2	2		
5	4		EBN	West
6	4		E½N	
7	5	4		
8	5			
9	5	4	East	WNW
10	5	3		
11	6	5	E½S	
12	7	4	ESE	West
1	8			
2	8			
3	8			
4	7			
5	7			
6	8			
7	9			
8	8	3	East	
9	7	5		
10	7	2		
11	7	5		
12	7	5		NNW

Light airs and hazey –

The Bill of Portland NEBN, 2 leagues

Dunnose NNW three miles –

Beachy Head NW Distance three leagues

Latitude 50:*42 North –

Remarks Thursday May 19 1768

H	K	F	Course	Wind
1	8		East	SE
2	7			SW
3				
4				WSW
5				
6				
7	5	5	EBN	
8	6	5		
9	4		ENE	SW
10	3	3		
11	4			
12	4			
1				
2				
3				
4				
5				
6				
7				NNW
8				
9				
10				
11				
12				

[559]Fresh breezes & squally.
Bro:^{t} too abreast of Fair Leigh
Distance 2 miles – I went on shore in the barge –[560]
The barge not returning, made sail –

Abrest of Dunginess
Moderate and cloudy

Dunginess Light WSW and South Foreland lights ENE – the South Foreland light at twelve ENE 5 miles

½ past 4 anchored in the Downs with the best b:^{r} in 8 fm: water & veer'd ⅔ of a cable –
The South Foreland SW
Warner Castle S.°66W
Deal Castle N84°W
Sand down Castle N38°W
North Foreland N12°E
Distance of shore 1½ miles
Got the sheet anchor over the side

Sam:l Wallis

---

559 The handwriting changes here. Wallis' signature appears at the end of this entry. The Hawkesworth account includes the following comments: "At half an hour after five, on the 13th, we saw the Islands of Scilly; on the 19th, I landed at Hastings in Sussex; and at four the next morning, the ship anchored safely in the Downs, it being just 637 days since her weighing anchor in Plymouth Sound. To this narrative, I have only to add, that the object of the voyage being discovery, it was my constant practice, during the whole time of my navigating those parts of the sea which are not perfectly known, to lie to every night, and make sail only in the day, that nothing might escape me."

560 Added in freehand : " – at Hastings & set out for London." FC.

We should not have dared to have made thus bold with you, had we not been encouraged by the humane and generous treatment we have so often experienced since we have had the happiness to be commanded by you – and thinks it our duty to return you our most sincere thanks for the many instances of that general treatment we have had from you – and as you are the only prop we have to depend on our hopes that the adress will not be without success – We humbly beg that you may recommend us to their Lordhips favour as it is certain that thro your goodness in so doing must depend our good or bad fortunes and as we came out in a state of uncertainty make us thus bold to solicit you in our behalf –
And may you live long & happy to be a service as well as an honour to your country are the prayers of sir your most obedient and most humble servants
The Dolphin[561]

This petition was given me as I was leaving the ship – I gave it the first Lord of the Admiralty who said it did me great honour and this was all wither they or I got by the voyage but much ill health & fatigue.

---

561 This transcription of the letter to Wallis from the crew of the Falmouth does not appear in the two other logs.

Week day	M.º Day	Wind	Remarks onboard the his Maj:ˢ Ship Dolphin[562]
May Friday	1768 20ᵗʰ	SW WSW	Moderate breezes and pleasant. P.M. at 4 veer'd away & moor'd ship a cable each way, bearings nearly as before, AM loos'd sails to dry, scrubb'd ship between wind & water & pay'd the wails PM pass'd by the Tweed frigate and a cutter for the river
Saturday	21ˢᵗ	SWerly	Moderate breezes and pleasant wːʳ Loos'd sails to dry
Sunday	22ⁿᵈ	NE.erly	Light winds and pleasant wːʳ P.M. cleared hawse AM washed between decks –
Monday	23ʳᵈ	NE.erly	The first and latter parts light winds and pleasant wea:ʳ the middle fresh breezes and cloudy.
Tuesday	24ᵗʰ	NE.erly	Light breezes and pleasant weather cleaned ship fore & aft came onboard the Clerk of the Chequer & muster'd the ships company –

---

562 These entries are in a different handwriting as compared to the rest of the ML. "At Anchor in the Downs." FC.

Wednesday	25th	NE ENE SE Nor	The first and middle parts light breezes & clear w:er the latter part mod & thick hazey w:er At 8 PM came onboard the Pilot & unmoor'd the ship. at 4 AM weigh'd and came to sail at noon abrest of Margate standing off and on waiting for the flood tide.
Thursday	26th	NE ENE North NNW North NNE	the first part light breezes & pleasant w:er the middle fresh and cloudy, the latter merate and clear. P.M. at 2 bore away and made sail, at 5 ran through the narrows and at 9 anch'd with the b:t b:r in 5½ fm and cleard 1½ of a cable, AM 3 weigh' & made sail, saw several Men of War off Sheerness – at 10 anchd with the best b:r in 8 fm about 2 m:s above Gravesend it being high water.
Friday	27th	E'erly	Moderate breezes and peasant at 4 PM weigh'd & came to sail and at 7 anchd in Longreach abrest of Purfleet, veer'd away & moor'd

			ship a cable each way, found riding here his Maj:ˢ ship Jason –
Saturday	28th	E:ᵗerly W:ᵗerly	Moderate breezes with some rain P.M. the guns and powder hoys alongside, cleared the ship of guns, powder & Gunners stores, unmoor'd ship & at 7 weigh'd & came to sail, at 10 anchor'd in the Galleons.[563]
			Sam:ˡ Wallis Note the ship was paid off at Deptford on the fourth day of June 1768 – she having been two years in commission – wanting ten days, being commissioned the nineteenth of June 1766 – Samˡ Wallis

563 "At 6 AM weigh'd & came to sail. At noon anchd the ship alongside the Surprize Deptford." FC. The FC continues:

29th May: "D:°W.r PM Unbent the sails and unreeved the running rigging, emp.d getting the stores of all kinds onshore. AM the people on shore to refresh."

30th May: "Light airs and clear weather. AM emp.d as before."

31st May: "Light airs & clear W:r Emp:d wholly as before."

1st June: "Moderate and clear W.r The people employed clearing the ship with all possible dispatch."

2nd June: "D:°W:r Employed as before."

3rd June: "D:°W:r employed getting out the ground lier and Pursers stores."

4th June: "Moderate and cloudy. Emp:d getting the anchor onshoar, unrigging the lower masts getting some provisions onshore."

5th June: "Light breezes and pleasant W:er Employed return all our stores and cleaning the ship."

6th June: "The winds, weather & employment as yesterday."

7th June: "Rainy weather. Employed as before and some hands cleaning the ship."

8th June: "D:°W:r and employment."

9th June: "First part showery the rem:r fine w:r finished returning the stores and cleared the ship."

10th June: "D:°w:r At 10 AM came down the Commiss:er and paid off the ship – struck the pennant."

The FC is signed by Samuel Wallis. The log ends with three pages of notes in freehand: "Character of Admiral Boscawen, by Beatty 1790 – This officer whose life had been dedicated to his profession, possessed from nature a warm temper and a good understanding his conduct corresponded with the vigour of his mind, making his friendships and enmities with the force of his character. But his ardour was tempered by humanity and guided by an affectionate regard for all the individuals intrusted to his management. To those who were more immediately under his eye his solicitude extended even to parental care, which was acknowledged by the strongest marks of grief among the seamen of the ships in which he had been embarked every man feeling the Admirals death as his own particular misfortune. Such were the peculiar characteristics which distinguished this great officer amont the seamen of Britain.

But as the active, the diligent, the intrepid servant of his country, he is exalted by all the talents of a distinguished chief. Consummate skill in his profession the most scrupulous fidelity which spurns at peculation, unbounded zeal and the most cool, the most collected, the most persevering courage, are some of the qualities which rendered Admiral Boscawen one of the greatest naval charcaters which this island ever produced – had this from Mr Boscawen 23 May 1790."

There then follows two pages of notes: "An account of what I delivered in at the Amdiralty on my arrival; A wreath of hair, one hundred pearls, bunches of feathers, numbers of fine pearl fish hooks, fine cloth and shells, – these were presented to her Majesty – draughts & perspective views of all the places we discovered with a map of the world & our run pricked off on it. A logbook

The bread fruit trees in general six feet girth and twenty to the branches, a soft wood & sap milky.

The apple trees from six to seven, and twenty feet to the branches, a harder wood than the bread fruit of the tree are their canoes built, and the planks in their houses made, there was ebony of which their staffs of honour were made, and the club that beat the bark whereof their cloth was made rose wood which they used to scrape into cocoa nut oil for anointing themselves with various other trees some very large were on the hils & mountains, which would be easily brought down in case they were wanted and saw mils might be easily erected as there is plenty of water comes from the mountains & might be easily diverted to whatever places one pleased it is now brought on by the inhabitants to water their plantations, & would answer for indigo & sugar or any thing else planters could wish –

with all the courses steered, weather remarks &:^{ce} during the whole voyage, a book of all the observations of longitude as observed by M:^{r} Maskeline's tables – with an observation of an eclipse which hapned while we were at Georges Island.

a Patagonian whip, pair of spurs, & slings –

a Bow & arrow with ornaments for the neck & head, used by the people in the Western parts of the Streights of Magellan

a stick of the winter bark

a canoe, tropic birds feathers and a shovel from Queen Charlottes Island.

A spontoon, drum, flute, conque, bow & casquett of arrows peice of cloth, with a twig & peice of rind it is made of with an instrument for making it, instruments for marking their backsides, a stone for bruising their bread a other fruit with a peice of rose wood, two breast plates, two hatchets, two hatchets (sic), a shark hook, other tools, & a fishing net from Georges Island – some oar found in Oznaburd Island &:^{ce}.

a club from Wallis Island

a great assortment of seeds from all the places we touched at.

All the forgoing were presented to the Museum, except the seeds & they were given to divers people particularly to the Princess Dowager of Wales's gardner at Kew. L:d Egmont S:^{r} Eds:^{d} Hawke, S:r Charles Saunders, S:^{r} Percy Brett, Adm:^{l} Keppel & many other great men besides to the Phisick Gardens, Oxford, Cambridge & Chelsea."

The FC thus comes to an end.

A	Aboa, Hog
B	
C	Cock or Hen, Moa
D	
E	Earings, Poeta
F	Father – Metua Fruit (amena, aoreda.) (Fish hook, Mattaw)
G	Girl, Aheyna
H	Husband, Tane
I	Images at their places of worship Tahowy
J	
K	
L	
M	Mother, Manacheyné. Married, Fahaney.
N	
O	Ouasou go to my hoise (ou, a po) goes onboard (ou, a tete, go onshoar)
P	
Q	
R	
S	Sleep – A bo, bo.
T	Tenhany – wife Tomorrow – Aheya – Mettawaugh
U	
V	
W	
X	
Y	
Z	

Annex L (FC) (Reproduced in Hawkesworth)

A Table of the Latitudes Observ'd and Longitudes West from London both by Account & Observation of all the Places His Maj:ˢ Ship was at, or saw in late Voyage in the Years 1766, 1767 & 1768

Names of Places	Time When	Lat:ᵈ In	Longitude supposed	Long:ᵈ obs:ᵈ by Doctor Maskeylyne's method	Variation
Lizard	August 22:ⁿᵈ 1766	50:°00' N	5:°14' W		21:°00' W
Funchall Road Madeira	Sept:ʳ 8:ᵗʰ 1766	32:°35' N	18:°00' W	16:°40' W	14:°10' W
Port Praja S:ᵗ Jago	Sept:ʳ 24:ᵗʰ 1766	14:°53' N	23:°50' W		8:°20' W
Port Desire	Dec:ʳ 8:ᵗʰ 1766	47:°56' S	67:°20' W	66:°24' W	23:°15' E
Cape Virgin Mary	Dec:ʳ 17:ᵗʰ 1766	52:°24' S	70:°04' W	69:°06' W	23:°00' E
Point Possession	Dec:ʳ 23:ʳᵈ 1766	52:°30' S	70:°11' W	69:°50' W	22:°40' E
Point Porpus	Dec:ʳ 26:ᵗʰ 1766	53:°08' S	71:°00' W	71:°30' W	22:°50' E
Port Famine	Dec:ʳ 27:ᵗʰ 1766	53:°43' S	71:°00' W	71:°32' W	22:°30' E
Cape Froward	Jan:ʳʸ 19:ᵗʰ 1767	54:°03' S			22:°40' E
Cape Holland	Jan:ʳʸ 20:ᵗʰ 1767	53:°58' S			22:°40' E
Cape Gallant	Jan:ʳʸ 23:ʳᵈ 1767	53:°50' S			22:°40' E
York Road	Feb:ʳʸ 4:ᵗʰ 1767	53:°40' S			22:°30' E
Cape Quod	Feb:ʳʸ 17:ᵗʰ 1767	53:°33' S			22:°35' E
Cape Notch	March 4:ᵗʰ 1767	53:°22' S			23:°00' E
Cape Upright	March 18:ᵗʰ 1767	53:°05' S			22:°40' E
Cape Pillar	April 11:ᵗʰ 1767	52:°46' S	76:°00' W		23:°00' E
At sea	April 21:ˢᵗ 1767	42:°30' S	96:°36' W	95:°46' W	12:°00' E
At sea	May 4:ᵗʰ 1767	28:°12' S	99:°00' W	96:°30' W	6:°00' E
At sea	May 20:ᵗʰ 1767	21:°00' S	110:°00' W	106:°47' W	5:°00' E
At sea	May 23:ʳᵈ 1767	20:°20' S	116:°54' W	112:°06' W	5:°00' E
At sea	June 1:ˢᵗ 1767	20:°38' S	132:°00' W	127:°45' W	5:°09' E
At sea	June 3:ʳᵈ 1767	19:°30' S	132:°30' W	129:°30' W	5:°40' E

EXPLORATION OF THE SOUTH SEAS

Names of Places	Time When	Lat:^{d} In	Longitude supposed	Long:^{d} obs:^{d} by Doctor Maskeylyne's method	Variation
Whitsunday Isl:^{d}	June 7:th 1767	19:°26' S	141:°00' W	137:°56' W	6:°00' E
Queen Charlotte's Island	June 8:th 1767	19:°18' S	141:°04' W	138:°04' W	5:°20' E
Egmont's Island	June 11:th 1767	19:°20' S	141:°27' W	138:°30' W	6:°00' E
Duke of Gloster's Island	June 12:th 1767	19:°11' S	143:°08' W	140:°06' W	7:°10' E
Duke of Cumberland's Island	June 13:th 1767	19:°18' S	143:°44' W	140:°34' W	7:°00' E
Prince William Henry's Island	June 13:th 1767	19:°00' S	144:°04' W	141:°06' W	7:°00' E
Osnaburg Island	June 17:th 1767	17:°51' S	150:°27' W	147:°30' W	6:°00' E
King George SE end	June 19:th 1767	17:°48' S	151:°30' W	149:°15' W	6:°00' E
The 3:rd Island SSW end	July 4:th 1767	17:°30' S	152:°00' W	150:°00' W	5:°30' E
Duke of York Is:^{d}	July 27:th 1767	17:°28' S	152:°12' W	150:°16' W	6:°00' E
S:^{r} Cha:^{s} Saunders Island	July 20:th 1767	17:°58' S	153:°02' W	157:°04' W	6:°30' E
Lord Howe's Is:^{d}	July 30:th 1767	16:°46' S	156:°38' W	154:°13' W	7:°40' E
Scilly Islands	July 31:st 1767	16:°28' S	157:°22' W	155:°30' W	8:°00 E
Boscawen's Island	Aug:^{t} 13:th 1767	15:°50' S	177:°20' W	175:°10' W	9:°00 E
Aug:^{s} Keppels Island	Aug:^{t} 13:th 1767	15:°50' S	177:°20' W	175:°13' W	10:°00 E
Wallis's Island	Aug:^{t} 17:th 1767	13:°18' S	100:°00' W	177:°13' W	10:°00 E
Piscadore S:°end	Sept:^{r} 3:rd 1767	11:°00' N	195:°00' W	192:°30' W	10:°00 E
Islands N:°end		11:°20' N	195:°35' W	193:°00' W	10:°00 E
Tinian	Sept:^{r} 30:th 1767	14:°58' S	215:°40' W	214:°10' W	6:°20 E
At sea	Oct:^{r} 17:th 1767	16:°10' S	218:°00' W	216:°25' W	5:°15 E
Grafton's Island	Oct:^{r} 29:th 1767	21:°04' S	239:°00' W	239:°00' W	1:°0 W
Pulo Aroe	Nov:^{r} 15:th 1767	2:°28' S	258:°00' W	255:°00' W	1:°00 W
Lucipera	Nov:^{r} 26:th 1767	4:°10' S		254:°46' W	None
Batavia	Dec:^{r} 1:st 1767			254:°30' W	1:°25' W
Princes Island	Dec:^{r} 16:th 1767	6:°41' S	256:°00' W	256:°30' W	1:°00' W
At sea	Jan:^{ry} 26:th 1768	34:°24' S	328:°00' W	323:°30' W	24:°00' W

Names of Places	Time When	Lat:ᵈ In	Longitude supposed	Long:ᵈ obs:ᵈ by Doctor Maskeylyne's method	Variation
At sea	Jan:ʸ 27:ᵗʰ 1768	34:°14' S	324:°00' W	323:°13' W	24:°00' W
Cape of Good Hope	Feb:ʸ 11:ᵗʰ 1768	34:°00' S	345:°00' W	342:°00' W	19:°30' W
At sea	March 15:ᵗʰ 1768	16:°44' S	3:°00' W	2:°00' W	13:°00' W
At sea	March 15:ᵗʰ 1768	16:°36' S	2:°00' W	2:°05' W	12:°50' W
S:ᵗ Helena	March 19:ᵗʰ 1768	15:°47' S	5:°49' W	5:°40' W	12:°47' W
Ascension	March 23:ʳᵈ 1768	7:°50' S	14:°18' W	14:°04' W	9:°53' W
At sea	March 24:ᵗʰ 1768	7:°28' S	14:°30' W	14:°38' W	10:°00' W
At sea	April 8:ᵗʰ 1768	15:°04' S	30:°00' W	34:°30' W	4:°40' W
At sea	April 11:ᵗʰ 1768	21:°28' S	36:°00' W	36:°37' W	4:°30' W
At sea	April 8:ᵗʰ 1768	33:°55' S	32:°00' W	33:°00' W	11:°34' W
At sea	April 21:ˢᵗ 1768	36:°15' S	30:°00' W	29:°31' W	14:°30' W
At sea	May 10:ᵗʰ 1768	49°438' S	6:°00' W	7:°52' W	22:°30' W
At sea	May 11:ᵗʰ 1768	48:°48' S	7:°30' W	8:°19' W	
S:t Agnus's Light House	May 13:ᵗʰ 1768	49:°58' S	7:°14' W	7:°08' W	20:°00 W